CURRICULUM PLANNING

Integrating Multiculturalism, Constructivism, and Education Reform

CURRICULUM PLANNING

Integrating Multiculturalism, Constructivism, and Education Reform

Kenneth T. Henson
Eastern Kentucky University

Boston   Burr Ridge, IL   Dubuque, IA   Madison, WI   New York   San Francisco   St. Louis
Bangkok   Bogotá   Caracas   Lisbon   London   Madrid
Mexico City   Milan   New Delhi   Seoul   Singapore   Sydney   Taipei   Toronto

McGraw-Hill Higher Education

A Division of The McGraw-Hill Companies

CURRICULUM PLANNING: INTEGRATING MULTICULTURALISM, CONSTRUCTIVISM, AND EDUCATION REFORM, SECOND EDITION

Published by McGraw-Hill, an imprint of The McGraw-Hill Companies, Inc., 1221 Avenue of the Americas, New York, NY 10020. Copyright © 2001 by The McGraw-Hill Companies, Inc. All rights reserved. Previous edition © 1995 by The Addison–Wesley Educational Publishers, Inc. All rights reserved. No part of this publication may be reproduced or distributed in any form or by any means, or stored in a database or retrieval system, without the prior written consent of The McGraw-Hill Companies, Inc., including, but not limited to, in any network or other electronic storage or transmission, or broadcast for distance learning.

Some ancillaries, including electronic and print components, may not be available to customers outside the United States.

This book is printed on acid-free paper.

1 2 3 4 5 6 7 8 9 0 QPF/QPF 0 9 8 7 6 5 4 3 2 1 0

ISBN 0–07–234610–8

Vice president and editor-in-chief: *Thalia Dorwick*
Editorial director: *Jane E. Vaicunas*
Sponsoring editor: *Beth Kaufman*
Developmental editor: *Cara Harvey*
Senior marketing manager: *Daniel M. Loch*
Project manager: *Mary Lee Harms*
Senior media developer: *James Fehr*
Senior production supervisor: *Sandra Hahn*
Coordinator of freelance design: *Rick D. Noel*
Cover designer: *Sheilah Barrett*
Cover image: *©SuperStock, Inc., Angel #2 by Diana Ong*
Senior photo research coordinator: *Lori Hancock*
Supplement coordinator: *Sandra M. Schnee*
Compositor: *David Corona Design*
Typeface: *10/12 Times Roman*
Printer: *Quebecor Printing Book Group/Fairfield, PA*

The credits section for this book begins on page 472 and is considered an extension of the copyright page.

Library of Congress Cataloging-in-Publication Data

Henson, Kenneth T.
　　Curriculum planning : integrating multiculturalism, constructivism, and education reform / Kenneth T. Henson — 2nd. ed.
　　　　p.　　cm.
　　　ISBN 0–07–234610–8
　　　1. Curriculum planning—United States—Case studies. 2. Multicultural education—United States—Case studies. 3. Constructivism (Education)—United States—Case studies. 4. Educational change—United States—Case studies. I. Title.

　　LB2806.15 .H47　　2001
　　375'.00'0973—dc21
　　　　　　　　　　　　　　　　　　　　　　　　　　　　00–036130
　　　　　　　　　　　　　　　　　　　　　　　　　　　　CIP

www.mhhe.com

Historically, every school has had a core of hardworking teachers who have been content to remain in their classrooms and devote their expertise and energy to educating their students. During times of emergency, such as preparing for accreditation visits, these teachers always surface as the leaders who do the job that must be done. Because these teachers provide the leadership for improving their schools, their efforts must be recognized.

But current reform movements in every state are demanding constant and total involvement of all educators. As in the past, teachers are giving time and energy to meet these demands. This book is dedicated to all the teachers who are giving their best to improve our schools and to all the tens of thousands of central office curriculum and instructional leaders, principals, and college and university professors who are dedicated to helping teachers meet this challenge.

B R I E F   C O N T E N T S

Preface   xvii
Acknowledgments   xxiii
To the Student   xxv

1   An Introduction to Curriculum Development   1

2   Social and Technological Foundations of Curriculum   36

3   Historical and Philosophical Foundations of Curriculum   80

4   Concepts, Theories, and Models   122

5   Designing and Organizing Curricula   172

6   Aims, Goals, and Objectives   208

7   Selecting Content and Activities   234

8   Helping People Change   282

9   Evaluating Instruction and the Curriculum   322

10   Planning and Converting Curriculum into Instruction   363

11   Current and Future Curriculum Trends   410

Glossary   461
Credits   472
Name Index   473
Subject Index   477

C O N T E N T S

Preface   xvii
Acknowledgments   xxiii
To the Student   xxv

CHAPTER 1

AN INTRODUCTION TO CURRICULUM DEVELOPMENT   1

Objectives   1
◆ The Case of Eastwood Middle School   2
The Interrelated Themes   5
Defining Curriculum   7
   Curriculum: A Program of Studies   8
   Curriculum: A Document   8
   Curriculum: Planned Experiences   8
   Curriculum: Social Implications   9
   Curriculum: Curriculum as an End   9
   Curriculum: Short and Long Definitions   9
   Curriculum: A Need for Uniformity   10
HIA: The Hidden Curriculum   10
   Impact on Multicultural Education   12
A Need for Reform   13
   A Look at Some Early Attempts at Education Reform   14
   A Look at a *Nation at Risk* and Its Impact on Other Reports   15
   A Positive Turn   17
   Narrow Views   18
   Overall Purposes   19
   Unsound Recommendations   19

Positive Outcomes   21
Administrators   21
Other Changes   22
Teacher Education   22
Identifying True Weaknesses   23
Learning Questions   31
Suggested Activities   32
Works Cited and Suggested Readings   33

CHAPTER 2

SOCIAL AND TECHNOLOGICAL FOUNDATIONS OF CURRICULUM   36

Objectives   37
◆ The Case of Linda Blevins and Marvin Watts   37
Part I: Social Foundations   39
Importance of Society-School Relationship   40
The School's Influence on the Community   42
How Society Influences Schools   44
Ways Society Affects the Schools: Forces that Affect the Curriculum   45
Future Effects   50
A Final Thought on Social Foundations   58
Part II: Technological Foundations   64
Technological Growth   64
The Computer   65
Meeting Multicultural Goals   66
Other Technological Developments   67
Chapter Summary   72
Learning Questions   73
Suggested Activities   74
Works Cited and Suggested Readings   75

CHAPTER 3

HISTORICAL AND PHILOSOPHICAL FOUNDATIONS OF CURRICULUM   80

Objectives   81
◆ The Case of Diane Worley   81
Part I: Historical Foundations of Curriculum   83
The Migrations   83
Early Schools   84
The Dame Schools   84
The Public School   86

Goals for Tomorrow's Schools   93
  The New Basics   93
  Goals for 2000   94
  Criticisms of the State-Level and National Standards   96
Part II: Philosophical Foundations of Curriculum   104
  Basic Philosophical Systems   105
  Influences of Philosophy on Education   112
Chapter Summary   114
Learning Questions   115
Suggested Activities   116
Works Cited and Suggested Readings   118

CHAPTER 4

CONCEPTS, THEORIES, AND MODELS   122

Objectives   123
◆ The Case of a Disappointed Student   123
The Role of Research   124
Lack of a Research Base   125
The Use of Common Sense   126
Science versus Common Sense   127
Word Traps   128
Concepts   129
Theories   130
  Sample Theories   132
Models   145
  The AIM Model   146
  Taba's Inverted Model   146
  Tyler's Ends-Means Model   148
  The Oliva Models   149
  The Saylor and Alexander Model   152
  Macdonald's Model   152
  The Zais Eclectic Model   154
Project ESCAPE   156
American Studies Program   162
  American Studies at Central High   162
Alverno College   164
Some Final Suggestions   164
Chapter Summary   167
Learning Questions   168
Suggested Activities   168
Works Cited and Suggested Readings   169

CHAPTER 5

DESIGNING AND ORGANIZING CURRICULA   172

Objectives   173
◆ The Case of the Little School that Grew   173
Curriculum Designs   176
The Subject-Centered Curriculum   178
   Strengths   179
   Weaknesses   179
The Broad-Fields Curriculum   180
The Core Curriculum   191
The Trump Plan   194
The Spiral Curriculum   195
Mastery Learning   196
Problem Solving   197
Selecting Curriculum Designs   198
Curriculum Design Qualities   199
   Scope   199
   Sequence   199
   Continuity   200
   Articulation   200
   Balance   200
A Final Note   201
Chapter Summary   202
Learning Questions   203
Suggested Activities   204
Works Cited and Suggested Readings   205

CHAPTER 6

AIMS, GOALS, AND OBJECTIVES   208

Objectives   209
◆ The Case of San Sona Elementary School   209
An Introduction to the Aims, Goals, and Objectives of Curriculum
   Development   210
   Aims   212
   Goals   213
   Objectives   213
   Criteria for Writing Performance Objectives   213
   Performance Objectives in the Three Domains   216
   Writing Objectives in the Cognitive Domain   216
   Writing Objectives in the Affective Domain   225
   Writing Objectives in the Psychomotor Domain   227

Chapter Summary   229
Learning Questions   230
Suggested Activities   230
Works Cited and Suggested Readings   232

CHAPTER 7

SELECTING CONTENT AND ACTIVITIES   234

Objectives   235
◆ The Case of Building Bridges to Reform   235
The Importance of Content and Activities Selection   241
   Arenas and Actors in Curriculum Planning   242
   Problems in Content and Activities Selection   248
   National Goals   250
   The Nature of Knowledge   251
   Selecting Activities   257
   Education Reform's Impact on Selection of Content and Activities   267
Checklist for Revising Curricula   271
Tables of Specifications   272
Chapter Summary   274
Learning Questions   277
Suggested Activities   277
Works Cited and Suggested Readings   278

CHAPTER 8

HELPING PEOPLE CHANGE   282

Objectives   283
◆ The Case of Regional University   283
Agents for Change   287
   A New Concept of Leadership   288
   A Need for Involvement   291
A Need to Go Beyond Current Horizons   310
School Culture and Climate   310
Forces that Promote and Impede Change   311
   Strong Leadership   312
Chapter Summary   315
Learning Questions   316
Suggested Activities   316
Questions on the Educational Excellence Laboratory Consortium   317
Works Cited and Suggested Readings   317

CHAPTER 9

EVALUATING INSTRUCTION AND THE CURRICULUM   322

Objectives   323
◆ The Case of an Accreditation Visit   323
The Significance of Evaluation   325
   Evaluating Instruction   326
   Evaluating the Curriculum   350
   Evaluating School Reform   355
Chapter Summary   357
Learning Questions   358
Suggested Activities   359
Works Cited and Suggested Readings   359

CHAPTER 10

PLANNING AND CONVERTING CURRICULUM INTO INSTRUCTION   363

Objectives   364
◆ A Wichita School Case   364
An Introduction to Converting the Curriculum   366
   Long-Range Planning   366
   Daily Lesson Planning   372
   Individualizing Instruction   385
Chapter Summary   400
Learning Questions   401
Suggested Activities   401
Works Cited and Suggested Readings   402

CHAPTER 11

CURRENT AND FUTURE CURRICULUM TRENDS   410

Objectives   411
Introduction   411
Trends across the Disciplines   411
   Safe Schools   411
   Home Schooling   412
   Multidisciplinary/Thematic Approach   412
   Reading and Writing across the Curriculum   414
   Alternative Assessment   415
   Performance Assessment   415
   Authentic Assessment   416
   Continuous Assessment and Progressive Reporting   416
   Self-Assessment   417

Tenure and Life Certification 417
Ethnic Diversity 418
Gender Equity 419
Geographic Stereotyping 420
Special Students 420
Inclusion 422
Gifted Students 423
Senior Citizens 424
Magnet Schools 424
Charter Schools 424
Business Partnership Programs 426
National Standards 426
Increased Parental Involvement and Control 428
A Move to Privatize Public Schools 430
The World of Work 430
Vouchers and School Choice 431
Cooperative Learning 432
Multiple Intelligences 433
Evaluating Textbooks and Ancillary Materials 434
Textbook Selection 435
Increased and Expanded Use of Technology 440
National Voluntary Testing 440
Summary: Trends across the Disciplines 440
Trends within the Disciplines 440
Mathematics 441
Science 442
Language Arts 449
Fine Arts 449
Foreign Language 450
English Language Arts 450
Social Studies 451
History 451
Geography 452
Civics 453
Health and Physical Education 453
Chapter Summary 453
Learning Questions 454
Suggested Activities 455
Works Cited and Suggested Readings 455

Glossary 461
Credits 472
Name Index 473
Subject Index 477

Approach

I consider myself among the most fortunate of educators, for I have spent the past decade in the middle of an unprecedented level of concentrated education reform in a state that places practice above rhetoric. Fortunate, too, because I have had colleagues who remain on the cutting edge of developments in their content fields and in pedagogy—educators who are enthusiastic about having the opportunity to raise the quality of curriculum and instruction to a new level.

As a graduate student, I found my curriculum texts to be among the most difficult of all my texts, not because the subject matter was inherently complex, but because these books were written in a jargon-laden, convoluted style that most of us found awkward, unclear, and sometimes even pompous. I wasn't impressed, and I always thought that I could do better. This text is part of my continuing attempt to do so.

Perhaps, like me, at some time in your life you have heard someone comment, "He (or she) must be really smart, because I listened to the whole presentation and didn't understand a single word." I believe that this type of thinking is wrongheaded. The best authors and teachers don't make things sound complicated; on the contrary, they do just the opposite, making complex subjects clear and easy to understand. Only then can the study of various disciplines become enjoyable. My goal for this text is to remove the mystery from curriculum development and make it a clear and exhilarating experience.

Many of the curriculum books I used had a second common weakness; they lacked currency. The twenty-first-century curriculum developer must have a firm grasp of the latest knowledge bases in curriculum study and its foundations. Major concepts, principles, and theories must be examined and explained, not to be memorized but to be used by today's educators to critically examine the many reform practices that are occurring in their local school districts. This book is well documented with the latest insights in the literature.

A Balanced View

My tone is intentionally encouraging, because lasting improvements in the nation's schools require the support of those of you enrolled in this course: designated curriculum directors, administrators, instructional supervisors, and teachers—especially teachers, because successful reform requires an unprecedented level of teacher involvement and leadership. But my encouraging language should not—must not—be interpreted as blind support for all education reform or as failure to recognize the many flaws and weaknesses that characterize many reform reports. On the contrary, my own concern for the many unsound practices recommended by the nation's many reform reports is clearly expressed in my *USA Today* article, "America's public schools: A look at the recent reports" (1986) and in the subsequent article, "Why curriculum development needs reforming." (*Educational Horizons,* Summer 1996).

Simple, quick-fix solutions usually occur only in an environment of ignorance and the effects of such changes usually disappear with equal speed. Sound curriculum development requires an awareness and understanding of theories based on a solid knowledge of educational foundations. Consequently, good curriculum development is seldom quick or easy. The overriding aim of this book is sound curriculum development for lasting improvement.

Themes of the Text

Education Reform

This book is written to help teachers and other educators meet the paramount challenge of twenty-first-century education, which is to help *all* students succeed, both academically and socially. This goal will require a special type of education reform. Because many reform practices are far from good, this book provides the foundations needed to make judicious decisions regarding the implementation of reform practices. Most reform practices have both strengths and limitations. The readers of this text are provided opportunities to review the merits and criticisms of each popular reform practice and are then pressed to weigh these carefully to make their own value judgments about the worth of each to their local school district. Good education reform is designed to help maximize the academic and social development of *all* students.

Multicultural Education

Throughout the country, teachers face students of widely varied backgrounds. Students from all cultural backgrounds leave their marks on the schools' honor rolls and lists of valedictorians and salutatorians; at the same time, because of language barriers and negative home environments, many youths from all cultures hold low expectations of themselves. Successful curriculum development in the twenty-first century must prepare teachers to help all students succeed. This book provides opportunities to apply curriculum foundations and practices to some of the many problem situations faced by today's students, situations that challenge all contemporary teachers. In a democracy, each student must be educated to his or her highest potential, and all citizens have a right to feel proud of their heritage. As used in this text, *multicultural education* refers to the establishing and maintaining of a classroom climate or culture in which students appreciate diversity and allow themselves to be enriched by the opportunity to work with students from many backgrounds, including differences in ethnicity, political affiliation, socioeconomical status, ability level, and religion.

Constructivism

The research has shown that the best teachers have a depth of understanding about a variety of curriculum theories and models, and are prepared to choose and use the combination that works best with the particular educator at a particular school at a particular time. Therefore, this book takes an eclectic approach, introducing a variety of curriculum and learning theories. Research has also shown that we learn best that which we are able to connect to our prior knowledge and use to create or "construct" new understanding.

Constructivists believe that true understanding happens only when we tie new information to previously acquired understanding and that the teacher's role is to help this happen. Each time we learn, we shape our existing understanding, making the current state of our knowledge temporary. Learning is the result of our discovering relationships between new and old information while confronting new information. Constructivists believe that this event (learning) happens best when learners help each other, motivated by an internal desire to learn. Russian psychologist Lev Vygotsky called the process of learning together "socially negotiating meaning." By the turn of the millennium, 80 percent of American teachers reported that they worked with small groups of students at least twice a week and with individual students at least once a week (see Henson & Eller, 1999).

Integration of the Themes

The themes of **education reform, multiculturalism,** and **constructivism** are woven throughout the content of each chapter. All three themes are addressed in the *Objectives, Learning Questions, Suggested Activities,* and *Summary* sections of each chapter as well. The following tables illustrate the integration of the themes. The numbers shown in each table represent the sequence in which the objective, question, or suggested activity refers to particular content found in the body of the respective chapter.

Education Reform

	Objective(s)	Learning Question(s)	Suggested Activities
Chapter 1	2	2, 3, 7, 8, 9, 10, 11, 12	6, 7
Chapter 2	6	6, 12, 13	10
Chapter 3	6, 7	11, 17, 19, 20	2, 3, 4, 19
Chapter 4	7	5	9
Chapter 5	2, 8, 9	7	4
Chapter 6	5	7	10
Chapter 7	3	7	6
Chapter 8	6, 7, 8	1, 3, 7, 8	1, 3
Chapter 9	1, 2	5, 15	6
Chapter 10	9	5	8
Chapter 11	1	2	1, 3

Multiculturalism

	Objective(s)	Learning Question(s)	Suggested Activities
Chapter 1	5	10, 11	9
Chapter 2	4, 6, 9	9	1, 2, 3, 8
Chapter 3	5	9	1
Chapter 4	5	6	7
Chapter 5	5	4	4
Chapter 6	6	4	8
Chapter 7	5	6, 7	7, 8
Chapter 8	5, 9	13	4, 5
Chapter 9	5	16	4,6
Chapter 10	5	8	2, 3
Chapter 11	6	6	4

Constructivism

	Objective(s)	Learning Question(s)	Suggested Activities
Chapter 1	6	13	3
Chapter 2	10	16	10
Chapter 3	4	7	20
Chapter 4	8	7	8
Chapter 5	10	1	6
Chapter 6	4, 7	4	9
Chapter 7	2	1	8
Chapter 8	9	13	6
Chapter 9	9	17	4
Chapter 10	3	2	6
Chapter 11	6	1	6

Case Studies

A special feature of this text is the inclusion of **case studies.** Each chapter begins with a short vignette entitled "The Case of . . ., and later in the chapter is a second case study, written specifically for the chapter in which it appears. Unlike the vignettes, which are based on actual events but perhaps are unintentionally embellished over time, **these case studies detail contemporary curriculum planning experiences occurring throughout the country.** Each is written by educators who are directly involved with the experiences described.

Each case study contains a description of the school and the surrounding community, which enables the reader to see how much the appropriateness of reform practices depends on the existing conditions at a particular school, in a particular community, or at a particular time. The case is then followed by a section entitled "Issues for Further Reflection and Application" that helps the reader examine the case information, focus on relevant issues, and practice making decisions about educational reform practices. The inclusion of the case studies is intended to give the reader an appreciation of the demands educators face, always requiring decisions and often without the availability of all the information needed to make wise decisions.

A C K N O W L E D G M E N T S

I would like to thank the following professors for providing feedback on the text and the manuscript during its development:

David M. Brown, *Texas A&M University, Texarkana*

Dennis C. Buss, *Rider University*

Christy Faison, *Rowan University*

P. Tony Graham, *James Madison University*

John P. Gustafson, *Winona State University*

Robert W. Johns, *University of Arkansas at Little Rock*

Angus J. MacNeil, *University of Houston, Clear Lake*

Larry Reck, *Indiana State University*

Timothy Riordan, *Xavier University*

Jay Thompson, *Ball State University*

Kim Truesdell, *University of Buffalo*

Newspapers, magazines, books, and reports regularly describe problems in our schools. In some places, legislators and educators are suing their states for failing to provide the type of education needed to prepare students for life and work in the twenty-first century. Schools and teachers are being measured, not by their own performance but rather by the performance of their students on national exams. The people are calling for a national curriculum. To say the least, these are exciting and challenging times.

As a twenty-first-century educator, you are no longer restricted to teaching the textbook content to the students in your class. The teacher's role has moved from the classroom to the total school (restructuring), to the community, and to the world (reform). Your job is to prepare your students to ask new types of questions, think new kinds of thoughts, dream new dreams, and reach new goals. In effect, you must play a major role in shaping the future.

To be sure, this new role requires mastering content, and knowledge of the principles of curriculum development is an indispensable part of this content. But, if indeed you are to use this course and this book to prepare the students at your school for the world, you will need content mastery *and more*. You must have the courage and stamina to ask yourself and seek the answers to many questions: What is it about education reform that perplexes me (after all, nobody fully understands all the reform elements)? Which reform practices in my district do I support? What insights about learners do I have that I can use to contribute to designing a new type of educational system? What is wrong with our current system? What is right with it? What is wrong with our world? How can I help change it? What are my strongest feelings? How can I use the answers to these questions to increase the impact I can have on shaping our schools and our world? What have been my greatest learning experiences? What made them so? Who is the best teacher I have ever had? Why? Exactly how did that teacher reach me? How can I help others use this teacher's strengths and methods? What is the difference between knowledge and wisdom? Why is this important to curriculum planners? What are my fondest memories from elementary school? Secondary school? What were my most traumatic educational experiences? How can I influence the shape of curricula to accentuate the former and eliminate the latter? How can I best use all of these memories and experiences to help others? How is each discipline different? Does each discipline have a best route to mastery? How can this route be discovered? For what disciplines is each teaching method best suited? What other kinds of questions should I be asking myself so that I can ride the crest of the reform wave and experience success instead of wallowing in dissatisfaction? How can I remain passionate about reform and yet avoid falling prey to the politicians' empty rhetoric and to the flawed recommendations that characterize so many of the reform reports? How can I keep my concern for the welfare of every student of every nationality and every social level as the reason and guide for all my decisions? How can I help all students realize their strengths, their self-worth, and their importance and obligations to the community? What is it about me that makes me different from any other human being who has ever lived, and how can I understand and harness this uniqueness to direct my energies and those of my colleagues to make a positive difference in our schools and in our world?

This book is not a tome filled with jargon and impressive, complex sentence structure. Rather, this book might raise more questions than it answers. The poet Antonio Machado once wrote, "Life is a path you beat while you walk it." Curriculum improvement is the same. There is no step-by-step manual, no algorithm or recipe. Instead, with each answer comes the arrival of new questions, if we keep our minds open. Does curriculum planning require a knowledge base and a depth of understanding? You bet. The challenge and fun remain hidden, waiting to be discovered, and therein also lie the excitement and fun. Never lose the excitement that comes from discovering a new insight. For, indeed, those who enjoy shaping the curriculum in their schools will tell you that the joy in the journey of curriculum improvement is to be found not only at the destination but also in the ongoing trip. Because I fully believe that neither you nor I will ever know all the answers, my advice is that you ask a lot of questions and, while you are seeking the answers, try to relax and enjoy the trip.

1 An Introduction to Curriculum Development

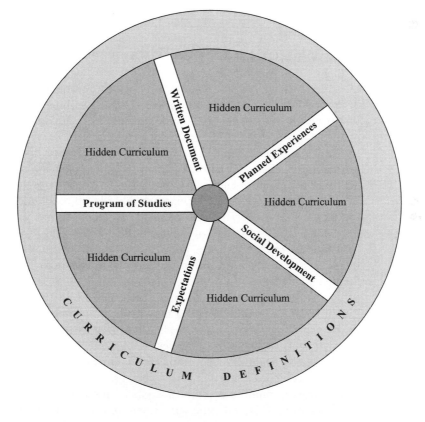

Objectives

This chapter will prepare you to:

- develop a working definition of curriculum.
- criticize the reform reports from an educational perspective.
- relate current literature on the knowledge base to curriculum development.
- describe some events that have led to an improved image of American education.
- improve your ability to influence your colleagues' perceptions.
- recognize the effects of your school's hidden curriculum.
- explain how the hidden curriculum can affect the academic and social development of all students.
- define constructivism.

THE CASE OF EASTWOOD MIDDLE SCHOOL

Eastwood Middle School is in many ways a typical American middle school. Its 26 teachers and 425 students in grades 5 to 8 make it average in size. Its culturally diverse student body and predominately white administration and faculty contribute to its typical qualities. Eastwood Middle serves a predominantly working-class population. The students do not always receive the level of encouragement needed to convince them to achieve their maximum potential. Those who do receive encouragement at home are often told to "get an education so you can get a good job." Unfortunately, like other communities, Eastwood has its share of broken homes, single-parent families, and latchkey children.

Eastwood is in the town of Madisonville, which has its right and wrong side of the tracks. There are several pockets of ethnic groups and Madisonville residents are stereotyped according to their subcommunities, each with its own ethnic culture.

As is true of schools throughout the country, Eastwood Middle School is the hub of the community, not in the sense of its being the meeting place for citizens to gather, but because it is the one place where the community's youth from all backgrounds come together.

Eastwood Middle School is located in a state where education reform is occurring at record speed, with each week bringing new dimensions of reform. In two years of rapid reform, the schools in this state have been introduced to such innovations as authentic assessment, curriculum alignment, nongraded primary curriculum, site-based decision making, alternative testing, performance evaluation, research-based teaching, educational technology, and valued outcomes. A new statewide tax increase has financed these and other changes.

To say that teaching at Eastwood Middle School during the last two years has been an exciting experience would be the understatement of the year. Highlighting the motivation for Eastwood teachers has been a series of articles in the local newspaper on a continuing "school reform" theme. Eastwood's senior faculty members remember times when the only news items on local schools were stories about the decline of local standardized test scores, the failure of the schools to enforce discipline codes, or an occasional drug bust. Drug problems initially shocked this small midwestern community, but as alcohol and drugs slowly invaded the town, their presence later became accepted as an unfortunate sign of the times.

In spite of these problems, good things have been happening at Eastwood, and recently even the television news programs have featured special stories on some of the curriculum reforms at Eastwood Middle. The senior faculty members agree that it is time for some positive stories about their school, and these reform stories are welcomed and appreciated by many.

Education reform at Eastwood Middle School has its detractors, and as with all schools, Eastwood Middle has its share of naysayers, faculty members who announce daily in the teachers' lounge that this new reform won't work. Some of the reasons they give for predicting the education reform movement's early demise include:

- "It will never work. Sure, all of the reform elements sound great in theory, but once they are removed from the master drawing board and put in the real world, they'll never work."

- "The recently generated monies fueling this education reform movement will soon run out, and when this happens the reform will stop."

- "This school reform movement is just another bandwagon fad. The legislators are using it to build their own support base. Once they stop getting publicity, they'll withdraw their support."

- "The principal is using the reform movement to get another feather in her hat. She'll press for its implementation just long enough to get all the media coverage she can get, and then she'll find another way to get publicity."

- "We teachers are being falsely enticed to go along with all the reform issues. We are receiving more and more work assignments with no more pay, and all of us are already overworked. Soon we'll come to our senses and say, 'Enough is enough.'"

- "This reform is holding us teachers accountable for the performance of *all* our students and, let's face it, some students will never succeed. The movement was doomed to fail before it started."

Although in numbers these naysayers are in the minority, they are a loud and determined group. The principal often muses over how much this group of teachers could contribute to reforming the school if only they would channel all of their energy positively.

Like most schools, Eastwood Middle also has its group of innovators who are standing ready to take on new challenges. These faculty members seem tireless. Instead of being exhausted from overwork, these teachers seem to get even more energy from working hard. Eastwood's principal wishes this group had more members.

Most of Eastwood's teachers are somewhere between these two extremes. They hear the rumblings, and they read and hear about the success stories. They are suspended between the two points of view, waiting to see whether they should invest their energy and time in the reform movement. They know that successful reform will require a big commitment of everybody's time and energy, and they want to improve their school, but since their schedules are already taxing, before making personal investments in reform they want to be sure the reform movement will not run out of steam or money before it succeeds.

Susan Carnes has just completed her undergraduate program and has accepted her first full-time teaching assignment at Eastwood Middle. After serving on this faculty for only two months, Susan can see the political forces at work. In addition to recognizing the distinct social groups, she has noticed that different individuals have their own reasons for wanting the education reform movement at Eastwood Middle to succeed or fail.

Carlos Garcia is a soft-spoken, polite science teacher who seems immune to the daily gossip. He is a good listener who seems to empathize with all the complainers, but he, himself, never complains. It seems clear that when the chips are down, Carlos will support the administration and the reform practices.

At the other extreme is Frances Watson, whose tongue seems to be loose at both ends. Frances is a large, boisterous teacher who demands everyone's attention wherever she goes, regardless of the purpose of the meeting. In faculty meetings when all 26 are present, Frances speaks every time anyone else speaks, as though she considers her ability to contribute to the conversation at least equal to that of the other 25 teachers combined. Susan is amazed that the rest of the faculty members permit one individual to dominate them. Apparently, they are willing to acquiesce to her overwhelming personality just to avoid the unpleasant complaining that would surely follow if she did not get her way.

This bothers Susan. After all, these are supposed to be professional people, and professional teachers are supposed to put the welfare of their students ahead of concerns for themselves and their colleagues. Susan doesn't see concern for the students as a force behind any of this faculty's decisions. In fact, she doesn't see any efforts being made to address the needs of the minority students.

Two months is a short time to be on a faculty, and Susan is sure that she has much more to learn about this school and her new colleagues. She can tell that success here will require her to learn more about both. Susan feels that as a professional, she must be committed to helping the local reform efforts succeed if, indeed, those efforts might improve the plight of the students at Eastwood. In any case, since implementing reform was the state's decision and she is a state employee, she has concluded that perhaps it is up to her to find ways to make the reform serve the students.

Susan wonders whether she should express her position on this local school reform issue and perhaps search out others who are also committed to its success. Also, Susan desperately wants to talk to someone about the school's multicultural needs. At this time, just having a peer to talk to and the ability to share her feelings would bring some much-needed relief, yet she wonders if this would lead to friction with those who oppose reform.

As reflected in this description of Eastwood Middle School, curriculum reform does not occur easily. Most faculties are divided over change of any kind, and reluctance is common, especially where heavy commitments of time and energy are required. Reform is energy-hungry, as reflected in John Goodlad's (1997, p. 102) comments, "Even with reform efforts close to and involving teachers from local schools, a major part of the net result appears to be added work and stress for teachers seeking to cope with matters that do not support their teaching." Intelligent schoolwide involvement in education reform will require a good grasp of the meaning of curriculum and will require familiarity with the development of the current wave of school reforms.

THE INTERRELATED THEMES

The three themes of this book, constructivism, multiculturalism, and education reform, are closely related. **Constructivism** is the belief that learning occurs only when the learner ties newly acquired information to previously gained understanding. **Multiculturalism** refers to establishing and maintaining a classroom climate where students with many differences in background, potential, and challenges learn to work with all of their classmates and learn to appreciate their uniqueness. **Education reform** refers to systematic approaches at the national, state, or local level to make significant improvements in education. Good education reform, as viewed by the author, uses practices or activities that help all students meet the goals of constructivists and multiculturalists.

One quality that aligns constructivism with multiculturalism is the common belief that *all students can and will learn.* Many teachers, even highly experienced teachers, find this concept difficult to accept, yet it is absolutely essential for maximum effectiveness in today's classrooms. Sooner or later, our basic beliefs translate into action. If teachers reject the postulate that all students can learn, these teachers will eventually, perhaps unwittingly, lower the expectations they hold for those students they perceive as less capable and as a result provide them less assistance. Teachers who believe that all students can succeed will never give up on or surrender their willingness to help any students to succeed to their maximum capacities.

As mentioned earlier, good education reform uses those practices considered essential by constructivists and multiculturalists. One of these common practices is the use of *small group assignments,* in which each member helps all other group members. The constructivists say that small group activities enhance learning. The multiculturalists say that small group activities enhance the development of social skills and even increase students' self-confidence because the value of each group member is recognized by all other members of the group.

Both constructivists and multiculturalists recognize that increased learning and socialization result only when all group members cooperate to help the other members of their group. Thus, another quality that ties constructivism to multiculturalism is *cooperation,* as opposed to the traditional belief that learning occurs best in a competitive environment. Banks (1999, p. 59) explains, "Multiculturalists believe that competition strengthens students' self-images. Research shows that achievement among Mexican-American students and African American students increases when cooperation rather than competition is fostered."

One quality that helps us understand the positive impact that cooperative, small-group work has on learning is *student discourse,* i.e., students talking and sharing teaching strategies. One contemporary educator has said that "Discourse in the classroom pulls together concepts, ideas, and conclusions" (Ballew, 1999, p. 115). Eminent Russian psychologist Lev Vygotsky (1896–1934) referred to small-group discussions as "negotiating understanding."

In contrast to traditional education, which depended on teacher-directed instruction with passive students, many contemporary education reform programs use *student-centered approaches.* For example, the most commonly used learning activity in constructivist classrooms is problem solving. Even the approaches used to solve problems have changed significantly. Instead of the traditional step-by-step, formula-driven problem solving, many contemporary education reform programs favor a more flexible, nonlinear approach because the nonlinear approach takes students from the simple, recall learning level to higher-order thinking (Ballew, 1999).

Another quality that ties the themes of this book together is the type of *assessments* used in many reform programs. During the early twentieth century, schools almost exclusively gave objective tests to hold students accountable for remembering "taught" information. To be candid, many contemporary education reformers have continued to use assessment to hold students, teachers, administrators, and even schools, districts, and state education systems accountable, but there is good news: many contemporary education reformers have endorsed the use of authentic assessments. The big difference is that authentic assessments require students to use the information they have learned to solve lifelike problems. Self-assessment has also become an accepted practice, using portfolios, exhibits, and other activities that require students to track their own progress. Furthermore, the assessment instruments are being used in a continuous manner, unlike the traditional practice of testing at the end of instruction, when it is too late to adjust methodologies to enhance learning.

Perhaps the most significant aspect of the change to continuous assessment is the purpose for which assessment is being used. As already pointed out, many contemporary education reform programs are using assessment to hold students, teachers, administrators, schools, and, in fact, educators at all levels accountable; however, contemporary educators are also using feedback from these continuous assessments to improve the curriculum, teaching, and learning.

Multiculturalists are quick to endorse practices that are used for the purpose of assisting students. Assistive instruction is often misinterpreted as making efforts to help by lowering the standards for challenged and non-mainstream students. In fact, multiculturalists encourage teachers to hold the same standards for all students and find ways to help students with special barriers, whether they are language barriers (for example, students who live in homes where English is not spoken), barriers resulting from homes or community cultures that may be dissonant to the school culture, or barriers caused by physical, mental, and/or emotional challenges.

Another quality tying the themes in this book together, and a reason for much hope, is the expansion of the learning arena. Formerly classroom-bound education has now expanded to become schoolwide, communitywide, and even worldwide education. *Partnerships* are being formed that include teachers, administrators, parents, and other community members. There is good news as the new millennium begins; there is evidence of decentralization, especially at the state and local levels (Day, 1999).

As the education arena has expanded, so has the power of each player, including students. Constructivists believe that students should be active participants in the shaping of their education. Teachers are being empowered by the late twentieth century invention of site-based school councils, which are often given power to make all types of important decisions, including major decisions about curriculum matters. Students, too, are being *empowered*. A major source of student empowerment is the constructivist belief that the only way to really understand is through solving problems, thereby creating new understanding. Thus, the realization that teachers cannot give understanding to passive students has also been a strong factor in efforts to purposefully empower students.

These are a few ways that this book's themes of *constructivism, multiculturalism,* and *education reform* are interrelated. As you read this book, learning about others' decisions and making decisions yourself, consider the effects that each decision will have on the goals of multiculturalism and constructivism.

DEFINING CURRICULUM

The importance of the curriculum for meeting the school's mission cannot be overemphasized. As Thompson and Gregg (1997, p. 28) state plainly, "The curriculum is the primary vehicle for achieving the goals and objectives of a school."

The term *curriculum* is a Latin word that originally meant "racecourse." When used in education, curriculum has many meanings. Traditionally, the term meant a list of courses, but through the years it has expanded, taking on several new meanings. Curriculum developers who have a clear mental grasp of several of these meanings can perform a wider range of curriculum development activities and can do so more effectively than those who have only a vague idea of what is meant when the word curriculum is mentioned.

Curriculum: A Program of Studies

In its early application to American education, curriculum meant a program of studies. Zais (1976) pointed out that when asked to describe a curriculum, a lay person is likely to list a sequence of courses. This view of curriculum is seen in most college catalogs, which often list a definite sequence of courses to describe a particular program of studies.

Curriculum: A Document

Some educators perceive the purpose of curriculum as being the improvement of instruction, and they define it accordingly. For example, James MacDonald defined curriculum as "planned actions for instruction" (Foshay, 1969). Such a definition implies that curriculum is a document. When an accrediting team makes a site visit, the chair or another team member may ask to see the science curriculum. Usually, this person would expect the school officials to produce a document describing the school's science program.

Curriculum: Planned Experiences

To other educators, the term curriculum means a school's planned experiences. Thompson and Gregg (1997, p. 28) have said that "Curriculum embraces every planned aspect of a school's educational program." Saylor and Alexander (1966, p. 5) distinguished between the school's actual activities and its planned activities: "Curriculum encompasses all learning opportunities provided by the school" versus "A curriculum plan is the advance arrangement of learning opportunities for a particular population of learners." Saylor and Alexander said that a curriculum guide is a written curriculum plan.

Others have also defined the curriculum as experiences:

> A sequence of potential experiences is set up by the school for the purpose of disciplining children and youth in group ways of thinking and acting. This set of experiences is referred to as the curriculum (Smith, Stanley, & Shores, 1957).

All the experiences that children have under the guidance of teachers (Caswell & Campbell, 1935).

The curriculum is now generally considered to be all of the experiences that learners have under the auspices of the school (Doll, 1989).

This change from an emphasis on content to an emphasis on experiences reflects a general change in thinking that occurred during the Progressive Education Era (the 1920s to the 1940s), when the curriculum emphasis shifted from being subject-centered to being student-centered.

Curriculum: Social Implications

By the 1980s, the concept of curriculum expanded even more, to include changes in social emphasis, for example:

[Curriculum is the] learning experiences and intended outcomes formulated through systematic reconstruction of knowledge and experience, under the auspices of the school, for the learners' continuous willful growth in personal-social competence (Tanner and Tanner, 1980).

If we are to achieve equality, we must broaden our conceptions of curriculum to include the entire culture of the school—not just subject matter content (Gay, 1990).

Curriculum as an End

The preceding definitions portray curricula as content to be learned or experiences to be had as a means toward an end. In contrast, other definitions present curriculum as an end unto itself:

Curriculum is all the planned learning outcomes for which the school is responsible (Popham and Baker, 1970).

Curriculum: Short and Long Definitions

Some definitions of curriculum are much more general than are others. This is even true for definitions written by the same author. For example, compare the following two definitions by Taba (1962):

Curriculum is a plan for learning.

A curriculum usually contains a statement of aims and of specific objectives; it indicates some selection and organization of content; it either implies or manifests certain patterns of learning and teaching, whether because the objectives demand them or because the content organization requires them. Finally, it includes a program of evaluation of the outcomes.

A Need for Uniformity

At this point, the logical mind strives to impose some order on the evolution of the meaning of the word curriculum. Unfortunately, this is not possible, because the development of curriculum theory has not followed a straight, logical path. Wiles and Bondi (1993, p. 15) offer the following explanation for the lack of systematic theoretical curricula evolution:

> As we approach the twenty-first century, theoretical dimensions of curriculum development remain suppressed by a dependence on economic sponsorship, political conservation, and the failure of educators to gain consensus for any significant change in the schooling process.

Instead of a clean definition of curriculum, we now offer a series of interpretations of curriculum given by Oliva (1997, p. 4) to conclude this discussion:

- Curriculum is that which is taught in school.
- Curriculum is a set of subjects.
- Curriculum is content.
- Curriculum is a program of studies.
- Curriculum is a set of materials.
- Curriculum is a sequence of courses.
- Curriculum is a set of performance objectives.
- Curriculum is a course of study.
- Curriculum is everything that goes on within the school, including extra-class activities, guidance, and interpersonal relationships.
- Curriculum is that which is taught both inside and outside the school directed by the school.
- Curriculum is everything that is planned by school personnel.
- Curriculum is a series of experiences undergone by learners in the school.
- Curriculum is that which an individual learner experiences as a result of schooling.

Figure 1.1 shows various definitions of curriculum categorized into thematic groups, showing some of the extremely diverse in ways that curriculum is viewed.

THE HIDDEN CURRICULUM

The curriculum that we have been attempting to define, though varied in many respects, has at least one implied commonality; it is visible. Whether it is a document or an ongoing set of activities, it is visible. But, like the moon,

FIGURE 1.1

Categorizing definitions

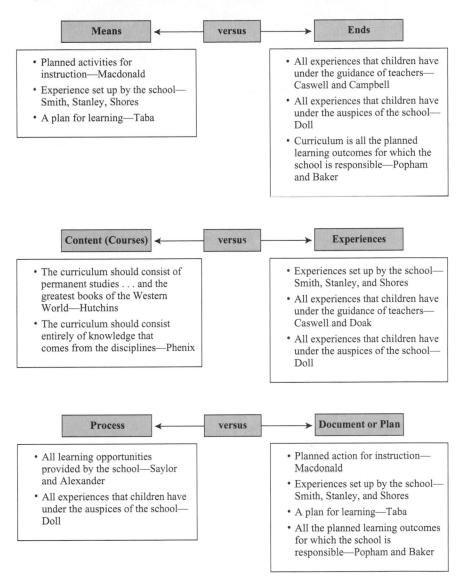

curriculum has a face that is never openly exposed; or, if you prefer, every curriculum has a hidden dimension. That more obscure, less visible part of the curriculum is referred to as the "hidden curriculum." Wiles and Bondi (1993, p. 9) refer to the hidden curriculum as the *unplanned* curriculum. Schubert (1986, p. 105) says that the hidden curriculum is that which is taught implicitly, rather than explicitly, by the school experience. McNeil (1990, p. 308) states, "The hidden curriculum refers to unofficial instructional influences. . . ."

The task of grasping a clear concept of the hidden curriculum is difficult. Not so difficult, though, is the ability to see that the hidden curriculum is a powerful force in any school, a force that may reinforce the school's, state's, and local reform efforts and the school's stated mission, or it may militate vigorously against the two, or it may support some parts of local reform practices and the school's mission and may work against other parts of the reform and mission.

The socialization process that comes from the school itself, as a community, is a significant part of the hidden curriculum. At some schools, this process teaches that competition is the road to success in the United States; at other schools, students learn that cooperation is preferred. At some schools students learn to appreciate diversity; at others, students learn to avoid students with different backgrounds. These are just two of the hundreds of lessons taught at every school by the hidden curriculum. As another example, Sautter (1994, p. 436) states, "The arts promote the 'hidden curriculum' of social behavior to improve self-discipline, self-motivation, self-esteem, and social interaction."

The nature of the hidden curriculum is more covert than overt, and this may or may not be intentional. Apple (1979, p. 14) defined the hidden curriculum as "the tacit teaching to students of norms, values, and dispositions that goes on simply by their living in and coping with the institutional expectations and routines of schools day in and day out for a number of years."

One part of the hidden curriculum is the dialogue that occurs among members of minority ethnic groups. Members of the mainstream may be critical of some minorities' tendency to gather in small groups. They may perceive such groups as prejudiced against the mainstream, never realizing that the minority group members are trying to satisfy some cultural and psychological needs (Banks, 1999; Tatum, 1997).

Impact on Multicultural Education

The hidden curriculum offers opportunities to communicate important positive multicultural messages. Through providing a positive role model, teachers can show their appreciation for the opportunities a multicultural class offers to enrich life experiences. All teachers who choose to can have multicultural classrooms, even teachers whose students are all white, all black, all Hispanic, or indeed any other ethnic background, or whose students are all male or all female, so long as the teacher leads students to tolerate, appreciate, and celebrate diversity (Davidman & Davidman, 1997).

In the absence of an appreciation for differences, unfortunately the hidden curriculum can also have a negative or prejudicial influence on students. Oliva (1997, p. 521) addresses this concern:

> Multiracial committees and entire faculties find that in order to eliminate negative attitudes and conflicts, they must analyze all aspects of the school, including the

'hidden curriculum'—the school climate, social relationships among individuals and groups, values and attitudes held by both students and faculty, presses on student conduct, unspoken expectations, and unwritten codes of conducts.

Martin Haberman expressed concern for what he considers severe hidden curriculum damage on a national level (see Haberman & Bracey, 1997, and Haberman, 1999). He argued that the 120 largest school districts in the United States offer curricula that unintentionally, and perhaps unknowingly, prepare students to fail in the workplace. For example, he says that in our efforts to be compassionate we often lead students to conclude that it is acceptable to be absent or tardy if you have a good excuse. Later, when these same students try this at the workplace, they are puzzled when they receive pink slips.

Haberman (1999, p. 73) asks the following questions:

1. Are we rewarding students on the quality of their excuses? Or are we rewarding students for making up work they have missed?

2. Are we rewarding students who do not like each other by separating them? Or are we rewarding students who show they can work with people they might not necessarily like?

3. Are we rewarding students for only working when a teacher is present? Or do we reward students for being productive without having direct supervision?

Haberman's concerns give credibility to the claim that the effect of the hidden curriculum is powerful, perhaps even more than that of the visible curriculum. Ask yourself, what experiences do I remember most from my school days? Were these planned activities or planned content or were they unplanned, such as important relationships between you and your teachers and classmates, the unwritten behavior code among students, or maybe just the overall culture of your school?

A NEED FOR REFORM

Curriculum development has been described as a messy process. Wynne and Ryan (1993, p. 135) wrote that "Curriculum is one of education's biggest, sloppiest, and slipperiest concepts." One reason that curriculum development is complicated is that it is aimed at facilitating teaching, and teaching itself is an enormously complex and fluid process. These barriers to curriculum change have contributed to a curriculum that many describe as archaic. Des Dixon (1994, p. 365) offers his description of today's curriculum:

> Today's curriculum is largely Victorian, a late nineteenth-century expression of the industrial revolution as applied to the education industry. We have tinkered with it but we have not changed it.

Another variable that complicates curriculum development is the environment in which it occurs, which is highly complex and forever changing. To remain effective, the curriculum must be designed and modified to reflect the changes in society at large, changes in the local community, changes in the local school, and changes in the students. Failure to consider and adjust for these changes would be tantamount to learning how to operate a car without ever putting it in traffic.

A Look at Some Early Attempts at Education Reform

Since the teachers' role in curriculum planning is expanding beyond their own classrooms, today's teachers cannot choose to ignore education reform. Therefore, it behooves all teachers to understand as much as possible about the overall national reform movement and about the specific reform elements (practices) that are occurring in their particular state. As Taba (1962, p. 9) pointed out:

> Decisions leading to change in curriculum organization have been made largely of pressure, by hunches, or in terms of expediency instead of being based on clear-cut theoretical considerations or tested knowledge.

Curriculum developers of the twenty-first century need an awareness of some of the history of the education reform movement of the 1980s and 1990s. This wave of education reform was started in a sporadic fashion with a few states introducing reform legislation. It has its origin in a climate of dissatisfaction and lack of confidence in local school boards and local educators (Des Dixon, 1994). This is not all bad; without a recognized need for change, there would be little improvement. Some people find it comforting to believe that this recent wave of reform had its origin in research, but nothing could be farther from the truth; the 1980s and 1990s reform wave was born in a climate of politics (Nelson, 1999). As Cook (1994, p. 48) says, ". . . this reform movement is all about power and who has it; those inside the schools or those outside." The good news is that: (1) to be effective, education programs must, and are, empowering teachers, and (2) all teachers can share this power and, in fact, must do so if education reform efforts are to be effective. Bernauer (1999, p. 69) says "Unless they [teachers] are empowered to deliver high quality, there is little chance that meaningful educational improvement will occur." Teachers need to be given control of their profession, and as Nelson (1999, p. 390) has written, this requires involving teachers with research:

> As in other significant professions, teachers should be prepared to be researchers into the practice that they control.

Actually, former governor William Winter of Mississippi is credited with having introduced the first bold statewide education reform movement. Governor Winter's major concern was with improving the state's economy, which he believed possible only through improving education. His Accountability in Instructional Management (AIM) program required all teachers to get together with fellow faculty members in their discipline and design a grade 1–12 curriculum. In every school and in all disciplines, each curriculum was to include objectives, content, teacher activities, student activities, materials, and test items *for every day's lesson.* Mississippi teachers were given five years to develop this new curriculum.

A Look at *A Nation at Risk* and Its Impact on Other Reports

Soon after the education reform process was underway in a few states, an explosion occurred. Dissatisfied with the performance of American students on standardized achievement tests, then secretary of education Terrel Bell initiated the National Commission on Excellence in Education. In 1983, this committee released its report, *A Nation at Risk,* to the president and to the public at large. Almost two decades later, the *A Nation at Risk/Goals 2000* agenda is, right or wrong, still at heart a movement founded on the establishment and broad implementation at the state and local levels of some form of nationally approved, uniform, world-class academic standards at all grade levels (Clinchy, 1998, p. 276; Borko & Elliot, 1999). Orlich (2000, p. 469–470) has summarized the report:

> *A Nation at Risk* recommended (1) a tougher set of academic basics for high school graduation, (2) higher standards for universities, (3) a longer school year and/or school day, (4) merit pay for top teachers, and (5) more citizen participation. Orlich also pointed out that this report was issued by a group that was dominated by people who did not work in the public schools. He also listed eight qualities of most reform reports:
>
> 1. The reforms are politically inspired and coerced by state governments.
> 2. The stress on higher student achievement is based on standards-based reports that were prepared by professional associations, not by local school boards.
> 3. Content standards tend to be collections of outcomes or student behaviors, assembled in a nonsystematic manner and without content hierarchies clearly shown.
> 4. Cost-benefit analyses are lacking from the reports on state school reforms.
> 5. Control of education has shifted to the national and state levels and away from localities.
> 6. The reform agendas, though fragmentary, are broad in scale and encompass most of the 50 states.
> 7. Politically inspired as the education reform movement has been, it must still be classified as being atheoretical—that is, its basic premises are

grounded not in empirically sound studies but rather in political enthusiasms and intentions.

8. Implied within these reforms is the conclusion that, as a consequence of standards and high-stakes state testing and assessment programs, there should be a dramatic increase in student achievement.

Orlich, D. C. "Education reform and limits to student achievement." Phi Delta Kappan, 81(6), 468–472.

Too much emphasis on standards and goals can shift the focus of education away from students; yet twenty-first century educators must keep the total welfare of students at the center of their thoughts and goals. Another way to express this common practice is to avoid putting concern for output above concern for input (or what happens to learners in the school). Nelson's comments (1999, p. 392) reflect this concern: "It is much healthier, less controlling, and more democratic to focus on the quality of what goes into the child than the quality of what comes out." For example, when comparing the test scores of American students to those of students in other nations, we must not assume that our schools have the same purpose as schools in other nations. While one might argue that we live in an international community and therefore must remain competitive in the world labor market, educators should ask themselves: Is this really the most important purpose of our schools? Is performance on such tests adequate for measuring the many functions of our schools?

The overemphasis on standardized test scores can take its toll on teachers. Vars (1997, p. 44) expresses concern over this outcome, stating, "Most of America's teachers today are anxious, if not paranoid, about preparing their students for state proficiency exams and other externally-imposed assessments."

Twenty-first century educators must avoid concluding that either the American schools or the work of American teachers has been inferior to schools and teachers in other nations based on standardized test scores when, in fact, the American students who have taken these tests have competed against the top few percent of selected students in other countries who have gone on to pursue formal secondary education programs. On the contrary, the proficiency demonstrated by American students is an accomplishment of great magnitude, and we should celebrate the work of twentieth-century teachers. Throughout the twentieth century, American schools have attempted to educate all of the country's youth. Granted, no country has reached perfection in this goal, but more importantly, until recently no other country had even aspired to this goal. Furthermore, our schools have been successful in retaining an increasing number of students. For example, in 1920 about 22 percent of the twenty-five to twenty-nine-year-olds were high school graduates, but by 1985, the proportion of students graduating had risen to 87 percent (Schlechty, 1990).

A third precaution that will serve twenty-first century teachers well is for educators to keep a balance in emphasis on all subjects. Tanner (1993, p. 296) addresses this concern. Referring to the reform reports, he notes that "our educational and curricular priorities are skewed to favor the development of an elite in the sciences and mathematics." Remember Sautter's comments (1994, p. 436) that it is not the sciences but the arts that contribute most to the development of positive personal traits: "The arts promote . . . social behavior . . ., self-discipline, self-motivation, self-esteem, and social interaction."

An additional precaution for future educators is to realize that lasting, meaningful reform must begin within the schools. Successful reform is something that teachers initiate. Unfortunately, as noted by Wagner (1998, p. 512), "Most approaches to systematic education reform are rooted in obsolete, top-down or expert-driven management beliefs and practices that reflect neither what we know about how people learn nor what we have come to understand about how organizations change." Failure to examine the reform process will lead to further disappointments (Hatch, 1998). There is, however, good news: A current inversion is sweeping the country, moving reform initiatives from state and federal bureaucracies to local districts and schools.

A final precaution is offered at this juncture: twenty-first century educators at all levels will need to be involved with research, which has been noticeably neglected by many educators. Bernauer (1999, p. 69) points out that "Initiatives supported by research offer the most promising ways to develop school-improvement programs." Examine the current reform practices in your local schools. Have they grown out of real teacher or student needs? Are these practices supported by research? Could/should the local teachers test them to see if they are working?

A Positive Turn

After a decade of negative reports, a couple of incidents occurred that have exposed the intentional misuse of testing to portray the schools negatively. Consequently, Gough (1993, p. 108) predicted an upturn in the public's perception of American education:

> But the public's perception of our profession took a turn for the better in 1991. That's when the first "Bracey Report" on the condition of education (titled "Why Can't They Be Like We Were?") appeared in the pages of the *Kappan*. That's also when the third draft of a report on the condition of American education, written by researchers at the Sandia National Laboratories, began to circulate informally throughout the education community—and then beyond it, to a broader audience.
>
> The Sandia researchers, employees of the Department of Energy, had no vested interest in defending education. . . . [They] found, in the process, essentially the same thing that Gerald Bracey had found: the schools were not in the state of collapse that some critics had claimed. . . .Thus, the Sandia study helped shift conventional wisdom. The "oh-ain't-the-schools-awful" refrain quickly began to give way to today's more realistic assertion that the schools are doing just about as well as they ever did. . .
>
> For years, the National Assessment of Educational Progress (NAEP) has been called "the nation's report card." Isolated results on this test have been used as

evidence of the deterioration of American schools. Yet, when viewed over a 20 year span, Bracey (1991) reported, "They are very stable." While the performance of white students has remained constant, the performance of Afro-Americans and Hispanics have actually risen.

With all the hoopla over our schools graduating illiterates, the writing scores on the nation's report card "have not changed since 1974." The greatest alarm set off in the bulk of the reform reports focuses on the declining math scores; yet, the NAEP math scores have remained constant since 1973. Science scores are slightly below their level at the time this testing began in 1969. Another major test of the performance of American schools is the Standardized Achievement Test. Bracey (1991) has said that, "Since 1977 when the National Center for Education Statistics (1990, Vol. I) reported the results as 'stagnation at relatively low levels' of achievement, every one- or two-point change in SAT scores has been front-page news. Less has been made of the fact that blacks, Asian-Americans, Native Americans, Mexican-Americans, and Puerto Ricans *all* scored higher on the SAT in 1990 than in 1975."

Another important fact that the public seldom sees is how the population who takes the SAT is determined. Since the test is taken voluntarily and since it is used for college admission, the annual audience is whoever shows up Saturday morning to take it. Considering the increase in the number and range of students who take this test, it is remarkable that the scores have held steady. For example, when the test was initiated in 1941, the subjects were 10,654 mostly white, male students headed for Ivy League and other prestigious private universities. During the 1988–90 school year, one and a quarter million students (1,025,523), of which 27 percent were members of minorities, took the test. Furthermore, 52 percent were females, and historically females have not scored as well as males on the SAT.

Narrow Views

Since the National Commission on Excellence (1983) released *A Nation at Risk,* over four hundred national- and state-level reform reports have followed. Most share the flaws that characterized their grandparent report, and most have additional flaws. Naturally, the reports represent the interests of their authors. Most reform reports have been written by committees whose interests or agenda ranged from economics to defense. Because the reports are written by special-interest groups and because most of the groups are politically based, many of these reports are narrow in their perspective. Whatever the purposes of our schools—and there is no implication that there is, could ever be, or should be universal agreement on their purposes—American schools do not exist with the sole purpose of producing competitive workers, or superior soldiers, or world-competitive economists. Thus, since many of the reports view the purpose of the schools in light of the mission of their interest group, the reports are too narrow.

Overall Purposes

Another flaw in many of the education reform reports concerns the overall intended purpose of the reports, that is, the reasons for their existence and their intended effects. The language used is significant. Some of the reform efforts use inflammatory language, which does not suggest an honest effort to inform or enlighten the public but rather may be an attempt to excite and alarm. For example, the grandparent report, *A Nation at Risk,* which set the tone for later reports, says, "If an unfriendly foreign power had attempted to impose on America the mediocre educational performance that exists today, we might well have viewed it as an act of war" (p. 5). This report also states that American schools are "drowning in a rising tide of mediocrity." Another major report, *Action for Excellence* (Education Commission of the States, 1983), which appeared at about the same time, speaks of "a need for survival" and uses such terms as "emergency" and "urgency." Intentional or not, the use of exaggeration and inflammatory language misleads the public.

This concern about the use of reform reports continues. As the 1990s were ending, Nelson (1999, p. 388) made the following criticism of reform that was underway in one state:

> In Minnesota, the governor, the majority in the legislature, the state board of education, the commissioner, and the homogenized educational bureaucracy have enacted, developed, sold, and defended the new Minnesota graduation rule that teachers are "to implement." Small wonder that teacher opposition to the reform has been, for the most part, muffled.

The act of planning reform at the state and national levels and then imposing it on local schools causes teachers and principals to further question the purpose of the reform.

Unsound Recommendations

Another common flaw in many education reform reports is in their recommendations. Because most of the reports were written by laypeople, most of whom are not educators, many of their recommendations are not educationally sound. For example, *A Nation at Risk* recommended both a longer school day and a longer school year. In other words, the critics were saying the performance of the schools is mediocre (meaning "very poor"), so give us more of it, which is illogical. Most of the reports call for more math and science at the expense of the arts and humanities. Most appear to address only the secondary curriculum, on the assumption that whatever is good for secondary students and teachers is good for their elementary counterparts.

Few of the earlier reports addressed the fact that a large number of students are on drugs. Few addressed the fact that teachers are overworked. Few mentioned the need to discover ways of motivating students. Until recently, few of the reports mentioned societal problems that must be addressed and overcome before the schools can reach their academic goals. Hodgkinson (1990, p. 10) lists some of these conditions:

- Since 1987, one-fourth of all preschool children in the United States have been living in poverty.
- Every year, about 350,000 children are born to mothers who were addicted to cocaine during pregnancy. Those who survive birth become children with strikingly short attention spans, poor coordination, and much worse. Of course, the schools will have to teach these children, and getting such children ready for kindergarten costs around $40,000 each   about the same as for children with fetal alcohol syndrome.
- Today, 15 million children are being reared by single mothers, whose family income averages about $11,400 in 1988 dollars (within $1,000 of the poverty line). The average family income for a married couple with children is slightly over $34,000 a year.
- Twenty percent of America's preschool children have not been vaccinated against polio.
- The "Norman Rockwell" family—a working father, a housewife mother, and two children of school age—constitutes only 6% of U.S. households today.

TABLE 1.1   Summary of Criticisms of Education Reform and Implication for Curricularists

Criticism	Implications for Curricularists
Faulty conclusions	Curricularists must expose the myths that commonly develop when people are misinformed.
Promotion of the narrow goals of reform committees	Curricularists must constantly remind the public that the goals of education are many and varied.
Educationally unsound recommendations	Curricularists must use the research and literature to expose recommendations that are educationally unsound.
Failure to involve teachers, administrators, and professors in the development of educational reform	Curricularists must find ways to become involved not only in the implementation of reform but also in the developmental stages. This includes lobbying local legislators, attending general sessions, and writing letters to offer time and expertise.
Lack of research base	Curricularists must use the research and literature to guide their own work. This requires being a wise consumer of others' research and being involved in research studies.

- One-fourth of pregnant mothers receive no physical care of any sort during the crucial first trimester of pregnancy. About 20% of handicapped children would not be impaired had their mothers had one physical exam during the first trimester, which could have detected potential problems.
- At least two million school-age children have no adult supervision at all after school. Two million more are being reared by neither parent.
- On any given night, between 50,000 and 200,000 children have no home. (In 1988, 40% of shelter users were families with children).
- In 1987, child protection agencies received 2.2 million reports of child abuse or neglect—triple the number received in 1976.

Positive Outcomes

Not all of the outcomes of education reform efforts have been negative. On the contrary, there is much good news to report, and it is growing daily. For example, the reports provided the education profession a great service in reaffirming in the public's mind the importance of education. Consequently, in several states the level of financial support has been raised. Equally important, this increased public awareness of the importance of education has raised the overall level of parental support. Increased parent participation is a necessity for maximum academic gains.

The education reform reports are also focusing teachers' attention on the broader curricula across the school (Hall, 1998). Historically, most teachers have not been involved with curriculum development beyond their own classroom. Until recently, most teachers have not been prepared or permitted to get involved with schoolwide planning. Involvement in their school's total curriculum should enable teachers to avoid or at least minimize disruptions and duplications between their classes and those of other teachers, particularly those classes that students take during the years just prior to and just following the teacher's classes.

Administrators

There is more good news; administrators, too, have become more involved with curriculum planning. During the 1980s and 1990s the level of involvement of school administrators in curriculum and instruction has reached heights unprecedented since the days of the one-room school. Research on effective schools has made educators aware of the need for administrators—particularly building principals—to be at the center of instructional and curriculum planning. Recognizing the need for administrators to be directly involved in instructional and curriculum planning, Terrel Bell (1993, p. 597) has said, "It is futile to even try to improve a school if the leadership is lackluster."

To serve students from a wide range of diverse backgrounds, administrators must make their schools inviting to everyone, taking a proactive stance and not just waiting for parents and other community members to become involved.

Other Changes

The reform movements are rapidly changing the roles and lives of teachers, administrators, parents, counselors, designated curriculum leaders, instructional supervisors, and students. Representatives from all of these groups are responding to the demands of education reform in many ways, ranging from desperate panic in efforts to meet the reform challenges to absolute refusal to comply with reform demands to unprecedented levels of enthusiasm, energy, and ownership over cutting-edge innovations.

Teacher Education

The focus of education reform programs of the 1980s and 1990s has been mainly on elementary and secondary schools; however, at the start of a new century, this focus is broadening to include the higher education institutions. Teacher education colleges and departments have three major responsibilities in the educational reform movements. First, they must prepare students to be knowledgeable about the major reform practices in their state and skilled in implementing these elements. Effective implementation of school reform will require that teachers, designated curriculum directors, instructional supervisors, administrators, parents, and counselors (1) be comfortable and confident in their ability to carry out reform, and (2) acquire and maintain a positive attitude toward the reform movement. Teacher education colleges and departments must provide students with opportunities to develop these necessary understandings, skills, and attitudes.

The second role of education colleges and departments is to help teachers assess the value of each reform practice for their school and students. Frankly, some of the reform practices should never have been implemented. Clark and Astuto (1994, p. 513) explain:

> Many of the reform initiatives that are currently most popular could be dismissed as ridiculous on their face if they were not devised and supported by apparently credible advocates.

Unfortunately, some of the earlier reform reports attempted to convince the public that the underlying cause of the perceived failure of American schools is weak teachers. The good news is that more modern reports have not reinforced that belief. A decade after *A Nation at Risk* was published, its initiator, former secretary of education Terrel Bell (1993, pp. 595, 597) wrote:

> We have foolishly concluded that any problems with the levels of academic achievement have been caused by faulty schools staffed by inept teachers and by fixing the schools we can attain the levels of success we so desperately need in this decade.

Mr. Bell continued by saying:

> We also know that teacher leadership of and involvement in school improvement must become a more integral part of our plans.

A third major role of teacher education colleges and departments in education reform is to help in-service teachers, administrators, curriculum developers, instructional supervisors, and counselors gear up to perform the reform requirements in their state. Teachers, particularly, hold the key to success or failure in reforming the schools. Clark and Astuto (1994, p. 520) explain, "No one can reform our schools for us. If there is to be authentic reform in American education, it must be a grassroots movement." This is precisely the viewpoint of this book. We hope to familiarize readers with the nature of the curriculum development process and the nature of education reform and to prepare them to apply sound foundations and principles of curriculum development to meet their responsibilities in implementing major education reform. Keep in mind at all times the two major purposes of U.S. schools: learning and socialization.

Identifying True Weaknesses

Current education reform efforts have resulted from perceived weaknesses in American schools. Although, as already stressed, some of these perceptions are dead wrong, some are not; some of the reform reports identify major weaknesses that permeate the schools. Separately and collectively, these weaknesses prevent American students from reaching their maximum potential. Correcting the condition will require some major curriculum adjustments within and beyond the classroom which, in turn, will require changing the ways teachers and other educators use the curriculum development process in their classrooms and in the school at large.

As you prepare to launch your own program to contribute to education reform, a logical way to begin your reform efforts is by examining the weaknesses in the current education system. The following paragraphs discuss some of the areas that many educators say need to be improved.

Failure to Use Research

At a time when the National Council for Accreditation of Teacher Education is requiring a sound knowledge base and a sound theoretical model, there is evidence that the public schools are ignoring these all-important issues. According to Egbert (1984, p. 14), "Teachers ignore research and overestimate the value of personal experience." When teachers ignore research, they forfeit the opportunity to bring maximum improvement into their classrooms (Nelson, 1999). Brown (1990) has said that teachers do not base their planning on the factors that affect achievement. Too often, the major goal of teachers is to cover the required topics. This attitude has carried over to the students. The teachers' desperation to cover the material does not go unnoticed by students. Stefanich (1990, p. 50) states that, "They (students) view learning only as the acquisition of knowledge."

These are, admittedly, broad generalizations and as such may often be erroneous assumptions. In fact, some teachers are actively conducting research. Some teacher education colleges and some departments, such as those found at Michigan State University and the University of Maryland, have histories of collaborating with local schools in conducting meaningful action research studies. If reform is successful, this practice will become commonplace in twenty-first century schools.

Teacher education colleges and departments must assume major responsibility for graduating students who are prepared as both conductors and consumers of research. These skills are prerequisite to developing an appreciation for research.

The relationship between the role of the schools and the way educators view research is ironic. From the perspective of the reconstructionist, a major role of the schools is to lead or shape society, yet society seems to be leading the schools in the use of research. It is unthinkable that the advancements made in industry, architecture, business, agriculture, engineering, medicine, or any other profession could have occurred without the major role that research plays in these professions.

Graduate curricula for educators reflect a recognition of the importance of research to education in that almost all graduate degree programs require one or more courses in research, and most advanced graduate programs require all candidates to conduct their own research studies, usually in the form of a major thesis or dissertation. Teacher educators must involve students in authentic problem solving to ensure that they view their research courses and assignments not as obstacles in their programs to be overcome but as powerful tools to be developed and used on a daily basis in the schools. It is perhaps even more critical that undergraduate teacher education programs engage all students in research, both as a subject to be studied and as a project to be carried out.

There is much reason for hope. A shift of teacher location from the isolated classroom to the broader school curriculum planning arena is occurring (Wang, Haertel, & Walberg, 1998). This movement is discussed further in Chapter 4. Later in this book you will also see that, ironically and unfortunately, the area of education where research lags most is the area where research could most improve education. Can you identify that area? You can test your hypothesis when we return to the topic in a later chapter.

To end this discussion on research on a negative note would be short-sighted, for the picture is rapidly changing; many schools are making remarkable progress with action research and, indeed are using action research to restructure their entire curriculum. The following case study by David Stine is a good model that other school faculties can follow.

Case Study

Action Research as an Instrument of Change

David Stine

Background Information

Many of the United States border states are confronted with a dramatic change in the demographics of students in the public schools. Increasing numbers of new students enroll with limited ability to read or speak the English language. Some arrive in the upper grades or even high school and have never been in a formal school setting. The newly enrolled students often represent a variety of the cultures from Asia, South and Central America, and Mexico. Teachers are faced with classes of students with a wide range of differences in their understanding of English and of American culture, and teachers in turn often have a limited understanding of the students' cultures.

In many schools there is no longer a predominant majority of any race of students, and there is a multiplicity of cultures and ethnic backgrounds to consider. Many schools are using the same textbooks, the same teaching methods, and the same assessment instruments in their classrooms that were introduced before these demographic changes occurred.

The Educational Community

With compulsory attendance policies in place and political pressure for minimal dropout rates ever present, schools are committed to providing appropriate education for all students, but class sizes are increasing and new funding is nonexistent. The faculty, administration, and staff are not sure how to cope with this changing student environment, and the community is concerned about dropping test scores.

At the state level there are debates in the legislature regarding the usefulness of bilingual education and of teaching English as a second language (ESL), how to teach reading, and even how to build student self-esteem. The state school board association also studies these problems, and the professors at the local universities can offer a variety of solutions to these concerns verified by their own research, but they seldom agree on any issue. The real challenge for the career educator is to determine what needs to be done to provide the most powerful teaching and learning environment for the students and then to take action.

(Continued)

The School

San Antonio High School is a large suburban comprehensive school of 3,000 students in grades 9 to 12. It is the original school in a union high school district that has spawned six other schools in neighboring communities and cities as the population has fled the urban center. Affordable housing, an increased service market, and major transportation links have made this area attractive for newcomers. A new principal has been hired to replace a retiring one and has been given the challenge to energize the faculty, assess the student needs, improve test scores, and build community relations.

The Principal

The new principal was the first administrator to be hired from outside the district in the last 12 years. The central administration and the board of education wanted to hire an experienced proven leader who had a track record of positive relations with faculty and a person who believed in a decentralized organization where teachers would be included in the decision-making process. The principal they chose had a demonstrated record of shared decision making and teacher empowerment in his previous schools. In addition, his references had praised his high energy and his work with parents and community. He was noted for his organizational ability and problem-solving skills.

The Case

Upon arriving on the job in the summer, when the faculty and students were enjoying vacation time, the new principal wanted to use this time to meet parents, get acquainted with local business owners, and invite faculty in for individual conferences. His intent was to discover the perceptions of the various stakeholders about the school. Two key questions he asked were, "What are you proudest of at SAHS" and "What needs our attention?"

In an effort to introduce himself to parents, the principal visited the local newspaper, and an article was published that profiled him and included his offer to meet with parents in their homes "any time—morning, noon, or night—during the first three weeks of August." Key parents who had held leadership positions or whose students were in leadership roles in school were also contacted individually. These key parents included booster club supporters, parents of scholarship winners, parents of student council members, and parents of incoming freshmen who had been active in the middle schools. The principal also held 17 coffee clatches, and their locations were recorded on a map of the school district that the principal later used for strategizing. The goal was to reach as many parents as possible and to learn about the demographics and living conditions of the students. This strategy also revealed the languages spoken in the homes. A guest book was available at each of the 17 homes where gatherings were held, and participants listed their names and the names and grade levels of their children in school. The mapping provided a geographic profile of the school district and clarified where centers of parent interest were and where additional outreach might be needed in the future. Four additional parent meetings were held after a second

(Continued)

list of invitations was extended to parents of special education students, Chapter 1 students, and bilingual students. The same two questions were asked at each meeting, and this completed the data gathering from the parents' needs assessment.

The principal also visited local businesses, service clubs, and special interest groups, including the Kiwanis, Rotary, Lions, Soroptomists, Toastmasters, American Association of University Women, Business and Professional Women, Veterans of Foreign Wars, American Legion, Chamber of Commerce, Hispanic Chamber, Salvation Army, and the local YMCA. The principal also contacted city and county governmental agencies, including the regional offices of elected state and county government office holders. At each visit the principal's message was similar: "I'm here and listening. What is good about our school, what needs attention, and how can we work together?"

About one-third of the faculty and staff accepted the invitation to come in and meet the new principal in an informal setting. After inquiring about their professional background, the principal asked about their current teaching assignment, about any extracurricular positions they might hold, and especially about any special interest or ability they might have. The purpose was to determine interest and ability to become involved in future changes at the school. After the preliminary conversation, the principal asked the same broad questions he had posed to parents and business owners, and then he did a lot of listening. This technique set the stage for collaboration and demonstrated a collegial approach to problem solving. An underlying message from the principal was his belief in the philosophy that "Power with is stronger than power over." Conversations with faculty included inquiry about what they felt needed "fixing" at the school and what contributions each might make. Much of the feedback from faculty could be summarized as, "Things are not the way they used to be. Changes are going to have to happen, and we are all part of the solution."

The stage was now set, with the initial information gathered and the climate for positive change in place, so that real collaborative research could be conducted with the administration and faculty working together. The ultimate goal was the improvement of teaching and increased learning for all students at the school. The faculty was ready to be included in the action research model of problem solving.

As the weeks of summer slipped away, more and more faculty and staff returned to work. As soon as the three co-administrators and the six counselors arrived, a half-day retreat was held. Again, the initial focus was to inquire about everyone's perceptions of the school and of what needed attention. After a period of brainstorming and summarizing, the new information was combined with the data gathered from parents, faculty, and other community members. During the last hour of the session, the members present explored what people, agencies, institutions, or other sources were available that could assist in interpreting all of the information that had been gathered. Responses included key personnel at other schools, district office staff, county educational office staff, and university professors. Members of the counseling staff and an assistant principal volunteered to work with faculty to assess previous test scores to diagnosis areas of weakness in student achievement. A second assistant principal took the leadership role in

(Continued)

working with department chairs, and especially with foreign language teachers and bilingual staff, to identify what curricular changes might be useful to assist students with special needs.

A powerful statement was issued which included the endorsement of the group and stated that there was substantial talent and competency within the faculty, and that they had been waiting to be asked for their input and to participate and to explore creative means to meet the new challenges with which they were being confronted. It was now time to open school and to begin the informal process of planning and continuing the action research already begun. Planning teams of volunteer faculty and department chairs began to review summaries of all the data that had been gathered. The principal introduced the teams to a seven-step model that included: 1. defining the problem, 2. proposing a method, 3. data collection, 4. data analysis, 5. reporting results, 6. action planning, and 7. evaluation. As faculty members discovered, action research is merely an organized step-by-step approach to solving a problem.

The initial step was to determine what was the most significant problem facing the school. After considerable deliberation, it was concluded that students with limited fluency in English needed extra help and a specialized program. With this focus it was then determined that an internal search for ideas and talent would be made to find the appropriate methods to solve this problem. Test scores were reviewed, specialists were consulted, and alternatives were considered. The data that had been collected were reviewed and analyzed to determine whether the school needed to be reorganized. The suggestions and results were then reported to the entire faculty and to the appropriate district staff to solicit their reactions and their suggestions. The final recommendation was to develop a "newcomers' school" on campus where students with limited English speaking proficiency would be placed for three periods per day. These students would attend regular classes for the remaining three periods. The core courses would include reading, writing, and speaking of English and would incorporate social science and mathematics. Students would be immersed with regular students in physical education and two elective classes. The basic classes would be limited to 20 students, and funds from various categorical programs would be utilized to finance the program. It was a clear consensus that the classes should be held on the regular campus and that the students should be a part of the regular student body. Evaluation would be key component, and records of tests given before and after participation in the program would be maintained. Routine assessment of student progress would be done on a weekly basis. Samples of student work would also be kept to verify progress, and a report to the board of education would be made at the end of the year.

With the program in place by the second semester, administrators, counselors, and faculty made special efforts to ensure accurate and thorough communication concerning student progress and overall program effectiveness. The faculty felt good about their participation in planning the program and recognized that they were an integral part of the solution. As a follow-up measure, plans were made to communicate to the community about the program and to invite parents to the school to observe the classes. Press releases would be written at regular intervals, and the total faculty would be kept apprised of the status and progress of the program.

(Continued)

Issues for Further Reflection and Application

1. How would you involve faculty members in the general data gathering stages?
2. What are some ways to involve students in the problem-solving process that may have been overlooked?
3. Do you think the action research model may have been short circuited in any way? If so, explain your answer.
4. Were the parents and community connected to the school by this process?
5. What is your assessment of the principal's utilization of time during the summer?
6. Would you object if your son or daughter were placed in this "newcomers' school"?
7. What might be the adverse consequences of a "school within a school"?
8. Could you use the action research model to solve a problem at your school? If so, describe the problem and how it might be solved.
9. What are some alternative problem-solving strategies that might have been used in this case?

Suggested Readings

Bichel, W. E., & Hattrup, R. A. (1995). Teachers and researchers in collaboration: Reflections on the process. *American Educational Research Journal, 32*(1), 35–62.

Johnson, C. C., et al. (1995). Using action research to assess instruction. *Reading Horizons, 35*(3), 199–208.

McLean, J. E. (1995). *Improving education through action research: A guide for administrators and teachers.* Thousand Oaks, CA: Corwin Press.

Sagor. R. (1993). *How to conduct collaborative action research.* Alexandria, VA: ASCD.

Wallace, M. (1987). A historical review of action research: Some implications for the education of teachers in their managerial role. *Journal of Education for Teaching, 13*(2), 97–115.

For example, the principal discussed in the case study took several initiatives to reach out and pull in members from various segments of the community. Do you think any of his strategies will be more effective than others? Which strategies would work best in your community?

Effective schools research has found that parent involvement is directly linked with academic success. Constructivists believe that each student must link newly acquired information to previously acquired understanding, but, as shown earlier in this chapter's case study, the principal and teachers do not have to prescribe a method for involving parents in the creation of new knowledge. Instead, this principal chose to use action research, letting the parents and other community members design their own strategies for helping students learn. What advantage do you see in this more open approach?

A major deterrent to teachers using research is fear. Many teachers feel insecure, perhaps believing they lack the skills required to conduct complex research studies, like the ones they studied in graduate school. As seen in this case study, however, teachers needn't conduct such complex studies, nor must they do their research alone. On the contrary, some of the best research that teachers do is in collaboration with their former professors and other teachers; collaboration is empowering. Also, some of the best studies are not highly complex studies. Rather, they are simple, practical studies about practical problems teachers have encountered. Did you notice that the teachers in this case study began simply by identifying a problem? What effect do you think this had on reducing their fear?

An Emphasis on Constructivism

Another positive reform quality is the emphasis on constructivism. Constructivists describe learning in terms of building connections between prior knowledge and new ideas and claim that effective teaching helps students construct an organized set of concepts that relates new and old ideas.

Teaching students to connect new information with existing understanding requires purposeful planning. Teachers must give assignments that require students to describe the process they use to explore new content as it relates to what they already know (Markle et al., 1990). Nicaise and Barnes (1996, p. 206) explain the role of constructivist teachers:

> The role of the teacher changes from information provider, sequencer of information, and test creator to guide, scaffolder, and problem or task presenter. Teacher responsibilities include creating information-rich environments where students think, explore, and construct meaning.

Although schools have many varied purposes (discussed in detail in Chapter 3), a universally recognized purpose is to educate. One perception of education is the process through which individuals learn to alter their environments and their own behavior to better cope with life situations. These goals require both academic and social growth. This process involves acquiring new information and changing it into meaningful knowledge. Indeed, as perceived by constructivists, this is the purpose of curriculum content. Content may even be defined as information that is selected to later be changed into useful knowledge. Similarly, activities are selected to become meaningful experiences to students. These processes will be discussed further in Chapter 7.

Summary

Traditionally, as applied to education, the term curriculum meant a "list of courses," but, through the years, it has come to mean many things to different people. To some, the curriculum is a written document that purports to guide students' learning; to others it is the activities themselves. Still others view the curriculum as a statement of objectives or expected outcomes.

Whatever the definition, educators agree that if it is to be worthwhile, the curriculum must be more than a document that is prepared, filed, and ignored. An awareness of the different definitions enhances the curriculum planner's ability to plan, execute, evaluate, and improve curricula. Furthermore, a sound, comprehensive understanding of curriculum is needed today to guard against the narrow view of some reformers who may aspire to use the curriculum to achieve their narrow goals.

The presence of a hidden curriculum, that is, the impressions and attitudes that arc taught implicitly, amplifies each teacher's need to have a firm grasp of the concept of curriculum. A sound understanding of curriculum will prepare teachers to better support positive reform changes while suppressing undesirable trends. Teachers in diverse settings have a special need to eliminate the negative effects of the hidden curriculum and to instead use the hidden curriculum to provide positive experiences for all students. To strengthen our youth and our nation, all teachers including those with homogeneous classrooms must prepare all students to live and work positively in diverse settings. Special effort should be made to involve parents from all segments of the community, thus developing a sense of ownership among all.

Many of the 1980s and 1990s reform reports followed the pattern set by *A Nation at Risk* in defining single-minded, self-centered goals for America's schools. Nevertheless, reform efforts overall have made citizens aware that teachers are the essential key to making major improvements in our schools and, as such, must be the leaders in reforming the curriculum. Twenty-first century educators will need good research skills and a sound understanding of curriculum if they are to be prepared to evaluate each reform report, support its positive goals, and avoid its pitfalls.

In the 1990s schools experienced a strong swing toward constructivism to meet higher standards set at national, state, and local levels. Parental involvement is essential for maximum academic and social achievement; essentially, learning must be the cooperative endeavor of teachers, students, and parents forming a learning community by solving problems cooperatively.

Learning Questions

1. What characteristics make some definitions of curriculum more useful in curriculum development than others?

2. What must teachers and others know about the process of curriculum development to enhance their school's reform efforts?

3. What must teachers and others know about school reform in their state to promote sound school reform through curriculum development?

4. Considering your experience in schools, the definitions in this chapter, and your role in education, how would you define *curriculum*?

5. What is the strongest evidence of the power of the hidden curriculum that you have witnessed?

6. What would you find helpful to your efforts to conduct research at your school?

7. What must teachers and others know about human behavior, politics, and the nature of schools to garner the support of their colleagues in education reform?

8. What political factors in your school might inhibit or promote reform?

9. Among the reform practices or policies in your state, what features can you identify that will serve student needs?

10. Can you identify features in local reform efforts that can be used to meet the special needs of minority students? If so, what are these features, and how can they be used more effectively toward this end?

11. Describe any elements in your school's hidden curriculum that work against minority students or education reform. For each element, tell how you might alter the effect of the hidden curriculum.

12. How can your faculty increase its political influence on education reform in your state and district?

13. What evidence of constructivism have you seen in school curricula?

Suggested Activities

1. Select a topic in your teaching field and identify and list the major concepts in a week's lessons.

2. Research the literature on effective schools and make a list of the qualities common to these schools.

3. Select an important concept in your teaching field and grade level, preferably one that students find difficult to comprehend, and devise a step-by-step method to help students relate this concept to prior knowledge.

4. Examine the list of definitions of *curriculum* in Figure 1.1. Create your own definition and use the definitions provided in the figure and text to support your definition.

5. Make a list of the major education reform practices in your state.

6. Assess your own reasons for taking this course and identify at least two important professional aims or goals that will give you direction and motivation throughout the course.

7. Examine the list of reasons the Eastwood Middle School naysayers gave as to why teachers resist education reform and restate each reason making it a reason to support education reform.

8. Interview a local school superintendent, principal, or counselor and get a list of the major education reform laws in your state. Select one or more of these practices that you would like to support. Between now and the end of this course, build a strong case of support for this reform practice.

9. Develop a strategy to increase your faculty's political influence in your community and state.

10. Design an activity to educate your students about contributions that each of several local cultures has made to the larger community or to the entire country.

Works Cited and Suggested Readings

Apple, M. (1979). *Ideology and curriculum.* Boston: Routledge & Kegan.

Ballew, H. (1999). "Mathematics in the next century." Chapter 10 in B. D. Day (Ed.) *Teaching and learning in the new millennium.* Indianapolis: Kappa Delta Pi.

Banks, J. A. (1999). "Multicultural citizenship education." Chapter 5 in B. D. Day (Ed.) *Teaching and learning in the new millennium.* Indianapolis: Kappa Delta Pi.

Beauchamp, G. A. (1981). *Curriculum theory* (4th ed.). Itasca, IL: Peacock Publishers.

Bell, T. H. (1993). Reflections one decade after "A Nation at Risk." *Phi Delta Kappan, 74*(8), 592–600.

Bernauer, J. A. (1999). Emerging standards: Empowerment with purpose. *Kappa Delta Pi Record, 35*(2), 68–70, 74.

Borko, H., & Elliott, R. (1999). Hands-on pedagogy versus hands-off accountability. *Phi Delta Kappan, 80*(5), 394–400.

Brown, D. S. (1990). Middle level teachers' perceptions of action research. *Middle School Journal, 22*(2), 30–32.

Bracey, G. W. (1991). Why can't they be like we were? *Phi Delta Kappan, 73*(2), 104–117.

Caswell, H. L., & Campbell, D. S. (1935). *Curriculum development.* New York: American Book Company.

Clark, D. L., & Astuto, T. A. (1994). Redirecting reform: Challenges to popular assumptions about teachers and students. *Phi Delta Kappan, 75*(7), 513–520.

Clinchy, E. (1998). The educationally challenged American school district. *Phi Delta Kappan, 80*(4), 272–278.

Cook, A. (1994, January). Whose story gets told? Rethinking research on schools. *Education Week, 13*(17), 48.

Davidman, & Davidman, P. T. (1997). *Teaching with a multicultural perspective* (2nd ed.). New York: Longman.

Day, B. (1999). "Participatory education: A proactive approach to U.S. education in the 21st century." In B. D. Day (Ed.) *Teaching and learning in the new millennium.* Indianapolis: Kappa Delta Pi.

Des Dixon, R. G. (1994). Future schools and how to get there from here. *Phi Delta Kappan, 75*(5), 360–365.

Doll, R. (1989). *Curriculum improvement: Decision making and process* (7th ed.). Boston: Allyn & Bacon.

Egbert, R. L. (1984). The role of research in teacher education. In R. L. Egbert & M. M. Kluender (Eds.), *Using research to improve teacher education.* Lincoln, NE: American Association of Colleges for Teacher Education.

Foshay, A. W. (1969). Changing interpretations of the elementary curriculum. In H. G. Shane (Ed.), *The American elementary school.* Thirteenth yearbook of the John Dewey Society.

Fullan, M. G. (1993). Why teachers must become change agents. *Educational Leadership, 50*(6), 12–17.

Gay, G. (1990). Achieving educational equality through curriculum desegregation. *Phi Delta Kappan, 72*(1), 61–62.

Goodlad, J. I. (1997). *In praise of education.* New York: Teachers College Press.

Gough, P. B. (1993). A view from the outside. *Phi Delta Kappan, 74*(9), 669.

Haberman, M., & Bracey, G. W. (1997). The anti-learning curriculum of urban schools. Part 1: The problem. *Kappa Delta Pi Record, 33*(3), 88–89.

Haberman, M. (1999). The anti-learning curriculum. Part 2: The solution. *Kappa Delta Pi Record, 35*(2), 71–74.

Hall, H. (1998). D. E. Pitton. Interview with Howard Hall, director of curriculum, District 191, June 5th.

Hatch, T. (1998). How comprehensive can comprehensive reform be? *Phi Delta Kappan, 79*(7), 518–522.

Henson, K. T. (1996, Summer) Why curriculum development needs reforming. *Educational Horizons, 74*(4), 157–162.

Henson, K. T. (1986). America's public schools: A look at the reports. *USA Today, 114,* 75–77.

Hodgkinson, H. (1990). Reform vs. reality. *Phi Delta Kappan, 73*(1), 9–16.

Hutchins, R. M. (1936). *The higher learning in America.* New Haven, CT: Yale University Press.

Markle, G., Johnston, J. H., Geer, C., & Meichtry, Y. (1990). Teaching for understanding. *Middle School Journal, 22*(2), 53–57.

McNeil, J. D. (1990). *Curriculum: A comprehensive introduction.* New York: HarperCollins.

National Center for Education Statistics, *The condition of education 1990, Vol. I. Elementary and secondary education.* Washington, DC: U.S. Department of Education, p. 9.

National Commission on Excellence in Education (1983). *A Nation at Risk.*

National Council for Accreditation of Teacher Education (1990). Standards, procedures, and policies for the accreditation of professional units. Washington, DC: NCATE.

Nelson, W. W. (1999). The Emperor redux. *Phi Delta Kappan, 80*(5), 387–392.

Nicaise, M., & Barnes, D. (1996). The union of technology, constructivism, and teacher education. *Journal of Teacher Education, 47*(3), 205–212.

Oliva, P. F. (1997). *Developing the curriculum* (4th ed.). New York: Longman.

Orlich, D. C. Education reform and limits to student achievement. *Phi Delta Kappan, 81*(6), 468–472.

Phenix, P. H. (1962). The disciplines as curriculum content. In Harry Passow (Ed.). New York: Columbia University Teachers College Press.

Pitton, D. E. (1999). Interview with Howard Hall, director of curriculum, District 191, 5 June.

Popham, W. J., & Baker, E. L. (1970). *Systematic instruction.* Englewood Cliffs, NJ: Prentice-Hall.

Sautter, R. C. (1994). An arts education school reform strategy. *Phi Delta Kappan, 75*(6), 432–437.

Saylor, J. G., & Alexander, W. M. (1966). *Curriculum planning for modern schools.* New York: Holt, Rinehart, and Winston.

Schlechty, P. C. (1990). *Schools for the 21st century: Leadership imperatives for educational reform.* San Francisco: Jossey-Bass Publishers.

Schubert, W. H. (1986). *Curriculum: Perspective, paradigm, and possibility.* New York: Macmillan.

Smith, B. O., Stanley, W. O., & Shores, J. H. (1957). *Fundamentals of curriculum development: Renewal.* New York: Harcourt, Brace, Jovanovich.

Stefanich, G. P. (1990). Cycles of cognition. *Middle School Journal, 22*(2), 47–52.

Taba, H. (1962). *Curriculum development: Theory and practice.* New York: Harcourt, Brace, Jovanovich, Inc.

Tanner, D. (1993). A nation "truly" at risk. *Phi Delta Kappan, 75*(4), 288–297.

Tanner, D., & Tanner, L. N. (1980). *Curriculum development: Theory into practice.* New York: Macmillan.

Tatum, B. D. (1997). *Why are all the black kids sitting in the cafeteria? And other conversations about race.* New York: Basic Books.

Thompson, S., & Gregg, L. (1997, May) Reculturing middle schools for meaningful change. *Middle School Journal, 28*(5), 27–31.

Van Gulick, R. (1990). Functionalism, information, and content. In W. G. Lylcan (Ed.). *Mind and cognition.* Cambridge, MA: Basil Blackwell.

Vars, G. F. (1997, March) Student concerns and standards too. *Middle School Journal, 28*(4), 44–49.

Wagner, T. (1998). Change as collaborative inquiry: A "constructivist" methodology for reinventing schools. *Phi Delta Kappan, 79*(7), 512–517.

Wang, M. C., Haertel, G. D., & Walberg, H. J. (1998). Models of reform: A comprehensive guide. *Educational Leadership, 55*(7), 66–71.

Wiles, J., & Bondi, J. (1993). *Curriculum development: A guide to practice* (4th ed.). New York: Macmillan.

Wynne, E. A., & Ryan, K. (1993). *Reclaiming our schools: A handbook on teaching character, academics, and discipline.* New York: Macmillan.

Zais, R. S. (1976). *Curriculum principles and foundations.* New York: Harper & Row.

2 SOCIAL AND TECHNOLOGICAL FOUNDATIONS OF CURRICULUM

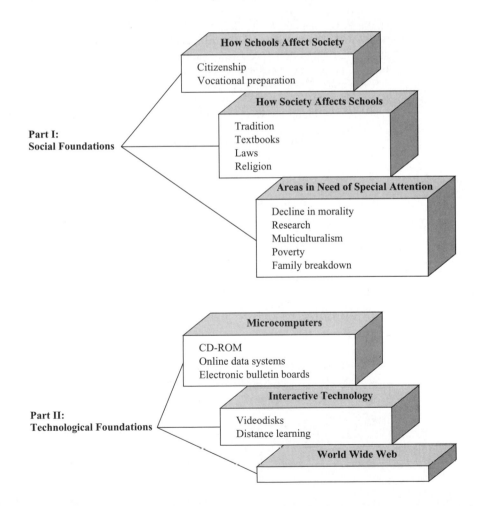

Part I:
Social Foundations

How Schools Affect Society
Citizenship
Vocational preparation

How Society Affects Schools
Tradition
Textbooks
Laws
Religion

Areas in Need of Special Attention
Decline in morality
Research
Multiculturalism
Poverty
Family breakdown

Part II:
Technological Foundations

Microcomputers
CD-ROM
Online data systems
Electronic bulletin boards

Interactive Technology
Videodisks
Distance learning

World Wide Web

Life at school and life outside school are simply too far apart. We need to go back, then, and build up anew from the foundations of democratic values, social realities, and our knowledge of human growth and development.
LOUNSBURY, 1991, p. 3

Objectives

This chapter should prepare you to:

- Apply the statement "The school is a microcosm of the community and of society at large" to curriculum development.
- Identify a unique goal of American schools and explain how this goal has helped shape curricula.
- Give an example of how a school's culture affects its curriculum.
- Defend the need for multicultural education in schools.
- Define cultural discontinuity and explain its effects on students.
- Explain how the education reform practice "teacher empowerment" has enhanced teachers' ability to change the entire school.
- Assess your technological comfort level.
- Broaden your ability to apply technology to curriculum development at your school.
- Apply technology to address multicultural concerns.
- Use the computer to help students tie new information to prior knowledge.

THE CASE OF LINDA BLEVINS AND MARVIN WATTS

Linda Blevins was in her senior year in college before she began to consider the job options that her major offered. She had chosen economics because she enjoyed studying the subject. Upon graduating, Linda accepted the first position for which she had been interviewed, in the home mortgage division of a local bank.

Linda found that her major had prepared her well for this job; from the beginning, she found the work easy. But by the end of her second year, she was extremely bored. Linda spent each day doing paperwork, and she missed being around people. She decided to return to school to pursue a master of arts in teaching (MAT) degree. Since she lived in the inner city and depended on the city buses for transportation, Linda felt fortunate that a university extension center was located only a few blocks from her apartment.

The program had a major classroom observation component that permitted students to observe in several different classrooms. In the first school she visited, 90 percent of the student body were members of minorities. About half of the students were African Americans, and other ethnic groups were also represented in most of the classes.

Linda was shocked by the first class she visited. The lack of order and control were alarming, and Linda was especially surprised by the teacher. Marvin Watts was a cigar-smoking, large white man who, Linda quickly deduced, had been hired because of his size and self-confidence. It was clear that the man feared nothing. In their first conference Marvin told her that his goal was simply to get through each day and each year. "You see," he said, "it would be different if these kids wanted to learn, but they don't. Hey, half of them are on dope or booze. The other half will drop out. Look at it this way, teachers are hired to keep these kids off the streets and out of the prisons which, as you know, are already overfull.

"Let me give you a little advice," he continued. "Nowadays you hear all this reform jargon. Let me tell you something: most of those reports were written by politicians who have no idea what the real world is like. I mean, have you seen the Goals for 2000? Give me a break. Half of these kids are on crack, and even they aren't as spacey as the president and governors responsible for that report. The schools will be drug-free by the year 2000! Yeah, sure they will. They talk about turning over the school to the parents and site-based councils. Hey, most of these kids don't *have* parents. Those that do don't speak enough English to order a meal at McDonalds. Could you imagine asking them if they think the curriculum should be integrated? They would probably think they had been insulted. And they're supposed to help the kids with their education. That's a joke. The kids who do have parents go home and help them!"

Linda noticed two Asian students who sat at the same table each day. Neither paid any attention to Mr. Watts as he lectured in a monotone. She could understand their choosing to ignore Watts, for that was her own method of tolerating his dull lectures, but she didn't understand why he was willing to ignore them, until she had an opportunity to ask.

"It's simple," Watts replied. "They don't understand a word of English. The sup will probably ship them to another school if he ever gets around to it. Right now, they're just as well off here as they would be anywhere else."

Linda was appalled at this attitude. At least Watts was honest, but how could he be so irresponsible? Linda was angry. Later, her shock and anger turned into concern. All she could think about were the waste of time and energy and the unfairness to these students. If they didn't prepare for the future while here at school, how would they ever improve their lot in life? Linda knew the answer to that question.

Linda also noticed that she could count the different ethnic groups in any room because the members of each group seemed to be drawn to each other like drops of oil on water. Mr. Watts showed no concern about this student-selected grouping.

Once she overcame her shock at the lack of respect these students showed to the teacher and to each other, Linda began to notice that none of the strategies she had learned about in her recent college courses were evidenced in any of the classrooms in this school. It was as though topics such as curriculum alignment, valued outcomes, research-based teaching, metacognition, research-based education, authentic assessment, performance evaluation, and, yes, cultural pluralism had never penetrated the walls of this school or the heads of any of its teachers.

Back at the university, Linda related each topic she studied to what she had observed in the classrooms. She could see that, once she graduated, if she decided to remain in this community (and that was a big if), the culture of the schools would work against any efforts she would make to implement the curriculum and instructional strategies she was learning. Although she wanted to help bring about change, she wondered whether she could fight the powerful forces of tradition that permeated this school and community.

Knowing that first-year teachers are often viewed with a jaundiced eye, Linda wanted to avoid being perceived as an overzealous novice who expects to save the world. She believed she needed a strategy that would provide gradual, long-lasting improvement for all students at this school without alienating her fellow teachers, but she didn't know how to begin developing such a plan.

Maximum effectiveness of all school personnel, including teachers and other curriculum developers, requires an understanding of the context in which a school resides. First, context refers to the school's physical surroundings. A school located in a small, rural community has potential advantages and disadvantages compared to an urban ghetto school. Maximum effectiveness in either setting requires planning to (1) capitalize on the resources of the community and (2) overcome the community's weaknesses.

PART 1: SOCIAL FOUNDATIONS

We are taught that a school is, theoretically, a microcosm of the local community and of society at large. Many teachers in urban schools find little comfort in this statement. Shouse (1992, p. 105) expresses this relationship another way by stating, "The world is an enlarged school, or the school is an epitomized world, as you please to say it." But, as Wood (1990, p. 33) reminds us, our schools are microcosms of good communities only when we work to make them so: "We take for granted that our schools are communities, when, in fact, they are merely institutions that can become communities only when we work at it."

Each school and each curriculum is unique. As Halperin (1996, p. 59) has said, "Curriculums are as unique as snowflakes." Although we may think of the uniqueness of each school as the differences in subjects taught and activities pursued, uniqueness comes from a much broader arena known as culture, and each school has its own unique culture. *Culture* has been defined as "an invisible framework of standards representing beliefs and values that are perceived as having worked well in the past" (Kowalski and Reitzug, 1993, p.159) and as simply, "The way we do things around here" (Tice, 1994, p. 48). Culture is the social glue that binds the many elements of a school or a society. A school's culture can make the school an enjoyable place to be or it can make some students' world a continuous nightmare. It can welcome ethnic diversity, or it can harbor and nurture prejudices. It can stimulate minds, or it can anesthetize entire beings.

Each generation must examine the culture of its schools and its communities. Experienced teachers realize that the school's culture and curriculum are tied to the culture of the community and society. Cohen (1990, p. 518) explains, "First, the curriculum has not just now gone public . . . political controversy over curriculum is as old as public education." Lieberman (1990) cautions educators to consider the effects that community changes have on the culture of a school and on the culture of the classrooms.

Importance of the Society-School Relationship

The relationship between the school and society is important in at least two general ways. First, many Americans believe that the school has some responsibility for shaping society, although they disagree on how much. Social reconstructionists believe that schools must completely reform society, while others question whether the school's role as an agent of change should be so extreme. At the opposite extreme are those who believe the school's primary role is to conserve society. These people would have society return to the "good ol' days." Whether one believes that schools should change society or preserve it, perhaps most people would agree that the schools should protect some qualities and change others.

The second major relationship between the school and society is the total of effects that society has on the schools. Goodlad (1997, p. 17) says that "Schools mirror society; they do not drive it." Oana (1993, p. 5) poignantly expresses the powerful influence the community has on the schools, stating, "The problem is, today's schools, no matter how much they change, cannot cope with all the social ills its clients bring to their doors each day."

Changes in the family are impacting student lives and must be addressed by the school's curricula. Erb (1997, p. 2) writes, "Emotionally-barren homes, unsafe neighborhoods, and the deprivation of property can leave some children scarred long before they enter a middle school." Unfortunately, many students arrive at school only to find themselves in an even more threatening world. Kenney and Watson (1996, p. 453) explain, "First, the most significant problems in our schools may not be as we often imagine them. Gangs, drugs, and armed agitators may receive the most attention; however, mostly the conflicts that surfaced . . . were related to everyday school reactions."

For teachers to think that it is possible to ignore society and shape their curricula as they, the professional educators, know it should be shaped is to be blind to reality. As Apple (1990, p. 526) has bluntly stated, "Whether we recognize it or not, curriculum and more general educational issues in the U.S. have always been caught up in the history of class, race, gender, and religious relations."

A clear understanding of the relationship between the schools and the society begins with the realization that the school is an institution that was created by and for society, and that the school is an institution that is supported by society. Trouble is inevitable for teachers who fail to recognize that the community owns and supports the schools. In his book *The Water Is Wide,* Pat Conroy (1972) describes his own failure to understand this relationship. While a first-year teacher, Conroy refused to heed the advice of his supervisor, who told him, "Son, I can replace you just as easily as replacing a light bulb." And he did. Conroy, an excellent teacher who loved his students and his job, was fired. Working in an institution that belongs to society, teachers and other school officials must work for and with the community.

It would be simple if the teacher's responsibility were only to his or her employer (i.e., society), but it isn't, because the school was also created for another purpose: to serve the students. Teachers have two masters to serve: the society and the students, and the two are not always compatible. On the contrary, serving society may be, and frequently is, in direct conflict with the teacher's responsibility to serve the students. For example, some schools are encouraged to change the curriculum to produce world-class workers, which may not be in the best interest of students. This conflict can be seen further by examining the school's purposes. Some of the traditional purposes of the school that remain important include citizenship, intellectualism, and vocational preparation (see Figure 2.1).

FIGURE 2.1

Some ways schools influence society.

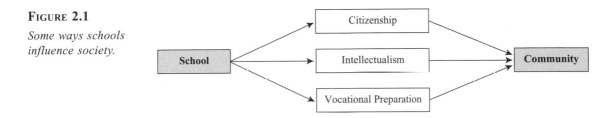

The School's Influence on the Community

Citizenship

More than two thousand years ago Aristotle stressed the need to guide the development of citizenship in youth. To Thomas Jefferson, an educated citizen was nothing less than indispensable to a democratic society. Remember Jefferson's famous admonition: "If a nation expects to be ignorant and free in a state of civilization it expects what never was and what never will be."

The need for teaching citizenship has not diminished over the years. Rappoport and Kletzien (1996, p. 26) emphasize the need for teaching citizenship in contemporary society when they state, "Teaching and enabling students to be responsible citizens is an essential mission of K–12 education in a democracy."

The Seven Cardinal Principles of Secondary Education, which also apply to elementary schools, affirm citizenship as an important aim for the nation's schools. Indeed, one of the seven important aims *is* citizenship. Although few people would question the value of this aim for American schools, many disagree about what the aim encompasses. Some of the more generally accepted responsibilities of schools in developing citizenship are the:

teaching of social studies

development of national allegiance

acquiring of skills

development of a desire to protect society

development of a desire to improve society

development of social responsibility

development of moral values.

Some of these responsibilities might be met indirectly through the hidden curriculum (discussed in Chapter 1).

Intellectualism

In his familiar quote, Jefferson used the word *ignorant,* the opposite of *knowledgeable* or *intellectual.* The pursuit of wisdom is as old as philosophy itself, and, as we shall see in Chapter 3, wisdom and philosophy are inseparable. During the golden age of intellectualism in Greece, the belief in the value of knowledge for knowledge's sake was common. Throughout most of the civilized world, intellectualism is still prized. In the United States, unfortunately, intellectualism is often viewed suspiciously unless it leads directly to practical ends.

Nevertheless, through the years, Americans have been dedicated to serving individual students. This desire is reflected in the high percentage of the nation's youths served by its schools, and in the wording of the Goals for 2000. The first of these goals is for *all* children in America to be ready for school, and the second goal is to raise the high school graduation rate to 90 percent by the year 2000.

Mary Antin, the daughter of European immigrants, understood this unique, education-for-all goal of American schools. Antin was unable to speak English, but that did not prevent her from attending the Boston public schools. Later, reflecting on her experience, she wrote, (1912, p. 186):

> Education was free . . . it was the only thing my father was able to promise us when he sent for us; surer, safer than bread or shelter. . . . No application made, no questions asked, no examinations, rulings, exclusions, no machinations, no fees. The doors stood open for every one of us.

This historically unprecedented commitment to all students, coupled with the belief that intellectual superiority is essential to maintaining national security and a strong economy, has given contemporary Americans a revived appreciation for the importance of intellectualism in the schools. The language used in the reform reports of the 1980s and 1990s has reflected this feeling; two of the most frequent words used in the more than 400 reports are *rigor* and *excellence.*

A poll of educational leaders (Elam, 1996) contained the question, "What do you consider to be the most important achievements of public education in America?" Most respondents cited the goal of maintaining and extending democracy as a way of life by providing free education without regard to race, class, religion, gender, or ideology. One of the poll's authors (Elam, 1996, p. 611) summarized, "We are one of a very few countries, said one leader, that attempt to teach all the children of all the people; against great odds, we have achieved almost universal education."

Vocational Preparation

The first American school was established to prepare young men for entrance into Harvard College, where they would study for the clergy. The vocational role of the school was reaffirmed in 1918 by the Seven Cardinal Principles of Secondary Education. In the United States, the vocational force is so strong that students at all levels often give as a reason for taking a particular class the fact that it is required for graduation, and their reason for wanting to graduate is to increase their ability to get a job and earn more money.

During the 1980s and 1990s, the impact of business and industry on the curriculum increased substantially. Apple (1990, p. 526) addresses this influence:

> The public debate on education and on all social issues has shifted profoundly to the right . . . (and) the effects can be seen . . . in the consistent pressure to make the needs of business and industry the primary concerns of the education system.

But the role of the worker has changed drastically in the last decades, shifting from Taylorism (breaking each job down into small parts and closely supervising the worker to ensure that each function is performed precisely according to instructions) to group problem solving. Arthur Wirth (1993, p. 1) describes a major contrast in the roles of educators during the 1990s and the world-connected, group-oriented, problem-solving skills that future work will require of employees. He says:

> Under Secretary Bennett's banner of "back to basics" and test score accountability, the 1980s produced the hyper-rationalization that Arthur Wise warned us about . . . the style of the 1980s was based, more than anything else, on control: "to control reading, to control language, to control learners, to control teachers. . . ." At the end of the 1980s Lauro Cavazos (Cooper, 1989), Bennett's successor, acknowledged, "We tried to improve education by imposing regulations from the top down, while leaving the basic structure of the school untouched. Obviously, that hasn't worked."

In contrast, modern businesses are turning away from the race to outperform the international competition and are using satellites, facsimile machines, and computer modems to solve problems. Robert Reich's book *The Work of Nations: Preparing Ourselves for 21st Century Capitalism* (1991, pp. 224–225) lists four worker skills that will be required in the future:

- **Abstraction**—the capacity to order and make meaning of the massive flow of information, to shape raw data into workable patterns
- **System thinking**—the capacity to see the parts in relation to the whole, to see why problems arise
- **Experimental inquiry**—the capacity to set up procedures to test and evaluate alternative ideas
- **Collaboration**—the capacity to engage in active communication and dialogue to get a variety of perspectives and to create consensus when that is necessary

How Society Influences Schools

Both society and the schools are in a continuous state of change. The relative power of social forces on the schools shifts, and the relative power that the schools have to shape society also waxes and wanes, requiring teachers, principals, and other curriculum directors to be constantly aware of the school's relationships within society. Although the relationship between the schools and society is symbiotic, the schools have the responsibility for monitoring the social forces that affect them and for seizing opportunities to impact the community. Stated differently, at any time, teachers, administrators, and other curriculum developers should be proactive and be able to foresee obstacles and opportunities; and change the curriculum accordingly.

Too frequently, educators have remained passive and reactive, going about their daily business without concern for the world around them. The result, of course, is that instead of presenting a steady positive image of their profession, educators always seem to be reacting and defending themselves and the schools.

Some important changes that curriculum developers should be concerned about include: (1) poverty, (2) breakdown of the family, (3) drug abuse, (4) multicultural issues, (5) opportunities to use classroom research, and (6) opportunities to use technology in the curriculum.

Society's impact on the schools is substantial. Darling-Hammond (1996, p. 5) explains, "Because rapid social and economic transformations require greater learning from all students, society is reshaping the mission of education." Consequently, education reform is making some long overdue improvements. Educators have an important responsibility to ensure that the changes intended in their schools are educationally sound; i.e., that they are validated by research. Consequently, several significant improvements are being made.

Solomon (1989, p. 63) has offered some specific suggestions for teachers to use to guide parents who want to provide help for their children. Referring specifically to helping parents help their children with their homework, Solomon states:

> Teachers should encourage parents to: (1) set a definite time for study each day with a beginning and ending time and no interruptions; (2) provide the proper environment; (3) provide the materials needed; (4) require the student to organize school materials including books, notes, assignments, and papers; (5) require a daily list of homework assignments, and (6) provide support and guidance if the child becomes discouraged or frustrated.

If parental involvement in curriculum development is to occur, it must be planned for from the outset.

For example, the roles of teachers and parents in curriculum planning are expanding. The benefit of involving teachers and parents is substantiated by research. O'Neal, Earley, and Snider (1991, p. 123) report that, "Research has constantly indicated that parent and family involvement is critical to the academic success of many children." Buttery and Anderson (1999, p. 113) say that, "Three decades of research have demonstrated that parental participation significantly contributes to learning."

Another example of a nationwide research-program improvement involves the creation of child care centers and teen centers. This approach is supported by research. Even the practice of validation through research is part of many reform programs. Some state reform programs require teachers to select and use methods that have been validated by research.

Ways Society Affects the Schools: Forces that Affect the Curriculum

A poll of educational leaders (Elam, 1996) found that one of the most frequent suggestions for improving the schools is for parents to take more responsibility for their children's schooling. However, this should not be interpreted to mean the more involvement, regardless of the circumstances, the better. Parents must consider the level of difficulty of the assignment, the ability level of the student, and the student's age. Generally, the older the student, the less help needed. The principal in the case study in Chapter 1 provided an excellent model to guide the involvement of parents in planning to improve the learning in their children's school, giving consideration to each parent's expertise and limitations. Cooper, Lindsay, and Nye (1998, p. 38) surveyed 709 parents and concluded that parental help can be detrimental if students don't need it. They point out, "Both teachers and parents appear to be aware that continued high levels of parent involvement throughout a child's school years could impede the child's acquisition of these (time management and study) critical skills." Educators bear the responsibility for communicating clearly with parents, which often is exceedingly difficult, especially when non-English speaking parents are involved. Buttery and Anderson (1999, p. 114) warn: "The problem of communications between teachers and non-English speaking parents may be underestimated." Teachers and administrators must ensure that parents and teachers are not asked to perform tasks, such as reading to their children, if the parents themselves are non-readers or very poor readers.

At any given moment, there are many forces working to keep the school curriculum the way it is and many counterforces aimed at changing the curriculum, including tradition, textbooks, laws, religious beliefs, multicultural concerns, poverty, the expansion of knowledge, and growth in technology (see Figure 2.2).

FIGURE 2.2

Some ways society influences schools.

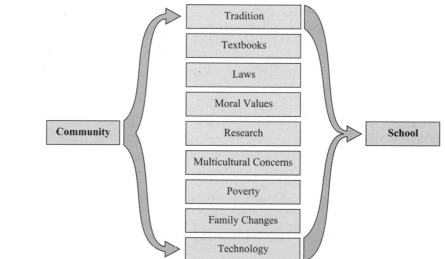

Tradition

One of the oldest and strongest forces in any society is tradition. The musical "Fiddler on the Roof" showed the powerful role that tradition played in nineteenth-century Russia. Tradition is a strong force in all societies, including our own.

When teachers try to introduce change at their schools, the first resistance they often hear is the voice of tradition:

"But we've never done that at this school."

"It will never work."

"They won't like it." (*They* is seldom defined)

"The administration will never buy it."

Tradition can be a stumbling block to progress when new ideas are not given a chance because of fear of failure or a fear of the unknown. Lowell C. Rose (1991, p. 128), former executive director of Phi Delta Kappa, pinpointed the paralyzing effect that tradition can have on schools when he said:

> Schools are cautious and confusing places where teachers, principals, and students try to create islands of safety and sanity for themselves and are reluctant to leave those safe shores for parts unknown.

Because teachers, principals, students, and even the school itself are part of the community at large, it is not surprising that the powers of tradition are at work inside the school as well as in the outside community.

Tradition also serves the schools in positive ways. It acts as a stabilizer, preventing "change for the sake of change"; in doing so, it protects the tried and proven. For example, consider the massive reform movements that are reshaping the curricula in all states. Some necessary questions are: Is this particular reform practice good? What evidence is available to show that it works? What evidence suggests otherwise? Do we really need this reform? Why? One commonly heard answer is, "Because the Japanese are doing it." After all, perhaps no other country has experienced such rapid improvement and earned the respect of the business world as completely as the Japanese. But is this a sound reason for change? In explaining the views of traditionalists, McNeil (1990, p. 4) tells us:

> Americans place a premium on innovation and creativity. Thus it is a mistake for educators in the United States to respond to competition from Japan by imitating the Japanese curriculum. . . . Instead of adopting curriculum so that pupils score higher on multiple-choice examinations, Americans should be concerned with maintaining their advantage in creativity, problem-solving skills, and innovation.

For further examination of change for the sake of change, see the case at the beginning of Chapter 5.

Textbooks

For almost four centuries the textbook has been the number one curriculum determiner in American schools. First, textbooks are highly accessible, making the issuing of reading assignments very easy. A second advantage that textbooks offer is organization, with the content in each chapter building on the content in previous chapters. This makes course organization easy. Even when a syllabus is required, the textbook often provides the pattern for the sequencing of the syllabus.

Textbooks allow teachers to demonstrate their knowledge of a subject. By mastering the stable content in the textbook and then lecturing, the teacher can demonstrate expertise in content and organization, and making students aware of the teacher's expertise gives the teacher expert power. Students expect and want their teachers to have mastery over the content they teach.

The textbook facilitates the alignment of instruction and assessment. By using the text to construct tests, a teacher can ensure coverage of the content studied. Even when the teacher fails to address some of the topics in class, content validity is enhanced by aligning the content on the test with the content in the text.

Laws

The power of legislation affecting schools is not constant. During one era, federal laws may be the dominating social force on schools. In another era, state laws, local developments, or other influences may dominate. For example, during the mid 1950s, the *Brown v. Board of Education* decision, which required integration in the public schools, was perhaps the strongest force affecting the curriculum. In 1975 Public Law 94-142, the Education for all Handicapped Children law dominated. During another era, increased funding or the absence of financial support may be the overriding force shaping the schools. For example, the Elementary and Secondary Education Act of 1965 was the most influential of any law on education in the 1960s.

Social Forces

A wide variety of social forces continues to dominate the shaping of schools. During the 1980s lack of funding forced a shorter school year in parts of West Virginia and Florida. The 1990s were characterized by politicians stressing "family values," but these values were not clearly defined. Such rhetoric, although empty, affects education. According to one writer, the 1990s gave "far too little attention to the ideas and ideals of democracy . . . and to the ideas and ideals of education" (Fenstermacher, 1994, p.1). As Goodlad (1997, p. 48) has said, the politicians used the family values jargon to garner votes, "leaving the listener to fill in the blanks with whatever beliefs she or he wishes justified."

Values

Because the first American school was established to prepare students for admission to a divinity college, values have been a force shaping the curriculum. At times, the question of how much influence religious institutions should have on the selection of values to be taught has caused controversy in communities. On some occasions, the controversy has been so extreme as to draw the attention of the entire nation. The most notable example was the Scopes trial (or the so-called "monkey trial") in Tennessee in 1925.

A deterioration of the moral fiber in the United States has made the moral responsibilities of schools a special concern to some educators. For example, John Lounsbury (1991, p. 5), a longtime leader in the National Middle Schools Association said:

> Unfortunately people continue to talk about training, performance on tests, mastery of discrete subjects, and grades, as if these were the beginnings and ends of education. Education in its fullest sense has to involve heart as well as mind, attitude as well as information, spirit as well as scholarship. That our nation is suffering from moral leukemia is hard to deny. . . . Eisenhower rightly warned us that "A people that values its privileges above its principles soon loses both."

Lounsbury is not alone in his perception of society's moral decline. The schools must share some of the blame because they no longer emphasize character development as they did for more than two hundred years. Audrey Cohen (1993, p. 791) notes, "Today, with parts of the American education system in disarray, the entire nation is politically, socially, and economically under siege. . . . The commitment to education as a training in character has vanished."

Lounsbury (1991, p. 5) gives some examples of values that are prized by civilizations throughout the world, values that he said should be everyday features in our schools; yet he warns against the schools dictating particular values.

> We need classrooms in which beauty is savored, truth honored, compassion practiced, and fellowship honored; classrooms where creativity is encouraged. . . . The school must not attempt to dictate a particular set of values, but must assist young adolescents in exploring their values, attitudes, and standards.

These comments exemplify the paradox involved in the curriculum planner's role in teaching values education. Morality is indispensable, and merely providing definitions of *value* is not enough. Theodore Roosevelt said, "To educate a man in mind and not in morals is to educate a menace to society.

G.A. Davis (1993, p. 32) gives credence to Lounsbury's words of caution:

> Schools always have taught values and always will. Values relating to patriotism, hygiene, and health, appreciation for the sciences, the arts, one's culture, and education itself are common substance for affective education in the classroom. Other values are equally non-controversial and warrant teaching: honesty, responsibility, trustworthiness, a sense of fairness, and respect for the rights and property of others.

Most teachers would probably agree that the schools share some of the responsibility for influencing these values.

At the beginning of the century, socialization was deemed by many to be a more important function of the schools than intellectual development. As Schlechty (1990, p. 18) says, "By the early twentieth century, and perhaps even more so by the 1930s, many thought that the 'real' purpose of schools was to serve as an engine of social reform." Certainly, some of the practices in many of today's schools would be shocking to those who hold the schools accountable for the welfare of society.

Future Effects

Research

This book stresses the need for research-based decisions in education, but therein lies a natural trap. The design of most educational studies is correlational, not causal. Consequently, research findings do not always lend themselves to linear application. A second trap can be the tendency of consumers to focus on research studies that support a favored practice. Special effort is needed to report and use those studies that question or contradict the favored positions.

Of equal concern is the contemporary practice of focusing most on those studies that examine effects on test scores. Interestingly, when W. J. Burke (1967) interviewed national teacher-of-the-year finalists over a seven-year period, he learned that all 54 finalists attributed their success to their relationships with students and, in particular, to their ability to transmit a sense of efficacy to each student. Burke (1967, p. 206) wrote, "My micro-scopic examination of fifty-four separate school systems encouraged me to believe that nothing in American life can match the vigor and importance of the classroom confrontation of minds. Therein lies our future."

The qualities that Burke describes do not appear on test scores. Such widespread testimony of the need to consider non-test-related measures of achievement is too convincing to be ignored.

Eisner (1985, p. 27) perceived the dependence on quantitative test scores to be so extreme that he referred to it as "scientism," the belief that unless something can be quantified it cannot be truly understood or known. Eisner listed "Faith in scientism as applied to education" as one of the six major forces affecting the curriculum.

Unfortunately, a broad focus will result only if curriculum workers insist on gathering and using qualitative data in their decision making. Every nation, every state, and every institution needs a stabilizer to keep it on course. A good example of an effective stabilizer would be the practice of researching each reform practice before permanently adopting it. Without such a stabilizer, we would discard the good along with the bad as we take up first one practice and then another.

Multicultural Concerns

In a democratic society, a major purpose of the schools, perhaps the most important purpose of all, is to promote and protect democracy. As Nelson (1999, p. 391) observes, "A truly democratic society . . . values diversity and requires dissent to maintain its vitality." One way to view the multicultural concerns of teachers is by recognizing that students from minority backgrounds live in two very different worlds. The lack of harmony between these worlds, or cultures, can cause continuous problems for minority students. Each culture has certain expectations and makes certain demands of the student, and these expectations and demands can be mutually exclusive, and they can be imposed directly or indirectly. Perhaps the worse of the two types is indirect expectations because they include conflicting forces, which make conflicting demands on students. Glatthorn (1993, p. 381) explains the results of these opposing or conflicting discontinuities:

> The best way to think about these children and youth is not to consider them "disadvantaged" or "culturally deprived," but to see them as individuals experiencing *cultural discontinuity.* As used by contemporary scholars, cultural discontinuity is the clash of two cultures: people with a particular set of cultural values and norms find themselves in an alien world with very different values and norms.

The degree of discomfort these students feel varies depending on their ages, gender, and the particular group to which they belong. To cushion the effects of cultural discontinuity, these students adjust their behaviors and develop protective images. Ross, Bondy, and Kyle (1993, p. 232) explain:

> In order to protect their sense of collective identity as a cultural group, the minority persons develop certain ways of behaving (i.e., walking, talking, dressing) which separate them from "white people's ways." Being successful in school is likely to be regarded as "acting white."

Teachers who understand that these conflicts exist can learn more about the difficulties these students face by helping them become involved with the curriculum and helping them to accept the curriculum by modifying it to make it resemble the "practical" learning that happens outside the school. As Darling-Hammond (1993, p. 755) explains, unless teachers understand that students' backgrounds, needs, and perspectives toward education are different, the needs of at-risk students will go unmet.

> Concerns about "at-risk" children—those who drop out, tune out, and fall behind—cannot be addressed without teachers who are prepared to understand and meet the needs of students who come to school with varying learning styles, and with differing beliefs about themselves and about what school means for them.

The movement toward multicultural education has grown rapidly and would have grown even faster were there not widespread confusion over the meaning of the term *multicultural.* Stringfield (1991, p. 262) expresses concern over the ambiguity in definitions of such terms in textbooks:

TABLE 2.1   Summary of Effects of Society on Schools

Elements in Society	Implications for Curricularists
Tradition	Impedes and deters change. Curricularists must find ways to protect cherished beliefs and yet to continue to improve the curriculum.
Laws	Introduce change. Curricularists are compelled to protect the rules of the school and the laws of the land
Religious beliefs	Protect accepted beliefs. Curricularists must assume that certain accepted values are promoted without imposing one denomination's beliefs or practices.
Research	Curricularists can use research to ensure that proposed changes are worthwhile.
Multicultural changes	Create a need for curricularists to make certain that the needs of minority students are met.
Poverty	Creates major learning obstacles for at least one-fourth of all students.
Changes in the family	The general deterioration of the family creates a need for the school to find other ways to motivate students and demonstrate the importance of education in today's world.

Upon examining seven textbooks in foundations, I found significant differences in terminology. Many terms in social foundations are confusing. . . . Terms such as "multicultural education," "multiethnic education," and "global education" are also unclear.

Whatever definitions are used, whenever students of any background perform below their potential, society suffers. Maximum human productivity requires tolerance, a quality that is still lacking in our society. Hugh B. Price (1992), the vice president of the Rockefeller Foundation, says that without the quality of tolerance, our society simply will not survive. The overlap among the social and nonsocial factors that pressure the curriculum is clearly and abundantly evident. By presenting simple stereotypes of members of minorities, textbooks retard curriculum changes needed to address ethnic and gender issues positively.

If tolerance is to be developed, our curricula must be adjusted to promote it. But the multicultural role of schools must go beyond the development of tolerance; future curricula must promote an appreciation for diversity. Each ethnic group should learn to value the uniqueness of other ethnic groups, and all groups must see the strength that diversity offers our nation.

Human rights must remain a major concern of all teachers, for all teachers share the responsibility for promoting among students an appreciation for others' rights. Students cannot be taught to appreciate and protect the rights of others through didactic methods, however. Ricardo Garcia (1994) suggests the use of social contracts such as the one shown in Box 2.1. He says that such a contract can be used like a blueprint to guide the management of classroom behavior.

Box 2.1

Social Contract

The classroom operates as a community of scholars who are engaged in learning. The individual's right to learn is protected and respected by all scholars. Scholars should initiate learning and teachers should initiate instruction, balancing the rights of individuals with the rights of other individuals in the community.

Right To Exist, or safe occupancy of space. The classroom is a physically safe learning environment. The teacher:

- does not allow students to physically harm each other or engage in other risky behavior that endangers any student.

Right To Liberty, or freedom of conscience and expression. The teacher:

- allows students to assert their opinions.
- fosters respectful student dissent as a means for rational understanding of issues and divergent opinions.
- fosters students' self-examination of their ethnic or cultural heritages. Teachers should help students become "ethnically literate" about their own individual cultural backgrounds and those of others.

Right To Happiness, or self-esteem: The classroom is an emotionally safe learning environment, fostering high self-esteem among students. The teacher:

- does not allow name-calling, elitist, racist, or sexist slurs, or stereotypical expressions in the classroom.
- disciplines students equitably ensuring that minority and majority group students are punished similarly for the same infractions.
- shows cultural respect by using linguistically and culturally relevant curriculum materials and instructional strategies, and telling the students that their languages and cultures are welcome in the classroom community.
- encourages students to understand their differences and similarities.

Kappa Delta Pi Record 30:21:70 © Kappa Delta Pi.

Evidence of Need

An examination of the demographic shift in cultures in the United States shows that there will be a new ethnic majority in the new millennium. Every major metropolitan area now has a "minority majority," but the teaching majority that has dominated the teacher ranks throughout the nation's existence continues to dominate.

A special handicap faced by many minority students is the language barrier. The United States trails most of the civilized world in the teaching of foreign languages. Ovando (1994) and Sizer (1990) recommend requiring that all students be proficient in two or more languages. Too often, foreign students are ignored because they speak little or no English. Perhaps the most urgent need of these students is a change in the attitudes of their teachers.

Several myths must be dispelled. For example, the common belief that learning an additional language interferes with one's native language must be disproved (Ovando, 1994). Another common myth is that success in learning a language is proportional to the time spent studying the language. Time-on-task is only one of many factors that affect learning a language.

In addition to fostering appropriate attitudes, schools should alter policies to promote language development and the academic success of students who are handicapped by a language barrier. For example, members of all ethnic groups should be held to the same academic expectations. Academic success requires a special kind of language development—that of an academic vocabulary, which requires about five to seven years to master. Policy should ensure that these students are given the necessary support during this developmental period.

Multicultural expectations can be met in a variety of ways. Scott (1993, p. 2) says that students need an opportunity to develop their own theories based on experiences in multicultural classrooms:

> What is needed for teacher evaluation is a conceptualization of teacher education pedagogy in which theory and practice are interactive. "Practices draws theory" as much as "theory draws practices." Such a pedagogy would require that prospective teachers have sufficient practice to build principles of action, an understanding by theory to guide decision-making, and the recognition that teaching situations are multi-faceted ones in which there is seldom a perfect match between theory and practice. By defining teaching as dilemma-driven, teacher educators can better prepare teachers to cope with situations where there is often no one right way, or even best way, to act.

During the 1980s and 1990s, feedback on effective school and teaching research prompted the use of direct instruction. Direct instruction is teacher directed and involves the whole class as opposed to individual or small-group assignments. Indeed, this approach was undeniably found to correlate with high achievement test scores. A table showing the effective practices used by a dozen researched-based education reform programs shows that over half (58%) of these current programs maximize the use of direct instruction (Wang, Haertel, & Walberg, 1998, p. 69). Some educators would argue that direct instruction does not lead to the type of thinking needed for twenty-first century living. Cohen (1993, p. 791) explains:

> And despite the lip service paid to the ideal of creating a spirit of inquiry, education is increasingly directed toward teaching students not how to inquire but rather how to digest the results of other people's inquiry.

So, educators must weigh the value of improvement on standardized tests against the value of learning to solve problems. Fortunately, many of the newer reform tests are beginning to focus on authentic problem solving.

Carnine, Grossen, and Selbert (1995, p. 147) use the bar graphs shown in Box 2.2 to show the relative effectiveness of direct instruction on standardized test scores as opposed to eight other instructional programs.

Box 2.2

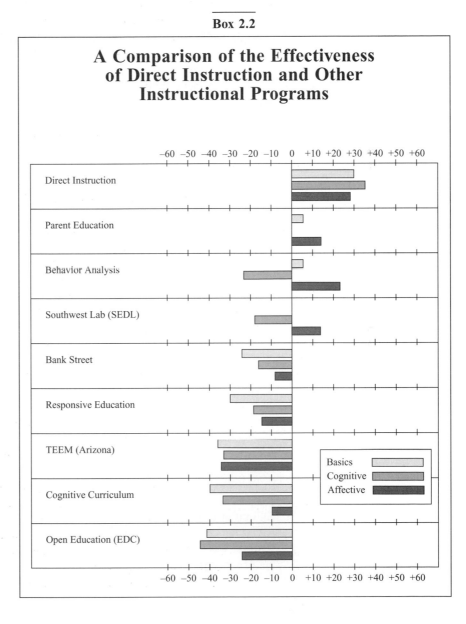

A Comparison of the Effectiveness of Direct Instruction and Other Instructional Programs

These authors summarize the findings about direct instruction as reported by impartial researchers as follows:

1. A greater measurable and educationally significant benefit of .6 to .8 grade equivalents is present at the end of the third grade for those students who received an extra year of direct instruction; that is, they began receiving direct instruction in kindergarten rather than in first grade.

2. Significant gains in IQ are found, which are largely maintained through third grade. Students entering the program with high IQs (>111) do not lose IQ points during the follow-through years, though one might expect some regression over time. And students entering with low IQs actually gain IQ points—entering K students with IQs below 71 gain 17 points, and entering first-grade students gain 9.4 points. Gains for the children with entering IQs in the 71–90 range are (first grade) 15.6 and (kindergarten) 9.2 points.

3. Studies of low-IQ students (<80) show that the program is clearly effective. In fact, these students gain nearly as much each year, in reading (decoding) and math, as do the direct instruction students with higher IQs. These gains are more than a year per year on the Wide-Range Achievement Test (WRAT) in reading and a year per year on the Miller's Analogy Test (MAT) Total Math.

4. Longitudinal studies of direct instruction and comparable nondirect instruction students have followed these students after leaving third grade. All the significant differences favored the direct instruction students: five on academic measures, three on attendance, two on college acceptance, and three on reduced retention rates.

5. Additional evaluation research is now showing that the model generalizes across both time and communities. The Department of Education's Joint Dissemination Review Panel validated direct educational programs as exemplary and qualified them for national dissemination. All twelve Direct Instruction Follow-Through projects were submitted for validation, eleven of which had eight to ten years of data on successive groups of children. Collectively, these projects' schools sampled a full range of students: large cities (New York, San Diego, Washington, DC), middle-sized cities (Flint, MI; Dayton, OH; E. St. Louis, IL); rural white communities (Flippin, AR; Smithville, TN); a rural black community (Williamsburg, SC); Latino communities (Uvalde, TX; E. Las Vegas, NM); and a Native American community (Cherokee, NC). One hundred percent of the projects were certified as exemplary in reading and mathematics for the primary grades.

Poverty

Throughout their existence American schools have been challenged by poverty. The Franklin Academy, with its practical and relevant curriculum, lost its position as the most popular school in the country because it charged tuition, and the vast majority of families could not afford to send their children to the academy. Throughout the twentieth century, many schools have been too poor to afford their students even such basic necessities as textbooks, pencils, paper, and chalk.

In the environments surrounding the schools, poverty has taken its toll on millions of children. Today, one child in four lives in poverty. Extreme poverty often manifests itself in malnourishment, high rates of mortality, and even suicide. The number of behavioral problems correlates with the degree of poverty (Williams et al., 1999).

One profound impact of poverty on youth is the incapacitating effect it has on the ability to read. In poor communities, many parents themselves are either illiterate or are busy working and thus cannot and do not model reading. As Krashen (1998, p. 19) notes, "Too many of our students, particularly those in high poverty schools' struggle to become fluent readers." This inability to read, in turn, restricts students' growth in all academic areas.

Such circumstances pressure educators to try to design the curricula to help our youth overcome the harm they suffer daily as a result of poverty. Knapp and Shields (1990) identify some ways that curricula in impoverished areas can be strengthened: (1) maximize time-on-task, (2) set high expectations, (3) strengthen the involvement of parents in the support of instruction, (4) plan content in small, discrete parts structured in sequence, (5) provide whole-group or small-group formats, and (6) integrate the curriculum, giving students in all subjects opportunities to write, read, and discuss.

Changes in the Family

Through the years, the family unit has been a profound strength in the American culture. The typical concept of family has changed radically in recent years, however. In 1989, a survey by the Massachusetts Mutual Life Insurance Company (Scligmann, 1989) asked 1,200 randomly selected adults what the word *family* meant to them. Only 22 percent picked the traditional definition of "a group of people related by blood, marriage, or adoption." About 75 percent selected "a group of people who love and care for each other."

Most of today's youths have no concept of the traditional family that existed throughout the first half of this century, that is, a mother and father, the father the breadwinner for his family and the mother a homemaker who did not have a job outside the home.

Contemporary curricula must reflect these changes. Homework assignments must be compatible with the realization that most of today's youths do not have the support of the traditional family and setting, for example, a quiet, lighted study area, ample time to give to homework assignments, and parents who are available, willing, and able to help students understand their assignments. Perhaps more important, most of today's youths have no adult role models at home who read books for information and pleasure, and many have no parents to encourage them and remind them of the importance of education.

Most contemporary youths do not receive strong motivation and encouragement outside the classroom, yet motivation is essential to learning. Campbell (1990) says that *motivation is more; it is learning.* Perhaps, more clearly stated, without motivation learning is impossible. Correctly designed, tests can be used to motivate students' interest in content. Markle et al. (1990, p. 56) have said, "The power of tests and other evaluation procedures to shape students' perceptions of their teachers' expectations cannot be overestimated." As teachers fulfill their new education reform roles—using valued outcomes, alternative assessment, performance evaluation, and portfolios—many new ways of motivating students will be available to those who are cognizant of the need to use evaluation and other means to motivate students.

A Final Thought on Social Foundations

As shown in Figure 2.3, a balance is maintained between the forces schools and their respective communities exert on each other. At any time, every community has forces that push against its schools. Some of the more influential of these forces include tradition, textbooks, laws, religious beliefs, research, multicultural concerns, poverty, family changes, and technology. At the same time, the schools exert pressure on their communities by preparing future citizens and promoting intellectualism. Ideally, a homeostatic balance is maintained. When this balance is lost, problems develop between the school and community.

FIGURE 2.3

A balance is maintained between the forces schools and communities exert on each other.

Case Study

Accessing the Internet

Bob Lucking

Background Information

Increasingly, teachers at all levels are feeling the need to use computers and related technology to a greater degree as a regular part of their instruction. They see an enormous explosion of business activity on the Internet and read stories in the press about vast storehouses of information becoming available "on the Web." Some college courses are being taught online, and libraries boast that their banks of electronic resources are much larger than their physical, on-location print holdings. Museums, art galleries, and historical sites are among the thousands of entities with information-filled websites welcoming visitors free of charge, offering rich repositories of textual material as well as images and even sound clips and movies useful to students of all ages. Teachers in K–12 schools, however, face many problems in gaining access to the Internet, effectively integrating its contents into their instruction, and monitoring students' use of appropriate subject matter. While these new sources of information have terrific appeal to educators, many issues regarding their use must be addressed by schools.

The Community

Seaside, a metropolitan area of 200,000 residents in the mid-southern region of the Atlantic seaboard, has developed a plan to help teachers make better use of technology. Seaside is urban in character, and its students span all economic levels. Many of these students will go on to college or the world of work where computer use is required. Two of the largest employers in the area are a maritime shipyard facility and an automobile assembly plant, both of which pride themselves in their high-tech facilities. The Department of Education in this state has recently announced with much fanfare that it will offer K–12 school programs that train students to be prepared for the technological demands of the future. Because Seaside is located near a large National Aeronautics Space Administration (NASA) facility, many of its residents are highly educated and technologically oriented, and some of these residents who are parents have convinced the school board that Seaside needs to take the state department initiative seriously. They have lobbied the school board to mandate that all students use computers regularly as part of their studies to the extent that students come to view cutting-edge technology merely as tools to accomplish academic and personal goals.

The School

Housing grades 9 through 12, Oscar Mason High School is located in the central part of Seaside and dates back to the 1920s. A new building was constructed in 1967, and although now dated, the school has been nicely maintained and is viewed

(Continued)

with pride by its 1,200 students. The student population is quite heterogeneous, reflective of the ethnic mix typical of urban schools today. For the past two years, the Oscar Mason football team has won the state championship, and school spirit has remained buoyed. The school's instructional program is comprehensive in nature, attempting to meet the needs of student interests ranging from vocational to college preparatory.

The Leaders

Roberto Geisera has taught English for fourteen years and is proud to be a teacher. Throughout his career, he has taught regular classes and occasional remedial classes, and during the past four years he has also taught a class of eleventh grade honors English. Seeking to broaden his skills, Roberto completed his masters degree, and as part of his program of studies he enrolled in two computer courses. During these courses, he became "hooked" on the power of computers and soon purchased a computer system for his home. In his spare time, he learned how to do desktop publishing, and he dabbled in Web design and telecommunications. Roberto began to use computers regularly in teaching his own classes and soon found that his colleagues sought him out whenever they had hardware or software problems.

Issues in Implementation

The school board, in consultation with the principals throughout Seaside, recognized that a schoolwide plan of implementing computer technology was the solution to utilizing the offers of the state and meeting the demands of the community. In its deliberation, the board concluded that the most effective way of integrating computer technology into the curriculum was through the use of computer labs placed in strategic locations in each school. All computers in each lab were to be linked via a local area network throughout the building, and each computer would have Internet access. However, the board recognized that someone would have to take responsibility for maintaining each of the labs and making sure that all hardware was working properly. Furthermore, someone would have to be placed in charge of providing training to other faculty to help them become accustomed to using the labs with students. After consulting with other area schools that had implemented computer plans, the board learned that on-location training was the most effective way to reach teachers. Since teachers would need only occasional access to the computers, the computer labs could be made available to be reserved on a first-come, first-served basis.

Having acknowledged this need, the administration created a new position for a computer resource teacher in each school and determined that the person who held this job would be released from teaching four periods a day to attend to the labs and help teachers. Even though some of Roberto's friends disapproved of positions that allowed for a diminished teaching load, Roberto applied for and received one of these posts. He recognized that some of his colleagues would have difficulty accepting him as their tutor, since the school culture dictated that all teachers were on an absolutely even plane.

(Continued)

Knowing that he would be under scrutiny in his new position, Roberto threw himself into the job. One of his first tasks was to train all of the teachers in four departments in the school. While most teachers were eager to broaden their range of skills, not all shared Roberto's enthusiasm about computers. Especially vociferous in their opposition was a contingent of math teachers who blasted the computer integration plan because they felt it overlooked the students' mastery of basic skills in computation. These teachers took note of the amount of money being spent on computer hardware when they were often restricted from buying workbooks and printed homework exercises. They argued that this new rush to technology was especially misguided in light of the constant emphasis on students' performance on mandatory tests of basic skills. The Department of Education's Test of Basic Competencies was the benchmark of all schools' success, and the faculty and administration at Oscar Mason had received substantial criticism when newspaper articles drew attention to a 7 percent decline of in student scores on the most recent administration of the tests. The resisting math cadre argued that the money spent on computers and network routers should go instead to commercially available test preparation materials. If the nation's media were going to measure school success in terms of standardized test scores, then Oscar Mason would be smart to respond accordingly, they felt.

Even some of Roberto's friends resisted the use of computers. Phil Bilgrim taught twelfth grade honors classes and an occasional elective in modern poetry, and he wanted little to do with discussions in the teachers' lounge about computers. He said that he did most of his best writing with a pencil in a dog-eared journal he carried with him, and he had two regional poetry recognition awards on his wall to prove that his method worked. He and a couple of teachers of a similar mind were not impressed with the school's interest in computers.

While Roberto was prepared for these concerns, he had not anticipated the complications that arose from trying to use the Internet for instructional purposes. One of the first issues that surfaced when teachers began discussing using the Internet with students was access to inappropriate material. Because the Internet spans all national boundaries and is available to persons with every interest, websites containing pornographic material are just as easily found as are those leading to the National Gallery of Art.

Early on, the school established a policy that only those students whose parents signed a permission form would be allowed to use the Internet in class. By requiring this signature, the school could lessen the likelihood that complaints would arise if students were to stumble across offensive sites. Most parents signed the forms and returned them quickly, but a substantial number were not returned. Teachers, therefore, had to devise two sets of learning activities so that those students who had not gotten approval for Internet work could carry out their learning in the back of the computer lab. It was a physically cumbersome arrangement at best. Roberto advised teachers to monitor the websites that their students visited while in the lab, but they found that students could, with the stroke of a few keys, do very successful searches for pornographic material.

Parental concern regarding inappropriate use of the Internet prompted the school's administration to assemble all computer resource teachers to establish a

(Continued)

plan to control students' access to the Internet. As a means of stopping misuse of the Web, the committee selected blocking software designed to stop users from entering undesirable sites based on key words or descriptors. Once this software was installed on the network, teachers were pleased to find that they could schedule the use of a computer lab and require their students to use the Internet to complete their assignments. Only occasionally did teachers find that their students were wandering off into forbidden sites not filtered by the blocking software; for instance, students in a social studies class found a racist site filled with hate messages. In another instance, a chemistry student found a site with detailed directions for making bombs. All in all, however, teachers found that they could monitor their students' diligence by remaining in the back of the computer lab and watching the screens of students as they did their work, and demand for time in the labs grew.

Although Roberto had worked through the difficulties of gaining teachers' acceptance of the Internet, he was not prepared for the fact that they were not all equally adept at integrating its use into their instruction. Pam Riley, for example, altered her entire home economics curriculum once she found a website on cooking in Puerto Rico. The site was actually an extended advertisement sponsored by a rice company, but it saved Riley from doing extensive lesson plans, since many elements of meal preparation and presentation were covered.

A second-year French teacher, Ted Gray, had particularly poor classroom management skills; his students' behavior nearly always bordered on revolt. Although Gray was one of the teachers Roberto least expected to use the lab, Roberto found that Gray signed up for lab hours for weeks at a time for his most unruly classes. Roberto stayed with Gray as he taught his classes and attempted to help his students while at the same time keeping order in the class. Since the students were officially in Gray's charge, Roberto was reluctant to offer more than a support function. Worse than his lack of control over students was Gray's choice of assignments for the use of the Internet. One Monday morning, looking particularly disheveled and disorganized, Gray brought his students to the lab and asked them to find "something about the south of France." One group of boys was soon looking at beach scenes at a site for a hotel in Cannes, but far more attention was being paid to the pictures of the women on the beach than to the language used in the ad. Another cluster of girls found the website of an American perfume producer with a product called Riviera in which all of the ad copy was in English. Unfazed, Gray sat in the back and graded papers, and Roberto shook his head at the wasted instructional time.

The growing interest in using the Internet led to other unpleasant exchanges among faculty over who should get to use the computer labs. Roberto's home department, the English faculty to whom he felt a great deal of allegiance, argued that they should be given priority in having access to the labs because they were using the computers for both Internet access and word processing. They were teaching students how to find information and how to give appropriate credit to the source, skills that are prerequisite to writing papers in all other disciplines, they posited. Further, they argued, students were taught the importance of rewriting and thus had an ongoing need to use the computers to update their drafts of

(Continued)

essays. Teachers in the social studies department disagreed. Social studies students, they contended, had the greatest need for Internet access because of all the historical documents and government information that was available. History, they argued, was best represented by the documents that recorded its details.

The problems created by the demand for access to limited resources continued to appear. Ben Hardy, who taught Advanced Placement (AP) physics courses, argued that the simulations available at a nearby university's website contributed most meaningfully to a student population more able to take advantage of the technology, that is, students bound for university classrooms. He maintained that universities were expecting their incoming students to possess a wide range of computer skills that could be acquired only after prolonged experience with computers. These students would be tomorrow's scientists and researchers and needed to work regularly with the tools necessary for their study and future profession, so clearly they should get extra time in the computer labs. The special education staff would hear nothing of this. They were quick to point to both state and federal laws mandating that special students not be impeded in their quest for an education equal to that of any other child.

Roberto saw that access to computers was going to be a difficult issue, but he kept his faith that these new challenges could also be met.

Issues for Further Reflection

1. To what extent should technology drive the nature of instruction in schools? Should teachers be required to use computer technology if they are reluctant to do so?

2. Should technology force teachers into new roles that do not require teaching? Will access to information through technology result in paraprofessionals managing instruction?

3. Given the unregulated nature of the Internet, how can parents be assured that their children will not be exposed to material the parents find offensive? How can teachers be prevented from using computer technology as a "baby-sitter"?

4. On what basis should educators decide equitable and fair access to limited technological resources? Should some students or some disciplines receive higher priority than others?

5. Does the change brought on by technology by its very nature violate tradition or confront the prevailing values of society? Will technology lead to the dehumanizing of education?

Suggested Readings

Banks, S., & Renwick, L. (1997, June 8). Technology remains promise, not panacea. *The Los Angeles Times,* pp. A1, A4.

Bradley, M. J., & Morrison, G. R. (1991). Student-teacher interactions in computer settings: A naturalistic inquiry. (Tech. Rep. No. 143). Memphis, TN: Memphis State University (ERIC Document Reproduction Service No. ED 343 565).

(Continued)

Chodorow, S. (1995). Educators must take the electronic revolution seriously. Alan
    Gregg Memorial Lecture. 106th Annual Meeting of the Association of American
    Medical Colleges, Washington, DC.
Conte, C. (1999). An education technology agenda. In *The Learning Connection:
    Schools in the Information Age* (on-line). Available at *www.benton.org/library/
    schools/home.html.*
Cravener, P. A., & Michael, W. B. (1996). Students use of adjunctive computer
    mediated communication. Paper presented at the Annual Conference of Distance
    Education, USA.
Means, B. (1993). Using technology to support education reform. Washington, DC:
    Office of Educational Research and Improvement (ERIC Document Reproduction
    Service, ED 364 220).
Mckenzie, J. (1998). Internet (and information) readiness. *From Now On, The
    Educational Technology Journal 6*(7) April 1998.
Mckenzie, J. (1997). Making the net work for schools. *From Now On. The Educational
    Technology Journal 7*(1) September 1997.
Neal, L. (1997). Virtual classrooms and communities. Proceedings of the ACM Group
    Conference, USA, 97, 1–13.
U.S. Congress, Office of Technology Assessment. (1995). *Teachers and technology:
    Making the connection* (OTA_EHR-616). Washington, DC: U.S. Government
    Printing Office.

PART II: TECHNOLOGICAL FOUNDATIONS

Technological Growth

The power of technology to change the curriculum is almost beyond comprehension, and the need for technologically induced changes in the curricula in
American elementary and secondary schools at the beginning of the millennium
is strong. Elam (1996) reports that one of the most frequent suggestions educational leaders make for improving today's schools is the integration of technology into the teaching and learning process. Nicaise and Barnes (1996, p. 207)
address the importance of technology in contemporary classrooms when they
state, "Technology (through simulations or microworlds) can facilitate learning,
especially the understanding of complex concepts. . . ."

According to a report of the U.S. Congress (1995), K–12 schools in this
country have acquired between 300,000 and 400,000 computers in each of the
last two decades, and three-fourths of all schools have access to telecommunications through local or wide-area networks. Over one-third of the schools have
access to the Internet. Unfortunately, teaching and learning with technology are
not so widespread (Northrup and Little, 1996, p. 213); yet, as reported by
Bernauer (1999, p. 70), "Findings confirm that motivation and achievement
improved after technology was integrated into the curriculum."

The Computer

In recent years, increased computer use has impacted heavily on curricula in secondary and elementary schools, characterizing the education reform movement in most states. Responding to an interviewer's question about areas of progress in education today (Dagenais, 1994, p. 52), Robert Anderson said, "Probably the most dynamic force impacting education today is the implementation of technological advancements." If educators take advantage of this development, it can be a great cause for celebration.

While most methods professors and students may feel they are overburdened, methods teachers should nonetheless attempt to gradually introduce technology by requiring teachers to write assignments that will require the use of problem-solving skills and creativity. For example, students can be taught to use the computer to create open-ended scenarios. Prospective English teachers might write the introduction to stories using word processing software to show to their students when they begin to teach in their own classrooms. Each scenario could be designed to help students develop particular skills, including advanced levels of thinking. Elementary science teachers might develop a story involving an imagined field trip to an unfamiliar environment. The introduction could stir students' imaginations, and they would then be encouraged to complete the story using their own embellishments. Such activities enable students to tie current information to prior knowledge.

A social studies teacher could begin a story about problems urban dwellers have because of their cultural differences. The software could be designed to help students analyze the problems from the viewpoints of different cultures. Once the stories are complete, role playing, simulations, and discussions placing students of varied backgrounds into cooperative working relationships can be next. A follow-up assignment might be for students to use the computer to develop a profile of their value systems, listing their own beliefs that came to light during the previous exercises.

Teachers who believe in integrating the disciplines know that such programs can be used in various disciplines. English writing assignments can easily focus on science, social studies, and other disciplines.

Chapter 6 discusses the various levels of the educational taxonomies and gives examples of objectives at each level in each domain. By designing computer activities at the upper levels of the taxonomies, teachers can effectively use the computer to meet one of the schools' most critical needs, that of raising the level of student thinking.

Future curricula must help teachers to assess software to ensure that it is educationally sound. Good software prompts students to produce charts, written responses, and other products that require higher-level thinking. Siegel and Davis (1986) say that commercial developers will probably not improve the quality of software as quickly as they should, as evidenced by the large number of computer books written to teach amateurs to program and the comparatively few books that tell how to select educationally sound software.

Curricula must also change to alter teachers' perceptions. According to Geisert and Dunn (1991, p. 223), "Some teachers acknowledge still having computer phobia and remain apprehensive about using computers as either an instructional or management tool." Curricula in the elementary and secondary schools must offer nonthreatening opportunities for teachers to develop computer competency and must give teachers the computer time needed to become comfortable using computers in their lessons.

Perhaps more important than the programs teachers choose to use is how the programs are introduced to students. The computer lab should be a place where students can explore without fear of criticism. Student self-concepts can be strengthened by involving students in the selection of computer activities.

Meeting Multicultural Goals

Computers can play several roles in developing and maintaining a classroom climate that encourages all students to accept, appreciate, and celebrate all types of differences. Many businesses have programs designed to enhance relationships among employees. Inviting guest speakers into the classroom who represent ethnic and gender diversity, who use computers to demonstrate their application, can expand students' application of computers while also providing positive role models.

There is also value in interacting with the community by sending teacher education students into schools with diverse populations. For at least three decades, teacher education colleges have been increasing the number of hours students spend in the schools. The University of Texas at Arlington, for example, requires that a minimum of 50 percent of the time in each course be spent in a related field experience (Patrick & Reinhartz, 1999). These experiences can be enriched by reflective assignments that prompt teacher education students to notice how computers are being used by a diverse body of students. Too often, we assume that our role is to know what students should be doing with computers and to guide them in that direction. But this is only partly true; we can and should also watch students to learn what they find attractive about computers. Given the opportunity to choose their own computer projects, what do they choose?

There is inherent value in using interactive strategies to enhance multicultural education (Nagel, 1998). Some programs partner students with counterparts in other counties for on going e-mail exchanges of information. Similar programs can be created within the students' own state, ensuring that students are paired with students with other cultural backgrounds and that assignments require students to reflect on and share the expectations of their culture. Autobiographic essays can be used to stimulate student reflections into their own cultures (Curtis, 1998). Such autobiographies can be shared by e-mail as well as with classmates and teachers within the same room.

Other Technological Developments

The microcomputer revolution is part of a much broader development that includes a number of other inventions. Several of these innovations are contributing to curriculum development and will certainly contribute more as newer developments occur. Paradoxically, although some schools cannot afford the expenses required to make their students technologically current, a significant advantage offered by that very technology is its ability to save money over time. Some of the more promising developments include CD-ROM, digital cameras, online data systems, electronic bulletin boards, interactive videos, interactive distance learning systems, and the World Wide Web.

CD-ROM

With CD-ROM enormous amounts of information can be stored on a small disk. Lack of adequate library facilities exacerbates rural teachers' responsibilities for accessing library materials for courses such as this curriculum course. Using CD-ROM technology, however, university extended campus centers can now make hundreds of journals available to local teachers. Such systems are incredibly user-friendly. A teacher can simply select a disk with the desired journal and immediately call to the screen any issue of the journal printed in the previous four or five years. Hard copies of appropriate articles can be printed. This useful innovation is already available at many university extended campus centers and in many school district curriculum centers.

Digital Cameras

Digital cameras use computers to create pictures, and thus are more convenient than traditional cameras. While the cost of digital cameras will prohibit their availability on some campuses, the cost is decreasing and many teacher education colleges now own digital cameras and color printers. Because these cameras do not use film (and thus no developing is required), they are much more user-friendly than traditional cameras. Prospective teachers can record what they observe during visits to school campuses for use in reports and in their portfolios. Teachers can also visit businesses and agencies in the community and record diverse community leaders using technology, thus connecting schools' use of technology to the use of technology by the outside community.

Digital cameras have unlimited uses. Accrediting agencies such as the National Council for Accreditation of Teacher Education (NCATE) require teacher education programs to promote diversity and multicultural education. With that goal in mind, teachers can use digital cameras to make a permanent visual record of activities that promote these values. The results can be made available on displays or in portfolios kept in the accreditation site team workroom. For example, if a college has minority student recruitment summer workshops, or an exchange program with a college with many students from different cultures, or if an institution holds multicultural or international events, these can be easily recorded using a digital camera.

Online Data Systems

Online data systems enable the user to access information from distant sources. Today, many online data systems are available through monthly subscriptions. An increasing number of local libraries subscribe to online data systems, making them accessible to virtually everyone.

In the near future, online data systems will use cable television lines and fiber optics. This will allow teachers in many school districts to make assignments on an almost unlimited array of topics (Armstrong et al., 1993).

Electronic Bulletin Boards

Electronic bulletin boards are bulletin boards connected to computers. Currently, many schools are providing their teachers with modems, permitting them to tie into electronic bulletin boards. This service will allow teachers to share information with other teachers at local schools and universities. For example, a university professor of science education would be able to share information with the science department in a public school. Consider the possibilities: Teachers and professors would be able to collaborate on classroom research, students at one school would be able to work with students at another school, and so on. Foreign language students are already using this system to post letters to their counterparts in other countries.

For several decades, British elementary and secondary students have shared their ongoing science projects through television. Electronic bulletin boards can provide American students a means of sharing their projects with other American students or, indeed, with students in countries throughout the world.

Electronic bulletin boards can be useful in strengthening communications among culturally different schools and universities. Stories in which students share their family values can become the topics of multicultural discussions.

Interactive Videos

In the wake of more recent advanced technology, teacher education programs may not be using video cameras and videodiscs as much as they once did. This is unfortunate, because prospective teachers need opportunities to critique their own behavior and that of their students.

Interactive video offers teachers an opportunity to involve students in curriculum development. Chapters 4, 7, and 10 stress the need for students to be involved in identifying major concepts in their subjects. By using interactive video, students can create scripts, edit material, and make presentations.

Consider the potential that this technology offers for bringing together students of varying ethnic backgrounds and students from different disciplines to work on cooperative assignments that are exciting to all students.

Interactive Distance Learning

Distance learning has been available in some school districts for over three decades. Early distance learning used satellite disks. A satellite disk was required on each end to provide an uplink for the sender and a downlink for the receiver. This system is still being used throughout the country.

Recently, the interactive dimension has been added to distance learning, allowing a two-way exchange of ideas. For example, extension courses have been taught extensively using distance learning. Now, many distance-learning classrooms have learner stations that enable students to communicate orally and visually with the instructor and with students at other locations.

The World Wide Web

Among the new technological developments redefining today's classrooms is the World Wide Web. Gagnon (1996, p. 3) explains:

> There's a revolution being waged by thousands of ordinary people doing extraordinary things with words, images, and sounds over the Internet. Using little more than their own talent and a few electronic tools, these individuals are creating, day by day, a new media for the twenty-first century. There's a simple name for the revolutionary new media . . . it's called the Web.

The Web offers connection to an unlimited number of information sources that can be useful to educators. As noted by Lucking in the case study in this chapter, some of this information can be detrimental and the introduction of computers and the Web may even cause dissension among the faculty, but the potential to gather good information is almost unlimited. For example, *http://www.neh.fed.us* will access the National Endowment for the Humanities and *http://www.nimh.nih.gov* connects to the Department of Health and Human Resources National Institute of Mental Health. These and hundreds of other Web sources put the information of the world in the hands of twenty-first century educators.

Many of the readers of this book are already knowledgeable consumers of technology. For those who have not caught the excitement offered by this rapidly developing field, remember the advice of Geisert and Dunn (1991), who said that the importance of knowing how to be an effective computer user in this day and age is too critical to let a lack of technological training get in the way; you are challenged to explore one or more of these or other technological advancements and the potential they offer for your future curriculum development activities.

Mecklenburger (1990), who directs the National School Boards Association Institute for the Transfer of Technology in Education, argues that teachers must think beyond just using new technology. Earlier in this chapter a need for curriculum stabilizers was stressed. Perhaps an emerging example in the twenty-first century is for teachers, principals, and other curriculum planners to continuously search their own minds for additional effective uses of technology to promote learning and other educational goals.

Impact on Learners

The very nature of technology will require changes in the ways learners think. Historically, curricula have been designed sequentially. For example, history courses have used timelines to align events chronologically to facilitate their recall; science content has been presented to show natural sequences (for example, the water cycle: rain, run-off, evaporation, condensation); and in English classes students have been taught to write phrases, clauses, simple sentences, compound sentences, paragraphs, and themes, with each skill depending on mastery of the ones preceding it. Each of these approaches is a linear process that facilitates recall. Cognitive mapping has been used to show the mental processes involved in learning. Often, the cognitive maps follow a general linear direction with only minor branching from the main path.

The nature of hypertext, however, is not linear, and natural patterns are not necessarily present on the Web. On the contrary, searches for information on the Internet can bounce in all directions as students use a hit-or-miss approach to surfing the seamless Web. Students will need help narrowing their searches, much as students of a half-century ago needed help from librarians when they walked into the library for the first time and felt overwhelmed by the ocean of information that surrounded them. Systems for simplifying searches will need to be developed, just as the Dewey Decimal System was developed to help twentieth century learners simplify their searches. Teachers may need to adjust the time expectations they hold for students, and teachers may need to devise methods to reduce the levels of frustration felt by students who may spend long periods of time searching for information without getting any human feedback or feeling sure of their progress.

Metacognition may be combined with journal keeping to enable students to trace their search methods and develop individual strategies that work for them. Such data could become useful in grouping students with similar learning approaches. Teachers may have to adjust their roles to spend more time working with small groups of students who share common interests, backgrounds, and talents.

Parental Involvement

Effective schools research has consistently shown that parental involvement has a powerful positive influence on learning. As seen in Chapter 11, at the end of the twentieth century, the favorite and most effective means of involving parents were newsletters and open houses.

Electronic bulletin boards and listservs can do anything a traditional newsletter could do, and do it much faster. In addition, computers can be used to individualize communication with parents. For example, individual academic computer files can be established, containing such items as individual education plans (IEPs) and academic contracts involving parents, making communications much more immediate and continuous. Because messages to parents would be accessible on the parents' computers, parents would have 24-hour access, which would sometimes free them of having to leave work to make school visits. Such approaches seem particularly attractive to many schools whose attendance at open houses has been declining over the past few decades.

Changes in technology will also require a reexamination of the role parents play in their children's education. In the past, beyond their role in providing students encouragement to do their homework assignments, parents were virtually shut out of their children's school time learning process, but now many parents have the ability and commitment to directly assist students with their assignments. How and how much these parents should contribute are questions that will need to be explored, now that the computer can make their children's assignments accessible to parents on a 24-hour basis.

This chapter should not end with tidy conclusions about how computers and other forms of technology should be used in classrooms because, although educators realize that technology has a powerful potential to enhance learning, it is still not entirely understood how technology should be used in schools. Nicaise and Barnes (1996, pp. 210–211) raise some of the many unanswered questions:

> What roles do students' goals and authentic tasks have on learning? How do complex and open-ended problems influence learning? What influence does technology have on interpersonal relationships? How can technology be used to promote learning?

This chapter also should not portray technology as the answer to all of our educational needs. On the contrary, some educators believe that the educational community should take a closer look at the limitations of technology. Pepi and Scheurman (1996, pp. 229–236) ask the following questions, which reveal some of these concerns:

> Just what do computers offer that those of us involved in elementary and secondary education really need? Are past, current, and anticipated uses of technology consistent with contemporary theories of learning? Is technology an effective catalyst for educational reform? Is using computers synonymous with good teaching? Does technology promote critical thinking? Does technology build cooperation? Is the appeal to a future dominated by computer technology a sufficient reason to give computer technology prominence in the public schools? How much information can we tolerate?

As seen in the case study, increased use of technology can actually cause problems. Roberto faced resistance at every turn, yet he remained undaunted, and his patience and persistence eventually led to success. Roberto's experience also provides insight into a major theme of this text, multiculturalism. Like technology, diversity among students presents teachers with an opportunity to enrich lessons and experiences almost beyond the imagination. Ironically, establishing a classroom that promotes diversity, including learning to respect all classmates and achieving a climate where all members will succeed, takes both of the strengths that Roberto so clearly exhibited—patience and persistence. Perhaps a prerequisite to developing either of these strengths is experiencing a strong sense of efficacy, a belief by the teacher that he or she and each student in class, by working together, can achieve the class goals.

The cooperative approach to learning reflects another major theme of this text, constructivism. Constructivists believe that students can learn better in a cooperative environment. The teacher establishes a positive, serious, yet enjoyable climate where individuals are encouraged and students are rewarded for helping others succeed. Roberto understands that to reach his school's technology goals he must establish and maintain a climate where his fellow teachers work cooperatively and positively to achieve these goals, and that yes, to a degree this responsibility belongs to everyone, including Roberto.

Chapter Summary

Every school has the potential to become a microcosm of the best features of the larger community of which it is a part. Like the community, the school has its own culture, which must be considered when curricula are developed. The curriculum developer must remember that the school is a creation of the community and is supported by the community, which means that the curriculum must serve the needs of the community.

Curriculum developers must also serve the needs of the students. With the breakdown of the traditional family and the increase in poverty and diversity in the late twentieth century, this job has become more challenging.

Forces are continuously at work in the schools and outside the schools; some forces pressure for change, while others press to maintain the status quo. Through the years, the textbook has been the major curriculum determiner, although it has many severe limitations. Recently, education reform laws have been a dominant force, introducing strategies that involve both parents and teachers and requiring teachers to use materials validated by research. Teachers and other curriculum developers must take the responsibility for examining local reform practices and for protecting the interests of their students.

Teachers attempting to promote multiculturalism recognize the need to protect cultural diversity, but confusion about relevant definitions has contributed to the ineffectiveness of their efforts. In democracies, people value diversity and individuals are encouraged to express dissent. The expression of individuality enhances feelings of self-worth, and this ultimately promotes success and increased productivity for the individual, which directly serves the country. Everyone in society suffers when some members of society do not contribute to their maximum potential. High but realistic expectations for all students can enhance academic achievement and eventual productivity and satisfaction in the workplace.

Constructivists emphasize the need to help students develop depth in understanding and tie newly acquired information to their existing knowledge base. Nicaise & Barnes (1996) report that technology can be used to increase depth in understanding. If technology is to be effective, similar connections must be made between the use of technology in the schools and the use of technology in the community. Teachers can help students make this connection by bringing business leaders and other leaders from the local community into the schools to show how the use of computers has improved their business or institution. Teachers can also give authentic, practical, real-world computer assignments in their classes. Because computers offer teachers the potential to improve learning in the classroom and at home, teachers will need to reexamine how students learn and what role parents play in their children's learning. The linear curriculum of the twentieth century may have to be replaced with a nonlinear approach to learning.

Education reform programs are pressing for educators to enhance students' appreciation of diversity. By including members of different ethnic groups and members of both sexes in the selection of consultants, teachers can enhance appreciation for diversity while reaching their technology goals.

Learning Questions

1. What do you believe Shouse meant when he said that the basic difference between the school world and the outside world is not in the activities themselves?

2. Why does a curriculum developer need to be familiar with a school's culture?

3. Should the fact that the community owns the schools give local citizens the right to dictate to the schools? If so, what types of issues should the community dictate, and what types should it not dictate?

4. In your opinion, what is the most important thing a school can do to develop good citizens?

5. What do you believe is the strongest force acting on school curricula? Explain your answer.

6. Should curriculum development courses focus on education reform? Why or why not?

7. How does tradition contribute to the schools positively? Negatively?

8. In what ways have teachers' technological needs expanded?

9. Describe one area in which educators' multicultural efforts need to be improved.

10. How can the curriculum developer adjust the curriculum to better meet the needs of children living in poverty?

11. What uncertainties do you have about making computer assignments?

12. How have education reform programs empowered teachers and parents to significantly change the schools?

13. If your school could influence the community to change in any way you wished, what change would you desire most?

14. If your school were a person, what do you think he or she would be feeling?

15. What does it mean to think of your school as a school as opposed to a training site or a factory?

16. How do the Goals for 2000 reflect constructivist theory?

Suggested Activities

1. Examine the course syllabi from all the courses you have taken, looking for multicultural objectives. Make a list of these objectives. Place an "x" by each objective you believe would be appropriate for future classes you will teach.

2. Study your school's community and make a list of multicultural resources. Include such items as field trips and guest speakers.

3. Research the literature for as many definitions as you can find for *cultural pluralism, cultural diversity,* and *multicultural education.* Using these definitions, write your own definition for each of these terms.

4. Interview a professor of computer education at your college. Make a list of the computer skills required for all undergraduate students in teacher education.

5. Interview two history teachers, asking them how they think the school can best develop citizenship in their students.

6. Select the method you prefer, for example, lecture, inquiry, discussion, simulation, or case study, and write an activity for your students to perform to develop good citizenship traits.

7. Develop a project to assign to your students to help them become more sensitive to world problems.

8. Write a computer assignment based on a multicultural problem in an urban setting.

9. Write a computer assignment that links your discipline to at least three other disciplines.

10. Choose a current reform practice at a local school and evaluate it in terms of constructivist theory.

Works Cited and Suggested Readings

Alessi, S. M., & Trollip, S. R. (1991). *Computer-based instruction, methods and development.* Englewood Cliffs, NJ: Prentice-Hall.

Antin, M. (1912). *The promised land.* Boston: Houghton Mifflin.

Apple, M. W. (1990). Is there a curriculum voice to reclaim? *Phi Delta Kappan, 71*(7), 526–530.

Armstrong, D. G., Henson, K. T., & Savage, T. V. (1993). *Education: An introduction* (4th ed.). Chapter 13. New York: Macmillan.

Barth, R. S. (1990). A personal vision of a good school. *Phi Delta Kappan, 71*(7), 512–516.

Becker, H. J. (1986). *Instructional uses of school computers: Report from the 1985 national survey.* Baltimore, MD: Johns Hopkins University, Center for Social Organization of Schools.

Berlinger, V. W., & Yates, C. M. (1993). Formal operational thought in the gifted: A post-Piagetian perspective. *Roeper Review, 15*(4), 220–224.

Berman, S. (1990, November). Educating for social responsibility. *Educational Leadership, 48*(3): 75–80.

Bernauer J. A. (1999). Emerging standards: Empowerment with purpose. *Kappa Delta Pi Record, 35*(2), 68–70, 74.

Brimfield, R. M. B. (1992, Summer). Curriculum: What's curriculum? *The Educational Forum, 56*(4), 381–389.

Burke, W. J. (1967). *Not for glory.* New York: Cowles Education Corporation.

Burrello, L. C., & Reitzug, U. C. (1993). Transforming context and developing culture in schools. *Journal of Counseling and Development, 71*(6), 669–677.

Buttery, T. J., & Anderson, P. J. (1999). Community, school, and parent dynamics: A synthesis of literature and activities. *Teacher Education Quarterly, 26*(4), 111–122.

Butzin, S. M. (1992, December). Interpreting technology into the classroom: Lessons from the Project Child experience. *Phi Delta Kappan, 74*(4), 330–333.

Campbell, L. P. (1990, September–October). Philosophy = Methodology = Motivation = Learning. *The Clearing House, 64*(1), 21–22.

Carnine, D., Grossen, B., & Silbert, I. (1995). "Direct instruction to facilitate cognitive growth." In J. H. Block, S. T. Everson, & T. R. Gusky (Eds.) *School improvement programs: A handbook for educational leaders.* New York: Scholastic, Inc.

Clark, S. N., Clark, D. C., & Irvin, J. I. (1997, May). Collaborative decision making. *Middle School Journal, 28*(5), 54–56.

Cohen, A. (1993). A new educational paradigm. *Phi Delta Kappan, 74*(10), 791–795.

Cohen, D. (1990). More voices in Babel? Educational research and the politics of curriculum. *Phi Delta Kappan, 71*(7), 518–522.

Conroy, P. (1972). *The water is wide.* (1991) Reprint. New York: The Old New York Book Shop.

Cooper, H., Lindsay, J. J., & Nye, B. (1998). *Homework in the home: How student, family, and parenting style differences relate to the homework process.* Research Report. Nashville, TN: Center for Research in Social Behavior, University of Missouri, and Center for Excellence for Research and Policy on Basic Skills, Tennessee State University.

Cooper, K. (1989). Education secretary calls for restructuring of public schools. *Center Daily Times,* May 23.

Curtis, A. C. (1998). Cultural reflections: The use of autobiography in the teacher education classroom. *Education, 119*(1), 28–30.

Dagenais, R. J. (1994). Professional development of teachers and administrators: Yesterday, today, and tomorrow/The views of Robert H. Anderson. *Kappa Delta Pi Record, 30*(2), 50–54.

Darling-Hammond, L. (1998). Teacher learning that supports student learning. *Educational Leadership, 55*(5), 6–11.

Darling-Hammond, L. (1996). The quiet revolution: Rethinking teacher development. *Educational Leadership, 53*(6), 4–10.

Darling-Hammond, L. (1993). Reforming the school reform agenda. *Phi Delta Kappan, 74*(10), 756–761.

Davis, G. A. (1993). Creative teaching of moral thinking: Fostering awareness and commitment. *Middle School Journal, 24*(4), 32–33.

Doyle, W. (1990). *Case methods in the education of teachers. Teacher Education Quarterly, 17*(1), 7–15.

Edwards, J. L. (1994). Get started on technology. *Education Digest, 59*(5), 46–47.

Eisner, E. W. (1985). *The educational imagination* (2nd ed.). NewYork: Macmillan.

Eisner, E. W. (1990). Who decides what schools should teach? *Phi Delta Kappan, 71*(7), 523–526.

Elam, S. M. (1996). Phi Delta Kappa's young leaders of 1980 tackle today's issues. *Phi Delta Kappan, 77*(9), 610–614.

Elam, S. M., Rose, L. C., & Gallup, A. (1994). The 26th annual Phi Delta Kappa/Gallup poll of the public's attitudes toward the public school." *Phi Delta Kappan, 76*(1), 41–56.

Erb, T. (1997, March). Student-friendly classrooms in not a very child-friendly world. *Middle School Journal, 28*(5), 2.

Fenstermacher, G. D. (1994, June 10). The absence of democratic and educational ideals from contemporary educational reform initiatives. Stanley Elam Lecture. Educational Press Association of America, Chicago.

Gagnon, E. (1996). *What's on the Web?* Fairfax, VA: Internet Media Corporation.

Garcia, R. L. (1994). Human rights in the pluralistic classroom. *Kappa Delta Pi Record, 30*(2), 70.

Geisert, G., & Dunn, R. (1991, March–April). Effective use of computers: Assignments based on individual learning style. *The Clearing House, 64*(4), 219–223.

Genesse, F., & Cloud, N. (1998). Multilingualism is a basic. *Educational Leadership, 55*(6), 62–65.

Glatthorn, A. A. (1993). *Learning twice.* New York: HarperCollins.

Goodlad, J. I. (1997). In praise of education. New York: Teachers College Press.

Goodman, K. S. et al. (1988). *Report card on basal readers.* Katonah, NY: Richard C. Owen.

Gough, P. B. (1990, June). Good news and bad news. *Phi Delta Kappan, 71*(10), 747.

Halperin, R. (1996). Exemplary curriculums cross national borders. *Educational Leadership, 53*(8), 59.

Hill, P. T. (1990, January). The federal role in education: A strategy for the 1990s. *Phi Delta Kappan, 71*(5), 398–402.

Hirsch, H. (1991, Spring). Book review. *The Educational Forum, 55*(3), 285–288.

Holt, M. (1993, January). The educational consequences of W. Edwards Demming. *Phi Delta Kappan, 74*(5), 382–388.

Kenney, D. J., & Watson, T. S. (1996). Reducing fear in the schools: Managing conflict through problem solving. *Education and Urban Society, 28*(4), 436–455.

Knapp, M. S., & Shields, P. M. (1990, June). Reconceiving academic instruction for the children of poverty. *Phi Delta Kappan, 71*(10), 753–758.

Kochan, F. K., & Herrington, C. D. (1992, Fall). Restructuring for today's children & strengthening schools by strengthening families. *The Educational Forum, 57,* 42–49.

Kowalski, T. J., & Reitzug, U. C. (1993). *Contemporary school administration: An introduction.* New York: Longman.

Kowalski, T. J., Weaver, R. A., & Henson, K. T. (1994). *Case studies on teaching.*

Krashen, S. (1998). Bridging inequity with books. *Educational Leadership, 55*(4), 18–21.

Lewis, A. (1994). Reinventing local school governance. *Phi Delta Kappan, 75*(5), 356–357.

Lieberman, A. (1990). Navigating the four C's: Building a bridge over troubled waters. *Phi Delta Kappan, 71*(7), 531–533.

Lounsbury, J. H. (1991). A fresh start for the middle school curriculum. *Middle School Journal, 23*(2), 3–7.

Markle, G., Johnston, J. H., Geer, C., & Meichtry, Y. (1990, November). Teaching for understanding. *Middle School Journal, 22*(2), 53–57.

McNeil, J. D. (1990). *Curriculum: A comprehensive introduction* (4th ed.). New York: HarperCollins.

Mecklenburger, J. A. (1990, October). Educational technology is not enough. *Phi Delta Kappan, 71,* 20.

Merseth, K. J. (1990). Case studies and teacher education. *Teacher Education Quarterly, 17*(1), 53–62.

Nagel, G. K. (1998). Looking for multicultural education: What could be done and why it isn't. *Education, 119*(2), 253–262.

National Council for Accreditation of Teacher Education (1990). *Standards, procedures, and policies for the accreditation of professional education units.* Washington, DC: National Council for Accreditation of Teacher Education.

Nelson, W. W. (1999). The emperor redux. *Phi Delta Kappan, 80*(5), 387–392.

Nicaise, M., & Barnes, D. (1996). The union of technology, constructivism, and teacher education. *Journal of Teacher Education, 47*(3), 205–212.

Northrup, P. T., & Little, W. (1996). Establishing instructional technology benchmarks for teacher preparation programs. *Journal of Teacher Education, 47*(3), 213–222.

Oana, R. G. (1993). *Changes in teacher education: Reform, renewal, reorganization, and professional development schools: A professional development leave report.* Bowling Green, OH: Bowling Green State University.

O'Neal, M., Earley, B., & Snider, M. (1991). Addressing the needs of at-risk students: A local school program that works. In R. C. Morris (Ed.) *Youth at risk,* pp. 122–125. Lancaster, PA.: Technomic Publishing Co.

Ovando, C. (1994, March 18). Curriculum reform and language minority students. Presentation delivered at the 1994 Professors of Curriculum meeting. Chicago.

Parker, W. C. (1990, November). Assessing citizenship. *Educational Leadership, 48*(3), 17–22.

Patrick, D., & Reinhartz, J. (1999). The role of collaboration in teacher preparation to meet the needs of diversity. *Education, 119*(3), 388–399.

Pepi, D., & Scheurman, G. (1996). The emperor's new computer: A critical look at our appetite for computer technology. *Journal of Teacher Education, 47*(3) 229–236.

Pipho, C. (1992, December). A decade of education reform." *Phi Delta Kappan, 74*(4), 278–279.

Ponder, G. A., & Holmes, K. M. (1992, Summer). Purpose, products, and visions: The creation of new schools. *The Educational Forum, 56*(4), 405–418.

Price, H. B. (1992). Multiculturalism: Myths and realities. *Phi Delta Kappan, 74*(3), 208 213.

Rappoport, A. L., & Kletzien, S. (1996). Kids around town: Civics lessons leave impressions. *Educational Leadership, 53*(8), 26–29.

Reed, D. F. (1994). Multicultural education for preservice students. *Action in teacher education, 15*(3), 27–34.

Reich, R. B. (1991). *The work of nations: Preparing ourselves for the 21st century capitalism.* New York: Knopf.

Ribas, W. B. (1998). Tips for reaching parents. *Educational Leadership, 56*(1), 83–85.

Riley, M. N. (1992, November). If it looks like manure. *Phi Delta Kappan, 74*(3), 239–241.

Rose, L. C. (1991, October). A vote of confidence for the schools. *Phi Delta Kappan, 73*(2), 121–128.

Ross, D. D., Bondy, E., & Kyle, D. W. (1993). *Reflective teaching for student empowerment.* New York: Macmillan.

Rothenberg, D. (1993). Multicultural education. *Middle School Journal, 24*(4), 73–75.

Rothstein, P. R. (1990). *Educational Psychology.* New York: McGraw-Hill.

Sagor, R. (1990, November). Education for living in a nuclear age. *Educational Leadership, 48*(3), 81–83.

Schlechty, P. C. (1990). *Schools for the 21st century: Leadership imperatives for educational reform.* San Francisco: Jossey-Bass Publishers.

Scott, P. (1993). Unpublished manuscript. Tallahassee, FL.

Seligmann, J. (1989, Winter Spring). Variations on a theme. *Newsweek, 22*(2), 38–46.

Shouse, J. B. (1992). The school has captured the world. *The Educational Forum, 57*(1), 104–106.

Siegel, M. A., & Davis, D. M. (1986). *Understanding computer-based education,* New York: Random House.

Sizer, T. R. (1990). *Horace's compromise: The dilemma of the American high school.* Boston: HoughtonMifflin.

Snider, R. C. (1992, December). The machine in the classroom. *Phi Delta Kappan, 74*(4), 316–323.

Solomon, S. (1989). Homework: The great reinforcer. *The Clearing House, 63*(2), 63.

Stinnett, T. M., & Henson, K. T. (1982). *America's public schools in transaction.* Columbia, NY: Teachers College Press.

Stringfield, J. K. (1991). The Humpty Dumpty school of communications in education. *The Educational Forum, 55*(3), 261–269.

Thompson, S., & Gregg, L. (1997, May). Reculturing middle schools for meaningful change. *Middle School Journal, 28*(5), 27–31.

Tice, T. N. (1994). Research spotlight. *Education Digest, 59*(5), 48–51.

Tishman, S., Jay, E., & Perkins, D. N. (1993). Teaching thinking dispositions: From transmission to enculturation. *Theory Into Practice, 32*(3), 147–153.

U.S. Congress. Office of Technology Assessment (1995). *Teachers and technology: Making the connection.* Washington, DC: U.S. Government Printing Office.

Wang, M. C., Haertel, G. D., & Walberg, H. J. (1998). Models of reform: A comparative guide. *Educational Leadership, 55*(7), 66–71.

Williams, P. A., Alley, R., & Henson, K. T. (1999). *Managing secondary classrooms.* Boston: Allyn & Bacon.

Wirth, A. C. (1993, January). Educational work: The choice we face. *Phi Delta Kappan, 74*(5), 361–366.

Wood, G. H. (1990, November). Teaching for democracy. *Educational Leadership, 48*(3), 32–37.

3 HISTORICAL AND PHILOSOPHICAL FOUNDATIONS OF CURRICULUM

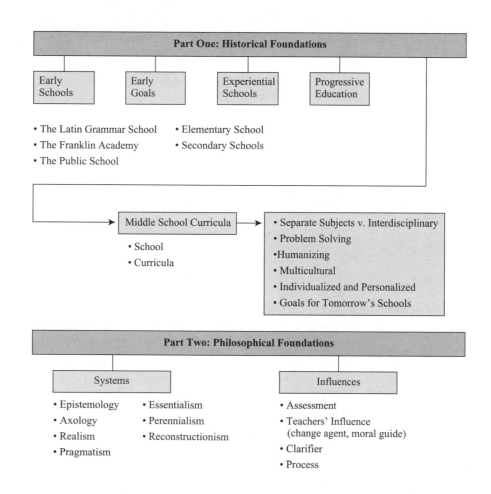

Part One: Historical Foundations

| Early Schools | Early Goals | Experiential Schools | Progressive Education |

- The Latin Grammar School
- The Franklin Academy
- The Public School

- Elementary School
- Secondary Schools

Middle School Curricula

- School
- Curricula

- Separate Subjects v. Interdisciplinary
- Problem Solving
- Humanizing
- Multicultural
- Individualized and Personalized
- Goals for Tomorrow's Schools

Part Two: Philosophical Foundations

Systems

- Epistemology
- Axology
- Realism
- Pragmatism

- Essentialism
- Perennialism
- Reconstructionism

Influences

- Assessment
- Teachers' Influence (change agent, moral guide)
- Clarifier
- Process

Objectives

- Evaluate the Seven Cardinal Principles of Secondary Education in terms of their relevance for today's schools.
- Discuss colonial legislation and its effect on today's schools.
- Give evidence of the Progressive Education Movement in today's curricula.
- Compare and contrast the influence of John Locke and John Dewey on today's curriculum.
- Discuss the role the curriculum must play in ensuring that the needs in multicultural classrooms are met.
- Trace the development of curricula from the colonial days to the present and relate this history to contemporary education reform.
- Give examples of three philosophical constructs in your fellow teachers' reactions to education reform.

THE CASE OF DIANE WORLEY

As Diane Worley completed her student teaching semester and her teacher education program, she reflected on the past four and a half years which she thought would take forever to finish but which surprisingly has passed so fast. At first she had been confused about the rumble over school reform in her state, but now she was glad that she had taken advantage of every opportunity to learn all she could about these activities. Having accepted her first teaching assignment and enrolled in her first graduate class, a curriculum development course, Diane was determined to use both her school experience and her curriculum course to continue learning about school reform.

Education 501, Foundations and Principles of Curriculum Development, proved to be an excellent setting in which Diane could pursue her newest professional goal. The course required each student to conduct an independent research project, prepare a written report, and make an oral presentation of this report to the rest of the class. The written report would be due two weeks prior to the final class meeting.

Diane had little difficulty in choosing her topic, "The Relationship Between the History of American Education and Contemporary School Reform." Her professor readily approved this topic.

As with most research studies, the first and most difficult task is delineating the project so that it is manageable. Diane considered the following issues:

- **The effect of American legislation on school reform.**   This would involve making a survey of such legislation as the Old Deluder Satan Act, the Kalamazoo case, and the Northwest Ordinance, examining the goals of these laws, and comparing these goals to the goals of current school reform.

- **The effect that textbooks have had on the curricula in American schools throughout their history and the effect they are now having in current reform efforts.**   This would include reviewing such books as the Bible, the McGuffey Readers, required classical literature, and the contemporary textbooks that Diane would use in her classes during her first year of teaching.

- **The Relationship between the Seven Cardinal Principles of Secondary Education and the Goals for 2000.**

- **The relationship between the goals of the Progressive Education Movement and those of contemporary school reform.**

- **The implications of the recommendations made at the Woods Hole Conference on current reform goals.**

- **The causes for the development of the junior high school and middle school and a comparison of these causes with the current school reform efforts.**

- **A comparison of the current priorities of middle-level education and the Goals for 2000.**

- **A survey of the major curriculum changes over the past 250 years and a comparison of these trends with the goals of current school reform.**

Diane found that just reflecting on these issues and the simple act of making the list were both stimulating. She imagined the many charts she could use to visually show relationships in new and interesting ways. This project would enable her to make a unique contribution to education reform in her school while equipping her with some of the tools needed to implement education reform.

Within a few days, Diane Worley had settled into her new school environment. She enjoyed each part of her new world. Naturally, this included the lunch period and breaks spent in the lounge, which provided about the only opportunities she had throughout the day to socialize with her fellow teachers. The lounge was especially interesting because of the differences she could see among her coworkers. Although she expected to see more agreement among professional teachers than she had seen among her fellow college students, such was not the case. In fact, compared to her college peers, these teachers seemed to have even more pronounced differences in opinions. But the part she liked most was that her new peers seemed free to express their views without fear of pressure to agree with their colleagues or without feeling that they needed their colleagues to agree with them.

Diane also enjoyed being treated as a professional. Her principal and the administrative staff treated her the same they treated teachers who had taught for many years. "What a contrast," she thought, "from the way I was treated as an undergraduate student." It was surprising to realize the degree to which others' perceptions of her had changed in only a few weeks.

To Diane, the best part of her new teaching career was the relationship she had with her students; nothing equaled the joy she felt from the meeting of minds engaged in purposeful learning. Soon though, Diane was to learn that not everyone shared her love of the pursuit of knowledge. Or perhaps the problem was that her love of her chosen methods of inquiry was grossly misunderstood.

The challenge came early in the first grading period when Diane introduced the term *concept*. Since some students seemed a little confused, Diane decided to give some examples. She carefully lifted her desk chair and placed it on the center of her desk. She began the inquiry by asking the students to name the object on the desk. Although several of the older students seemed embarrassed about responding, everyone eventually said it was a chair. Then she asked the students how they knew it was a chair. The students began naming its parts: "It's a chair because it has a seat, four legs, and a back." "What would it be if these parts were disassembled?" Diane asked. After a lengthy discussion, the students concluded that it would no longer be a chair but just a collection of chair parts. "Then, a chair is more than something physical?" Diane concluded, with a questioning tone. The students agreed. Diane felt that she was really getting the idea of a *concept* over to these students; however, the district instructional supervisor happened to pass by Diane's classroom. Seeing the chair on the desk, the supervisor decided to pause long enough to see what was going on.

The supervisor, Ms. Sterling-Austin, was more than intrigued by this novel approach. In fact, after the lesson, she questioned this teaching style very rigorously.

Many teachers have lost the passion for teaching that Diane feels. Negative reform reports, articles, and radio and television programs on education reform have caused many contemporary teachers to feel underappreciated. An awareness of the history of American schools and an ability to apply history and philosophy to curriculum development should help readers assess local reform practices.

PART ONE: HISTORICAL FOUNDATIONS OF CURRICULUM

The Migrations

Certainly one of the most colorful characters in history was England's King Henry VIII, noted for his political cunning, lust, bad temper, and selfishness among other qualities. When the Roman Catholic Church refused to sanctify Henry's marriage to Anne Boleyn, he established his own church, the Church of England, which today is still the major denomination in England. When James I became king in 1603, he made life difficult for certain Protestant churches. After resisting his pressures for seventeen years, one Protestant group went to

Holland. Meeting even greater opposition there, they soon left for America. By this time a second group of Protestants had left England for America, and by 1630 both groups had arrived in the area that was to be named Massachusetts.

Contrary to popular belief, these people, known as the *Puritans,* were not seeking religious freedom for all—they were seeking religious freedom for the Puritans. According to their strict laws, the role of the church was to interpret the will of God, and the role of the state was to enforce it. The church building commonly served also as the courthouse where civil laws were made and offenders were tried and sentenced. Since the civil law and the church were inseparable and since obedience to God required a knowledge of His laws, an institution was needed to guarantee that each citizen possessed this required knowledge.

Early Schools

The Latin Grammar School

In 1635 the first Latin grammar school, forerunner of our modern schools, appeared (Armstrong et al., 1997). Designed after the English schools, Latin grammar schools aimed at preparing select young men for entrance to an elite college that opened in 1636 in Massachusetts. Among the Puritan immigrants were more than a hundred graduates of Oxford and Cambridge universities. Steeped in a tradition that prized quality education, these highly educated settlers were determined to provide equally excellent educational opportunities for their sons. Thus, the General Court of Massachusetts appropriated approximately $1,000 for a new college.

Soon afterward, a young minister who was dying of tuberculosis willed his 400 books and half of his estate (worth almost $2,000) to the new college. This gift by John Harvard prompted the renaming of the institution to Harvard College.

The Dame Schools

By 1642 every home was required to teach reading, Puritanism, and the laws of the colony (Armstrong et al., 1997). Thus the first American "public schools" were not really schools at all, at least not in the sense of having a schoolhouse with professional teachers. Although they were commonly called *dame schools* or *kitchen schools,* they were actually citizens' homes. Some wealthy citizens met the requirements of the law by hiring English tutors and transporting them to America to work. But since this option was unaffordable for most people, many of the early settlers got together and designated one of the women to teach the neighborhood children. Because household help was expensive and the teachers' pay was meager or nothing at all, these "dames" often taught the children at the kitchen table while also preparing the family meals. Thus came the names dame school and kitchen school. The curriculum for these schools often consisted of no more than a few simple laws of the colony, a few Biblical rhymes, and some Biblical readings. Inspectors visited each house to ensure that this teaching was being done. Because this system was expensive and ineffective, it was soon replaced by the public school.

The main motivation for the Puritans' long, expensive, and dangerous journey to the New World was their desire to build a new community to worship God. Worried that the devil was constantly engaged in efforts to take advantage of their children's ignorance and mislead them, the Puritans wasted little time before passing a law to help their children escape the devil's snares or delude the devil. The law, called the *Old Deluder Satan Act,* passed in 1647, required Massachusetts towns to erect and maintain schools. Communities of 50 or more families had to teach reading and writing; those with 100 or more families had to establish a Latin grammar school and hire a teacher. The curriculum of this school was highly classical and dominated by Latin and Greek.

The Franklin Academy

The following century was characterized by expansion; surveyors were needed to build roads, navigators were needed for the expanding trade industry, mathematicians were needed for growing businesses, and so on. Soon a need developed for a very different type of school, one with a less classical and more practical curriculum. Benjamin Franklin responded to this need by opening the Franklin Academy in Philadelphia. In many ways the academy was the very opposite of the Latin grammar school: the academy was both secular and practical, offering subjects such as mathematics, astronomy, surveying, bookkeeping, and navigation. Because of its practical emphasis, by the end of the Revolutionary War, schools modeled on the Franklin Academy had replaced the Latin grammar school as the most common type of secondary school in the United States. The content, strengths, and weaknesses of the three types of early schools are summarized in Table 3.1.

TABLE 3.1   Curricula of Early Schools

	Dame School	*Latin Grammar School*	*Franklin Academy*
Content	Puritanism, colonial law, reading	Latin, Greek, religion	Astronomy, bookkeeping, mathematics, navigation, surveying
Outstanding Strength	The only school available	Availability	Practical
Outstanding Weakness	The teachers were not trained professionals	Impractical curriculum	Charged tuition

The Public School

The Franklin Academy's practical curriculum enabled it to replace the Latin grammar school (Armstrong et al., 1997), but it had one weakness—it was private and many parents could not afford its tuition. The Revolutionary War kindled a spirit of freedom and caused citizens to realize the value of education to a democratic society. Thomas Jefferson eloquently expressed this idea when he declared, "If a nation expects to be ignorant and free in a state of civilization it expects what never was and what never will be." In 1779, Jefferson proposed three years of free public education to all citizens of Virginia. Unfortunately, however, another 42 years passed before the Boston School Committee established the country's first public high school, in 1821. The Boston English Classical School, later named the Boston English High School, was developed to prepare youth for employment. For many of its students, it served as an entry to the university. Since early high schools served these two distinctly different purposes, the curricula in individual schools varied greatly; most were very pragmatic, but some, located in college communities, were highly classical.

By 1860, half of the nation's children were in school. The commitment of the government to education was reconfirmed in 1787 by the Northwest Ordinance, which reserved a parcel of land in every township to be sold to finance public education. Further support came in 1874 in the Kalamazoo case, which gave citizens in every town the right to levy taxes to support their secondary schools.

Goals for the Early Elementary School

Since the time of the establishment of the forerunners to modern elementary schools, the curriculum has been continually expanding. The first Latin grammar schools had the single purpose of preparing elite young men for Harvard and the ministry, and the dame schools continued this religious emphasis, but their curricula broadened to include colonial law and reading. These changes were not as bold as they might sound, since the colonial law and God's word were one and the same, and since the reason for adding reading was to prepare the youth to read the Bible.

Goals for the Early High School

The last quarter of the nineteenth century set some definite trends that are still prevalent in high school education. The once small schools began to grow in enrollments. Teachers and administrators joined to form the first unified coalition of organized educators, the National Education Association (NEA). The NEA assumed leadership in determining the goals for the early high schools, and in 1892 its Committee of Ten stated that the purpose of the school was to prepare students for life, yet recommended that all students be taught the college

preparatory subjects. Three years later the NEA reinforced the college preparatory goal with its Committee on College Entrance Requirements. During this
same quarter century, regional associations were formed to inspect and accredit
high schools.

The new century brought further clarification of the goals of the high school.
In 1918 the NEA's Commission on the Reorganization of Secondary Education
listed the following seven principles, formally known as the Seven Cardinal
Principles of Secondary Education, as the main goals for both secondary and
elementary schools:

1. Health

2. Command of fundamental processes (development of basic skills)

3. Worthy home membership

4. Vocational efficiency

5. Citizenship

6. Worthy use of leisure time

7. Ethical character

Many educators consider this list of broad goals for high schools as the
most important aims ever set forth for American education. The goals in fact
apply to both elementary and secondary schools. While the list contains only
seven entries, the breadth and nature of the goals have caused them to remain
relevant even though society has constantly changed.

Experiential Education

From the beginning of public schools in America until 1875 (about 250 years),
the school curricula have been largely determined by one type of textbook or
another. Initially, the main texts were the Bible and the hornbook, a slate with
a sheet of parchment or paper, used in the dame schools, covered with hornlike
(or bonelike) material to protect the paper from becoming soiled, so it could be
used repeatedly.

In the 1690s the first basal reader, called the *New England Primer,* was
published. It, too, was a blend of religion and morals. Rhymes, called *catechisms,*
were used to teach religious doctrine and language skills. Walker (1976, p. 6)
described the primer's contents: "The sin of man, the wrath of God, the judgment of a fiery hell, and the salvation of a resurrected Christ permeated it from
cover to cover." In 1782 Noah Wester's book, known as the *Blue Back Speller,*
was published, adding spelling to the curriculum. During the next 60 years, 24
million copies of the speller were sold. The intentions of the book were to provide moral and nonsectarian religious guidance, to provide valuable knowledge,
and to motivate the students' interest.

During these first 250 years, instruction centered on recitation. Students
studied, memorized, and recited their lessons until the material was committed

to memory; those who failed received corporal punishment. In 1875 this method was openly challenged by Colonel Francis Parker, who had been orphaned at the age of 8 and apprenticed to a farmer until the age of 21. Parker had discovered that life on the farm was very educational, but he had found school to be so hateful and unbearable that he attended it only about eight weeks every year. Instead of turning his back on education, however, Parker decided to try to improve it. He believed that if education could be acquired pleasantly in the fields, woodlands, and pastures, it could also be enjoyed in the schools. His dream was to become a great teacher; little did he know that the fulfillment of his dream would result in a revolution of American education.

In 1875 this huge bearded man was elected as superintendent of schools in Quincy, Massachusetts, a suburb of Boston. Parker established teachers' meetings where he gave to his 40 teachers not advice and knowledge but questions and demonstrations. He did not tell them how to teach; he showed them. He gave them not only a technique but also a spirit; he made them want to put life into their curriculum. To create a natural learning environment, Parker substituted games and puzzles for recitation and rote memorization. In the lower grades he instituted singing, playing, reading, counting objects, writing, and drawing. Above all, he wanted the experiences at his schools to be happy ones. Reversing the traditional teaching process, which began with rules and definitions, he gave students real-life problems that made them seek out the rules or generalizations.

This system, which became known as the *Quincy System,* gained national attention. In his own words Parker told how enthusiastic the community had become over its schools: "Throughout the centuries of Quincy's history, its people have ever manifested a deep interest in education, and I believe that I am right when I say that at no time in the past has this interest been greater than it is in the first year of the new century [of Independence]" (Campbell, 1967, p. 83).

The Quincy System was the forerunner of other innovative experiments in education, including the Gary Plan, the Dalton Plan, and the Winnetka Plan. The *Gary Plan* was developed by William A. Wirt, the superintendent of schools in Gary, Indiana, where the elementary and high schools were designed as miniature communities. Unlike the other schools which had self-contained classrooms, the Gary Plan was open; students moved freely from one place to another throughout the day in platoons. Like Parker's system, this system was experimental and student-centered. The *Dalton Plan,* developed in Dalton, Massachusetts, in 1919, was significant in that it was a highly individualized program. Using contracts, students followed their own program. This plan involved students and teachers in the development of curricula. The *Winnetka Plan,* developed in 1919 by Carleton Washburne, superintendent of schools at Winnetka, Illinois, was also a highly individualized program. Stressing self-expression and creativity, it even used self-instructional materials to teach the fundamentals. The features of these experimental student-centered curricula are shown in Table 3.2.

TABLE 3.2   Early Twentieth-Century Student-Centered Curricula

Quincy System	Gary Plan	Dalton Plan	Winnetka Plan
Games and puzzles	Miniature communities	Student contracts	Self-instructional materials
Student and teacher involvement in planning	Platoons	Student and teacher involvement in planning	Self-expression and creativity

These programs were important in two ways: First, they changed the way Americans thought about education, which no longer had to be textbook-oriented and dominated by recitation. Students could become the center of the learning experience, and school could be enjoyed, since student activity was not stifled but encouraged. The belief of the seventeenth-century philosopher John Locke—that experience is the basis of all understanding—was finally being implemented. Second, these programs were important because they led to several national movements in education.

In a survey of 149 principals in Minnesota and Indiana, Kowalski (1994) found that involvement in curriculum development leads teachers to assume higher levels of responsibility. Sixty-one percent of the respondents said that it brought significant improvements to their programs. In recent years, site-based management has significantly increased the level of teacher involvement in schoolwide curriculum planning. Wohlstetter (1997) concluded that the ability of site-based management to bring lasting change to the curriculum must be complemented by (1) organizational conditions that encourage interactions among stakeholders, and (2) far-reaching curricula and instructional reforms that can guide those interactions. After reviewing the research on site-based management, Latham (1998, p. 86) concluded that "To be considered truly successful, site-based management must be tied to real reforms in how educators interact with one another and how they teach their students."

Progressive Education

The experienced-based movement that Francis Parker had started in 1875 moved vigorously into the twentieth century. Before his death in 1902, Parker took a position as head of a normal school in Chicago, which later merged with the University of Chicago, where John Dewey was head of the philosophy and psychology department from 1894 to 1904. Professor Dewey established a school on the university's campus to serve as an experimental laboratory to study education processes. This laboratory school was like any other school except that it was accessible to the university professors and students to conduct on-site research on teaching practices. Within a few years, almost every state in the nation had at least one university laboratory school.

Fifty years later, most of these laboratory schools were still operating, but recently most of them have eliminated the high school grades. As the century ended, all but about one hundred of the laboratory schools had closed. Ironically, many of the surviving schools are now playing a major role in education reform by being forerunners in implementing school reform in their states, by serving as professional development schools, and by acting as role models through implementing education reform practices.

During the first quarter of the twentieth century, true concern for the student was evident. The Progressive Education Movement was child-centered, as opposed to subject-centered. Though often confused with permissive education, the Progressive Education Movement did not espouse permissiveness. The concept of progressivism is much more akin to pragmatism, for during this era secondary school curricula became much more practical, offering agriculture, home economics, and other vocational subjects.

Progressivism meant more than practicality; it also meant that students helped plan the curriculum and sometimes selected their own individualized learning activities. The arts, sports, and extracurricular activities were added to the school program. Progressive educators' belief in the democratic process led them to involve parents, students, and teachers. For 50 years the progressive trend was well accepted by students, who perceived the curriculum as highly relevant. From 1933 to 1941 the Progressive Education Association sponsored the Eight-Year Study, a survey of the effects of such a general education on learners. Conducted by Harvard University, the study followed students of 30 experimental high schools through high school and college. The graduates of the experimental school equaled their counterparts in the attainment of subject matter, and they outperformed them in attainment of academic honors and grades. Furthermore, students who had had freedom of choice in their curricula proved to be significantly superior in intellectual curiosity, creativity, drive, leadership, and extraclass activities. They also proved to be more objective and more aware of world events. Unfortunately, because of timing alone, the results of the Eight-Year Study were lost in history; they were made public just as the country plunged into World War II.

Separate Subjects vs. Interdisciplinary Approach

By the middle of the twentieth century, the question of how content should be structured had become a hot issue. The Progressive Movement had blended the various disciplines in the belief that more understanding would result. For example, the "core curriculum" had become very popular: a core of common experiences was believed to be essential for all students, and some of these experiences were interdisciplinary. But interdisciplinary movements were criticized severely by educators such as Arthur E. Bestor (1953), who believed that they had weakened the curricula. Bestor and others criticized schools severely for this "anti-intellectualism."

Curricula That Promote Inquiry

In the 1950s, urged on by such critics as California's superintendent of education, Max Rafferty, and U.S. Navy Admiral Hyman Rickover, the American public reexamined its schools. There was a general attitude of disappointment, culminating in the Russians' successful launching of the world's first satellite in 1957. Harvard University's president, James B. Conant, had already been insisting that the secondary school curricula should be more rigorous. He especially urged that stronger minimum requirements be made of all students and that even more requirements be made for the academically gifted.

As a result, a special committee convened in Woods Hole, Massachusetts, in 1959 to design a better system for educating America's youth. The 35 leaders in education, government, industry, and science concluded that education should be built around broad theories and concepts. The following year, Woods Hole Conference committee member Jerome S. Bruner (1960, p. 33) reported the general conclusions of the study in his book *The Process of Education*. One of his often-quoted statements in that book expresses the emphasis that this committee placed on structuring knowledge so that it can be more easily learned. Said Bruner, "I hypothesize that any subject can be taught effectively in some intellectually honest form to any child."

The 1960s saw a veritable alphabet soup of programs that often integrated two or more disciplines in an attempt to help students learn to inquire and discover relationships. Some of the more popular programs were the SMSG (Science-Mathematics-Study Group), ESCP (Earth Science Curriculum Project), BSCS (Biological Sciences Curriculum Study), PSSC (Physical Science Study Committee), and ISCS (Intermediate Science Curriculum Study). Another contribution was Benjamin Bloom's Taxonomy of Educational Objectives, which enabled teachers to build learning experiences on increasingly higher levels of the thought processes. With advances in technology came another reason for structuring learning experiences: students needed to be stimulated to think through processes and to establish relationships themselves, not just to remember facts but to use those facts to solve problems.

Even when efforts are made to integrate the disciplines, however, some teachers have a way of resisting changes that they think might weaken teaching of their discipline. Often they insist on teaching only their own discipline, in which they find familiarity and comfort. Thompson and Gregg (1997, p. 30) noted this protective trait of teachers, stating, "In fact, most interdisciplinary teams operate as multidisciplinary teams with each teacher on the team responsible for his or her own content area."

This recognition of teachers' tendency to teach only their own disciplines does not dissuade some educators from promoting the benefits of integrating the disciplines. Clark, Clark, and Irvin (1997, p. 55) cited several advantages of involving teachers in collaborative planning: "The research on collaborative decision making suggests that teacher participation does positively affect the school climate. Better communication and increased involvement and empowerment are constantly reported."

Teachers can also be taught valuable inquiry skills, which can improve teachers' ability to reach all students, including students of other cultures. As Darling-Hammond (1998, p. 9) noted, "Training in inquiry also helps teachers learn how to look at the world from multiple perspectives and to use this knowledge to reach diverse students."

Curricula That Humanize

An important goal of today's schools is to humanize the school environment. The country's first high schools were typically one-room buildings designed to accommodate at most a few dozen students, but during the early 1950s there was a national trend to consolidate small schools. This resulted in larger and larger schools, until today a school of 2,000, 3,000, or 4,000 students is common. The advantage is that a greater diversity of subjects is possible; the disadvantage is the resulting impersonal, dehumanizing environment.

As you continue to study curriculum planning, think about ways you can make learning more personal, more meaningful, and more enjoyable for your students. This topic will be revisited in Chapter 5.

Multicultural Curricula

Beginning teachers are often nervous or concerned about facing multicultural classes without the skills to help students of varied backgrounds meet their needs (Wilson, Ireton, & Wood, 1997). Researchers are trying to determine the most effective ways to teach in multicultural settings and to design curricula that promote an appreciation for diversity. The area of concern is expanding to include groups that have traditionally been ignored even when attention was given to other minority groups.

Effective management of multiculturalism will require each administrator and each faculty member to invent curriculum and instructional approaches to meet the needs of the unique student body at each school and the needs of each unique classroom. Student involvement in the development of multicultural curricula, individualization, and personalization is indispensable.

Curricula That Individualize and Personalize

The 1960s saw much attention being placed on individualizing the curriculum, and some very good programs were developed. Individualized Guided Education (IGE), a program developed in Wisconsin, and Individually Prescribed Instruction (IPI) developed at the University of Pittsburgh, are two of the most successful. The competency-based movement of the 1970s introduced individualization into American schools at all levels, elementary through university. The competency-based programs have made significant contributions to individualizing education but, ironically and often justifiably, have been labeled "dehumanizing." It is becoming increasingly obvious that mere individualization is not enough (Kohl, in Scherer 1998). Our huge contemporary schools with their complicated schedules (many running on double shifts) need more. They need ways of personalizing all aspects of the schooling process. Koba (1996, p. 17) has said that "(A curriculum grounded in the lives of students) would enable them to more easily learn meaningful content and skills and to focus on their own needs and the needs of their community."

Twenty-first century schools must address students' social needs. Academic success cannot come in an environment that ignores students' personal needs. Erb (1997, p. 2) expresses this sentiment, saying, "While the public and legislatures may be mandating evaluation only in academic areas, success there can only come if the young adolescents we teach are socially and emotionally healthy as well."

One approach to helping students cope with their personal and social problems is by offering conflict resolution experiences in their curricula. Currently, over two thousand schools conduct conflict resolution programs, which permit students to role-play their problems (Houck & Maxon, 1997). Cherniss (1998, p. 28) reports that "Increasingly, schools are providing students with opportunities for social and emotional learning."

GOALS FOR TOMORROW'S SCHOOLS

The New Basics

How can anyone know what needs the future will bring and what goals future schools will have? The task is not as impossible as it sounds; in fact, there are some clear goals. The late Dr. Harold Shane of Indiana University called the goals "the new basics" for our secondary schools. These goals include the need to (1) learn how to live with uncertainty, complexity, and change; (2) develop the ability to anticipate; (3) adapt to new structures, new constraints, and new situations without emotional drain and emotional collisions; (4) learn how to learn, that is, learn how to search out contradictions in one's values and understandings; (5) see relationships and be able to sort and weigh them; (6) understand the facts of life (realities) and become aware of alternatives; (7) learn to analyze the consequences of one's choices; (8) learn how to make choices; and (9) learn how to work together to get things done. For example, youth must learn how to reach compromises and how to accept compromises with honor.

Certainly, the new basics for the twenty-first century must include appreciating multiculturalism, including the study of foreign languages. Genesee and Cloud (1998, p. 62) state, "Basic education in the next millennium must include competence in second and even third languages." The Council for Basic Education advocates studying the arts, learning about metacognition, and reaching a greater depth of understanding of the core subjects. Cross and Applebaum (1998, p. 74) agree that "Basic education today includes the arts, as well as thinking processes and understanding."

Goals for 2000

The Goals for 2000, established by the president and the state governors were discussed in Chapter 1. The public's opinions about these goals are shown in Table 3.3.

The public has some major concerns about the feasibility of these goals. These concerns are shown in Table 3.4. In summary, the public strongly supports these goals but it is skeptical about the likelihood of their attainment.

TABLE 3.3   The Public's Priorities for Goals for 2000

Goal	Very High, %		High, %		Low, %		Very Low, %		Unknown, %	
	1991	*1990*	*1991*	*1990*	*1991*	*1990*	*1991*	*1990*	*1991*	*1990*
A	52	44	38	44	6	6	1	2	3	4
B	54	45	37	42	5	8	1	1	3	4
C	55	46	35	42	6	7	1	2	3	3
D	43	34	41	42	11	16	2	3	3	5
E	50	45	36	37	9	11	2	3	3	4
F	63	55	23	26	6	9	5	6	3	4

TABLE 3.4   The Public's Assessment of Likelihood of Attainment of Goals for 2000

Goal	Very Likely, %		Likely, %		Unlikely, %		Very Unlikely, %		Unknown, %	
	1991	*1990*	*1991*	*1990*	*1991*	*1990*	*1991*	*1990*	*1991*	*1990*
A	10	12	37	38	33	33	14	12	6	5
B	6	10	36	35	39	37	14	12	5	6
C	6	9	36	38	36	36	15	12	7	5
D	4	6	22	23	45	41	23	24	6	6
E	6	7	25	25	41	42	23	21	5	5
F	4	5	14	14	38	40	39	36	5	5

Interstate New Teacher Assessment and Support Consortium (INTASC)

Many turn-of-the-century education programs seek to improve teaching by increasing performance standards. During the 1980s and early 1990s this approach was focused primarily on student performance. The 1990s brought an increased emphasis on teacher preparation. One of the earliest of these programs was the Interstate New Teacher Assessment and Support Consortium (INTASC). Whereas most 1980s education reform had focused on strengthening teacher preparation in the content areas (particularly science and mathematics), INTASC was aimed at improving teachers' ability to integrate their content knowledge with pedagogical knowledge (INTASC, 1999).

INTASC developed the following set of core standards designed to be used as a framework in teacher preparatory programs:

1. The teacher understands the central concepts, tools of inquiry, and structures of the discipline(s) he or she teaches and can create learning experiences that make these aspects of subject matter meaningful for students.

2. The teacher understands how children learn and develop and can provide learning opportunities that support their intellectual, social, and personal development.

3. The teacher understands how students differ in their approaches to learning and creates instructional opportunities that are adapted to diverse learners.

4. The teacher understands and uses a variety of instructional strategies to encourage students' development of critical thinking, problem solving, and performance skills.

5. The teacher uses an understanding of individual and group motivation and behavior to create a learning environment that encourages positive social interaction, active engagement in learning, and self-motivation.

6. The teacher uses knowledge of effective verbal, nonverbal, and media communication techniques to foster active inquiry, collaboration, and supportive interaction in the classroom.

7. The teacher plans instruction based upon knowledge of subject matter, students, the community, and curriculum goals.

8. The teacher understands and uses formal and informal assessment strategies to evaluate and ensure the continuous intellectual, social, and physical development of the learner.

9. The teacher is a reflective practitioner who continually evaluates the effects of his/her choices and actions on others (students, parents, and other professionals in the learning community) and who actively seeks out opportunities to grow professionally.

10. The teacher fosters relationships with school colleagues, parents, and agencies in the larger community to support students' learning and well being.

In the late 1990s, INTASC began developing a similar set of standards for each of several content areas. In several states INTASC personnel have joined efforts with the respective state departments of education to enhance teachers' understanding of the INTASC standards and to improve teachers' ability to design portfolios to support this goal.

National Board for Professional Teaching Standards

The National Board for Professional Teaching Standards (NBPTS) is a 63-member board of teachers, administrators, and other citizens (mostly teachers) developed in 1987 to identify the standards teachers need to fulfill the following propositions:

1. Teachers are committed to students and their learning.
2. Teachers know the subjects they teach and how to teach those subjects to students.
3. Teachers are responsible for managing and monitoring students' learning.
4. Teachers think systematically about their practice and learn from experience.
5. Teachers are members of learning communities.

The NBPTS has developed rigorous standards used to assess teachers' fulfillment of these propositions. Portfolio development is an important part of this program. By applying and paying a fee, individual teachers can apply for state-issued NBPTS certification. While NBPTS certification is far more rigorous than state-level certification, it does not replace state certification. Like the INTASC model, NBPTS officials work closely with state-level education officers. Additional information about NBPTS can be found at the following website: *http://www.nbpts.org/.*

Criticisms of the State-Level and National Standards

By the end of the 1990s more than forty-five states were requiring that all students meet standards (Schomoker & Marzano, 1999). The reactions to the creation of national standards have been mixed. Some educators agree with the feelings of the reformers who took the initiative originally; put succinctly, these educators feel that state and national standards were long overdue. Other educators are dissatisfied with the new standards. A major concern is that the standards cover too much material, perhaps two or three times as much as can be handled (Schmidt, McKnight, & Raizen, 1996). Others are concerned that there are "enormous differences in what teachers teach in the same subject at the same grade level in the same school . . . forcing teachers to select or to omit different topics haphazardly" (Schmoker & Marzano, 1999, p. 19). Another concern is that the choice of language and the way some of the standards are written make their coverage so difficult that it would be impossible to cover them in the time teachers are afforded to teach their subjects (Wolk, 1998).

Having reviewed the development of American schools, now let's examine the philosophical beliefs that undergird the curricula in these schools. Initially, you may find the case study by Haffner, Kaplan, and Kirby disconcerting, but they deliver some important messages, and one of these is that to meet the needs of twenty-first century students, teachers must come out of their comfort zones. You may want to take a deep breath before you begin reading this case.

Case Study

Curriculum for the Real World

Janet E. Haffner
Retired Principal of the Accelerated Academics Academy. Visiting Professor, School of Education, University of Michigan, Flint. Currently, principal of the DuKette Catholic School, an inner city mission school.

Leonard Kaplan
Professor of Curriculum and Instruction, College of Education, Wayne State University, Detroit.

Kathleen L. Kirby
English Department Chairperson, Creator of Central Project Career Academy Interdisciplinary team block.

Background Information

"Funerals are so depressing. They say it was drug related. Two bullets to the head while he was kneeling, but it was a week before he died. Just like Ron last month, shot in his sleep, muffled by a pillow. These boys were 13 and 14 and never were children, playing grown-up since they were six. I wonder if John's trial will be over this summer? He's probably going to get life. The prosecutor wants to try him as an adult. What's a life sentence when you're twelve? We've got our jobs cut out for us again this year. Just once I'd like to start the year problem-free."—Principal of the Accelerated Academics Academy.

Many of our urban "dropouts" never "dropped in" in the first place. To a great extent this may be due to an environment viewed as demeaning, even threatening, and seldom receptive to learners. Particularly in the middle school, where the

(Continued)

dropout and attendance rates show a dramatic change from those at the elementary school, students fear or distrust both a curriculum that may be alien to their perceived needs and a faculty whose personal values conflict with their sense of right and wrong. The Accelerated Academics Academy was created five years ago to address these problems. As a result it has become possible for discouraged learners to achieve success.

The Community

In Michigan the curriculum is affected by several major legislative factors. To begin with, the school taxes are no longer property based but are state controlled on a per-pupil basis. Furthermore, the legislature has mandated "choice" (the ability to attend any public school in the state), is promoting charter schools, and requires a satisfactory score on a statewide assessment test for public school diploma endorsement. Finally, the legislature is conducting an overhaul of the welfare program, resulting in substantial funding cuts to adult education and at-risk student programs. The state education department is presently writing curriculum standards for each grade and every subject. This is a strong union state that promotes academic freedom and the professionalism of teachers and teaching.

The school district cited in this case study is located in a mid-size urban setting of approximately 138,000 people with the majority of its population being African American. It is undergoing major upheaval; there is a new superintendent, the school board members are often at odds with each other and with members of the community, the district is undergoing restructuring—in short, chaos abounds. Conversely, this is a district that has historically been a nationally recognized innovator in school, community, and educational projects and practices. Indeed, it continues to forge ahead in that leadership role despite current problems.

A thriving manufacturing center for over a century, this community has, during the past 25 years, become a victim of urban decay due to business and middle-class flight. It now faces the task of reinventing itself while dealing with gang problems, young people's feelings of hopelessness, frequent street violence, and rampant teen pregnancy.

As with many poor, urban districts plagued with violence and safety issues, the schools in this community are equipped with surveillance cameras and metal detectors. Each secondary building is staffed with uniformed security during school hours, and a police liaison officer is assigned to each school.

On the positive side of this picture, community leaders are actively involved in developing programs that enhance both the quality of life in the city and the education of residents' children. An extensive cultural center boasts an art institute, a large concert hall, a smaller theater, a museum, and a planetarium as well as a music, art, and drama schools, all of which attract people from a tri-county area and are highly utilized by the city's schools.

The School

The Accelerated Academics Academy is an urban dropout intervention program for 210 discouraged learners. The academy was initially funded by a federal grant but is now beginning to be funded through the public school system. Most of the

(Continued)

students entering the academy have failed twice somewhere before reaching the sixth grade. The most commonly failed grades were kindergarten and first grade. Interviewed at the end of fifth grade, these students never go to sixth grade but instead enter the academy as seventh graders. These young people actually get the gift of a year back. The hope is that after spending two years at the academy they will then be ready to enter high school. Though the age range of academy students is between 12 and 16, the average entering scores in reading and math competency fall between 3.5 and 4.3 grade equivalency on the Iowa Test of Basic Skills (ITBS). Many who come to the school have missed as many as 60–70 school days the previous year. The majority of academy students (42 percent) attended between three and six schools during the elementary grades. Others attended elementary programs but seldom passed.

Children in the urban setting who have failed once have only a 50 percent change of graduating, and those held back twice have little, if any, chance to graduate (Gastright 1989); however, at this program students come and they stay. While students in the district's other middle schools missed an average of 32 days per year, academy students averaged only 14.6 missed days over the last three years.

The academy staff presently consists of ten full-time and one half-time teacher, one social worker, two student advocates, a secretary, one security person, and the principal. Five of the teachers have less than four years experience while the other half are seasoned veterans. The half-time teacher also serves as the Title I facilitator.

The key to making a difference with academy students is a group of sharing, caring adults. Every staff member at the academy is there because he/she wants to be. They are selected because of their outstanding skills and demonstrated commitment to students. Their professionalism is demonstrated by the time spent in developing curriculum and preparing lessons, by the degree of pride they exhibit in the accomplishments of their students, and by a "can do" attitude.

The Principal

The principal of this program is an energetic woman with an extensive background in working with students with learning disabilities and at-risk students. She holds a doctorate in Curriculum and Instruction and two masters degrees, one in Educational Leadership and the other in Learning Disabilities. This is her first administrative position after 17 years in the classroom.

The principal makes decisions based upon in-depth reading of the research and educational journals followed by discussions with teachers. For example, research on block scheduling was debated and adopted. Weekly discussions on brain-based learning techniques are held, but this principal also supports staff members who are trying innovative activities in the classroom. Teachers are continually encouraged to reflect on their daily teaching activities in order to become more effective.

Extensive data is collected and kept to demonstrate to the staff and the community what works and what needs adjusting. The central district administrators are kept apprised of attendance, activities, and academic gains. Extensive records are kept on the students who have graduated from the academy and high school.

(Continued)

The Case

During a recent lesson in social studies, a teacher discussing the Boston Tea Party explained that it was a "street fight" involving seven or eight people in which Crispus Attucks, "a brother," was the first to get shot. The kids can relate.

Developing classroom curriculum and instruction that will meet the needs of these discouraged students is a formidable task, but it allows for creativity. Most teachers are competent in their content areas, but due to gaps in the students' learning, the teaching staff must stretch out of their comfort zone. Since the students have very low reading and math skills, they may not respond to traditional textbook instruction, so teachers construct curriculum that is grade-level relevant through discussion, demonstration, and focus on high-interest subject matter. Thus students can still be successful while developing competency.

Before the academy's instructional curriculum could be developed, several issues needed to be addressed. First, it was decided that all staff must present a united front when dealing with discipline; therefore, a structured disciplinary plan and a list of expectations were developed. After trying several different approaches to discipline, it became apparent that an authoritarian mentality did not work at the academy. The staff then decided that the students and staff responded most positively to Dr. William Glasser's choice theory (Glasser, 1994).

Long-held traditional views of instructional delivery and classroom management were also beginning to be held suspect because of the lack of academic success these students had previously experienced. Discomfort with the notion of each teacher doing their own thing led teachers and administrators to an exploration and discussion of brain-based learning techniques (Caine, 1991; Jensen, 1995). Not only did these techniques and the theory behind them help in structuring learning activities, but it became clearer why many of the techniques used previously were or were not successful. The entire staff continues to attend seminars and workshops in an attempt to bring stability and structure to what could be a chaotic setting.

Teachers develop integrated units knowing that learners need to see how subjects are interconnected rather than compartmentalized. It is understood that students must interact with the learning experience and be able to relate it to their own environment or prior knowledge. Finally, the teaching staff attempts to make learning enjoyable and nonthreatening.

Since the ability to read is the major key to success, curriculum across disciplines is developed to foster reading skills. However, textbooks and computers are used as supplements to the curriculum, not as the curriculum itself. The basic question is, Are we doing this for kids or because it is easier for us? Staff convenience is categorically rejected in favor of the learner, and curricular decisions are regularly reviewed and adjusted.

Many academy students are observed coming to school late, hungry, unprepared, and carrying so much emotional baggage that before they can even get to their first-hour class they are already defeated. A breakfast program was established, and homeroom was redeveloped into a first-hour class called Family. Family consists of the first 45 minutes of every morning. Every available adult on the staff is assigned approximately 10 students. The curriculum deals with

(Continued)

developing a strong sense of self, learning collective values, and observing, on a daily basis, an adult modeling caring and concern. This is the epitome of *in loco parentis*. Students are assisted with homework, and Family leaders attempt to handle the "baggage" that the students need to talk about before they go to their academic classes.

The staff works to develop situations within Family that make each student feel a part of the school community. Awareness of others' cultures, a dress code, logos, and awards are all forms of group identity in this strong multicultured curriculum. Celebrating cultural holidays such as Kwanzaa, honoring birthdays, having special breakfasts for Family members, taking your Family to lunch, and bringing in treats are all encouraged. Each Family selects a college or university as their group identity; they develop a motto, a logo, and an oath. Fun competition between Families is a regular activity. The Family leaders encourage their charges to become involved with school activities such as talent shows, girls' club, competitive sports, science club, writers' club, art projects, and musical productions. Not only does this build confidence, but it also addresses the varied intelligences of the students (Gardner, 1985).

Students remain with the same Family leader for the two years they are at the academy. The leader serves as surrogate mother, father, mentor, and model, but most of all, friend. The Family leader contacts parents and runs interference if one of their students has a problem with another staff member. Everyone on the staff believes that Family is one of the academy's most powerful teaching tools, since building trust and caring is a cornerstone of the program.

Instructors are constantly redesigning their classrooms to create a safe, accepting place where students feel comfortable about learning. The staff and student body jointly developed a fair discipline policy and behavior management approach that allows for choices. They mutually developed peer mediation groups, a student court, and student monitors. Ideally, the right choices are the responsibility of the students.

Staff members encourage students to take risks and stress that it is acceptable to make mistakes. In a survey (Haffner, 1994) the question was posed, "Do you ask for help when you need it?" Eighty-nine percent of the students at the academy responded affirmatively, compared to 58.8 percent of the students in a control group. The staff consistently allows for correcting and revising for quality academic work. As the saying goes, nothing succeeds like success.

Each teacher has the responsibility of helping each student understand the short- and long-term goals of the curriculum as they relate to success, careers, and community. For many students these connections have never been made. To that end, each student is required to have one community service project per year. These projects include participating in the adopt-a-highway program, making regular visits to a nursing home (reading to the residents, singing, or helping with crafts), assisting the elderly in the neighborhood, working in the local soup kitchen, helping in the school's child care center during parent meetings, or assisting elementary teachers in a nearby school. Several academy students have been hired by the YMCA for their summer camp program. Academy students have also been guest speakers at symposiums on violence, at the state education association meeting, and at several service organizations.

(Continued)

In a unit developed by the teachers with support from the business community, students generate and manage a budget. Part of the assignment involves simulated experiences in hunting for an apartment, shopping for groceries, buying clothes, and purchasing a car. Students go into the community with their assignments and are assisted by community members. The students have reported that they are treated as if they are adults and are actually renting their first apartment or buying their first car.

Perhaps the most exciting activity is winter camp. All students and staff attend winter camp for three days and two nights. The curriculum is developed jointly by the schools' support staff and members of the YMCA camp staff. Activities include identifying winter birds, doing science projects, cross country skiing, practicing outdoor survival skills, and participating in outdoor group team activities called "low ropes." For most students, it is the first time they have been away from their families and out of the city. The camping experience is also a bonding time for the academy staff.

Within subject areas the school begins the year by developing "learning how to learn" activities. Skills such as note taking, mind mapping, organizing notebooks, setting goals, reading strategies, test-taking strategies, and developing good homework habits are stressed and highly tuned. Students are encouraged to show what they know. Teachers explain that their purpose is to assist students to discover their strengths, improve their weaknesses, and ensure their success.

The teaching staff and the social worker begin to build a composite written profile of each student. By the end of the first five-week marking period all students are tested to pinpoint their learning styles and their reading and math levels. A general picture of students' strengths and weaknesses is then identified. The social worker holds weekly sessions with the teacher teams to give teachers ideas for how best to work with individual students in ways appropriate to the social and emotional needs of that student.

Every morning the whole staff meets for fifteen minutes to be briefed about any useful district information, touch base on the Family activity for the day, and discuss situations that may cause concern for the student body. This time generally affords space for staff to share news and support each other. A sense of collegiality continues to grow at the academy that will in the long run make a difference for the students and the community. The greatest challenge this program faces is to continually rethink what culturally responsive, noncoercive, nonmanipulative teaching should look like and to offer developmentally appropriate choices.

Issues for Further Reflection and Application

1. This curriculum combines both cognitive and affective approaches. What makes it work? Is it measurable?

2. The curriculum focuses on a unique population of students. How could it be adapted to other settings?

3. List the factors you believe make the program a success.

4. If you were a curriculum planner, how would you choose staff for an alternative program such as this?

(Continued)

5. How important is the leadership at the school level and district level when developing curriculum?

6. Much has been said about relating subject to student experience. Is this practical? Important? Possible?

7. In this program the teaching staff is responsible for developing the schedule and the discipline policy. What are the strengths and weaknesses of this total staff involvement?

8. What is your response to the Family curriculum and all that it entails?

9. Community service is part of this school's requirements. How do you see that as a benefit or hindrance for these particular students? What are some precautions to take in implementing such off-campus experiences?

10. Many would say that Winter Camp is a frill. How could you defend the Winter Camp experience as a viable part of the curriculum?

11. If you had a chance to create a program like this or to teach in such an environment, would you? What do you see as problems, pitfalls, and pluses?

12. There is an intense focus on developing self-esteem in this program. How can this be defended as a viable curricular component?

Suggested Reading

Association of Teacher Educators. (1992). *Education and the family.* Kaplan, L. (Ed.). Boston: Allyn & Bacon.

Association of Teacher Educators (1996). *Teachers for the new millennium.* Kaplan, L., & Edelfelt, R. (Eds.) Thousand Oaks, CA: Corwin Press.

Caine, N., & Caine, G. (1991). *Making connections: Teaching and the human brain.* Reading, MA: Addison-Wesley.

Connelly, M., & Clandinin, D. (1998). *Teachers as curriculum planner: Narratives of experiences.* New York, NY: Columbia University, Teachers College Press.

Costa, A. L. (1991). *The school as a home for the mind.* Arlington Heights: IL: IRI/Skylight Training and Publishing.

Gardner, H. (1993). *Multiple intelligences: The theory in practice.* New York: Basic Books.

Glasser, W. (1986). *Control theory in the classroom.* New York: Harper & Row.

Haffner, J. (1994). *Twice retained: A study of the middle school students who have failed twice.* Doctoral Dissertation. Detroit: Wayne State University.

Jacobs, H. (1989). *Interdisciplinary curriculum: design and implementation.* ASCD.

Jensen, E. (1995). *Brain-based learning and teaching.* Oakland, CA: Turning Point.

Jensen, E. (1998). *Teaching with the brain in mind.* Oakland, CA: Turning Point.

Kaplan, L. (1986). *Asking the next question.* IN: College Town Press.

Kovalik, S. (1994). *Integrated thematic instruction: The model.* Kent, WA: Susan Kovalik & Associates.

McGeehan, J. (1998). *Transformations: Leadership for brain compatible learning.* Kent, WA: Books for Educators.

Rodriguez, E., & Bellanca, J. (1996). *What is it about me you can't teach?* An Instructional Guide for the Urban Educator. Arlington Heights, IL: IRI/Skylight Training and Publishing, Inc.

Perhaps you will remember from Chapter 1 that schools with high achievement rates have a high degree of parent involvement. The authors of this case study say that "The real key to making a difference with these kids is a group of sharing, caring adults," referring to the school's faculty and staff, who "are there because they want to be."

Teachers promoting multiculturalism are concerned with helping each student feel capable and worthwhile. Authors of this case say, "The curriculum (at this school) deals with developing a strong sense of self. . . ." Interestingly, this school uses a "family" approach to achieve this goal. Is it only coincidental that "staff members encourage students to take risks and stress that it is acceptable to make mistakes" and that risk-taking and mistakes are characteristic of good problem solving, which is the main methodology used in constructivist classes?

A final link between this case and the success of this school and constructivism is the thought expressed in the last sentence of the case study, "The greatest challenge this program faces is to continually rethink what culturally responsive, noncoercive, nonmanipulative teaching should look like." Continually rethinking suggests a steady state of flux. Remember that constructivists view all knowledge as being temporary. In essence, not only do we teachers not always have the correct answers but our curricula and methodology, too, must keep changing as we continue to learn more about the nature of learning and teaching.

Part Two: Philosophical Foundations of Curriculum

Having reviewed the development of American schools, let us now examine the philosophical beliefs that undergird these schools' curricula.

When Pythagoras (we are told) was asked what he meant by calling himself a *philosopher,* he replied as follows:

> Men enter their lives somewhat like the crowd meets at the festival. Some come to sell their merchandise, that is, to make money; some come to display their physical force in order to become famous; while there is a third group of men who only come to admire the beautiful works of art as well as the fine performances and speeches. In a similar way we meet each other in this life of ours; it is as if each of us were coming from afar, bringing along his own conception of life. Some desire nothing except money; some only strive for fame; while a few wish nothing except to watch or to contemplate the most beautiful things. But what are the most beautiful things? Certainly the universe as a whole and the order according to which the heavenly bodies move around are beautiful. But their beauty is merely a participation in the beauty of the first being which can only be reached by thought. Those who contemplate this first being [which Pythagoras seems to have described as the number and the proportion constituting the nature of all things] are the philosophers, the "lovers of wisdom." For wisdom is the knowledge of things beautiful, first, divine, pure, and eternal.
> (Lobkowicz, 1967, pp. 5–6)

The Oxford English Dictionary defines philosophy as "the love, study, and pursuit of wisdom, or of knowledge of things and their causes, whether theoretical or practical." Regardless of the source of the definition, philosophy always involves thinking and is not limited to any subject. It usually is concerned with asking questions that are general and difficult, such as: What is the purpose of life? What is good? What is truth?

Philosophy can also be applied to various disciplines or to specific areas of thought. For example, natural philosophy is what we know as science. Philosophy can also be applied to the study of education, thus the school of educational philosophy or philosophy of education.

Basic Philosophical Systems

For over twenty-two centuries, philosophers have grappled with the many types of questions such as the ones mentioned. These efforts have led to the formulation of several basic philosophical systems, including epistemology, logic, idealism, axiology, realism, pragmatism, essentialism, existentialism, perenialism, progressivism, and reconstructionism.

Philosophies can be distinguished from one another according to the *major* questions that philosophy poses. *Major* is emphasized here because no question is beyond the realm of philosophy. Examples of major questions are: What is real? (metaphysics), What is true? What is the nature of knowledge? (epistemology) What is good? (axiology).

Epistemology

Epistemology is the branch of philosophy that seeks the truth about the nature of knowledge. Epistemologists might ask, does each discipline have its own unique structure, and therefore should it be taught or explored in unique ways? A central purpose of the Woods Hole Conference, discussed earlier, was to identify the special structures of disciplines, particularly the sciences, mathematics, and foreign language.

Epistemologists might ask educators, Is one method of learning better than another? Are teaching and learning methods situation specific? Is the scientific method superior to others? Educators who think so are likely to include more of the hard sciences in the curriculum; those who accept other learning processes are apt to include more of the humanities in the curriculum. Is giving students information inferior or superior to helping them discover it? Is insight better than inquiry? Is knowing more or less important than learning? How teachers answer these questions inevitably affects the kinds of curricula they establish in their classrooms.

Epistemology and the Themes

While the role of epistemologists is not to dictate or to recommend one learning theory over another, they would be pleased that this book recommends an eclectic approach to studying and applying learning theory, and they would also be pleased that one of the major themes of this book (constructivism) is a study of how students learn.

An education reform practice that is currently growing in popularity is the study of the disciplines to determine whether each discipline holds its own secret, a best method for studying it. Epistemologists would advise curriculum developers to keep this question at the forefront when participating in local school reform.

These questions can also serve teachers as they make decisions about how much and in what ways they will use technology in their classrooms. Do some subjects, more than others, lend themselves to being studied through the use of technology? Should technology be used to advance higher-level thinking more in some subjects than in others? Does the integration of some subjects enhance the use of technology?

Axiology

Axiology is the school of philosophy that deals with values and ethics, raising such questions as What is good? What is valuable? What is right? What is wrong? Is pleasure-seeking wrong? Asking such axiological questions helps teachers understand the role of ethics and values in the curriculum. This chapter mentioned the role that religion had in colonial curricula. Although the church has been legally separated from state-supported schools, some contemporary educators and citizens at large still believe that the study of morality is as important now as it was in colonial America—maybe more important.

Axiology and the Themes

Axiologists would not tell us what values the curriculum should promote, but they would remind us to think about this role of the curriculum. What effect, if any, does dispensing condoms in high school have on student values? Should the curriculum be changed to promote school safety? If so, how?

Realism

Realists believe that humans should seek the truth. They believe in rational explanations, and they believe that the scientific method should be used to discover the rationality of the universe. Formalized during the sixteenth and seventeenth centuries by the English philosopher Francis Bacon, the *scientific method* consists of the following steps:

1. Define the problem
2. Formulate a hypothesis
3. Gather data

4. Interpret the data

5. Use reason to draw a conclusion

6. Test your conclusion

To the realist, the truth is to be limited to that which can be tested and proven empirically (using the five senses). John Dewey (1939, p. 111) said that the "scientific method is the only authentic means at our command for getting at the significance of our everyday experiences of the world in which we live."

Some important contributors to realism include Aristotle (384–322 B.C.), St. Thomas Aquinas (1225–1274), Francis Bacon (1561–1626), John Locke (1632–1704), Johann F. Herbert (1776–1841), and Alfred North Whitehead (1861–1947).

Realism and the Themes

The realist is likely to believe the sciences and mathematics should dominate the curriculum. Certainly, such thinking is common among contemporary education reformers. They also believe that students should be taught to use logic and the scientific method. Unlike many contemporary education reformers, however, the realists believe that these subjects should remain separated, as opposed to being part of interdisciplinary programs. The realist searches for the natural order in all things, including content generalizations such as concepts, principles, axioms, and theorems.

Another popular education reform practice is to implement authentic curricula. Proponents of realism would argue that our schools should build the curriculum around real-life problems. The current emphasis on integrated curriculum, conceptual themes, and problem-solving reflect this philosophy. Critics would argue that teachers just don't have time to assign problems and wait for students to discover the answers. These teachers will say that they barely have time to cover the necessary content, even when using the most economic instructional strategies.

Pragmatism

The philosophical structure called *pragmatism* had its origin in the sixteenth and seventeenth centuries. Its major contributors include the English philosopher Francis Bacon (1561–1626) and the German philosopher Immanuel Kant (1724–1804), who coined the term *pragmatism,* which means practical. Pragmatists ask the questions, What is it good for? How can it be applied? Although pragmatism began in Europe, its growth has been led by American philosophers such as Charles Pierce (1839–1914), William James (1842–1910), and John Dewey (1859–1952).

Unlike the idealists and the realists, the pragmatists do not seek universal truths. Rather, they view the world as a world of change. English poet John Wilmont expresses this pragmatist's view of the world: "Tis nature's way to change. Constancy alone is strange."

Since the world is ever-changing, humans must constantly examine their own desires. Information that is useful to help people reach their desires is valuable.

To the pragmatist, the role of education is to help students learn how to discover themselves, and the best way to do this is through direct experience. This means the curriculum should be learner-centered and experience-based, full of problem-solving activities, the type of curriculum that dominated the Progressive Education Era.

Pragmatism and the Themes

Since the development of the Franklin Academy, the curricula in American schools have been heavily influenced by pragmatism. Contemporary education reform practices are rich with pragmatism as well. For example, many education programs stress authentic activities, that is, hands-on activities that cause students to apply theory and knowledge to solve real-life problems. The discovery learning practices, which characterize many of today's education programs, are endorsed by pragmatists.

Constructivism is based on the premise that it is better to understand a little than to recall a lot without understanding it. This, too, is a pragmatist belief. The methods used by constructivist teachers are encouraged by pragmatists. Indeed, pragmatists believe changing and improving are natural processes.

Essentialism

In rebuttal to the Progressive Education Movement, William Bagley organized a new philosophical structure called *essentialism*. Bagley believed that the purpose of schools is to stabilize society by teaching that knowledge which is essential. This would require mastery of subjects such as reading, writing, arithmetic, history, and English, which are essential to prepare students for productive lives. The teaching of these subjects should be organized from the simple to the complex and from the concrete to the abstract.

Clearly, the curriculum for essentialists has no room for frills or individualizing or for nonessential, "popular" courses. Academic rigor must be the standard for all if the essential intellectual and practical goals are to be reached.

Essentialism and the Themes

Essentialists support such contemporary programs as school-to-work and service learning so long as they are subject-based. They are concerned that the trend toward using multidisciplinary approaches will weaken the disciplines. They have little concern for programs that attempt to meet individual needs, such as multiple intelligences and styles matching. Diversity is of little consequence to essentialists. Computer use is supported, but only when it is in the service of mastering the essential subjects.

Perennialism

Perennialism emphasizes that knowledge which has endured through the years. Americans Robert Hutchins and Mortimer Adler introduced perennialism during the twentieth century. Perennial subjects include classical literature, philosophy, science, history, and the fine arts. The goal of the perennialist is to develop and challenge the intellect—to prepare students for life by teaching them to think. The perennial curriculum emphasizes the humanities and the three R's.

Opponents of perennialism would argue that the purpose of schools is to teach students to think. The perrenialists agree but believe the best way to achieve his lofty goal is through studying a combination of classical subjects (including the humanities and the fine arts) and the basics.

Some critics of perennialism argue that students cannot be prepared for the changing world by studying age-old subjects. Many parents believe the main purpose of education is to prepare students to get good paying jobs. These parents won't settle for their children just gaining knowledge; that might be nice, but it isn't as important as knowing how to earn a living.

Herein lies a natural conflict between perennialist teachers and parents who hold a more conservative "earn a living" attitude. In college most teachers learn to appreciate the arts and literature. They may want more for their students than the parents want.

Perennialism and the Themes

In looking at today's education reform issues, it is possible to find practices that perennialists endorse. For example, they support contemporary critics' cries for more science and mathematics. It is much easier to identity reform movements that the perennialists view at frills, such as constructivism and metacognition. Perennialists clearly favor the classical curriculum that characterized our first schools over these contemporary programs. Computers are fine so long as they help students master the essential subjects. Using computers for drill and practice would be fine with perennialists, and this is the very use of computers some contemporary educators oppose.

Diversity is not a major concern for perennialists because they believe that the classical subjects are good for everyone.

Reconstructionism

Like pragmatism and perennialism, *reconstructionism* is considered an American structure. Reconstructionists believe that the schools should be reconstructed to remove from our society such cultural crises as poverty, racism, ignorance, and war.

Reconstructionists are quick to remind us that most teachers come from middle-class families and therefore have a propensity to protect the society they have always known. Reconstructionists say that because of their middle-class backgrounds, most teachers don't know about poverty and unemployment.

Reconstructionist-based curricula focus on the major problems of society and prepare students to make critical analyses. Emphasis is placed on the behavioral sciences, and students are taught to influence the community.

Some major contributors to reconstructionism include Plato (427–347 B.C.), St. Augustine (354–430), John Dewey (1859–1952), George Counts (1889–1974), and Brameld (1904–).

Reconstructionists believe that society has lost its way (Armstrong et al., 1993), and they believe that society has traveled too far down its misguided path to be corrected by tinkering; correcting its problems will require major reform. Reconstructionists believe that the role of the school is to empower citizens with the capacity to ensure that democratic principles will be followed, bringing equity to all areas of society.

Reconstructionists believe that a major responsibility of the schools is to teach students to analyze and question practices that they perceive as unfair to individuals or groups, and that perhaps schools' foremost responsibility is to motivate students to take action to correct inequities.

George S. Counts and Harold Rugg were major leaders in the development and growth of reconstructionism. In his book *Dare the Schools Build a New Social Order?* Counts (1932) answered his question with a resounding yes.

Reconstructionists have always been concerned with the mission of the school's curriculum, which, to them, is clear: to redesign a society that has become inequitable. Modern reconstructionists are keenly focused on the Goals for 2000 and on the direction of education reform programs. Students, they believe, should be given social problems to analyze and correct. Some contemporary topics that concern constructionists are AIDS, pollution, immorality, inhumanity, world hunger, crime, and war. These topics are especially important because they are worldwide; reconstructionists believe that the curriculum should cover global problems.

Reconstructionists believe that the curriculum should enlighten students politically. They would quickly recognize and take action to correct any perceived failure of educators to promote the cause and value of education to the masses.

The reconstructionism philosophy, which is deeply concerned with the welfare of society and espouses action to improve the community and society, should not be confused with *revolutionism,* which holds that the only way to improve society is to destroy the existing system. The concept of reconstruction has appealed to a wide range of personalities and fostered a number of subphilosophies. For example, some educators and philosophers consider Francis Parker and John Dewey as superb exemplars of reconstructionism, while others, for example, George S. Counts, perceived them and other progressivists as failures. Viewing progressive educators as weak and ineffective, Counts (1932, p. 259) called on the progressivists to:

. . . Face squarely and courageously every social issue, come to grips with life in all of its stark reality, establish an organic relation with the community, develop a realistic and comprehensive theory of welfare, fashion a compelling and challenging vision of human destiny, and become somewhat less frightened than it is today at the bogeys of imposition and indoctrination. In a word, Progressive Education cannot build its program out of the interests of children: it cannot place its trust in a child-centered school.

Obviously, Counts was more radical in his beliefs and the ways he communicated them than were the progressivists.

Reconstructionism and the Themes

Many local education reform movements are headed by committees of noneducators who believe there is a need for people like themselves who can take an objective look at education (a task they believe is impossible for teachers because teachers are too close to the process to be objective) and plan strategies to adjust education to make it serve society's greatest needs. Equity is an important goal of reconstructionists; therefore, diversity becomes a major goal for the schools.

During the twenty-first century, every school in the United States will continue to be affected by education reform. In some ways most schools are contributing to the reform movement, but the nature of reform from one school to another differs immensely. Some faculties embrace reform, viewing it as an opportunity to improve education for their students; other see it as an imposition on their time and energy. Because reform is being forced rapidly by outside change agents, many highly professional, energetic, and dedicated teachers find it impossible to avoid feeling imposed upon by state and local reform programs.

The varying cultures in the surrounding communities partially explain the differences in the ways members of various faculties feel. The local school administration and policies can also be strong forces shaping the ways faculty members feel and react to reform policies.

Each school's faculty is made of individuals, some of whom are reconstructionists, and some of whom are not. Among those who are activists, each can be placed on a linear scale based on the intensity with which they share their beliefs. Some fall on the mild side with Dewey and Parker, while others belong on the strong side along with Counts. As each of us looks at the school with which we are most familiar, it is easy to identify the extremists, but sometimes it is not so easy to know where others stand who may covertly express their philosophies.

Some individuals may question the value of studying philosophies in a curriculum course. If we remember to think of philosophies not merely as statements in dusty books but rather as the beliefs of people we know, and if we can consider the tremendous influence that some of our fellow teachers have in every meeting in which they engage, from planning for an accreditation visit to deciding how to use this year's in-service planning days, then perhaps we can see that our individual and collective philosophies determine how we behave in regard to all issues. Our philosophies determine how we feel about issues and about other people. In no other philosophical structure is this more obvious than it is in reconstructionism.

Now that you have read about several philosophies, how would you categorize the philosophy of the principal in the case study of the Accelerated Academics Academy? Was she an idealist? a realist? pragmist? existentialist? essentialist? perennialist? reconstructionist?

Influences of Philosophy on Education

Assessment

The philosophy of education is concerned with abstract and difficult questions such as, What are the purposes of education? Familiarity with the philosophy of education helps in the establishment of long-range objectives.

An analogy may help to explain this major function of the philosophy of education. A traveler had been lost for several hours. After escaping from a series of traffic jams which had left him feeling quite exasperated, he finally found the open road. As he continued driving happily and rapidly, a passenger asked if he weren't still lost. "Well, yes," he replied, "as a matter of fact I am still lost, but we are making excellent time, aren't we?"

Educators can make good time and yet be lost and without any long-range goals. Curriculum developers must know what to teach and what effects they want schooling to have on students. They must know what they would have students become. For these answers, curriculum developers must turn to the philosopher; for the philosopher will force them to formulate a system of values and decide which values are more important than others. Armed with a system of values, curriculum developers can then adjust teaching methodology and curriculum in accordance with their ultimate educational objectives. As one philosopher, Herbert Spencer, said, "In determining a curriculum, our first step must be to classify, in order of their importance, the leading kinds of activity which constitute human life."

Since the value systems of no two people are the same, there will always be conflict. Our values are continually changing, and we must continually readjust our school programs to align them with our current value system.

The Teacher's Influence

The second contribution philosophy makes to education is through the influence of the teacher. Thought inevitably leads to action; the way teachers think influences the way they act. Our values and our views of the totality of existence will affect our relationships with others. If the teacher has good rapport with students, the teacher's own beliefs and value system will affect those of the pupils.

Teachers often find themselves in a seemingly impossible position when trying to teach about such controversial issues as abortion, drug use, and war. Students inevitably ask questions to learn their teachers' points of view. If teachers reveal their opinions, many students will accept them without questioning their validity. This is perhaps the worst thing that could happen because it prevents the students from engaging in the process of reasoning. Ideally, the teacher's desire for students to engage in this reasoning process will eclipse the teacher's desire to have pupils accept the teacher's views. However, this does not suggest that teachers should have no influence on the students. It does suggest that teachers have a particular type of influence, that they will encourage students to think independently rather than blindly accepting the opinions of others.

An Agent of Change

What role does the philosophy of education play in changing education? Some philosophers view philosophy as a theoretical activity that follows its own disciplinary rules and is not in itself practical or reforming. If you accept this point of view, you must believe that it is not the purpose of the philosophy of education to change education. However, it is essential that the person who philosophizes about education care intensely about the practice and improvement of education. Notice that the word *improvement* implies change. Although philosophers are unlikely to suggest specific needed changes in our schools, they are likely to affect teachers so that the teachers will be stimulated to make changes, of the need for which the philosopher may be quite unaware.

With regard to the role that the philosophy of education plays in changes, some things are clear: (1) The philosophy of education does contribute to change, but only when such change is needed; (2) the contribution may be more indirect than direct, and (3) the types of change caused by the philosopher deal with the important values of life and, therefore, are likely to be monumental changes. Currently, there exists an urgent need for educators to look at the whole education process in totally new ways, to explore the subconscious part of behavior, and to consider the basic overall changes in society when designing school curricula. This seems to illustrate the type of change that the philosopher is likely to stimulate—major change brought about indirectly as a result of the philosopher's help in sorting out the more valuable things in life.

A Moral Guide

Should our curriculum teach ethics? If so, what role does philosophy play in moral education? If we believe that no knowledge exists merely for its own sake, and all knowledge must in some way affect conduct, the answer to these questions is that teachers cannot avoid teaching ethics. This issue is vital, because education in any society serves to help initiate its young into its culture, and certainly the moral beliefs are a large part of any culture.

But educators must do more than just hand down the ethics of former generations to newer generations. As our culture changes, so do our moral standards. In ancient Greek, *heritage* meant "process"; later it meant "content." Now it means the whole intellectual, moral, and cultural setting into which we are born.

By *ethical and moral foundations* we refer to how our society answers the basic question Are there relationships that are right and relationships that are wrong? The answer is not clear. In the western world there are two opposing positions: the Christian tradition, which possesses beliefs of absolute right and wrong, and the Greek view that humans, through their own reasoning, make their own morals. This places teachers in a difficult position. How can they transmit such conflicting information to students?

As previously noted, some educators believe that education must strive to enable pupils to think for themselves and make up their own minds. Most modern educators would agree that the curriculum must respect students' intellectual integrity and promote their capacity for independent judgment.

With respect to the moral role of philosophy in education, we can state that: (1) education has a moral responsibility to its pupils, (2) teachers should teach the morals of the society to their pupils, and (3) teachers must not impose their beliefs on their pupils, but must encourage them to apply their own intellectual ability to reason out their own modes of behavior.

A Clarifier

Philosophy has yet another role in education: to help clarify concepts such as *cause, self, mind,* and *good.* By doing this, philosophers will inevitably help to clarify the relationships of these abstractions to each other, which will lead to the informed analysis of current educational theories.

A Process

The preceding paragraphs have presented philosophy as a thinking process for answering the most abstract, the most general, and certainly the most difficult types of questions. Immanuel Kant (1724–1804) told his pupils, "You will not learn from me philosophy, but how to philosophize, not to repeat, but how to think. Think for yourselves, inquire for yourselves, stand on your own feet." An important role of educational philosophy is to make us aware of the need for asking questions.

Chapter Summary

Formal education in America began in the homes, where teaching of reading, Puritanism, and colonial law was required. In 1635 the forerunners of our current high schools appeared; similar to the English schools, they were designed to prepare the elite for the university. Because their curricula were dominated by classical Latin and Greek, they were called Latin grammar schools. Because of their impracticality, they soon gave way to very practical curricula based on the Franklin Academy, founded in 1750. These schools were private, and many people could not afford them. The first public high schools, called the Boston English High Schools, appeared in 1821. The schools varied. Some were very pragmatic, but some were just the opposite.

In 1918 the NEA appointed a commission to identify the goals of secondary schools. Their findings, called the Seven Cardinal Principles of Secondary Education, are equally applicable today. The twentieth century brought the Progressive Education Movement, which emphasized the practical, child-centered curriculum for 50 years until it gave way to a subject-centered curriculum. This conservative, subject-centered curriculum yielded to a process-centered curriculum following the launching of *Sputnik* in 1957.

All teachers have philosophies, and their personal philosophies inevitably affect their teaching behavior. By examining their beliefs, teachers and other curriculum developers can use these beliefs to design curricula to achieve their overall aims. An awareness of all of the major philosophical structures empowers teachers to use their preferred structures to design curricula. Employing the original philosophy of John Locke, who espoused experience-based, learner-centered curricula, Colonel Francis Parker was the first administrator to involve teachers and students in curriculum development.

Many philosophical structures have certain concepts in common, but in other respects, they differ totally. An awareness of the similarities and differences of these philosophies is essential if teachers are to maximize their contributions to education reform in their schools.

As noted throughout the chapter, each of these philosophical structures has particular potential for serving the schools' constructivist and multicultural goals, helping all students achieve their potential and succeed as capable learners and worthy individuals.

Learning Questions

1. Why should the textbook be one of several curriculum determiners?
2. Why did the Latin grammar schools become obsolete?
3. Why did the Franklin Academy lose popularity?
4. What is the significance of the dame schools?
5. What qualities of the Seven Cardinal Principles have made these principals endure?
6. Why has the textbook been the single greatest curriculum determiner throughout the history of American schools?
7. What is the significance of such curricula as the Quincy System, the Gary Plan, the Dalton Plan, and the Winnetka Plan? How does each relate to constructivist theory?

8. If the Progressive Education Movement curricula were so successful, why did this era end?

9. What was meant by the statement, "Effective management of multiculturalism will require each faculty and each faculty member to invent curriculum to meet the needs of each student body"?

10. What is the significance of the Old Deluder Satan Act?

11. What relationships can you see between events in the history of American schools and the current education reform efforts in your district?

12. What is the relationship between the study of the history of our schools and efforts to determine what contemporary curricula should achieve?

13. Suppose you could use only two of the philosophical structures introduced in this chapter. On which two structures would you base your curriculum? Why?

14. Which is a more useful strategy to use when teaching your subjects, inductive logic or deductive logic? Why?

15. How does philosophy give direction without dictating directions? (*Hint:* At this moment, how is the author of this book influencing or directing your thinking?)

16. Why are philosophers always long on questions and short on answers?

17. Why must education work to stabilize society and also work to change society?

18. Why do teachers have no alternative but to affect the values and morals of their students?

19. Name three qualities in contemporary society that you believe are worth protecting and three qualities you think should be abolished. Justify your choices.

20. What is your most strongly held philosophical belief? How can you use this strength of belief to contribute to your district's school reform movement?

Suggested Activities

1. Name one goal or aim that you feel is of utmost importance to today's schools. Explain how you can work toward achieving that goal.

2. Make a list of the legislated reform elements in your district. This may require interviews with some of your education professors and/or a visit to your library's reference room and government documents department.

3. Interview three teachers and ask each to identify strengths and weaknesses in local school reform. Make a chart showing these strengths and the weaknesses.

4. Interview one or more education professors and ask them what changes education reform has stimulated in the classes they teach.

5. How would you explain the continued relevance of the Seven Cardinal Principles of Secondary Education?

6. Compare and contrast the Seven Cardinal Principles and the Goals for 2000.

7. Make a list of the unique characteristics of transessence, and for each characteristic describe one way the curricula can be changed to meet this need.

8. Examine the legislation described in this chapter and list one purpose for each law. Tell how effectively you think current school curricula meet each purpose.

9. What precautions can you take to ensure that your own future curricula are not textbook dominated?

10. Make a list of the major concepts presented in this chapter.

11. Describe one characteristic of modern classrooms (physical, emotional, psychological, or other) that resulted from the influence of the Progressive Education Movement.

12. Explain and defend the statement, "Curriculum development should take a philosophically eclectic approach." Now challenge this position.

13. Research the topics of values and morality in education.

14. For the school with which you are most familiar, describe features in that school's curriculum that reflect various philosophical structures introduced in this chapter.

15. Read the book *Summerhill* by A. S. Neill, and write a brief paper describing the philosophy upon which that school operates.

16. Interview three teachers, asking them what they perceive as the number one purpose of schools. Contrast these responses with the Goals for 2000 and with the Seven Cardinal Principles of Secondary Education.

17. Read the book *Emile* by Jean Jacques Rousseau, and write a paper describing Rousseau's philosophy as it is expressed in the book.

18. List a school's three most important purposes, and describe at least one student activity you might assign to achieve each purpose.

19. Philosophy is the love of the pursuit of wisdom. Describe a strategy for designing your curricula to lead your students to love the pursuit of wisdom.

20. Review the philosophical structures discussed in this chapter, and then examine the elements of school reform that are impacting your district. Describe any needs that you see for your district's reform efforts to use a defined philosophical structure in designing future reform activities.

21. Disregarding your physical appearance, identify your most pronounced personal strength and your most important weakness. Explain how you can modify or shape your curricula to capitalize on this strength and compensate for this weakness.

Works Cited and Suggested Readings

Alexander, W. M., & George, P. S. (1981). *The exemplary middle school.* New York: Holt, Rinehart and Winston.

Alexander, L. (1986, November). Time for results: An overview. *Phi Delta Kappan, 68,* 202–204.

Archambault, R. D. (1964). *John Dewey on education.* New York: Random House.

Armstrong, D. G., Henson, K. T., & Savage, T. V. (1993). *Education: An introduction* (4th ed.). New York: Macmillan.

Armstrong, D. G., Henson, K. T., & Savage, T. V. (1997). *Teaching today: An introduction to education* (5th ed.). Upper Saddle River, NJ: Merrill.

Backbone (1991, April). Essential for survival on the troubled journey. (1991, April). *A quarterly information resource on Issues facing children, adolescents, and families, 7*(1), 1–3.

Bestor, A. E. (1953). *Educational wastelands.* Urbana, IL: University of Illinois.

Bonar, B. D. (1992, Fall). The role of laboratory schools in American education. *National Association of Laboratory Schools Journal, 17*(1), 42–53.

Brendtro, L. K., Brokenleg, M., & Van Bockern, S. (1990). *Reclaiming youth at risk, our hope for the future.* Bloomington, IN: National Education Service.

Bruner, J. S. (1960). *Toward a theory of instruction.* Cambridge, MA: Harvard University Press.

Campbell, J. K. (1967). *Colonel Francis Parker: The children's crusader.* New York: Columbia University Teachers' College Press.

Carbone, P. F., Jr. (1991, Summer). The teacher as a philosopher. *Education Reform, 55*(4), 319–332.

Carroll, L. (1898). *Alice's adventures in Wonderland.* London: Oxford University Press.

Cherniss, C. (1998). Social and emotional learning for leaders. *Educational Leadership, 55*(7), 28–29.

Clark, S. N., Clark, D. C., & Irvin, J. I. (1997). Collaborative decision making. *Middle School Journal, 28*(5), 54–56.

Coles, R., & Geneve, L. (1990, March). The moral life of America's school children. *Teacher Magazine.*

Counts, G. S. (1932). *Dare the schools build a new social order?* New York: John Day.

Cremin, L. A. (1976). *Public education.* New York: Basic Books.

Cremin, L. A. (1961). *The transformation of the school: Progressivism in American education, 1876–1957*. New York: Knopf.

Cross, C. T., & Applebaum, K. (1998). Stretching students' minds is basic education. *Educational Leadership, 55*(6), 74–76.

Darling-Hammond, L. (1998). Teacher learning that supports student learning. *Educational Leadership, 55*(5), 6–11.

Davis, O. L., Jr. (Ed.). (1976). *Perspectives on curriculum development 1776–1976*. Washington, DC: Association for Supervision and Curriculum Development.

Dewey, J. (1939). *Experience and education*. New York: Macmillan.

Eichorn, D. H. (1980). The school. In M. Johnson (Ed.), *Toward adolescence*. 79th Yearbook of the National Society for the Study of Education. Chicago: University of Chicago Press.

Epstein, H. T. (1976). A bibliography based framework for intervention projects. *Mental Retardation, 14*, 26–27.

Erb, T. (1997, March). Student-friendly classrooms in a not very child-friendly world. *Middle School Journal, 28*(5), 2.

Genesee. F., & Cloud, N. (1998). Multilingualism is basic. *Educational Leadership, 55*(6), 62–65.

Hall, G. S. (1904). *Adolescence, its psychology, and its relations to physiology, anthropology, sociology, sex, crime, religion, and education*. (Vols. I and II.) New York: Appleton.

Henson, K. T. (1986, April). Middle schools: Paradoxes and promises. *The Clearing House, 59*, 345–347.

Henson, K. T. (1996). *Methods and strategies for teaching in secondary and middle school* (3rd ed.). New York: Longman.

Holt, J. (1971). *How children fail*. New York: Pitman.

Houck, J. W., & Maxon, S. (1997). The role of teachers and the schools in assisting children who live with violence. *Education, 117*(4), 522–529.

Hudson, L. (1966). *Contrary imaginations: A psychological study of the English schoolboy*. Middlesex, England: Penguin.

Jones, V. (1991). Responding to students' behavior problems. *Beyond Behavior, 2*(1), 17–21.

Klingele, W. E. (1979). *Teaching in middle schools*. Boston: Allyn & Bacon.

Koba, S. B. (1996). Narrowing the achievement gap in science. *Educational Leadership, 53*(8), 14–17.

Konopka, G. (1973). Requirements for healthy development of adolescent youth. *Adolescence, 8*, 2.

Kowalski, T. J. (1994). Site-based management, teacher empowerment, and unionism: Beliefs of suburban school principals. *Contemporary Education, 65*(4), 200–206.

Latham, A. S. (1998). Site-based management: Is it working? *Educational Leadership, 55*(7), 85–86.

Lobkowicz, N. (1967). *Theory into practice*. Notre Dame, IN: University of Notre Dame Press. (Cicero, Tusc. v.3, 8–9; Jamblichus, DeVita Pyth.) 58–49.

Meyersohn, M. (1950). *The Wit and wisdom of Franklin D. Roosevelt*. Boston: Beacon Press.

National Education Association (1923). *Research bulletin*.

National Education Goals Panel (1991). *Goals report*. Washington, DC: United States Government Printing Office.

Neimark, E. (1975). In F. D. Horowitz (Ed.), *Review of child development research* (Vol. 4). Chicago: University of Chicago Press.

Nord, W. A. (1991). Teaching and morality: The knowledge most worth having. In D. D. Dill et al. (Eds.), *What teachers need to know.* San Francisco: Jossey-Bass.

Offer, D. (1969). *The psychological world of a teenager.* New York: Basic Books.

Onions, C. T. (1933). *The shorter Oxford English dictionary.* Oxford: Clarendon Press, p. 1488.

Ozmon, H. A., & Craver, S. M. (1997). *Philosophical foundations of education* (6th ed.). Columbus, OH: Merrill.

Perkins, D. (1994). Do students understand understanding? *Education Digest, 59*(5), 21–25.

Peters, R. S. (1966). *Ethics and education.* Atlanta: Scott, Foresman, p. 125.

Phenix, P. H. (1961). *Philosophy of education.* New York: John Wiley, p. 56.

Reinstein, D. (1998). Crossing the economic divide. *Educational Leadership, 55*(4), 28–29

Renner, J. W., Bibens, R. F., & Shepherd, G. D. (1972). *Guiding learning in the secondary school.* New York: Harper and Row.

Rousseau, J. J. (1950). *Emile.* Great Neck, NY: Barron's Educational Series.

Rousseau, J. J. (1979). *Emile.* Translated by Alan Bloom. New York: Basic Books.

Scherer, M. (1998). The discipline of hope: An interview with Herbert Kohl. *Educational Leadership, 56*(1), 8–13.

Schmidt, W. H., McKnight, C. C., & Raizen, S. A. (1996). Splintered vision: An investigation of U.S. science and mathematics education: Executive summary. Lansing, MI: U.S. National Research Center for the Third International Mathematics and Science Study, Michigan State University.

Schmoker, M., & Marzano, R. J. (1999). Realizing the promise of standards-based education. *Educational Leadership, 56*(6), 17–21.

Shannon, R. L., & Shannon, D. M. (1991, Fall). The British Infant School. *Educational Forum, 56*(1), 61–70.

Sizer, T. R. (1992). *Horace's compromise: The dilemma of the American high school.* Boston: Houghton Mifflin.

Smart M. S., & Smart, R. C. (1978). *Adolescence* (2nd ed.). New York: Macmillan.

Smith, F. R., & Cox, C. B. (1976). *Secondary schools in a changing society.* New York: Holt, Rinehart and Winston.

Smith, T. L. (1912). *The Montessori system.* New York: Harper and Brothers.

Snodgrass, D. M. (1991). The parent connection. *Adolescence, 26,* 83–87.

Spencer, H. (1960). *Education: Intellectual, moral and physical.* New York: D. Appleton, pp. 17–18.

Standing, E. M. (1962). *The Montessori revolution in education.* New York: Shocken Books.

Steeves, F. L., & English, F. W. (1978). *Secondary curriculum for a changing world.* Columbus, OH: Charles E. Merrill.

Stefanich, G. P. (1990). Cycles of cognition. *Middle School Journal, 22*(2), 47–52.

Stinnett, T. M., & Henson, K. T. (1982). *America's public schools in transition: Future trends and issues.* New York: Columbia University Teachers' College Press.

Swaim, J. H. (1991, March). Reform of teacher education: Implications for the middle level. *Middle School Journal, 22*(4), 47–51.

Thayer, V. T. (1965). *Formative ideas in American education.* New York: Dodd, Mead.

Thompson, S., & Gregg, L. (1997). Reculturing middle schools for meaningful change. *Middle School Journal, 28*(5), 27–31.

Van Til, W. (1978). *Secondary education: School and community.* Boston: Houghton Mifflin.

Walker, B. F. (1976). *Curriculum evolution as portrayed through old textbooks.* Terre Haute, IN: Curriculum Research and Development Center, Indiana State University.

Wilson, B., Ireton, E., & Wood, J. A. (1997). Beginning teacher fears. *Education, 117*(3), 396–400.

Winn, D. D., Regan, P., & Gibson, S. (1991, March–April). Teaching the middle years learner. *The Clearing House, 64,* 265–267.

Wohlstetter, P., Van Kirk, A. N., Robertson, P. J., & Mohrman, S. A. (1997). *Organizing for successful school-based management.* Alexandria, VA: Association for Supervision and Curriculum Development.

Wolk, R. (1998). Doing it right. *Teacher Magazine, 10*(1), 6.

Wynne, E. A., & Ryan, K. (1993). *Reclaiming our schools: A handbook on teaching character, academics, and discipline.* New York: Macmillan.

Zirpoli, T. J., & Melloy, K. J. (1993). *Behavior management: Applications for teachers and parents.* New York: Macmillan.

4   CONCEPTS, THEORIES, AND MODELS

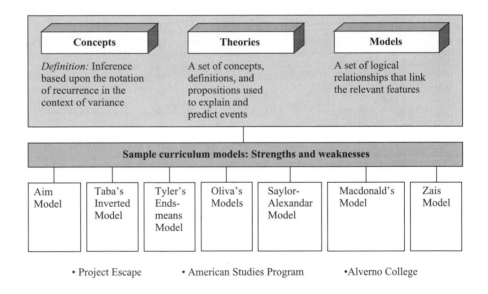

Concepts

Definition: Inference based upon the notation of recurrence in the context of variance

Theories

A set of concepts, definitions, and propositions used to explain and predict events

Models

A set of logical relationships that link the relevant features

Sample curriculum models: Strengths and weaknesses

| Aim Model | Taba's Inverted Model | Tyler's Ends-means Model | Oliva's Models | Saylor-Alexandar Model | Macdonald's Model | Zais Model |

• Project Escape   • American Studies Program   •Alverno College

Objectives

This chapter should prepare you to:

- Describe the role that concepts play in learning.
- Contrast the roles of theories and models in curriculum development.
- Correct two misconceptions about theory.
- Describe students' relationships with theory.
- Discuss the role of cultural heritage in multicultural classes and describe a program model for meeting these needs.
- Criticize the strengths and weaknesses of six curriculum development models.
- Describe an experientially based education reform program.
- Understand and appreciate the role of experience in constructivism.

No man claiming to be practically versed in a science can disdain its theory without exposing himself as an ignoramus in his field.
Immanuel Kant

The Case of a Disappointed Student

Next semester I will be a senior; my grade point average is 3.73—and I feel as if I know nothing. In almost every class I attend, I get nothing but information. I've heard that great minds discuss ideas, but my college classes are like petrified forests: the ideas may be there, but they are viewed only as objects of curiosity, too long ago buried under the tons of information built up over the centuries. Long ago the simple-minded pleasure of giving precise answers to precise questions replaced the hard work of intellectual endeavor. This didn't happen overnight; it took a long time, and now here we are, in the petrified forest of education.

Why can't educators see that there is simply too much information to learn? It is important to use the mind. It is important to be able to deal with ideas. It is important to be aware of the changing world. Here is the frustration: we constantly look backwards in order to invent the future. It is not that we do not need information, but must we spend all our lives just accumulating information?

I believe intellectual curiosity is the only constant in education, and unless that curiosity is awakened, no education will, or indeed can, take place. And this awakening does not come from gathering information; ideas awake the intellect. I realize that *ideas* is an abstract term. That is precisely why it is so important.

Ideas are concepts, and as students deal with them, as they try to bring them to concreteness, as they focus their minds on them, they are truly becoming educated. Again, I grant that information is a necessity, but it is gained throughout a lifetime. Unless educators see the difference between wisdom and knowledge and begin dealing with the mind rather than just with information, the classroom will continue to be a sea of mediocrity.

In trying to get an education, I feel like a nonswimmer who dived into the deep end of the pool. The problem is that my instructors do not know how to swim either. They know all about the right strokes; they know all about the proper breathing procedures; but they have never been in the pool. It isn't that they don't want to help—they just don't know how. The best they can do is stand at the edge of the pool and throw me the empty container that used to hold the life preserver.

I don't want to just criticize—this is a plea. One day soon, I will be a teacher. What am I to do? I can't go back, since I am already in the water. I can't go forward, because I cannot swim. There is only one answer: I must learn to swim—even if only enough to stay afloat. I dare not struggle back to the edge; if I do, I will only become one of the nameless faces that throw out the empty containers.

As you read this bored and disappointed student's view of contemporary education, you may have found issues that were overstated and perhaps others that were totally inaccurate, but you should recognize the truth in the student's concern for the shallowness that characterizes what goes on in many classrooms. As one educator has noted, "Understanding is not a private possession to be protected from theft but, rather, a capacity developed through the free exchange of ideas" (Wiske, 1994, p. 19). This chapter examines this problem and discusses ways that teachers and other curriculum developers can put meaning into education.

THE ROLE OF RESEARCH

This chapter focuses on concepts, theories, and models. Constructionists emphasize the importance of using concepts to build the curriculum for each course. Theories are important because they expand concepts into broader themes. Models are important because they provide examples that can be followed. While it is not important to try to understand all of the relationships among concepts, theories, and models, educators should understand that the main power of each is its generalizability, a quality that is important to all curriculum planning because it increases applicability while encouraging the curriculum developer's creativity.

In defining professionalism, Kowalski and Reitzug (1993, p. 25) list several qualities of professionals and add, "Research is another characteristic commonly used to identify professions." Yet educational psychologists and other educators report that generally teachers do not use research to guide their practice. Egbert (1984, p. 14) says, in reference to teachers' planning, "Teachers ignore research and overestimate the value of personal experience." Brown (1990) echoed this concern, saying that teachers usually do not base their planning on the factors that affect achievement. Nelson (1999, p. 390) expressed the need to use research simply but effectively, "As in other significant professions, teachers should be prepared to be researchers in the practice that they control." When Marshall (1991, p. 227) asked teachers why they used traditional methods, that is, students seated in rows, quiet classrooms, teacher-dominant, textbook-oriented, paper and pencil instruction, her responses were:

- "It's the way I was taught."
- "It's the way I learned."
- "It's the easiest [most expedient] way to cover the material."

The absence of theory utilization extends to all phases of teaching including how teachers manage their classrooms. Martin (1997, p. 6) says, "Traditionally, educators have learned to manage classrooms from each other where the focus is on practice rather than theory. When classroom management is taught in this manner, we run the risk of making the same mistakes without realizing why."

Bellon et al. (1992, p. 3) acknowledge teachers' failure to know about and use research: "Many experienced teachers are not conversant with the research on teaching. . . . Teachers will adopt new approaches without understanding the underlying principles and assumptions. . . . Most teachers, however, are interested in the research and would like to make selected applications of research findings." Teachers have their own theories based on their personal experiences, and they are reluctant to give up these theories even when physical evidence contradicts them (Woods, 1994). Furthermore, students' theories are often very different from what their teachers think they are (Heckman, Confer, & Hakim, 1994).

LACK OF A RESEARCH BASE

Until recently, teachers had both an excuse and a reason for ignoring the research: very little research on teaching was available. But during the second half of the twentieth century, research on teaching increased rapidly. Good (1990, p. 17) explains:

> In the past twenty years, improved research and research methodology have increased dramatically our knowledge of teaching. . . . What was once a very limited collection of results of various studies that did not combine to form easily interpretable patterns has become an increasingly integrated knowledge base that includes a sizable collection of replicated correlational findings, many of which have been validated experimentally.

According to Good, prior to the 1980s the research on curriculum and instruction was fragmented. The scattered studies were isolated, and they provided only microscopic glimpses of segments of the educational process. But with a newly acquired knowledge base, educators can more effectively use the data to make instruction-related decisions.

During the past two decades, we have learned a great deal about instruction in American schools. Sophisticated observational research has yielded more knowledge about schooling than had been obtained in the previous 85 years. There is now an extensive quantitative and qualitative database to help educators understand classroom problems and make decisions about instructional issues.

One promising development that has been pulling teachers back into the center of schoolwide curriculum development and giving teachers a renewed interest in curriculum research and development is teachers' participation in action research projects (discussed further in Chapter 8). Such research appeals to twenty-first century education reformers because it is authentic; it focuses on real-life problems and is aimed at improving current conditions.

The involvement of teachers in research ranges from micro (classroom level) projects to macro (schoolwide) restructuring projects. Action research projects usually involve more than one teacher, may or may not involve university staff members, and usually begin with the perception of a gap between the current state of affairs and a more desirable state (Bracey, 1991).

Students should also be involved in research. Rappoport and Kletzien (1996, p. 28) explain, "It's a disservice to students to expect them to express opinions on matters they have not researched." Reform programs of the late twentieth and early twenty-first centuries are bringing teachers out of their classrooms and involving them with the rest of the school's curriculum planning, and this broader involvement has led to an increased use of research by teachers. Wang, Haertel, and Walberg (1998, p. 68) have noticed this difference: "The comprehensive school reform programs generally include more research-based practices than the curriculum focused programs." Ironically, and unfortunately, though, education reformers have neglected to continue researching the most important variable of all, which is the amount of learning associated with these various programs (Wang, Haertel, & Walberg, 1998).

THE USE OF COMMON SENSE

Another reason some educators reject research is because they tend to rely on common sense, but common sense isn't reliable. For example, when inexperienced drivers enter a foggy area, they almost invariably turn their lights on high beam. Common sense has told them that the high beams will help them see better, but they don't. In fact, because of increased reflection, the high beams can be blinding to the driver. To use another driving example, when a car skids, common sense tells the driver to turn the wheel in the direction opposite to the skidding. But doing this intensifies the problem.

Readers who have taken a physics course may remember the problem that involves simultaneously shooting a rifle horizontally and dropping a bullet vertically. The problem is to determine which bullet will hit the ground first. Common sense says the dropped bullet will hit the ground first because the distance it travels is so much shorter. In fact, the two bullets land simultaneously. A basic principle of gravitation says that free-falling bodies travel at a velocity of 96 ft/sec^2, regardless of their horizontal speeds.

SCIENCE VERSUS COMMON SENSE

Kerlinger (1973, pp. 3–5) used the work of Whitehead (1911) and Conant (1951) to show that, although science can be misleading, it differs from common sense in important ways:

> Whitehead has pointed out that in creative thought common sense is a bad master. "Its sole criterion for judgment is that the new ideas shall look like the old ones." This is well said. Common sense may often be a bad master for the evaluation of knowledge. . . .
>
> Science and common sense differ sharply in [several] ways. . . . First, the uses of conceptual schemes and theoretical structures are strikingly different. While the man in the street uses "theories" and concepts, he ordinarily does so in a loose fashion. He often blindly accepts fanciful explanations of natural and human phenomena. . . . The scientist, on the other hand, systematically builds his theoretical structures, tests them for internal consistency, and subjects aspects of them to empirical test. . . . Second, the scientist systematically and empirically tests his theories and hypotheses. The man in the street tests his "hypotheses" too, but he tests them in what might be called a selective fashion. He often "selects" evidence simply because it is consistent with his hypothesis. . . . [The scientist] insists upon systematic, controlled, and empirical testing of these relations. A third difference lies in the notion of control. . . . The scientist tries systematically to rule out variables that are possible "causes" of the effects he is studying other than the variables that he has hypothesized to be the "causes." [The layman] tends to accept those explanations that arc in accord with his preconceptions and biases. . . .
>
> A final difference between common sense and science lies in different explanations of observed phenomena. The scientist, when attempting to explain the relations among observed phenomena, carefully rules out what have been called "metaphysical explanations." A metaphysical explanation is simply a proposition that cannot be tested.

According to Ozmon & Craver (1999, p. 298), historically teachers have treated information as have laypersons:

> Teachers constantly call for practical solutions to educational problems. But this concern with "practicality" is itself open to analytic inquiry: just what does "practical" mean in this instance? Often, the "practical" teacher wants a technique, a

gimmick, to apply to and solve a problem. It is reasonable, however, to observe that such "practical" solutions are often theoretical in the worst sense. Techniques are sometimes used indiscriminately. They are applied generally and universally in situations for which they were not designed; however, they are deemed "practical" because their mechanics are known and they are capable of being acted upon.

WORD TRAPS

Chapter 1 contained some criticisms of current education reform practices. Paramount among these practices are the overreliance on achievement tests scores and the careless use of terminology. This concern appeared again in Chapter 2, in reference to the awkward and careless way writers use such terms as *multicultural education* and *pluralistic education.* Ozmon and Craver (1999, p. 298) explain the danger in the overuse and misuse of the word *practical:*

> "Achievement" is a talisman by which many educators swear, and the worth of any educational activity is judged on students' achievement scores. "Achievement" in such instances is usually understood to be a "practical" outcome of one's education, but such emphasis may serve to retard one's education if the meaning of achievement is vague and unclear. Suppose one wants to learn how to play the piano, and the educator says that the "practical" approach is to proceed by achievement in learning to play scales. Such a method may result in the student's learning to play scales but not in developing [an] ability to play the piano or in sustaining [the student's] interest. We may pose the question: how "practical" is this approach?

Criticism of theory is not new. Practitioners have always been critical, especially when the theory doesn't work when applied to practice. Two centuries ago Kant (1793, p. 41) had a good response for the critics of his day: "Thus, when the theory did not work too well in practice, the fault lay, not in the theory, but rather in there not being enough theory which a man should have learned from experience."

Recall the student's plea at the beginning of this chapter. Too often, educators attend to the specifics at the cost of ignoring the meanings that these specifics could have if students are prepared to make generalizations and apply these generalizations to their own lives and to the world around them. Perkins (1994, p. 23) expresses this concern:

> Knowledge tends to get glued to the narrow circumstances of initial acquisition. But an understanding of performance virtually by definition requires a modicum of transfer because it asks the learner to go beyond the information given, tackling some task that reaches further than the textbook or lecture.

Learning without application tends to be useless. As expressed by Eggebrecht, Dagenais, Dosch, Merczak, Park, Styer, and Workman (1996, p. 5) "If learning has value, students should be able to transfer the knowledge they acquire in school to the world beyond the classroom."

Words seem to be a common trap for educators and students alike. Too often, the aim is "achievement," but when measured by pencil and paper tests, that achievement amounts to no more than memorizing words or facts. To get beyond these facts, teachers need three tools: (1) concepts, (2) theories, and (3) models.

CONCEPTS

Tyson and Carroll (1970, p. 25) define *concept* as follows: "A concept is an inference based upon the notation of recurrence in the context of variance which enables one to order and organize experience." Put simply, unlike facts, a concept has a recurring quality that gives the concept a very special power, "generalizability." The recurring quality may be a physical property such as the four legs and flat surface that recur among tables, or the recurring pattern could be in other properties such as utility, which reoccurs in the case of all tools. Or the recurring quality can be an abstraction, as reflected in such feelings as love, hate, doubt, or curiosity.

The power of the concept in learning must never be underestimated. Einstein (1951, p. 7) said that it is the very essence of all thinking:

> What precisely is "thinking"? When at the reception of sense-impressions, memory-pictures emerge, that is not yet "thinking." And when such pictures form series, each member of which calls forth another, this too is not yet "thinking." When, however, a certain picture turns up in many series, then—precisely through such return—it becomes an ordering element for such series, in that it connects series which in themselves are unconnected. Such an element becomes an instrument, a concept. I think that the transition from free association or "dreaming" to thinking is characterized by the more or less dominating role which the "concept" plays in it.

Ward (1969, p. 423) describes the concept's special power of generalization:

> You enter the old kitchen, in which there is a blazing hearthfire complete with bubbling, boiling teakettle. Oh, it's always there anyway; you've seen it before. Besides, your mind is on something else. Your quaint kitchen is pretty well tuned out by you, or you only perceive it at the (blob) level. Wait, something focuses your attention on the event system that is the boiling kettle. You've noticed. Now you are beginning to operate. You've noticed something, and something is happening. The lid jumps up and down. You wonder why. Ah, cause, the why sets you to scrutinizing relationships. First you attend, focus, observe, isolate. Next, you want the cause of something. Establishing tentative cause gets you to infer a low-level generalization. "That lid will move because steam is pushing it up and down. If that particular kettle is put on that fire and it boils, then its lid will jump up and down" is a relatively low level of abstraction because the particulars of the scene are still involved. The next level of abstraction, of generalization, will take you to a point of thinking, "When a kettle is placed on a fire, the water will boil and cause a loose lid to move."

This illustrates how concepts can be discovered and formulated by students. Some of the current education reform programs stress the significance of identifying major concepts in each discipline. In contrast, other programs (particularly authentic, performance-based ones) stress method to the degree that content is downplayed, the argument being that if the process is right the content will come automatically. These reformers argue that education is an emotional, learn-from-the-gut experience.

Most contemporary reformers embrace the teaching/learning style reflected in the teakettle scenario, the discovery method. Constructivists argue that direct involvement in identifying concepts enables students to tie the major content generalizations in the lesson to previous understanding.

Stefanich (1990, p. 48) writes that the curriculum should be carefully designed to help students see the relationships among concepts:

> Students tend to deal with concepts in isolation. They cannot effectively consider a number of isolated examples and apply these to general theory or principle. They cannot effectively apply a general principle to a number of instances or examples. They are unable to cognitively process variable time frames or situations which require simultaneous consideration of multiple characters or events.

Students tend to be unaware of the major concepts in each lesson, and, furthermore, there is evidence that teachers are aware of this oversight and are unwilling to make the adjustments needed to correct this flaw (Perkins and Blythe, 1994). Because students tend to deal with concepts in isolation, the teacher's job of getting the students to see the relationships among concepts may be made easier by explaining the tentative nature of concepts. The boundaries of all concepts are tentative. Even all disciplinary boundaries are tentative (Gardner and Boix-Mansilla, 1994).

Authentic problem solving, a popular technique found in today's education reform programs, can be a useful strategy for teaching concepts. As Prescott, Rinard, Cockerill, and Baker (1996, p. 11) explain, "For those students who do not think and learn in a predominantly abstract way, teaching science concepts in context provides a concrete and familiar framework for new ideas. This helps them comprehend and retain the information and gives them a rationale for doing so." These authors are referring to the Applications in Biology/Chemistry (ABC) curriculum program, which is designed for the middle 50 percent of the secondary student population.

THEORIES

Once students understand concepts, these concepts can be assembled to form even more powerful mental tools: theories and models. Kerlinger (1973, p. 9) gives the following definition of a *theory:*

> A theory is a set of interrelated constructs (concepts), definitions, and propositions that present a systematic view of phenomena by specifying relations among variables, with the purpose of explaining and predicting the phenomena.

Martin (1997, p. 6) expresses the indispensable value that theory holds for teachers when he states, "Without theory, we are left with a bag of tricks."

Philosophy can help the educator use theories. An educator can begin by formulating a theory of education. Although many educators have tried unsuccessfully to formulate such a theory, this poor record should not preclude teachers from writing their own philosophies of education. On the contrary, curriculum coursework should prepare teachers to formulate their own theories and philosophies about education. All teachers must take time to reflect and reinvent. Systematic and ongoing inquiry must be a routine part of our roles as teachers and learners (Stallworth, 1998).

The relationship between philosophy and educational theory was explained by John Dewey in 1916. Ozmon and Craver (1999, p. 7) explain:

> According to Dewey, the theory of education is a set of "generalizations" and "abstractions" about education. Many people probably think that abstraction is useless when dealing with practical matters, but Dewey maintained that it can serve a very useful purpose. . . . Things are generalized so they may have broader application. A theory of education contains generalizations that are applicable to many situations.

To many, the term *theory* may conjure up images of scientists working in laboratories. People tend also to believe that theories, when followed precisely, will lead to the correct solution. These common views of theory have some basic problems. First, scientists are not the only people who theorize. At one time or another, all of us have used theories. As Ozmon and Craver (1999, p. 8) explain:

> Experienced teachers do this quite often. They exchange ideas and methods that they have found fruitful in achieving certain educational goals. In this sense, they are theorizing or building theory, even though the theory may not be very sophisticated. One person tries another's approach, and afterward discusses it. Experienced teachers find ways to redefine goals and to vary, expand, or redirect the approaches for future use; hence, very "practical" approaches and goals are generalized, abstracted. These approaches and goals have been tested and found successful, or they have been altered, improved, or discarded. . . . In this way theory and practice may build upon each other.

Second, theorizing occurs both inside and outside the laboratory. In reference to action research, Bernaur (1999, p. 69) writes, "Theories are grounded in classroom experiences rather than theoretical premises." We also theorize outside the classroom. Each time we buy a new automobile or dishwasher, we theorize about its future performance and its durability.

Finally, theories do not always produce correct answers, and they never tell us what we should do. Although some theories have predictive powers and can tell us what will very likely happen if we do this or that, the decision to choose one alternative over another is ours. So the role of the theory is not to guide our behavior; rather, it is to help guide our thinking. More accurately, theory is one of several forces that work together to guide our thinking. For example, our emotions and our value systems also play important roles in our decisions to behave in certain ways.

Theories are never final, because science is fluid in nature. The more we learn, the more we are able to learn. Learning is like stepping on a rock to see farther, then stepping on another, larger rock, and then another. Or, it is like the work of an astronomer. Each time a more powerful telescope is invented, our knowledge of the universe expands, and often our theories must be changed to accommodate our new understandings.

Applied to curriculum development, theories cannot tell teachers and other curriculum developers to develop curricula a particular way. But theory can guide the curriculum developer's thinking, which can indirectly improve curriculum design.

To be useful, an educational theory doesn't have to be proved. Some theories are used to predict; others are used to explain. Pratt (1971) explains, "What theory provides is order and intelligibility out of miscellaneous and unrelated profusion of phenomena."

Another misconception is that theories must be complicated, esoteric, and pedantic. Obviously, theories cannot be of value if they are obscure. Ozmon and Craver (1999, p. 10) advise, "If a theory does not help us communicate in a better or more advantageous way, criticize our assumptions and actions, gain perspective, seek out new possibilities, order and direct practice, then we had better let it go or revise it in new directions."

Sample Theories

Following are sample theories from the four major content areas. This material is from *Conceptual Tools for Teaching in Secondary Schools* (Tyson & Carroll, 1970).

1. Science: The total amount of energy is not affected by energy transformation.
2. English: Effective writing is a function of clear, concise sentences.
3. Social Studies: Attitudes are a function of group affiliation.
4. Mathematics: In a right angle the square of the hypotenuse is equal to the sum of the squares of the other two sides.

Some of these theories are familiar because we memorized them in high school. We still use them, but perhaps only rarely (for example, the Pythagorean theorem). Other theories guide our daily thinking. Using a theory requires awareness and understanding, not memorization. As you continue through this book, your goal should be to understand and recall the relationships among the curriculum development theories.

Ensuring that the major concepts and theories in each discipline become the focus of the curriculum requires a carefully planned schoolwide strategy. These major content generalizations should rest on a solid foundation that includes knowledge of the latest database on brain research, matching teaching/learning styles, local and state guidelines or benchmarks, and the learned societies' guidelines. The following case study by Bolinger and Thompson reports on a school that has used such a comprehensive strategy to significantly raise the academic performance of its students.

Case Study

Angola High School

Dr. Rex Bolinger
Principal, Angola High School

Dr. Jay Thompson
Dept. of Curriculum and Instruction, Ball State University

Background Information

Angola High School is an example of a school that has gone through effective change. Using both micro and macro research to guide its restructuring efforts, the teachers and administrators at Angola High School have made significant improvements in student learning. The school has won several awards since the results of the restructuring efforts have been made public. Significant improvements have been sustained into the fourth year of restructuring. Angola High School was named an Indiana Academic Improvement School in 1995 by the Indiana Department of Education, Indiana's Most Outstanding Successful High School by the Indiana Association of Teacher Educators and the Indiana Association of Colleges of Teacher Education in 1996 and 1998, and an Indiana Blue Ribbon School by the Indiana Department of Education and the U.S. Department of Education in 1997.

Curriculum development and alignment have been the foundation of the success achieved at Angola High School. In 1989, the entire school adopted Thomas Guskey's model of curriculum development, which focuses on establishing what teachers want their students to learn and what teachers expect their students to be able to do with what they have learned. This was done by developing what Guskey referred to as "Tables of Specification" (Guskey, 1985). The tables allow teachers to develop guides for units of study that outline a program that begins with knowledge of terms and progresses to higher-level activities requiring a synthesis of material learned previously. Teachers used curricular materials from the Indiana Department of Education, learned societies such as the National Council of Teachers of Mathematics, and other resources to determine what they believed were the

(Continued)

critical elements of the curriculum. Materials covered in the new statewide graduation exam were also examined carefully. This process established consistency with vertical and horizontal articulation. The Guskey model, with its emphasis on mastery, allows schools to have a clearly focused direction in curricular content and instruction.

The Case

In addition to curriculum development at Angola High School, a massive restructuring was necessary to affect instruction and assessment practices within the school if there was to be real and lasting improvement. Flexible scheduling became the vehicle and catalyst for change at AHS. The Carnegie Foundation report on high schools, *Breaking Ranks: Changing an American Institution,* became the guiding set of principles for change. A 4x4 intensive block schedule was adopted, which meant teachers were given longer periods of time to work with students daily. Teachers' daily class loads were reduced to half the numbers of students they had traditionally seen. Extensive amounts of teacher in-service and professional development activities were provided. Peer coaching teams formed around Bruce Joyce's models of teaching (Joyce, 1996), which helped faculty members to understand the need to engage active learners. William Glasser's work and Howard Gardner's research on how people learn helped the faculty understand the need for changes from traditional instructional patterns. Perhaps the most important reference for the faculty was *Teaching in the Block: Strategies for Engaging Active Learners* by Robert Lynn Canady and Michael Rettig. Each teacher received a copy of this book, and copies were placed in the school's professional library. Peer coaching teams used it as a regular resource, and it has become a source of regular teaching discussions. The book explains teaching models and strategies in easily understood terms. It guided teachers through the processes of using a strategy that perhaps was new to them.

Assessment and evaluation strategies were the third critical element in the Angola High School reform effort. Time was spent with faculty members regarding authentic assessment techniques, and strategies to incorporate these principles into the classroom were also discussed. Portfolios and student-generated technology presentations were two very visible results of these efforts; however, the schoolwide action research efforts around assessment were the most critical elements in evaluating, reporting, and communicating positive changes in student learning. An assessment team led by Mr. David Snyder, research biology teacher, put in place a credible research study around collectable data within our school. Both qualitative and quantitative materials were studied. His two-year case study was presented in 1997 at the Annual Meeting of the Midwest Educational Research Association in Chicago, Illinois. The data continue to garner national recognition and can be viewed on the AHS home page at: *www.msdsteuben.k12.in.us/ahs/ahs.htm.* Copies of the report may be obtained by sending requests to Angola High School, 755 S. 100 E., Angola, IN 46703.

The following graphs depict the baseline data prior to reforms and the three years of data available following the restructuring. A fourth year of data reflects positive sustained results as well.

(Continued)

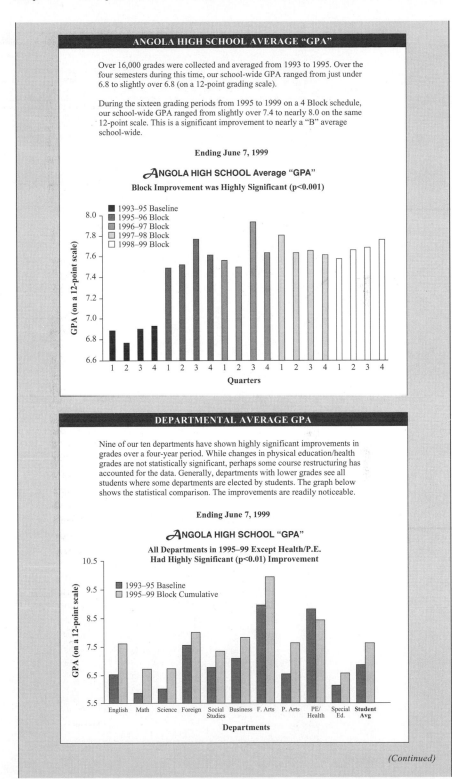

ANGOLA HIGH SCHOOL AVERAGE "GPA"

Over 16,000 grades were collected and averaged from 1993 to 1995. Over the four semesters during this time, our school-wide GPA ranged from just under 6.8 to slightly over 6.8 (on a 12-point grading scale).

During the sixteen grading periods from 1995 to 1999 on a 4 Block schedule, our school-wide GPA ranged from slightly over 7.4 to nearly 8.0 on the same 12-point scale. This is a significant improvement to nearly a "B" average school-wide.

Ending June 7, 1999

***A*NGOLA HIGH SCHOOL Average "GPA"**

Block Improvement was Highly Significant (p<0.001)

DEPARTMENTAL AVERAGE GPA

Nine of our ten departments have shown highly significant improvements in grades over a four-year period. While changes in physical education/health grades are not statistically significant, perhaps some course restructuring has accounted for the data. Generally, departments with lower grades see all students where some departments are elected by students. The graph below shows the statistical comparison. The improvements are readily noticeable.

Ending June 7, 1999

***A*NGOLA HIGH SCHOOL "GPA"**

All Departments in 1995–99 Except Health/P.E. Had Highly Significant (p<0.01) Improvement

(Continued)

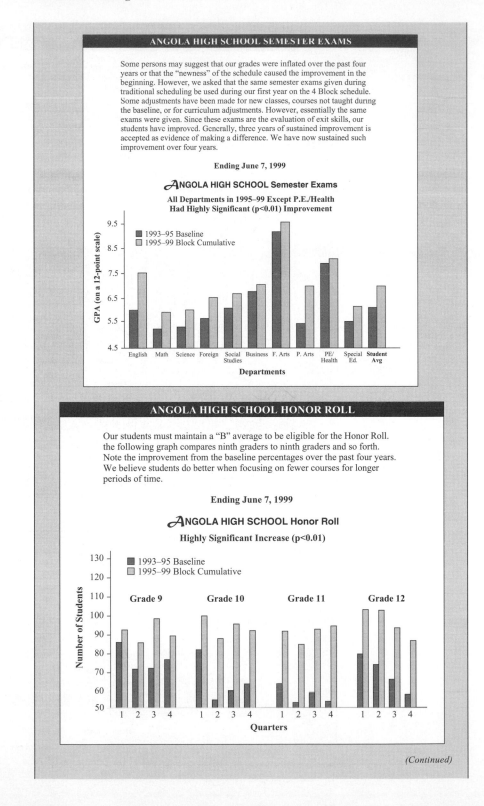

ANGOLA HIGH SCHOOL SEMESTER EXAMS

Some persons may suggest that our grades were inflated over the past four years or that the "newness" of the schedule caused the improvement in the beginning. However, we asked that the same semester exams given during traditional scheduling be used during our first year on the 4 Block schedule. Some adjustments have been made for new classes, courses not taught during the baseline, or for curriculum adjustments. However, essentially the same exams were given. Since these exams are the evaluation of exit skills, our students have improved. Generally, three years of sustained improvement is accepted as evidence of making a difference. We have now sustained such improvement over four years.

Ending June 7, 1999

ᴀNGOLA HIGH SCHOOL Semester Exams

All Departments in 1995–99 Except P.E./Health
Had Highly Significant ($p<0.01$) Improvement

ANGOLA HIGH SCHOOL HONOR ROLL

Our students must maintain a "B" average to be eligible for the Honor Roll. the following graph compares ninth graders to ninth graders and so forth. Note the improvement from the baseline percentages over the past four years. We believe students do better when focusing on fewer courses for longer periods of time.

Ending June 7, 1999

ᴀNGOLA HIGH SCHOOL Honor Roll

Highly Significant Increase ($p<0.01$)

(Continued)

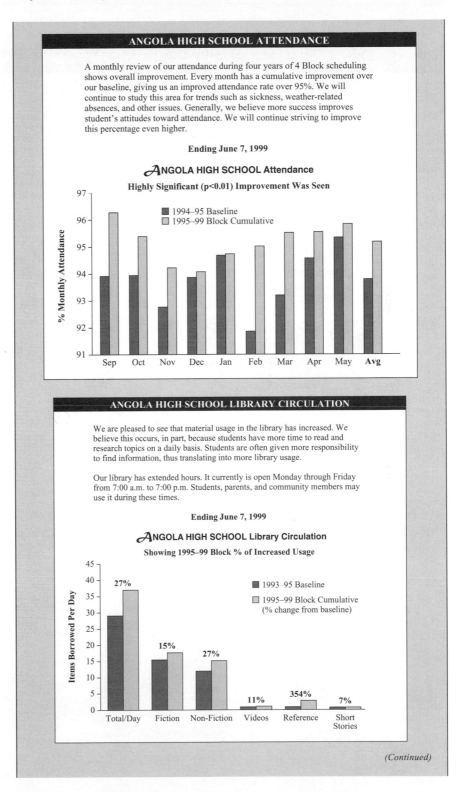

ANGOLA HIGH SCHOOL ATTENDANCE

A monthly review of our attendance during four years of 4 Block scheduling shows overall improvement. Every month has a cumulative improvement over our baseline, giving us an improved attendance rate over 95%. We will continue to study this area for trends such as sickness, weather-related absences, and other issues. Generally, we believe more success improves student's attitudes toward attendance. We will continue striving to improve this percentage even higher.

Ending June 7, 1999

𝒜NGOLA HIGH SCHOOL Attendance

Highly Significant (p<0.01) Improvement Was Seen

- ■ 1994–95 Baseline
- ☐ 1995–99 Block Cumulative

ANGOLA HIGH SCHOOL LIBRARY CIRCULATION

We are pleased to see that material usage in the library has increased. We believe this occurs, in part, because students have more time to read and research topics on a daily basis. Students are often given more responsibility to find information, thus translating into more library usage.

Our library has extended hours. It currently is open Monday through Friday from 7:00 a.m. to 7:00 p.m. Students, parents, and community members may use it during these times.

Ending June 7, 1999

𝒜NGOLA HIGH SCHOOL Library Circulation

Showing 1995–99 Block % of Increased Usage

- ■ 1993–95 Baseline
- ☐ 1995–99 Block Cumulative (% change from baseline)

(Continued)

ANGOLA HIGH SCHOOL TESTING
ISTEP+ (Indiana Statewide Test of Educational Progress)
SAT, ACT, & AP SCORES

The ISTEP+ has been given to sophomores throughout Indiana from the fall of 1995 to the fall of 1998. Our results have been very high. Last year's scores from Angola High School sophomores were some of the highest in our area and ranked very high among Indiana's high schools. However, we expect fluctuations from year to year. Thes scores vary from group to group, often based upon numerous factors beyond the type of schedule a school follows. We are pleased with our results.

We have shown improvement over the past three years with SAT and ACT scores. Our cumulative scores were above both state and national averages in the verbal and math sections. The number of students taking Advanced Placement (AP) courses has risen while the percentage of scores at "3" or higher has increased. However, a similar response will be given as with ISTEP+ scores. We believe additional years of review will be necessary to draw any general conclusions regarding these scores and our daily schedule.

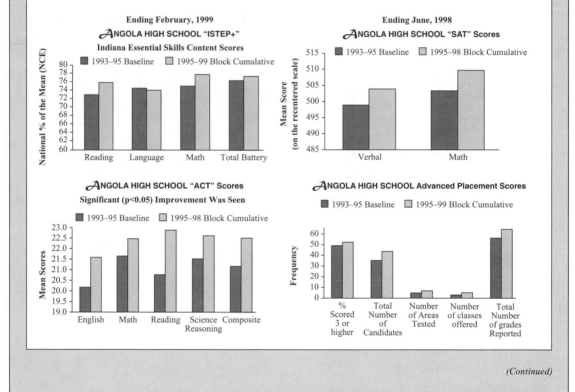

(Continued)

ANGOLA HIGH SCHOOL SUSPENSIONS, EXPULSION, GRADUATION, AND DROP OUT RATES

In-school suspension rates (ISS), out-of-school suspension rates (OSS), and expulsions have decreased during the four years of block scheduling compared to our baseline. With fewer class changes and potential for problems, issues seem to decrease. Attempts to personalize our classrooms, opportunities for cooperative activities, and the creation of a peer mediation program are factors in these positive statistics. Note the increase in graduation rates and decrease in drop out rates over the past four years. These are encouraging statistics.

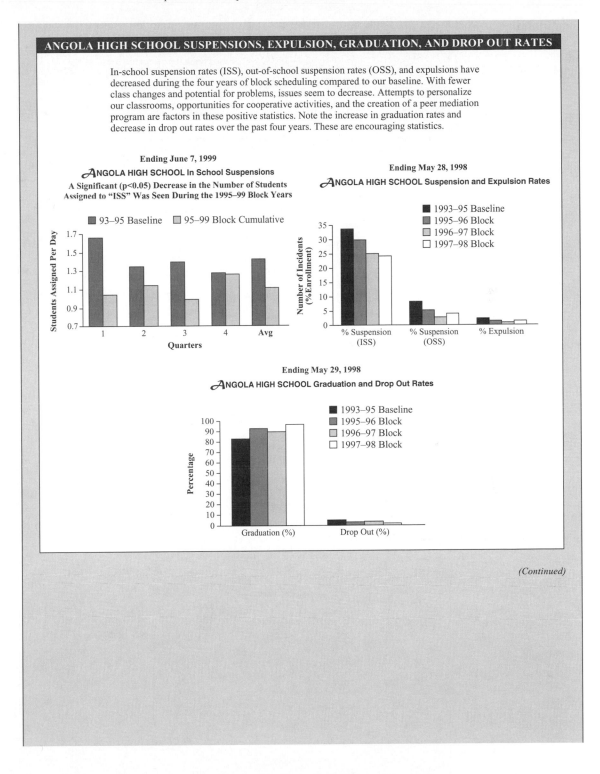

Ending June 7, 1999

ANGOLA HIGH SCHOOL In School Suspensions

A Significant (p<0.05) Decrease in the Number of Students Assigned to "ISS" Was Seen During the 1995–99 Block Years

Ending May 28, 1998

ANGOLA HIGH SCHOOL Suspension and Expulsion Rates

Ending May 29, 1998

ANGOLA HIGH SCHOOL Graduation and Drop Out Rates

(Continued)

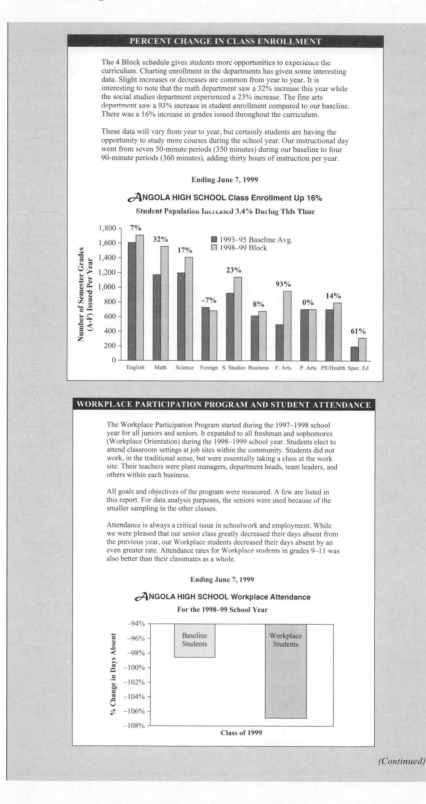

PERCENT CHANGE IN CLASS ENROLLMENT

The 4 Block schedule gives students more opportunities to experience the curriculum. Charting enrollment in the departments has given some interesting data. Slight increases or decreases are common from year to year. It is interesting to note that the math department saw a 32% increase this year while the social studies department experienced a 23% increase. The fine arts department saw a 93% increase in student enrollment compared to our baseline. There was a 16% increase in grades issued throughout the curriculum.

These data will vary from year to year, but certainly students are having the opportunity to study more courses during the school year. Our instructional day went from seven 50-minute periods (350 minutes) during our baseline to four 90-minute periods (360 minutes), adding thirty hours of instruction per year.

Ending June 7, 1999

𝒜NGOLA HIGH SCHOOL Class Enrollment Up 16%

Student Population Increased 3.4% During This Time

WORKPLACE PARTICIPATION PROGRAM AND STUDENT ATTENDANCE

The Workplace Participation Program started during the 1997–1998 school year for all juniors and seniors. It expanded to all freshman and sophomores (Workplace Orientation) during the 1998–1999 school year. Students elect to attend classroom settings at job sites within the community. Students did not work, in the traditional sense, but were essentially taking a class at the work site. Their teachers were plant managers, department heads, team leaders, and others within each business.

All goals and objectives of the program were measured. A few are listed in this report. For data analysis purposes, the seniors were used because of the smaller sampling in the other classes.

Attendance is always a critical issue in schoolwork and employment. While we were pleased that our senior class greatly decreased their days absent from the previous year, our Workplace students decreased their days absent by an even greater rate. Attendance rates for Workplace students in grades 9–11 was also better than their classmates as a whole.

Ending June 7, 1999

𝒜NGOLA HIGH SCHOOL Workplace Attendance

For the 1998–99 School Year

(Continued)

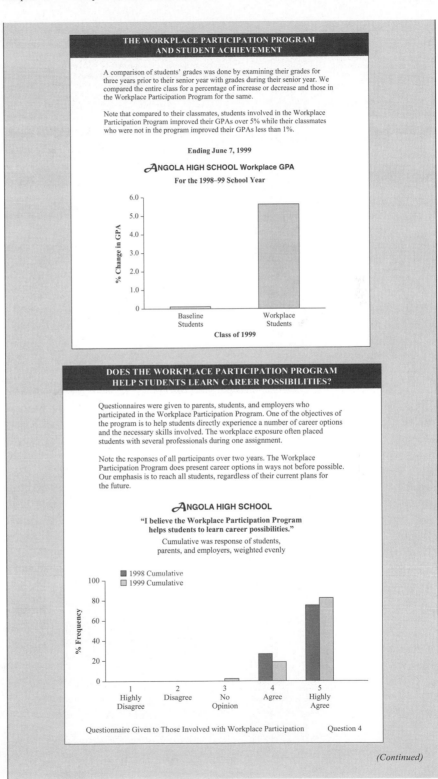

**THE WORKPLACE PARTICIPATION PROGRAM
AND STUDENT ACHIEVEMENT**

A comparison of students' grades was done by examining their grades for three years prior to their senior year with grades during their senior year. We compared the entire class for a percentage of increase or decrease and those in the Workplace Participation Program for the same.

Note that compared to their classmates, students involved in the Workplace Participation Program improved their GPAs over 5% while their classmates who were not in the program improved their GPAs less than 1%.

Ending June 7, 1999

𝒜NGOLA HIGH SCHOOL Workplace GPA

For the 1998–99 School Year

(bar chart: % Change in GPA vs Class of 1999; Baseline Students ≈ 0.1, Workplace Students ≈ 5.6)

**DOES THE WORKPLACE PARTICIPATION PROGRAM
HELP STUDENTS LEARN CAREER POSSIBILITIES?**

Questionnaires were given to parents, students, and employers who participated in the Workplace Participation Program. One of the objectives of the program is to help students directly experience a number of career options and the necessary skills involved. The workplace exposure often placed students with several professionals during one assignment.

Note the responses of all participants over two years. The Workplace Participation Program does present career options in ways not before possible. Our emphasis is to reach all students, regardless of their current plans for the future.

𝒜NGOLA HIGH SCHOOL

**"I believe the Workplace Participation Program
helps students to learn career possibilities."**

Cumulative was response of students,
parents, and employers, weighted evenly

(bar chart: % Frequency vs responses 1 Highly Disagree, 2 Disagree, 3 No Opinion, 4 Agree, 5 Highly Agree; legend 1998 Cumulative, 1999 Cumulative)

Questionnaire Given to Those Involved with Workplace Participation   Question 4

(Continued)

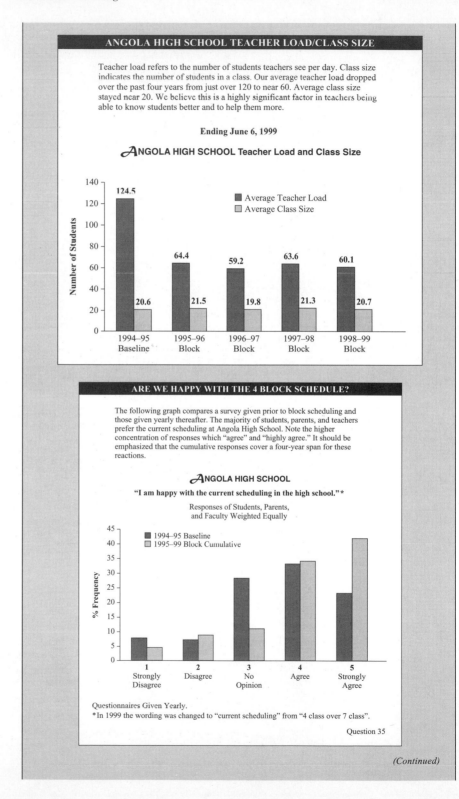

ANGOLA HIGH SCHOOL TEACHER LOAD/CLASS SIZE

Teacher load refers to the number of students teachers see per day. Class size indicates the number of students in a class. Our average teacher load dropped over the past four years from just over 120 to near 60. Average class size stayed near 20. We believe this is a highly significant factor in teachers being able to know students better and to help them more.

Ending June 6, 1999

ANGOLA HIGH SCHOOL Teacher Load and Class Size

Average Teacher Load
Average Class Size

Number of Students

124.5 | 20.6 — 1994–95 Baseline
64.4 | 21.5 — 1995–96 Block
59.2 | 19.8 — 1996–97 Block
63.6 | 21.3 — 1997–98 Block
60.1 | 20.7 — 1998–99 Block

ARE WE HAPPY WITH THE 4 BLOCK SCHEDULE?

The following graph compares a survey given prior to block scheduling and those given yearly thereafter. The majority of students, parents, and teachers prefer the current scheduling at Angola High School. Note the higher concentration of responses which "agree" and "highly agree." It should be emphasized that the cumulative responses cover a four-year span for these reactions.

ANGOLA HIGH SCHOOL

"I am happy with the current scheduling in the high school." *

Responses of Students, Parents,
and Faculty Weighted Equally

% Frequency

1994–95 Baseline
1995–99 Block Cumulative

1 Strongly Disagree
2 Disagree
3 No Opinion
4 Agree
5 Strongly Agree

Questionnaires Given Yearly.
*In 1999 the wording was changed to "current scheduling" from "4 class over 7 class".

Question 35

(Continued)

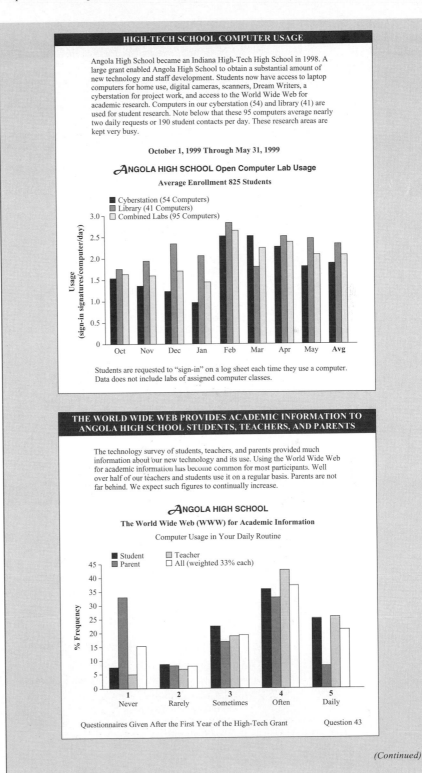

HIGH-TECH SCHOOL COMPUTER USAGE

Angola High School became an Indiana High-Tech High School in 1998. A large grant enabled Angola High School to obtain a substantial amount of new technology and staff development. Students now have access to laptop computers for home use, digital cameras, scanners, Dream Writers, a cyberstation for project work, and access to the World Wide Web for academic research. Computers in our cyberstation (54) and library (41) are used for student research. Note below that these 95 computers average nearly two daily requests or 190 student contacts per day. These research areas are kept very busy.

October 1, 1999 Through May 31, 1999

𝒜NGOLA HIGH SCHOOL Open Computer Lab Usage

Average Enrollment 825 Students

- Cyberstation (54 Computers)
- Library (41 Computers)
- Combined Labs (95 Computers)

Students are requested to "sign-in" on a log sheet each time they use a computer. Data does not include labs of assigned computer classes.

THE WORLD WIDE WEB PROVIDES ACADEMIC INFORMATION TO ANGOLA HIGH SCHOOL STUDENTS, TEACHERS, AND PARENTS

The technology survey of students, teachers, and parents provided much information about our new technology and its use. Using the World Wide Web for academic information has become common for most participants. Well over half of our teachers and students use it on a regular basis. Parents are not far behind. We expect such figures to continually increase.

𝒜NGOLA HIGH SCHOOL

The World Wide Web (WWW) for Academic Information

Computer Usage in Your Daily Routine

- Student
- Parent
- Teacher
- All (weighted 33% each)

Questionnaires Given After the First Year of the High-Tech Grant   Question 43

(Continued)

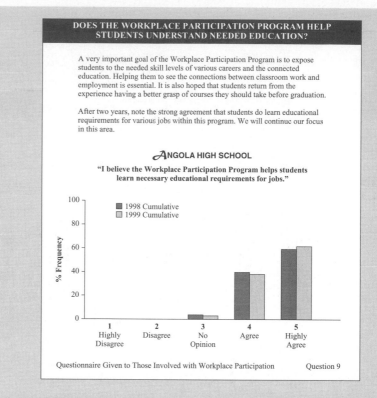

DOES THE WORKPLACE PARTICIPATION PROGRAM HELP
STUDENTS UNDERSTAND NEEDED EDUCATION?

A very important goal of the Workplace Participation Program is to expose students to the needed skill levels of various careers and the connected education. Helping them to see the connections between classroom work and employment is essential. It is also hoped that students return from the experience having a better grasp of courses they should take before graduation.

After two years, note the strong agreement that students do learn educational requirements for various jobs within this program. We will continue our focus in this area.

*A*NGOLA HIGH SCHOOL

**"I believe the Workplace Participation Program helps students
learn necessary educational requirements for jobs."**

Questionnaire Given to Those Involved with Workplace Participation   Question 9

The success at AHS is due partly to others' understanding of the change process. Michael Fullan's work on change is worthy of study. Dr. Jay Thompson, professor of Ball State University, helped AHS in countless ways in dealing with change. Thomas Sergiovanni's (1996) work in school leadership is some of the most significant research affecting the climate and culture at Angola High School.

The Angola High School model of success has incorporated aspects of curriculum development, appropriate instruction, and evaluation which combine to create a successful academic environment for student learning. Effecting change involves more than simply developing new curriculum. It involves professional development, teaching that engages active learners, strong leadership, and an effective evaluation procedure to obtain and study results. These characteristics have caused Angola High School to be considered an outstanding successful high school.

Issues for Further Reflection and Application

1. Angola High School used tables of specifications to restructure its curriculum. How can such tables be used to align a school's curriculum with the new minimum standards set by such learned societies as the National Science Teachers Association and the National Council for Social Studies?

(Continued)

2. Block scheduling is often criticized for allowing students to waste time that should be used receiving direct instruction.
    A. What advantages does block scheduling offer to offset this loss?
    B. What, if any, should be the role of direct instruction when using block scheduling? Should direct instruction during block scheduling be used more or less than in traditional 50- to 60-minute classes?

Suggested Readings

Canady, R. L., & Rettig, M. D. (1996). *Teaching in the block: Strategies for engaging active learners.* Princeton, NJ: Eye on Education.
Guskey, T. R. (1985). *Implementing mastery learning.* Bellmont, CA: Wadsworth.
Joyce, B., & Weil, J. (1996). *Models of teaching* (5th ed.). Needham Heights, MA: Allyn & Bacon.
Sergiovanni, T. J. (1996). *Leadership for the schoolhouse.* San Francisco: Jossey-Bass.
Snyder, D. (1997). *4-Block scheduling: A case study of data analysis of one high school after two years.* Forum paper, Midwest Educational Research Association, annual meeting.

MODELS

The third special tool that teachers need is models. Rivett (1972) has defined *model* as "a set of logical relationships either qualitative or quantitative, which will link together the relevant features of the reality with which we are concerned."

Compare this definition with Beauchamp's (1981, p. 27) description of the role of the model, "Functionally, models are used to represent events and event interactions in a highly compact and illustrative manner."

It should be noted that a model is not reality. Rather, like a painting or a story, it is a visual or written description of someone's perception of reality. It is told that, during an exhibition of Matisse's works, a woman criticized one of the drawings, saying, "The hand doesn't look like a hand." Matisse replied, "It's not, madam. It's a drawing of a hand." Like theories, models help their authors explain various related concepts and the relationships among the various parts of the models. Puryear (Hill, 1986, p. 57) addresses the purpose of models:

> The purposes of a model are to help us organize what we already know, to help us see new relationships, and to keep us from being dazzled by the full-blown complexity of the subject. A model is not intended to be a picture of reality but a tool for thinking.

Like theories, models are imperfect. As more knowledge is gained about what a model portrays, the model becomes weaker, projecting a less complete image. This nature of models requires modifying them from time to time. Currently, there is no adequate theory of education. Because curriculum theory is a subtheory of educational theory and curriculum models represent curriculum theory, it follows, then, that no curriculum model can be perfect, and no curriculum theory can be totally adequate until a satisfactory theory of education has been developed. Meanwhile, teachers and other curriculum workers will continue to benefit from learning all they can about a variety of curriculum models. Following are some models, with strengths and weaknesses noted. As noted earlier in this chapter, education reformers have increased the use of research; however, they have failed to study the most important variable of all, the effects of each program on student learning (Wang, Haertel, Walberg, 1998).

The AIM Model

The first governor's education model for reforming the curriculum was described in Chapter 3. Figure 4.1 shows the legislation that required developing a new 1–12 curriculum in all of Mississippi's schools.

The AIM model is simple and clear. It begins with objectives and moves in the single direction shown by the arrows. It includes both student activities and teacher activities, but it offers no foundation elements and no philosophy statement.

Taba's Inverted Model

Taba's approach to curriculum development is referred to as an inverted model because it begins in the classroom with the teacher, as contrasted with other models which begin in the district office, in state department offices, or in federal offices. This method has eight steps. Step 1 is diagnosing needs, using a needs assessment tool. Step 2 is formulating specific objectives, including concepts and attitudes to be learned, ways of thinking to be enforced, and habits and skills to be mastered. Step 3 is selecting content, by carefully choosing topics, and writing a rationale to support each choice.

Table 4.1 shows the psychological stages in Piaget's developmental hierarchy reached by the majority of students at each age. Teachers should be careful to select content and activities that parallel students' developmental levels; however, as Perkins (1994, p. 23) cautions, "Teachers teaching for understanding do well to bear in mind factors like complexity, but without rigid conceptions of what students can and cannot learn at certain ages."

FIGURE 4.1

The AIM curriculum model.

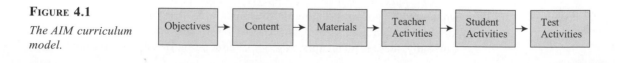

_____

Table 4.1   Percentage of Individuals in Piagetian Stages

Age (Years)	Preoperational	Concrete Onset	Concrete Mature	Formal Onset	Formal Mature
7	35	55	10		
8	25	55	20		
9	15	55	30		
10	12	52	35	1	
11	6	49	40	5	
12	5	32	51	12	
13	2	34	44	14	6
14	1	32	43	15	9
15	1	14	53	19	13
16	1	15	54	17	13
17	3	19	47	19	12
18	1	15	50	15	19

SOURCE: G. P. Stefanich (1990, November), Cycles of cognition. *Middle School Journal,* 22(2), p. 49. Used with permission from G. P. Stefanich and *Middle School Journal.* Originally taken from H. T. Epstein, "Brain growth and cognitive learning." *Colorado Journal of Educational Research,* 3, 1979.

Step 4 is organizing the content, beginning with the simple topics on the list, exploring them in greater depth, and moving to the more difficult topics, noting the essential learner activities. (The idea is to also peek at the generalizations to be developed instead of just listing the generalizations for students). Steps 5 and 6 are selecting and organizing experiences, ensuring that each activity has a definite function, and looking again at the developmental level of the students. What kinds of activities are needed by a given age group to develop the understandings sought? These steps include multipurpose activities that can help students achieve more than one objective. The activities must be ordered to make continuous and accumulative learning possible by connecting new information to previous experiences. Involvement in activities can help students see the relevance and meaning in the content they are studying. Nicaise and Barnes (1996, p. 206) explain, "Because tasks help students to implement knowledge in genuine ways, they may also help students become aware of the relevancy and meaningfulness of what they are learning."

Step 7 is evaluating the unit continuously, noting the students' likes, and Step 8 is checking for balance and sequence, ensuring that the activities provide opportunities to learn how to generalize, that the content sequence flows, that there is balance between written and oral work and research and analysis, that different forms of expression are possible, and that the organization is open-ended, allowing students to open up and talk.

As mentioned in Chapter 1, Taba's model has several unique strengths. Its inverted dimension involves teachers in its development, which gives them a level of commitment and ownership not common to other models and which prepares teachers to implement the model. Its unit base ties curriculum to instruction. Since "curriculum" is often interpreted to mean a document, as separate from instruction, too often curriculum development is thought of as disconnected from teaching. By bringing together curriculum and instruction, the model ties theory to practice.

Tyler's Ends-Means Model

Tyler's ends-means model introduced a revolutionary idea to curriculum planning. He said that the curriculum developer should start by deciding what purposes the curriculum is to have and then plan accordingly. Today, this approach seems embarrassingly simple, but it was revolutionary at the time, since no curriculum developer had ever presented such a model. See Figure 4.2 for a summary of Tyler's model. Tyler suggested that several ends, which he called goals, educational objectives, and purposes, be identified by examining three elements: the learners, life in the community, and subject matter.

The Student as a Source

Tyler believed that a broad and comprehensive analysis of the student should be made. The curriculum developer should determine the learner's needs and wants, since that information can help educators in motivating the student to learn. The students' abilities must also be considered.

Society as a Source

Tyler believed that the process of generalizing was central to all learning. Since the learner needs to understand the environment, interacting with others is essential. This makes the local community and society at large the students' learning laboratory. By studying the community and the society, the student can find problems to solve and ways of solving them.

Subject Matter as a Source

Tyler was heavily influenced by John Dewey, who stressed learning by doing. He was also influenced by Jerome Bruner (1966), who wrote about the structure of knowledge. They said (and Tyler agreed) that, to master a subject, one must understand its underlying structure.

FIGURE 4.2

Tyler's ends-means model.

Philosophy as a Source

According to Tyler, sound curriculum development begins with sound thinking and that sound thinking begins by formulating a philosophy. He believed it is necessary to define a school's philosophy. If Tyler were to lead others in curriculum development, he would insist that teachers spell out their own individual philosophy and also that of their school. In this respect, Tyler's model reflects the axiom "To understand others, you must first understand yourself. To serve others you must understand both the serving agency [the school] and yourself."

Psychology as a Source

Tyler believed that effective curriculum development requires understanding the learners' levels of development and the nature of the learning process. This understanding helps to refine the list of objectives. According to Oliva (1997), Tyler would have curriculum workers use philosophy and psychology as "screens," filtering out objectives that were beyond the student's capacity to attain and those that run counter to the faculty's philosophy.

   The case study earlier in this chapter described Angola High School, whose strengths were attributed to its curriculum and the alignment of its content with "what we want our students to learn and what we expect students to be able to do with what they have learned." Aligning content with expectations reflects the constructivist philosophy. We have just examined several aspects of Tyler's philosophy. His ends-means theory involved beginning with what we want the students to know and be able to do and then designing the content and activities accordingly. Might we say that teachers should begin designing every lesson by examining their own philosophies? Each of us can use our unique philosophy and expectations to design goals, content, and activities.

The Oliva Models

Oliva first introduced a curriculum development model in 1976 (see Figure 4.3). In 1992 he expanded this model, as shown in Figure 4.4. He explains these models as follows.

> Some years ago I set out to chart a model for curriculum development that met three criteria: the model had to be simple, comprehensive, and systematic. . . . Although this model represents the most essential components, it can be readily expanded into an extended model that provides additional detail and shows some processes that the simplified model assumes.

FIGURE 4.3

Oliva's 1976 model for curriculum development. Reproduced by permission of Longman.

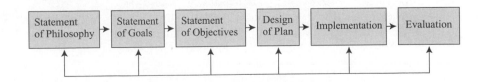

The Twelve Components

Figure 4.4 shows a comprehensive, step-by-step process that takes the curriculum planner from the sources of the curriculum to evaluation. In the figure, the squares represent planning phases; the circles, operational phases. The process starts with component I, at which time the curriculum developers state the aims of education and their philosophical and psychological principles. These aims are based on beliefs about the needs of our society and the needs of individuals living in our society. This component incorporates concepts similar to Tyler's use of philosophy and psychology as "screens."

Component II requires an analysis of the needs of the community in which the school is located, the needs of students served in that community, and the exigencies of the subject matter that will be taught in the given school. Sources of the curriculum are seen as cutting across components I and II. Whereas component I treats the needs of students and society in a more general sense, component II introduces the concepts of needs of particular students in particular localities, because the needs of students in particular communities are not always the same as the general needs of students throughout our society.

FIGURE 4.4

Oliva's 1992 model for curriculum development.

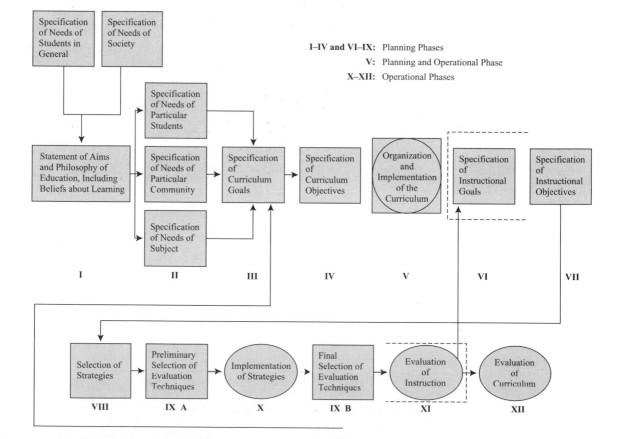

151

Components III and IV call for specifying curricular goals and objectives based on the aims, beliefs, and needs specified in components I and II. A distinction that will be clarified later with examples is made between goals and objectives. The tasks of component V are to organize and implement the curriculum and to formulate and establish the structure by which the curriculum will be organized.

In components VI and VII an increasing level of specification is sought. Instructional goals and objectives are stated for each level and subject. A distinction between goals and objectives is visually portrayed.

After specifying instructional objectives, the curriculum worker moves to component VIII, and chooses instructional strategies for use with students in the classroom. Simultaneously, the curriculum worker initiates the preliminary selection of evaluation techniques, phase A of component IX. At this stage, the curriculum planner thinks ahead and begins to consider ways to assess student achievement. The implementation of instructional strategies—component X—follows.

After the students have been provided appropriate opportunities to learn (component X), the planner returns to the problem of selecting techniques for evaluating student achievement and instructor effectiveness. Component IX, then, is divided into two phases: the first precedes the implementation of instruction (IX A), and the second follows the implementation (IX B). The instructional phase (component X) provides the planner with the opportunity to refine, add to, and complete the selection of means to evaluate pupil performance.

Evaluation of instruction is carried out during component XI. Component XII completes the cycle, with evaluation not of the student or the teacher but rather of the curricular program. In this model, components I to IV and VI to IX are planning phases, whereas components X to XII are operational phases. Component V is both a planning and an operational phase.

Like some other models, this model combines a scheme for curriculum development (components I to V and XII) and a design for instruction (components VI to XI).

The feedback lines that cycle back from the evaluation of the curriculum to the curriculum goals and from the evaluation of instruction to the instructional goals are important features of the model. These lines indicate the necessity of continuous revision of the components of their respective subcycles.

Use of the Model

The model can be used in a variety of ways. First, it offers a process for the complete development of a school's curriculum. By following the model, the faculty of each special area, for example, language arts, can fashion a plan for the curriculum of that area and design ways in which it will be carried out through instruction. Or the faculty can develop schoolwide, interdisciplinary programs that cut across areas of specialization such as career education, guidance, and extraclass activities.

Second, a faculty can focus on the curricular components of the model (components I to V and XII) to make programmatic decisions. Third, a faculty can concentrate on the instructional components (VI to XI).

Summary of the Oliva Model

A particular strength of the Oliva model is its inclusion of foundations. The original model requires a statement of philosophy, which is extremely important and, unfortunately, is not common among curriculum documents. Oliva's revised model includes societal and student needs, which are also invaluable parts of curriculum models.

The Saylor and Alexander Model

Saylor and Alexander (1966) introduced a curriculum model that has very strong foundations (see Figure 4.5). This model was designed to suggest a process for selecting learner activities. A special strength of this model is its comprehensiveness. In a sense, it connects the curriculum with instruction by showing that teaching methods and strategies result from the curriculum plan. Another major strength of the model is that all steps in its suggested curriculum development process are grounded in social, philosophical, and psychological foundations.

Macdonald's Model

Macdonald (1965) perceived teaching as a personality system (the teacher) acting in a professional role and learning as a personality system (the student) performing task-related (learning) behaviors. He defined instruction as the social system within which formal teaching and learning take place, and curriculum as the social system that eventuates in a plan of instruction. Macdonald used a Venn diagram (see Figure 4.6) to illustrate the model's parts and their relationships. He defined the intersecting parts of the diagram as follows:

   V. Concomitant learning
  VI. Behavior modification through teacher feedback
 VII. In-service experiences
VIII. Supervision experiences
  IX. Pupil-teacher planning experiences
   X. Pupil-teacher planning experiences

A strength of Macdonald's model is in its presentation of the relationships among the model's various elements. Such relationships are essential if curriculum is a structural series of intended learning outcomes, as he perceived.

FIGURE 4.5

The Saylor and Alexander curriculum model.

The Basic Determinants of the Curriculum

> **The Philosophical and Psychological Foundations of the School**
>
> > **Factors Influencing the Design of the Curriculum**
> >
> > > **The Curriculum Plan**
> > >
> > > > **Strategy for Teaching**
> > > >
> > > > > **The Curriculum**
> > > > > The actual experiences provided pupils by the school for the realization of goals
> > > >
> > > > a. Methods of teaching
> > > > b. Units of work
> > > > c. Plans for developing experiences
> > >
> > > a. Classroom program: courses and offerings
> > > b. Extra classroom activities
> > > c. Services of the school
> > > d. Social life and interpersonal relationships
> > > e. Organization of the school
> >
> > a. Decisions of the U.S. Supreme Court
> > b. State laws
> > c. State department of education regulations
> > d. Requirements of colleges and occupations
> > e. The nature of the community and the neighborhood
> > f. Tradition
> > g. Resources, facilities, and materials
> > h. Social pressures and expectations
> > i. Research and experimentation
> > j. Proposals of leaders and scholars
>
> a. The aims of the school: changes in behavior potential
> b. The functions of the school in democratic America
> c. Principles of learning
> d. Knowledge and the disciplines: content to be transmitted
> e. Social conditions: the nature of the times

a. Social values, ideals, and beliefs to be perpetuated
b. Pupil capacities and potentialities to be developed and needs, aspirations, and motivations to be served

FIGURE 4.6

Macdonald's curriculum model. Reproduced by permission from James B. Macdonald's (1976). Educational models for instruction. In James B. Macdonald and Robert R. Leeper (Eds.), Theories for Instruction. *Alexandria, VA: Association for Supervision and Curriculum Development.*

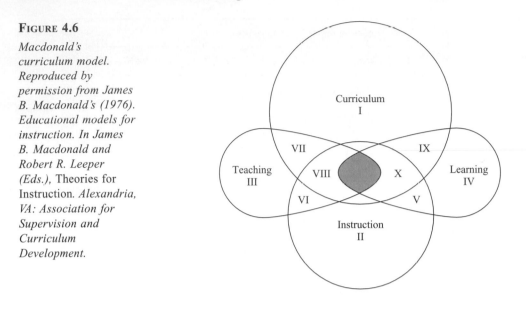

The Zais Eclectic Model

Figure 4.7 is a simple eclectic model developed by Zais that attempts to portray in static terms the components of the curriculum and the principle forces that affect its substance and design. The model is not concerned with processes—of curriculum construction, development, or implementation—or even with design per se. Its purpose is to portray graphically the principle variables, and their relationships, that planners need to consider in curriculum construction.

The curriculum is shown in the model as a somewhat formless entity girdled by a double line. This indicates that, although the boundaries of the curriculum (as we currently understand them) are somewhat ill-defined, it is essentially an integrated entity. Within the double line the components that make up the curriculum (aims, goals, objectives, content, learning activities, and evaluation) are separated by jagged lines. This is meant to emphasize the relatedness of each component to all the others and to suggest that, as in a jigsaw puzzle, all the pieces should fit precisely to produce a coherent picture.

The shaded area that joins the four foundation blocks to the curriculum indicates the influence of curriculum foundations on the content and organization of curriculum components (i.e., the curriculum design). In other words, we might say that the foundation blocks represent the soil and climate which determine the nature of the curriculum "plant." Each foundation block is joined to the others by double-headed arrows, suggesting the interrelatedness of all the

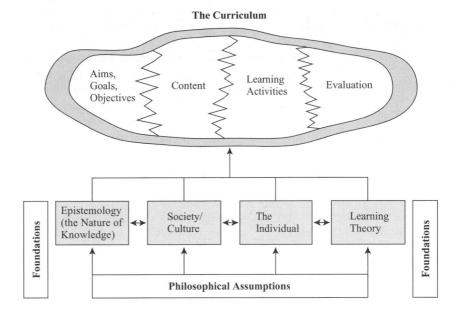

areas. Although intimately connected, however, the foundation blocks do not, as do the curriculum components, form a unified whole. Undergirding the four foundation blocks is the broad area of philosophical assumptions. This aspect of the model indicates that, consciously or unconsciously, basic philosophical assumptions influence value judgements made about the foundations.

Summary of the Zais Eclectic Model

The Zais eclectic model, dealing only with the static nature of a portion of the curriculum enterprise, is quite modest. Yet it is highly significant because it addresses probably the most crucial curriculum issues: the nature of the curriculum and the forces that determine its content and organization. It is interesting to note in this regard that far more attention has been paid in the literature to prescribing processes of curriculum development and change than to developing an understanding of the bases and nature of the curriculum itself. This typically American emphasis on activity and "how to do it," however, does not seem to have borne much fruit. Experience shows that in spite of a surplus of instruction and of activity in the processes of curriculum improvement and change, the curriculum remains controlled for the most part by the forces and events of historical accident, to say nothing of the influences of fashion and fad. In short, superficial understanding has apparently generated superficial strategies that get superficial results.

PROJECT ESCAPE

Although much disagreement on the pros and cons of education reform can be found among educators at all levels, most educators agree that there is always room for improving school programs. Constant improvement depends on a constant flow of credible ideas and innovations. Since part of the responsibility for introducing effective innovations must be borne by teacher education programs, the continuous flow of elementary and secondary school curriculum innovations requires a continuous flow of innovations among teacher education programs. In other words, our teacher education institutions must be wellsprings of curriculum improvement. A program that reflects much of the current thinking among both educators and layperson critics is described below.

With its origins as a normal school, the School of Education at Indiana State University has a history of developing innovative programs and offering them as models to other teacher preparation programs throughout the nation. One such program is called Project ESCAPE, an acronym for Elementary and Secondary Cooperative Approach to Performance Education. This program was created to provide an alternative to offer to those education students who prefer classroom-based programs over traditional university-based programs.

A major difference between this program and traditional teacher education programs is its competency base, but perhaps its most profound difference is that all of the competencies are developed in elementary and secondary classrooms instead of in traditional teacher education courses.

The program began with the identification of 25 elementary master teachers and 25 secondary master teachers, selected by their principals. These teachers examined their own classes and identified the one major area of teacher skills that would profit most from improvement. Then the teacher was given the sample learning module shown in Table 4.2 and asked to develop a learning module. The only restrictions were that the module should be highly tactile, visual, and activity-based and should not require extensive reading.

Once developed, each module was assessed to determine the approximate number of hours required to complete it. These contact hours were divided by 15 to arrive at a comparative number of semester credit hours. For example, a module that required 45 hours to complete was assigned 3 credit hours. The lengths of those 48 ESCAPE modules ranged from 0.5 credit hours to 3.5 credit hours.

Each module was supported by a rationale designed to inform students of the benefits it offers, to encourage students to choose the module. A sample rationale statement is shown in Table. 4.3.

As shown in Figure 4.8, each module is accompanied by a flowchart to help guide the student. Each module has a self-evaluation and a preassessment (which is the same as the post-assessment). If a student passes the preassessment, the student receives credit and is not required to complete the module (see Table 4.3).

TABLE 4.2   Sample Learning Module: Spelling Words with *ie* and *ei*

Objectives

The purpose of this module is to focus attention on commonly misspelled ie/ei words. Completion of the following specific objective is required for satisfactory demonstration of this competency.

Spell correctly 100 percent of the words in the list containing the *ie/ei* element.

Rationale

To be considered an educated person, a student must spell correctly. This judgment may be illogical, but it is inescapable. Of course, spelling is of itself essential to good writing.

Module Guide

1. Read the objectives and the rationale.
2. Take the preassessment. If you score 100 percent, you have completed the module.
3. Do the instructional activities.
4. Take the post-assessment.

Preassessment

Ask someone to dictate to you the words listed in the post-assessment. Try to write them correctly. If you score 100 percent, you have completed the module.

Instructional Activities

1. Memorize the following rhyme:
   I before e except after c
   or when sounded like a
   as in neighbor or weigh

2. Memorize the following exceptions to the rhyme:
   a. Leisure   c. Seize   e. Their
   b. Neither   d. Weird

Post-assessment

Have someone dictate the following list to you. Try to spell the words correctly. A score of 100 percent is required for completion of the module.

a. achieve	e. ceiling	i. freight	m. seize
b. apiece	f. conceited	j. heinous	n. their
c. belief	g. deceived	k. neighbor	o. veil
d. neither	h. received	l. reign	p. weigh

Remediation

If you have scored less than 100 percent on the Post-assessment, repeat the Instructional Activities with the help of your module resource person.

A list of the 48 different modules is given in Table 4.4. Some modules focus on skills and content that are considered indispensable for all teachers; these modules are required of all students. Other modules are optional, and individual students must choose from among the optional modules to obtain enough credits to fulfill their state's teacher certification requirements.

TABLE 4.3   Sample Rationale Statement

When teachers begin to plan for the learning activities of their pupils, they assume roles of decision makers as to what and how curriculum content is to be taught, as well as to what activities and behaviors will be engaged in by the pupils and teachers. These decisions cannot be guided alone by their preferences. There are certain rules and regulations that are imposed by the state, the school corporation, and the local school that limit their complete autonomy in these matters. To ensure secure legal positions in their classrooms, the teachers must have a knowledge of these rules and regulations and must work within the framework imposed by these regulations.

Today, teachers are being held accountable for the educational decisions that they make. More and more teachers are having to defend their actions in court. There are at least three reasons why this is true: the decline in reliance on the doctrine of "sovereign immunity" of school districts, students' increasing knowledge of these legal rights coupled with changing attitudes toward teachers and schools and the decline of the acceptance of *in loco parentis* as a legal theory.

It is well worth noting that much court litigation that resulted in severe penalties for the teacher might have been avoided had the teacher had knowledge of the law. Hill (1973) claimed that the teachers generally are not aware of their legal responsibilities and limitations. Teachers are presumed to know the statutory laws of individual states that may require or prohibit certain behavior or acts and to know the rules and regulations established by their local boards of education. Yet Hill conducted a study in which he compared teachers' knowledge of the law with that of people in other professions. He found that teachers ranked last in their knowledge about pertinent legislation that was passed. He noted that teachers make decisions in education as if legislation does not exist. Since ignorance of the law is not a valid defense, knowledge of rules and regulations that limit teacher decisions is necessary for all teachers.

SOURCE: *A module on modules.* Elementary and Secondary Education Act of 1963. Terre Haute, IN: Vigo County School System/Indiana State University.

FIGURE 4.8

Module guide for students.

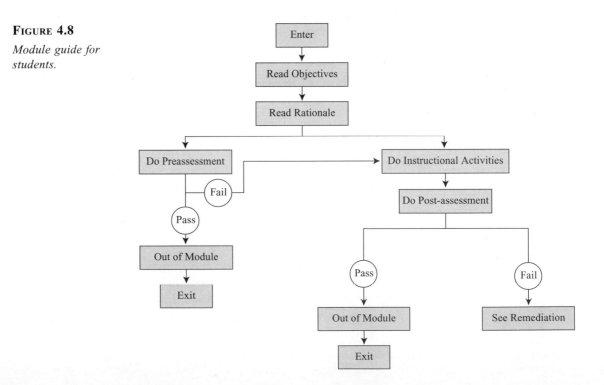

TABLE 4.4   **ESCAPE Modules**

I. Organizing and Teaching Subject Matter

   A. Planning

      101—Curriculum—fitting the curriculum of a subject or grade level into the total academic program

      102—Planning and Teaching a Unit—developing, executing, and evaluating plans with a central theme

      103—A Daily Lesson Plan—developing, executing, and evaluating a daily lesson plan

      104—Conference Planning—familiarizing the student (teacher) with procedures and organization of conference planning for an entire class

   B. Techniques for Teaching Subject Matter

      111—Principles of Reinforcement—identifying and applying various reinforcement methods in the classroom

      112—Asking Questions—asking higher-order questions

      113—A Module on Modules—identifying parts of a module

II. Human Dynamics of Teaching

   A. Teacher-Pupil Interaction

      201—Motivation—using Maslow's Hierarchy of Human Basic Needs to assist motivational learning activities

      202—Consistency—demonstrating using consistency with pupils in and out of the classroom

      203—Classroom Management—demonstrating skills and techniques utilizing the democratic process in the classroom

      204—Reinforcement Techniques in Written Work—using written reinforcement techniques on written work

      205—Handling Discipline Problems Objectively—recognizing and handling discipline problems

      206—Humor in Education—demonstrating a sense of humor in the classroom

   B. Diagnosing Classroom Climate

      211—The sociogram: Social Isolates—using the sociogram to identify social isolates and prescribing a suitable remedy

      212—Learning Difficulties—diagnosing learning difficulties and prescribing appropriate teaching-learning strategies

      213—Children's Misbehavior Goals—identifying and dealing with children's misbehavior goals as described by Adler

   C. Teacher-Pupil Relationships

      221—Empathetic Responses—aiding in developing empathetic responses

      222—Group Structure and Dynamics—reviewing group processes and their effects upon dynamics and task achievement

      223—Attitude Feedback—measuring and finding a means to a positive attitude

      224—Value Clarification—defining values and related behavioral problems

      225—Recognizing Enthusiasm—identifying verbal and nonverbal behaviors which demonstrate enthusiastic teaching and assessing the consequences of those behaviors

III. Developing Teaching Skills

   A. Technical Skills of Teaching

      301—Handwriting—demonstrating the ability to form letters according to the curriculum guide of the student's (teacher's) school

(Continued)

TABLE 4.4   ESCAPE Modules *(Continued)*

302—Use of Instructional Media—developing and executing an instructional presentation demonstrating the proper operational techniques of audio-visual media

303 Plan Book Grade Book: Development and Utilization—developing and using a plan book and a grade book to meet the needs of a student's (teacher's) teaching situation

304—Utilizing and Supplementing Cumulative Records—familiarizing the student (teacher) with ten pupils through cumulative records, observations, and interviews

305—Parent Conferences—conducting a parent-teacher conference

306—Field Trips—planning and/or executing a field trip

B. Varied Approaches to Teaching

311—Individualizing Instruction—demonstrating techniques of individualizing instruction

312—Guided Discovery—using the guided discovery technique

313—Problem Solving—using the problem-solving technique

314—Performance-Based Education in the Classroom—preparing and implementing a performance-based lesson plan identifying specified skills or competencies

315—Creativity—describing and demonstrating the humanistic teaching technique of creativity

316—Individual Needs—using activities for meeting individual performance levels

C. Verbal Communication in Teaching

321—Enunciation—focusing attention on and corrective measures for commonly mispronounced words

322—Communicating on the Pupil's Level—restating a school directive at the pupil's level of understanding

323—Voice Simulation—using voice simulations in story telling, story reading, and role playing

324—Listening Skills—using listening variables and reacting to pupil comments to facilitate better pupil understanding

325—Lecture and Demonstration—describing and practicing lecture and demonstration techniques

IV. Professional Responsibilities

A. Policies and Regulations for the Classroom

401—Rules and Regulations—familiarizing the student (teacher) with state and local regulations, requirements, and curriculum policies

402—Emergency Preparedness—demonstrating knowledge of and developing a plan for federal, state, and local Emergency Preparedness Plans

403—School Policy—demonstrating knowledge of local policies and procedures as presented in policy handbooks

404—Good Health—demonstrating the importance of a working knowledge of health factors in education

B. Professional Contributions of the Classroom Teacher

411—Professional Organizations—learning about professional educational organizations

412—Code of Ethics—demonstrating a knowledge of ethical behavior

413—Legal Responsibility of the Teacher—demonstrating legal responsibility

414—School Communication and the Community—demonstrating the ability to communicate with the community through various media

415—Co-Curricular Activities—identifying common problems of and participating in activities not part of the regular academic program

416—Professional Growth—demonstrating a knowledge of professionalism, an awareness of impedances to it, opportunities and resources for growth, and professional responsibilities

All ESCAPE program graduates are given a computer printout showing the particular competencies they have completed. The printouts begin with personalized statements (see Table 4.5). Following this opening statement is a list of the competencies the student has mastered. The intent is to provide a competency-based testimony to perspective employers.

A final note of interest to curriculum workers is the module evaluation instrument (see Table 4.6). Particular attention should be paid to the fact that this instrument is not designed to measure student performance; its purpose is to provide ongoing quality control for the module.

TABLE 4.5   Competencies Printout Used in Interviews

The purpose of this printout is to attest to the fact that [name of student] has demonstrated a mastery level of competence in the following teaching behaviors:

In the area of PLANNING, [name of student] has demonstrated a mastery level of expertise in [for students who completed Module 101] fitting the curriculum of a subject or grade level into the total academic program; [for students who completed Module 102] developing, executing, and evaluating plans with a central theme; [for students who completed Module 103] developing, executing, and evaluating a daily lesson plan; and [for students who completed Module 104] planning and organizing a conference planning session for an entire class.

In the area of TEACHING STRATEGIES, [name of student] has demonstrated a high level of competence in. . . .

TABLE 4.6   Module Evaluation Instrument

	Unsatisfactory (0 points)	Satisfactory (1 point)	Very Satisfactory (2 points)	Not Applicable
1. Was the format easily read?	_____	_____	_____	_____
2. Were the Objectives stated in behavioral terms?	_____	_____	_____	_____
3. During the initial introduction of the lesson, was adequate attention given to the review of facts and concepts learned in the previous lesson?	_____	_____	_____	_____
4. Were key questions listed in order to determine the pupil's comprehension and application of the concept reviewed?	_____	_____	_____	_____
5. Were the concepts, facts, or examples relating to the achievement of the objectives listed?	_____	_____	_____	_____
6. Was the step-by-step development of the lesson clearly outlined?	_____	_____	_____	_____
7. Was a variety of activities provided to meet individual differences in needs, interests, and abilities of the pupils?	_____	_____	_____	_____
8. Were the pupils' learning activities meaningful enough to be conducive to achieving the objectives?	_____	_____	_____	_____
9. Was the summary complete enough to ensure a basis for the next lesson?	_____	_____	_____	_____
10. Were provisions made for flexibility?	_____	_____	_____	_____

AMERICAN STUDIES PROGRAM

One of the most promising yet underused types of curricula which is equally attractive to all subject areas and all grade levels is experiential curriculum. Students enjoy experiential programs because of the opportunities they give students to be involved in "real-life" activities; teachers appreciate experiential programs for their power to motivate students. Following is a description of a successful experientially based program.

American Studies at Central High

What can a school do to generate enthusiasm among students for nonbasic courses? In the American Studies Program at Central High School in Tuscaloosa, Alabama, students look forward to going to jail.[1]

The American Studies Program was conceived in response to a federal court ruling that achieved racial desegregation by pairing two recently built segregated high schools. Although this measure eliminated segregation in the schools, many people felt that it did so at the expense of the students' community identity. And many students did indeed respond negatively to the ruling. The level of participation in school activities decreased, while absenteeism soared.

A committee of teachers, administrators, and faculty members from the University of Alabama concluded that participation in community life would diminish feelings of alienation among the students. The American Studies Program they designed is housed in the Old Jail, which is located in Tuscaloosa's historical district. The program provides students with a sense of community, gives them a reason to explore their different heritages, involves them in preservation of the area's history, and requires them to participate in the political life of the city.

The program began in 1980 with 145 juniors and seniors and has continued to grow. The staff consists of a director and three teachers who team-teach in a four-hour block each morning. The students return to the main campus for classes each afternoon.

Flexible scheduling allows students to attend town meetings, seminars, and labs and to participate in extended field trips. Films, lectures, and performances in the program are followed by seminars attended by 25 to 30 students. The labs are designed to focus on the skills in reading, writing, speaking, and problem solving that are required for specific tasks.

The courses for the juniors—American history, American literature, writing, and environmental science—emphasize historical preservation. The students are encouraged to familiarize themselves with the many resources available

---

[1] This program description first appeared as a *Phi Delta Kappan* article written by Jane Ingram, Kenneth T. Henson, and Adolph B. Crew.

through the University of Alabama and the local junior college and from the citizens of Tuscaloosa. Some students research local history, using genealogies, oral histories, and data from their own archeological survey. Another group forms the staff of *Timepiece,* a student publication that features project-related articles, interviews, family stories, and local tall tales.

Students also visit Tanglewood, a 480-acre plantation donated to the university in 1949. The mansion, built in 1858, contains documents dating back as far as 1819 that provide fascinating insights into the history of a southern family. The original land grant, signed by President Martin Van Buren, hangs on one wall beside two original bills of sale for slaves. Students camp out on the grounds of the estate, using only equipment that would have been available in the mid-nineteenth century. Such activities encourage cooperation and a sense of community among the students.

The seniors' course of study is broader. It revolves around participation in the national political process. Students form their own government and explore such themes as the struggle to survive (frontier and wilderness), the struggle to cooperate (the formation of government, with emphasis on the executive branch), the struggle to create (the legislative branch), and the struggle to justify (the judicial branch).

Significant contemporary events are used as peak experiences in the curriculum. Local, state, and national elections provide students with a variety of opportunities through which they can investigate the American political process. Some students volunteer to work in the campaign headquarters of the political party or candidate of their choice. Candidates and their campaign organizers visit the classroom and describe the electoral process to the seniors. Appropriate literature, such as Robert Penn Warren's *All the King's Men,* helps to relate classroom work to field study.

The seniors also study and employ propaganda techniques in a mock debate and election. They learn to analyze the arguments offered on opposing sides of controversial issues and to write position papers on the issues. As a community service, on the day after an election, students collect every visible campaign poster within the city limits. The culminating experience of the senior semester is an extended field trip to Washington, D.C.

There are many important advantages to the American Studies Program. Perhaps the most important is that it provides an opportunity for personal growth. Students learn to look at experience as multifaceted, to make judgments from a broader base, and to bring their own heritage into clearer focus. For many, this method of perceiving experience and making judgments will become a habit. The experiential nature of the program necessitates firsthand learning by the students. Because they are given tasks that require cooperation, they have developed a sense of community by the end of the semester. At the same time, their personal investment in these tasks motivates students to improve their basic skills in reading, writing, speaking, and problem solving.

Thanks to its popularity and record of success, the American Studies Program has become a permanent part of the Tuscaloosa curriculum. An officer of the Southeastern American Studies Association described Tuscaloosa's program as "the most extensive and challenging application of American Studies in the high school that has ever been attempted anywhere in the country." The team of American Studies teachers at Central High School has found the experience both time- and energy-consuming but professionally fulfilling. The students, too, have found that the program requires extra time and effort. But there is general agreement among all the participants that the quality of the experience makes it worthwhile.

ALVERNO COLLEGE

Another innovative teacher education program is located in Milwaukee, Wisconsin. Like Project ESCAPE, the Alverno College program is outcomes-based and performance-based. Figure 4.9 shows the general abilities required of Alverno students and their respective levels of mastery.

An important feature of the Alverno program is continuous self-assessment. Many contemporary K–12 education reform programs require students to assess their own progress. Another important feature of the Alverno program is the recognition that students can achieve at various levels of mastery. As Alverno students increase their levels of mastery, they earn more units of credits. All students are required to earn high levels of mastery in some areas of performance.

SOME FINAL SUGGESTIONS

Before studying these models, you were advised to keep in mind each model's potential to affect student learning. To a large degree, the outcome will depend on the effectiveness of the communications among all parties involved in the model's implementation. The teachers at Anzar High School in California developed a set of guidelines that they use to guide their team leadership model, and according to these teachers (Barnett, McKowan, & Bloom, 1998), good communications is the key. In addition to being respectful of each other, these teachers commit to being true to themselves by being honest and speaking their ideas.

Here are two final suggestions about using models. First, use them. Second, be fluid with their use. Farson (1997, p. 35) once said, "Once you've found a management technique that works, give it up." Perhaps even better advice to those who work with curricula is to use models and to continuously revise and reinvent them.

FIGURE 4.9

*Alverno
competencies.*

Abilities and Developmental Levels

1. Develop communication ability (effectively send and respond to communications for varied audiences and purposes)

   Level 1— Identify own strengths and weaknesses as communicator

   Level 2— Show analytic approach to effective communicating

   Level 3— Communicate effectively

   Level 4— Communicate effectively making relationships out of explicit frameworks from at least three major areas of knowledge

   In majors and areas of specialization:

   Level 5— Communicate effectively, with application of communications theory

   Level 6— Communicate with habitual effectiveness and application of theory, through coordinated use of different media that represent contemporary technological advancement in the communications field

   IN WRITING, READING, SPEAKING, LISTENING, USING MEDIA, QUANTIFIED DATA, AND THE COMPUTER

2. Develop analytical capabilities

   Level 1— Show observational skills

   Level 2— Draw reasonable inferences from observations

   Level 3— Perceive and make relationships

   Level 4— Analyze structure and organization

   In majors and areas of specialization:

   Level 5— Establish ability to employ frameworks from area of concentration or support area discipline in order to analyze

   Level 6— Master ability to employ independently the frameworks from area of concentration or support area discipline in order to analyze

3. Develop workable problem-solving skill

   Level 1— Articulate and evaluate own problem-solving process

   Level 2— Define problems or design strategies to solve problems using discipline-related frameworks

   Level 3— Select or design appropriate frameworks and strategies to solve problems

   Level 4— Implement a solution and evaluate the problem-solving process used

   In majors and areas of specialization:

   Level 5— Design and implement a process for resolving a problem which requires collaboration with others

   Level 6— Demonstrate facility in solving problems in a variety of situations

4. Develop facility in making value judgments and independent decisions

   Level 1— Identify own values

   Level 2— Infer and analyze values in artistic and humanistic works

   Level 3— Relate values to scientific and technological developments

   Level 4— Engage in valuing in decision-making in multiple contexts

   In majors and areas of specialization:

   Level 5— Analyze and formulate the value foundation/framework of a specific area of knowledge, in its theory and practice

   Level 6— Apply own theory of value and the value foundation of an area of knowledge in a professional context

   (Continued)

Figure 4.9

*Alverno
competencies.
(Concluded)*

5. Develop facility for social interaction

   Level 1— Identify own interaction behaviors utilized in a group problem-solving situation

   Level 2— Analyze behavior of others within two theoretical frameworks

   Level 3— Evaluate behavior of self within two theoretical frameworks

   Level 4— Demonstrate effective social interaction behavior in a variety of situations and circumstances

   In majors and areas of specialization:

   Level 5— Demonstrate effective interpersonal and intergroup behaviors in cross-cultural interactions

   Level 6— Facilitate effective interpersonal in intergroup relationships in one's professional situation

6. Develop global perspectives

   Level 1— Assess own knowledge and skills to think about and act on global concerns

   Level 2— Analyze global issues from multiple perspectives

   Level 3— Articulate understanding of interconnected local and global issues

   Level 4— Apply frameworks in formulating a response to global concerns and local issues

   In majors and areas of specialization:

   Level 5— Generate theoretical and pragmatic approaches to global problems, within a disciplinary or professional context

   Level 6— Develop responsibility toward the global environment in others

7. Develop effective citizenship

   Level 1— Assess own knowledge and skills in thinking about and acting on local issues

   Level 2— Analyze community issues and develop strategies for informed response

   Level 3— Evaluate personal and organizational characteristics, skills and strategies that facilitate accomplishment of mutual goals

   Level 4— Apply development of citizenship skills in a community setting

   In a majors and areas of specialization:

   Level 5— Show ability to plan for effective change in social or professional areas

   Level 6— Exercise leadership in addressing social or professional issues

8. Develop aesthetic responsiveness: involvement with the arts

   Level 1— Articulate a personal response to various works of art

   Level 2— Explain how personal and formal factors shape own responses to works of art

   Level 3— Connect art and own responses to art to broader contexts

   Level 4— Take a position on the merits of specific artistic works and reconsider own judgements about specific works as knowledge and experience change

   In majors and areas of specialization:

   Level 5— Choose and discuss artistic works which reflect personal vision of what it means to be human

   Level 6— Demonstrate the impact of the arts on your own life to this point and project their role in personal future

As seen in earlier chapters, there is currently a strong perceived need to personalize curricula. Consider the effects that performance-based programs such as Project ESCAPE and the Alverno program have on personalizing student experiences.

Chapter Summary

According to the literature (Egbert, 1984; Brown, 1990; Marshall, 1991), most teachers teach the ways they were taught, ignoring the research. But during the past two decades, a strong knowledge base on teaching has been developed.

Teachers rely on common sense, but common sense is not always reliable. Science has given us a more reliable system that includes concepts, theories, and models.

Many current education reformers are constructivists. Both the focus on major content generalizations (concepts) and the use of activities that let students discover these concepts are qualities of constructivists.

Currently, there is no complete, perfect theory of education, but there are opportunities to contribute to the development of such a theory.

Teachers often criticize theory, saying that it is unrelated to practice. Actually, theory is not supposed to dictate practice. The role of theory is to guide our thinking. Thus, theory, plus several other factors including our emotions and our value systems, determines our behavior.

There are two types of models: descriptive and predictive. Descriptive models explain the relationships among their parts. Predictive models help us predict future consequences. Two of the most influential curriculum models are Tyler's ends-means model and Taba's inverted model. Tyler's model proposes that we begin curriculum development by identifying desired outcomes and design the curriculum accordingly. Taba's model is called an inverted model because, unlike traditional models which were developed at the district, state, and federal levels, it begins in the classroom with teachers. Because of this, teachers are more effective in implementing the new curriculum.

The value of any model or theory hinges on the degree to which its users understand the purpose of models and theories and the users' willingness to revise the model or theory as their local community, school, and students change. Confidence in models and theories and the skills required to use them effectively require a climate that makes teachers feel comfortable enough to put aside their dependence on the security they have when their only purpose is to help students remember facts. Put simply, effective use of theories and models requires a climate that encourages experimentation and tolerates errors.

This chapter included a description of block scheduling and its unique potential to contribute to the constructivist and multicultural themes of this text. Future teachers can expect increased diversity at their schools. It is imperative that these themes are remembered and that the welfare of all students remain paramount when all types of educational decisions are made.

Learning Questions

1. Why is just teaching concepts inadequate?

2. What is the purpose of models?

3. What is the relationship between concepts and theories? Between theories and models?

4. In what ways can the scientific method be superior to common sense at times?

5. What evidence can you offer to show that current education reformers have used research? Have ignored research?

6. Would you classify the statement "There are more differences within cultures than between cultures?" as a concept, a theory, or a model? Explain your choice.

7. How can the interdisciplinary approach to multicultural education be defended? *Hint:* Consider the Stefanich quote in this chapter.

This chapter began with a statement describing a student's pessimism and anxiety about a career in teaching. This chapter dealt in part with the role that generalizing plays in learning. The following questions are intended to help you make some generalizations about the important relationships between the student's comments and the chapter content.

8. The student's plea for meaning that goes beyond the accumulation of disjointed facts contains a powerful sentence: "To me, intellectual curiosity is the only constant in education." What does this statement mean?

9. What is the real difference between wisdom and knowledge?

10. What is the essence of this student's plea?

11. Are contemporary educators addressing this student's concern?

12. How can this student's claim that educators look at the past to build the future be applied to our school's failure to address growing social problems, such as the needs of minority students?

13. How can teachers help students focus on ideas as opposed to facts?

14. What can teachers and other curriculum developers do to respond to the growing body of information?

Suggested Activities

1. Select two curriculum models and contrast them.

2. Explain why all curriculum developers need to begin by stating their educational philosophies.

3. Contrast the Taba model with other models. List at least two unique strengths of each model.

4. Explain what is unique about the Tyler ends-means model.

5. Describe your strongest-held belief about: (a) the nature of youth, (b) the role of the school in social development, and (c) the nature of learning.

6. Design a curriculum model that represents your own unique philosophical, social, and psychological beliefs.

7. Describe the biggest change that has occurred in society during your lifetime, and explain how that change has or should have influenced school curricula.

8. Examine the Perkins quote on page 128. Explain how this quote supports the constructivist philosophy.

9. Choose an approach used in the American Studies program and use it to bring reform to your local school.

Works Cited and Suggested Readings

Barnett, D., & McKowen, C. (1998). A school without a principal. *Educational Leadership, 55*(7), 48–49.

Beauchamp, G. A. (1981). *Curriculum theory* (4th ed.). Itasca, IL: Peacock Publishers.

Bellon, J. J., Bellon, E. C., & Bank, M. A. (1992). *Teaching from a research knowledge base.* Columbus, OH: Merrill.

Bernauer, J. A. (1999). Emerging standards: Empowerment with purpose. *Kappa Delta Pi Record, 35*(2), 68–70, 74.

Black, J. H., Efthim, H. E., & Burns, R. B. (1989). *Building effective mastery learning schools.* New York: Longman.

Bracey, G. W. (1991). Teachers as researchers. *Phi Delta Kappan, 72*(5), 404–405.

Brandwein, P. F. (1966). *Concepts in science.* New York: Harcourt, Brace, p. 12.

Brown, D. S. (1990). Middle level teachers' perceptions of action research. *Middle School Journal,* pp. 30–32.

Bruner, J. S., Goodnow, J. J., & Austin, G. (1965). *A study of thinking.* New York: Science Editions, p. 45.

Bruner, J. S. (1966). *Toward a theory of instruction.* Cambridge, MA: Harvard University Press, p. 78.

Carson, T. (1990). What kind of knowing is critical action research? *Theory into Practice, 29*(3), 67–173.

Conant, J. (1951). *Science and common sense.* New Haven, CT: Yale University Press.

Cooper, L. R. (1991). Teachers as researchers. *Kappa Delta Pi Record, 27*(4), 115–117.

Cornett, J. W. (1990). Utilizing action research in graduate curriculum courses. *Theory into Practice, 29*(3), 185–193.

Dewey, J. (1916). *Democracy in education.* New York: Macmillan.

Dill, D. (1990). *What teachers need to know.* San Francisco: Jossey-Bass.

Egbert, R. L. (1984). The role of research in teacher education. In R. L. Egbert & M. M. Kluender (Eds.), *Using research to improve teacher education.* Lincoln, NE: American Association of Colleges for Teacher Education.

Eggebrecht, J., Dagenais, R., Dosch, D., Merczak, N. J., Park, M. N., Styer, S. C., & Workman, D. (1996). Reconnecting the sciences. *Educational Leadership, 53*(8), 4–8.

Einstein, A. (1951). Autobiographical notes (P. A. Schilpp, Trans.). In P. A. Schilpp (Ed.), *Albert Einstein: Philosopher-scientist* (p. 7). The Library of Living Philosophers (Vol. VII). New York: Tudor.

Farson, R. (1997). *Management of the absurd.* New York: Simon & Schuster.

Fullan, M. (1998). Breaking the bonds of dependency. *Educational Leadership, 55*(7), 6–10.

Gardner, H., & Boix-Mansilla, V. (1994). Teaching for understanding: Within and across the disciplines. *Educational Leadership, 51*(5), 14–18.

Glaymour, C. (1980). *Theory and evidence.* Princeton, NJ: Princeton University Press.

Good, T. (1990). Building the knowledge base of teaching. In D. D. Dill (Ed.), *What teachers need to know.* San Francisco: Jossey-Bass.

Heckman, P. E., Confer, C. B., & Hakim, D. (1994). Planting seeds: Understanding through investigation. *Educational Leadership, 51*(5), 36–39.

Hill, J. C. (1986). *Curriculum evaluation for school improvement.* Springfield, IL: Charles C. Thomas.

Hurlocke, E. (1925). An evaluation of certain incentives used in schoolwork. *Journal of Educational Psychology, 16,* 145–159.

Kant, I. (1793). (E. B. Ashton, Trans.). *On the old saw: That may be right in theory but it won't work in practice.* Philadelphia: University of Pennsylvania Press.

Kerlinger, F. (1973). *Foundations of behavioral research* (2nd ed.). New York: Holt, Rinehart, & Winston.

Kowalski, T. J., & Reitzug, U. C. (1993). *Contemporary school administration: An introduction.* New York: Longman.

Marshall, C. (1991 March–April). Teachers' learning styles: How they affect student learning. *The Clearing House, 64*(4), 225–227.

Macdonald, J. B. (1965). Educational models of instruction. In J. B. Macdonald and R. R. Leeper (Eds.), *Theories of instruction.* Washington, DC: Association for Supervision and Curriculum Development.

Martin, N. K. (1997 March). Connecting instruction and management in a student-centered classroom. *Middle School Journal, 28*(5), 3–9.

McElroy, L. (1990). Becoming real: An ethic at the heart of action research. *Theory into Practice, 29*(3), 209–213.

Nelson, W. W. (1999). The emperor redux. *Phi Delta Kappan, 80*(5), 387–392.

Newsome, G. L. (1964). In what sense is theory a guide to practice in education? *Educational Theory, 14,* 36.

Nicaise, M., & Barnes, D. (1996). The union of technology, constructivism, and teacher education. *Journal of Teacher Education, 47*(3), 205–212.

Oliva, P. F. (1976). *Supervision of today's school.* New York: Harper & Row, p. 232.

Oliva, P. F. (1992). *Developing the curriculum* (3rd ed.). New York: HarperCollins.

Oliva, P. F. (1997). *Developing the curriculum* (4th ed.). New York: HarperCollins.

O'Neil, J. I. (1997). Building schools as communities: A conversation with James Comer. *Educational Leadership, 54*(8), 6–10.

Ozmon, H. A., & Craver, S. M. (1999). *Philosophical foundations of education* (6th ed.). Columbus, OH: Merrill.

Perkins, D. (1994). Do students understand understanding? *Education Digest, 59*(5), 21–25.

Perkins, D., & Blythe, T. (1994) Putting understanding up front. *Educational Leadership, 51*(5), 4–7.

Pratt, R. (1971). *Contemporary theories of education.* Scranton, PA: International Textbook.

Prescott, C., Rinard, B., Cockerill, J., & Baker, N. (1996). Science through workplace lenses. *Educational Leadership, 53*(8), 10–13.

Rappoport, A. L., & Kletzien, S. (1996). Kids around town: Civics lessons leave impressions. *Educational Leadership, 53*(8), 26–29.

Rivett, P. (1972). *Principles of model building.* New York: John Wiley.

Sanger, J. (1990). Awakening a scream of consciousness: The critical group in action research. *Theory into Practice, 29*(3), 174–178.

Saylor, J. G., & Alexander, W. M. (1966). *Curriculum planning for modern schools.* New York: Holt, Rinehart, & Winston.

Stallworth, B. J. (1998). Practicing what we teach. *Educational Leadership, 55*(5), 77–79.

Stefanich, G. P. (1990). Cycles of cognition. *Middle School Journal, 22*(2), 47–52.

Taba, H. (1962). *Curriculum development: Theory and practice.* New York: Harcourt, Brace.

Tripp, D. H. (1990). Socially critical action research. *Theory Into Practice, 29*(3), 158–166.

Tyson, J. C., & Carroll, M. A. (1970). *Conceptual tools for teaching in secondary schools.* Boston: HoughtonMifflin.

Wang, M. C., Haertel, G. D., & Walberg, H. J. (1998). Models of reform: A comprehensive guide. *Educational Leadership, 55*(7), 66–67.

Ward, M. W. (1969). Learning to generalize. *Science Education, 53,* 423–424.

Whitehead, A. N. (1911). *An introduction to mathematics.* New York: Holt, Rinehart, & Winston, p. 157.

Woods, R. K. (1994). A close-up look at how children learn science. *Educational Leadership, 51*(5), 33–35.

Zais, R. S. (1976). *Curriculum principles and foundations.* New York: Harper & Row.

5 DESIGNING AND ORGANIZING CURRICULA

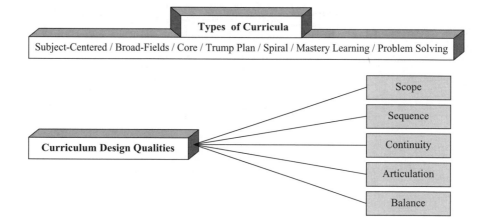

Types of Curricula

Subject-Centered / Broad-Fields / Core / Trump Plan / Spiral / Mastery Learning / Problem Solving

Curriculum Design Qualities

Scope

Sequence

Continuity

Articulation

Balance

Objectives

This chapter should prepare you to:

- Give two reasons why the traditional 6–3–3 school grade pattern changed.
- Describe three effects that *Sputnik* had on curricula in American schools and compare the impact of *Sputnik* to the impact of current education reform.
- Discuss the strengths and weaknesses of the subject-centered curricula.
- Choose a curriculum design, diagram it, and criticize it.
- Explain the relative growth of social problems among middle-class white and other communities.
- Contrast the Trump Plan with the core curriculum.
- Discuss mastery learning research and give three unique qualities of mastery learning.
- Discuss the potential of the curriculum design models discussed in this chapter for improving learning for all students.
- Identify strengths and weaknesses among the curriculum design models discussed in this chapter for developing social skills.
- Use curriculum design qualities to critique those reform practices with which you are familiar.
- Discuss the need for local reform.
- Compare mastery learning theory to constructivism
- Define confluency and discuss its appropriate influence on curriculum planning.

THE CASE OF THE LITTLE SCHOOL THAT GREW[1]

Once upon a time in a land not too far away, a few townspeople got together and decided that the time had come to develop a system to educate their children. Every parent in town pitched in to build a schoolhouse; many rural people even walked into town to assist. Once the building was completed, a teacher was appointed. This teacher was a real leader of children. They knew he was really interested in them and aware of the things that meant the most to them. He knew that these were the things that could help or hurt them most.

A second group gathered to develop a curriculum. Since the parents were busy caring for their children, only the people without children could spare the

---

[1] Taken from the author's article "The Little School That Grew" which appeared in the *Journal of Teacher Education,* Spring 1975, *26*(1), 55–59.

time to develop the new school's curriculum, so a few merchants, a few craftspeople, and a few of the elite, well-to-do fathers in town comprised the first curriculum committee. (This practice of putting business people in charge of education may have given rise to the current practice in school reform.)

The meeting began with a decision about what courses should be taught. The merchants made certain that mathematics was included. The craftspeople wanted a vocational program to teach adolescents a trade so that the common eight year apprenticeship would not be necessary. Through a rigid bargaining process, the well-to-do group gave in to the inclusion of a vocational course only because, in turn, they were promised a complete fine arts program of painting, sculpture, and music. Everyone was quite pleased, even the teacher, although he had no voting power on curriculum decisions (this was before teacher unions and site-based councils).

The Little School Begins

The first day of school proved to be typical of many days that followed. With only one room in the schoolhouse, the older children helped the younger ones with their lessons. The teacher understood that self-fulfillment comes most easily through helping others. Perhaps the ease with which these youngsters of varying ages and ethnic backgrounds got along could be attributed to the teacher, who seemed to care immensely for each child.

At the back of the room on a large table were glasses of watercolors, a large pork-and-beans can full of brushes, and a stack of white paper. This was the art "program." No class hour was set aside for art. As the children finished their lessons, they were free to go to the back of the room and try out their skills. In fact, there was no planned instruction in art. The teacher was available when a child asked for help, but even then, little instruction was provided; mostly the child got encouragement. The room was encircled with paintings attached to a line by clothes pins. On any day a production from each child was displayed, representing as many subjects as there were students.

As you may have suspected, the physical education program was not well organized. At recess, the children went to the ball field for a game of shove-up, a game the teacher knew was remarkable because no side choosing is necessary—no child has to suffer being chosen last. Each player has an equal opportunity to play each position. Most important, each child can experience success and failure without disappointing teammates, since when someone strikes out, only that one child is out. This vigorous game was always enjoyed by all.

The noon hour was a daily highlight. Paper sacks blossomed to give forth smells of sandwiches made from home-cured ham or sausage. Exchanges of sandwiches were common, since most kids brought two identical sandwiches and welcomed the variety. But taste was not as important as was the opportunity to enjoy the food as the children sat beneath a large oak (some had favorite seats up in the tree where they enjoyed their noon meal). On hot days, the cool, shady cement doorstop of the schoolhouse always attracted a few diners.

For many years, the little school continued to offer these uniquely human activities, and everyone assumed that the school's first teacher was doing a fine job and that it was a fine little school, until a certain event changed their minds.

Change Comes to the Little School

While visiting the adjacent community, a school board member found a larger, more sophisticated school with many fine qualities not found in the little school. When the board member returned, a board meeting was immediately called and the other members were informed of the many good qualities of the newer, larger school. When it was mentioned that School X had a lunchroom, someone asked, "Why can't our school have a lunchroom?" When the board was informed that the uniformity and structure in School X's curriculum was made possible by multiple classrooms and a bell system, someone asked, "Why can't our school have separate classrooms and a bell system?" Each time an advantage was noted at School X, the notation was followed by the question, "Why can't our school have that?"

Immediate plans were begun to implement these innovations. A larger two-story schoolhouse was constructed. An electric bell system made possible the dividing of the curriculum into many subject units and the development of grades and grade levels. Content specialist teachers were hired. The students readily accepted change, for it meant freshness—a way to escape the present school program. From listening to their parents, they had learned that their school curriculum had gradually become dull, routine, and traditional.

The first year of the new curriculum seemed an overwhelming success. The students were getting expert instruction and were motivated by a real sense of competition. Class times were regulated by a bell system, and a new lunchroom provided a hot lunch for each student.

But as time passed, these innovations brought some unforeseeable changes. The grouping based on age, grade, and ability level caused the more capable students to develop an attitude of superiority, and they had little tolerance for slower learners. The slower students knew they had been singled out as "average" (meaning below average) or low achievers. In other words, they had been labeled "failures."

A real difference could be seen in the way students moved about. Children who had once gaily skipped off to recess or leisurely wandered at will to the back of the room to paint pictures were now literally running from room to room. When the bell system was installed, five minutes was allotted between periods. Later this was decreased to three minutes, then two.

Thirty minutes was provided for lunch. The lunch period bell sent each student running at top speed. The lucky few who captured positions at the head of the line were too excited to eat; the slower runners found themselves with only five to ten minutes to bolt down their food. The time of day that had once meant complete relaxation had now disappeared.

Inside the classrooms, the new teachers presented eloquent lectures and held all students accountable for attaining set objectives, each having a minimum acceptable level of performance and specific conditions under which it was to be demonstrated. Each art student was carefully instructed on matters of content and technique. No longer could they waste time dabbling in watercolors, creating meaningless paintings that were often crude and ugly.

On the playgrounds a highly structured and competitive program was installed for those students who excelled in physical skills and endurance.

The little school had come a long way. Its administrators and faculty were proud. Parents knew from hearing teachers' comments that it must be one of the most progressive and innovative schools because its curriculum had been completely restructured to meet the demands of the times. Student complaints reinforced the faith in the new curriculum, because everyone knows that kids never like anything that is good for them.

As you continue reading this chapter, remember that curriculum changes are made every day and that teachers are involved in the decisions to change and how to change. This chapter will review some of the basic curriculum designs that have become standard over the years, and it will also introduce curriculum dimensions that provide ways of examining the curriculum, such as scope, sequence, articulation, and balance. Think critically about your own philosophy of education, the major purposes of schools, the major flaws and shortcomings in today's curricula. As a curriculum planner who will be involved in schoolwide planning, you can significantly influence the quality of your school. This chapter will provide some of the concepts that you will need to achieve this goal.

CURRICULUM DESIGNS

Through the years, curricula have been tailored, modified, and shaped to fit the needs of a changing society. The curriculum for the first American schools was simple and straightforward because the purpose of those first schools was simple and straightforward—to prepare students for admission to Harvard College, a school of divinity.

But during the almost 400 years since then, different demands have been placed on the schools. Each added purpose has required an adjustment to the curriculum. John Dewey (1916, p. 409) expressed the need for continuous curriculum design when he said,

Democracy has to be born anew in each generation, and education is its midwife.

Almost a century has passed since Dewey made this statement, and educators are still worried that "A good deal of the typical curriculum does not connect—not to practical applications, personal insights, or much of anything. It's not the kind of knowledge that would connect, or it is not taught in a way that would help learners make connections" (Dewey, 1916, p. 24). Pennsylvania teacher of the year, Howard Selekman (1999, p. 59) says, "Teachers seek to establish any connections, connections that are meaningful to us and our students."

This chapter chronicles some of the most important curriculum designs. These designs are grouped according to the age level of the students they serve (elementary, junior high or middle level, and high school) and according to patterns that recur among them. Within each level, the major curriculum designs are discussed. These are shown in Table 5.1. For certain, many of these divisions are not as distinct and separate as Table 5.1 might suggest. For example, it is common for a school at any level to have a combination of several designs. But separating the designs enables us to discuss and understand the unique needs and characteristics of each design.

Since schools typically start at the kindergarten level and go through grade 12, several patterns are common. Originally, the schools were designed for age 6 through about age 15. Later, as the school curriculum was extended to grade 12, the schools were divided into two areas: elementary (grades 1–6) and secondary (grades 7–12). But, at the secondary school the development range was too broad. Some students hadn't reached puberty; others were young adults. For

TABLE 5.1   Common Curriculum Designs at Various Grade Levels

Level	*Common Curriculum Designs*
Elementary	Graded Open education Nongraded Cooperative learning Integrated
Junior high	Graded Core curriculum Open education Cooperative learning Integrated
Middle school	Graded Nongraded Open education Cooperative learning Integrated
High school	Graded Subject matter Broad fields Alternative Cooperative learning Integrated

TABLE 5.2   Changes in Grade Groupings

Years	Grade Levels Represented		
1835–1847	Nongraded		
1848–1909	1–12		
1910–1950	1–6–6		
1951–Present	K–6,	7–9,	10–12
	K–5,	6–8,	9–12
	K–5,	6–9,	10–12
	K–4,	5–8,	9–12

this reason and for administrative convenience, the junior high school was formed. This became the 6–3–3 curriculum design.

As more knowledge about the effects of maturity on student behavior became available, it became apparent that the preadolescent age-group was very different from the younger and older students. Educators also learned that American youth were aging socially more rapidly than their predecessors had. It was decided that a special school was needed for this age-group; it became known as the *middle school.* The ages represented in middle schools vary; the most common are ages 11 to 14 and 11 to 15. The curricula for the systems that have these schools are 5–3–4 or 5–4–4. Since the kindergarten is common among curricula today, the patterns are often represented by K–5–3–4 or K–5–5–4. Table 5.2 shows the changes in grade groupings through the years.

Although the number of curriculum designs that can be used at each level is almost unlimited, each design is associated more with some levels than with others. Some of the more popular curriculum designs that have had an impact on the schools at various times include subject-centered, broad-fields, core, Trump Plan, spiral, mastery learning, open education, and problem solving.

The Subject-Centered Curriculum

The first curricula of the Latin grammar schools were composed of religion, Latin, and Greek. Thus, the first American school curriculum design was the subject-centered design. *Subject-centered* does imply that the curriculum is built around one or more subjects, but it also implies more. Throughout our schools' history, subject-centered curricula have been complemented by a particular teaching style, the lecture. The objective of subject-centered curricula is to learn the subject, that is, the content.

The subject-centered curriculum is the oldest curriculum design in the world (Armstrong et al., 2001). It isn't surprising to learn that subject-centered curricula are surrounded by tradition. In fact, the subject-centered content itself is traditional content, that is, content which over the years has been accepted.

As mentioned earlier, the major delivery system for subject-centered curricula is the lecture, itself the most traditional teaching method. Even the objective of subject-centered curricula is the traditionally accepted goal of accumulation of information.

Strengths

The subject-centered curriculum design has several features that cause proponents to favor it. The continued use of this design through the years means that people are familiar with it and comfortable using it. Furthermore, its long use gives a sense of "tried and proven," or, "It was good enough for me; therefore, I trust it for my children."

A more tangible quality of the subject-centered curriculum is its tight organization. The content is rigidly sequenced. When using this design, teachers can, and almost always do, follow the sequence of the textbook. This makes the task of keeping track of where each lesson ends and where the next one begins easy. This tight organization helps the teacher avoid accidental duplication of content and makes the testing simple. Easy design of tests was mentioned earlier as a strength of the textbook. Since the subject-centered design is characterized by use of textbooks, it benefits from the strengths and suffers from the weaknesses of textbooks.

The tightly organized subject-centered curriculum is easy to implement. Courses can be added to or deleted from a school's program (or even added to or deleted from a student's individual curriculum). Thus transferring from one school to another, and even from one state to another, is easy. This advantage is realized by high school students who go on to colleges out of state. Of course, for transfer students the college may stipulate a particular additional course or courses.

Still another advantage of the subject-centered curriculum design is its efficiency. The well-organized, compact curriculum enables students to cover a lot of content in a short time. This advantage becomes clear when contrasted with an inquiry curriculum (which requires students to discover relationships for themselves before they learn them), with case studies (which require students to sift relevant information from irrelevant information), with simulations and games (which are student-paced), with mastery learning (which permits students to remediate and recycle), or the discussion method (which also requires much more time to cover the material).

Weaknesses

Among the limitations of the subject-centered curriculum are its failure to consider the unique needs and interests of students and its detachment from contemporary events in the world. Perhaps the most severe criticism against the subject-centered curriculum is the effect it has on learners. Although it is satisfying to the teacher, the subject-centered design is a poor motivator for students. Interestingly, the lecture is favored by poorer students because it places less classroom responsibility on learners. Too often, the goal is to be able to recall information rather than to attempt to understand it. Audrey Cohen (1993, p. 792) explains:

> Subject-oriented learning has combined with the increasing fragmentation of knowledge to create an information mania in our schools that makes simply digesting facts a priority and eliminates consideration of the goals to which facts and ideas might be applied.

Success in reaching the underachievers requires special effort from the teacher. O'Neal, Earley, and Snider (1991, p. 122) explain:

> Research indicates that while many underachieving students have poorer auditory and visual skills, their kinesthetic and tactile capabilities are high. Implications are that teachers may need to use a greater variety of instructional methods.

Geisert and Dunn (1991, p. 223) say that "difficult material needs to be introduced through each student's strongest perceptual modality (preferred learning style) and then reinforced through supplementary modalities." Obviously, the subject-centered curriculum design makes comparatively little use of such necessary reinforcement.

The subject-centered curriculum can be effective when used by those teachers who are willing to alter their teaching styles and lower the level of instruction to the point at which the student can become a successful learner. But to assume that teachers will make this change is perhaps a mistake. Marshall (1991, p. 226) explains teachers' reluctance to leave the security of the subject-centered curriculum:

> Consequently, for teachers to change their teaching styles, to understand and risk planning instruction on the basis of learning style patterns of students—and, therefore, to teach successfully a wider range of learners—they must come to recognize, respect, and support the learning differences of students. If students do not learn the way we teach them, then we must teach them the way they learn.

THE BROAD-FIELDS CURRICULUM

Realizing that the neat containers called *subjects,* that had been designed to hold and dispense knowledge had limitations, educators decided to enlarge the containers. The results were referred to as the *broad-fields curriculum.*

An important goal of this design, devised around the turn of the century, was to reduce the propensity that students in subject-centered curricula had for memorizing fragmented facts. The broad-fields curriculum would solve this problem by broadening such subjects as history, geography, and civics into a curriculum category—social studies. Instead of studying reading, writing, literature, and speech, students would study language arts. Instead of taking physics and chemistry, students would take physical science. Instead of taking botany, anatomy, physiology, and zoology or biology, students would take biological science. These larger categories (biological sciences, earth sciences, and physical sciences) were expanded to form general science.

Unfortunately, the broad-fields curriculum design has not always been effective. A major cause for its shortcomings is the way the curriculum has been delivered. For example, some teachers ignored the broad content generalizations that the creators of this design sought to help students develop. Other teachers taught the generalizations, but as facts to be memorized; and as Harrison (1990, p. 503) cautions, this won't achieve the goal of having students understand the generalizations:

> Instruction must focus on the use of the concepts (content generalizations) and the context in which they occur in order to ascertain their practical connections.

Furthermore, success requires good note taking, and under the best conditions only 52 percent of the major ideas are captured in students' notes (Maddox and Hoole, 1975). When recording lectures, students focus more on less important points while missing the more important general understandings. King (1990, p. 131) reports:

> Researchers have found that when students take notes during a lecture they are far more likely to record bits and pieces of the lecture verbatim or simply paraphrase information rather than organize the lecture material into some sort of conceptual framework or relate the new information to what they already know.

Because the lecture affords teachers the opportunity to demonstrate their expertise, many teachers depart on an ego trip, leaving the confused students behind. Stefanich (1990) said that this practice leads to failure: "In order to be successful teachers, we must be prepared to lower the level of instruction to the point where each student becomes a successful learner."

The broad-fields curriculum was an attempt to use an integration of traditional subjects to help students develop broad understanding in all areas. This curriculum design has survived for over half a century: the approach enjoyed a resurgence during the early 1960s, stimulated by *Sputnik* and the Woods Hole Conference. Bruner chaired this conference and proposed the use of integrated themes. His words were misinterpreted (see Orlich, 2000) having an even greater effect on the rapid development of this integrated theme approach. Fortunately, the revival addressed the delivery system which had caused much failure when the broad-fields design was first implemented. Content generalizations such as concepts, principles, and themes were the organizing elements that were coupled with inquiry and discovery learning methods in the 1960s designs. The dependence of this curriculum design on its delivery system for success reflects the inextricable and interdependent relationship between curriculum and instruction in general. The dependence on the teacher for the success of this curriculum can be generalized to all curricula. Eisner (1985, p. 195) explains:

When the curriculum development movement got underway in the early 1960s, there was talk about the desirability of creating "teacher proof" curricula. That aspiration has, through the years, given way to the more realistic view that teachers are not mere tubes for curriculum developers. Teachers cannot and should not be bypassed.

As Darling-Hammond (1996, p. 5) explains, "Educational reform was 'teacher proofed' with hundreds of pieces of legislation and thousands of discrete regulations prescribing what educators should do." This is most unfortunate because, as Nelson (1999, p. 392) observes, "In each classroom in this county there is a highly educated adult with the potential for creating meaningful learning environments that address the needs of every student."

The following case study clearly shows the important role that teachers can and must play in working directly with students and parents to get students vested in the curriculum so that all students will feel a sense of ownership of their curriculum.

Case Study

An Interdisciplinary Team Approach

Irma N. Guadarrama
University of Houston

Background Information

In recent surveys, the nation's public school population tallies reveal dramatic increases among Hispanic youth, an important statistic for many educators in light of the group's overall pervasive academic failure as demonstrated in school performance and standardized test score indicators. While graduation rates have increased for whites and blacks, the drop-out rates for Hispanics have remained at a staggering rate, up to 35 percent but no less than 27 percent from 1975 to 1996 (National Center for Educational Statistics, 1995). These are sobering statistics when one takes into account the ever-increasing growth in population among Hispanics. The March 1993 Current Population Survey by the U.S. Census Bureau (Pinal, 1998) estimates the number of Hispanics in the United States to be 22.8 million (excluding Hispanics in Puerto Rico), which is 8.9 percent of the total U.S. population. It is a young population with a median age of 26.7 years, 9 years younger than the non-Hispanic population median age. By the year 2050, the projected population for Hispanics in the United States is estimated to be 23 percent of the total population (U.S. Census Bureau, 1995).

The total drop-out rates for Hispanics born outside of the United States is 43 percent. The drop-out rate for second-generation Hispanics is higher, at 24 percent, than that for native-born Hispanics, which is 17 percent.

The 1994 National Assessment of Educational Progress (NAEP) reported that Hispanic students' academic performance on reading and subject matter tests

(Continued)

remain significantly lower, at least two grade levels lower, than that of their Anglo student counterparts. Scores on writing proficiency tests for Hispanics have remained relatively unchanged since 1984, and the average scores for white students were higher than those for Hispanics at all grade levels (NAEP, 1998). Hispanic students score well below their Anglo counterparts on the SAT and ACT college entrance assessments, with only minor improvement in scores during the last decade (Duran, 1994).

Language diversity is a major characteristic among minority youth, and Spanish is the language spoken by the majority of this population. According to the U.S. Census Bureau of 1990, approximately 6.3 million children ages 5 to 17 speak a language other than English at home, some 325 languages including about 175 spoken by Native Americans (Crawford, 1997). However, in comparison to reports submitted by each state's education department, the census totals represent an undercount of at least 1.4 million language minority students, and possibly as many as 3.7 million. Even though the language minority student population is distributed throughout the country, the bulk of the students, about 70 percent, live in states that receive the most immigrants, Texas being one of them (Crawford, 1997). In 1993–94, the total public school enrollment in Texas was 3.6 million, of which 35.5 percent were Hispanic. (Anglo students totaled 47.7 percent, black students 14.2 percent, and Asian Americans 2.2 percent.) This case study highlights a high school's efforts to address the educational issues of Hispanic students in an urban school district.

The Changing Landscape

Situated on a modest hill dotted with huge trees, one of the city's oldest high schools commands a majestic presence that, underneath a gray, aging veneer, still bears a hint of elegance with its spacious stairs leading to a towering building. Indeed, the main entry hall, which showcases numerous trophies, plaques, and other mementos amid clusters of photographs of athletic teams, seems more like a monument in honor of the "glory days" of Northwest Side High than simply a chronicle of the school's achievements. In the '50s, '60s, and part of the '70s the area's well-off families sent their children to this high school, and some of them in turn became second-generation Northwest Side High graduates. The demographic landscape began to change in the latter part of the '70s, when large numbers of Mexican American families settled in the neighborhood, purchasing homes left behind by aging couples or young families who moved to more economically advantaged areas. Today, the sprawling residential area is almost exclusively populated by Mexican American families, one of the largest communities of its kind in a city of 485,000, where Hispanics make up 22 percent of the total population. The adjacent businesses, partially located in the tourist center of the city, abound with goods and services that cater mainly to Spanish-speaking clientele.

The First Team

It is Fall 1994, and for about 150 freshmen at Northwest Side High (50 percent of the total freshman class), school life seems a little different than from the rest of the student body. The Mexican American youth (and one African American) are

(Continued)

in a "special" program, but no one is quite sure why or what the novelty is about. They're members of an "interdisciplinary team," and some are upset over rumors that they have been chosen to participate because they may have been perceived as discipline problems. Their teachers explain that they were randomly selected and not because of a discipline issue, but that good behavior is definitely a prerequisite for staying in the program. Nevertheless, the ninth graders are often taunted by their peers, and many parents have called the principal to find out how and why their children have been "disciplined." However, by mid-term a completely different picture emerges. Instead of being critical, many nonparticipating students request admission into the program, and inquiring parents want to know how their children can get involved. Mr. T, the principal, patiently tells parents and students alike about the school's new pilot program, how it would benefit the students, and how the program solicits an increased involvement by parents.

During the two-year period that the interdisciplinary team approach was first implemented (1994–1996), Northwest Side High (NSHS) had an average of 1300 students, and 99 percent were Hispanic. While the enrollment figures have fluctuated in the last five years, the percentage of Hispanic students has remained stable. When Mr. T arrived as principal in 1992, he found two contrasting academic components. One was the magnet program called the High School for Medical Professions, consisting of a small group of teachers and about 300 students who successfully worked together to produce a high-quality curriculum that steered students toward careers in science and/or medicine-dominated fields. Their teaming approach impressed him, even when "teaming" was not yet an educational strategy. This faculty had almost complete autonomy in selecting the curriculum and discipline policies, as well as their own self-contained governance structure that was facilitated by a program coordinator. Mr. T recognized the benefits of this approach for students and their parents as well as how it empowered the faculty.

However, the majority of students who didn't attend the magnet school were not performing at an acceptable academic level, as indicated in the criterion-references, state-required test scores. Nor were the students achieving acceptable passing rates in their classes, and the high drop-out rate was alarming. But if the students' academic performance was a source of frustration for the principal, the resistance toward change exhibited by some of his faculty members was even more problematic:

> The faculty that I inherited was a veteran staff that really didn't want to do a lot of nontraditional things; they had done the same thing for 10 years. My second year there I changed the schedule from an eight-period day to a six-period day with a 90-minute block. It drove some of them nuts. I did that because our scores had been so flat and our program had become so stagnant. We had teachers who taught the same class 10 years in a row. Never looked at a different lesson plan. They just did the same thing over and over. I wanted to change that.

The Principal

A native of the high school's city, Mr. T received an undergraduate degree from a local, private university. He graduated from a high school in the same school district as NSHS. Almost all of his professional work had been in various schools

(Continued)

in his school district. His assignment as principal at NSHS was for six years. Prior to that he had been an assistant principal at a middle school for two years and at a high school for three years. He was a high school English teacher for nine years before he earned his master's degree and a middle-management certificate.

Mr. T selected the interdisciplinary team approach when NSHS became part of a consortium of a dozen high schools across the state to pilot innovative educational strategies based on the High Schools That Work concept. He had learned in workshops about the concept's underlying principle, namely, to build communities of learning that engaged teachers in collaborative teams and addressed the specific issues of their students. At the workshops he met with other principals who shared similar frustrations and visions. There were three main goals behind the interdisciplinary team approach: (1) increase the student retention rate; (2) increase graduation rates; and (3) improve all test scores, including the TAAS and the SAT. Mr. T envisioned students as active participants in their classrooms and in extracurricular activities such as student organizations and athletics; he wanted them to have ownership of the program. Specifically targeted were ninth graders, who often experience difficulty in adjusting to the transition to high school. He also believed that students' academic success during the first two years of high school is crucial to improving their chances to graduate.

Selecting Teachers

The first order of business was the selection of the four core curriculum teachers to teach science, history, math, and English. Mr. T deliberated carefully before he made his final selection:

> I selected teachers really for two reasons: first of all, all the teachers are quality. I knew that the teachers I selected had the background in teaching skills to be successful. But I needed teachers that I knew enjoyed being with students and were willing to get out of the box. I wanted teachers to talk to the students and call the parents, for instance. Normally, in a traditional high school, everybody has the same tardy policy. You get three tardies and you get an infraction, and you do after-school detention; then, the cycle starts over again. Well, I needed teachers who could counsel the kids. The other issue was finding teachers who were willing to work together, because in interdisciplinary teaming, unless I had teachers willing to coordinate together, it wasn't going to work. These teachers were able to meet and discuss profiles of the students, and I gave them the complete autonomy in working with the interdisciplinary team of kids. In other words, I didn't want them sending kids to the vice-principal. I wanted them dealing with the discipline issues; I wanted them meeting with the parents. We wanted them to bond with the students and become the chief persons and the focus in the lives of those kids.

As a participating school in the High Schools That Work consortium, NSHS was allocated state funds for staff development and instructional materials. To help teachers learn about their new roles, Mr. T planned staff development retreats, providing them with the opportunity to work through their inhibitions and to assess their personal attributes and learn about group dynamics. The extra funds also allowed teachers from a variety of content areas to attend ongoing training sessions with teachers from other high school programs on interdisciplinary team techniques.

(Continued)

Accepting the Challenge

According to Mr. T, the faculty as a whole was convinced that something different had to be done, especially with the ninth-graders, but he was asking the teachers to take huge, additional steps beyond that. They had to accept the challenge and "get out of the box," to get out of the traditional ways of teaching and work collaboratively to help students. This seemed like a tall order, especially for a faculty that "never really saw each other."

A few of the teachers were more willing than others to take up the challenge. One of them was Ms. G, an English teacher who opted to accept Mr. T's request to join the interdisciplinary team:

> The reason I like teaching outside of the textbook is that the kids cooperated a lot better when they knew it wasn't part of the textbook. If you walked into my classroom, unless you understood what was going on, you'd think my classroom management skills were lacking because you'd see a lot of talking, a lot of groups, a lot of noise, a lot of movement.

One of the projects completed in Ms. G's class was on "Making Choices." Students researched teen violence, and each student developed a brochure, one of which would be published and distributed to the rest of the student body. She guided students to research the traditional and alternative sources. They used the library, surveyed their classmates throughout the school, invited speakers such as police officers to speak at the school, and talked among themselves and community members. Why had Ms. G decided to select such a nontraditional project?

> At the time there was a lot of teen violence. Teens started getting ahold of more guns; there were more killings, especially among gang members, and there were a lot of statistics about gangs and guns. . . . I remember reading in the paper that this was becoming alarming and it was going to get worse before it got better. I think part of it was my own interest and how I thought that as a teacher we can't go there because it's going to affect me as well as my kids. What I found out about our kids, living in this demographic area and with their background, is that it really was no big thing to them; it was almost like, well, it's just like part of life, unfortunately. They've seen their own friends getting killed and so forth due to gang violence or just guns. At the same time they saw whom they could possibly help. . . . If I had chosen another type of project—say, they had to read the novel *To Kill a Mockingbird* and then write a paper on it—I don't think they would have been as thrilled.

Ms. G, a Mexican American, grew up in the neighborhood. She was identified by her colleagues as the teacher who could "handle the students." In response to why students could relate well to her she underscored the importance of understanding them:

> I think they related to me better because I better understood, and it could have been because I used to be where they were. But I think the relationship you establish with your students is very important. I would like to think that they looked at me as a role model. I was able to relate to them so well because I was one of them. My standards were high, but I don't think they were out of reach. I respected them, their culture, where they were from. I think they saw that and in return they respected me. And it's just the rapport that you establish with these kids. The fact that I gave them freedom, choices. Even though I would say, "This is what has to be done today, this is what we have to do, which one do you want to do first. . . ." I gave them certain choices. They made up

(Continued)

their own rules when we did the projects—these are the do's these are the don'ts—I let them come up with their own, with maybe make a few changes here and there. A lot of it is to give them ownership and they will respond to you better because they don't see it as so teacher centered; they feel like they have a say in this. I think that's very important in their decision making. They have to have the freedom to make decisions, and they have to have the freedom to make mistakes, too.

According to Ms. G, the team was most successful in building consensus, especially as it concerned students who experienced difficulty in school. During the teachers' common planning period, the team took the opportunity to discuss the students' progress and determine a plan of action for those falling behind or needing extra help. Usually, parent conferences were organized as part of the remedial help, although parents were also informed when their children were doing well. The teachers collaborated in writing individual letters to parents, personalizing their method of communication. The second year was especially productive in terms of team collaboration.

Assessing the Program

Mr. T was satisfied with how teachers worked together, combining classes and doing things they hadn't done before. He observed the interdisciplinary team making a concerted effort to ensure success for every student: "I think students were showing success because these teachers were making sure they were going to be successful not by watering down the curriculum but by simply letting them know that we cared about them, that we believe they could be successful."

The quality and quantity of parent involvement were also perceived by Mr. T as indicators of success. The interdisciplinary team teachers engaged more parents in conferences. The strategy of requiring parents to pick up their child's six-week report card seemed to enhance communication between teachers and parents.

Students in the interdisciplinary team participated more in extracurricular activities such as athletics, band, and cheerleading than did the rest of the student body. Student attendance was higher and the overall passing rate surpassed that of the other students at NSHS. Mr. T described the team as a sort of family.

The interdisciplinary team approach seemed to improve the quality of educational experiences for both teachers and students. Ms. G reported that overall the teachers in the team seemed to "enjoy the kids better."

Mr. T and Ms. G expressed very similar ideas concerning the program goals, the roles of teachers, and the program's effectiveness. There were no noticeable points of disagreement or contradictions. Both principal and teacher emphasized the importance of ownership. Mr. T expressed the importance of convincing teachers of their uncompromising acceptance of the program philosophy and goals. Unless teachers experienced a genuine and total integration of the program with their teaching, the results would lack the positive impact hoped for. Ms. G seemed to accept the program in its entirety. Perhaps, this is because she is a risk-taker, as she describes herself. However, she also expects her students to claim ownership in their learning process. She begins by giving them choices, but ultimately, to be responsible for their own learning and academic achievements, students must make the choice.

(Continued)

Addressing the Students' Self-Esteem

Perhaps one area that was interpreted in slightly different ways by the principal and the teacher was in the perception of self-esteem. Mr. T felt that the students' self-esteem was elevated by experiencing success in their academic performance. Certainly, no one can argue that success may result in increased self-confidence, particularly success in school performance. However, Ms. G had a different view of the students' self-esteem. She expressed this view as she described the students:

> You had those who were still struggling with English, those who were newer to the country, but those students for the most part worked very hard to get better. On the other hand, you had those who were born here—second, third generation. They resisted the Spanish language. When I would try to talk to them or say something in Spanish, they would say, "What? What are you saying? I don't understand. . . ." I think for the most part some of them would be embarrassed to say or to speak Spanish or they would be embarrassed about their parents who only spoke Spanish. I think that throughout their lives and maybe their parents', if you knew only Spanish you were labeled, and those kids hated to be labeled. Unfortunately, they were labeled low skilled, low class, so they resisted. But, if you put them in a setting where they have the opportunity to go with the Anglos, they would still stick with their own. There was a lot of pride among themselves and among the culture. They love the Spanish music, they would go to the dances, and they would have all the top Spanish singers and bands; but if you try to talk to them directly in Spanish or try to talk to them about the culture associated with Mexico, they didn't like that. It's really strange, yet they were very proud. But I'm hoping that later on as they get older that they'll start appreciating and become more proud of their culture and more part of it.

As expected, the students' scores on the state criterion-referenced test improved. Mr. T noted that 75 percent of the interdisciplinary team group members were successful, compared to the previous ninth graders who had a 40 to 50 percent success rate. Even though 25 percent of the students were not successful, he believes that they had made some important gains.

The pressure to increase student scores on this test is not always compatible with the type of teaching promoted in the interdisciplinary team approach according to Ms. G, who comments on the problems with TAAS, the state-mandated test:

> Unfortunately, another barrier to this type of teaching method is the TAAS. There is so much pressure on us as teachers for our students to do well on the TAAS that it's really hard not to have that in the back of your mind. In math, the students are so low in math that, even though [the math teacher is] a great teacher, I don't think she felt very comfortable because there was so much pressure on her. And she cared about whether the kids passed the TAAS. There are ways, I'm sure, that you can still teach TAAS objectives, but we needed more time to experiment, and that's something they didn't give us.

Furthermore, it is common knowledge among experienced faculty members that principals such as Mr. T who successfully implement innovative programs are usually rewarded with a promotion that removes them from the school. But a promotion and removal of the principal from the school can interrupt a successful attempt to maintain a quality program. A new principal usually signals a new and frustrating beginning for teachers, students, and parents. Ms. G was not surprised.

(Continued)

She said, "Who can blame the principal for being promoted and removed? It's a hard job being a principal; I certainly don't want to be principal." As anticipated, Mr. T was promoted, much to the disappointment of many in the NSHS community. Only one of the four teachers in the interdisciplinary team remains at NSHS.

Suggestions for Improvement

Mr. T offers several excellent suggestions on how the interdisciplinary team approach could be improved. For example, he would allow teachers to have more input regarding the design and organization of the program. The incoming ninth graders would be carefully assessed to determine how their needs can be better met. Furthermore, he would extend the program to include juniors and seniors. The program assessment component would be better designed and implemented. He would organize his administrative team in ways that would offer more technical assistance to the team staff. In essence, the spiral curriculum would have a deeper base and be extended further while still addressing as well as possible the needs of students and aligning their achievements with curriculum standards.

Mr. T's Leadership

The leadership style of Mr. T seems to complement well the interdisciplinary team approach. He perceives himself as a visionary leader with a consistent and well-developed plan. He plays the role of a resourceful colleague who supports teachers in every way possible. His willingness to submit to regular assessment procedures reveals a committed, selfless professional.

The experiences at NSHS had a personal and professional impact on Mr. T. He explained how the experience changed him:

> I became better at understanding curriculum. It made me want to understand how kids learn, for instance. It forced me to do that, so I became much more comfortable understanding the academic areas and the needs of kids as well as teachers. It also helped me to better understand why kids were not being successful, their inability to set goals. I learned how to develop processes to help kids with that component. It made me more of a student again; I spent a great deal of time reading the material and visiting and networking with principals in other schools. It really helped me a lot.

Ms. G's Transformation

The experience also impacted Ms. G in profound, positive ways. She described how her teaching is now more student-centered:

> I like to see students come up with their own answers or go to their peers for solutions, suggestions, or ideas. I now use some of those methods in my classroom. I'm not up there lecturing so much; I let them work in groups, collaborate, I let them have peer responses. You walk into my room and you'll see kids in little groups, you'll see them on the floor, you'll see them reading each other's papers; you'll see them goofing off, too.

(Continued)

Conclusion

The question remains whether the interdisciplinary team approach is specifically appropriate for NSIIS or whether it should be implemented in all high schools. Educators who believe that high schools should strive to meet the needs of all students will advocate for at least one interdisciplinary team component. However, parents would be more apt to favor this approach for their children, especially in a rapidly changing society that conveys vague and conflicting values about what education is about, what important skills are needed for participation in the future workforce, and how their children's well-being may be sustained beyond their teenage years. Ms. G's assessment of the program in the following comment is a strong statement about the appropriateness and effectiveness of the interdisciplinary team approach: "I think that students got the best of what we could possibly offer them . . . they got a little bit of the icing on the cake because of the program."

Issues for Further Reflection and Application

1. Discuss whether you think the interdisciplinary team approach should be implemented in all high schools. Discuss whether this approach would work in your school. What do you think are the most common issues associated with implementing this approach?

2. What indicators pointed to the success of the interdisciplinary team approach in this case study?

3. What role did Ms. G play in the interdisciplinary team, and how would you assess her performance in this role?

4. Describe the teacher qualities that contribute to the interdisciplinary team teaching and some teacher qualities that inhibit this approach.

5. Describe Mr. T's leadership abilities and style and state whether you think they are appropriate or not for providing leadership in an interdisciplinary team approach.

6. Do you think that the students' self-esteem was addressed adequately in the program? What else could have been done to raise students' self-esteem?

Suggested Readings

Crawford, J. 1997. *Best evidence: Research foundations of the Bilingual Education Act.* Washington, DC: National Clearinghouse for Bilingual Education.

Durán, R. 1994. Hispanic Student Achievement. In M. J. Justiz, R. Wilson, & L. Bjork (Eds.), *Minorities in higher education.* Phoenix, AZ: American Council on Education and the Oryx Press, pp. 151–172.

National Assessment of Educational Progress. 1994. *Academic achievement.* Washington, DC: U.S. Department of Education.

National Center for Educational Statistics. 1995. *Dropout rates in the U.S.* Washington, DC: U.S. Department of Education.

Pinal, J. 1998. *The Hispanic population.* Washington, DC: U.S. Census Bureau

U.S. Census Bureau. 1995. *Population projections of the United States by age, race, and Hispanic origin: 1992–2050.* Washington, DC: U.S. Census Bureau.

As shown in this case study, a positive self-concept is a prerequisite to sustaining a continuing record of academic success. Many minority group members have barriers that are unique to them, barriers that make this prerequisite especially difficult for these students to attain. Following is a discussion of several types of curricula, including the core curriculum, the Trump Plan, the spiral curriculum, mastery learning, and problem solving. As you read about each of these curriculum designs, consider its unique opportunities for enhancing students' self-concepts.

THE CORE CURRICULUM

Near the turn of the century, some innovative curriculum directors, such as Francis Parker, who was described in Chapter 3, began searching for a way to escape the fragmentation that characterized the traditional (subject-centered) curricula. The result was a design called the *core curriculum*. The theory behind the development of this approach begins with the realization that some content is indispensable for all students. This content would become the core. See Figure 5.1.

FIGURE 5.1

Structure of the core curriculum design.

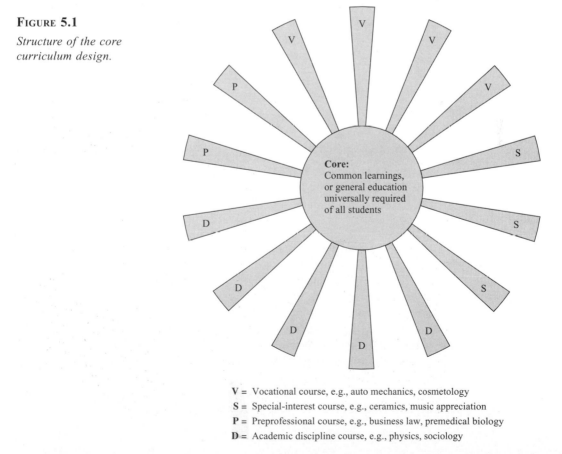

V = Vocational course, e.g., auto mechanics, cosmetology
S = Special-interest course, e.g., ceramics, music appreciation
P = Preprofessional course, e.g., business law, premedical biology
D = Academic discipline course, e.g., physics, sociology

Around the core are a number of spokes. These different spokes represent academic discipline courses (D), professional courses (P), special-interest courses (S), and vocational courses (V).

The core curriculum has a dimension of versatility that makes it attractive to advocates of a variety of philosophies. For example, core curricula are characterized by high expectations for students, frequent high-quality academic interactions among teachers and students, and direct instruction (Wang, Haertel, & Walberg, 1998). Essentialists can use the core to ensure coverage of the essential subjects. At the other extreme, the progressive educator can assign both content and activities to ensure that individual students' needs are met. In between, the pragmatists can use the core to ensure the coverage of practical curricula.

Zais (1976, p. 423) identified six types of curricula as core curricula: (1) the separate subjects core, (2) the correlated core, (3) the fused core, (4) the activity/experiences core, (5) the areas-of-living core, and (6) the social problems core.

The core curriculum represented the second attempt to integrate learning. Contemporary, real-life problems were used for organizing the curricula. Typically, core programs are organized into blocks of time, often two or three successive periods, during which the teacher or a team of teachers integrates two or more subjects or disciplines. Oliva (1997, p. 277) lists six characteristics of core curricula:

1. They constitute a portion of the curriculum that is required of all students.

2. They unify or fuse subject matter, usually English and social studies.

3. Their content centers on problems that cut across the disciplines; the primary method of learning is problem solving using all applicable subject matter.

4. They are organized into blocks of time, usually two to three periods under a "core" teacher (with the possible use of additional teachers and others as resource persons).

5. They encourage teachers to plan with students.

6. They provide pupil guidance.

The 1980s and 1990s saw an increased interest in the core curriculum of English, science, social studies, and math. Its new use was a response to the call for accountability. See Figure 5.2.

The core curriculum has been best received at the junior and senior high levels, but it has never been universally accepted even at these levels. As with other innovative curricula, the success of the core curriculum, regardless of the version used, hinges on the ability and willingness of teachers to make it work. Most teachers are ill-prepared to implement problem-centered approaches or to integrate subjects and activities to achieve the comprehensive understandings sought by the core curricularists, because most teachers, themselves, were educated in textbook-oriented, subject-centered curricula.

FIGURE 5.2

Percentage of high school graduates completing a core curriculum.

Did you know?

HIGH SCHOOL STUDENTS ARE TAKING TOUGHER COURSES.

THE FACTS

As a result of the education reforms of the 1980s, which focused on increasing the coursework requirements for high school students, more students today are taking tougher courses than were their predecessors in the early 1980s. This is true across racial and ethnic groups.

NEXT STEPS

All students should be required to complete more stringent coursework in order to graduate from high school. States and school districts should eliminate the "general track" or make the general track coursework requirements more stringent so that all students graduate from high school having completed four years of English and three years of social studies, science, and mathematics.

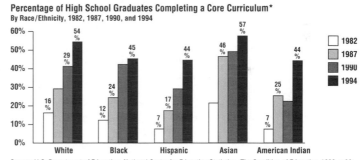

Percentage of High School Graduates Completing a Core Curriculum*
By Race/Ethnicity, 1982, 1987, 1990, and 1994

Source: U.S. Department of Education, National Center for Education Statistics. *The Condition of Education*, 1996, p.98.
*The "core curriculum" consists of four years of English and three years each of social studies, science, and mathematics.

REALITY CHECK

Many people believe the public schools are failing. Public schools must become better, but there have been major improvements in public education since the early 1980s. In the current atmosphere, the negative is being emphasized and the positive pushed aside. These one-page policy briefs are meant to show the improvements that have occurred in public education while urging persistent efforts to bring better education to more children.

THE CENTER ON EDUCATION POLICY is the independent advocate for public education and for more effective public schools. The Center works to help Americans better understand the role fo public education in a democracy and the need to improve the academic quality of public schools. We do not represent any special interests; instead, we try to help citizens make sense of the conflicting opinions and perceptions about public education and create the conditions that will lead to better public schools. The Center receives its funding from charitable foundations such as The Pew Chantable Trusts, The George Sund Foundation, The Joyce Foundation, and Phi Delta Kappa International.

1001 Connecticut Avenue N.W.
Suite 519
Washington, DC 20035
Phone: 202-822-8065
Fax: 202-822-6008
E-mail: ctred@ctredbol.org
WEBSITE: www.ctredbol.org

STAFF: John F. Jennings, *Director*; Diane Starx Renner, *Associate Director*; Toni Panter, *Administrative Assistant*

THE TRUMP PLAN

Throughout the twentieth century, grouping of students was a topic of study and debate among educators and researchers. The results of such studies have been mixed. For example, Good, Reyes, Grouws, and Molryan (1990–1991) report that, in groups with a wide range of ability, the better students dominate the others. Yet Calfee and Brown (1979), say that when grouped homogeneously, low-ability students perform even less well. Centra and Potter (1980) found that the amount of time students spend in direct instruction is directly related to their level of achievement. Yet Julik (1981) reviewed more than 40 studies and reported that grouping had a strong motivating effect on students. Garmston and Wellman (1998, p. 33) offer four skills that can enhance group work:

1. Knowing one's intentions and choosing congruent behavior.
2. Setting aside unproductive patterns of listening, responding, and inquiring.
3. Knowing when to self-assert and when to integrate.
4. Knowing and supporting the group's purposes, topics, processes, and development.

The Trump Plan recommended grouping students in small groups (15 or fewer students) and in large groups of 100 to 300 students. Students would spend part of each day in small groups and part of each day in large groups. They would spend the remainder of the day studying alone or in small groups according to each student's preference. As shown in Figure 5.3, Trump had definite ideas about how much time should be allotted to these arrangements.

FIGURE 5.3

The Trump Plan.

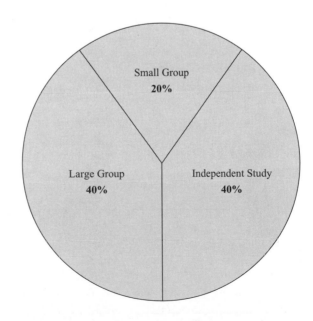

Small Group
20%

Large Group
40%

Independent Study
40%

A strength of the Trump Plan is its variety: something for everyone. Evidence of this model is seen through our nation's schools. At the turn of the century nearly 100 percent of teachers used whole-group instruction at least once a week, over 90 percent worked with individuals at least once a week, and at least 80 percent used small groups at least once a week (Meek, 1998). Furthermore, this plan specified a variety of teacher or discussion leader activities and a variety of media for the large groups. Small-group work provided a variety of activities involving all students. Independent study time also afforded students a high level of involvement while performing laboratory experiments, problem solving, reading, listening to tapes, or pursuing a variety of creative activities. The ability that this curriculum design provides for meeting the unique needs of diverse students has extended its use in schools at a time when education reformers are dedicated to ensuring that each student can and will learn.

One feature of the Trump Plan, introduced over 30 years ago, is variable scheduling, not only during the school day but throughout the year. Another feature of The Trump Plan was year-round instruction. The January 23, 1993, *Richmond Register* daily newspaper carried an article headed "Ft. Knox pupils begin year-round school." The article noted that "year-round school is practiced in over 2000 school districts in the United States and it's growing rapidly."

In an era of unprecedented pressure to prepare students to score well on education reform initiated exams, some may consider the Trump Plan dated, but a recent study of America's teachers (Meek, 1998, p. 15) revealed several facts that validate this model for use in the twenty-first century:

- Nearly 100 percent of teachers reported using whole-group instruction at least once a week.

- More than 90 percent of all teachers reported working with individual students at least once a week.

- 80 percent of teachers report working with small groups at least once a week.

THE SPIRAL CURRICULUM

Throughout the twentieth century, connectionist psychologists insisted that when learning occurs, it occurs in steps, each part building on simpler content learned earlier. Constructivists agree that each part of the content should be tied to prior learning. Markle, Johnston, Geer, and Meichtry (1990, p. 53) explain:

> Constructivists describe learning in terms of building connections between prior knowledge and new ideas and claim that effective teachings help students construct an organized set of concepts that relates new and old ideas.

The *spiral curriculum* takes connectionism one step further, recommending that the same topics be returned to the curriculum at a later date, sometimes at a higher grade level. Having gained in maturity and in the accumulation of prerequisite knowledge, students will be able to develop understandings that were beyond their capacity when simpler elements of the topic were introduced earlier.

The repetitive nature of the spiral curriculum is viewed by some as a strength and by others as a weakness. Some contemporary educators attribute the success of Asian students at least in part to the fact that, unlike American students who confront the same material repeatedly, Asian curricula address each topic at only one level, providing time needed to pursue each topic in depth (Lewis & Tsuchida, 1990).

MASTERY LEARNING

In 1963 an article in the *Teachers College Record* (Carroll, 1963) described a curriculum designed to ensure that all students could succeed. Rejecting the work of E. L. Thorndike, which correlated students' success with their IQ, Carroll said that all students could learn if certain curriculum and instructional adjustments were made.

First, this new program, called *mastery learning,* would incorporate flexible time, as much as each individual needed. Second, students who failed to master the content and objectives on the first attempt could recycle without penalty. Remediation using a variety of different learning styles would be provided between testing cycles. Formative evaluation, not the traditional summative evaluation, would dominate. *Formative evaluation* is given in small steps throughout the teaching unit. Its purpose is to promote learning by using test scores to improve both instruction and the curriculum. Formative test scores are never used to determine grades.

As to letter grades, which most schools require, mastery learning typically uses A's, B's, and I's; there are no C's, D's, or F's. Students who score below the level set for mastery (usually 80 percent) must remediate and recycle.

Like all other curriculum designs, mastery learning succeeds or fails depending on its application. Cunningham (1991, p. 84) explains:

> There are two essential elements of the mastery learning process. The first is an extremely close congruence between the material being taught, the teaching strategies employed, and the content measured. The second essential element is the provision of formative assessment, opportunities for students followed by feedback, corrective and enrichment activities.

There are basically two types of mastery learning: (1) teacher-paced and group-based, and (2) student-paced and individual-based (Block & Henson, 1986). Most mastery learning programs are student-paced; that is, the students set their own pace (Guskey & Gates, 1986). Most are individual-based; that is, individual students pursue the content independently. This quality enables students to tie new information to previously learned knowledge and, in this sense, reflects the constructivist theory. Obviously, modern reformers who are committed to meeting the diverse needs of all students and those who adhere to the constructivist approach to learning find mastery learning appealing. Though mixed, the results of studies of the effects of mastery learning programs are encouraging. The first studies (Bloom, Hastings, & Madaus, 1981) found that at least 95 percent of all high school students could master all school objectives. Burns (1979) reviewed 157 such studies. Although in one-third of his studies (47) no differences in achievement were found, in two-thirds of the studies, (107) mastery learning students significantly outscored their traditionally taught counterparts. In only 3 of the 157 studies did mastery learning students achieve less than their counterparts. Burns' review covered 3,000 schools and spanned over 15 years.

Guskey and Gates (1986) reviewed 25 studies of group-based and teacher-paced mastery learning programs in elementary schools and secondary schools. In all 25 studies, the students in mastery learning groups outlearned their counterparts.

But mastery learning is not without critics. Arlin (1984) described mastery learning as a "psychological trap," lacking a proper conceptual basis. Slavin (1989, p. 79) says:

> If school districts expect that by introducing group-based mastery learning . . . they can measurably increase their students' achievement, there is little evidence to support them.

PROBLEM SOLVING

The problem-solving curriculum became popular during the Progressive Education Era (from about 1925 to 1945) because of the emphasis during that time on learner-centered curricula. What better way to involve students and provide a means for connecting new information to prior understanding than to give them problems to solve? Problem solving received a rebirth in the 1960s, when the post-*Sputnik* scare was at its peak. Realizing that American students were long on facts and short on the ability to apply these facts, curriculum designs cast the new interdisciplinary curriculum in the form of problems.

These new programs were identified by acronyms and titles, many which reflected their developers. For example, Harvard had its Project Physics, and Boulder, Colorado, had its Earth Science Curriculum Project (ESCP). There was a Science and Mathematics Study Group (SMSG). These curricula were three-dimensional.

Typical of laboratory schools and other innovative schools during this era, the P. K. Younge Laboratory School at the University of Florida was equipped with a room full of objects, including a set of scales, tension springs, a toy truck, an inclined plane, and dozens of other gadgets. This was the hardware required to implement one of the new problem-solving curricula. By requiring students to use this hands-on equipment to solve problems, these curricula forced students to apply their acquired knowledge.

Problem solving is still a valued curriculum design because many people maintain that this skill is a necessity for coping in the future. A national panel reporting to the National Center for Educational Statistics known as the Special Study Panel on Education Indicators to the Acting Commissioner of Education Statistics (1991, p. 65), says that people need the ability to integrate information from all disciplines and use integrative reasoning to solve problems:

> Integrative reasoning is essential in modern life and today's workplace. It represents not the ability to recall bits and pieces of information, but the "things" one can demonstrate one can do. These include communication, using technology and information effectively, and proficiency in working in a problem-solving capacity either alone or in teams.

The need for curricula to be offered in a risk-free environment has been mentioned throughout this book. At no place is this need greater than in a problem-solving classroom. Martinez (1998, p. 609) explains,

> Errors are a part of the process of problem solving, which implies that both teachers and learners need to be more tolerant of them. If no mistakes are made, then almost certainly no problem solving is taking place. Unfortunately, one tradition of schooling is that perfect performance is often exalted as an ideal. Errors are seen as failures, as signs that the highest marks are not quite merited.

Providing students with opportunities to solve problems can make the difference between their dealing with the content superficial and their developing in-depth understanding of the content and learning how to apply it to solve authentic problems. Alper, Fendel, Fraser, and Resek (1996, p. 19) explain, "By solving a variety of problems, students deepen their understanding, and they begin to abstract the concepts and refine the techniques needed to apply to the complex original problem."

At the turn of the millennium, education reformers' heavy emphasis on constructivism has again rekindled the passion that educators have for problem solving. The need, when problem solving, to connect to previous understanding and learn in depth continue to make problem solving popular in American schools.

SELECTING CURRICULUM DESIGNS

Since each curriculum design has a unique combination of strengths and weaknesses, curriculum developers who are aware of these designs can match them with the needs of their schools. For example, the many schools that are now being required by reform practices to implement integrated thematic units can benefit from the broad-fields design. Schools seeking ways to improve educational opportunities for minority students may choose to implement mastery learning because it gives students the time they need to master each concept and because it provides students with opportunities to remediate and recycle without penalty. Multicultural classes may choose the Trump Plan or problem-solving curricula because they provide students with opportunities to participate in cooperative group projects.

Students of all backgrounds, including white middle-class students, face increasing obstacles in their communities. In recent years, the greatest increase in the incidence of social problems has been in white middle-class communities (O'Neil, 1998). Education reform programs in many states are requiring their primary teachers to abolish the early grade levels. Teachers who have taught in open classrooms will have developed many prerequisite skills such as team teaching and continuous progress records keeping. Teachers wishing to increase the level of understanding in their classes or wishing to ensure that concepts are remembered in higher grades may choose the spiral curriculum. Teachers who are sensitive to the need for a solid set of content and experiences for all students while providing different tracks to meet their students' varying vocational ambitions may vote for the core curriculum.

CURRICULUM DESIGN QUALITIES

None of these curriculum designs is unique. Rather, each design shares some common qualities. Examples of features include: scope, sequence, continuity, articulation, and balance.

Scope

Curriculum scope refers to the breadth of the curriculum at any level or at any given time. For example, the breadth of eighth grade science refers to the variety of science topics covered during the eighth grade. Because scope concerns only one point in time, it is called a *horizontal dimension.*

Sequence

Curriculum sequence is concerned with the order of topics over time. For example, in biology, students might study the cell and then tissue, organs, and systems. Because it examines the curriculum over a period of time, curriculum sequence is called a *vertical dimension.*

TABLE 5.3   **Sequence versus continuity**

Curriculum A	Curriculum B	Curriculum C
H	H	II
G	G	G
F		F
E	E	E
D	D	C
C		D
B	B	B
A	A	A

Continuity

Continuity refers to the smoothness or the absence of disruptions in the curriculum over time. A curriculum might have good sequence but might also have disruptions. That curriculum would lack continuity. For example, as shown in Table 5.3, curriculum A has good sequence and good continuity. Curriculum B has good sequence but lacks continuity. Curriculum C has poor sequence. Also, even though no topics are missing, the lack of order creates disruptions; therefore, curriculum C lacks continuity. So, sequence without continuity is possible, but continuity without sequence is not.

Articulation

Articulation refers to the smooth flow of the curriculum in both dimensions, vertical and horizontal. Vertical articulation is called continuity. Its horizontal counterpart has no name.

Balance

Another important curriculum feature is *balance.* Frequently, the layperson speaks of a "well-rounded education," implying that an individual is getting, or a school program is offering, a curriculum with balance between the arts and sciences, or with balance between college prep subjects and vocational subjects.

The Role of Emotions in Learning

Now, let's reflect on the confluency concept and the recent brain research discoveries (LeDoux, 1996; Wolfe & Brandt, 1998) about the role emotions play in learning. How can curriculum planners use this information to improve the curriculum's balance? One way to ensure a balance between the cognitive and the affective role in each lesson is to plan activities that you know most students will enjoy. Perhaps some clues as to how this can be achieved are found in the words of some former teachers of the year who give testimony to the importance of the joy in learning (Henson & Eller, 1999).

- "I believe that working and learning at school can and should be fun. I joke and laugh freely with my students." Duane Obermier, former Nebraska Teacher of the Year.
- Cynthia Lancaster, former Washington State Teacher of the Year, tells beginning teachers that setting clear behavior roles early in the year is a good way to provide an atmosphere that allows the teacher and students to have fun.
- Susan Lloyd, former Alabama Teacher of the Year suggests that the best fun a teacher can plan is the joy of learning, and says that in planning for this to happen in her classes, she spends most of her time learning, attending lectures, reading, and discussing current issues. She uses "fascinating facts and thought-provoking questions" to kick-start their brains.
- Marilyn Grondel, former Utah Teacher of the Year says, "I believe that wonder and joy are always in the attic of one's mind." She shares a few of techniques she uses to bring joy into her classes. First, she looks to the community. Since her school is in a rural setting, she uses stories of horses to get students' attention. Next, she models: when she has reading class, for instance, she takes her turn and reads and writes along with the students. She also brings in community leaders for career day. Finally, she shares her techniques with fellow teachers: "A successful teacher becomes more successful by dialoguing with colleagues and sharing ideas and materials."

A FINAL NOTE

Some of these programs are more student focused than others. I believe the goal of all curriculum designs should be to keep the focus on the students. Kowal (1991, p. 269) has reminded curriculum designers that keeping the student in the center of attention does not imply that students should always get what they want. Student wants and student needs may be two entirely different things:

> The task is not to design a . . . program based on who yells the loudest or the longest or to use compromise as a rationale for curriculum design. The basis of an appropriate rationale is centered on the student; how students can be best prepared for a future, which is at any given time unknown.

Designing curricula to meet the future needs of students is an ongoing challenge that educators must meet.

Most schools use modifications of several of these curriculum designs. In fact, because of the effect of the culture of the school and the culture of the local community, all curriculum designs must be modified so that they can adapt to the unique characteristics and needs of each particular school.

Chapter Summary

The subject-centered curriculum is the oldest curriculum design. Teachers like it because it employs textbooks and the lecture method. The textbook provides specific, tightly organized content, enabling teachers to show off their expertise. Students like subject-centered curricula because of the specific content and tight organization and because they can remain passive while in the classroom.

Near the turn of the twentieth century, educators became concerned that the subject-centered curricula led only to the memorization of disjointed facts and bits of information. As a result, this curriculum was replaced in many schools by broad-fields curricula, which integrated the subjects to produce broader understanding.

By the 1920s the educators of the Progressive era wanted curricula that would enable them to serve each individual student's needs. They devised the core curriculum to achieve this goal. Other groups used it to achieve other goals. The many variations of core curricula had two things in common: (1) a common core of content required of everyone, and (2) a combination of content and activities used to meet particular goals.

Many modern education reformers believe that the subject-centered curriculum approach restricts learning. Thus, multi-disciplinary curricula have regained popularity in schools throughout the country. Current reformers who push to have all children succeed like the individual emphasis given by the broad-fields and multi-disciplinary approaches introduced by progressive educators.

During the late 1950s, the Trump Plan was developed. This design was different from existing designs because it focused on grouping. Students were required to spend 40 percent of their time in large groups, 20 percent in small groups, and the remaining 40 percent in independent study or in small groups if they preferred.

Like the core curriculum, the Trump Plan had strength in its variety. The Trump Plan included variation in methods, materials, and even in the length of the school day and the school year, including year-round curricula. Its emphasis on individual and small-group work appeals to current educators. Eighty percent of today's teachers use small-group assignments weekly, and 90 percent work with individual students weekly.

The spiral curriculum is built on two psychological foundations: connectionism and constructivism. It also employs developmentalism, recognizing that students are not ready to study certain concepts until they reach the required level of development and until they have had the necessary experiences.

Mastery learning is a curriculum design that purports to offer the opportunity for all students to succeed by giving individual students all the time they need to master the objectives, by affording them opportunities to remediate and recycle without penalty, and by using formative evaluation which is given during instruction, not to assign grades but to improve learning by improving the curriculum and instruction. Obviously this dedication to meeting the diverse needs of all students appeals to those contemporary educators who are dedicated to meeting the needs of students from all cultural backgrounds.

The problem-solving curriculum has long been a favorite design for educators who espouse learner-centered education. The launching of *Sputnik* gave problem-centered curricula a boost. It was hoped that, by discovering the answers to problems, students would more thoroughly understand the broader content generalizations required to master a discipline. The problem-solving curriculum has received a renewed level of interest in American schools because it enables students to learn the topics at a greater depth and affords them opportunities to tie new information to prior understanding.

Most mastery learning programs are individually based, making them attractive to those teachers who are dedicated to meeting the needs of diverse groups of students.

These curriculum designs are all different, but they all have certain features in common, such as scope (breadth), sequence, continuity, articulation, and balance. Success with any of these designs depends on teachers understanding the underpinning philosophies and on the quality of instruction used with the designs.

Learning Questions

1. What qualities in the Little School That Grew are examples of constructivist theory?

2. Can you identify any practices in contemporary education reform that parallel the forces that caused the Little School to lose some of its valuable qualities?

3. What curriculum designs were reflected in this curriculum of the Little School before and after its changes?

4. Can you think of ways to make the changes the Little School made and yet avoid the losses that it suffered?

5. Which of the curriculum designs presented in this chapter do you see evidenced most in your own school? Why do you think this design dominates at your school?

6. To what extent is formative evaluation (compared to summative evaluation) used in your school? Why do you think this is so?

7. What kinds of balance do you think your own college curriculum should strive to maintain? Examples: humanities versus sciences, general studies versus major subjects.

8. Do you believe it is important for teachers to understand a program's underlying philosophy? Why or why not?

9. Do you think the American culture has any qualities that cause teachers to implement practices without fully understanding their philosophies? Name some of these qualities.

10. Which is worse in curriculum design, poor sequence or poor continuity? Why?

11. Do the current education reform practices in your school have sound philosophical and theoretical bases? Explain your answer.

12. What is the best way you know to make school enjoyable to all students?

Suggested Activities

1. Select a curriculum design from this chapter and research its (*a*) philosophical and psychological bases, and (*b*) its degree of success as reported in the research and other literature.

2. Examine your own school (or visit a local school) and see what evidence you can find for each of these designs. Don't be surprised if you learn that the school uses a combination of several designs rather than a single "pure" design.

3. Get a copy of your state's curriculum guide from your library or from a local school counselor. Choose a discipline and grade level. For your chosen discipline and grade level, describe the program in your state's curriculum guide in terms of (*a*) how the content is sequenced, (*b*) the scope of the content, and (*c*) the balance between the sciences and the arts and between required subjects and electives.

4. The success of any curriculum design depends on the teacher's ability to implement the design. Select a design and describe how you could help teachers prepare to use it successfully.

5. Make a list of the reform elements under way in your district. Now compare the curriculum designs in this chapter with the items in your list. What designs offer the best opportunities to meet some of the local reform goals?

6. Examine your school's curriculum plan and identify signs of constructivist theory.

Works Cited and Suggested Readings

Alper, L., Fendel, D., Fraser, S., & Resek, D. (1996). Problem-based mathematics—Not just for the college-bound. *Educational Leadership, 53*(8), 18–21.

Arlin, M. (1984, Spring). Time, equality, and mastery of learning." *Review of Educational Research, 54,* 71–72.

Armstrong, D. G., Henson, K. T., & Savage, T. V. (2001). *Teaching today* (6th ed.). Upper Saddle River, NJ: Merrill.

Benning, J. (1990). The connection between learning environment. In E. Herbert & Meels (Eds.), *Children learning and school design: A first national invitational conference for architects and educators.* Winnetka, IL: Winnetka Publishing School.

Block, J. H., & Henson, K. T. (1986, Spring). Mastery learning and middle school instruction. *American Middle School Education, 9*(2), 21–29.

Block, J. H., Efthim, H. E., & Burns, R. B. (1989). *Building effective mastery learning schools.* New York: Longman.

Bloom, B. S., Hastings, J. T., & Madaus, G. F. (1981). *Evaluation to improve learning.* New York: McGraw-Hill.

Brophy, J. (1998). *Motivating students to learn.* Boston: McGraw-Hill.

Burns, R. B. (1979). Mastery learning: Does it work? *Educational Leadership, 37,* 110–113.

Calfee, R., & Brown, R. (1979). Grouping students for instruction. *Yearbook of the National Society for the Study of Education, 78* (Part II), 144–148.

Centra, J., & Potter, D. (1980). School and teacher effects: An interrelational model. *Review of Educational Research, 50,* 273–291.

Carroll, J. B. (1963). A model of school learning. *Teachers College Record, 64,* 723–733.

Cohen, A. (1993). A new educational paradigm. *Phi Delta Kappan, 74*(10), 791–795.

Cunningham, R. D. Jr., (1991, September). Modeling mastery teaching through supervision. *NASSP Bulletin, 75*(536), 83–87.

Darling-Hammond, L. (1993). Reforming the school reform agenda. *Phi Delta Kappan, 74*(10), 756–761.

Darling-Hammond, L. (1996). The quiet revolution: Rethinking teacher development. *Educational Leadership, 53*(6), 4–10.

Darling-Hammond, L. (1997). *The right to learn.* San Francisco: Jossey-Bass.

Dewey, J. (1916). The need of an industrial education in an industrial democracy. *Manual Training and Vocational Education, 16,* 409–414.

Eisner, E. W. (1985). *The educational imagination* (2nd ed.). New York: Macmillan.

Garmston R., & Wellman, B. (1998). Teacher talk that makes a difference. *Educational Leadership, 55*(7), 30–34.

Geisert, G., & Dunn, R. (1991, March). Effective use of computers: Assignments based on individual learning style. *The Clearing House, 4*(4), 219–223.

Glasser, W. W. (1997). A new look at school failure and school success. *Phi Delta Kappan, 78,* 596–602.

Goleman, D. (1995). *Emotional intelligence: Why it can matter more than I.Q.* New York: Bantam.

Good, T. L., Reyes, B. S., Grouws, D. A., & Molryan, C. M. (1990–91). Using work groups in mathematics instruction. *Educational Leadership, 47*(4), 56–62.

Grondel, M. (1999). In K. T. Henson & B. F. Eller (Eds.), *Educational psychology for effective teaching.* Belmont, CA: Wadsworth.

Guskey, T. R., & Gates, S. L. (1986). Synthesis of research on the effects of mastery learning in elementary and secondary classrooms. *Educational Leadership, 45*(8), 73–80.

Hansen, J. M., & Childs, J. (1998). Creating a school where people like to be. *Educational Leadership, 56*(1), 14–16.

Harrison, C. J. (1990). Concepts, operational definitions, and case studies in instruction. *Education, 110*(4), 502–505.

Henson, K. T. (1975). The little school that grew. *Journal of Teacher Education, 26*(1), 55–59.

Henson, K. T. (1979, Winter). Why our open classrooms fail. *Educational Horizons, 35,* 82–85.

Henson, K. T., & Eller, B. F. (1999). *Educational psychology for effective teaching.* Belmont, CA: Wadsworth.

Herbert, E. A. (1998). Design matters: How a school environment affects children. *Educational Leadership, 56*(1), 69–70.

Julik, J. A. (1981, April). The effect of ability grouping on secondary school students. Paper presented at the American Educational Research Association, Los Angeles.

King, A. (1990, November–December). Reciprocal questioning: A strategy for teaching students how to learn from lectures. *The Clearing House, 64*(2), 131–135.

Kowal, J. (1991). Science, technology, and human values: A curricular approach. *Theory Into Practice, 30*(4), 267–272.

Lancaster, C. (1999). In K. T. Henson & B. F. Eller (Eds.), *Educational psychology for effective teaching.* Belmont, CA: Wadsworth.

LeDoux, J. (1996). *The emotional brain: The mysterious underpinnings of emotional life.* New York: Simon & Schuster.

Lewis, C., & Tsuchida, I. (1998). The basics in Japan: The three C's. *Educational Leadership, 55*(6), 32–37.

Lloyd, S. (1999). In K. T. Henson & B. F. Eller (Eds.), *Educational psychology for effective teaching.* Belmont, CA: Wadsworth.

Maddox, H., & Hoole, E. (1975). Performance decrement in the lecture. *Educational Review, 28,* 17–30.

Markle, G., Johnston, J. H., Geer, C., & Meichtry, Y. (1990, November). Teaching for understanding. *Middle School Journal, 22*(2), 53–57.

Marshall, C. (1991, March–April). Teachers' learning styles: How do they affect student learning? *The Clearing House, 64*(4),225–227.

Martinez, M. E. (1998). What is problem solving? *Phi Delta Kappan, 79*(8), 605–609.

Maslow, A. (1973). What is a taoistic teacher? In L. J. Rubin (Ed.), *Facts and feelings in the classroom.* (pp. 149–170). New York: Walker.

Meek, A. (1998). America's teachers: Much to celebrate. *Educational Leadership, 55*(5), 12–16.

Nelson, W. W. (1999). The emperor redux. *Phi Delta Kappan, 80*(5), 387–392.

Obermier. D. (1999). In K. T. Henson & B. F. Eller (Eds.), *Educational psychology for effective teaching.* Belmont, CA: Wadsworth.

Oliva, P. F. (1997). *Developing the curriculum* (4th ed.). New York: HarperCollins.

O'Neal, M., Earley, B., & Snider, M. (1991). Addressing the needs of at-risk students: A local school program that works. In R. C. Morris (Ed.), *Youth at risk,* (pp. 122–125). Lancaster, PA: Technomic Publishing Co.

O'Neil, J. (1998). Why are all the black kids sitting together? *Educational Leadership, 55*(4), 12–17.

Orlich, D. C. (2000). Education reform and limits to student achievement. *Phi Delta Kappan, 81*(6), 468–472.

Perkins, D. (1994). Do students understand understanding? *Education Digest, 59*(5), 21–25.

Purkey, W. W., & Novak, J. M. (1996). *Inviting school success.* Belmont, CA: Wadsworth.

Rathbone, C. H. (1971, September). The open classroom: Underlying premises. *Urban Review, 5*(1): 4–10.

Rubin, L. (1977). Open education: A short critique. In L. Rubin (Ed.), *Curriculum handbook: The disciplines, current moments, and instructional methodology.* Boston: Allyn & Bacon, p. 375.

Scherer, M. (1998). A conversation with Herbert Kohl. *Educational Leadership, 56*(1), 8–13.

Selekman, H. R. (1999). A teacher's class. In K. T. Henson and B. F. Eller (Eds.), *Educational psychology for effective teaching.* Belmont, CA: Wadsworth.

Slavin, R. E. (1989, April). On mastery learning and mastery teaching. *Review of Educational Research, 50,* 77–79.

Special Panel on Education Indicators for the National Center for Education Statistics (1991, September). *Education counts.* Washington, DC: U.S. Department of Education.

Stefanich, G. P. (1990, November). Cycles of cognition. *Middle School Journal, 22*(2), 47–52.

Trump, J. L., & Baynham, D. (1961). *Focus on change: Guide to better schools.* Chicago: Rand McNally.

Wang, M. C., Haertel, G. D., & Walberg, H. J. (1998). Models of reform: A comparative guide. *Educational Leadership, 55*(7), 66–71.

Wolfe, P., & Brandt, R. (1998). What do we know from brain research? *Educational Leadership, 56*(3), 8–13.

Zais, R. S. (1976). *Curriculum: Principles and foundations.* New York: Harper & Row.

6 AIMS, GOALS, AND OBJECTIVES

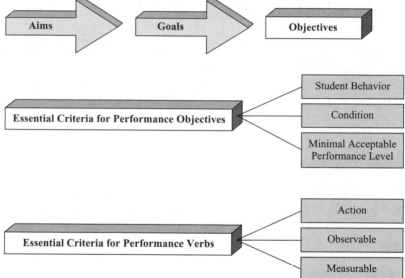

Objectives

This chapter should prepare you to:

- Differentiate among the uses of education aims, goals, and objectives.
- Write an objective for each level of the three domains.
- Explain how objectives fit into the total curriculum.
- List three ways to involve students in curriculum planning.
- Name two basic needs of all limited proficient language students.
- Tell what the teacher can do to use objectives in a positive way to support education reform.
- Draw a model to show your interpretation of constructivism.

THE CASE OF SAN SONA ELEMENTARY SCHOOL

San Sona Elementary School has the reputation of being one of the most innovative, experimental, and advanced schools in its district. The many oil wells in the area make financing one of the least of the principal's worries. The state's education reform program has been pressing all of the schools to increase their students' level of achievement.

When Sondra Bell became principal last year, she promised the board members that, with their support, she would lead the school to even greater heights.

As Sondra planned her annual report, she realized that the board members had lived up to their part of the bargain, but she wondered whether they felt as positive about her. The report was to contain two parts, "In Retrospect" and "In Prospect." Because she thought that the first part was a little weak, Sondra decided to compensate by planning an impressive "In Prospect" section.

She began by spelling out her objectives for the coming year. Could she impress the board by planning everything for the coming year around the performance objectives that she would set for the students? This seemed like a logical approach, so she pulled out a taxonomy of educational objectives from the notes in her curriculum course. For each daily lesson, she wrote an objective at each level of the cognitive domain. But when she began writing objectives for all levels of the affective domain, her task became more difficult. Although she had initially planned to write objectives that represented all levels of all three domains, Sondra gave up in despair long before the task was completed.

Rather than admit failure, Sondra appointed a committee consisting of the department heads and one or two members of each department. She assigned them exactly the same task—to write sample objectives at all levels in all domains for each subject in the entire school curriculum. The faculty was not at all happy with this request. Most teachers were already using objectives in planning their lessons, but they thought this was going too far.

Sondra heard some of the teachers' complaints so often that she almost suspected a conspiracy. Most teachers insisted that the implementation of the education reform practices had already made their workload almost impossible. Sondra supposed they were telling the truth, because a new performance evaluation system required all teachers to develop portfolios for all their students and forbade the use of paper tests. In addition, soon all tests would have to be aligned with the state's 150 new valued outcomes. As Sondra reflected, she realized that, indeed, the new education reform requirements were truly overloading her faculty.

Another complaint that was voiced daily questioned the value of stating everything in terms of objectives. Some teachers speculated that it was just another policy imposed on them from the outside and written by nonteachers who had little or no experience in writing objectives for classroom use. Other teachers said that they thought that trying to write everything in terms of objectives would restrict classroom activities and make lessons seem overstructured or prefabricated. Some said that the use of objectives would lead to totally depersonalized teaching.

As Sondra considered these complaints, she wondered whether there might be a more acceptable way to convince the faculty to use objectives with all lessons.

An Introduction to the Aims, Goals, and Objectives of Curriculum Development

Curriculum developers at all levels share some common roles. Today, as never before, reform programs hold teachers, instructional supervisors, administrators, and curriculum specialists responsible for student achievement. Although most of the reform reports speak of "quality," an amorphous term, former deputy secretary of the U.S. Department of Education David Kearns (1994) says, "Quality is not the ends—it is the means." Siegel and Byrne (1994, p. 2), both officers at the National Alliance of Business, are clear about their perception of the school's role:

> The primary objective of the current education restructuring movement is to improve learning.

Terms such as *performance evaluation, alternative assessment,* and *valued outcomes* reflect the determination of education reformers to hold educators responsible for ensuring that their students are making satisfactory academic progress. Teachers are caught between two very different mandates and are working to make both the trip (education) and the destination (improved test scores) happen. Goodlad (1997, p. 116) describes the fact that this is a common part of being a modern educator, stating, "It is the rare schoolteacher who does not experience several times in a decade being part of an exercise in stating educational goals."

Curriculum alignment, another popular term of the 1990s, is another reminder that educators have the responsibility of ensuring the academic success of their students. Haberman (1992, p. 11) says, "All schools offer four curricula: What's in the textbooks, what the teachers actually teach, what the students learn, and what is included on tests." Curriculum alignment means adjusting the planned curriculum so that the taught curriculum will parallel the tested curriculum (English, 1992) (see Figure 6.1).

Bill Zlatos (1994, pp. 26–27) said that *outcomes-based education* (OBE), which he describes as defining clearly what students are to learn (desired outcomes), measuring their progress in terms of actual achievement, meeting their needs through various teaching strategies, and giving them enough time and help to meet their potential, is the fastest-growing education reform practice of the '90s. Although critics challenge the effectiveness of OBE, Connecticut, the first state to adopt statewide goals, has experienced increases in the percentage of students graduating and the percentage of students going to college as well as higher average reading and math scores. Unfortunately, as discussed elsewhere in this book, the OBE concept evokes resentment among many. Zlatos (p. 28) concludes that, "Up to now, the consensus is that opponents have been winning the skirmishes on OBE."

Ideally, curriculum development should begin by examining the desired outcomes. Such formative assessment will be discussed in Chapter 9. The purpose is simply to know what the curriculum, and hence the instruction that follows, is trying to achieve. Many states are developing new tests that all schools within the state must administer periodically. Obviously, curriculum developers should examine these desired outcomes and design the curriculum accordingly.

Increased accountability requires a cooperative approach to curriculum development. Essex (1992, p. 231) expresses this concept this way: "Subject matter teachers should meet at regular intervals to discuss and plan curriculum and to develop sound strategies designed to achieve quality standards." In an interview, Anderson (see Dagenais, 1994, p. 53) expresses concern for teachers' failure to interact with other teachers:

> I think that the most disabling tradition in America and, in fact, world education is the self-contained classroom. Teachers work by themselves and are insulated from intervention by the four walls of their room and the tradition of being fully in charge.

The statement made earlier, "Ideally, curriculum development should begin by examining the desired outcomes," begins with an important conditional, "ideally." As practitioners very well know, most curriculum development doesn't

FIGURE 6.1

The relationships between aims, goals, and objectives.

occur under ideal conditions. While recognizing the ideal can help one to grasp an understanding of the curriculum development process, most curriculum developers find themselves revising existing curricula, which may be far from ideal. Former Teachers of the Year tell how important collaboration with colleagues is to them. Marilyn Grondel (Henson & Eller, 1999, p. 317) states, "I believe that a successful teacher does not keep ideas and materials secret. A successful teacher becomes more successful by dialoguing with colleagues and sharing ideas and materials." Howard Selekman, former Pennsylvania Teacher of the Year (Henson & Eller, 1999, p. 59) says, "My best teaching occurs when my opportunities to meet, talk, plan, implement, and evaluate with my colleagues are frequent." Teachers must also involve students and parents in reshaping the curriculum. Current reform seems to demand a holistic approach. Siegel and Byrne (1994, p. 2) explain,

> The key relationships in restructuring education are the ones between students and those with whom they interact most closely: their teachers, parents, and peers. Seen in this light, learning is a shared responsibility and is the chief product of these relationships.

Teacher empowerment is another term associated with education reform. Haberman (1992, p. 11) says, "I believe that classrooms, by controlling their teaching behavior, still retain the most powerful influence on students' learning and can serve as curriculum leaders." Teacher empowerment can be further enhanced when teachers increase their involvement in planning the school's curriculum (Clark, Clark, & Irvin, 1997). The extent to which teacher empowerment has increased in recent years is perceived differently by teachers and their principals. Only about 35 percent of teachers responding to two studies said that they have a great deal of influence over their school's curriculum; in contrast, 62 and 75 percent of principals in the same two studies said their teachers had a great deal of influence in shaping their school's curricula (Shen, 1998). Curriculum developers need to differentiate among the aims, goals, and objectives used to express desired outcomes.

Aims

Of the different types of educational expectations, aims are the most general. Educational aims are lifetime aspirations that provide long-term directions for students. Most aims are written for groups rather than individuals. A good example of educational aims is the following "Seven Cardinal Principles of Secondary Education," discussed in Chapter 3:

1. Health
2. Development of moral character
3. Worthy home membership
4. Citizenship

5. Worthy use of leisure time

6. Vocational efficiency

7. Development of the fundamental processes

Like a cross-country road map, aims help us guide our lives in general, desirable directions. They can never be fully attained. For example, one aim might be to design and maintain a curriculum that promotes multiculturalism. Another aim could be to construct and use a curriculum that exhibits constructivist learning theory. Neither of these aims can ever be fully met, because there will always be room for improvement.

Goals

Like aims, education goals are also expectations of groups, and they may take weeks, months, or even years to attain. By definition, goals differ from aims in that goals are attainable, even though many go unattained. A particular high school may have as one of its goals that the mean achievement scores for all classes tested in the next year will equal to or exceed their counterparts' scores on this year's tests. Because goals are group-oriented, the successful attainment of goals does not require every student to succeed.

Because group projects can contribute to students' social growth, which is often one of a school's aims, students should be involved in setting goals. Such involvement can also enhance multicultural goal attainment. Vars (1997, p. 45) insists that student involvement occurs early: "Involving students in goal setting should begin on the very first day of class, as students and teachers get acquainted and share their hopes for the coming year."

An example of a multicultural goal might be to have all students working cooperatively on small group assignments with all their classmates by the end of the first grading period. A constructivist goal might be to have all students by the end of the first week of school write their individual perception of how they learn best, naming at least three conditions that they find supportive.

Objectives

To avoid confusion, this book will use the term *objectives* to refer to what is expected of students daily. We could also call these *performance objectives,* since each objective refers to the ability of students to perform selected tasks in one or more specific ways.

Performance assessment is not always easy. As Vars (1997, p. 46) explains, "Even experts on educational measurement continue to wrestle with how to make performance assessment valid and reliable, not to mention 'honest' and 'fair.'"

Returning to the road map analogy, objectives are like statewide maps in that they chart the course for each day. Many educators have insisted that all worthwhile expectations that schools hold for students should be stated in objectives. The author disagrees and maintains that some of the most valuable services provided by schools, some of the most important effects of schools and teachers, may never be stated in terms of objectives. For example, by definition, objectives must be measurable, but how can you measure the growth of a student's self-concept or appreciation for learning?

Attempts to state all of a school's business in terms of objectives have been made, and they have failed. One teacher education faculty attempted this feat and produced over 2,500 objectives to be met by each student majoring in teacher education. The cause of this problem is not the objectives but rather their misuse. Such findings do not negate the importance of appropriately used objectives.

Objectives clarify the expectations teachers hold for student performance. As Wulf and Schane (1984, p. 117) have said, when objectives are used "there are no unexpected or surprise results since both parties have agreed upon the end product." When students know the expected outcomes, they usually become more involved in their assignments (Unger, 1994). Because performance objectives are the most specific of all expressions of education expectations, they must be written with great precision and in detail. The following sections introduce techniques for writing performance objectives.

Criteria for Writing Performance Objectives

The exact steps that teachers use when writing objectives may vary according to the preferences of their administrators and according to the content being studied. Most authorities appear to agree that all statements of performance objectives must meet at least three criteria, as follows:

1. Objectives must be stated in terms of expected student behavior (not teacher behavior).

2. Objectives must specify the conditions under which the students are expected to perform.

3. Objectives must specify the minimum acceptable level of performance.

Stating objectives in terms of expected student behavior rather than teacher behavior is important because all lessons are developed for students. For each student the success of each lesson depends on appropriate student involvement. For example, rather than saying, "The teacher will teach verb conjugation," the objective would read, "Students will conjugate verbs."

Reform efforts are bringing pressures on educators from many directions. The emphasis is usually on test scores, pressuring teachers to raise the scores of their students. Some educators feel that our nation has gone overboard with accountability and testing. LaBonty and Everts-Danielson (1992, p. 186) state, "We are, in fact, a nation engulfed in testing." Educators must remember that schools exists for students, not educators or even parents. Cole and Schlechty (1992, p. 11) express this concern:

> Students, and the work students are expected to do, should be the focus of all school activity. Schools should, therefore, be organized around the work of students, not around the work of teachers, administrators, or the particular interests of school boards, political factions, or interest groups.

To be more precise, the school exists to change the behavior of students— mentally, physically, socially, emotionally, and even morally. When teachers state all objectives in terms of desired student performance and use specifics that are observable and measurable, they and their students more clearly understand what is expected and the degree to which these expectations are being met. The lists of terms in Table 6.1 shows types of verbs that describe specific, observable, and measurable actions (see the Yes column) and those that are too general and vague to be accurately observed and measured (see the No column).

Because students can grasp only a limited number of major ideas in a period of 45 or 50 minutes, the daily lesson plan for a given period should contain only four or five major ideas. Suppose an English teacher wants to teach composition writing. That teacher could select four or five of the most important ideas about

TABLE 6.1   Performance Objective Terms

Yes (Specific and measurable)	No (vague and not measurable)
Build	Appreciate
Classify	Consider
Contrast	Desire
Demonstrate	Feel
Distinguish	Find interesting
Evaluate	Have insight into
Identify	Know
Interpret	Learn
Label	Like to
List	Love to
Match	Really like to
Measure	Recognize
Name	Remember
Remove	See that
Select	Think
State	Understand
Write	Want to

capturing and holding the reader's attention. These would become the content for the first day's lesson in a unit titled "Composition Writing." Suppose the teacher determines that five ideas are essential to capturing the reader's attention and that, once captured, four ideas are essential to holding it. If so, the teacher could plan one lesson on how to capture the reader's attention and a subsequent lesson on how to hold the reader's attention.

Since objectives should be written in terms of desired student behavior, the emphasis should not be "Today I'll teach" but "As a result of the lesson, each student will. . . ." Teachers should also state the conditions under which the students are expected to perform ("When given a list containing vertebrates and invertebrates, . . ."). Teachers should also state the expected level of performance ("with 80 percent accuracy" or "without error"), and they should avoid using verbs that cannot be observed or measured, such as *appreciate, learn, know,* and *understand* (see Table 6.1). Such general verbs should be replaced with specific, action-oriented verbs such as *identify, list, explain, name, describe,* and *compare.*

Performance Objectives in the Three Domains

Some education aims and goals deal with thinking (for example, command of the fundamental processes), others involve attitudes (for example, development of moral character), and still others focus on physical skills (for example, competency in art, music, and sports). Many educators say that teachers should write performance objectives in each of these domains (cognitive, affective, and psychomotor) for each class. Although this may not always be practical or sensible, perhaps you will agree that teachers should be able to do this and should also be able to write objectives at varying levels of difficulty in each domain.

Writing Objectives in the Cognitive Domain

The first real systematic approach to helping teachers write objectives at specified levels came in 1956, when Benjamin S. Bloom and a group of students at the University of Chicago developed a taxonomy of educational objectives in the cognitive domain that included the following six levels (Bloom, 1956):

Level 1: Knowledge

Level 2: Comprehension

Level 3: Application

Level 4: Analysis

Level 5: Synthesis

Level 6: Evaluation

Involving students in tasks that require them to operate at these different levels requires the ability to write objectives for each level.

Level 1: Knowledge

Mastery of facts and concepts is a prerequisite for performing higher mental operations. For example, many mathematics problems require students to multiply. Learning the multiplication tables can probably best be done by simple rote memorization. Objectives that focus on memorization are the easiest to write. Unfortunately, many lessons fail to go beyond this most elementary level. Some assignments or tasks at the knowledge level are essential, but they should not dominate the curriculum.

An example of an objective written at the knowledge level would be: "When given a list of adjectives, verbs, and adverbs, the student will correctly identify 8 of the 10 adverbs and 8 of the 10 adjectives." This objective begins with a statement of the conditions under which students are expected to perform the task ("When given. . . ."), and it is written in terms of desired student performance ("the student will. . . ."). In addition, the objective contains an action-oriented verb that can be observed and measured ("identify"), and it ends with a statement of the minimum acceptable level of performance ("8 of the 10").

Level 2: Comprehension

Comprehension-level objectives are more demanding than are knowledge-level objectives. Comprehension objectives require students to do more than memorize; they require students to translate, interpret, or predict a continuation of trends (Bloom, 1956).

Today many teachers are teaming with teachers of other disciplines. A history teacher who wants students to know the differences between simple and compound sentences may set the following objective: "When given a paragraph containing compound sentences and simple sentences, the student will correctly underscore the simple sentences using a single line and underscore the compound sentences using double lines."

You should also tell your students the level of performance you are willing to accept. Must it be 100 percent? Is 90 percent acceptable? 80 percent?

Since the comprehension level requires students to translate, interpret, and predict, student activities that require the use of charts, maps, graphs, and tables are useful when writing objectives at the comprehension level.

Level 3: Application

Principles (or content generalizations) are at the center of application-level objectives. These objectives require students to use principles or generalizations to solve a concrete problem. For example, an art teacher might write the following objective for painting students: "Given the definition of the golden triangle, the student will use the golden triangle to assess the balance of colors or shapes used in a picture." Or an English teacher might write the following objective: "Given the beats and measures in iambic pentameter, the student will write a five-verse poem in iambic pentameter without missing more than one beat per verse."

A professor at St. John's University who teaches a writing for publication class to doctoral students requires each student to prepare an article for one journal and then rewrite it to make it suitable for another journal. This is an excellent example of the use of an application-level objective.

Level 4: Analysis

Analysis-level objectives also require students to work with principles, concepts, and broad generalizations. In this case, students are required to break down the concepts and principles in order to better understand them, and to do this they must understand not only the content but also its structural form.

For example, a government teacher might write the following objective for a class that is studying how a bill becomes a law: "Given a particular law, students will trace its development from the time it was first introduced as a bill, listing every major step without missing any." A teacher of auto mechanics might write the following objective for a group of students who have been studying the electrical system in an automobile: "Starting with the positive battery terminal, the student will trace the electric current throughout the automobile until it returns to the negative battery terminal, stating what happens in the coil, alternator, distributor, and condenser without getting more than one of these steps out of sequence." A biology teacher might ask students to trace the human circulatory system in a similar manner.

Level 5: Synthesis

Unlike analysis objectives, which require students to take principles apart, synthesis requires students to take several parts of something and put them together to make a whole. Synthesis-level objectives are more demanding because they require students to form a new whole, requiring students to think in new ways and to be creative. For example, a science teacher might require students to design a toy machine that could climb a set of stairs. Because of their divergent and creative nature, synthesis-level questions are difficult to write. Generally, practice is a prerequisite to competence in writing objectives at this level.

At the beginning of Chapter 4, a quote by John Wright expressed his concern over what he perceived as shallow teachers using shallow lessons that produce shallow learning. The need for teachers to be able to write higher-level objectives is great. Without such objectives, classroom thinking will remain dominated by rote memorizing. Stefanich (1990, p. 49) warns:

Higher-level thinking cannot be demanded. We must learn it through nurturing a series of successfully more advanced learning tasks until the student reaches the desired level of performance.

Level 6: Evaluation

The evaluation level is the highest level in Bloom's cognitive domain. Evaluation-level objectives require students to make judgments based on definite criteria, not just opinions. Evaluation-level objectives contain various combinations of elements of the first five levels of objective types.

A speech teacher might use the following objective with students who are studying diplomatic and persuasive techniques: "While viewing a video recording of a public figure's two most recent public addresses, each student will rate the speeches in terms of tact and persuasion, pinpointing in each address at least three areas of strength and three areas of weakness." Or a physical education instructor who is teaching bowling may want to write an objective that involves evaluating a participant's starting position, delivery, and follow-through.

The ability to write objectives at each cognitive level is crucial, since this is the only way to be sure that students will learn to develop intellectual skills at each level. Because this is the most important work a teacher does to effect learning, teachers must be able to state objectives clearly.

Not all educators agree that such distinct steps parallel the actual development of youths. One skeptic is Donald Orlich (1991, p. 160), who says,

> For over a quarter of a century, I have assumed and taught my students that the four upper levels of the taxonomy had to be taught in a sequence. But the more that I observed young students in hands-on classes . . . the less support I found for the linear assumption. . . . I can no longer assume a linear connection to the four upper levels of the cognitive taxonomy. Nor can I support the idea of hierarchical arrangement of the entire model!

Orlich uses the following quote from John Goodlad's 1984 study, *A Place Called School* (p. 236), to say that other educators also have concerns over the levels of objectives that are represented in high school curricula:

> Only rarely did we find evidence to suggest instruction [in reading and math] likely to go much beyond merely possession of information to a level of understanding its implications and either applying it or exploring its possible applications. Nor did we see activities likely to arouse students' curiosity or to involve them in seeking a solution to some problem not already laid bare by teachers or textbook. . . . And it appears that this preoccupation with the lower intellectual processes pervades social studies and science as well. An analysis of topics studied and materials used gives not an impression of students studying human adaptations and exploration, but of facts to be learned.

Others criticize the use of goals and objectives because of a concept called "goal displacement." Faidley and Musser (1991, p. 24) explain this criticism:

It is a commonly known and widely studied phenomenon in organizations that when people are given a specific objective, they will often reach that objective at the expense of the overall purpose (that) that objective was established to attain.

If students are to reach the upper levels of the taxonomy it will be the result of purposeful planning by the teacher, yet teachers often hold expectations that are beyond students' levels of development. As you already know, success is more likely to come when the entire school and community are involved early and often. The following case study by Thompson and Fillion outlines a strategy used by an inner-city elementary school to elicit the cooperation of various members of the school and community.

Case Study

Developing Aims, Goals, and Objectives for an Afrocentric Elementary School

Dr. Johnnie Thompson
Wichita State University

Dr. Bryant Fillion
Wichita State University

Background Information

This case study describes the transition of a respected inner-city traditional elementary school into a highly successful Afrocentric theme school that has received citywide and national recognition for excellence in student academic achievement and community collaboration. It demonstrates the efficacy and power of widely shared and clearly articulated affective aims and goals to enlist the active support and involvement of parents and the community in curriculum development and school reform. It also illustrates the problems of inner-city schools attempting to design culturally relevant curricula for minority student populations.

In this case study, the school is given the fictitious name "Basie," but all information is factually accurate, drawn from a study of one actual inner-city school in a major Midwestern city school district.

In 1988, Basie elementary school (grades K–5) was one of a diminishing number of inner-city "traditional" elementary schools in a system that was moving toward establishing magnet schools in an attempt to attract students from majority ethnic/racial groups. The school system was comprised of 80 percent "single race minority" schools. The city's school population was approximately 70 percent African American.

During the 1988–89 school year, Basie responded to district encouragement to establish a clear focus and requested approval to become an Afrocentric magnet

(Continued)

school. The district administration discouraged this request, stating that such a focus would be unlikely to attract members of other ethnic groups. However, with strong leadership from the school principal and staff and support from the African American community, in September 1992 the school received approval to become the city's first Afrocentric "theme school."

Since then, the school has helped students improve their test scores and gained enthusiastic support from parents, the neighborhood, and the African American community. The school was cited favorably in a 1994 *Newsweek* article and recognized in 1995 as a U.S. Department of Education "Certificate of Merit Award Winner." In 1996, owing partly to the school's success, a middle school, a high school, and a second elementary school in the city were designated as Afrocentric theme schools.

The Community

Basie is located in a neighborhood that is 99 percent African American, as are approximately 98 percent of its students, drawn from various areas around the city. It became a full Chapter 1 school in 1992. The faculty at Basie school is 60 percent minority and 40 percent nonminority, which conforms to federal guidelines regarding staffing.

The School

Even before its designation as a theme school, Basie had an established record of academic achievement and enjoyed a reputation in the community as an excellent school. Iowa Test of Basic Skills (ITBS) scores for the school were at or above national norms in reading, language, and mathematics. The school always had a waiting list of students far in excess of the 330 spaces available.

Following the mandate to develop an Afrocentric theme school, the school staff, with strong community support and involvement, confronted the task of designing and organizing the school's curriculum, of translating aims, goals, and objectives into school and classroom realities. The traditional elementary school organization by grade levels and individual classrooms was maintained, as was the emphasis on core curriculum support for academic achievement in reading, language, and math.

Committees and working groups were strongly encouraged to use a wide range of information and resources related to Afrocentric themes and the reform of inner-city schools. They were also influenced by the concept of SETCLAE (self-esteem through culture leads to academic excellence), which maintains that for African American students the Afrocentric emphasis will improve students' academic performance and competence, as well as promoting the values, attitudes, and behaviors most highly valued by the larger society.

Student attitudes and behavior are a central and specific concern of Basie's curriculum and the instructional program. The creation of an exciting, motivating, and emotionally safe school environment has been a primary focus of program development. Student pride, confidence, self-management, positive behavior, self-discipline, and community awareness are directly and systematically addressed

(Continued)

throughout the program. The SETCLAE materials are used to promote students' positive applications of the cultural heritage they are studying.

Parents and leaders from the African American community joined the Basie staff in a task force to promote acceptance of the Afrocentric concept by the district's administration and to develop a school improvement plan that focused on (1) students' academic and social development; (2) African-centered values and interactive/cooperative learning methods; (3) staff development; (4) community involvement of parents and elders, and the provision of community services; (5) school management that involved the total staff along with parents and community members; and (6) evaluation that used African-centered perspectives and methods.

Following African educational concepts, the school was seen as an integral part of the community, a "village school of learning," rather than just a school coexisting in the community. The school's systematic involvement of parents and community was developed to give practical expression to the concept that "It takes an entire village to raise a child." This approach was consistent with other community involvement initiatives in the United States, such as the James Comer School Development Approach for use in low-income communities.

Afrocentric subject matter was not entirely new to most elementary teachers, who had been teaching elements of such a curriculum every February, as part of Black History Month. Afrocentric materials such as those developed in the Portland, Oregon, schools had become increasingly familiar to inner-city teachers. Distinctly African components of the revised Basie program included the study of particular African countries and history, the use of terms from Kiswahili, a pan-African language, and some instruction in Kiswahili. African stories, songs, poems, and proverbs were introduced in schoolwide and classroom meetings (termed *Harambee,* which is Kiswahili for "coming together") and used throughout the curriculum. The extensive use of oral language and oral traditions in Harambee was based on African educational practices, as was the extensive use and encouragement of artistic expression. The school adopted a "value system restructuring" approach based on the systematic introduction and use of the seven African principles of Nguso Saba (unity, self-determination, collective work and responsibility, cooperative economics, purpose, creativity, and faith).

In an ongoing attempt to monitor and assess progress, teachers and committees generated, considered, and reported data on student achievement and behavior, as well as on staff, parent, and community involvement in the school. Student test results from district and state assessments were consistently monitored.

Basie school continues to meet the directives of the school district and maintain its academic standing in test scores. Students' high achievement on the district and state examinations offers strong support for the community and staff contention that the infusion of new or distinctive material into the school program has not diminished students' achievement of academic skills or displaced subject matter knowledge expected from all students in the state and district. Basie students' behavior, attitudes, and academic performance appear to support the belief that African American studies do not denigrate the culture of others.

In its initial four years using an Afrocentric theme, the school has also been cited for students' exemplary behavior. Visitors to the school invariably remark

(Continued)

on the courtesy, discipline, and enthusiasm of the students, and the ease and confidence with which they converse with adults. A report from the district's evaluation office during the 1993–94 school year said, "Student behavior is a hallmark of this school . . . While children still squirmed and fidgeted in the chairs, students were never seen disrupting their class or acting out in the hallway."

Today, every Basie student and staff member can quote and explain the school motto: "On time, on task, on a mission." The mission statement, also known to the staff and most students, says "[Basie] School aspires to be a national model of academic excellence in school reform, educating the whole child through culturally appropriate programs and instructional methods based on the highest African-centered perspectives and values to develop a strong sense of self-worth, appreciation for others, social responsibility, health, and leadership in an atmosphere of high expectations designed to teach the child how to learn, how to apply knowledge to real life situations, and to develop a desire to make learning a way of life."

Parents, "community elders," and volunteer mentors are actively involved in Basie's school advisory council. Weekly progress reports and monthly newsletters are sent to parents. The school building is open from 7:30 A.M. until 10:00 P.M. daily as well as for Saturday school programs and for an extended summer school. It is also a Center for Learning and Neighborhood Services, including child care, a school-based health center, various social services, and a cooperative produce market.

The Principal and Educational Leaders

In 1988, and throughout the school's transition to an Afrocentric school, Basie had as its principal a dynamic, charismatic, and knowledgeable instructional leader with an unquestioned devotion to the school's students and their families. She had lived in Africa for two years during her service in the Peace Corps and believed firmly that effective schools must be integral parts of the communities they serve. She has been highly effective in enlisting parent and community support.

The principal's personal commitment of her time and energy was an inspiration to parents, students, and most teachers. However, as the new school program expanded to include systematic after-school tutoring, evening programs, a "Saturday Academy," an extensive summer school program, and community outreach activities, teachers' schedules extended well beyond the traditional school day. Some teachers were unable or unwilling to make these additional investments of time and energy.

The principal's leadership style included extensive use of faculty and community involvement on committees and working groups for program and staff development.

Clearly, Basie's Afrocentric curriculum neither begins nor ends at the door of the school. For those who maintain that a school's concern is, or ought to be, exclusively academic, or competitive, or culturally neutral, the Basie program raises important and difficult issues.

(Continued)

Issues for Further Reflection and Application

1. How might a school's faculty and administration resolve an apparent conflict between larger social goals (such as school integration) and the needs and interests of the students and their community? (*Hint:* Could the curriculum be made more relevant to the particular students actually being served?)

2. Should a public school program ever be targeted exclusively to the needs and interests of any one racial/ethnic group?

3. How might a school's curriculum promote students' ethnic/racial awareness and pride without denigrating other cultures and groups?

4. Do you agree with the SETCLAE contention that self-esteem through culture leads to academic excellence?

5. As a program expands beyond the traditional school day, how can administrators balance the needs of the students and program against the needs and expectations of teachers?

6. To what extent should student attitudes, behavior, and values be directly addressed by the school's curriculum? How might the program achieve a balance between these concerns and the need for academic achievement?

7. How might a school's generation and use of data be used to support and improve its program?

8. What outside community factors should be used to determine a school's curriculum?

Suggested Readings

Comer, J. P. (1980). *School power: Implications of an intervention project*. New York: Free Press.

Kunjufu, J., & Prescott, F. M. (1989). *SETCLAE*. Chicago, IL: African American Images.

Levine, D., & Eubanks, E. (1990). Desegregation and regional magnetization. In T. Estes, R. Levine, & G. Waldrip (Eds.), *Magnet schools: Recent developments and perspectives*. Austin, Texas: Morgan Printing and Publishing, pp. 48–58.

Portland Public Schools. (1987). *African American baseline essays*. Portland, OR: Multnomah School District 1J.

Traub, J. (1991). Ghetto blasters: The case for all-black schools. *The New Republic, 204,* 21–23.

As we saw in this case study, the intent of the faculty at Basie School was to reshape its curriculum to increase student pride, self-confidence, and self-management, a prominent goal of multiculturalism classrooms. We also were told that this faculty had received a mandate to develop an Afrocentric theme and, even prior to the mandate, had begun to redesign and improve its already effective curriculum. Do you think the fact that the faculty was already committed to this goal influenced its success?

Throughout recent years, Basie's students have been repeatedly cited for their exemplary behavior. The recent reform program at Basie reaches far into the community. Can you think of a way to link these two seemingly unrelated characteristics in a way that will enhance the program's success? Could the school's excellent reputation be used to motivate community members to get involved? People want to be associated with success; it is a good reflection on them. What can you say about the principal's philosophy of community involvement with schools?

Writing Objectives in the Affective Domain

As addressed in Chapter 3, teachers have no choice but to affect students' values, and teachers are responsible for teaching certain values such as honesty and citizenship. An important role of the school and the teacher in the realm of values is to help students become aware of their own values, to question these values, and to discover the basis for those values, be they factual and logical, or prejudiced and illogical.

Krathwohl and coworkers developed a system known as the affective domain to categorize values. The outcome was the following hierarchy of objectives in the affective domain (Krathwohl et al., 1964):

Level 1: Receiving

Level 2: Responding

Level 3: Valuing

Level 4: Organizing

Level 5: Characterizing

Level 1: Receiving

Receiving refers to students' awareness of new information or experiences. Students receive information in varying degrees. In a single class, some may not receive the information at all, while others attend or receive at a low level of awareness, and still others are very selective, paying attention only to the things that are most meaningful to them. Of course, students can be encouraged and taught to develop their attention skills.

Level 2: Responding

At the *responding* level, the student reacts to whatever has attracted his or her attention. This requires physical, active behavior. Some responses may be overt or purposeful behaviors, as contrasted to the simple, automatic responses. A student who becomes involved at the responding level might, at the teacher's instruction or even voluntarily, go to the library and research the issue further, or the student may choose to obey the rules set forth in the class.

Level 3: Valuing

A *value* is demonstrated when someone prizes a behavior enough to be willing to perform it even in the face of alternatives. A value is not necessarily reflected when a person reacts without having had time to think. In other words, if people really value a behavior they are likely to perform it repeatedly regardless of the results it may bring (Simon, Howe, & Kirschenbaum, 1972).

For example, a mathematics teacher whose students are learning to use simulation games might write the following valuing objective: "When given free time next week at the end of each period to read, play simulation games, talk to friends, or sleep, each student will choose to play simulation games at least two out of the five days." Note that the objective asks students to choose a certain behavior individually of their own free will and to repeat that choice. Also notice that there are other alternatives from which to choose.

Level 4: Organizing

The *organization* level of behavior requires individuals to bring together different values to build a value system. Whenever there is conflict between two or more of their values, they must resolve the conflict. For example, elementary through high school students constantly encounter conflicting expectations of friends and parents. As students mature, their behavior should be influenced less by the expectations of the people they are with at the moment; they should learn to combine the two different sets of values with their own existing beliefs and knowledge about themselves. They will respond to the orderly composite of the combined values, developing their own value systems. At this level students may change their behavior or defend it. For example, a teacher might assign students to defend opposing positions on a controversial issue. By defending both sides, each student will, in effect, compare the two points of view and may even devise a compromise between the two extremes.

A teacher of a class in U.S. government might introduce a hypothetical bill and have students form two teams, one composed of those who favor the bill and one team composed of those who oppose it. The objective might read: "After having had the opportunity to support the bill, and the opportunity to try to defeat it, the students will consider all the information and write a statement that expresses their feelings for and against the bill. Given the opportunity, the students will choose to modify the bill to make it reflect their own value systems."

Level 5: Characterizing

At the *characterization* level, students have already developed their own value systems. Their consistent behavior is predictable. At this level, students also demonstrate a degree of individuality and self-reliance.

An example of an objective written at the characterization level is: "Each student will bring one newspaper article or news report to class and explain at least two ways in which the article caused the student to change his or her mind from a previously held position on a controversial issue." Does this objective prove that the student has really changed values? What if the student just says that the change has occurred? At the moment the student may believe this, but what about a week from now or a year from now? This objective could be rewritten so that this doubt would be removed or reduced, should the teacher wish to do so.

Writing Objectives in the Psychomotor Domain

The psychomotor domain involves the development of physical skills that require coordination of mind and body. This domain has always been especially relevant to such courses as physical education, art, drama, music, and vocational courses; the current emphasis on interdisciplinary, integrated curricula and performance evaluation makes the psychomotor domain particularly relevant.

Although this domain was the last to have a taxonomy developed for it, at least two scales have now been developed. The following taxonomy is based on a scale developed by E. J. Simpson (1972):

Level 1: Perception

Level 2: Set

Level 3: Guided response

Level 4: Mechanism

Level 5: Complex overt response

Level 6: Adaptation

Level 7: Origination

Level 1: Perception

Purposeful motor activity begins in the brain, where phenomena received act as guides to motor activity. The performer must first become aware of a stimulus, pick up on cues for action, and then act upon these cues. For example, a writer discovers that she is separating her subjects and verbs with too much descriptive material, thus diluting the impact of her themes. Or a baseball batter notices himself flinching and taking short steps away from the plate when striking, causing him to miss the ball. A piano student may learn that he is failing to maintain a steady tempo when playing quietly.

A sample objective at the perception level would be: "Following a demonstration, a geometry student who has been confusing the x and y axes in plotting graphs will notice that the x axis always runs horizontally and the y axis always runs vertically."

Level 2: Set

In the psychomotor domain, *set* refers to an individual's readiness to act. It includes both mental readiness and physical and emotional readiness. For example, a high-diver is always seen pausing before a dive to get a psychological, emotional, and physical set. Emotionally she must feel confident about her ability to make a safe and accurate dive. Although she may have performed the same dive hundreds of times, she still takes the time to think through the sequence of steps before each dive. Physically, she must ready her muscles in order to respond quickly and accurately. On a less dramatic scale, a student preparing to take notes or do a writing assignment may be seen flexing his fingers or rubbing his eyes—in short, getting set to perform at his best.

An example of a psychomotor objective at this level for piano students is: "Upon the signal 'ready,' each student will assume proper posture and place all fingers in the correct keyboard position." Is there a minimum level of performance specified in this objective?

Level 3: Guided Response

Once the students perceive the need to act and ready themselves to act, they may find that whenever the act involves complex skills they will need guidance through their first few responses. For example, students in the photography club may need oral guidance as they process their first negatives.

An example of an objective to enhance the development of these skills would be: "When given step-by-step directions in the darkroom, each student will open the film cylinder, remove the film, and, without touching the surface of the film, wind the film on a spool so that the surface of each round does not touch previous rounds."

Level 4: Mechanism

This level involves performing an act somewhat automatically without having to pause to think through each separate step. For example, the photography teacher might want students eventually to be able to perform the entire sequence of development operations while simultaneously counting the number of seconds required to wait following each step. Or a chemistry teacher might write the following objective at the mechanism level: "Given a series of compounds to analyze, the student will operate the electron microscope without having to pause even once to think about the sequence involved in mounting the slide, focusing the projector, and changing the lens size."

Level 5: Complex Overt Response

The level of complex overt response is an extension of the previous level, but it involves more complicated tasks. For example, a driver education teacher may write an objective at this level such as: "When given an unexpected and abrupt command to stop, the student will immediately respond by checking in the rear-view mirror, applying the correct amount of pressure to the brakes, giving the correct signal, and gradually pulling off the road."

Level 6: Adaptation

At this level the student is required to adjust performance as different situations dictate. For example, to allow for an icy surface the driver would adjust her brake pressure and steer into a skid if needed. Or a cook would adjust the cooking time when going from an electric stove to a gas stove. A boxer would alter his style to adjust for a left-handed opponent.

An example of a psychomotor objective at the adaptation level is: "When dancing the tango, the student will insert the fan at three appropriate places."

Level 7: Origination

At the origination level, the highest level of the psychomotor domain, the student creates new movement patterns to fit the particular situation. For example, the cook adds his own touch of genius, and the pianist alters her style or the music itself.

An art teacher might write the following objective: "Given a mixture of powders and compounds of varying textures, the student will use these to accentuate the feeling he is trying to communicate in an oil painting."

As seen in this chapter, clearly worded objectives are essential in all classes to clarify teacher expectations.

Chapter Summary

Throughout the country, education reform efforts have increased the level of accountability of teachers, administrators, and other curriculum developers, making them responsible for the academic success of their students. By learning to write aims, goals, and objectives, educators can improve the level at which they support the reform efforts in their state.

The production of aims, goals, and objectives also supports the constructivist approach to education because by nature constructivism is criterion referenced. Writing aims, goals, and objectives also serves other education reform goals, including curriculum alignment, cooperative learning, and restructuring. Many education reform movements focus on empowering teachers to become more involved in the total school activities. Expertise in writing aims empowers teachers to become involved at a higher level in setting their school's mission.

Constructivist teachers consider objectives to be essential if teachers are to succeed in carrying the more theoretical aims and goals to their practical attainment. Objectives should always be expressed in terms of individual student performance, and they should always specify the conditions under which the student must perform and the minimal acceptable level of performance. Objectives should use only verbs that are observable and measurable.

Not everyone supports the use of objectives. Critics believe that some of the most important functions of schools cannot be expressed in terms of objectives. Some critics say that setting objectives lowers students' levels of aspirations. Still other critics question the traditionally held belief that the levels of the taxonomies must be taught in sequence.

Expectations must not be considered only as expectations others hold for us. Rather, these aims, goals, and objectives are powerful tools that we can use to help all students overcome adversity and succeed academically and socially, tools we can use to meet the multicultural and constuctivist goals endorsed by this text.

Learning Questions

1. What implications does education reformers' increased emphasis on academic accountability have for teachers' competence in writing aims and goals?

2. If education aims can never be reached, then why are they needed?

3. How can tests be used to raise students' levels of thinking?

4. Why should and how can teachers involve students in planning?

5. Do you believe that educators have gone too far in using objectives? If so, what are some effective teacher responses to the requirement that every class have objectives?

6. Why should teachers include affective and psychomotor objectives in their curricula?

Suggested Activities

1. Select an education film, videotape, or book and write one aim, two goals, and five objectives for the lesson accompanying this medium.

2. What one thing would you most like to change in the world? Write one objective in each of the domains that will help make this change.

3. Check the personal philosophy statement you wrote while studying Chapter 3, or write a statement of your beliefs about the main purpose of schools. Based on this statement, write one affective goal. Next, write at least two affective objectives to help your student reach this goal.

4. Make a list of observable, measurable verbs to use when writing objectives.

5. Examine the example psychomotor objective at the end of the section entitled "Level 2: Set." Can you rewrite this objective to assess behavior in a more meaningful way? Taking a moment to think about this objective, list two ways you could establish minimum levels of performance. Does either of your objectives explain what is meant by "correct posture" or "correct keyboard position"? Do both of your suggested changes help make the act measurable?

6. Suppose you are teaching the circulatory system to a biology class. See if you can write an objective that will measure whether students understand the sequence in which the blood travels throughout the body. (*Hint:* You may want to designate one of the heart's chambers as a beginning point.) Check your objective to see whether it includes the three designated criteria: Is it written in terms of expected student performance? If so, underscore the part of the objective that identifies both the performer and the performance. Does the verb you used express action? Can it be observed or measured? Does your statement of conditions accurately describe the conditions under which you expect the student to perform? Circle it. Did you begin the objective with a statement such as "Given. . . ." or "When given. . . ."? (This is an easy way to be sure you have included a statement of conditions in each objective.) Is your statement very general, such as "When given a test" or "Following a lesson"? Can you make it more specific? Can you think of a way to alter the tack, making it easier to perform, simply by changing the conditions? Finally, examine your objective to see whether it includes a statement of the minimum acceptable level of performance. Draw a box around this statement. Does it tell the student exactly how accurately the task must be performed before it will be acceptable? Does it contain a percentage or fraction, such as "with 80 percent accuracy" or "four out of five times"? Can you think of other ways to express your concept of the minimum acceptable level of performance without using percentages or fractions?

   By now you probably would like to start over and rewrite your original objective, improving each part. Do so. Then examine your evaluation-level objective. Does it require that the judgment be based on supportive data or on internal or external standards?

7. Because of the lack of emphasis on concepts and the lack of opportunities to develop concepts, principles, and other content generalizations in school work, American students often fall short in their ability to grasp the structure of the disciplines. Suppose you are an art teacher. In your class, you have studied such concepts as cubism (using cubes to form objects) and pointillism (using points to form

shapes). Can you write an objective at the synthesis level? (*Hint:* You might begin by identifying a particular effect, feeling, or mood that you would like your students to achieve through the use of cubism and pointillism.) One example of such an objective might be as follows: "While looking at examples of cubism in Picasso's paintings and at pointillism in some of Renoir's paintings, the student will combine these two techniques (adding a personal technique if desired) to express at least three of the following feelings: happiness, surprise, sadness, anger, love." At the synthesis level, the objective should provide enough structure to make the assignment meaningful and yet allow students enough freedom to put themselves into the work.

8. Write a multicultural aim and then write three or four goals to help students pursue that aim.

9. Make a list of verbs that describe constructivist behaviors.

10. Explain the relationship between outcome-based education and education reform.

Works Cited and Suggested Readings

Bloom, B. S. (1956). *Taxonomy of educational objectives. The classification of educational goals, Handbook I. Cognitive domain.* New York: McKay.

Bushman, J. H. (1991). Reshaping the secondary curriculum. *The Clearing House, 65*(2), 83–85.

Clark, S. N., Clark, D. C., & Irvin, J. I. (1997). Collaborative decision making. *Middle School Journal, 28*(5), 54–56.

Cole, R. W., & Schlechty, D. C. (1992). Teachers as trailblazers in restructuring. *The Education Digest, 58*(6), 8–12.

Dagenais, R. J. (1994). Professional development of teachers and administrators: Yesterday, today, and tomorrow/The views of Robert H. Anderson. *Kappa Delta Pi Record, 30*(2), 50–54.

English, F. (1992). *Curriculum alignment.* An Eastern Kentucky University/Phi Delta Kappa Conference. Richmond, KY.

Essex, N. L. (1992). Educational malpractice: The price of professionalism. *The Clearing House, 65*(4), 229–232.

Faidley, R., & Musser, S. (1991). National educational standards: The complex challenge for educational leaders. *NASSP Bulletin, 75*(537), 23–27.

Fillion, B. (1998). Breaking the bonds of dependency. *Educational Leadership, 55*(7), 6–10.

Gay, G. (1980). Conceptual models of the curriculum planning process. In A. W. Foshay (Ed.), *Curriculum improvement.* Alexander, VA: Association for Supervision and Curriculum Development, p. 120.

Goodlad, J. I. (1984). *A place called school.* New York: McGraw-Hill.

Goodlad, J. I. (1997). *In praise of education.* New York: Teachers College Press.

Haberman, M. (1992). The role of the classroom teacher as curriculum leader. *NASSP Bulletin, 76*(547), 11–19.

Henson, K. T. (1976). Behavioral objectives: Over light. *Contemporary Education, 47,* 250.

Henson, K. T., & Eller, B. F. (1999). *Educational psychology for effective teaching.* Belmont, CA: Wadsworth.

Kearns, D. T. (1994). Foreword to Siegel, P., & Byrne, S. *Using quality to design school systems.* San Francisco: Jossey-Bass.

Krathwohl, D. R., Bloom, B. S., & Masia, B. B. (1964). *Taxonomy of educational objectives: The classification of educational goals. Handbook II: The affective domain.* New York: McKay.

LaBonty, J., & Everts-Danielson, K. (1992). Alternative assessment feedback techniques in methods courses. *The Clearing House, 65*(3), 186–190.

Orlich, D. (1991). A new analogue for the cognitive taxonomy. *The Clearing House, 64*(3), 159–161.

O'Neil, J. D. (1997). Building schools as communities: A conversation with James Conner. *Educational Leadership, 54*(8), 6–10.

Ornstein, A. C. (1992). Essay tests: Use in development and grading. *The Clearing House, 65*(3), 175–178.

Scherer, M. (1998). A conversation with Herbert Kohl. *Educational Leadership, 56*(1), 8–13.

Shen, J. (1998). Do teachers feel empowered? *Educational Leadership, 55*(7), 35–36.

Siegel, P., & Byrne, S. (1994). *Using quality to design school systems.* San Francisco: Jossey-Bass.

Simon, S., Howe, L. W., & Kirschenbaum, H. (1972). *Values clarification.* New York: Hart.

Simpson, E. J. (1972). The classification of educational objectives in the psychomotor domain. In *The psychomotor domain,* Vol. 3. Washington, DC: Gryphon House.

Stefanich, G. P. (1990). Cycles of cognition. *Middle School Journal, 22*(2), 47–52.

Unger, C. (1994). What teaching for understanding looks like. *Educational Leadership, 51*(5), 8–10.

Vars, G. F. (1997). Student concerns and standards too. *Middle School Journal, 28*(4), 44–49.

Wulf, K. M., & Schane, B. (1984). *Curriculum design.* Glenview, IL: Scott, Foresman.

Zlatos, B. (1994). Outcomes-based outrage runs both ways. *Education Digest, 59*(5), 26–29.

7 SELECTING CONTENT AND ACTIVITIES

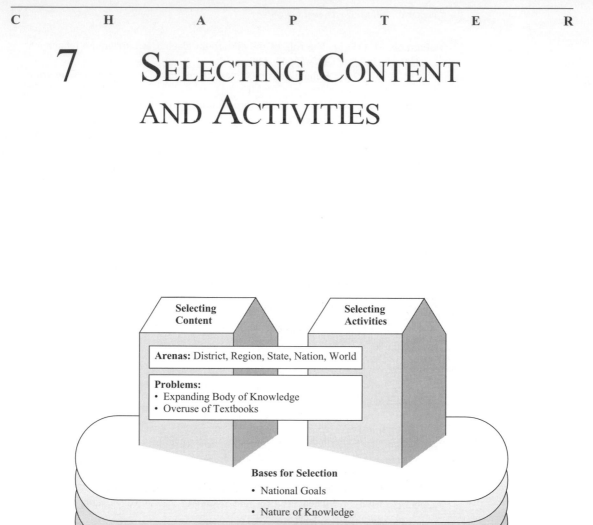

Selecting Content

Selecting Activities

Arenas: District, Region, State, Nation, World

Problems:
• Expanding Body of Knowledge
• Overuse of Textbooks

Bases for Selection
• National Goals
• Nature of Knowledge
• Society's Needs
• Student Needs
• Human Development
• Education Reform Goals

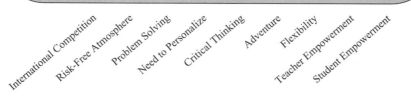

International Competition · Risk-Free Atmosphere · Problem Solving · Need to Personalize · Critical Thinking · Adventure · Flexibility · Teacher Empowerment · Student Empowerment

Objectives

This chapter should prepare you to:

• . Develop a multipurpose activity to achieve two objectives that you consider important.

• Justify the sacrifice of content and class time used for problem solving.

• As a curricularist, defend education reform's goal to empower teachers.

• Give two reasons for including problems when selecting curriculum content and activities.

• Defend the inclusion of multicultural content in the curriculum.

• React to the statement "In selecting content, more is less."

• Develop a table of specifications to achieve a goal that you consider important for one of your courses.

THE CASE OF BUILDING BRIDGES TO REFORM[1]

Wednesday is a special day at Model Laboratory School in Richmond, Kentucky. Walk the halls, and you will see a bustle of educational activity, indicating that something exciting is going on. A group of students sits on the floor in a classroom working on a weather map that shows lows, highs, and fronts. But upon closer inspection you will realize that all the words on the map are in Spanish and that this is a Spanish class for young children. In the cafeteria, students are participating in a simulation that challenges them to consider the relationships between power and authority in a democratic society. In one of the school's three computer labs, other students are learning the intricacies of the WordPerfect word processing program. In the chemistry classroom, teachers, playing the roles of pharmacists, clerks, and sales representatives in a simulation, are questioned by students using forensic chemistry to sort out facts in a "murder case." The two school administrators, the librarian, the gifted coordinator, and the two counselors are teaching today. A local college dean and a mystery writer from the college's English department are team-teaching a Writing for Publication class to high school sophomores, juniors, and seniors.

What's happening at Model Laboratory School is one attempt to reform a school program at the grassroots level. The impetus for the Wednesday activities was provided by the passage of a reform act known as the Kentucky Education

---

[1] Appreciation is given to Dr. Bruce Bonar, the director of Model Laboratory School, for providing the information for this case.

Reform Act of 1990. The state's supreme court declared the state's entire public school system unconstitutional, based upon a case claiming that the state's educational funding was insufficient and that the funds were being distributed unfairly among the school districts. The result was the passage of legislation that created a new way to fund and run schools, different ways to measure student progress, and different techniques for teaching kids.

With a proclivity toward experimentation, the Model Lab teachers were inclined to embrace the school reform movement. As members of an institution whose aims are to test and disseminate innovative projects, the faculty at Model jumped onto the reform bandwagon with vigor. The laboratory school formed a site-based council during the first year after KERA was passed, and it began the first nongraded primary program in the area. As part of a grant, a writing resource teacher worked with faculty to facilitate the writing process in all subjects, the goal being to train all faculty to teach writing.

The faculty received enormous amounts of training both within and outside the school building. The primary teachers attended a total of 80 workshops in preparation for teaching nongraded classes. All faculty were trained in performance-based instruction and academic theme building. Other teachers and administrators attended meetings on portfolio construction in math and language arts, assessment, and technology. All teachers and administrators attended a five-day curriculum alignment workshop.

After receiving this extensive reform training, the laboratory school teachers searched for ways to put the training into practice. During the early days of reform, there were no KERA reform models in Kentucky schools, and it seemed as if every few days, a new element (or required practice) in the reform law would appear. Implementing Kentucky education reform during its development was characterized by one educator as "building an airplane while you're flying it."

Despite the demands of KERA and the extensive training of the faculty, the structure of the high school and middle school remained unchanged. Teachers began to develop event and portfolio tasks that demonstrate student competency in learning, either individually or within a group. Some teachers joined with colleagues to teach integrated units and tasks. Still, the reform attempts remained sporadic, with some teachers more readily aligning their classes with the KERA curriculum elements while others remained tied to more traditional educational practices.

The state education reform legislation encouraged the development of alternative curricula. The Wednesday classes were designed to meet this need. The new curriculum, called the *alternative schedule,* caused everyone at this school to focus on reform. This program has given teachers an almost threat-free environment in which to try new curricula, experiment with reform, and cover topics inadequately covered in the traditional curriculum.

The decision to implement the alternative schedule was made by the teachers and endorsed by the school's site-based decision-making council. The program requires teachers to construct courses that run for nine consecutive Wednesdays, with some classes meeting for one hour and others meeting for two consecutive hours. The courses are designed to fulfill at least one of four reform criteria:

1. Meet the needs of students who work at different learning rates (the reform act states that *all* children can and will learn).

2. Integrate learning experiences with the real world.

3. Demonstrate performance-based learning and evaluation.

4. Increase social awareness and cooperative behavior.

Teachers submitted proposals that were reviewed by faculty and evaluated based on the efficacy of the offering and its match to the criteria. Parents assist teachers in some classes; in others, parents teach and faculty serve as supervisors. Courses are designed in two-hour blocks for high school students. Middle school students take classes that last for one hour, except for those students taking high school offerings.

Teachers, working with administrators, use student choices and faculty recommendations to set up class schedules. Students needing remediation and those needing accelerated curricula are assigned to the same offerings, particularly labs in math, social studies, and language arts. Students receive most, but not all, the classes they request. In the middle school, students have fewer choices, and some of the younger children are required to take certain classes in math. The Wednesday schedule is shown in Figure 7.1.

Evaluations were carried out after the first year of the Wednesday classes. More than 90 percent of the students enthusiastically endorsed the project. Only 3 of the school's 25 faculty members opposed the alternative schedule. Many parents commented positively about the minicourses, stating that children seemed more enthusiastic about school on Wednesday. School attendance records indicated that, on the average, 98 percent of the students came to school on Wednesdays as compared to the overall 95 percent daily rate. Teachers reported that students seemed to be more productive on Fridays while the alternative schedule was in place, perhaps because of the variety they experienced in their weekly schedule.

The alternative schedule is an attempt by one school to cope with the demands of local school change. Whether this program remains intact and becomes institutionalized or whether the ideas in the alternative schedule become incorporated into a larger and more comprehensive restructuring of the school remains to be seen. For the moment, the teachers and students at Model Laboratory School are looking forward to Wednesdays.

FIGURE 7.1

Courses offered in the Wednesday Alternative Curriculum at Model Laboratory School.

Block A

APPLIED PROBLEM-SOLVING:
The students will have the opportunity to use many types of media and machine or processes to solve problems by designing and building a prototype. GEVEDON

DATABASES AND SPREADSHEETS:
This course will explore uses of databases and spreadsheets. Students will create, edit, and update data and investigate given sets of data for research and finance problem. FIND OUT WHY DATABASES AND SPREADSHEETS SPARKED THE PC REVOLUTION! CYRUS

HISTORICAL RESEARCH;
Students will explore a topic of history, using secondary and primary resources. Students will produce a product depicting some aspect of the topic. WHAT DO YOU KNOW ABOUT LIFE ON THE FRONTIER IN MADISON COUNTY 200 YEARS AGO? DR. BONAR

THE INKWELL:
This is a practical, hands-on course in the production of a student magazine. Students will write, select, edit, and use desktop publishing technology, including the scanning of images and artwork. RHODUS/CARTER

Block B

AMERICAN STUDIES LAB:
Offers opportunity for study in topics of interest in American culture, whether historical, literary, or pop. A variety of interests and purposes will be tolerated and encouraged. Students requiring additional time and/or guided practice in reading, notetaking, or communicating may be assigned to laboratory on a contract basis, with improved performance keyed to grades in regular classes. ROBERTS

ATHLETIC TRAINING:
Students will be familiarized with trainer's techniques for prevention of sports injuries and will have the opportunity to learn basic equipment, safety tips, and taping procedures. Students will study topics related to elite athletes and athletic performance. GALLOWAY

CHORUS:
Students will learn and perform choral music with a concert October 15th and 7:30 in Edwards Auditorium. Everyone join! Everyone attend! HENRICKSON

CREATIVE FOODS:
This course includes the study of planning, preparing, serving, and eating regional and foreign foods, for occasions such as holidays, receptions, and

Block C

ACADEMIC TEAM:
Think you're smart? Wish you were? Or just want to set around and watch a bunch of people who arc? Take Academic Team and you will have time to study areas of strength or weakness, to develop the all-important coordination of your right hand (beep, beep!), and to interact with some of Model's most interesting people. ROBERTS

ART APPRECIATION & STUDIO WORK:
FEE: $6.
Students will explore a different type of art each week. Learn about famous artists and different cultures and then create an art project that uses similar ideas, materials, and techniques. ISAACS

DIPLOMACY:
Diplomacy is a role-playing board game of skill and cunning in which chance plays no part. Game recreates events in pre-WWI Europe. Tests ability to plan a campaign and outwit one's fellow in negotiation. Students of Machiaveli's Prince should enjoy this game! Only 18 high school students can participate in teams of three. STEPHENS

(Continued)

FIGURE 7.1

(Continued)

Block A

LAB SKILLS:
Required of all freshman science students and all new sophomores. Students will learn and practice skills required for success in labs in earth science, biology, chemistry, and physics. ALEXANDER & SHUTTLEWORTH

MATHEMATICS LABORATORY:
Students will be allowed extra computer time and assistance in exploring mathematics and computer topics of interest. Students experiencing difficulty in math classes may be placed into the lab with contract tying improved performance back to the classroom grade. ALLEN

MOCK TRIAL, AN INTRODUCTION:
Students will receive an in-depth introduction to the mock trial and will participate as attorneys or witnesses in several "class" mock trials. Interested students will be encouraged to try out for Model's immensely successful Mock Trial Team. **Not open to students who took this class last year.** DR. EDWARDS

THE OBSERVER:
Monthly newspaper—works with everyone/every aspect of the school! Must be able to sell ads, write articles, do layouts, take and print pictures, and meet deadlines. COMBS

Block B

company meals. A $20 fee will be required to cover the cost of foods. WHERE ELSE CAN YOU GET 8 OR 9 MEALS FOR $20! ADKINS

"HERSTORY": WOMEN IN HISTORY
It is said that "The hand that rocks the cradle rules the world!" Join Herstory and examine the impact the hands of women have had throughout history. SIMS

INSTRUMENTAL MUSIC:
If you never started on a band instrument but would like to, or you started and dropped but would like to try again, or scheduling kept you out of Band, or you are in Band and would like to learn a different instrument, this course is for you! Course teaches basics of instrument and music reading, enabling students to develop skills leading to performance with the Band.
REQUIRED: You must have your own band instrument to use! STEPHENS

MATHEMATICS LABORATORY:
Students will be allowed extra computer time and assistance in exploring mathematics and computer topics of interest. Students experiencing difficulty in math classes may be placed into the lab with contracts keying

Block C

FROM EXECUTIONS TO EXPLORATIONS: MEDIEVAL AND RENAISSANCE WORLD
It is better to be beheaded with a sword or an axe? Did Robin Hood fear the Black Death? Did knights wear clothing under their armor? Can you turn other metals into gold? Were damsels really in distress? What would have happened if Columbus had stopped and asked for directions? The answers to these and other exciting questions will be explored by students through films, readings, guest speakers, music, discussions, projects, role-playing, and games. Activities will culminate with a schoolwide Renaissance fair. SHUTTLEWORTH & SIMS

INTRODUCTION TO WORD PERFECT:
This word processing course will meet in the high school computer lab and will teach beginning or advanced students how to create letters and other personal-use documents using Word Perfect. DR. EDWARDS

LIGHTS, CAMERA, ACTION: BEGINNING VIDEO PRODUCTION
The students will be actively involved in the proper usage of the camcorder, and will plan and produce a video. MCILVAIN

(Continued)

FIGURE 7.1
(*Continued*)

Block A

RED, YELLOW, BLACK
AND WHITE:
EXPLORING
CULTURAL
DIVERSITY:
This class will explore
the cultural diversity of
the United States and the
world through a variety
of experiences. Students
will read both fiction and
nonfiction, view films/
movies, participate in
role-playing games, meet
guest speakers from
diverse cultures, and visit
the displays of the
Cultural Festival at EKU.
JACOBS

SOCIAL STUDIES—
CAFETERIA STYLE!
Students will be free to
select from a variety of
experiences in the rich
world of social studies.
CAMPAIGN '92 students
will study and debate the
issues American **should**
be talking about and
have the opportunity to
get involved in the
election. **1792–1992**—
students interested in
Kentucky's **only**
Bicentennial will be able
to study issues of local
or statewide interest.
Students will be
encouraged to produce
scholarship-winning
products for the
Kentucky Junior
Academy of History.
ROBERTS & SIMS

WEIGHT TRAINING:
An introduction to and
application of weight
training principles. Avoid
HEART ATTACKS!
GET YOUR IRON THE
SAFE WAY—PUMP IT!
AMBROSE

Block B

improved performance
back to the classroom
grade. CYRUS

SEIKO YOUTH
CHALLENGE:
Would you like to solve
a real environmental
problem in our
community? In this class
we will form teams who
will then identify,
investigate, and prepare a
solution to be entered
into the Seiko Youth
Challenge competition.
WOLFE

SPEECH LEAGUE:
This class will offer
students the opportunity
to explore their public
speaking and dramatic
talents by participating in
the Kentucky High
School Speech League.
Students may choose
from a variety of
categories, such as
Oratory, Debate,
Extemporaneous
Speaking, Radio
Broadcasting, Duo
Interpretation, Dramatic
and Humorous
Interpretation,
Storytelling, Poetry,
Prose, etc. This offering
will require students to
participate in two Speech
League competitions at a
small entry fee. JACOBS

WEIGHT TRAINING:
An introduction to and
application of weight
training principles. GIVE
YOUR BODY A
WEIGHT BREAK!
TAKE YOUR IRON THE
HEALTHY WAY—
PUMP IT! AMBROSE

Block C

PUBLIC SERVICE
COOPERATIVE:
Students will be placed
in a public work setting,
attend seminars, and
participate in field trips,
to increase social
awareness and allow
career exploration
through interaction with
the public. Students
should increase their
understanding of the
importance of
community service and
of the diversity of the
community. ADKINS

TEST PREPARATION:
THE PSAT
Students will have pre-
and post-assessments
with the PSAT. Use of
test scores, strategies for
testing, and content area
review will be the major
focus of the course.
RECOMMENDED FOR
ALL JUNIORS AND
THOSE SOPHOMORES
PLANNING TO TAKE
THE PSAT THIS YEAR.
MCCREARY

WINDOWS ON
ARCHAEOLOGY:
This nine weeks students
will examine the basic
tools and techniques of
field archaeology,
including the study of
rock formations,
artifacts, fossils, carbon
dating, statistical
methods of "dig" site
identification, layout of a
"dig" site. Students will
participate in a "dig" at
an artificially "salted"
site. They will have field
trips to the Universities
of Kentucky and
Cincinnati where they
will see museums and

FIGURE 7.1
(Concluded)

Block A	Block B	Block C
AMATEUR RADIO: Operate Model's Amateur Radio Station. Current equipment puts us on 80, 40, 20, 15, and 10 meters, capable of 180 watts CW or SSB, and 150 watts AM phone. We plan to expand to 160 meters and into VIIF range as equipment and antennas become available. Must have valid amateur radio license on file with Mr. Stephens and be checked out on equipment. STEPHENS **All Blocks All Day**	WRITER'S WORKSHOP: Students will increase their writing skills in a broad range of areas, from writing mechanically correct, killer themes to creative writing. RHODUS	archaeology departments. This project, partially funded by a grant from GTE, will offer students exciting, in-depth exploration of archaeology and will develop skills and attitudes crucial to success in science in today's world. ALEXANDER & ALLEN *THE EXEMPLAR:* This course is for the yearbook staff which will have the practical experience of designing and producing another outstanding, award winning, annual for the school. Students will write copy, work on layouts, use computer equipment, and meet deadlines—all valuable experiences today. COMBS

THE IMPORTANCE OF CONTENT AND ACTIVITIES SELECTION

Almost 150 years ago, at the beginning of the Civil War, British educator Herbert Spencer (1861) posed the simple, yet profound and enduring question, "What knowledge is of most worth?" Before Spencer's question can be answered, other questions must be asked: "Of most worth for what? Of most worth for whom?" We can begin to find the answers to these questions by examining the purposes of our schools. Although these questions are, by their very nature, philosophical, they have highly practical implications. Selecting content and activities is a responsibility shared by all teachers. Since different individuals and groups hold different opinions regarding the purposes of schools, the job of selecting content and activities is not simple. Before reviewing the purposes of schools, let's look at some current practices that contribute to the complexity of content and activities selection.

Curriculum development, if it is effective at all, is an ongoing activity, every day throughout the year. Even so, most schools lag in their effort to provide relevant content and activities. Anderson and Pavan (1993, p. 207) explain:

> Even though the review and revision of curriculum is a perennial and essential task in every school district, it is probable that 99 percent of American school districts are significantly behind schedule in so far as updating is concerned.

This constant demand for updating requires teachers and other curricularists to stay on top of the job. At a time when the political leaders in many states are pressing for education reform, the importance of selecting the most appropriate content for K–12 classrooms cannot be overstressed. As expressed by Anderson and Pavan (1993, p. 190):

> The K–12 curriculum is in almost desperate need of streamlining and reform. The question "What should be taught?" and the even more relevant question, "What must be learned?" deserve top priority on every campus.

Arenas and Actors in Curriculum Planning

Curriculum planning occurs at several levels, including the classroom, school, school district, region, state, nation, and world. Each level has its own set of actors. Following is a discussion of each of these levels, each with its own actors and their means of influencing the curriculum.

The Classroom

Teachers have always played an important role in the shaping of classroom-level curricula. As the type of curriculum itself has shifted (for example, from content-centered to student-centered and vice versa) and the nature of the teacher's role has changed, teachers' influence has remained significant, both overtly and covertly. For example, in most schools teachers are permitted to add their own objectives, content, and activities to their syllabi (overt influence), and the way teachers behave can also heavily influence the curriculum (covert influence).

An advantage of classroom-level curriculum planning is the significant influence of teachers, since teachers largely determine the amount of learning that occurs (Bellon, Bellon, & Blank, 1992). Classroom-level planning also benefits from teachers' increased level of commitment and resulting clarity that can result from their direct involvement.

Classroom-level curriculum planning also has limitations. Teachers whose involvement with the curriculum is limited to their classrooms may focus their curricula on instruction, with little or no thought to long-term outcomes or to other parts of their students' curricula.

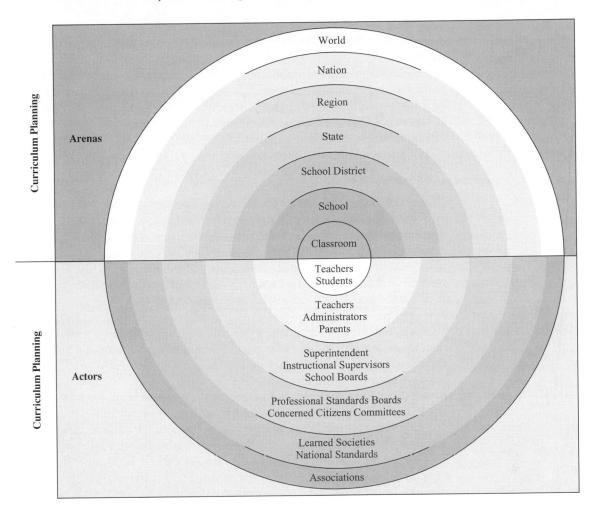

World

Nation

Region

State

School District

School

Classroom

Teachers
Students

Teachers
Administrators
Parents

Superintendent
Instructional Supervisors
School Boards

Professional Standards Boards
Concerned Citizens Committees

Learned Societies
National Standards

Associations

Arenas

Actors

Curriculum Planning

Curriculum Planning

Arenas and actors in curriculum planning.

School

Schoolwide curriculum planning has several advantages. To expand their curriculum planning arena beyond their own classrooms, teachers must increase their interactions with other teachers. Of particular value is their increased awareness of their students' curriculum scope, sequence, and articulation, that is, they are no longer concerned only with what happens to students in their own classrooms. They become committed to helping shape the school's curriculum to promote student success throughout their school years, and in all subjects.

Another advantage of schoolwide curriculum planning is that increased interaction with fellow teachers causes teachers to reflect on their practices and share these with their coworkers. As Garmston & Wellman (1998, p. 30) have said, such conversation can occur at the dialogue level, producing collective meaning and shared meaning, and at the discussion level, which involves decisions.

Perhaps the greatest advantage of schoolwide planning is its contribution to the forming of a learning community, where all professionals at a school work together to create understanding. It was this advantage that led Manning and Saddlemire (1996) to say that the school is the perfect arena for curriculum planning.

School District

During the early twentieth century, the nation's population grew until there were so many schools that state department educators began to worry that they could not control all the schools in their respective states. This concern led to the development of school districts. Thus, the school district is actually a tool for management or control, rather than a body developed primarily to conduct research and development on curriculum design and/or instruction. School districts were created not to help schools improve but to require them to maintain a desired level of quality.

School districts differ greatly from state to state. Traditionally, the size and number of districts within states were determined by the size and number of counties. Often, each county had one school district office. As town populations grew, many towns began forming their own school districts. Thus a county might have a district office to serve rural students, and one or more towns within the county would have their own district offices. In many instances the influence of population growth on the decision to form town or city school districts was secondary to the residents' desire to have their own football or basketball district.

Mentioning the influence of sports on school districts does not imply that there is a total lack of concern in these districts for the improvement of the quality of education; however, it does say that in some locations concern for quality education is shared and in some instances is overshadowed by other concerns.

The key players at the district level are the superintendent and the school board (often called the board of education or board of trustees). Superintendents may be either elected by popular vote or appointed by the school board. In either instance, they are accountable to the school board. Some school boards give their superintendent a budget and almost total latitude to use it as she or he sees fit; other school boards are much more restrictive. Curriculum planning is one of several roles of most district boards. Other roles include providing necessary finances and faculties, ensuring that schools meet state mandates, and curtailing drug abuse (Kowalski & Reitzug, 1993).

Other important players at the district level include such experts as psychologists, psychomotrists, special educators, curriculum developers, and instructional supervisors (Oliva and Pawlas, 1999). The curriculum developers and instructional supervisors are the most influential with regard to improving the schools' curricula. Traditionally, teachers held periodic districtwide in-service meetings to address curriculum and instructional concerns. In recent years, in many districts the district expert has moved the in-service support to the school campuses, recognizing the advantages that schoolwide collaborate planning has over planning at other levels.

Region

Several states have chosen to create regional education offices. The reasons for this choice may differ from one state to another; often it results from a concern over disparity of financial funds for schooling among schools and districts. Put simply, some geographic areas are so poor that they need help to provide quality education to their children. Other states are so populous or so large geographically that they become extremely awkward to manage.

Regional centers are sometimes referred to as "services centers" because they provide a range of services to their members. Some states require all schools or school districts to hold membership in a regional center, while other states (example, Indiana) make the choice optional. The services provided by regional centers are varied. Some centers provide staff development, which helps large states such as Alaska or Texas, which would find it time-consuming and expensive to either send consultants or transport teachers across the state for faculty development.

The recent expansion of the use of technology has made regional centers more advantageous, for purposes of staff development. Equally important, regional centers have a history of providing their members help with purchasing. Acting as a co-op, the centers can save their members a lot of money by setting up bidding among competing companies. The state of Kentucky directs each district to hold membership in a regional co-op, which may be operated by the state department, a higher education institution, or a private (commercial) organization. These regional co-ops provide both faculty development services and purchasing.

Regional education systems are usually run by school boards made up of superintendents of the districts that hold membership in the regional system.

State

The U.S. Constitution gave the states power to run their schools. During the 1980s and 1990s, an increased emphasis on accountability intensified the role the states play in controlling such issues as the curriculum and testing to ensure that all schools provide quality education for all students.

Traditionally, states have exerted control of curricula through such efforts as setting certification standards for teachers, administrators, counselors, and other professional educators. The goal of educating all children, emphasized during the 1980s and 1990s, increased the production of individual curricula through the use of individualized education programs (IEPs).

As expectations for schools grew, the 1990s also brought an increase in the number of educational professional standards boards, whose job was to ensure the upgrading of elementary and secondary education. Some states identified master teachers (often called distinguished educators) who were assigned to help faltering schools improve their curricula and instruction.

Nation

Although the amount of financial support for education coming from the national level traditionally has been small (below 10 percent), this amount has been large enough to heavily influence the curriculum at most schools. The 1990s brought an increased emphasis on national curriculum standards (discussed further in Chapter 11). Federal legislation has always emphasized those values that are paramount at the time. The 1960s and 1970s brought a deluge of prepackaged programs developed by federally funded regional research and development programs; the 1970s and 1980s brought an emphasis on bilingual curricula. The 1970s and 1980s also brought a swing in emphasis to more traditional or basic curricula, and the 1990s witnessed a shift toward educating all students, including minorities and special students. Paradoxically, as the 1980s and 1990s brought these increased federal interests, the Reagan administration also made a commitment to decreased federal intervention in education. Whenever national security seems threatened or when the national economy falls behind that of any of the world's leading nations, a clamor for increased federal control develops, and vice versa; therefore, the role of federal influence on curricula waxes and wanes.

Another major player in national influence on schools is the group of organizations known as the *learned societies,* including such societies as the National Council for the Teachers of English, the National Council for the Teaching of Mathematics, and the National Science Teachers Association. As the 1990s came to an end, each of these organizations was exerting a major influence on school curricula through its recently developed minimum standards.

Although the idea of national standards continued to grow throughout the twentieth century, and such lists eventually became a reality, the use of national standards continues to be controversial. Some opponents object on a constitutional basis for, indeed, the use of national standards takes the right to control education away from the state and local governments. Other objectors point to a flaw in the use of minimum standards, doubting the assumption that setting minimums can and will force higher levels of performance on students. Darling-Hammond and Falk (1997, p. 191) point out that the use of minimum national standards could increase failure, and increased retention seldom increases learner success. On the contrary, as these authors point out, "Dozens of studies over the past two decades have found that retaining students contributes to academic failure and behavioral difficulties rather than to success in school."

World

Although the national or federal level is often considered the highest level of influence on the curriculum, some individuals and organizations are committed to making worldwide improvements to curricula. For example, such organizations as the Fulbright Association and the Peace Corps are dedicated to improving relationships of people of all nations throughout the world. These associations sponsor international exchanges of teachers and support travel for educators who are committed to improving international relations and raising teaching standards.

Such associations as the Association for Supervision and Curriculum Development, Kappa Delta Pi, and Phi Delta Kappa, International, are also committed to the improvement of relations among cultures. These organizations provide speakers and conferences to achieve this goal, and use their professional journals to promote multiculturalism.

Pressure Groups

As shown in Box 7.1, at each level, from the classroom to the world, pressure groups are at work that are committed to influencing the curriculum. Some pressure groups are loosely organized and work informally to shape the curriculum. Others are highly organized groups with carefully outlined strategies. These groups often use such public media as television, radio, and newspapers to publicize their views through ads and editorials to increase their influence. They may also carefully plan to get on the programs of educational boards. Particularly at the state and higher levels, pressure groups often target legislators, governors, and other politicians in an attempt to alter laws.

Box 7.1

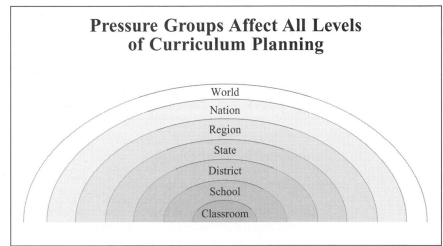

Box 7.2

Pressures Help Shape the Actual Curriculum

pressures at The School	pressures at The State

Formal Aims → Goals → Objectives = The Actual or Living Curriculum

pressures throughout The Region	pressures throughout The District	worldwide Pressure groups

---

Nowhere and at no time has the work of pressure groups been more prevalent than at the present in education reform. Every state has a number of pressure groups, some with little power and some with enormous influence. In many states, pressure groups exert a major impact at the state level through media ads, the presence of pressure groups at state meetings, and memberships on statewide committees, and through their individual and collective influence on legislators.

Collectively, the influence of pressure groups on the curriculum is powerful. The efforts of some pressure groups support those of others, although some pressure groups work to suppress or overcome the pressure of other groups. As shown in Box 7.2, the actual curricula in the classrooms is the product of all these pressures and the expectations and plans of educators.

Problems in Content and Activities Selection

Knowledge Explosion

A major problem that has persisted through the years and that has accelerated in recent years is the amount of information from which curriculum developers must choose. The "knowledge explosion" highlights the lack of a rational system for selecting content and activities.

Reliance on Textbooks

As mentioned earlier, the number one curriculum determiner throughout the history of our schools has been the textbook. Applebee, Langer, and Mullis (1987, p. 2) reviewed the results of several studies on the extent to which textbooks shape the curriculum and report that "Numerous studies report that textbooks structure from 75 to 90 percent of classroom instruction."

This reliance on the textbook would be more acceptable if the textbook writers and publishers used a logical system to select content, but they do not. Consequently, the content in textbooks is usually a hodgepodge of topics. Referring to the constant adding of content to textbooks, Tyson and Woodward (1989, p. 15) state, "It is not surprising then, that American textbooks have become compendiums of topics, none of which are treated in depth."

Another problem with letting the textbook determine the curriculum is the failure of textbooks to cover pertinent concepts, that is, material whose understanding is a prerequisite to understanding the discipline being studied. And another serious problem with letting the textbooks determine the curriculum is their failure to promote higher levels of thinking and understanding. Davis and Hoskins (see Orlich, 1980) found that over 85 percent of textbook content is written at the recall level. Trachtenberg (1974) analyzed more than 61,000 questions in workbooks, texts, and teachers' manuals accompanying nine world history textbooks and reported that 95 percent of those questions were simple recall and other questions requiring only lower-order thinking.

Personal Preference

Another variable that affects, indeed often dictates, content selection is personal preference. A team of researchers (see Berliner, 1984, p. 53) reported that an elementary teacher who enjoyed teaching science taught not only two or three times as much science as a fellow teacher who said that she did not enjoy teaching science, but 28 times as much time teaching science.

The search for the best content and activities for curricula of any era must be ongoing. Consequently, the search for the best system for selecting content and activities must never stop. It is clear that such determiners as the textbooks and personal preference fall short in the search for an answer to Spencer's question "What knowledge is of most worth?"

In any era, a search for the best content should include, as a minimum, a consideration of (1) the known information, that is, the body of knowledge the curriculum developer has available, (2) society's needs (including current trends and perceived future needs), (3) the needs and interests of learners, and (4) the state of human development (what has social worth). See Figure 7.2.

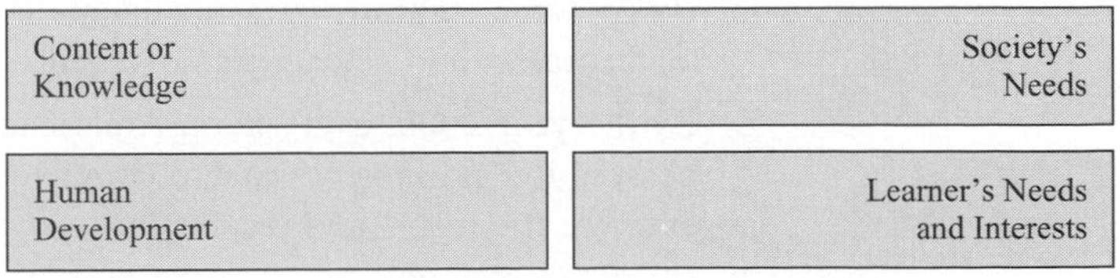

FIGURE 7.2

Foundations for selecting content.

Content or Knowledge	Society's Needs
Human Development	Learner's Needs and Interests

National Goals

Since curriculum development is a continuing process, and since the purposes of schools change, the selection of content should begin by considering the existing aims and goals. For example, the Seven Cardinal Principles of Secondary Education, which have already been listed twice in this book, may be revisited:

1. Health
2. Command of the fundamental processes (development of basic skills)
3. Worthy home membership
4. Vocational efficiency
5. Citizenship
6. Worthy use of leisure time
7. Ethical character

The importance of these goals for today's schools has already been discussed. Another source for a search for a system to guide the selection of content and activities is the more recent Goals for 2000.

Goals for 2000

A. By the year 2000, all children in America will start school ready to learn (i.e., in good health, having been read to and otherwise prepared by parents, etc.).

B. By the year 2000, the high school graduation rate will increase to at least 90% (from the current rate of 74%).

C. By the year 2000, American students will leave grades 4, 8, and 12 having demonstrated competency in challenging subject matter, including English, mathematics, science, history, and geography. In addition, every school in America will ensure that all students learn to use their minds, in order to prepare them for responsible citizenship, further learning, and productive employment in a modern economy.

D. By the year 2000, American students will be first in the world in mathematics and science achievement.

E. By the year 2000, every adult American will be literate and will possess the skills necessary to compete in a global economy and to exercise the rights and responsibilities of citizenship.

F. By the year 2000, every school in America will be free of drugs and violence and will offer a disciplined environment conducive to learning.

G. By the year 2000, each school will promote partnerships that will increase parental involvement and participation in promoting the social, emotional, and academic growth of children.

By the end of the 1900s, every state in the nation—every state legislature, every state board of education, and every state department—had adopted these goals (Clinchy, 1998).

An examination of the Seven Cardinal Principles and the Goals for 2000 shows that both hold the schools responsible for serving both the society and the students.

We have identified four important factors in the selection process for the best content: knowledge or information, the needs of society, student needs, and human development. Now let's examine each of these factors.

The Nature of Knowledge

Many criticisms are heard today about the schools' failure to teach students how to master the subjects they study. Nationally normed standardized tests show that an alarming number of students fail to develop a clear understanding of the content they encounter in their classrooms.

Because the subject-centered design has dominated the curricula in American schools throughout their existence, concern for content mastery has always been present. Initially, there was little question of what content was most important. The Puritans created the schools to teach the laws of the colony (which the Puritans defined as God's laws), which were determined by the Scriptures. This curriculum quickly gave way to the practical curriculum of the Franklin Academy. The English secondary schools' curricula seemed to take over and serve the schools for many decades. In fact, little formal attention was given to content prior to the 1960s.

Content plays a dominant role in subject-centered curricula. First, *information,* often in the form of seemingly unrelated facts, is selected for inclusion in the curriculum. Once selected, this information becomes curriculum content. *Content* is defined as the information selected to be part of a curriculum. The aim is for this content to become knowledge. *Knowledge* is defined as the content that students have connected to their previous experiences. The relationship between information, content, and knowledge is shown in Figure 7.3. Although the differences between these three terms may appear slight, their effects on students make the difference between memorizing and understanding.

FIGURE 7.3

The relationship between information, content, and knowledge.

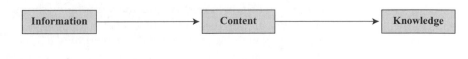

Constructivists (King and Rosenshine, 1993, p. 127) stress the importance of students being able to relate newly acquired information to previously acquired understandings:

> According to constructivist views, when presented with new information individuals use their existing knowledge and prior knowledge to help make sense of the new material.

Markle, Johnston, Geer, and Meichtry (1990, p. 53) further explain:

> Constructivists describe learning in terms of building connections between prior knowledge and new ideas and claim that effective teaching helps students construct an organized set of concepts that relates old and new ideas.

Teachers generally recognize the importance of students learning the main concepts in each lesson; yet Perkins and Blythe (1994, p. 4) report that students do not clearly understand the major concepts:

> Teachers were all too aware that their students often did not understand key concepts nearly as well as they might. Research affirms this perception. A number of studies have documented students' misconceptions about key ideas in mathematics and the sciences, their parochial views of history, their tendency to reduce complex literary works to stereotypes, and so on.

This concern was further expressed by Gardner and Boix-Mansilla (1994, p. 14) who said:

> While students may succeed in "parroting back" phrases from lectures and texts, they often falter when asked to apply their understanding to new situations.

Nicaise and Barnes (1996, p. 206) summarize the constructivist viewpoint:

> In sum, constructivists embrace social collaboration on and in important and authentic activities in which students have control and self-initiated direction. Teachers create learning environments containing multiple viewpoints. Rich resources become available for student exploration and integration into a personal construction of meaning. Teachers create authentic tasks or problems and support student learning through coaching, prompting, challenging, and fading.

Society's Needs

From the time of the development of the English classical school until *Sputnik* (1957), curriculum content received little attention. In fact, throughout our nation's history, unfortunately, the schools have been taken for granted, except in times of national emergencies. After the launch of *Sputnik,* the next national "emergency" came in the early 1980s when it became obvious that the nation's dominant position in world productivity was being seriously threatened. For the first time, it was recognized that other nations could mass-produce higher-quality automobiles and equally good electronics at prices that were competitive in the national and international markets. To the writers of many education reform reports, this constituted a national emergency, and the schools were to be held accountable for putting the nation in jeopardy. Consequently, the education reform movement exemplified society's perceptions of its needs.

John Dewey believed that each generation brings on a new culture. If this is so, then with each new generation a new curriculum must be developed to serve the unique needs of the new culture.

Learners' Needs

To understand the needs of learners, curriculum developers can begin by examining their most basic beliefs about the youths they know. Although this list is far from exclusive, the following questions might be asked. By nature, are young people:

- Social?
- Curious?
- Self-centered?
- Active?
- Passive?
- Competitive?
- Cooperative?

These traits can be studied merely by observing the behavior of a group of young people. If left to choose, will most young people work with others or will they work alone? Do most have more questions than answers?

Although most young people are social, are they not also self-centered? Do they not perceive the world as revolving around them and their wants? As they mature, many young people are taught by their parents or peers to be more considerate of others. Are not young people both cooperative and competitive? These paradoxes (social, yet self-centered; cooperative, yet competitive) allow for curriculum developers to choose. For example, suppose that a teacher believes that young people are basically social. Then suppose that this teacher notices that the behavior of a group of children contradicts this assumption. The curriculum must be adjusted to correct this behavior.

Among learners' needs is the need to explore their interests. Rousseau's book *Emile* stressed the need to give students complete freedom. This meant that they could study what they pleased. A. S. Neil (1960) described his school, Summerhill, as giving students the freedom to study what they wished and the freedom to attend only the classes that interested them. The Progressive Education Movement gave students choice of content. Contemporary curriculum leaders stress the need to involve students in the selection of content.

In selecting content, teachers and other curricularists must remember to look for content that students will find interesting. Rinne (1998, p. 621) provided encouragement by stating:

> Almost all subject matter, no matter how dull, mundane, or prosaic it may seem at first, has latent intrinsic appeals that our most effective teachers have learned how to reveal to students.

Human Development

John Dewey believed that the schools had a responsibility for improving human-kind. Newton (1989, p. 91) said:

> According to Dewey, "The aim of education is not merely to make citizens of workers, but to make human beings who will continuously add to the meaning of their experience and to their ability to direct subsequent experience." He wanted each generation to go beyond its predecessors in the quality of behavior it sought to nurture in children.

Thus, some content should (must) be selected on the basis of its potential for helping improve the quality of thinking and the quality of behavior of hu-mankind. The definition of philosophy as the "pursuit of wisdom" (see Chapter 3), coupled with the definition of wisdom as the "knowledge of things beautiful, first, divine, pure, and eternal," seems to guarantee a place in the curriculum for the study of philosophy, values, and the arts.

The Comprehensive High School

One of the most far-reaching efforts to ensure that schools develop the full potential of their students occurred in the late 1950s when James Conant, who had been a chemistry professor and later was president of Harvard University, began openly expressing his dissatisfaction with the American high school. He put his concern in print in his book *The American High School* (1959), in which he defended the concept of large, comprehensive schools with core curricula. He especially wanted the schools to offer vocational and precollege programs along with a strong general studies program. The comprehensive high school, which was first recommended in 1918 by the NEA Commission on the Reor-ganization of Secondary Education, publishers of the Seven Cardinal Principles of Secondary Education, had come under major attack

Through his contributions as a chemist, writer, researcher, and president of Harvard, Conant had earned the respect of the public at large and especially the scientific community. He was commissioned by the Carnegie Corporation to write *The American High School,* a report designed to strengthen the education of all students. The report was highly prescriptive, requiring of all students four years of English, three or four years of social studies, one year of math, and one year of science. A heavier curriculum was prescribed for gifted students. The report recommended both heterogeneous groupings (homerooms) and ability groupings. It also set a minimum number of hours of homework. To achieve currency and to respond to the nation's needs, he recommended requiring all seniors to take a course on American problems. Conant's critics questioned that a single course could achieve so much, especially since a large portion of students dropped out before reaching the senior year. However, Conant's recom-mendations were widely adopted, reaffirming the credibility of the comprehen-sive school and the Carnegie unit.

Personalizing the Curriculum

This book embraces and endorses the development of classrooms in which everyone cares about the feelings of others. Because of their home and neighborhood environments, many students may experience cultural shock in such a classroom. Initially, some students may resist such personalized environments, in the same way some students are ashamed of earning good grades. Nevertheless, most people want others to respect and care for them. Wolfgramm (1993, pp. 102–103) explains:

> Students must know that they are valued as individuals. Their needs are important. They are not pawns in an international game of economic survival. The question "For whom are our schools?" must be central to the debate on school reform. Educational environments that stress student interest, personal choice, first hand experience, thoughtfulness, and humanness need to be encouraged.

Unfortunately, many young people grow up on the streets or in homes where the first and only rule is survival. In such environments, youths appear to have no choice but to be tough, if, indeed, they are to survive. But, given a choice, many—perhaps all—of these youngsters would prefer a safer climate such as that offered by the schools. Harkins (1992, p. 62) said this quite effectively:

> Despite widespread portrayals of schools as deserts, the local school is for many youngsters an oasis. At least it has that possibility. A safe, consistent, and caring school setting is for many students a complete contrast from life at home or in the neighborhood.

Referring to their vision of what schools can be, Ponder and Holmes (1992, p. 409) describe the ideal relationship between teachers and students:

> Children will feel close to their teachers and will "experience teachers enjoying them and enjoying being with them." Teachers will be involved with kids both educationally and personally and "they will value their relationships with the kids. . . . In this ideal school, being a content expert is not enough"—"teachers need to be good at relating."

Such curricula will require a combination of the educational domains. Ponder and Holmes (1992, p. 409) state:

> Teachers must be knowledgeable about people and not just subjects, and they must have counseling and social work skills. Humor, openness, and energy are the instructional tools these teachers will use to build relationships with everyone.

This personal approach includes respecting students' perspectives. As Fielding and Pearson (1994, p. 66) said, "Recently, the process of allowing students to build, express, and defend their own interpretations has become a revalued goal of text discussions."

Some programs individualize curricula for students. These programs may personalize or depersonalize the curriculum, depending on the circumstances. Kohl (see Scherer, 1998, p. 12) explained the difference between individualized education and personalized education:

> Individualized-learning programs are often a series of tracks for children, suggesting that they all are trying to get to the same place but at different speeds. Whereas in personalized learning, the goals may be the same, but the paths may be different. In personalized learning there's a personal relationship between teacher and child. As a teacher you respect the unique way a child perceives the world and, accordingly, shape the way a child is going to learn. And you respect the learner as a person who is connected to a family, the world, and larger things in life.

It is interesting to note that at a time when many reformers compare our schools unfavorably with Asian schools because of differences in standardized test scores in mathematics and foreign languages, Japanese elementary teachers rank students' personal growth and fulfillment as a top education priority, self-understanding and human relation skills as the second-highest priority, and academic excellence seventh (Lewis & Tsuchida, 1998).

Nowhere in the accountability-based, content-focused education reform reports is anyone likely to find suggestions for developing personalized curricula; yet for proactive teachers the opportunity is there.

At-Risk Students

One condition of modern society with which future curricula must deal in order to remove a major learning barrier is the growing number of at-risk students. *At-risk students* are more likely than average students to drop out of school. Wanat (1992) said that the school is a refuge for these children because it provides them needed stability; these youths know that the schools and teachers can be counted on. If students obey the policies, they can expect to get along fine. If they put forth the required effort, the chances are good that they will succeed in the school environment. This is far from the case in other aspects of their lives. Also, unlike the families of a large percent of today's youths, the school is not going to fall apart; it is not subject to divorce. In discussing what this comforting quality of consistency means to children of divorces, Wanat (1992, p. 59) says, "Schools provide structure and stability and maintain a foundation that's not going to come apart like the family came apart."

Unlike the competitive, norm-referenced systems used in many traditional schools, a system using clear, criterion-based objectives that specify definite results of specific behaviors instills a sense of security in students. A curriculum that supports reasonably high expectations of all students communicates that the school has confidence in students' capabilities.

Selecting Activities

For the sake of simplicity, the early part of this chapter was limited to a discussion of the importance of content and the need for curriculum developers to use a logical strategy to select the best content for their schools. In reality, of course, to separate content from the activities students need in order to master this content is to take a superficial approach. If educators accept John Locke's concept of *tabula rasa* (that everyone is born with a blank mind and the only way to put anything on it is through experience), or if educators accept John Dewey's philosophy of "learning by doing," then the fact that content and activities are inseparable is evident.

The process of selection of content, then, is meaningless unless it includes the selection of activities through which that content can become meaningful. Yet, educators focus on content while ignoring activities. For example, although the textbook remains the dominant curriculum determiner, and although many studies have analyzed textbook content, unfortunately, few studies analyze the uses that teachers make of textbooks (Garcia, 1993). Educators need to conduct more investigations on both planned teacher activities and student activities. Such investigations should include determining which instructional methods are best suited to specific disciplines. As Gardner and Boix-Mansilla (1994, p. 18) explain:

> Different disciplines call on different analytic styles, approaches to problem solving, and findings, temperaments, and intelligences . . . effective teachers should help youngsters to appreciate that what counts as cause and effect, data and explanation use of language and argument, varies across the disciplines.

Consider, for example, the kind of activities that can be used to help students appreciate diversity. By assigning group projects, teachers can let students experience other cultures firsthand. For example, groups of students from varied cultures could be assigned to examine newspapers, textbooks, videotapes, computer software, and other materials for possible use in their classroom.

Another approach to dealing with prejudice is through conversation. Most people lack the communication skills needed to hold such directed conversations, however. Information on holding conversations to reduce prejudice can be obtained by contacting:

Study Circles Resource Center
P.O. Box 203, 697
Pomfret, CT 06258
Tel: 203-928-2616
Fax: 203-928-3713.

As new content and activities are selected, and disciplines are integrated to strengthen the curriculum, a key to success is collaboration. The following case study by MicKovich and Evans provides some practical and useful suggestions.

Case Study

The Role of Collaboration in Curriculum Decisions

Mrs. Alice K. Mikovch and Dr. Sam Adams

Background Information

Selecting content and activities appropriate for inclusion in classrooms where the nature of knowledge, the national goals, and the needs of both society and students are considered is complex and challenging. One model embraced by the proponents of educational reform efforts endorses collaboration. Collaboration is a team approach where school personnel are involved in planning, teaching, coaching, assessing of student progress, and problem solving to ensure a quality education for all children. Collaboration promotes the development of classrooms where teachers share in the task of creating a climate in which all students can be successful and learn.

When the Kentucky State Supreme Court declared the state's educational system unconstitutional for failing to provide adequate financial support and for distributing the support inequitably, the legislature responded by enacting an Education Reform Act. This reform impacted all grades, kindergarten through twelfth. A major top-down change was the Primary School Program. The State Department of Education identified seven critical attributes or curriculum components of these nongraded classrooms. In September 1992 all elementary schools in the state were required to begin piloting the new program.

Mandated changes required that school personnel redefine their curriculum in the primary grades and that teachers learn to collaborate in the decision-making process. As is typical with the threat of change, the idea was met with resistance from all levels. The degree of resistance was often determined by the leadership of individual schools. Some schools addressed the regulation with extensive professional training of all school personnel; others chose to bury their heads and pray that the requirements for change would go away.

The following case discusses the transition to a collaborative model implemented by Bonnie and Judy, a team of teachers in one primary school, and the impact this transition will have on the school's curriculum. The team has since been recognized statewide as an exemplary model for collaboration. Recently, Bonnie and Judy were asked to serve the school in different capacities. Judy will become a resource teacher, and Bonnie will continue in the classroom with a new team teacher. This case examines decisions facing the committee chosen to hire the new teacher and the decisions Bonnie and Judy will make in order for the transition to proceed as smoothly as possible without changing the quality of the program.

The Community

The school in this case study is in a mid-sized city in Kentucky. Historically, the area has been primarily agricultural. For the last ten years, the area has been experiencing moderate growth and a strong economy, and this trend is expected

(Continued)

to continue. Manufacturing accounts for 55 percent of the employment. Over half of the products produced are durable goods such as machinery and transportation equipment.

The community is home to a large regional university that has substantial economic impact in the area. In addition, the university has provided many area residents the opportunity to become first-generation college graduates. This opportunity has altered career choices that once were limited to occupations in agriculture or in unskilled labor positions. The university has taken a leadership role in implementing state-mandated educational reform and has worked closely with educators to provide needs assessment and training for school personnel.

The area chamber of commerce takes a great deal of pride in promotion of the city. It provides many incentives for industry to settle in the area. One important element in relocation decisions rests with the reputation for academic excellence in the schools. The student scores in most schools in this community reflect an above average track record, although three of the city's schools were listed among the lowest in recent state test results. Residents of the area have access to a regional shopping center and to a larger metropolitan area.

The School

The school is located in a district that includes three high schools, three middle schools, and fourteen elementary schools. The school has approximately 600 students, employs 20 classroom teachers and 11 special teachers, and serves preschool to sixth grade students. The students represent diverse socioeconomic levels from migrant, manufacturing, farming, and professional families. This elementary school is considered to be academically strong. The retention rate for teachers is high, and many preservice students from the local university request to student teach at the school because of its reputation for excellence in teaching and for being innovative in its choice of curriculum.

The Principal

Mrs. Smith has been the principal at this elementary school for several years. She credits her decision to enter the education field to tremendous teachers who shared their enthusiasm and joy for learning with her. The first opportunity she had to help a group of children learn to read convinced her that she truly had been given a gift to teach.

At one point in her career, she left the classroom to become a representative for a major education publishing firm. She considers this time to be the greatest learning experience she has had. The opportunity to visit many schools and communities on the national as well as the international level and to touch the lives of children by field testing materials has altered how she views education. She has learned that schools do not have to be run today as they were run in the '50s and '60s. Mrs. Smith believes institutions of instruction have to be empowered to do the things that are best for the children in the community.

These progressive beliefs are reflected in the vision Mrs. Smith has for her school. When the state legislators passed the education reform bill requiring all elementary schools to restructure, she had already begun the process. She had initiated a site-based council to make administrative decisions. Her teachers had visited a well-regarded primary program that incorporated multi-aged/

(Continued)

multi-ability classrooms, and she had convinced two of her teachers, Judy and Bonnie, to volunteer to pilot a similar program. In her school, Mrs. Smith recognized that teaching practices and curriculum needed to change, and so her staff received training in innovative teaching programs. Reform was not a threat to Mrs. Smith nor the staff; reform meant that the curriculum they had been investigating now became regulation. For Mrs. Smith, educational reform is an exciting time. She hires her teachers with the understanding that they have the responsibility to teach children in accordance with educational reform.

One aspect of reform clearly modeled in Mrs. Smith's school is collaboration on all aspects of education. Mrs. Smith defines collaboration as a management vehicle whereby all school personnel enter into a contract to plan the curriculum and to meet the needs of children. They began by developing the following transformation plan based on state regulations. Thematic units are written by teams of teachers that will ensure the educational goals are met and the lives of students are enriched. All faculty are required to implement the instructional program on which they as a staff have collaborated. Every teacher, including Mrs. Smith, works with children in the classrooms, and Mrs. Smith sees that the necessary teacher training and classroom materials are provided when needed. Some teaching is done individually, but more often teams work together, and members of the community often assist in classrooms. When collaboration was first initiated by the principal, teachers made remarks such as, "You mean other teachers are going to come in and teach with me or they're going to be in my room while I'm teaching?" Now the remarks are: "I'll take this group of ten to work on regrouping in subtraction and you take the rest to finish that writing piece," and "What can I do to help?"

Mrs. Smith insists on knowing all that is going on in her building. She listens to suggestions from the staff but admits to controlling the outcome when possible. In her words, she gets aggravated and testy when challenged. When the staff feels she has overstepped her bounds, they come to her office, close the door, and present their case. She backs off if it is in the best interest of the teachers.

Mrs. Smith is generous, bright, hard working, and fun loving. When she finds material to aid with instruction or to improve the atmosphere in classrooms, she buys it, often from her own pocket. Every new educational program with merit will be tried at this school before it appears at the other elementary schools in the area. When remodeling at the school threatened to interfere with the first day of school, Mrs. Smith stayed at the school all night several nights working to ensure that the building was ready and that the atmosphere was inviting for her students and staff. She mixes humor with work. At one faculty meeting, she attended as an oversized puppet representing a gold medal swimmer complete with bikini and with medals for each staff member.

The Teachers

Bonnie and Judy have been collaborating in a multi-age classroom of kindergarten, first grade, and second grade students for the last four years. Bonnie had been a very traditional classroom teacher for 30 years. Judy, on the other hand, was a recent graduate of a university where she received state-of-the-art training in educational reform. For two years, she worked in a fourth grade to practice what she had studied. She implemented the use of portfolios, performance events,

(Continued)

open-ended questions, and journals before these were widely accepted. She chose her curriculum from a variety of sources, always keeping in mind the needs and interests of her students.

Even though their teaching experiences differed, both teachers loved the challenge of their classrooms serving as pilot sites for innovative programs. Each of them knew that they, along with their local school, would benefit from the training that would proceed the innovation. For example, Judy received extensive training on collaboration from the State Department, which proved to be invaluable when piloting the primary program. Bonnie tested a new assessment instrument used to determine if third graders should move to the fourth grade. It came as no surprise that these teachers were asked to work together when the subject of collaboration was introduced. Although neither has any regrets about her decision to be part of a team, Judy admits she was unsure she wanted to share the fresh ideas she had. Bonnie on the other hand recognized something was missing in her teaching. She says her last four years have been her best yet in the classroom.

Collaboration has changed what is being taught and how it is taught in their classroom. Much more attention is given to making natural connections within the curriculum and to meeting the needs of the children in the room. Art, music, physical education, special education and Title 1 teachers also work with Bonnie and Judy. These professionals combine their teaching expertise, their knowledge of content, and their resources to plan meaningful, challenging learning experiences for students. For instance, because Judy has had extensive training with the writing process, she takes the lead in teaching composition during language arts instruction. Bonnie provides basic skills training, but not in the traditional mode using reading charts and skills out of context. Instead she incorporates children's literature to teach the skills. Basal readers are used as a resource, and teachers find it interesting that students often take these basal readers home for recreational reading. Special education teachers assist with developing and implementing teaching strategies appropriate for students with exceptional needs. Children diagnosed as having emotional problems and who exhibit inappropriate behaviors in the classroom are handled competently by Judy and Bonnie because of the guidance they have received from the special education teacher. All students, as well as teachers, benefit from these exchanges of ideas.

Bonnie and Judy credit their successful collaboration to several factors. They recognize that fear of the unknown is often worse than the change itself and that the training they received on collaboration was essential. They also admit that the "pushing and pulling" Mrs. Smith does to encourage her teachers to become risk takers pays high dividends. These women believe the more open the communication among team members and the better teachers know each other, the more successful the collaboration will be. Judy and Bonnie compare their working relationship to a marriage. They say they have to listen, be open to suggestions, and learn to accept criticism. They have reached a point where they often seem to "read each other's minds." Another critical factor requires that teachers become facilitators rather than lecturers. Many teachers have difficulty empowering students; they want to make the decisions and call the shots. Learning to collaborate can help teachers overcome such rigidity.

Judy and Bonnie will no longer have responsibility for the same classroom of children. Judy has been appointed as an instructional resource teacher and will be collaborating with all the teachers in the building. Bonnie will remain in the

(Continued)

classroom and work with a new teacher. Both women have genuine concerns as to what this move will mean for the program. They recognize that there are key issues that will impact this tradition.

One issue important to Bonnie is that her new partner be hired as promptly as possible. She believes the new teacher and she need to get to know each other quickly so they can build on their combined strengths to mesh as a team. She fervently hopes the site-based council will hire a "people person," because she feels that particular personality type lends itself better to collaboration. She hopes the new person will be mature and have sufficient self-confidence to offer suggestions on curriculum issues, classroom climate, and management concerns. Bonnie is looking forward to teaching with someone who has creative, fresh ideas for curriculum development. Judy is going to be available for continued collaboration, but Bonnie plans to involve her new partner in all classroom decisions that need to be made before school begins. She wants to determine early when to take the lead and when to step back. Bonnie knows from experience that all team members must carry their weight in order to avoid conflict.

A second issue involves choosing a new staff person that can meet the standards set by the principal. Mrs. Smith openly admits to being a manipulator and to being assertive. The teachers accept this and are the first to say she never asks more of her teachers than she asks of herself. Recently, a young teacher interviewing for a position stated, "You know, Mrs. Smith, you have a reputation of being really hard to work for." Mrs. Smith replied, "I am. I am hard to work for." For her, there is always another joy around the corner, another program, another grant. She prides herself on being current with everything. If a new program is on the market and she feels it will help even one child in her school, she goes after the training, and she expects her teachers to implement the curriculum in as professional a manner as possible. Both Judy and Bonnie have seen new teachers in tears because they have not met Mrs. Smith's standards.

A third concern is whether the new teacher will help maintain the professional relationship that has been developed with the community and the state. The staff takes great pride in the support it receives. Last year 750 hours of parent volunteer time were logged at the school. Preservice elementary majors from the local university complete extensive field placements here. In addition, a major industrial plant has formed a business partnership with the school. School districts across the state send teams of visitors to the school regularly. The principal and staff will not tolerate a loss of community support because of a weak teacher.

Judy and Bonnie have been invited to serve on the teacher selection committee to hire the new teacher. As the committee convenes to generate a list of qualities they will be looking for in the new teacher and to formulate questions they hope to have answered in the interview, it becomes clear that the position will need to be filled by a special candidate.

Issues for Further Reflection and Application

1. What characteristics of change are reflected in this case study?
2. In what ways would the selection of curriculum be compounded by the collaborative model?

(Continued)

3. If you were to be assigned to a team of teachers with differing views on curriculum, how would you address the issue?

4. Develop a case for convincing your team that your choice of curriculum is appropriate for students in your classroom.

5. What are some changes in teaching behaviors that must occur before collaboration on curriculum can be successful?

6. Having read a description of the principal, Mrs. Smith, what would be your initial reaction to the prospect of working on her staff? How could you expect to change as a professional?

7. If you had accepted a position with a new school district and knew you would be expected to do extensive collaboration on curriculum issues, what steps would you take to prepare yourself?

8. Consider a possible discussion the selection committee might have as they prepare to interview perspective candidates for Judy's former position. Formulate questions they might ask in the interview and possible responses the candidate might make.

9. Describe the ideal candidate for Judy's former position. In what ways can the staff determine if the candidate is genuine?

10. Discuss the pros and cons of hiring an experienced teacher versus an inexperienced teacher with regards to collaboration on curriculum issues.

11. In the case study, Bonnie is concerned with filling the new position quickly. In that same paragraph is the statement, "Judy is going to be available for continued collaboration." How can you interpret this statement?

12. How could you convince coworkers to support curriculum decisions if they were adamantly opposed to the decisions?

13. Judy and Bonnie effectively modeled collaboration on curriculum issues in a primary classroom. In what ways would collaboration differ in a middle school or high school setting?

14. Innovations in educational reform are seldom new. Predict changes you are likely to experience during your professional career. How do you picture yourself adjusting to the changes?

Suggested Readings

Costa, J. L. (1995). Teacher collaboration: A comparison of four strategies. *Alberta Journal of Educational Research, 41*:4.

Johnston, S., & Hedemmann, M. (1994). School level curriculum decisions—A case of battling against the odds. *Educational Review, 46*:3.

Kentucky Department of Education. (1996, April). *Primarily yours: Ideas and information for teaching Kentucky's primary children.* Frankfort, KY: Author.

Little, M. (1995). Classroom collaboration: Making it happen. *Learning Disabilities Forum, 20*:4.

Schrag, F. (1995). Teacher accountability: A philosophical view. *Phi Delta Kappan, 76*:8.

Van Allen, L. (1995). Middle school teachers are different (middle ground). *English Journal 84*:5.

Whinery, B., & Faircloth, C. (1994). The change process and interdisciplinary teaching. *Middle School Journal, 26*:2.

This case study has presented the concept of collaboration as an effective approach to curriculum reform. The primary change agent is the principal, Mrs. Smith. Let's examine this person's philosophy. She is tough to work for, demanding of everyone, including herself, and insists on being on the cutting edge of knowledge in her field. She is a risk taker who pushes her teachers to also take risks.

Now let's examine Mrs. Smith's philosophy as it relates to the multicultural theme of this book. Too often, educators believe that they should vary the demands made on students based on the challenges they face as members of minorities. The literature tells us that this is a mistake. Instead of lowering the bar for a student who speaks little or no English, or who has a physical, emotional, or mental challenge, or who comes from a home where the importance of education takes second place to immediate survival needs, I believe all teachers should follow Mrs. Smith's model, scouring the professional journals and attending professional workshops to learn how to help students overcome these barriers.

We saw that Mrs. Smith is very demanding of everyone, including herself. Students are much more accepting of demands when teachers place themselves under the same demands, and students are more likely to take risks when the teacher takes risks. We also know that risk taking is part of problem solving, the main methodology used in constructivism.

The Knowledge Base

In a chapter written for an Association for Supervision and Curriculum Development (ASCD) yearbook, Hopkins (1990, pp. 64–65) concluded with the following message:

> We now know a great deal about the conditions that make for high school achievement and what a school is like that is dedicated to the learning of both students and teachers. We need to use this knowledge creatively, and humanely to create the vision we now know is possible.

Hopkins suggests that we employ our accumulated knowledge to uncover the conditions that lead to increased learning. It becomes more important to do this as our teaching knowledge base increases. Within the past few years, researchers have collected more information about effective teaching than had been accumulated over the previous two centuries. This fact alone demands that, when selecting teacher activities and learner activities, teachers make full use of the existing knowledge base, keep abreast of the findings reported monthly in professional journals, and whenever possible contribute to the knowledge base. However, caution should be used to avoid the temptation to overgeneralize data and draw unfounded conclusions. Joyce (1990, p. 26) explains:

> It is easy to underplay the research base and fail to locate some of the solid material that has been accumulated. On the other hand, it is equally easy to make too much of some provocative but thin findings and imbue them with qualities of substance that are not yet warranted.

The message in Joyce's words seems to be that teachers should be encouraged to use the knowledge base when selecting teacher activities and learner activities, but to proceed with caution. An equally strong suggestion can be found in these words for teacher education programs. To be capable of achieving the desired balance, that is, to select and use valid research without imbuing the findings with unwarranted substance, requires knowledge of and skills in using research. Teacher education programs, undergraduate and especially graduate, should include research across the curriculum. Without a research component, the potential for in-service faculty development programs to help teachers build the necessary research skills—indeed, the potential of a single research course to achieve this goal—is extremely limited.

Problem Solving

Since the Woods Hole Conference in 1959 (discussed in Chapter 3), problem solving has been emphasized in curricula in both elementary and secondary schools. Its heavy emphasis in the early 1960s was predicated on its effectiveness in helping students understand the content they studied. Richards (1993, p. 29) stressed the acuteness of this need in the 1990s:

> It only makes sense in a world that encourages problem solving, more corporate decisions being reached through employer-employee think tanks, and doctors including their patients in their diagnosis process, that students should be encouraged to be more actively involved in their own educational pursuits; in order to make them more capable, proficient, and responsible for the employment work.

When students solve problems in a cooperative manner, additional benefits accrue: they can achieve several goals simultaneously. Cooperation leads to increased and deeper understanding (O'Donnell & Dansereau, 1993). After studying the cognitive effects of guided cooperative questioning, King and Rosenshine (1993, p. 143) reported:

> Results of this study show that children at fifth-grade level can be trained to use the highly elaborated question stems to generate thought-provoking questions about material presented in classroom lessons.

Since many problem-solving situations are open-ended, students learn from dealing with them that knowledge seeking does not stop with a single answer. Often one answer may lead to additional questions. Knovac (1993, p. 53) agrees with this perception, stating, "And students need to know that understanding is never complete. It is an iterative process where the learner moves gradually toward greater understanding."

Some teachers have mistakenly thought that effective use of activities requires choosing one activity to help students meet one objective; they have assumed that there should be a separate activity for each objective in their curriculum. But this is not so: carefully designed, a multipurpose activity can serve several objectives. Dormody (1991, p. 4) discusses this advantage of multipurpose activities when he addresses some of the benefits of group problem solving:

> Group problem solving has something for everybody, and can motivate different students in many different ways. While solving group problems, students can learn about teamwork, leadership, the subject matter area of the problem and problem solving itself.

Problem solving is so entrenched in today's curricula that Zubrick (1991, p. 3) apologized for having to remind readers of its importance:

> Given the eminence of problem solving as an accepted teaching methodology and the fact that the ability to solve problems is a nearly universally acknowledged outcome for all educational programs, it seems sacrificial to question problem solving in an education journal.

In summary, problem solving is a strategy that offers tomorrow's citizens opportunities to prepare for the type of lifestyle that will require critical thinking and problem-solving abilities. Alvarez (1993, p. 13) states, "If we expect critical thinking to take place, we need to provide students with problem solving lessons in meaningful learning contexts." Alvarez suggests that one viable context in which students can develop critical thinking skills is the case study method: "Self-selected cases spurred curiosity and invited students to initiate critical and imaginative thinking" (p. 14). Cases provide an open invitation to generalize (Biddle & Anderson, 1986), and they allow students to be creative and imaginative (Kowalski, Henson, & Weaver (1994).

Internationalization

Chapter 1 discussed a high level of panic expressed in the education reform reports of the 1980s and 1990s. Setting the pattern, the title of the report, *A Nation at Risk,* suggested a crisis, speaking of "a rising tide of mediocrity." That concern over the ability of United States citizens to compete internationally suggests how important it is for American students to be knowledgeable about the world at large. King (1991, p. 18) stresses this need:

> The infusion of international knowledge, skills, and attitudes should take place at all levels and within all courses in the curriculum. International concepts should be integrated directly into subject matter.

If a school's curriculum is to serve society by providing leadership, it must incorporate technological developments and international trends and must include content and activities to prepare the current generation of youth for their contemporary and future roles in the community and in the world.

To survive, all societies depend on the cooperation of the rest of the world. As this dependency increases, another responsibility of the curriculum is to recognize, and help others recognize, the importance of global awareness. Decker (1992, pp. 5–6) says, "A sound source of impact is recognition of the vital role of education in helping members of all societies understand and discharge their global responsibilities." There is evidence that an increased global awareness can help prepare students to make better decisions about world issues. Denee (1993, p. 368) explains:

> Incorporating a global perspective into your curriculum is both practical and beneficial. By recognizing our increased worldwide independence and by developing empathy with humankind, we develop the ability to make intelligent decisions regarding our world.

Education Reform's Impact on Selection of Content and Activities

Throughout the country, education reform is causing educators to alter the selection of curriculum content and activities. The curriculum has always attracted reformers. Cuban (1993, p. 183) addresses this irresistible quality of the curriculum: "Hence, changing the official curriculum is the bright brass luring reformers. Such issues fire passions, grab headlines, and lead off the evening news." The *official curriculum* is the planned curriculum. That the curriculum will be altered significantly is fact; how curricula will be altered depends on teachers. The point here is that teachers need not, and indeed must not, wait to see how tomorrow's content and activities will look; rather, responsible teachers must take a proactive stance and shape the new curricula by choosing the content and activities needed to prepare students for the twenty-first century. Recognizing the need for ongoing improvement does not imply that all change or all reform is good. Teachers should not blindly accept all reform as improvement; rather, they should continually evaluate the worth of new as well as old practices.

A Need for Increased Flexibility

Taking a proactive role will require teachers to think and even feel in different ways. In the past, the curriculum demanded compliance from students, but this approach does not always work in today's schools. Brimfield (1992, p. 386) explains:

> For many children the curriculum is neither the content, nor the one of compliance which I experienced as a student. It is a curriculum of endurance and apathy. They simply do not care about what is happening in their classes either because its value has not been emphasized at home or because their own needs for survival must take precedence.

The time is ripe for contemporary teachers to ask what they want of tomorrow's schools. Although this Tylerian (ends-means) approach is sometimes criticized, it is an excellent beginning. The reform reports call for more science and mathematics and for students to develop the ability to apply their knowledge in their adult lives. These reports call for American students to be able to achieve the highest scores on national achievement tests and to outperform their counterparts internationally. Although these goals may have merit, teachers must look beyond them, for, by themselves, the goals do not address the need to prepare students for the future. For example, the new century will require high levels of flexibility—in thinking, in accepting the differences between people, in accepting the ideas of others, and in relating to errors (that is, accepting mistakes as a part of the learning process). As role models, teachers must excel in their flexibility, and curricula must be designed to nurture these flexible behaviors.

In their article "Purpose, products, and visions: The creation of new schools," Ponder and Holmes (1992, p. 414) describe their concept of the ideal curriculum for tomorrow's schools:

> Risk taking will be supported and rewarded; mistakes will be expected as a natural by-product of experimentation. . . . Like an experienced traveler, teachers will know many different routes to each learning destination. Teachers will look to each student's unique needs to determine which route is best. They will consider different cognitive styles and modality preferences. They will design activities that appeal to both left and right brain learners. They will also vary the pace at which they drive students toward the learning objectives.

Flexibility must go even further: teachers who use authoritarian methods must learn to relinquish some of their authority; they must learn how to feel comfortable in letting students set some of their own objectives, knowing that these will be different for different students and knowing that many mistakes will be made.

Robert Anderson (Dagenias, 1994, p. 53) offers his vision of the school climate of the future, and his thinking parallels that of Ponder and Holmes:

> The school environment must become and remain dynamic. There must be a feeling of adventure in the air. Learners, adults as well as children, must behave like explorers in the risk-taking sense. . . . The culture of the school must be such that there is a maximum(s) of opportunity for working together, sharing, trading secrets, and celebrating.

The expansion of flexibility must be a personal goal of experienced and new teachers alike, and a curriculum goal for students. Chapter 10 discusses Abraham Maslow's view that a human being's cognitive and emotional selves are inseparable. Interestingly, Maslow became increasingly aware of this relationship in his later years. In fact, he wrote the quote cited in Chapter 10 just weeks before his death. Piaget's thinking paralleled that of Maslow, and not long before his own death, Piaget also wrote about the inseparable connection between the cognitive self and the emotional self.

Teacher Empowerment

Current education reform efforts emphasize the need to empower teachers. Teachers who traditionally have remained in self-contained classrooms must assume a larger role in the entire operation of the school if, indeed, education reform efforts are to succeed.

Teacher empowerment is more than a fad of current education reform, and its purpose goes beyond the securing of higher pay and better working conditions for teachers. As much as higher pay and better working conditions may be needed, some educators believe that teacher empowerment is indispensable to meaningful reform. Ayers (1992, p. 260) shares this perception:

> In a sense, all education is about power—its goal is for people to become more skilled, more able, more dynamic, more vital. Teaching is about strengthening, invigorating, and empowering others.

As reported in the previous chapter, the extent to which teacher empowerment has increased in recent years is perceived differently by teachers and their principals. Shen (1998, p. 36) studied teacher empowerment practices and concluded that "Despite today's rhetoric of teacher empowerment and decentralization, empowerment thus far appears to have gone to principals." Teacher empowerment requires teachers to develop greater expertise in curriculum development. Klein (1992, p. 196) emphasizes the role of knowledge in this empowering act:

> If teacher empowerment extends to curriculum decision making, as some leaders propose, the need for teachers to become more knowledgeable about and sophisticated in the field of curriculum—including theories and alternative ways of conducting classroom practice—becomes critical.

Notice how in this discussion it is virtually impossible to distinguish between curriculum content and curriculum activities. Teacher empowerment requires the ability to select both content and activities to promote the empowerment of students.

Student Empowerment

Like teachers, if students are to become creators of knowledge, they must be empowered to take risks. Constructivist teachers create classroom environments where students can hypothesize without fear of being ridiculed. In such classrooms students learn to view mistakes as doorsteps to success. Constructivist teachers recognize that they must not let tradition dictate the selection of content and activities. Problem solving is a timely process, but the benefits justify the extra time that must be allotted for this purpose.

A safe classroom climate provides a learning community where students and teachers can work together to create understanding. Martin (1997, p. 9) emphasizes the importance of both the learning community and its safe climate:

> If learning is fostered by a student-centered environment, then quality instruction requires the creation of a "learning community" within the classroom. In such a community, students feel intellectually safe to explore, to try, to make mistakes, and explore again.

The Need for Security

Teacher empowerment also requires a safe climate. As Greenlaw (1993, p. 120) says, "Some teachers do not have the confidence in themselves or the courage to act to make empowerment work." The best confidence builder is acceptance, and self-acceptance is best achieved through success. Too often, education reformers and reform policies unintentionally and unknowingly send the message that teachers' prior efforts have been futile. For example, consider what happens when, without their involvement in and input into the decisions to alter the curriculum, teachers are told to replace existing practices with new ones. A common interpretation of this directive is that someone—usually an outsider who knows little about the characteristics and needs of students and the community—has decided that the current practices are all wrong, which means that teachers have failed. The harm that this conclusion brings to schools can easily be avoided by involving teachers in decisions to change and by letting teachers know that reform can occur by building on the existing curriculum; indeed, destroying or replacing an existing curriculum is seldom, if ever, necessary or desirable.

For example, during a workshop designed to help teachers develop an integrated curriculum, one teacher was overheard saying, "When we collapsed four subjects to form a central integrated theme, and designed 120-minute periods, some of the teachers insisted on having 30 minutes to devote exclusively to their discipline." Although success with integrated programs requires teachers to give up the idea of having time exclusively for their discipline, reprimanding a teacher who balked at this would gain nothing. A far better approach would be to compliment such teachers on their level of dedication to their discipline and explain that they will not have to give up their level of commitment to their subject but will be required to forgo spending their time exclusively on their discipline.

Because constructivism involves problem solving, and because problem solving requires more time than do direct methods of instruction, students in constructivist classes may spend time on fewer types of activities, which they explore in greater depth. The case study in Chapter 4 described block scheduling at Angola High School and how such scheduling is linked to constructivism. Another quality that makes block scheduling useful in constructivist classrooms is the opportunity it gives teachers to blend two or more disciplines. Integrated themes open up a curriculum, giving students freedom to head in many directions and take many risks, as they search for answers.

Both teachers and students need confidence-building activities. As future citizens, students need the self-confidence required to live in a future that will place new demands on all citizens. One of these demands will be to deal with uncertainty. Eisner (1992, p. 723) said it clearly: "Education is about learning how to deal with uncertainty and ambiguity."

Feeling uncertain is being in a zone of high discomfort. As seen in Chapter 2, in the past, schools have been bastions of tradition protecting teachers from the unknown. Like other adults, many teachers fear uncertainty because when they went to school, they were punished for making errors. Of course, the all-too-logical conclusion is that the best way to avoid errors is to avoid experimenting with new approaches. This condition can be rectified for both the teachers and their students by curricula that make mistakes acceptable. The best way to drive out fear of the unknown is to make the unknown familiar; in the classroom this means taking risks, making mistakes, and using mistakes, instead of hiding from them. You will see that the home economics teacher in Chapter 10 exemplifies this strategy by using sugarless cookies to explore taste and texture.

Another way to help teachers overcome their fear of reform is to assure them that they have the time needed to implement reform. Unfortunately, the tone of urgency expressed in some of the reform reports has intensified teachers' anxieties; yet curricularists know that significant educational change comes slowly. A timetable can be used to assure teachers that they are making progress at a rate that is both reasonable and acceptable.

Still another way to build self-confidence is through helping others increase their self-esteem. Canfield (1990, p. 49) offers nine suggestions for teachers to use to help their students develop self-esteem. The teacher:

1. Accepts total responsibility for the learner's self-concept.

2. Focuses on the positive.

3. Monitors his or her comments.

4. Uses student support groups in the classroom.

5. Identifies strengths and resources.

6. Clarifies the learner's vision.

7. Sets goals and objectives.

8. Takes appropriate action.

9. Responds appropriately to feedback.

The curriculum should offer an effective route whereby students can succeed, and self-esteem should come from self-improvement rather than from self-concept development programs that rely on telling students that they are important.

Checklist for Revising Curricula

The Association for Supervision and Curriculum Development (1992, p. 137) offers the following questions that can be used as a checklist when revising curricula. Does your curriculum:

1. Provide a balanced core of common learning?

2. Focus on results with multiple assessments?

3. Integrate subject areas?

4. Involve students in learning?

5. Recognize and respect student diversity?

6. Avoid tracking plans?

7. Develop student thinking skills?

In one or more ways, most of these questions relate directly to the selection of content and activities. By planning activities to help their students increase their self- esteem, teachers can enhance their own self-concepts, and by covering all the reform practices endorsed by their district, teachers can feel more comfortable about education reform. A description of a system teachers can use to ensure that they are achieving local education reform expectations follows.

Tables of Specifications

Because curriculum development is a complex process, and because it is rapidly becoming more complex (through the pressure of education reform), including the most important content in the curriculum has become a formidable challenge. A system is needed to ensure that the most important content and activities are being covered so that the expectations of the curriculum are met. One such system is a *table of specifications.*

The concept of tables of specifications was introduced in Chapter 4. Angola High School used tables of specifications to raise learning units to higher levels. Tables of specifications vary, but their principle is constant. Each table uses a matrix. The columns and lines are labeled. For example, Table 7.1 is a sample table of specifications designed to ensure that the local education reform practices are being covered in a teacher education curriculum.

In this example, the teacher education courses are listed horizontally across the top of the chart, and the reform elements are listed vertically at the left.

The table of specifications can be used in two ways. First, the left side of the matrix can be used as a point of origin. For example, this approach would be used if you wanted to know how thoroughly a particular reform element is being covered. Or you might wish to know how comprehensive a particular course is in covering education reform. You can determine this by using the top as your point of origin; locate the course in question and move down the column to see how many reform elements are addressed in this course. This particular matrix goes further: a 1 to 3 numbering system is assigned to show the depth to which a particular reform element is covered. Coverage at level 1 is an introduction; level 3 is mastery; level 2 is between introduction and mastery.

On a smaller scale, a table of specifications can be designed for each course. Across the top you can list the objectives you want students to master. The first column can list the content generalizations (concepts) needed to achieve these objectives. Once the top row and the first column are filled in, you can use the chart to check each objective to determine whether the content needed to achieve the objective is covered. Table 7.2 is a sample table of specifications for a high school class in world history.

TABLE 7.1   Table of Specifications for Educational Reform

KERA topics	Courses in the Program Area											
	ELE 361	ELE 262	ELE 445	ELE 446	ELE 490	ELE 491	ELE 492	ELE 493	ELE 499	ELE 530	ELE 541	ELE 551
1. Curriculum goals	2	2	1	2	1	3	3	2	3	2	1	2
2. Performance-based student assessment	1	2	0	2	2	3	1	2	2	1	2	1
3. Nongraded primary	2	1	0	2	3	3	1	2	2	2	1	1
4. Site-based decision making	1	0	1	1	1	2	1	1	1	0	1	0
5. Instructional uses of technology	1	0	1	1	1	3	2	1	2	0	1	1
6. Research-based instructional practices	3	1	1	2	3	1	3	2	2	2	1	3
7. Extended school program	0	0	0	2	1	0	0	0	1	1	1	0
8. Motivating students of diverser cultures	3	1	1	1	1	1	2	2	3	3	2	3
9. School finance	0	0	0	0	0	0	1	0	1	0	0	0

Rating scale: 1—Awareness of topic; 2—topic is reinforced; 3—mastery of topic is achieved.

TABLE 7.2   Table of Specifications to Ensure Content Coverage for All Objectives

Content generalizations	Obj. 16	Obj. 17	Obj. 18	Obj. 19	Obj. 20	Obj. 21	Obj. 22	Obj. 23	Obj. 24	Obj. 25	Obj. 26	Obj. 27
1. Concept of power and authority and law and order												
2. Generalizations on social orders of feudal classes												
3. Little representation of lower classes												
4. Foundations of democracy laid in medieval period, quality of life and secularism increased		✔		✔	✔						✔	✔
5. Value of art created by many great artists during this period		✔	✔	✔	✔		✔		✔	✔	✔	✔
6. Even though centuries pass, life remains the same	✔	✔		✔	✔		✔	✔	✔	✔	✔	
7. Past contributions relate to total picture of history		✔	✔	✔	✔	✔	✔			✔	✔	✔

Similar tables of specification can be developed to ensure coverage in the affective and psychomotor domains. An advantage of tables of specification is that they can be used to ensure coverage of objectives at varying levels of the three domains of the educational taxonomies. See Table 7.3, a table of specifications for an art class.

Still another use of the table of specifications is to ensure that a curriculum contains activities covering each major concept or objective. List the objectives or concepts on one axis and the activities on the other. When the table is used for this purpose, one activity should correspond to each objective or concept, although the same activity may be assigned to more than one objective or concept.

For example, Table 7.4 shows a table of specifications for a grade 4–6 unit on weather. Major concepts are expressed in 1–3 words so that they will fit in the table. Whenever possible, concept statements should be kept to simple sentences.

The number of ways teachers can use tables of specifications is limited only by teachers' imaginations. Certainly, discovering creative applications of this instrument to solve contemporary problems epitomizes the exhilarating nature of curriculum improvement and the challenges that face today's teachers. As teachers' roles in curriculum development grow, so will the need to be skilled in discovering new ways to use this and other versatile instruments.

Chapter Summary

According to the many contemporary educators who hold constructivist beliefs, a major role of the curriculum is to help students make meaning out of newly acquired information. Achieving this goal requires the ability on the part of teachers to make careful selections of content and activities. Yet, in the past, most teachers have not selected content and activities logically. The textbook, a very poor source for determining content, remains the dominant curriculum determiner, followed closely by another equally poor curriculum determiner, personal choice.

Constructivists believe that the only way to make sense of newly acquired information is by integrating it into previously acquired understandings. This requires using concepts and themes and selecting appropriate student activities to enable students to use the new information.

The curriculum should serve the student and the society. Content selection should use human development (the improvement of society through improving individuals) in the selection of content. Multipurpose activities serve a multiple number of objectives. Problem solving is an excellent form of multipurpose activity, since the future will require individuals to solve more problems.

Current world events, current education reform goals, and the future welfare of students should govern the selection of content and activities. Many

TABLE 7.3   Table of Specifications to Ensure Coverage of All Levels of the Three Domains

The levels of each domain are arranged in a hierarchy from left to right at the top. Each level assumes inclusion of lower levels. The highest targeted level is checked.

	Cognitive						Affective					Psychomotor						
	Knowledge	Comprehension	Application	Analysis	Synthesis	Evaluation	Receiving	Responding	Valuing	Organization	Characterization	Reception	Set	Guided Response	Mechanism	Comp. Overt Resp.	Adaption	Origination
1. Name materials	✔						✔						✔					
2. Select materials		✔					✔						✔					
3. Identify terms	✔						✔						✔					
4. Spell terms			✔				✔								✔			
5. Name design element	✔						✔						✔					
6. Name design principle	✔						✔						✔					
7. Identify design element				✔			✔											
8. Identify comprehension principle				✔			✔											
9. Identify comprehension areas				✔			✔											
10. Identify comprehension in pictures				✔			✔						✔					
11. Mix colors: hue			✔						✔						✔			
12. Create: tint, shade					✔					✔								✔
13. Create: mood					✔					✔								✔
14. Create: design element					✔					✔								✔
15. Compare pictures				✔						✔			✔					
16. Compare sculpture, pictures				✔						✔					✔			
17. Use technique			✔				✔						✔					
18. "Wait turn"				✔			✔											
19. Choose for group				✔						✔						✔		
20. Properly use material and equipment	✔		✔				✔									✔		
21. Construct 3-D objects				✔						✔								✔
22. Store materials				✔			✔								✔			
23. Store equipment							✔								✔			
24. Share with instructor							✔							✔				
25. Share with group							✔							✔				
26. Share with the class							✔							✔				
27. Display, classroom						✔				✔								
28. Display, other						✔				✔								
29. Prepare display		✔							✔						✔			
30. Select group				✔						✔				✔				
31. Show followership				✔						✔				✔				
32. Show leadership						✔			✔					✔				
33. Accept others' work						✔					✔	✔						
34. Evaluate products						✔				✔							✔	
35. Evaluate process						✔				✔							✔	
36. Work alone, cooperate		✔					✔							✔				
37. Cooperate in group		✔					✔							✔				
38. Adapt techniques						✔				✔								✔

TABLE 7.4   Table of Specifications for a Unit on Weather

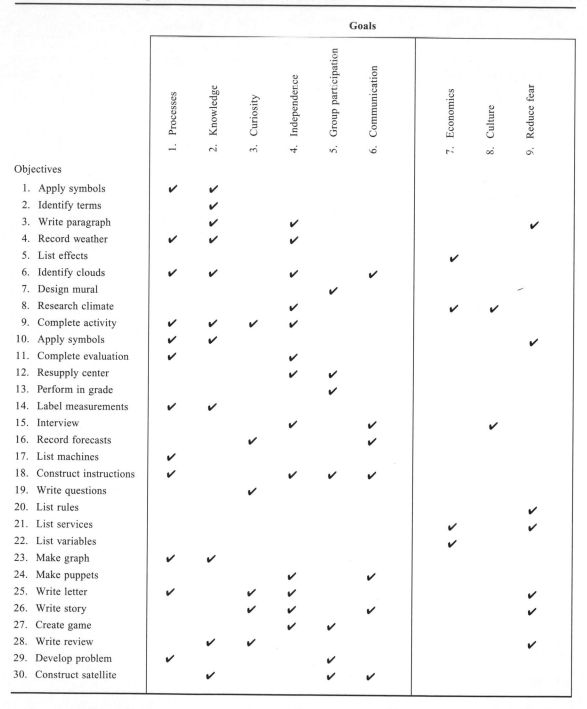

Objectives	1. Processes	2. Knowledge	3. Curiosity	4. Independence	5. Group participation	6. Communication	7. Economics	8. Culture	9. Reduce fear
1. Apply symbols	✔	✔							
2. Identify terms		✔							
3. Write paragraph		✔		✔					✔
4. Record weather	✔	✔		✔					
5. List effects							✔		
6. Identify clouds	✔	✔		✔		✔			
7. Design mural					✔				
8. Research climate				✔			✔	✔	
9. Complete activity	✔	✔	✔	✔					
10. Apply symbols	✔	✔							✔
11. Complete evaluation	✔			✔					
12. Resupply center				✔	✔				
13. Perform in grade					✔				
14. Label measurements	✔	✔							
15. Interview				✔		✔		✔	
16. Record forecasts			✔			✔			
17. List machines	✔								
18. Construct instructions	✔			✔	✔	✔			
19. Write questions			✔						
20. List rules									✔
21. List services							✔		✔
22. List variables							✔		
23. Make graph	✔	✔							
24. Make puppets				✔		✔			
25. Write letter	✔		✔	✔					
26. Write story			✔	✔		✔			✔
27. Create game				✔	✔				
28. Write review		✔	✔						✔
29. Develop problem	✔				✔				
30. Construct satellite		✔			✔	✔			

contemporary educators are convinced that less is more, preferring schools to cover fewer topics but in greater depth, a practice that characterizes Asian curricula. Curricularists are encouraged to use a criterion-referenced, approach, that is, to first select the desired outcomes and then select the appropriate content needed to achieve these outcomes. These outcomes must include the desire for all students, regardless of their ethnic background, to succeed to their maximum capacity. Curricularists are reminded of the need to use their judgment and weigh the relative importance of content against its contributions to the aims, goals, and objectives of the school and the classroom.

As our society becomes increasingly diverse, we must not exempt students whom we might consider less capable or under special challenges from meeting class expectations. Rather, we must attend workshops and read professional literature to continue discovering ways of helping all students reach national, regional, and local standards and goals. Attaining this goal of including all students when making decisions about the curriculum will require taking risks; therefore, we must create a climate where experimentation is valued and mistakes are expected and accepted as necessary steps to growth.

Learning Questions

1. How should one's knowledge of constructivism affect the selection of content and activities?
2. What is the difference between *content* and *knowledge,* and what can the curriculum developer do to alter this relationship?
3. Which of the four major factors—society's needs, knowledge, student needs, or human development—do you think is most important to curriculum development? Why?
4. Which should receive more emphasis in curriculum development, the present or the future? Why?
5. How does knowledge about other cultures affect appreciation for diversity?
6. How is education reform in your school affecting students' appreciation for diversity?

Suggested Activities

1. Research the topic "human development." Begin by finding three definitions of this term, and then write your own definition. Next, make a list of actions you can take to help achieve this goal as you plan curricula.

2. Choose one lesson that you enjoy teaching. List and describe one activity that you might include in that lesson to address human development.

3. Write a one- or two-page statement describing your beliefs about the nature of youth. Include your perceptions of young peoples' nature to be (*a*) curious or apathetic, (*b*) active or passive, (*c*) cooperative or competitive, (*d*) self-centered or social, and (*e*) honest or dishonest.

4. With regard to John Dewey's admonition to redesign our curricula to fit the rebirth of a new culture with each generation, make a list of important factors in the lives of contemporary youths that are unique to this generation.

5. Develop a system that you can use to gather information about student preferences.

6. Examine a state study guide or your state's reform program. Then select two or three goals and develop a multipurpose activity to serve the goals.

7. Develop a group assignment whose goal is to increase appreciation for diversity. *Hint:* Critique curriculum materials regarding their portrayal of minorities.

8. Develop an activity that will enable students to use their previous multicultural experiences as building blocks to gain an even greater appreciation for diversity.

Works Cited and Suggested Readings

Alvarez, M. C. (1993). Imaginative uses of self-selected cases. *Reading research and instruction, 32*(2), 1–18.

Anderson, R. H., & Pavan, B. N. (1993). *Nongradeness: Helping it to happen.* Lancaster, PA: Technomic.

Applebee, A. N., Langer, J. A., & Mullis, I. V. S. (1987). *The nation's report card: Literature and U. S. history.* Princeton, NJ: Educational Testing Service.

Association for Supervision and Curriculum Development. (1992). *ASCD curriculum handbook.* Alexandria, VA: Author.

Ayers, W. (1992). The shifting ground of curriculum thought and everyday practice. *Theory into practice, 31*(3), 259–263.

Bellon, J. J., Bellon, E. C., & Blank, M. A. (1992). *Teaching from a research knowledge base.* New York: Macmillan.

Bellon, J. J., Bellon, J. I., & Blank, M.A. (1992). *What really works: Research based instruction.* Knoxville, TN: Bellon & Associates.

Bellon, J. J., Bellon, E. C., & Burns, M.A. (1992). *Teaching from a research knowledge base.* Columbus, OH: Merrill.

Berliner, D. C. (1984). The half-full glass: A review of research on teaching. In. P. A. Hosford (Ed.), *Using what we know about teaching.* Alexandria, VA: Association for Supervision and Curriculum Development.

Biddle, B., & Anderson, D. (1986). *Theory, methods, knowledge, and research on teaching.* In M. Wittrock (Ed.), Handbook of research on teaching (3rd ed.). New York: Macmillan, pp. 230–252.

Brimfield, R. M. B. (1992). Curriculum! What's curriculum? *Educational Forum, 56*(4), 381–389.

Canfield, J. (1990). Improving students' self-esteem. *Educational Leadership, 48*(1), 48–50.

Clinchy, E. (1998). The educationally challenged American school district. *Phi Delta Kappan, 80*(4), 272–277.

Conant, J. B. (1959). *The American high school.* New York: McGraw-Hill.

Cuban, L. (1993). The lure of curricular reform and its pitiful history. *Phi Delta Kappan, 75*(2), 182–185.

Dagenais, R. J. (1994). Professional development of teachers and administrators: Yesterday, today, and tomorrow/The views of Robert H. Anderson. *Kappa Delta Pi Record, 30*(2), 50–54.

Danzberger, J. P., & Friedman, W. (1997). Public conversations about the public schools. *Phi Delta Kappan, 78*(10), 744–748.

Darling-Hammond L., & Falk, B. (1997). Using standards and assessment to support student learning. *Phi Delta Kappan, 79*(3), 190–195.

Decker, L. E. (1992). Building learning communities: Realities of educational restructuring. In L. E. Decker & V. A. Romney (Eds.), *Educational restructuring and the community education process.* Alexandria, VA: National Community Education Association.

Dennee, J. (1993). Developing a global perspective through cooperative learning. *Contemporary Education, 66*(6), 367–369.

Dormody, T. J. (1991). Getting the most out of group problem solving. *The Agricultural Education Magazine, 64*(3), 4, 10.

Eisner, E. (1992). The federal reform of schools: Looking for the silver bullet. *Phi Delta Kappan, 73*(9), 722–726.

Erb, T. O. (1991) Preparing middle grades teachers to understand the curriculum. *Middle School Journal, 23,* 24–28.

Fielding, L. G., & Pearson, P. D. (1994). Reading comprehension: What works. *Educational Leadership, 51*(5), 62–68.

Fogarty, R. (1992). Ten ways to integrate curriculum. *Education Digest, 57,* 537.

Garcia, J. (1993). The changing image of ethnic groups in textbooks. *Phi Delta Kappan, 75*(1), 29–35.

Gardner, H., & Boix-Mansilla, V. (1994). Teaching for understanding within and across disciplines. *Educational Leadership, 51*(5), 14–18.

Greenlaw, M. (1993). Do teachers really want to be empowered? *Contemporary Education, 64*(2), 119–122.

Garmston, R., & Wellman, B. (1998). Teacher talk that makes a difference. *Phi Delta Kappan, 55*(7), 30–34.

Harkins, W. (1992). A practical approach to organizing curriculum. *NASSP Bulletin, 76,* Fall, 54–62.

Hopkins, D. (1990). Integrating staff development and staff improvement: A study of teacher personality and school climate. In B. Joyce (Ed.), *Changing school culture through staff development.* ASCD Yearbook. Arlington, VA: Association for Supervision and Curriculum Development, pp. 41–67.

Joyce, B. (1990). The self-education teacher: Empowering teachers through research." In B. Joyce (Ed.), *Changing school culture through staff development.* ASCD Yearbook. Arlington, VA: Association for Supervision and Curriculum Development, pp. 26–40.

King, D. R. (1991). Changing the curriculum: Will it never end? *Agricultural Education Magazine, 63,* 18–19.

King, A., & Rosenshine, B. (1993). Effects of guided cooperative questioning on children's knowledge construction. *The Journal of Experimental Education, 61*(2), 127–148.

Klein, M. F. (1992). A perspective on the gap between curriculum theory and practice. *Theory into Practice, 31*(3), 191–197.

Knovac, J. D. (1993). How do we learn our lessons? (Helping students learn how to learn). *The Science Teacher, 60*(3), 50–55.

Kowal, J. (1991). Science, technology, and human values: A curricular approach. *Theory into Practice, 30*(4), 267–272.

Kowalski, T. J., Henson, K. T., & Weaver, R. A. (1994). *Case studies of beginning teachers.* New York: Longman.

Kowalski, T. J., & Reitzug, U. C., (1993). *Contemporary school administration.* New York: Longman.

Lewis, C., & Tsuchida, I. (1998). The basics in Japan: The three c's. *Educational Leadership, 55*(6), 32–37.

Manning, M. L., & Saddlemire, R. (1996). Developing a sense of community in secondary schools. *NASSP Bulletin, 80*(584), 41–48.

Markle, G., Johnston, J. H., Geer, C., & Meichtry, Y. (1990). Teaching for understanding. *Middle School Journal, 22*(2), 53–57.

Martin, N. K. (1997). Connecting instruction and management in a student-centered classroom. *Middle School Journal, 28*(5), 3–9.

Matthews, D. (1997). The lack of a public for public schools. *Phi Delta Kappan, 78*(10), 740–743.

National Education Goals Panel (1991). *Goals report.* Washington, DC: United States Government Printing Office.

Neil, A. S. (1960). *Summerhill.* New York: Hart.

Newton, B. T. (1989). Democratic aims of education—Revisited. *Education, 110*(1), 87–93.

Nicaise, M., & Barnes, D. (1996). The union of technology, constructivism, and teacher education. *Journal of Teacher Education, 47*(3), 205–212.

O'Donnell, T., & Danserau, D. F. (1993). Learning from lectures: Effects of cooperative review. *The Journal of Experimental Education, 61*(2), 116–125.

Oliva, P. F., & Pawlas, G. E. (1999). *Supervision for today's schools, 5th ed.* New York: John Wiley.

Orlich, D. (1980). *Teaching strategies: A guide to better instruction.* Lexington, MA: D. C. Heath

Perkins, D., & Blythe, T. (1994). Putting understanding up-front. *Educational Leadership, 51*(5), 4–7.

Ponder, G. A., & Holmes, K. M. (1992). Purpose, products, and visions: The creation of new schools. *The Educational Forum, 56*(4), 405–418.

Richards, P. M. (1993). A step beyond cooperative learning. *Middle School Journal, 24*(3), 28–29.

Rinne, C. H. (1998). Motivating students is a percentage game. *Phi Delta Kappen, 79*(8), 620–628.

Rioux, J. W., & Berla, N. (1993). *Innovations in parent and family involvement.* Princeton, NJ: Eye on Education.

Scherer, M. (1998). A conversation with Herbert Kohl. *Educational Leadership, 56*(1), 8–13.

Scheville, J., Porter, A., Billi, G., Floden, R., Freeman, D., Knappan, L., Kuhs, T., & Schmidt, W. (1981). Teachers as policy brokers in the content of elementary school mathematics. In L. S. Schulman & E. G. Sykes (Eds.), *Handbook of teaching and policy.* New York: Longman.

Schomoker, M. (1990). Sentimentalizing self-esteem. *The Education Digest, 60*(7), 55–56.

Shen, J. (1998). Do teachers feel empowered? *Educational Leadership, 55*(7), 35–38.

Spencer, H. (1861). *Education: Intellectual, moral and physical.* New York: D. Appleton.

Taba, H. (1962). *Curriculum Development: Theory and practice.* New York: Harcourt Brace Jovanovich.

Trachtenberg, D. (1974). Student tasks in text material: What cognitive skills do they tap? *Peabody Journal of Education, 52,* 54–57.

Tyson, H., & Woodward, A. (1989). Why students aren't learning very much from textbooks. *Educational Leadership,* 14–17.

Wanat, C. L. (1992). Meeting the needs of single-parent children: School and parent views differ. *NASSP Bulletin, 76*(543), 55–60.

Weil, R. (1997). The view from between a rock and a hard place. *Phi Delta Kappan, 78*(10), 760–764.

Wiske, M. S. (1994). How teaching for understanding changes the rules in the classroom. *Educational Leadership, 51*(5), 19–21.

Wolfgramm, H. F. (1993). For whom are our schools? *Contemporary Education, 64*(2), 99–103.

Woods, R. K. (1994). A close-up look at how children learn science. *Educational Leadership, 51*(5), 33–35.

Zubrick, P. R. (1991). Problem solving? *Agricultural Education Magazine, 63*(12), 3 & 11.

8 HELPING PEOPLE CHANGE

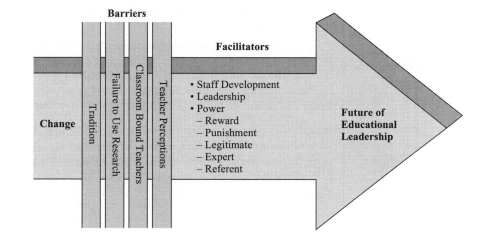

Barriers

Change

Tradition

Failure to Use Research

Classroom Bound Teachers

Teacher Perceptions

Facilitators

- Staff Development
- Leadership
- Power
  - Reward
  - Punishment
  - Legitimate
  - Expert
  - Referent

Future of Educational Leadership

Objectives

This chapter should prepare you to:

- Explain how the curriculum role of the educational leader has changed in recent years.
- Tell why teachers need to conduct research.
- Describe the change in the need for teacher involvement in schoolwide curriculum matters.
- Explain the effect that education reform has had on teacher involvement in schoolwide matters.
- Discuss the effect of teacher involvement in classroom assignments on student behavior in multicultural classes.
- Describe how education consortia can contribute to school reform.
- Justify teacher empowerment as a prerequisite to (a) improving a school's curriculum and (b) implementing education reform.
- Discuss the use of power in education reform.
- Describe some of the benefits of teacher involvement in research.
- Explain the implications that research has for constructivism and multiculturalism.

THE CASE OF REGIONAL UNIVERSITY

In a state where education reform was raging, no money had been appropriated for higher education institutions to enable them to provide help to the public schools, yet some of the state universities and colleges had a long-standing record of providing faculty development and other services to the schools. These educators had a deep commitment to helping the schools reform. Furthermore, the leaders at these colleges and universities anticipated that their institutions would be held accountable for the schools' success or failure in implementing the new laws.

Like a number of other state universities, Regional University has a fully staffed Office of Field Services and Professional Development. For 12 years Regional University has hosted the monthly meetings for about 40 public school superintendents. In addition, Regional's, in-service director has met regularly with the superintendents and instructional supervisors in the 22 counties in its service region and has provided numerous staff development workshops. Other universities in the state have similar arrangements and a history of providing strong support to the schools in their respective regions.

When the winds of school reform began blowing across the state, Regional's president and its education dean spent time in the capitol with the general assembly at open debates on education. As radical change became imminent,

Regional was self-designated as a leader in mapping the state's school reform, and its College of Education was named as the organizer and leader for the university. As soon as the education reform bill was drafted, Regional began holding trainer-of-trainer workshops on major reform issues contained in the bill, such as nongraded primary curricula, valued outcomes, alternative curricula, integrated curricula, portfolios, alternative assessment, performance evaluation, multicultural education, curriculum alignment, site-based decision making, educational technology, and research-based teaching. It was expected that, as new reform elements were introduced, new workshops would be developed.

With the news that the state was appropriating additional funds to the public schools for education reform (increased dollars based on average daily attendance), but that no additional money would be provided to the universities, Regional University made the following proposal to the school districts in its service region.

Educational Excellence Laboratory
A Proposed Staff Development Consortium
Proposal Abstract[1]

The State General Assembly, as a part of its education reform package, has identified staff development as a serious need in improving the state's public schools and has recommended that regional centers and consortia be established to address this need. In response to this recommendation, it is proposed that a staff development consortium, the Educational Excellence Laboratory, be established at Regional University. The Educational Excellence Laboratory would utilize the existing facilities and expertise of the university to provide effective staff development programs targeted to the identified needs of the participating school districts.

Statement of Need

1. Many state school districts lack the fiscal resources to provide staff development activities that have the necessary breadth and depth to effect change.
2. The districts lack a sufficient number of supervisory personnel necessary to plan and manage long-range staff development programs.
3. Many districts are in remote and isolated areas, far removed from access to exemplary programs. More programs, addressing areawide concerns, need to be located in the various areas.
4. Assistance in the design, analysis, and application of school-based research, addressing local problems, is critical.

---

[1] Special thanks to Dr. William R. Thames for his development and leadership with the Education Excellence Consortium.

Regional's Role

Regional University has a definite role to play in this effort to enhance staff development activities in the public schools. An office to assist the schools in staff development already exists in the College of Education. The faculty members of the College of Education have close, trusting relationships with the teachers and administrators in the schools. Regional's leadership role in teacher education, both preservice and in-service, is recognized and accepted.

Goals

The Regional University Educational Excellence Laboratory will revitalize school districts in the consortium through programs designed to provide continuous in-depth professional development opportunities. Extensive assessment will determine local needs related to the recommended educational reforms. Utilizing the nursery through 12th grade laboratory school at Regional, along with on-site assistance, Regional will help local districts improve their staff development programs through:

1. *Staff development:* Continual training will be offered to effect positive school changes.
2. *Curriculum and instruction research:* This will focus on assessing local needs and on designing and conducting research related to effective instructional techniques and curricula.
3. *Technology services:* The future of education reform is related to the efforts of schools to use computers as instructional and administrative tools.
4. *Diagnostic, assessment, and assistance services:* Students placed at risk or with handicapping conditions are in need of diagnoses and assessments for individualized educational plans.
5. *Learning resource center:* Teachers need accessible locations where they can review materials, create instructional materials, and share ideas.
6. *Needs assessment and evaluation:* Continued progress in education requires assessing needs and evaluating expected outcomes in order to tailor the professional development program to the school level.
7. *Professional renewal opportunities:* Practicing teachers and administrators need opportunities for professional renewal which will motivate them and bring about their commitment to educational reform.

Organizational Structure

The proposed Educational Excellence Laboratory consortium would provide professional development services at several sites on the Regional campus and in the field. The consortium would be operated through the existing Office of Field Services and Professional Development located in the College of Education. This office has the responsibility for assisting the school districts in the planning, implementation, and delivery of quality staff development activities. The director of this office would serve as the director of the consortium under the guidance of a steering committee composed of representatives from participating school districts.

The Educational Excellence Laboratory consortium would have five sites, each with a distinct function in professional development. The sites and their functions would be as follows:

1. *Assessment and evaluation site:* Located in the College of Education's Office of Research and Planning, this site will conduct needs assessments, long-range planning, and program evaluation.

2. *Training sites:* Located at Regional's off-campus center and at the on-campus Sam Ervin Center, these sites will provide easy access for training that reflects the best practices and is responsive to participant needs.

3. *Demonstration site:* The laboratory school, located on Regional's campus, will serve as the demonstration site for innovative approaches to instruction and curriculum.

4. *Resource sites:* The off-campus facility and the Horns Library will provide instructional materials libraries for use by participating districts. Other sites to be utilized would be the Tri-Lakes Environmental Center, the Planetarium, the Department of Special Education (with its communication disorders laboratories), the College of Allied Health and Nursing, and the Department of Health Education.

5. *Research and development site:* Located within the laboratory school, this site will provide assistance in identifying the best developing instructional practices and assistance in conducting research with and disseminating results to participating school districts.

The establishment of the Regional University Educational Excellence Laboratory, as outlined above, would result in more effective professional development and improvement of instruction for school districts participating in the consortium.

Educational Excellence Laboratory
Proposed Initial Funding

Funding for the initial activities of the consortium would be provided jointly by Regional University and the participating school districts. Regional University will seek outside funding for its initial share, and participating districts will match that amount dollar for dollar. The exact amount required from each participating district will depend upon the amount of outside funding secured by Regional and the number of school districts participating in the consortium.

Funding for the continuing operation of the consortium would come from the monies provided to the districts through the reform package in the following manner:

Year 1	$1 per child
Year 2	$5 per child
Year 3–5	$25 per child

Twenty-one school districts joined the new consortium, each agreeing to pay a fee based on the number of students in its region. After two years, the consortium expanded its services to include purchasing goods (food, instructional supplies, and cleaning materials). During the following year, purchases of goods exceeded $2 million, saving the districts thousands of dollars.

During the second half of the consortium's third year (June through December) 598 reform workshops were provided to 15,990 teachers. Most of the workshops were delivered on site in the local districts.

AGENTS FOR CHANGE

Improving schools involves changing the curriculum and changing the behavior of those who implement the curriculum. It is a long-standing axiom that good leaders are good agents for change (Oliva & Pawlas, 1999). Making changes can be slow and awkward at first (Laud, 1998), but the good news is that it is now clear that administrators and teachers can effectively be taught the issues and process of making changes (Anderson, Rotheiser, & Gordon, 1998).

Historically, the appropriate leadership role in the schools has been that of ridding schools of their problems. Responsibility for providing this leadership belonged to the principal and the principal's assistant. Basically, the charge of these administrators was to fix or have fixed whatever went wrong, from leaky roofs to student behavior, sometimes even teacher behavior. The need for preparing teachers to be change agents in the twenty-first century is expressed by Claus (1999, p. 5): "A growing literature articulates the need to educate preservice teachers as effective agents of change in pursuit of more democratic schools and social reform."

A New Concept of Leadership

These perceptions have changed. First, the charge is no longer to maintain the status quo. The academic expectations of all schools have been raised, making the curriculum the center of attention. Second, the administrator is very much in the center of efforts to improve curriculum and instruction. Third, the curriculum is being improved on a continuous, nonstop basis; curriculum improvement does not wait until "problems" are identified.

Many changes in today's schools have an impact beyond traditional classroom-level curriculum. In fact, the most common change today is to restructure the organization. *Restructuring* means comprehensive curriculum change to attain the school's mission. Education reform is a major catalyst for much of this change. Fullan and Stiegelbauer (1990) say that, without question, education reform and the process of change are intertwined. In fact, change is a prerequisite for meeting any of the elements of education reform. Because of this dependency on change, Kowalski and Reitzug (1993, p. 305) stress the need for educators to pursue further study to learn more about the way organizations change. They say:

> Without question, the goal of reform and the process of change are intertwined. For this reason, a clear perspective of the former cannot be achieved without an understanding of how the latter does or does not occur. Your understandings of organizations at the early stages of professional study are critically important.

Resistance to Change

Changing organizations is difficult because organizations have a built-in resistance to change. Because of their fundamental nature, schools are especially resistant to change. Fullan and Stiegelbauer (1990, p. 12) describe this property of schools:

> On the one hand schools are expected to engage in continuous renewal, and change expectations are constantly swirling around; on the other hand, the way teachers are trained, the way schools are organized, the way the hierarchy operates, and the way political decision makers treat educators result in a system that is more likely to retain the status quo.

Thus, teachers themselves are responsible for much of the reluctance of schools to change. Thompson and Gregg (1997, pp. 29–30) mention this effect that teachers have on maintaining the status quo, pointing to "even middle schools that organize the curriculum in a way that separates the disciplines." Teachers are reluctant to get involved with changes that are prescribed (Nelson, 1999) and with changes that are likely to be short-lived. Referring to teachers, Wolf and McIver (1999, p. 406) observe, "They refused to invest in a reform that might not last."

Tyack (1990) points out that most of the changes that have occurred in the schools over the past 30 years have not resulted from local initiation; most important changes in our schools have been unplanned and have been stimulated by external forces such as federal laws. Fullen (1999, p. 25) agrees, "Most outside forces threaten schools, but they are also necessary for success." Kowalski and Reitzug (1993) devised a chart to show some of the forces that lead to change and how most schools change (see Figure 8.1). The left side of Figure 8.1 lists the ways most schools have changed; the right side lists behaviors that are foreign to many of today's schools.

FIGURE 8.1

Conditions leading to education change.

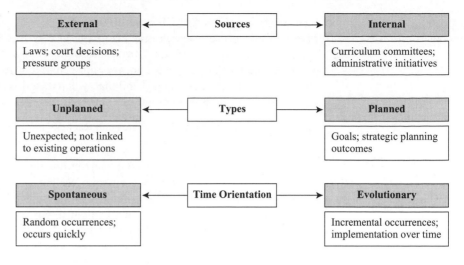

Some Barriers to Change

Changing the behavior of organizations requires changing the behavior of individuals in the organizations. It is an accepted and well-documented fact that teachers have historically avoided involvement in the organization in which they work.

Barrier 1: Failure to Use Research

Chapter 1 identified one of the barriers that keep teachers from getting involved with organizational change: most teachers do not use research (Egbert, 1984; King, 1991). An examination of the reasons why teachers choose to ignore research might give some clue as to how the problem could be corrected. King (1991, p. 43) says that the reasons teachers give for not using research are:

1. Lack of confidence in their ability to understand the studies reported in research publications.
2. Confusion over contradictory research results.
3. Inability to apply research findings immediately in the classroom.

An examination of these reasons suggests that teachers may have little choice; many teachers don't use research because they can't. Bellon et al. (1992, p. 3) agree: "Many experienced teachers are not conversant with the recent research on teaching." Consider the limits that teachers' failure to use research has had on promoting such learning theories as constructivism. Teachers who regularly read professional journals, and who conduct action research studies, are more aware of the benefits and techniques of establishing and maintaining constructivist classrooms.

Barrier 2: Teachers Are Classroom-Bound

The inability to use research may also explain why teachers shun curriculum planning at levels beyond their own classroom. Young (see Haberman, 1992, p. 15) concludes that most teachers are ambivalent toward curriculum development beyond the classroom level and that, when they do develop curricula, they stay at the classroom or instructional level:

> The data presented clearly indicates that teachers' primary interest was in translating curriculum into instruction.

The idea that teachers tend to shun curriculum involvement at levels beyond their own classrooms is reinforced by Young (1985, p. 14) who discovered that the degree to which teachers feel alienated from the decision-making hierarchy relates directly to their sense of involvement in curricular decisions at a level beyond the classroom. Perhaps Eisner (1990, p. 525) says it best when, referring to teachers, he says simply, "We do what we know how to do."

Consider the negative effect that this classroom-bound tendency has had on any attempts that schools may have made to promote multiculturalism. Teachers who stay away from other teachers cannot become role models who demonstrate the positive outcomes of working with members of other cultures.

Barrier 3: Perceptions of Teachers

Teachers' proclivities to avoid research and schoolwide involvement have caused other educators, and perhaps even teachers themselves, to view teachers as incapable of contributing meaningfully to schoolwide change. To a degree, this result has been a self-fulfilling prophecy.

The evidence that teachers prefer not to get involved with curriculum development outside their classrooms and that they purposely avoid dealing with research is convincing; yet one should not conclude that teachers cannot or should not be prepared for using research and working with the total curriculum. Haberman (1992, p. 17) discusses how teachers are perceived and alludes to how this view must change:

> Another barrier to change in schools has been the perception that teachers are part of the existing problems and that any successful attempt to improve the schools must first be teacher-proof. . . . Classroom teachers must be viewed as part of the solution, never as the problem.

Teachers' reluctance to change perhaps can be attributed, at least in part, to the failure of schools to involve teachers in change. Barth (1990, p. 513) discussed this reluctance and some possible consequences when teachers do get involved:

> The lives of teachers and principals more closely mirror the cultivation of mushrooms: "You're kept in the dark most of the time, periodically you're covered with manure, and when you stick your head out it gets chopped off.

Apparently, major education reform is required to involve teachers and administrators in change.

A Need for Involvement

Staying in the classroom and attending only to instruction and other "classroom matters" seemed appropriate until states and school districts began gathering research data on effective schools. These data indicated that changing ineffective schools into effective schools requires teacher involvement with the total school, especially with curriculum matters. Haberman (1992, p. 14) explains:

> Recently, more attention has been given to the concept of the teacher as a professional with specialized knowledge and a pragmatic approach to curriculum planning that is derived from classroom experience. At the classroom level, the teacher would carry out action research to provide knowledge about the needs of students and their relationship to the curriculum.

There are several reasons why contemporary educators insist that teachers should be involved in changing the curriculum at levels beyond their own classroom. Cuban (1993, p. 182) says that improving schools requires more than just changing the curriculum; it also requires changing people, which is neither simple nor easy:

> It is humbling to realize how little each generation learns from the experience of its equally earnest forebears about just how crude a tool curriculum change is for transforming student knowledge and behavior.

Kirk (1988) reports that teachers who are directly involved in curriculum development tend to shift their teaching style from prescriptive to interactive, causing them to increase their interactions with students and more effectively evaluate the needs of their students. Haberman (1992, p. 15) confirms this:

> As teachers feel more involved in the development of curriculum, it is clear that their personal commitment will be a primary factor in motivating the student to be more interested in the material being presented. Further, improvements in teacher-student relationships will not only enhance teaching, but will be evidenced in student achievement as well. Thus, curriculum development becomes curriculum renewal as the chain of communication from student to teacher to curriculum committee becomes a continuous cycle of analysis and problem solving.

When teachers are encouraged to become involved and to contribute to curriculum improvement at levels beyond the classroom, they influence the degree to which their peers accept change. It is not surprising that teachers are willing to follow the lead of their peers rather than mandates imposed by outsiders. Ambrosie and Hanley (1991, p. 78) discovered that when change comes from the central office, teachers react positively 38 percent of the time; when the impetus for change comes from other teachers they react positively 86 percent of the time.

Ways of Involving Teachers

Educators (Kirk, 1988; Haberman, 1992; Ravitch, 1992; Fullan, 1993) agree that in the future teachers should and must be involved more in curriculum than they have in the past. In an article titled "Why teachers must become change agents," Fullan (1993, p. 17) states:

> In the future the teacher must be equally at home in the classroom and in working with others to bring about continuous improvements.

Similar reports of the power of involvement in changing behavior have come from programs designed to diminish misbehavior and improve children's willingness to work with peers from other cultures (Wade, 1997).

The literature provides suggestions as to how teachers can best be enticed to get involved. Early involvement, that is, during the planning stage, is especially important. Ravitch (1992) said that teachers should be involved in setting high standards and in rethinking the school's curriculum. This suggestion seems timely, since the U.S. Department of Education is now issuing grants to several agencies to support the development of national education standards. Haberman (1992) suggests that all persons who work on curricula have responsibility for communicating the new curriculum to their peers and to the community at large.

The Use of Incentives to Involve Teachers

Persuading teachers to expand their levels of involvement in curriculum matters will require special incentives, and although more money may contribute to this persuasion, money is not always the strongest motivator. Wright (1985) found that of the several incentives used to motivate teacher involvement, the most frequently identified incentives are intrinsic rewards, such as increased self-confidence, a sense of achievement or challenge, or the opportunity to develop new skills. Young (1985, p. 14) agrees that the power of intrinsic motivators is important, reporting that the number one motivator for teachers to become involved in curriculum development is their desire for personal involvement in decision making.

It should not be surprising that intrinsic motivators are influential on teachers' involvement in curriculum development within or outside their school; Maslow's hierarchy of needs clearly explains the force of such motivation. Yet one should not conclude that extrinsic motivators are unimportant. Psychologist Frederick Herzberg (Herzberg, Mausner, & Snyderman, 1959) uses the diagram in Figure 8.2 to show the relationships between factors that prevent workers from being dissatisfied and factors that motivate individuals to do their best.

Through a series of teacher interviews, Young (1985) learned that lack of compensation for extra time spent working on committees and the absence of released time deterred teachers from considering involvement in curriculum development. Klein (1992, p. 96) said that one of these types of support-staff development is very important and explains why:

> Teachers will become more involved in curriculum decision making, which will require significantly more curriculum development skills and knowledge than they typically now have.

FIGURE 8.2

Model of Herzberg et al., Two-Factor Motivation Theory.

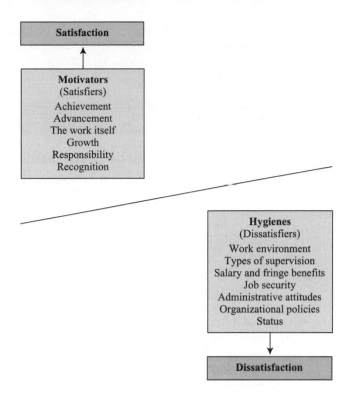

A major factor that inhibits many teachers from expanding their involvement arena is their uncertainty about what activities and behavior are appropriate for teachers. Obviously, as the teacher's role rapidly changes, the array of appropriate teacher activities increases. A review of the literature (Joyce 1990; Little 1989; Rosenholtz 1989) suggests that most teacher behavior is individualistic, dealing with day-to-day operations because the culture of schools supports it. Yet Joyce (1990, p. 33) warns, "Without a balance between operations and the study of teaching and curriculum, the school is liable to drift toward obsolescence and fail to adapt to the needs of the surrounding society."

Schwahn and Spady (1998, pp. 45–47) offer the following rules for effecting change:

1. People don't change unless they share a compelling reason.

2. People don't change unless they have ownership in the change.

3. People don't change unless their leaders model that they are serious about the change.

4. People are unlikely to change unless they have a concrete picture of what the change will look like for them personally.

5. People can't make a change—or make it last—unless they receive organizational support for the change.

These suggestions can and should be used daily by all educators to make improvements more effective and enjoyable. Only then, will the levels of teachers' and students' resistance be lowered.

Teachers as Researchers

From its inception until the mid-twentieth century, the American school was the hub of all sorts of community activities. Cake walks and fish fries were common means of raising money for the schools; the money in turn was given to the teachers to buy supplies to help develop the curriculum. In rural areas, the school building was the meetinghouse for the vocational associations (Farm Bureau, Future Farmers of America, Future Homemakers of America, and 4-H Clubs), and in town the schoolhouse was used by civic groups. In both rural and urban settings, schools have served as polls. A special meeting at school brought in not only mom and dad but the entire extended family including the grandparents, uncles, aunts, and cousins. Involvement of parents and other community members can increase a school's academic gains (Day 1999; Fullan 1999).

During this time, the one-room schoolhouse put teachers in charge of the entire curriculum. But increased urbanization, school growth and consolidation, and forced busing destroyed the concept of the school as the hub of the community. Federal and state curriculum mandates reshaped the curricula. By the early 1960s, prefabricated curricula were being manufactured at research and development centers and sent to the schools. The results of these changes have been (1) a diminishing of the *level* of the teacher's responsibility for curriculum development, and (2) a reduction in the *range* of teacher involvement in curriculum development, from schoolwide control to projects that are limited to their own classrooms.

Removing teachers from the center of schoolwide curriculum development has isolated them from research activities and kept them from seeing the need to verify their practices. It has also left teachers feeling left out of schoolwide decisions. Carson (1990, p. 167) expresses the problem this way:

> Rather than being active participants in school change, teachers have found themselves on the receiving end of criticism, new regulations, having to implement new programs, answering to external evaluations, and being responsible for more layers of bureaucratic management.

On the positive side, there have been some recent increases in the level of teacher involvement with research. Claus (1999, p. 13) warns, "Teacher educators must educate pre-service teachers to consult and conduct research relevant to the issues they wish to address and the goals they hope to achieve." A review of the literature shows that as early as 1908, concrete efforts were being made to involve classroom teachers in research (Lowery, 1908; Henson, 1996). The purpose of this early research conducted by teachers was to develop curricula (McKernan, 1988), and this purpose has remained constant throughout the century, although a new term, *action research,* has become popular in recent years. McCutcheon and Jung (1990, p. 144) define action research as "inquiry teachers undertake to understand and improve their own practice." When conducting action research, teachers may work alone or collaborate with others (Shalaway, 1990).

This enduring involvement by some teachers in research should not be interpreted to mean that all or even most teachers have been conducting research. On the contrary, most teachers have purposefully avoided research, and for a number of reasons. For example, teachers often perceive research topics as too theoretical and too superficial (Chattin-McNichols & Loeffler, 1989). This perception may result, at least in part, from the different natures of the teacher's world and the researcher's world. Cuban (1992) contrasts the two worlds, saying that the teacher's world is characterized by action and concrete facts, whereas researchers deal with abstractions and theory. Teachers want concrete answers to questions such as "What should I do?" Researchers are comfortable exploring possibilities.

When teachers do become involved with research several significant gains are realized. For example, their own teaching often improves. Kirk (1988) said that as teachers become involved with research, their style shifts from prescriptive to interactive. Stevens, Slaton, and Bunny (1992) said that through involvement with research, teachers experience a renewed desire to stay current (see Sardo-Brown, 1992). As Boyer (1990, p. 57) expressed it, "As teachers become researchers they become learners." Nixon (1981, p. 9) says that "Action research serves primarily to sharpen perceptions, stimulate discussion, and energize questioning."

After becoming involved in conducting research, teachers become more critical, questioning their own beliefs and the assertions of others (Neilsen, 1990). Involvement with research makes teachers more reflective, a critical trait for contemporary teachers. Lytle and Cochran-Smith (1990, p. 101) state:

> As teachers begin to participate in the generation of knowledge about teaching, learning, and schooling, they become more critical of both university-based research and standard school practices. They challenge taken-for-granted assumptions about theory and practice.

Improved teacher attitude is another benefit that arises from teacher involvement with research, and one common result of improved attitude is increased teacher effectiveness. Bennett (1993, p. 69) says:

> I noted that teachers went into the research component of the program feeling anxious and hostile, but emerged feeling positive about the experience and their newly found identities as teacher-researchers.

An important dimension in many contemporary educational reform efforts is *teacher empowerment.* According to Carson (1990, p. 167), "Action research has been seen as a way of giving teaching back to teachers." Current education literature often reports on how involvement in action research increases teachers' self-development (Bernauer, 1999). As Tripp (1990, p. 165) says, "Action research enables teachers both to formulate and act upon their own concerns, thereby personally and professionally developing themselves within and through their practice."

Action research brings both perceptual and phenomenological benefits to teachers. First, involvement in research makes teachers more aware. One way to think about perceptual benefits is to consider what happens to teachers' perceptions when they are not involved in ongoing research. Sanger (1990, p. 175), says, ". . . as teachers, we gather to ourselves that which confirms our deepest underlying prejudices and attitudes."

Involvement in action research can move teachers beyond their perceptions, into their understandings and feelings about themselves and how they relate to their work. It can help teachers understand that, although they often pretend to have all of the answers needed in their daily work, they never really do. Each of us interprets the world about us in unique ways. Involvement in research can help us view our professional role open-mindedly. As Carson (1990, p. 172) explains, "This requires an openness to our own experience and the experience of others, putting aside dogmatic arguments and preconceived opinions."

Increased understanding about ourselves in relation to the world around us opens the path to clearer, more honest relationships with others. Most current action research projects are collaborative efforts, and, even more collaboration between schools and universities is needed, as Stroot et al. (1999, p. 39) state: "We encourage collaborative research projects, especially in areas where all will benefit." McElroy (1990, p. 209) says that, "Being authentic (or real), for example, in our relationship with another is at the heart of collaborative action research, and is at the heart of a matter of ethics." He reports that his collaborative research efforts have caused him to replace his concern for self with a greater connection, a freeing to experience more authentically: "This ego-less is not weakening; rather, it provides a feeling of strength, of standing firmly on a formless, shifting ground."

As faculties throughout the country are being "forced" to implement education reform, it is evident to the outside observer that egos are threatened. Much, if not most, resistance comes from the threat teachers feel from the forced changes. When told that we must change, we infer that we have been doing something wrong; the message is that our performance is unacceptable. Few forces can fire the level of resistance that follows when individuals are told, either overtly or covertly, that they are unworthy. If, indeed, involvement in collaborative action research can free teachers from some of their need to protect their egos, then it may be paving the road to progress for school reform. For a more complete review of research on teachers as researchers, see Henson, 1996.

Like theory, research and development are not linear, problem-answer processes. Since the goal is often to change the infrastructure of the school's curriculum, and since lasting change is a slow process, action research requires patience and commitment. Sanger, an action research trainer (1990, p. 175) says, "The deepest and least changeable levels seem to accrete slowly through experience. Rather like a coral reef, 'significant' bits are drawn down from the surface of daily events and settle and fuse with deeper layers. They add to and complement what is already there."

There is evidence that involvement with research prepares teachers for future change by making them more flexible and accepting to change. Bennett (1993, p. 69) addresses this idea:

> As teachers gained experience and success with research, their attitude toward research greatly improved. Teacher-researchers viewed themselves as being more open to change.

New ways to involve teachers in action research are continually being sought. Often we hear teachers say they would be eager to get involved in schoolwide planning if only they had time. In fact, teachers everywhere are struggling with heavy workloads. The following case study by Granada and Lapan shows how a good organizer can help busy colleagues find the time and energy required to make significant changes in the school curriculum.

Case Study

Teaming and Collaborating for Change

Jim Granada
University of Texas, San Antonio

Stephen D. Lapan
Northern Arizona University

Background Information

Change is an issue teachers must face from the day they enter a teacher training program until the day of the retirement party. Change comes in many forms, from curriculum reform to state competency mandates to changes in personnel. Very often in the education world, change is imposed on, rather than initiated by, classroom teachers. The result is generally a reluctance to embrace change and often a resistance to changes being proposed. If teachers are to accept and support change, they must have a complete understanding of the proposed changes and the change process. Acceptance and support at the classroom and building levels come much easier when the agents of change are classroom teachers.

Teaming and collaboration foster innovation and change. The utilization of the talents of two or more individuals enhances the change process and provides the opportunity to explore a variety of ideas and options. Discussion among team players allows for a greater depth of understanding, particularly when the focus of discussion is related to a proposed change. This teamwork and collaboration can be between teacher and student, teacher and parent, teacher and colleague,

(Continued)

and/or teacher and administrator. Collaboration toward change provides a sense of ownership to the players. Reluctance and resistance tend to fade as collaborators explore the possible outcomes of proposed changes, improving their understanding of the meaning of reform and the change process. When presented with change that would result in limitations rather than benefits, the collaborators can explore alternatives together for an improved change plan.

In the summer of 1991, fifteen potential change agent teachers arrived on the campus of Northern Arizona University (NAU) to become participants in a training project funded by a Jacob Javits grant.[1] The goal of the training project was to prepare teams of classroom teachers, over a period of ten weeks, to develop and implement programs of gifted education for underrepresented populations in their school. Schools had been approached by NAU project directors earlier in the year, with specific focus on sites that served a large number of ethnic minority students. Administrators expressing an interest in project involvement followed up the visit by soliciting volunteers for training. The fifteen training participants had agreed to devote a large part of their summer to become agents of change. Each school site involved agreed to send at least two teachers who would serve as the returning change agent team.

These teacher teams faced ten weeks of intensive training that included practice in teaching methods, lesson and unit development, and analysis of their own teaching. They would be expected to learn how to identify underserved minority gifted youth and to develop a faculty collaboration and program plan to implement upon their return to school in the fall. While the road ahead would be a rocky, frustrating one for these potential change agents, the NAU project staff hoped that the teachers would learn to work together as they never had before.

The stories of the 15 participants during the course of training and school year implementation are as unique as the school sites they represented. Levels of success were varied as well. One particularly successful site was an elementary school in the southwest area of Arizona, an oasis in the middle of the desert regions near the border of Mexico. This is that school's story.

The Community

The community has a population approaching 55,000, a medium-sized city by Arizona standards. Agriculture, through irrigation of the desert area, is a part of the lifeblood of the economy. A significant number of Mexican families, representing more than 33 percent of the community's population (all Hispanics represented nearly 36%) were drawn to the city, either due to the proximity of its location or the job opportunities that beckoned. The impact of the Mexican culture was prevalent throughout the area, most notably in the schools. Large numbers of Mexican and Mexican-American students ascended the public schools. The community struggled with providing the best educational programs possible for these students; a disproportionately high dropout rate of Hispanic students was an indicator that much more needed to be done.

---

[1] The project reported in this case study was supported under the Javits Act Program (Grant No. R206A90087) as administered by the Office of Educational Research and Improvement, U.S. Department of Education. Professors S. Lapan and P. Hays directed this NAU project.

(Continued)

The School

The elementary school site that was selected as part of the training project was a relatively new building in a growing section of the city. Socioeconomic diversity was apparent as one drove around the neighborhood. The student population was relatively large, serving grades K–6, and portable classrooms were being used to accommodate numbers. The staff, including the principal, was primarily female, with several teachers at each grade level. An absence of diversity on the staff was quite obvious when compared with diversity in the student population; only one of 40 staff members was Hispanic while the school had a 52 percent Hispanic enrollment. The presence of bilingual office staff was a positive, not only in terms of translating communications but also serving somewhat in the role of "liaisons" for the Spanish-speaking community.

The school offered a gifted education program that was similar to many across the state. State-mandated intelligence and achievement tests were used as criteria for placement, and the program focused on acceleration and enrichment. Very few minority students had been identified for this program.

The Players

The key players in the NAU project training were Melinda, a fifth grade teacher, Bart, a sixth grade teacher, and Kelly, the school principal. Melinda had not been teaching long, but her classroom was very organized and structured. Routines were well established, and the room environment was quiet and orderly. Bart had taught at the school for a few years and was known for his success with challenging students. It was no surprise to walk in his classroom and find a large number of boys (and a few girls) who had the potential to be very disruptive. Bart's classroom was very different from Melinda's; noise was quite common, and the approach used was only moderately structured. Bart's laid-back, carefree attitude was in direct contrast to Melinda's stoic approach to teaching. Kelly had been the building administrator for a few years and steered her faculty and staff smoothly and efficiently. You knew where you stood with Kelly, and she ran the school's business with fair yet demanding expectations. Principal Kelly was the kind of person you could have a serious educational debate with during lunch, then meet for dinner and talk about the best places to eat in the casino haven of Laughlin, Nevada. The personalities of these three individuals were enough alike that they could laugh together at times, yet different enough that decisions would rarely be made without extensive discussion.

Bart was the renegade of the trio, the prankster, the jokester, the "I've seen it all" kind of guy. His East coast upbringing gave him an air of worldliness as well as a bit of a hard edge. Bart cared about his students but gave the impression that he wouldn't be particularly nurturing (in the traditional sense) in the classroom. Bart was actively involved in sports, both as a participant and spectator, and had "coach" ingrained in his personality. Bart was married with three sons. His wife was pursuing a teaching degree.

Melinda was the organizer. With her quiet leadership she was able to reign in Bart's spontaneity when decisions had to be made. Melinda was efficient and linear in many aspects of her life. She had high expectations for herself, her

(Continued)

students, and those she worked with. A natural at nurturing, Melinda was also very perceptive about her students' special needs, and she would do whatever was necessary to provide for her students or secure whatever they needed that she could not provide. Her second life revolved around her husband and two dogs.

Kelly was a natural administrator. She was a "no-nonsense" kind of decision maker when situations called for a "the buck stops here" kind of solution. Kelly also was an innovative instructional leader; she recognized many needs not being met in her school and explored creative ways to meet those needs under the funding constraints of the district. Well informed about the educational literature and trends of the day, she contemplated pursuing of a doctorate in school administration. Kelly provided the wisdom of her years of experience and the support of her position as building administrator to the team.

The Case: Part One—The Training

Melinda and Bart arrived on campus at Northern Arizona University in June 1991 along with the other project participants from across the state. The two teachers spent the first few days attending intensive full-day sessions that provided experiences in knowledge acquisition, reflective thinking, self-evaluation, critical thinking, and collaboration. As the training progressed, Melinda seemed to become more quiet, more serious, and more efficient. Bart became far more outgoing and, some would say, outlandish in his behavior.

The first opportunity for direct collaboration among participants was also an exercise that focused on trust and openness. Groups were assigned to assess videotaped teaching lessons. Taping of lessons was not new to these two; a prearrival requirement of the project had been to tape a lesson at school and mail it to the project staff. However, this was the first time either of the two had had their teaching analyzed by peers and followed up by a roundtable discussion of what was observed and recorded about the lesson. As would be expected, all the teachers were anxious about the revelations that were forthcoming.

Early in the training, teams from each of the project sites were prepared for the curriculum and program planning that would take place as the training progressed. A site plan was to be developed, in collaboration with the building administrator, for a gifted education delivery model that would identify and provide programming for underrepresented populations at each school. These site plans were highly specific to the needs of the school community and culture.

Melinda and Bart were very effective in developing their site plan. Having full support and continuous communication with Kelly, their principal, they designed a plan that would focus on identifying students with potential in the areas of leadership and creativity. They both saw this as a program needed by the students they worked with. They determined that the most effective initial implementation of their design would be in two stages. Initially, they would go into classrooms at their assigned teaching levels (Melinda at fifth grade, Bart at sixth grade) and teach whole-class lessons designed to tap the creative and leadership talents of students. Together with the regular classroom teacher, they would begin collecting data to help them determine which students might benefit from a gifted program focusing on leadership and creativity.

(Continued)

Phase two of their program implementation would be to jointly select students who had demonstrated potential in either the leadership or creativity areas and meet with the identified students on a regular basis by pulling them out of classes at scheduled times (this is called a pull-out model in gifted education), Bart working with sixth graders and Melinda with fifth graders. With the help of teaching colleagues, they would identify students from all of the classrooms (including their own) who were not currently a part of the traditional gifted program, paying particular attention to finding untapped talent among minority students, girls, and underachievers. This two-phase design seemed manageable within the first year of implementation and would be a step in the right direction toward meeting some of the recognized limitations of the offerings currently in place.

The Case: Part Two—Fall Semester, 1991

Sometimes agents of change must make sacrifices for the sake of an innovation. Such was the case with Melinda and Bart. They, as well as Principal Kelly, knew they had a very good plan, but they wondered how there would be time to implement it. They all knew, after ten weeks of reflection, that this was something the students would benefit from, and they were committed to making it work, so, together, they sat down to look at the dreaded "master schedule."

What resulted from hours of reconfiguring was a give-and-take outcome: Melinda and Bart would give of their talents to students and staff and take from their individual schedules a portion of the all-too-few planning times they were allotted. Kelly mapped out the most advantageous times for each to do so, and the first major logistical obstacle had been overcome. They hoped that the rest of the staff, recognizing the efforts being made by Melinda and Bart, would be supportive of whatever scheduling changes needed to be made that would affect them.

In August, the first order of business was an optional in-service/orientation with teachers whose students might be selected for participation in the program. An information session was held early one morning during "prep" week, with Melinda, Bart, and an NAU project staff member presenting an overview of the year ahead. The turnout for this optional session was reflective of site support. In attendance were Kelly, the district gifted program teacher, all fifth and sixth grade teachers, and two of the fourth grade teachers. In the presentation, much emphasis was placed on the importance of the role of the classroom teacher. Bart and Melinda left the presentation feeling pleased about the interest demonstrated by their peers.

Initially, the project site team had planned to ease into implementation, starting out with demonstration lessons in classrooms. Once again, the teachers on the team were charting unfamiliar territory. The idea of peer modeling is not new, but it was new in their building. The demonstration lessons would have a variety of targeted outcomes. Bart and Melinda would provide teachers with lesson models that would foster creative responses from students in the regular classroom setting. It was hoped that teachers would be motivated to incorporate similar types of lessons into their daily teaching. A direct outcome of the lessons would be opportunities for Bart and Melinda to interact with students and list those students who might benefit from inclusion in the alternate gifted program. Melinda and

(Continued)

Bart hoped that more of these potential students would be recognized and that more dialogue would take place regarding them.

Although the original intent of the demonstration lessons had been broader, Bart and Melinda chose to focus on the use of the lessons as a means of identifying gifted students. The classroom teachers for the most part shared this goal. In addition, a sixth grade teacher saw a global purpose for the demonstrations. She saw the lessons as a means of expanding her students' reasoning and their ability to perceive things differently than they might in a typical classroom. The lessons were viewed more as mind expansion than as teaching definite skills. A fifth grade teacher, having experienced the lessons, recognized Melinda and Bart's new expertise in identifying the creative talent in kids. She recognized her own limitations, and was very pleased that the two were able to share this expertise with her.

The Case: Part Three—Spring Semester, 1992

When the second semester began, it was time to test the planned pull-out program. This would be a real test of collaboration, support, and teamwork for Melinda and Bart. They planned on meeting with newly identified students on a weekly basis.

During the second month of the pull-out, Bart shared these observations:

> We're getting a lot of cooperation from our staff. The kids that we have in the program are real excited about it and they make a big deal about going, and we have lots of other students who have requested to be in the program and they don't understand why they're not. You know we've made positive strides.

Melinda shared a regret that she and Bart had related to an original component of the site plan:

> I think we had hoped to involve our [district] gifted program, tie them more in with ours, and I don't think we're doing that, and, again, it's because of all the different schedules we're on. And to actually sit down and say, "Let's plan something for both groups to do," we don't do that. And I think we'd hoped we could do that more.

As the semester progressed, a few more students were identified, and students were involved in a number of projects in the pull-out program that tapped both their creative potential and their critical thinking skills. Students shared their enthusiasm for being in the program with classmates and classroom teachers. They said they enjoyed the chance to use their imaginations, and some said that their enthusiasm for being involved with the program had extended to their families. One student stated that when he talked about the program, his parents would "stop what they were doing and listen to me." He added that his parents contributed ideas related to specific projects he was working on in the program.

Two students in the program shared some interesting insights. The first, in response to being asked why the program was being implemented, responded:

> Because they [Bart and Melinda] felt that there was a need to get something because there were a bunch of kids being neglected. Nothing was being done with them, and they were not even ever thought of that way [being gifted].

(Continued)

The second student recognized the extended benefits of being involved:

> You do activities to make you feel not that you're more special than another person, but to bring out your ideas. That way you get a better understanding, and then when you go to your regular class you can participate more and express your ideas in a way someone wouldn't.

Not only was the impact of the new program being felt at the building level, but Bart and Melinda's work was being recognized throughout the district. They had met with the director of gifted programs in the district early in the second semester to update her on the progress of the program. The director had then contacted Bart and Melinda a few times, including requests for conference presentations, and she appeared to want both teachers to stay actively involved in gifted education at the district level.

In-services were an additional opportunity for the novice change agents to spread the good word about their successful program. Melinda commented about two specific in-service opportunities she and Bart had the pleasure of being involved with:

> We did a half-day in-service with the gifted teachers from the whole school district. We presented different types of materials and just shared with them parts of the summer training. We gave them some examples of work and lesson plans that we had.

> The whole district had an afternoon in-service on the Hispanic culture. We got to do a presentation on our program there. Our focus was on minority gifted, targeting minority students for gifted programs. Quite a few teachers came to that one.

An air of confidence was very much present as the two shared their experiences among the network of project staff and participants. They became quite eager to tell the story of their program and, specifically, the success stories of the students they were serving.

As the school year drew to a close, both teachers finished up projects not only in the pull-out program but in their own classrooms as well. Plans had to be made not only for the summer but for the unique challenges of a dual-track school the following year. As the three team members—the principal, the fifth grade teacher, and the sixth grade teacher—looked back at the year that had gone by so quickly, they began to reflect on the changes that had taken place.

Throughout the school year, and particularly during the second semester, Melinda and Bart worked closely together. Initially they had planned how the implementation would take place and prepared demonstration lessons. As the year progressed, their collaborative effort grew as they focused on identifying students for the program, developing activities for the pull-out sessions, and providing in-service programs and consulting for staff and district personnel. You might be curious to know how the two teachers viewed such a close partnership, since more often than not teachers perform their daily teaching duties in the isolation of a self-contained classroom. Looking back at the year, Melinda and Bart had only positive remarks to make about their year-long collaboration.

One indication that this was a successful collaboration was the impact the two teachers, with the support and guidance of the principal, had at the building level.

(Continued)

Principal Kelly noted the positive effects the implementation had on her school community:

> I think it's been very creative, very beneficial to the students. It's created a lot of parent interest, and I think the neatest thing I've seen happen is the interest the other teachers now have in developing upper-level thinking skills. . . . I think the teachers were excited to know that Melinda and Bart were willing to come into their rooms and actually model lessons.

At year's end, Kelly shared these additional impressions, from the perspective of being the building principal:

> They [students] felt like they were important, like they were being considered. A lot of the students that Bart and Melinda had been working with I had seen [in] a negative [way because of] discipline problems, [but] those decreased. They turned into the kinds of students that would come in and ask questions like, "Why aren't we doing more recycling? What can we do about recycling?" Instead of being frustrated out on the playground and getting in trouble, they were learning to take questions they had and try to find solutions for the questions.

Beyond the immediate changes they saw in the students and in their teaching, Bart and Melinda saw changes in their roles at the building level, too. They saw their program as taking the first steps toward at least a preliminary solution to the gang problems that were facing their community. Identifying kids that could "get lost in the cracks and maybe not even finish high school" and recognizing and valuing their talents might have long-range effects. They also saw the program's impact on the teachers, many of whom were rethinking what "giftedness" meant. Both teachers saw themselves being recognized as leaders in the building and in the district. The opportunities to serve as in-service presenters was new to each of them, but they quickly grew comfortable with the new roles.

The Case: Part Four—Some General Outcomes

The year of change resulted in a number of outcomes, anticipated and otherwise. What was targeted by the team was successfully accomplished, in spite of the challenges and limitations. But some not-so-obvious changes also resulted from the multiple levels of collaboration that took place.

Classroom teachers, though not always active players, began to have a heightened awareness of what the term "gifted" really means, and how often talent is hidden. Teachers began generating "waiting lists" of kids they had begun to see in a very different way. In one instance, a classroom teacher anticipated a future placement of a student who had just been moved into her classroom from an ESL (English as a Second Language) setting, which was a new way for the building staff to look at a non-English-speaking child, and credit for the teacher's heightened sensitivity goes to Bart and Melinda.

Teachers of younger students were also influenced by the program's implementation. Fourth grade teachers, not directly involved in the current configuration, had been approaching Melinda regarding future placement of students. Melinda, after a number of conversations with the fourth grade teachers, felt they

(Continued)

were not only gaining information through these interactions, but they were also beginning to justify their own hunches about students they had who did not meet district criteria for placement.

Finally, the district itself was beginning to evaluate gifted education. Melinda offered this perception:

> I think we've probably stirred them [district] up a little. I think we've gone in and we've asked questions that they couldn't answer. So I think they're looking at trying to answer those questions on change. It may be slow in coming, but they're aware that they've got to do something, and I'd like to think that we've helped them become aware.

Melinda, Bart, and Kelly had a lot to be proud of as the year ended. Most of their plan had been successfully implemented, they had been able to overcome the challenges of scheduling, and they had provided a special year for two groups of students. But they were all aware that, even as a threesome, they could not have done it unassisted. Melinda summed up what all agreed was the key to success:

> I think you need support from your staff and administration to help with your plan. I think you need to start small and then build up toward big. I think if you take on too much too soon, you'll fail. I think having a team was great because you've been there to help each other out the whole way. You can ask each other questions like, "What are you doing?" and "How did this work?" and "Have you tried this?" Or you remind each other of things. Being in constant communication with others lets you know you're not alone.

The Case: Part Five—The Epilogue

This program was implemented during the academic year 1991–1992. So what does it prove? What does something that happened a few years ago, in some unknown to most of us place, have to do with education reform now?

If nothing else, perhaps the reader of this success story can see that more is happening in the public school than what is often so negatively portrayed in the media. Perhaps one can see a bit of themselves in Melinda, Bart, or Kelly. Maybe someone reading this will think back on a situation or setting very similar to the one presented. Maybe that someone can make a difference themselves.

This case is not a story of great political changes or sweeping educational reform. This isn't a story that will someday become a blockbuster movie or a best seller. This is a testimonial to the hard work of a trio of everyday educators who, with some training and support, demonstrated how positive change can happen by using a team approach and collaboration with colleagues and a school principal.

Issues for Further Reflection and Application

1. What are the advantages and disadvantages of working with no-nonsense, linear thinkers when changes are being made?

2. Change often brings varying degrees of discomfort if not downright pain to people having to adjust to new circumstances. Can innovators be conditioned to accept and overcome the discomfort that change brings?

(Continued)

3. What role does flexibility play in change leadership?

4. What steps can agents of change take to ensure that students will not feel left out or ignored?

Suggested Readings

Amabile, T. M. (1988). A model of creativity and innovation in organizations. *Research in Organizational Behavior, 10,* 123–167.

Barth, R. S. (1990). *Improving schools from within.* San Francisco: Jossey-Bass.

Day, B. M. (1999). *Teaching and learning for the millennium.* Indianapolis, IN: Kappa Delta Pi.

Fullan, M. (1993). *Change forces: Probing the depth of educational reform.* Bristol, PA: Falmer Press.

Fullan, M. (1999). Participating education: A proactive approach. In B. M. Day (Ed.), *Teaching and learning for the millennium.* Indianapolis, IN: Kappa Delta Pi.

Hodgetts, R. M. (1996). *Modern human relations at work.* Fort Worth, TX: Dryden Press.

Speck, M. (1999). *The principalship: Building a learning community.* Upper Saddle River, NJ: PrenticeHall.

The authors of this case study began by saying that collaboration is based on trust and openness. At different phases of the project, the authors explain how they altered their plans at the last moment, adjusting their approach to make the students more comfortable. Such flexibility is characteristic of successful teachers in multicultural classrooms and of teachers in constructivist classrooms. When plans are altered based on need, one might conclude that the planning was wasted time, but such a conclusion overlooks the purpose of planning. Good planning helps teachers organize the lessons in their minds. Once the organization is made, teachers are freed from the intense fear that can result from not knowing what to do. Good planning doesn't close the door on alternatives. On the contrary, it frees the teacher to pursue different directions.

Such flexibility is essential in constructivist classes, for a common characteristic of teacher behavior and one of the most frequently made mistakes of constructivist teachers is a tendency to rush students. Problem solving takes time, much more time than more direct instructional methods. Making errors and exploring alternative solutions takes time, but making errors is an essential part of the learning process in problem solving, constructivist classes. Flexibility is equally important in diverse classrooms, where teachers must be devoted to the concept that all students can and will learn. Finally, flexibility is an essential quality for anyone attempting to help people change, whether students or teachers.

Helping Teachers Become Researchers

Teacher research occurs in many different ways. One variable among organizational structures of research activities is the teacher's role, which can range from that of a passive assistant to that of an independent researcher or a full partner in research.

Not all teachers want to conduct research; therefore, success in promoting teacher research depends on the selection of appropriate teachers, that is, teachers who possess the desire and qualities conducive to conducting research. Teachers who try out a new method in their classroom and compare its results with previously used methods are engaging in action research (Oliva & Pawlas, 1999). An obviously necessary quality for successfully using action research is curiosity; teacher researchers must have questions for which they want answers—questions about their own teaching.

Another quality that facilitates the conducting of research is the habit of constant reading. Teacher researchers must read professional journals in their fields. As Shalaway (1990, p. 37) says, "Teacher researchers agree that all teachers can benefit by keeping up with the professional literature." This practice is essential because regular reading of the professional literature keeps teachers current in their field and reflects an attitude of intellectual flexibility (Hattrup & Bickel, 1993).

An analysis of the benefits teachers derive from being involved with research found that most of the benefits are realized only when teachers are involved at the highest level. This type of involvement occurs only when teachers identify a problem that is important to them. As Chattin-McNichols and Loeffler (1989, p. 21) explain, identifying an important problem is easy:

> Classroom teachers are faced, on a daily basis, with questions that puzzle and concern them in their interactions with children. Many of these questions provide appropriate material for microresearch projects for teachers to carry out in their classrooms.

Once a problem is selected for study, the investigator must define the problem. Part of this identification might include establishing a baseline, which the Reading/Language in Secondary Schools Subcommittee of the International Reading Association (1989) says is essential. A baseline or benchmark level provides a starting place for measuring improvement. A baseline can be established by using a pretest or simply by gathering data.

Once the baseline is established, the investigating teacher(s) should implement the change strategies and then follow up by testing to determine the amount of progress. Chattin-McNichols and Loeffler (1989) stressed the importance of full teacher involvement in every stage of the research. Maria Cardelle-Elawar (1993) developed the model for initiating teacher research shown in Figure 8.3.

Consortia

Several professional organizations—especially state education association chapters—are dedicated to helping teachers become empowered and prepared to assume greater curriculum leadership roles. Many workshops are required to prepare in-service teachers and administrators for the reform challenges in their state, but even the best workshops are no better than the degree to which the objectives, content, and skills they cover match the needs of the teachers and

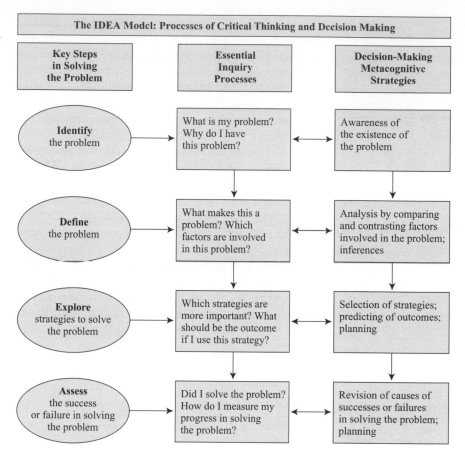

administrators who attend the workshops. One organizational structure used to assume this match is the consortium.

An *educational consortium* is a formal coalition of two or more school districts designed to aid them in achieving common goals. Educational consortia work much like traditional agricultural and vocational education cooperatives. Member school districts pool their resources to purchase services that no district could afford by itself.

Staff Development Problems

Staff development makes specific demands of its leaders. When those demands are not met, problems arise. Reporting on a study by the Southern Education Consortium, Purvis and Boren (1991, p. 21) identified three major problems related to staff development: "(1) Incentives for attendance are lacking,

(2) programs are not related to teachers' needs and interests, and (3) staff development programs are not well organized and thought out carefully enough."

Myrick and Jones (1991, pp. 3–6) suggest the following roles and responsibilities of staff development leaders:

- Leaders must be aware of new practices in curriculum and instruction.
- Leaders must help develop a vision for their school.
- Leaders must communicate the school's or department's mission and goals.
- Leaders must be team members.
- Leaders must secure financing.
- Leaders must conduct assessments.
- Leaders must value growing.
- Leaders must earn trust.
- Leaders must remain open-minded.
- Leaders must recognize contributions by others.

Interestingly, some of these responsibilities seem to apply to any educational leader, not just to the staff development leader. Clearly, the education reform reports have changed the role of educational leaders quite dramatically, making it broader and increasing their management responsibilities. Education reform has pressed for participation in management as a means of empowering teachers because, as indicated earlier, there is evidence that successful involvement of teachers in managing the schools is essential to maximum educational improvement.

Poplin (1992) discusses this shift in the role of educational leaders, making several points that deserve repeating. First, the role of educational leaders has, indeed, changed, becoming much broader. Because of school-based management, the teacher must be prepared to manage a broad spectrum of the school's business, including financial and curriculum decisions, heretofore outside the teacher's purview. Second, today's leaders must provide a climate that lets teachers expand their horizons. Third, the contemporary leader must help teachers develop skills they can use to evaluate their own performance. Fourth, today's leader must protect teachers' time. (This translates into providing released time from regular assignments.) In short, Popin describes today's leader as a highly skilled manager, able to provide latitude, freedom, support, and encouragement for teachers to grow and become less dependent on their leadership.

All curriculum leaders, including department and grade-level chairs, need these types of skills. For many leaders, the greatest challenge may be to bring about the changes in attitude that will be required to provide leadership or managership while working alongside other teachers.

A Need to Go Beyond Current Horizons

This chapter has stressed the need to examine the teacher's work environment and to provide fiscal and physical support to curriculum leaders and to their colleagues as they work together to improve the curriculum. This kind of support is essential for effective leadership, but success requires more. Curriculum leaders must be motivated to achieve beyond their previous levels. Remember John Dewey's human development goal: that each culture would be elevated above its previous culture through the development of individuals. In other words, as essential as the tools needed to do the job are, success requires more: teachers must be motivated to want to exceed the accomplishments made by the previous generation.

School Culture and Climate

Anyone who has worked with schools knows that each school has its own culture, its own ethos. Schools are like homes: some make you feel welcome; others don't. Some schools send a message that they are exciting places to be. Some schools are threatening; others offer security. Some are as dead as a petrified forest; others are like a freeway during rush hour—people have places to go, and they are eager to get there. As McNeil (1990, p. 196) says, "The idea of a school having an ethos, being distinct from other schools, and subjecting all aspects of school life to this quality is powerful."

Kowalski and Reitzug (1993, p. 311) use the diagram shown in Figure 9.2 to show the relationship among a school's climate and the variables that interact to form its climate: culture, milieu, ecology, social system, and organization. They explain the interactions among these factors:

> There are three common perspectives of how change occurs in organizations. The first is a technical view erected on an assumption that increased knowledge and technical assistance produce change. This approach assumes rationality and focuses on the nature of the innovation (e.g., a new program). The second perspective accounts for power and influence that may be used by groups and individuals to support or ward off change. The focus is political behavior, and attention is given to both the innovation and the context of the organization. The third perspective looks at the shared values, beliefs, and norms of the organization. It is identified as the cultural perspective and emphasizes the importance of organizational context. After more than ten years of attempted reform, educators and the general public are recognizing the limitations of the first two approaches. Hence, more recent reform efforts have focused largely on the third category. More precisely, second wave change efforts are inquiring about the ways in which culture produces barriers that prevent change.
>
> Imagine a situation in which a third-grade teacher is considering whether to administer corporal punishment to a disruptive student. What factors affect the decision? First, the teacher's behavior is influenced by personal values, experiences, and beliefs regarding the moral and practical dimensions of hitting a child.

Additionally, the teacher hopefully considers whether corporal punishment is acceptable professionally and legally. The third, and often most influential, component is the teacher's perception of what the school expects from him or her. In other words, the teacher considers the school's norms. Do other teachers use corporal punishment? Does the principal advocate it? In some combination, the teacher weighs personal considerations (e.g., personal beliefs, motivations), legal and professional dimensions, and school-specific norms. Thus, even though the teacher may reject the use of corporal punishment, both personally and professionally, the act still may be carried out because of social pressures maintained by the school.

Sagor (1992) testifies to the importance of school culture and to the contribution that good leaders make to their school's culture. Sagor says that good principals use three building blocks of transformational leadership: (1) a clear and unified focus, (2) a cultural perspective, and (3) a constant push for improvement.

Good leaders may have very different styles, but they also have some qualities in common. According to Sagor, good leaders never quit asking questions about practices that affect learning, and they give their teachers latitude and meaningful personal support.

A school's culture can facilitate or impede change. Showers and Joyce (1996, p. 16) point out, "A cohesive school culture makes possible the collective decisions that generate schoolwide improvement efforts."

Forces that Promote and Impede Change

A look at the factors reminds the reader that at any school, forces within each of these factors work to improve the schools, and other forces work to impede change. Basom and Crandall (1991, pp. 74–75) have identified seven common barriers to change:

- A discontinuity of leadership deters change (many schools have frequent changes in personnel in key leadership positions).

- Many educators view change as unmanageable (administrators and teachers do not believe they can bring about purposeful change).

- Educators have not been properly prepared to deal with the complexity of restructuring schools (administrators and teachers know little about organizational behavior, conflict management, and other related topics).

- In following a "top-down" approach to making decisions, educators have not relied on research and craft knowledge to inform their decisions (decision makers have not been required to justify their decisions).

- Educators are conditioned and socialized by the format of schooling they experienced and understand (they believe that school structure is not the problem).

- There are conflicting visions of what schools should become (teachers and administrators cannot agree on what changes are needed or what goals should be established).
- Time and resources have been insufficient (time and money are not available to conduct necessary staff development).

As you read this list, perhaps you noticed that some are conceptual, relating to traditional ideas about the schools and how improvement should occur (e.g., the top-down approach) and some are actual barriers (e.g., lack of funds, hopeless attitude). Other barriers result from the newness of restructuring, and these can be reduced as the knowledge base on restructuring grows. Twenty-first century educators should, by now, realize the importance of collecting data and writing cases that reflect the problems they face, and they should acknowledge the victories they have won in overcoming these barriers as they accept new challenges such as restructuring. For example, leaders often need help in convincing their peers that their school really does have a problem, and leaders need the skills to lead their teachers to develop a clear mission and goals.

Strong Leadership

Good leaders recognize that if schools are to remain functional in a rapidly changing community they must grow and develop just as individuals grow and develop (Oliva & Pawlas, 1999). Good leaders are dreamers, yet they also have the capacity to go beyond their own dreams and help teachers exceed the leader's imagination. Tewel (1991, p. 13) explains that the leader should:

- Offer a menu of ideas.
- Encourage teachers to plan new initiatives on their own.
- Reward teacher independence and creativity.
- Decentralize decision making.

All designated curriculum directors, principals, vice principals, department and grade level chairs, and individuals designated or elected to effect changes in the curricula at some point must deal with diversity among their team members, the teachers. The emerging natural leaders who stand like the U.S. Marines, ready to go into action at any moment, are an asset to any organization, but their value is defined by the support they receive from the established leaders. The naysayers, who have perhaps the clearest vision of their role in life—to share their cynicism, doubts, and complaints with anyone who will listen—have the power to sabotage almost any operation, if they are neglected by the school's leaders. The contributions of the members of the critical mass, who absorb conflicting messages from the other groups as they wait to do what they must, will be determined by the leadership they receive. Left alone, the majority will do little or nothing; correctly motivated, they often surprise even themselves with their contributions.

No leader knows exactly how much time and energy to assign to these different groups, but experienced leaders know that because the naysayers are the loudest they often get the most attention. The "squeaky wheel" often forces leaders to focus their attention, and to use most of their time and resources, to try to redirect, appease, or subdue this group. This is usually a mistake, since this group can seldom be redirected or subdued.

Although the naysayers seem aggressive, and aggressiveness suggests self-confidence, they may actually be suffering from low self-esteem. Research (Csikszentmihalyi, 1990) has suggested that the best way to help individuals improve their self-esteem is to direct them to goal-oriented activity that is linked to some social or positive purpose (Schomoker, 1992, p. 94). Although this approach sounds logical, and simple, building self-esteem is not easy. Research done by the California Task Force (Obispo, 1993) shows that self-esteem programs are largely ineffective.

Using Power

Leaders have several types of power at their disposal. By being aware of the sources of power, leaders can often increase their power and improve the ways they use it. Steers, Ungson, and Mowday (1985) have identified five types of leadership power: (1) reward power, (2) punishment power, (3) legitimate power, (4) expert power, and (5) referent power.

Reward power and *punishment power* are often combined and collectively called *coercive power*. Reward power is the more appropriate power to wield when dealing with professionals. Merit pay is an example of the use of reward power. Many current state school reform programs are using punishment power to increase academic achievement. Baselines for performance are established for each school. If the achievement scores fall significantly below the baseline, the school may be put on warning or probation and given a designated time to raise its achievement scores to an acceptable level. If the school fails, a variety of punishments may be implemented, including removal of the local governing body. In other words, the local administrators may be fired.

Current education reform programs are also using reward power. These same programs may set levels above the baseline at which the local school can earn a specified number of dollars for each point achieved above the baseline. In some instances, this money can even be used as bonus pay for teachers.

Legitimate power is power sanctioned by an organization. For example, the chair of the high school science department has power simply because of holding this position.

Educational leaders rely heavily on *expert power,* derived from having special knowledge and skills, and *referent power,* which comes from the ability to get others to identify with their leader and imitate their leader. As teachers themselves become empowered and educational leaders become better managers, referent power grows increasingly indispensable for educational leaders.

Expert power, too, is indispensable for educational leaders. But the type of expertise required of educational leaders has changed. More than ever before, this expertise comes not so much from acquired cognitive knowledge but from growth in the affective domain. Future educational leaders will have to be experts in coping with the unknown. Much security is relinquished as fellow teachers are placed in leadership roles. A power shift occurs when site-based decision-making teams (often called *school councils*) take on problems and make decisions that a single individual (for example, the principal or superintendent) lacks the expertise to handle. Bernauer (1999, p. 70) points out that one way teachers can become empowered with expertise is through conducting action research: "Specific features of action research can lead to empowerment."

Another type of expertise that is quickly becoming indispensable for the educational leader is consensus development. No longer can the leader make unilateral choices; rather, a leader must lead the team to consensus. Interestingly, as a local decision-making team perfects this skill, the team also gains power. Steers, Ungson, and Mowday (1985, p. 436) acknowledge this type power:

> In general, the more cohesion and homogeneity a group or collection of groups has on a particular issue, the greater its influence.

Of the various types of power, several are derived from the organization and some are inherent in the leader. True leaders always depend on expert, referent, and consensus-building power. Steers, Ungson, and Mowday (1985, p. 307) state that "Leadership exists when subordinates *voluntarily* comply because of something the leader has done."

The Future of Educational Leadership

Predicting the future is always risky, but leaders have the responsibility to do just that. The risk can be reduced by gathering as much information as possible and using that information in predicting. Notice that the task is to predict the future of educational leadership, not to predict what type of leadership the future will bring. There is a subtle but powerful difference between the two concepts. The latter assumes that educational leaders will exist in some form; the former makes no such assumption.

There is reason to consider the possibility that educational leadership is becoming moribund, and education reform is the likeliest culprit. Holzman (1992, p. 36) asks, "Are we sure that leadership itself and the cult of personal leadership are not in large measure the problem with public education in the United States today?" There has been a radical shift in the role of the leader, away from leadership as we have known it.

Sergiovanni (1992, pp. 41, 42, 45) says that teachers become more committed and self-managing when schools become the committees, freeing principals from the burden of trying to control people. He blames leadership for standing in the way of an exploration of alternative ways to run the schools. He also points out that leadership is something that someone does to others, whereas the greatest improvement in our schools and teachers is likely to come from within the teachers. Although he never says it, Sergiovanni "leads" his readers to suspect, if not conclude, that leadership also hampers professionalism:

> Both professionalism and leadership are frequently prescribed as cures for school problems, but in many ways two concepts are antithetical. The more professionalism is emphasized, the less leadership is needed. The more leadership is emphasized, the less likely it is the professionalism will develop.

Sergiovanni concludes by saying, "In time, direct leadership will become less and less important, self-management will take hold, and substitutes for leadership will become more deeply embedded in the school."

Chapter Summary

The role of educational leaders is changing dramatically and rapidly. In the past, these leaders served as curriculum troubleshooters who located and fixed problems. Now, curriculum development is a continuing process that doesn't require the occurrence of problems to get attention. Education reform has brought curriculum development to the center of attention. Effective schools balance top-down and bottom-up reform (Fullan, 1999), and empower their teachers to manage both types.

Traditionally, most teachers have handicapped themselves by avoiding involvement with research and with the rest of the school outside their classroom. However, to bring student performance to the levels called for in the reform reports will require teachers to become involved with the total curriculum.

Successful teacher involvement in restructuring will require teachers to develop skills in research, in curriculum development, and in working cooperatively with other teachers, administrators, and parents. The leader must help by providing staff development and by managing teams of teachers as they work on the curriculum. Such successful management will require skills in using power, especially expert power and referent power. As teachers become empowered, educational leaders will no longer be able to depend on traditional types of powers (legitimate and coercive), but they will be required to become more proficient in developing and using referent power.

Another responsibility of contemporary and future leaders is to determine the needs of individuals and faculties and arrange for staff development that addresses these needs. One method that has proven effective is the consortium.

In the future, educational leaders, as they have been viewed in the past, may no longer be in demand. If the term *leader* continues to be used in this context, the "leaders" will have to be adept in management skills and will have to trust their colleagues to set goals and make all types of important decisions.

This chapter has endorsed collaboration and flexibility, two qualities that constructivist teachers in diverse settings can use to help all students succeed. The chapter has also stressed organization. Future educators will experience an increased need to be able to develop organized strategies to meet the increasing academic and social needs of their increasingly diverse classes. Remember the constructivist and multicultural themes of this book as you examine the following questions, and consider the potential that such concepts as research and student empowerment have for helping students reach these goals.

Learning Questions

1. How are educational research and education reform related?
2. Why do teachers avoid research?
3. Why does education reform require teachers to expand their horizons?
4. What are some intrinsic motivators that can be used to help teachers become involved in improving their schools?
5. How can educational leaders ensure that staff development workshops will match the teachers' needs?
6. What are some responsibilities of staff development leaders?
7. How have the education reform reports altered the role of educational leaders?
8. Why is teacher empowerment a major goal of education reform?
9. How does Herzberg's two-factor theory relate to educational leadership?
10. What types of power do educational leaders need most? Why?
11. Why must educational leaders change their perception of their need for security?
12. How does individuals' reluctance to change affect their cultural perceptions?
13. How should research help teachers develop and maintain multicultural and constructivist classrooms?

Suggested Activities

1. Curriculum change has become a continuous process. Develop a calendar you can use to help fellow teachers make curriculum improvements throughout the year. Designate times for: (1) developing a needs assessment, (2) conducting a needs assessment, (3) setting goals, (4) planning workshops, (5) advertising workshops, and (6) giving the workshops.

2. The success of an educational consortium depends on a match between the staff development offered and the needs and desires of its members. Design a system that will communicate the relevance of programs offered throughout the year and that will show the relationships between the goals of the workshops and the needs of the consortium members.

3. As leaders prepare for their new roles as managers, their success requires good human relations skills. Choose a current education reform practice from the list on page 285, and prepare a presentation to use during an open house to convince parents of the importance of this reform element.

4. Design an assignment that permits your students to "show off" the mutlicultural progress of their class.

5. Create an assignment that requires students to research and list strengths of the various cultures represented in your classroom.

6. Research the topic "constructivism," and plan a lesson that uses several constructivist principles.

Questions on the Educational Excellence Laboratory Consortium

1. What responsibility do you believe the directors of such consortia have for determining the most critical needs of their clients?

2. How do you think consortia directors can learn what services a district needs most?

3. Most of the workshops given by this consortium were given on site in the respective school districts. How important is this? Why?

4. Each school district's membership cost is based on the number of its students. Why is this important?

5. How can a consortium afford services that a district cannot afford? After all, the consortium gets no funding beyond that given to the schools.

Works Cited and Suggested Readings

Ambrosie, F., & Hanley, P. W. (1991, October). The role of the curriculum specialist in site-based management. *NASSP Bulletin, 75*(537), 73–81.

Anderson, S., Rotheiser, C., & Gordon, K. (1998). Preparing teachers to be leaders. *Educational Leadership, 55*(5), 59–61.

Barth, R. S. (1990). A personal vision of a good school. *Phi Delta Kappan, 71*(7), 512–516.

Basom, R. E., & Crandall, D. P. (1991). Implementing a redesign strategy: Lessons from educational change. *Educational Horizons, 69*(2), 73–77.

Bellon, J. J., Bellon, E. E., & Blank, M. A. (1992). *Teaching from a research knowledge base.* New York: Macmillan.

Bennett, C. K. (1993). Teacher-researchers: All dressed up and no place to go. *Educational Leadership, 51*(2), 69–70.

Bernauer, J. A. (1999). Emerging standards: Empowerment with purpose. *Kappa Delta Pi Record, 35*(2), 68–70, 74.

Boyer, E. (1982). A conversation with Ernest Boyer. *Change, 41*(1), 18–21.

Boyer, E. (1990). *Scholarship reconsidered.* New York: Carnegie Foundation for the Advancement of Teaching.

Bracey, G. W. (1991). Teachers as researchers. *Phi Delta Kappan, 72*(5), 404–405.

Brown, D. S. (1990). Middle level teachers' perceptions of action research. *Middle School Journal,* pp. 30–32.

Bushman, J. H. (1991, November–December). Reshaping the secondary curriculum. *The Clearing House, 65*(2), 83–85.

Cardelle-Elawar, M. (1993). The teacher as researcher in the classroom. *Action in Teacher Education, 15*(1), 49–57.

Carson, T. (1990). What kind of knowing is critical action research? *Theory into Practice, 29*(3), 167–173.

Chattin-McNichols, J., & Loeffler, M. H. (1989). Teachers as researchers: The first cycle of the teachers' research network. *Young Children, 44*(5), 20–27.

Claus, J. (1999). You can't avoid the politics. *Journal of Teacher Education, 50*(1), 5–16.

Conley, D. T. (1991, September). Eight stops to improved teacher remediation. *NASSP Bulletin, 75*(536), 26–39.

Cooper, L. R. (1991). Teachers as researchers. *Kappa Delta Pi Record, 27*(4), 115–117.

Cornett, J. W. (1990). Utilizing action research in graduate curriculum courses. *Theory into Practice, 29*(3), 185–193.

Csikszentmihalyi, M. (1990). *Flow: The psychology of optional experience.* New York: Harcourt Brace.

Cuban, L. (1992). Managing dilemmas while building professional communities. *Educational Researcher, 21*(1), 4–11.

Cuban, L. (1993). The lure of curricular reform and its pitiful history. *Phi Delta Kappan, 75*(2), 182–185.

Darling-Hammond, L. (1993). Reframing the school reform agenda. *Phi Delta Kappan, 74*(10), 753–761.

Day, B. (1999). Participatory education: A proactive approach to U.S. education in the 21st century. In B. Day (Ed.), *Teaching and learning for the millennium.* Indianapolis: Kappa Delta Pi.

Egbert, R. L. (1984). The role of research in teacher education. In R. L. Egbert & M. M. Kluender (Eds.), *Using research to improve teacher education.* Lincoln, NE: American Association of Colleges for Teacher Education.

Eisner, E. W. (1990). Who decides what schools teach? *Phi Delta Kappan, 71*(7), 523–526.

Enns-Connolly, E. (1990). Second language curriculum development as dialectic process. *The Canadian Modern Language Review, 46,* 500–513.

Fullan, M. G. (1993). Why teachers must become change agents. *Educational Leadership, 50*(6), 12–17.

Fullan, M. G. (1999). Education reform on the move. In B. Day (Ed.), *Teaching and learning in the millennium.* Indianapolis: Kappa Delta Pi.

Fullan, M. G., & Stiegelbauer, S. (1990). *The new meaning of educational change* (2nd ed.). New York: Teachers College Press.

Garrison, J. W. (1988). Democracy, scientific knowledge, and teacher empowerment. *Teachers College Record, 89*(4), 487–504.

Haberman, M. (1992, November). The role of the classroom teacher as a curriculum leader. *NASSP Bulletin, 76*(547), 11–19.

Hattrup, V., & Bickel, W. E. (1993). Teacher-researcher collaboration: Resolving the tensions. *Educational Leadership, 50*(6), 38–40.

Henson, K. T. (1996). Teachers as researchers. Chapter 5 in J. Sikula, T. J. Buttery, & E. Guyton (Eds.), *Handbook of research on teacher education* (2nd ed.). Arlington, VA: Association of Teacher Educators.

Henson, K. T., & Saterfiel, T. H. (1968, June). These schools join forces to share the research load and their findings. *The American School Board Journal, 173*(6), 40–42.

Herzberg, F., Mausner, B., & Snyderman, B. (1959). *The motivation to work.* New York: John Wiley.

Holzman, M. (1992, February). Do we really need "leadership"? *Educational Leadership, 49*(5), 36–40.

Houser, N. O. (1990). Teacher-researcher: The synthesis of roles for teacher empowerment. *Action in Teacher Education, 12*(2), 55–60.

Joyce, B. (1990). The self-educating teacher: Empowering teachers through research. In B. Joyce (Ed.), *Changing school culture through staff development.* In the 1990 ASCD Yearbook. Arlington, VA: Association for Supervision and Curriculum Development.

Kant, I. (1973). E. B. Ashton (Trans., 1974), *On the old saw: That may be right in theory but it won't work in practice.* Philadelphia: University of Pennsylvania Press.

Kearney, K., & Tashlik, P. (1985). Collaboration and conflict: Teacher and researchers learning. *Language Arts, 62*(7), 765–769.

King, M. (1991, September). Cooperative planning workshops: Helping teachers improve. *NASSP Bulletin, 75*(536), 42–46.

Kirk, D. (1988). Ideology and school-centered innovation: A case study and a critique. *Journal of Curriculum Studies, 20,* 449–464.

Klein, M. F. (1992, Summer). A perspective on the gap between curricula theory and practice. *Theory into Practice, 31,* 91–97.

Kowalski, T. J., & Reitzug, V. C. (1993). *Contemporary school administration.* New York: Longman.

Laud, L. E. (1998). Changing the way we communicate. *Educational Leadership, 55*(7), 23–25.

Little, J. (1989). The persistence of privacy: Autonomy and initiations in teachers' professional relations. Paper presented at the annual meeting of the American Educational Research Association in San Francisco.

Lowery, L. (1908). *The relation of superintendents and principal to the training and professional improvement of their teachers.* Seventh yearbook for the National Society for the Study of Education. Part I. Chicago: University of Chicago Press.

Lytle, S. L., & Cochran-Smith, M. (1990). Learning from teacher research: A working topology. *Teachers College Record, 92*(1), 83–103.

McCutcheon, C., & Jung, B. (1990). Alternative perspectives on action research. *Theory into Practice, 29*(3), 144–151.

McElroy, L. (1990). Becoming real: An ethic at the heart of action research. *Theory into Practice, 29*(3), 209–213.

McKernan, J. (1988). Teacher as researcher: Paradigm or praxis. *Contemporary Education, 59*(3), 154–158.

McLaughlin, H. J., Hall, M., Earle, K., Miller, V., & Wheeler, M. (1995). Hearing our students: Team action research in a middle school. *Middle School Journal, 26*(3), 7–12.

McNeil, J. D. (1990). *Curriculum: A comprehensive introduction* (4th ed.). New York: HarperCollins.

Myrick, P., & Jones, R. (1991, September). How instructional leaders view staff development. *NASSP Bulletin, 75*(536), 1–6.

Neilsen, L. (1990, November). Research comes home. *Reading Teacher, 44*(1), 248–250.

Nelson, W. W. (1999). The emperor redux. *Phi Delta Kappan, 80*(5), 387–392.

Newsome, G. L. (1964). In what sense is theory a guide to practice in education? *Educational Theory, 14,* 36.

Nixon, J. (1981). *A teacher's guide to action research.* London: Grants McIntyre.

Obispo, S. L. (1993, February). Go slow on self-esteem. *Phi Delta Kappan, 74*(6), 504.

Oliva, P. F., & Pawlas, G. E. (1999). *Supervision for today's schools* (5th ed.). New York: John Wiley.

Poplin, M. S. (1992, February). The leader's new role: Looking to the growth of teachers. *Educational Leadership, 49*(5), 10–11.

Purvis, J. R., & Boren, L. C. (1991, September). Planning, implementing a staff development program. *NASSP Bulletin, 75*(536), 16–24.

Ravitch, D. (1992, December). National standards and curriculum reform: A view from the Department of Education. *NASSP Bulletin, 76*(548), 24–29.

Reading/Language in Secondary Schools Subcommittee of the International Reading Association. (1989). Classroom research: The teacher as researcher. *Journal of Reading, 33*(3), 216–218.

Reis, S. M., & Renzolli, J. S. (1992, October). Using curriculum compacting to challenge the above average. *Educational Leadership, 50*(2), 51–57.

Rosenholtz, S. J. (1989). *Teachers' workplace: The organization of schools.* White Plains, NY: Longman.

Russell, B. (1958). *Religion and science.* Oxford: Oxford University Press.

Sagor, R. D. (1992, February). Three principals who make a difference. *Educational Leadership, 49*(5), 13–18.

Sanger, J. (1990). Awakening a scream of consciousness: The critical group in action research. *Theory into Practice, 29*(3), 174–178.

Sardo-Brown, D. (1992). Elementary teachers' perceptions of action research. *Action in Teacher Education, 14*(2), 55–59.

Schomoker, M. (1992, November). What really promotes self-esteem? *Educational Leadership, 50*(3), 94.

Schubert, W. H. (1986). *Curriculum: Perspective, paradigm, and possibility.* New York: Macmillan.

Schwahn, C., & Spady, W. (1998). Why change doesn't happen and how to make sure it does. *Educational Leadership, 55*(7), 45–47.

Sergiovanni, T. J. (1992, February). Why we should seek substitutes for leadership. *Educational Leadership, 49*(5), 41–45.

Shalaway, L. (1990). Tap into teacher research. *Instructor, 100*(1), 34–38.

Showers, B., & Joyce, B. (1996). The evolution of peer teaching. *Educational Leadership, 53*(6), 12–16.

Steers, R. M., Ungson, G. R., & Mowday, R. T. (1985). *Managing effective organizations.* Boston: Kent.

Stefanich, G. P. (1990). Cycles of cognition. *Middle School Journal, 22*(2), 47–52.

Stevens, K. B., Slaton, D. B., & Bunny, S. (1992). A collaborative research effort between public school and university faculty members. *Teacher Education and Special Education, 15*(1), 1–8.

Stroot, S. A., Fowlkes, J., Langholz, J., Paxton, S., Stedman, P., Steffs, L., & Valtman, A. (1999). Impact on a collaborative peer assistance and review model on entry-year teachers in a large urban school setting. *The Journal of Teacher Education, 50*(1), 27–41.

Taba, H. (1962). *Curriculum development: Theory and practice.* Orlando, FL: Harcourt Brace..

Tewel, K. J. (1991, October). Promoting change in secondary schools. *NASSP Bulletin, 75*(537), 10–17.

Thompson, S., & Gregg, L. (1997). Reculturing middle schools for meaningful change. *Middle School Journal, 28*(5), 27–31.

Tripp, D. H. (1990). Socially critical action research. *Theory into Practice, 29*(3), 158–166.

Tyack, D. (1990). Restructuring in historical perspective: Tinkering toward utopia. *Teachers College Record, 92*(2), 170–191.

Wade, R. K. (1997). Lifting a school's spirit. *Educational Leadership, 54*(8), 34–36.

Wolf, S. A., & McIver, M. C. (1999). When process becomes policy: The paradox of Kentucky state reform for exemplary teachers of writing. *Phi Delta Kappan, 80*(5), 401–406.

Wright, R. (1985). Motivating teacher involvement in professional growth activities. *The Canadian Administrator, 5,* 1–6.

Young, J. H. (1985). The curriculum decision-making preferences of school personnel. *The Alberta Journal of Educational Research, 25,* 20–29.

9   Evaluating Instruction and the Curriculum

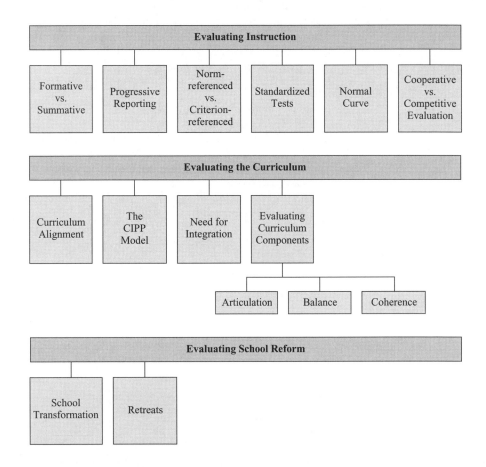

Objectives

This chapter should prepare you to:

- Discuss the impact of education reform on curriculum evaluation.
- Explain the role of curriculum alignment in education reform.
- Give an example of progress reporting and either challenge or defend its use in the schools.
- Differentiate between the use of norm-referenced evaluation and criterion-referenced evaluation in elementary and secondary schools.
- Contrast the effects of competition and cooperation on mainstream cultures.
- Write a brief mission statement for a school and use this statement to write three aims for the school.
- Describe two ways that curriculum balance should be evaluated.
- Give an example of the proper relationships among curriculum articulation, continuity, and scope.
- Evaluate a curriculum to determine its constructivist strengths and weaknesses.

THE CASE OF AN ACCREDITATION VISIT

By Sunday afternoon, cars from across the state and a few from out of state begin converging at a local motel. The next three days will be grueling for these university professors, public school administrators, and teachers, for as a regional accrediting team, these 12 educators each morning will arrive by 7:30 A.M. at Hillsboro Middle School, where they will visit classes, study records, and interview administrators, teachers, counselors, and students. Even the custodians and lunchroom workers will not escape their scrutiny. Each day, at about 4:00 P.M., the team members will reassemble in their designated workroom at the school, drive back to their motel, have an hour for dinner, and begin discussing what they saw and making plans for the next day. If all goes well, they will be able to retire each evening by about midnight. If not, they will work until 2 or 3 o'clock in the morning. Each member knows what lies ahead. They also know that, if they are lucky, there will be some good humor along the way. But the real reward for working these long hours without pay will come from knowing that, by conducting a thorough evaluation of the entire school, they will be helping this school improve itself.

The next two days prove to be both successful and enjoyable. Team members who are teachers spend several hours in classrooms watching teachers in their respective disciplines teach. Teachers rarely have an opportunity to see how other teachers organize their curricula and manage their lessons, so this classroom time is one of the professional benefits of participating on such a team. The counselor and two administrators on the team also spend time with their counterparts at Hillsboro Middle School.

But the classroom and office visits are only part of the overall observations of this school. As these team members walk down the halls, and even during lunch, they constantly observe the teachers and students. Several team members notice that the school's faculty had practically no minority members. The minority student representation at Hillsboro is also extremely low, and this, too, concerns some of the team members.

Because of their hectic schedule, Wednesday comes faster than the team thought possible and the visit is complete, except for the detailed written report that the chair must prepare and mail to the principal. As the team anticipated, the work was hard, but they did enjoy some humorous moments. Mr. Sims, a team member, is a veteran superintendent who is proud of his school district and likes to talk about his schools. But during their initial meeting, the team chair had made a rule that any members who talked about their own professional experiences would have to put a quarter in the kitty. At the end of the visit, the money would be used to buy refreshments for the group to enjoy while celebrating the completion of the evaluation.

Each time Mr. Sims started to talk about his schools, he was interrupted and reminded to put a quarter in the pot. At one meeting, after he had deposited three quarters, he became so frustrated that he raised his hand to silence everyone, reached into his wallet, took out a $10 bill, and, dropping it into the kitty, said, "Now all of you are going to shut up until I finish my story." And they did! After that, Mr. Sims received a lot of respect.

Accreditation visits can have some surprises. On this visit, the surprise came early. Sunday evening was special because the administrators and the school board had an opportunity to express their appreciation to the team members for giving their time and energy to the important goal of helping the school improve. The dinner itself was very nice. But it was the entertainment that surprised the team members most. First, they were surprised to be entertained by an orchestra. Even more surprising was the fact that the school's students were the orchestra musicians. None of the evaluators had ever known of a middle school that had an orchestra, and these youngsters had performed like professional musicians.

Accreditation visits usually reveal some weaknesses, too, and this visit was no exception. Apart from the lack of minority representation, the greatest disappointment was with the science department. More accurately, it was the absence of a science department, since there was none. Actually, the entire three grades offered only one course in science, and that course wasn't required of all students. This meant that some graduates of the school entered high school having had no science in their program. On the positive side, a closer look revealed that the school's outstanding music curriculum was complemented by a superb art curriculum. In summary, the school had an outstanding fine arts curriculum at the expense of having no science program.

One of the team members, a professor of curriculum and instruction, was assigned the task of coordinating the part of the report that focused on the school's instructional program. She referred to her notes as she described her impressions of the English curriculum:

> The English curriculum has a purposeful sequence. Within the year, each topic leads to the next, and each year builds on the preceding year.
>
> Within and between years, the content is continuous and free of disruptions. I would say that the English curriculum has excellent sequence and continuity.
>
> I do question the scope of this curriculum. It seems a little skewed, a little narrow in that there is more literature than composition. I wonder whether this arrangement is used to raise the achievement test scores. As you know, each year this school ranks near the top on the state achievement test scores.
>
> As for the social studies curriculum, it seems to be in good shape. It has both good scope and good sequence. Nothing major is missing. The math curriculum is about the same. I did see one thing that bothered me, which is the absence of integration. For example, I didn't find any trace of math in the social studies department, and vice versa. I wonder why the math department doesn't have assignments that address social problems. I didn't see much in the way of writing assignments being required outside the English Department. Thus I would say that the curriculum lacks integration. I believe that many of these shortcomings could be overcome if the school's curriculum had a more contemporary focus. More topics such as urban living and cultural pluralism are needed.
>
> I also examined the testing program. The curriculum content and the tests are aligned with the state's valued outcomes. In other words, the taught curriculum is tied to the tested curriculum. I'm sure this contributes to the success the students have on the state's achievement tests.

When all reports are completed, the team chair will have the responsibility of writing the summary report. This task will require checking the individual reports to determine whether any elements are missing from the major curriculum. He will then consolidate the reports and add his own observations on the major components of the curriculum.

THE SIGNIFICANCE OF EVALUATION

Historically, teachers have been responsible for using measurement and evaluation in their classes to assess the outcomes of their instruction; however, most teacher preparation programs have not required a course designed to prepare them for this important task. Furthermore, when a course in evaluation is required, the emphasis is invariably on standardized tests. In reality, teachers spend much more of their planning time and classroom teaching time preparing, administering, and scoring tests they create themselves than they spend on standardized tests. This statement is not intended to downplay the need teachers have for understanding standardized tests but, rather, to point out a serious failure in most teacher education curricula to prepare teachers to develop, administer, and score teacher-made tests.

A second major curriculum shortcoming in many teacher education programs is the failure to offer instruction on testing, measurement, and evaluation. At both the college and the K–12 level, the overwhelming emphasis has been placed on summative evaluation while ignoring formative evaluation.

A third concern, which makes evaluation more significant than ever as a topic for teachers and all curriculum workers to study, is the emphasis that education reform is placing on evaluation and the manner in which it is using evaluation to determine progress in education reform.

All of these concerns focus on instruction and learning. As mentioned in earlier chapters, perhaps through no fault of their own, historically teachers have limited their involvement in the schools to their own classrooms, and they have limited their attention to that part of the education process with which they are most comfortable—instruction. Administrators have accepted this limitation of teacher involvement and, in fact, have often promoted it (Habermann, 1992). Yet, as pointed out in Chapter 1, maximum success with education reform will require teachers to become intensely involved with the total school program, including its evaluation.

Given the history of teachers' isolation from the school outside their own classroom, it is not surprising that they have not been involved in curriculum evaluation. Yet there is a special need for teachers to be involved with the whole school curriculum. Oliva (1997, p. 437) addresses this need:

> [M]ost valuative studies must be and are conducted by the local curriculum planners and the teachers. The shortage of trained personnel and the costs of employing specialists are prohibitive for many school systems. Even in large systems that employ curriculum evaluators, many curriculum evaluation tasks are performed by teachers and curriculum planners.

Only when teachers are involved in designing the curriculum are they capable of implementing it, and only when they are involved with developing the curriculum are they committed to working to make it succeed (Nelson, 1999; Pitton, 1999). Reconstructionists are calling for teachers to become intensely involved in redesigning the entire school structure. But successful contribution to the restructuring of school programs will require skills that most teachers currently lack. Central to these necessary skills is the ability to evaluate the school's curriculum. The following definition of curriculum evaluation should help clarify the need for all teachers to develop skills in curriculum evaluation (Hill, 1986, p. 5):

> Curriculum evaluation gathers evidence and promotes understanding of how to bring about the optimum arrangement of the curriculum, the most skillful facilitation of instruction, and the potentials of learners in order to increase, extend, and deepen the learner's ways of knowing, valuing, acting, and growing. It is not a procedure focused only on the identification of curriculum materials and textbooks or the assessment of learner achievements according to program objectives. Rather,

it is the meaning making technology which is applied to the curriculum, instruction, and learning potentials of a school. These three—curriculum, instruction, and learning—are inseparably linked in synergy as a whole system. They are the core technology, the productive functions, which are the work of the school. This comprehensive definition of curriculum evaluation is basic to conceptions of curriculum development.

The first part of this chapter examines the roles of testing, measurement, and evaluation in instruction, reviewing the past and current roles of these processes in instruction. The second part examines the role that evaluation must play in curriculum. Finally, several models for evaluating the curriculum will be examined.

Evaluating Instruction

A Look at the Past

The literature sends a convincing message about the ways teachers have misused and underused evaluation (Frymier, 1979; Fielding and Shaughnessy, 1990; Nelson, 1999; Parsons and Jones, 1990; Wiggins, 1989; and Winton, 1991). All who have come through the American educational system know how frequently tests are used as instruments to enforce good behavior and punish misbehavior. Winton (1991, p. 40) addresses this concern:

> Teachers sometimes use grading to motivate, punish, or control. In this they frequently have parents as allies. It is assumed that students with poor grades will naturally work harder to achieve better grades. Good marks become the objective of learning. Grades become the currency which students, teachers, and parents may use for different purposes.

Others have noticed further misuses of evaluation. One concern is the record teachers have of ignoring the knowledge base on evaluation. Parsons and Jones (1990, p. 17) state clearly that we fail to use all that we know about evaluation: "Unfortunately, the litany of our knowledge about classroom evaluation does not match our usual practices as teachers." Teachers' failure to use the existing knowledge base on evaluation and testing is pervasive, and the potential that tests offer to improve instruction is being wasted. Fielding and Shaughnessy (1990, p. 90) say, "The gap between the potential of testing as a teaching-learning tool and the reality of current practice is wide."

The failure to use current knowledge on evaluation and testing parallels their failure to use research in general (Egbert, 1984; Brown, 1990), and this failure can be attributed to those same reasons that teachers give for ignoring the research (Marshall, 1991). Another factor that contributes to teachers' failure to use the available data is their misconceptions about the proper use of evaluation and testing. For example, many teachers are criticized for "teaching to the test," but, as Wiggins (1989, p. 41) states, "To talk with disdain of 'teaching to the test' is to misunderstand how we learn."

Just how pervasive is the practice of adjusting curricula and instruction to help students score higher on the exams? A survey of 1,200 teachers from throughout the country found that fewer than 20 percent report having made no changes in their teaching as a result of standardized tests. Thirty percent said they place more emphasis on basic skills, and one-fourth said the exams prompt them to emphasize paper and pencil computation. About a fourth (24 percent) reported that they spend more time studying the topics that are covered on the test (Chambers, 1993, p. 80). Is this practice bad? Good? Consider these questions as you continue this study of evaluation.

A Need for Formative Evaluation

Initiated by Carroll (1963) and promoted by Bloom, Hastings, and Madaus (1971), and Block, Efthim, and Burns (1989), *formative evaluation* is now receiving a resurge of attention stimulated by the current education reform efforts. Unlike its counterpart, *summative evaluation,* which is used to determine grades and to differentiate between passing students and failing students, formative evaluation has one ultimate purpose—to promote learning. It achieves this goal through improving study habits, instruction, and the curriculum.

Dagley and Orso (1991, p. 73) note the purpose of formative evaluation: "Formative evaluation is an ongoing process, designed to improve the teacher's performance." Formative evaluation enables teachers to monitor their instruction and keep it on course (Oliva, 1997). Also, Block & Henson (1986, p. 24) state, "If any student cannot learn excellently from the original instruction, the student can learn excellently from one or more correctives." Put simply, students often need a chance to test their knowledge without penalty so they will know how to adjust their study techniques. According to Markle, Johnston, Geer, and Meichtry (1990), tests can become strong clarifiers of teacher expectations, thereby guiding students toward expected outcomes. Although most teachers agree that going over test answers in class can help some students learn more about the material, they are aware that this approach is not likely to result in total mastery of the material. In essence, formative evaluation works because it enables teachers to better serve learners and, as Nelson (1999, p. 392) attests, this is the ultimate test of any education reform practice: "When assessment is used to control outcomes rather than to identify needs and when test results, rather than learning, become the goal, the education system serves the controller, not the learner."

Students do not usually see the potential that tests have for promoting learning. At least this is what their behavior after they complete a test suggests. According to Stefanich (1990, p. 50), "After a test is finished, it is time to shut down the schema. Teachers are sometimes frustrated because students do not exhibit any interest in reviewing their tests." A much more systematic use of evaluation is needed, one that will separate evaluation from grading, a system that is aimed only at promoting learning.

Progressive Reporting

Letter grades are being replaced with *progress reports,* which can be far more revealing than traditional grades. Winton (1991, p. 40) explains:

> The use of progress reporting is a viable alternative since it imparts information— information about what is being taught, alternative activities the student has completed, and how he or she is coping with the course. No individual letter grade can do this. Direct conferences supplement narrative reports and a portfolio of student work is much more revealing and reliable.

Another advantage of progress reporting is its ongoing nature. Unlike traditional exams, which give only one-time results, ongoing testing produces a much more comprehensive view of student progress, which often varies continuously. As Perrone (1994, p. 13) says, "Ongoing assessment is critical."

Take-Home Tests

One example of formative evaluation is the use of *take-home tests.* This type of test gives students access to more information sources and provides students with more time to internalize that information. According to Parsons and Jones (1990, p. 17): "Take-home tests can provide an answer for teachers who wish to evaluate student progress with longer and more complex problem situations."

Summative Evaluation

Dagley and Orso (1991, p. 73) present one use of summative evaluation: "The purpose of summative evaluation is to decide if the teacher meets minimal accountability standards." Summative evaluation is also used to measure student performance to determine such major decisions as grades, passing, and failing.

Because teachers have used tests almost exclusively for the purpose of determining student grades, it might be assumed that, with all that practice, teachers are systematic in the way they convert raw scores into letter grades. But this is not so; each teacher seems to have an individual system, and many teachers use a different system from one grading period to the next. Why? Because most teachers never find a system with which they are satisfied. There is no single system that is right for evaluating all classes. An awareness of the strengths and weaknesses of various grading systems empowers teachers to choose wisely.

Norm-Referenced versus Criterion-Referenced Evaluation

Evaluation systems that force a student to compete with other students are called *norm-referenced,* and those that do not require interstudent competition but instead are based on a set of standards of mastery are called *criterion-referenced.* Traditionally, by using norm-referenced evaluation, our schools have required students to compete with their classmates. Many teachers believe that competition among students is necessary for motivating, but classroom competition is often damaging, especially when the competition is excessive and when students of unequal abilities are forced to compete. Winton (1991, p. 40) expresses concern over excessive use of competition: "Over and over again in homes and in schools we set up situations which guarantee that children will feel defeated and inept." Winton challenges this practice: "Evaluation should be for the purpose of promoting further learning. It should be a positive, supportive experience."

Standardized Tests

Education reform has increased the use of *standardized tests*. Standardized tests have several features in common. First, they are based on norms derived from the average scores of thousands of students who have taken the test. Usually these scores come from students throughout the nation, so each student's performance is compared with that of thousands of other students.

Standardized tests are usually used to measure or grade a school's curriculum. Seeking to make teachers more accountable, state officials have forced schools to give standardized tests to students to measure both student success and teacher success. On the one hand, standardized tests provide a means of comparing local performance with state and national means; on the other, standardized tests may unintentionally shape a school's curriculum. Most educators think that several other factors should also be major influences in shaping the curriculum.

Misuse of standardized test scores has always been a problem. Unless teachers and other curriculum directors work to prevent such misuse, education reformers' emphasis on increased accountability, as measured by standardized tests, will intensify this problem.

The Normal Curve

A second use of tests that requires students to compete with one another is the *normal curve* (also called the *normal probability curve* or the *probability curve*). The curve could just as well be called the *natural curve* or the *chance curve,* because it reflects natural or chance distribution. This distribution is shown in Figure 9.1.

The normal curve is divided into equal segments. The vertical line through the center (the mean) represents the average of a whole population. Each vertical line to the right of the mean represents one average (or standard) unit of deviation above the mean. Each vertical line to the left of the mean represents one standard unit of deviation below the mean. As the figure shows, about 34 percent of the population is within one standard deviation unit above the mean, and about 34 percent of the population is within the one standard deviation unit

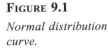

FIGURE 9.1

Normal distribution curve.

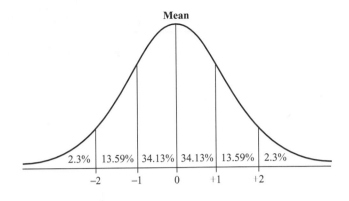

below the mean. Only about 14 percent of the population is in the second deviation range above the mean, and about 14 percent is in the second deviation range below the mean. A very small portion of the population (approximately 2.3 percent) deviates enough from the mean to fall within the third unit of deviation above the mean; an equal portion deviates three standard units below the mean.

Teachers who use the normal curve to assign grades in a school classroom make several bold assumptions. First, like other evaluation schemes that are based on competition among students, the normal curve rests on the assumption that the level of a particular student's performance compared with that of the average of a group of students (usually the student's classmates) is important. Second, use of the normal curve assumes that all students have an equal opportunity to succeed—as though all have equal study opportunities, equal encouragement and help from home, and equal potential, which is extremely unlikely. Third, the use of the normal curve assumes that the number of students used as a norm is large enough to reflect the characteristics of all students at a particular grade level. Unless the class size exceeds 100 students, this is a bold assumption, indeed. The use of the normal curve assumes that 68 percent of the students will earn C's, 13.5 percent will earn B's, and another 13.5 percent D's, and that 2.5 percent will earn A's and 2.5 percent will fail. Its use is appropriate only to the degree to which these percentages actually reflect the subjects' distribution.

Box 9.1 shows how standardized test scores can have a very high error rate, using an example of standard error in the field of geology.

Stanine Scores

Stanine (from *standard nine*) *scores* are derived by using the normal distribution curve to group test scores into nine categories (see Figure 9.2). This modification of the normal curve eliminates the A's, B's, C's, D's, and F's. An advantage of stanine scores is that they remove the stigma associated with letter grades.

Box 9.1

A Very Standard Error

Let's Ponder

The following passage illustrates the magnitude of the standard of error in geology and demonstrates why standardized test scores often have an equally alarming high standard error.[1] Read the passage, then think about this as you respond to the questions below.

A Very Standard Error

My friend was a geologist. We were in his backyard, expressing awe at the majesty of the Rocky Mountains. The monstrous flat sloping rocks that are the hallmark of Boulder, Colorado, were the subject of our conversation.

"Do you know how old those rocks are?" my friend inquired.

"I have no idea at all," I replied.

"They are about four hundred million years old," he said, "give or take a hundred million years."

1. Do you think the general public is aware of the large standard of error common to many standardized test scores? What evidence can you offer to support your answer?
2. What do educators do that suggests that they do not consider the fallibility of standardized test scores?
3. Realizing that standardized tests frequently have large standards of error, how do you think this should affect a teacher's use of standardized test scores? Why?

---

[1] The passage is from J. Frymier (1979). On the way to the Forum: It's a very standard error. *Educational Forum, 36,* 388–391.

Another advantage stanine scores have over the normal curve is the use of nine categories instead of the normal curve's five categories, giving the teacher more groups in which to place projects that must be subjectively evaluated. Stanines may become more useful as education reform programs press for the use of more self-evaluation instruments (such as portfolios) and for other qualitative evaluative instruments.

Schoolwide Standards

Even more popular than the normal curve is the practice of schools setting their own standards. Most teachers are undoubtedly familiar with the system shown in Box 9.2.

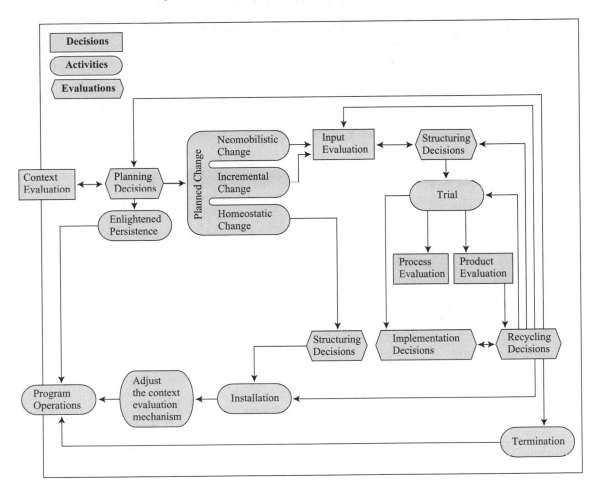

FIGURE 9.2

The CIPP model.

<hr>

Box 9.2

Traditional Grading Scale

Score		*Grade*
90 percent and above	=	A
80–89 percent	=	B
70–79 percent	=	C
60–69 percent	=	D
Below 60 percent	=	F (Failure)

This type of evaluation makes an important and often false assumption: that the level of difficulty of the test fits the abilities of the students exactly. Student teachers usually realize this error as they begin marking their first set of papers, discovering that most of their students have failed the test. Although the exact percentage used to define the boundaries of each grade may vary from school to school, the system remains a common method of evaluation.

The Case Against Competitive Evaluation

Researchers and educators have recently discovered much evidence that grading in the high school should be strictly an individual concern involving the teacher and the student. Fantini (1986, p. 132) states, "Criterion-referenced tests (which do not force competition among students) contribute more to student . . . progress than (do) norm-referenced tests." Once it was thought that competition for grades was necessary because it motivated students to do their best. This may be true for students who have the most ability, but forcing the less capable students to compete with their more academically capable classmates can discourage the less capable students, causing them to concentrate on their inadequacies. Competition can also be bad for the more capable student in that it can cause them to have a superior attitude toward their less capable classmates. Teachers can reduce these problems by refraining from making test scores and grades public.

Many contemporary educators believe that grades should reflect a student's effort—that no one should receive an A without really trying, and that no students who are exerting themselves to their full potential should receive an F. These teachers hold that the purpose of grading is not to acknowledge high ability levels and not to punish those who do not have high ability; rather, each grade should reflect the degree of progress a student makes relative to that student's ability. Consider the following report (Brogdon, 1993, p. 76):

> An accrediting team member reports being approached by a student named Darlene. "Is it fair for them to keep my diploma?" she asked, fighting back the tears. She talked about kids who fought and sassed the teachers, who cut class and took dope, who acted up and interfered with instruction, lazy kids who refused to do homework. After each example, she would say, "I didn't do that; I did what they told me to do." Three times during our conversation she sobbed, "I know I'm in special education and we're slow. But I tried hard and did my work. I didn't cause trouble . . ."
>
> Darlene's counselor supported her: "She tried so hard and worked so hard; she came early and stayed late on test days." Near the end of the conversation, the counselor talked about Darlene's strengths. "She knew how to get along with people. Her clothes were always clean and ironed, and that's impressive, especially for a student as poor as Darlene. (She lived in a run-down mobile home with her mother and several brothers and sisters). The kindergarten teachers who supervised her in the program loved her. She would have a diploma and a job if it weren't for that stupid test."

Although she started to school at age 7 and repeated the first grade, Darlene made good grades in every subject, except social studies, throughout elementary and middle school. Her high school grades were low average.

The counselor reminded her colleagues of a similar student who now holds a responsible position with a national firm. "Like Darlene, Suzanne, too, could barely read, but she worked hard and she got along. She got the opportunity to work there because she got a diploma. Suzanne probably couldn't read above the 4th grade level, but she has kept a job because of other traits; being responsible, courteous, dependable, and hardworking."

To realize how far we have come with testing, contrast Darlene's case with the type of teacher certification evaluations that were conducted a century earlier (Huggest & Stinnett, 1958, p. 416):

> Grandfather was on the school board in the little rural community in which he lived. He and another board member had in mind a young man named Matthew as a teacher of their school. Matthew had little "book larnin." He attended church regularly and his character seemed to be quiet satisfactory. So far as was known he did not use intoxicating beverages . . . But he had only attended and finished the local one-room school. The certification law at that time stated that all candidates must be examined in respect to character, ability to teach, and soundness of knowledge of the subject taught . . . Matthew was examined by Grandfather—who commanded him to open his mouth. . . . Grandfather peered inside the tobacco stained cavity and then ran his fingers over the blackened teeth. Grandfather said to the other member of the board . . . "Write Matthew out a certificate to teach. . . . I find him sound in every way."

The Impact of Competition on At-Risk Students

The need for continuous curriculum evaluation has already been emphasized. Because local communities and the American society change continually, teachers and the curricularists must align the curricula with the environment and with the school's mission. For example, the curricula and practices at many schools do not make a connection between the classroom and students' lives in their homes and communities. Failure to tie school experiences to nonschool experiences causes dissonance, which is counterproductive to achieving schools' instructional goals and social goals. Cognitive achievement is made more difficult for students who force incongruence between their school life and home life (Delgado-Gaitan, 1991).

Competition also impedes the attainment of current multicultural goals. Banks (1993, p. 26) expresses this concern:

> Cultural conflict occurs in the classroom because much of the personal/cultural knowledge that students from diverse cultural groups bring to the classroom is inconsistent with school knowledge and with the teacher's personal cultural knowledge. For example, research indicates that many African American and Mexican American students are more likely to experience academic success in cooperative rather than in competitive learning environments.

To succeed, students of many different backgrounds must figure out the rules of the school's culture. Without a curriculum that provides assistance, many minority students will not be able to cross this bridge to academic success. Continuous curriculum evaluation is needed to ensure that this assistance is being provided.

Portfolios

A *portfolio* is a collection of tangible products that provides evidence of a student's skills. It is also a collection of information about a teacher's practice. Of course, good folios also reflect student behavior. Many educators believe there are advantages in involving students in their own ongoing evaluation. By 1998, half of America's teachers had begun using portfolios in their classes (Meek, 1998, p. 15). The success of portfolios is contingent upon establishing the purpose of the portfolios when they are assigned. Barton and Collins (1993, p. 202) explain:

> The first characteristic of our portfolio development is explicitness of purpose. Teachers by themselves and teachers and learners together must explicitly define purposes of the portfolio so that learners know what is expected of them before they begin developing their evidence file.

The need to define the purposes of portfolios is made clear in a Kentucky teacher's comments (Borko & Elliott, 1999, p. 399):

> [Ann and Kay] continued to wonder whether portfolios could serve both pedagogical and accountability purposes. Ann ruminated, "Is this an instructional tool or is it an assessment tool? I think there's still a big question in my mind as to whether it should be both.

According to Pratt (1980, p. 258), "Many schools allow students to write their own self-appraisal. . . . This encourages students to reflect on their own learning." Portfolios also have the power to motivate students. Portfolio development shifts the ownership of learning to students (Wiggins, 1992; Barton and Collins, 1993). Portfolios should include writing across the curriculum projects. As Perrone (1994, p. 13) points out, "If students are not regularly writing across a variety of topics and in a variety of styles for diverse purposes, then promoting self-evaluation has limited value."

The use of portfolios embraces the idea that students' judgment should be sought and used in determining their grades. A couple of relevant questions commonly asked about student portfolios are, "How do you believe the quality of your present work compares with your previous work?" and "Do you believe this sample of your work represents the best you can do?" Of course this approach requires that the teacher know each student, not merely as a recognizable face but as a developing, growing person.

Portfolios function much as a commercial artist's portfolio shows the artist's skills in several related areas. The portfolio requirements shown in Box 9.3 are typical in that they cover a variety of skills such as writing, artwork, and oral performance. Requiring such a variety of products is a common strength of portfolios. Perhaps you noticed that this portfolio requires the same skills as the goals required for high school graduation in Wisconsin. Since a portfolio is part of a student's curriculum, this quality makes this portfolio a good example of curriculum alignment.

Box 9.3

A Sample Portfolio

The Rite of Passage Experience (R.O.P.E.) at Walden, Ill, Racine, Wisconsin[1]

All seniors must complete a portfolio, a study project on U.S. history, and 15 oral and written presentations before a R.O.P.E. committee composed of staff, students, and an outside adult. Nine of the presentations are based on the materials in the portfolio and the project; the remaining six are developed for presentation before the committee. All seniors must enroll in a yearlong course designed to help them meet these requirements.

The eight-part *portfolio,* developed in the first semester, is intended to be "a reflection and analysis of the senior's own life and times." The requirements include:

- a written autobiography
- a reflection on work (including a résumé)
- an essay on ethics
- a written summary of coursework in science
- an artistic product or a written report on art (including an essay on artistic standards used in judging artwork)

The *project* is a research paper on a topic of the student's choosing in American history. The student is orally questioned on the paper in the presentations before the committee during the second semester.

The *presentations* include oral tests on the previous work, as well as six additional presentations on the essential subject areas and "personal proficiency" (life skills, setting, and realizing personal goals, etc.). The presentations before the committee usually last an hour, with most students averaging about 6 separate appearances to complete all 15.

A diploma is awarded to those students passing 12 of the 15 presentations and meeting district requirements in math, government, reading, and English.

Note: This summary is paraphrased from both the R.O.P.E. Student Handbook and an earlier draft of Archbald and Newmann's (1988) *Beyond Standardized Testing.*

---

[1] *From G. Wiggins (1989, April). Teaching to the authentic test.* Educational Leadership, *46(7) pp. 4–47.*

Another example of a portfolio is shown in Box 9.4. This is an oral history project for ninth graders designed by Albin Moser at Hope High School, Providence, Rhode Island. This project has two outstanding strengths: it requires the student to reflect and to be creative.

As stated earlier, most portfolios require a variety of products from the students, and this is considered a strength. Not all portfolios are multidisciplinary, however. Some portfolios focus only on an activity required to develop

---

Box 9.4

An Oral History Project for Ninth-Graders[1]

To the student:

You must complete an oral history based on interviews and written sources and then present your findings orally in class. The choice of subject matter is up to you. Some examples of possible topics include: your family, running a small business, substance abuse, a labor union, teenage parents, and recent immigrants.

Create three workable hypotheses based on your preliminary investigations and four questions you will ask to test out each hypothesis.

Criteria for Evaluation of Oral History Project

To the teacher:

Did student investigate three hypotheses?

Did student describe at least one change over time?

Did student demonstrate that he or she had done background research?

Were the four people selected for the interviews appropriate sources?

Did student prepare at least four questions in advance, related to each hypothesis?

Were those questions leading or biased?

Were follow-up questions asked where possible, based on answers?

Did student note important differences between "fact" and "opinion" in answers?

Did student use evidence to prove the ultimate best hypothesis?

Did student exhibit organization in writing and presentation to class?

Note: This example is courtesy of Albin Moser, Hope High School, Providence, Rhode Island. To obtain a thorough account of a performance-based history course, including the lessons used and pitfalls encountered, write to Dave Kobrin, Brown University, Education Department, Providence, RI 02912.

---

[1] *From G. Wiggins (1989, April). Teaching to the authentic test.* Educational Leadership, *p. 44.*

Box 9.5

The Writing Portfolio

The writing portfolio used in Vermont schools at grades 4 and 8 includes two types of products: (1) a collection of six pieces or writing done by the student during the academic year; and (2) a "uniform writing assessment," a formal writing assignment that is given by all teachers to all students in the grade level.

Examining a student's writing portfolio reveals the following:

1. a table of contents
2. a "best piece"
3. a letter
4. a poem, short story, play, or personal narrative
5. a personal response to a cultural, media, or sports exhibit or event *or* to a book, current issue, math problem, or scientific phenomenon
6. one prose piece from any curriculum area other than English or language arts (for fourth-graders) and three prose pieces from any curriculum area other than English or language arts (for eighth-graders)
7. the piece produced in response to the uniform writing assessment, as well as related outlines, drafts, etc.

---

a particular skill. For example, Abruscato (1993) describes a portfolio used in Vermont schools in grades 4 and 8 that is designed to enhance the development of writing skills (see Box 9.5). Effectiveness in the use of portfolios requires continuous reflection by their owners (Van Wagenen & Hibbard, 1998).

A Need for Complementary Grading Systems

A strength of many education reform programs is the fact that they require a combination of types of measurements of student performance. Epstein and MacIver (1990, p. 39) recommend blending performance evaluation and progress grades: "A school that officially rewards improvement by using progress grades along with performance grades can expect at least 1.7 percent fewer of its male students to eventually drop out."

A Need for Multicriteria Grading

Although some reform programs are strengthened by the use of nontraditional evaluations, a major weakness in other education reform programs is their exclusive use of standardized test scores to hold teachers and administrators accountable for student performance. No test has the ability to accurately measure student progress in all desired learner outcomes.

Although the terms *grading* and *testing* are often used synonymously, this is a mistake. Most teachers believe that a student's grade should reflect more than test scores. Fantini (1986, p. 112) states, "No test reveals all there is to know about the learner, and no test should be used as an exclusive measure for any student's capacity." Because no single test can measure all a student knows about any topic, and some things other than the acquisition of knowledge are important in school, a variety of measurements is needed. For example, teachers are responsible for seeing that each student develops certain behavioral patterns and attitudes, such as honesty, promptness with assignments, the ability to work with others, and respect for others. Therefore, each of these traits should be reflected in a student's grade. Evaluation of these qualities is essentially subjective, and to avoid becoming prejudiced, teachers should decide at the beginning of the year just how much weight these parts of the total evaluation have and take care not to depart from the guidelines they set.

Grades should represent all the major activities a student engages in while in the classroom. Daily work and term projects may, and perhaps should, carry as much weight toward the final grade for the term as do the tests. The use of several tests (weekly or biweekly), daily assignments, term projects, and daily discussions provides more satisfactory material on which to base the final grade. Winton (1991, p. 40) gives a good summary of the use of multicriteria grading: "Good middle school philosophy limits competition and substitutes direct conferences and written evaluations for formal grading systems."

Assignments for Extra Credit

To challenge the most capable students, some teachers include a bonus question on every major test. This is fine if those who do not choose to answer this question and those who answer it incorrectly are not penalized. Some teachers offer extra credit to students who attend special sessions and complete extra assignments in areas in which they are having difficulties. This practice can also be helpful in motivating students.

When a student asks for an assignment for extra credit at the end of the grading period, however, the student may be less interested in learning than in raising a grade. The student may really be asking, "Will you extend an assignment that failed to motivate me the first time I was confronted with it so that my grade can be elevated?" Sometimes such requests prompt teachers to assign additional problems that the student already knows how to work, or they may prompt the teacher to assign the task of copying hundreds of words from an encyclopedia, library book, or magazine without requiring the student to understand or use the content. This practice is most undesirable, for it encourages some students to procrastinate until the last minute and then subject themselves to X amount of punishment rather than attaining X amount of understanding. Students may also associate the undesirable assignment with the subject and learn to dislike the subject that produced the meaningless assignment.

Decisions on whether to honor students' requests to do extra work for credit should be based on the probability that the student will learn from the task. More aware teachers may ask the students what type of assignment they propose to do and what they expect to learn from it. If the students can convince their teacher that they can and will learn as a result of the task, the assignment may be warranted.

Grading Systems

Since most teachers have considerable latitude in choosing whatever criteria they use to assess grades, all grading, including criterion-referenced systems, is essentially subjective. One question should preface all grade assignments: What grade will be the best for this student? The answer will be determined, at least in part, by each individual student's ability and by the level to which the student applies this ability. To assign a grade that is higher than deserved is certainly not good for the student, nor is assigning a grade lower than the student has earned.

Obviously, each teacher's philosophy on grading shapes the teacher's choice of grading systems, but having a philosophy of grading is not enough. Teachers must base their choice of a grading system on the information they have at hand, and although this choice significantly shapes the teacher's instructional program, it is seldom appreciated. Pratt (1980, p. 259) explains, "Grading is a sensitive area, one in which the teacher can feel uncomfortably exposed and can be subject to powerful pressures to make decisions that are in conflict with the educator's professional judgment."

Too often teachers rely on test scores alone to determine student grades. As Parsons and Jones (1990, p. 20) explain, there is strength in using a variety of criteria to assign grades: "In fact, the more diverse and imaginative the evaluation activities used by the teacher, the more all-encompassing and valid the evaluation is likely to be."

Ideally, teachers have a variety of activities upon which to base each grade. For example, there may be class projects, presentations, classwork, homework, and tests. Some examples of student performance that could be used to assess the grade at the end of a six-week grading period include:

Six weekly tests

One final exam

One term paper

One oral presentation or term project

One group project

Thirty homework assignments

Twenty classroom assignments

In order to arrive at a single grade for the six-week period, the teacher can assign equal or varying values to each item on this list. Consideration should be given to the amount of time the student has spent on each activity. Ranking these elements according to the time invested in each, as shown in Box 9.6, may simplify this process.

The activities in Box 9.6 required 49 hours of student time. To simplify the process, an additional hour of credit can be added to represent classroom participation. With a total of 50 hours, each hour spent in an activity could account for 2 percent of the grade. Thus the percentage assigned to each activity could be as shown in Box 9.7.

Box 9.6

Grade Relative to Time

Activity	*Time Required*
Homework 30 × 40 minutes	20 hours
Classwork 20 × 30 minutes	10 hours
Group project	6 hours
Six weekly tests at 50 minutes	5 hours
One term paper	4 hours
Oral presentation of project (including preparation)	3 hours
One final exam	1 hour

Box 9.7

Relative Weights of Grade Determiners

Activity	*Percentage of Grade*
Homework	40
Classwork	20
Group project	12
Weekly tests	10
Term paper	8
Oral presentation	6
Final exam	2
Classroom participation	2

Suppose the teacher of this class is not happy to have the final exam count only 2 percent against 20 percent for classwork. This is no problem—the distribution can be changed (10 percent to the final exam and 12 percent to classwork or 5 percent and 17 percent, and so on).

The distribution will not be identical from one teacher to another. This does not matter, so long as each grade is based on the chosen system. Criteria other than the time spent on each activity may also be considered when determining the value of each activity, for example, the degree of emphasis given to each topic in class and the degree to which the student has cooperated with other students.

Traditionally, most schools have required students to earn a designated percentage of the possible points to receive an A, a B, a C, or a D. Contemporary educators question this rigid approach, wondering whether such systems will meet the needs of future citizens. Smith (1991, p. 21) comments: "Traditional evaluation . . . is not likely to provide the clarity and focus students need."

Performance-Based Assessment

According to Guskey (1994, p. 51), "Few innovations in evaluation have caught on as quickly as performance-based assessment." However, there is no unanimity of agreement on its definition (Kennedy, 1992). Performance-based assessment requires students to create an answer or a product (Fever & Fulton, 1993). It is not a new idea. Winograd and Jones (1992, p. 37) say that "Historically, good teachers have used performance assessment to monitor the progress of their students." Education reformers of the 1990s place much confidence in performance-based assessment as a means of motivating teachers and students to increase the level of academic attainment. As Aschbacher (1992, p. 51) explains, "The current enthusiasm for performance assessment reflects a hope that it can drive school reform and improvements in student performance, particularly complex thinking skills."

Performance-based assessment exists in many forms. It can require verbal performance (e.g., a voice music major's recital or an oral dissertation defense), writing (e.g., an essay exam), or of manipulative skills (e.g., a science laboratory assignment). Fever and Fulton (1993, p. 478) say that "It [performance evaluation] is best understood as a continuum of formats that range from the simplest student-constructed response to comprehensive demonstrations or collections of large bodies of work over time."

Another form of performance-based assessment is exhibitions between students or between groups of students. For example, a simulation baseball game can be used in any subject at any grade level.

Performance-based assessment can be defended by the fact that it requires students to go beyond simple recall of knowledge, requiring them to use the newly acquired knowledge. At a higher level, performance-based assessment, as Goldberg (1992) said of the arts, can provide opportunities and motivation for students to transform meaning.

Guskey (1994, p. 51) says that the value of performance-based assessment goes further:

> Some educators have carried this vision a step further, suggesting that authentic, performance-based assessments could actually drive instructional improvements. This approach is called measurement-driven-instruction or MDI.

Offering such meaningful advantages as it does, one might think that performance-based assessment would be universally accepted, but it is not. Because performance-based assessment sparks competition, it also sparks controversy. Worthen and Leopold (1992, p. 1) discuss its controversial nature:

> Despite the surge of interest in alternative assessment (alternative ways of assessing student performance), criticism of this movement by those who favor more traditional means of assessment create a strong undertow.

Outcomes-Based Education

No reform practice has drawn more controversy than *outcomes-based education (OBE)*. Although to most educators it means simply that educational planning should begin by determining the desired outcomes and should end by having students perform the activities needed to achieve those outcomes, not all people see it so simply. Buschee and Baron (1994, p. 193) say that "outcome-based education is a student-centered, results-oriented design based on the belief that all individuals can learn." However, OBE opponents are concerned that the approach may be lowering the standards for good students. Towers (1994, p. 627) voices this concern stating, "To a degree OBE may be allowing our best and brightest future teachers to go unchallenged, drifting aimlessly from one undemanding task to the next." Towers (see Brandt, 1994, p. 5) says that the OBE controversy itself is confusing because the term means different things to different people. As Spady (1994) has said, the disagreement is not so much over whether to target outcomes as it is over *what* outcomes we should have.

The fear of failing to challenge students includes the failure to challenge not only their intellect as measured by standardized education reform tests but also the failure to challenge students' creativity. Likewise, teachers' creativity is a human resource that some people fear is being taken from teachers by reformers' testing programs. Nelson (1999) expresses this concern:

> In each classroom this country there is a highly educated adult with the potential for creating meaningful learning environments that address the needs of every student. Those adults should be supported and empowered so they can be the "origins" of practices that meet the needs of their very singular classroom communities.

Adding clarity, and therefore meaning, to our teaching, although very important, is just one advantage of using OBE. Marzano (1994, p. 44) says, "One common argument for their increased use is that many provide information about students' abilities to analyze and apply information—their ability to think."

With the recent emphasis on promoting higher-order thinking, this goal itself is enough to garner the support of many for OBE.

Authentic Tests

Tests designed to cause students to develop those skills measured by standardized tests are called *authentic tests.* Authentic tests get their name from the fact that they test for valuable understanding and that the test activities themselves are valuable (Guskey, 1994). The Special Study Panel on Educational Indicators for the National Center for Education Statistics (1991) says that *authentic, alternative,* and *performance* are all terms applied to emerging assessment techniques. Whatever names they go by, their common denominator is that they call on students to apply their thinking and reasoning skills to generate often elaborate responses to the problems put before them. Authentic tests can increase both teacher and student creativity. Looman deWijk (1996, p. 51) explains: "Authentic or performance-based assessments bring integrity to the learning and are flexible enough to encourage teacher and student activity." Successful authentic testing requires teachers to (1) begin planning by examining the types of skills they wish their students to have, (2) design their tests to meet these aims, and (3) teach accordingly.

Case Study

Integrating and Assessing Critical Thinking across the Curriculum

Christy L. Faison
Rowan University

Background Information

In the mid 1990s a small northeastern state attempted to address the challenge of providing a thorough and efficient education for all children while allowing the many independent school districts to maintain local control. Educators from around the state joined with education department officials to develop content standards that would be applied to grades K–12 in all districts. This comprehensive curriculum guide was meant to serve as a source of expectations for individual districts to follow at all grade levels, not as a state-mandated curriculum. In addition to content-specific standards, the state developed five cross-content standards, one of which was "the ability to learn, to reason, to think creatively, to make decisions, and to solve problems." (This standard will be the focus of this

(Continued)

case study.) To evaluate the attainment of these expectations, the state also developed a series of required assessments to be given at the fourth, eighth, and eleventh grade levels. Classroom teachers, principals, and curriculum specialists all over the state are now having lively discussions about classroom instruction and how to assess student learning in light of the implementation of these new standards. This case study gives you the opportunity to "eavesdrop" on one such discussion and, like the teachers, debate relevant issues with regard to the use and evaluation of statewide standards.

The Community

The case study takes place in a large suburban district recognized for its educational excellence. The district has experienced rapid growth in the past five years. Due to a very supportive community, the district has been able to match this growth with additional classroom space and personnel. The residents of the district are predominantly professionals who commute to nearby urban areas to work. Many residents are also employed by a local university. The average household income is approximately $55,000. Housing costs range from $60,000 to close to $1,000,000. The population is 48,000, and about 12 percent of the residents are members of minority groups.

The School

This discussion of standards takes place at a local elementary school (grades 1–5) within the district, which has an enrollment of approximately 600 students. English is the primary language in 95 percent of the homes. The school enjoys high attendance and low mobility rates. Twenty-seven percent of the faculty hold graduate degrees. Information regarding previous testing at the fourth grade level is not available due to the newness of the assessment requirement. The school has a dynamic principal known for her instructional leadership, an active site-based council which makes school-level decisions, and a district supervisor of curriculum who is readily available to the teachers.

The Case

Once the state-initiated standards became official, a great deal of focus was placed on understanding them in their entirety as well as at each specific grade level in many districts throughout the state. As a result, numerous in-service sessions, curriculum meetings, and faculty meetings were spent attempting to coordinate efforts for addressing and assessing the standards at the classroom level. To support teachers in this endeavor, state frameworks were created to assist in implementing the standards in each subject area. Not surprisingly, one focus of discussion among teachers throughout the state was the changes in the tests at the fourth, eighth, and eleventh grade levels as well.

Even though teachers began integrating the subject-specific standards into their thought processes regarding planning and teaching, what seemed to be left

(Continued)

out of the initial discourse were the five standards that were to be addressed across all subject areas and at all grade levels. At our chosen school, a third grade teacher and a fourth grade teacher were discussing these cross-disciplinary standards to identify what their two grades were covering in relation to the expectations for these standards. The district curriculum supervisor was in the building that day, and she joined in on the discussion. They concluded that this discourse should occur among all faculty members.

After consultation with the principal, an ad hoc committee was formed with one staff member from each grade level (first through fifth) and one representative from among the special area teachers. The principal agreed to sit in on these meetings as a participant rather than its organizer or leader. She believed that the group's potential for success was much greater because the group was started by teachers and run by teachers. The fourth grade teacher volunteered to organize the meetings; her motivation came in part from her concern that state testing based on the new standards would have a major impact at her grade level. The following description summarizes the first four meetings of this group.

The committee quickly realized that meeting the standards to be addressed in all disciplines and across all grade levels would require a schoolwide effort. They decided to begin with the standard that addressed critical thinking, decision making, and problem solving. They spent the first session discussing the stated expectations of students, sharing examples of critical thinking and creative thinking activities already a part of teaching and learning in various classrooms. Two points emerged. The first was that teachers were already providing instruction across the grade levels in higher-level thinking exercises, but it was rarely in any uniform manner. The second was that this group should identify a focus of specific topics for future meetings. They generated the following list for discussion at future meetings, knowing that as they progressed, other topics and tangents might seem appropriate to add to the list:

1. What is involved in critical and creative thinking? Do these terms have the same meaning in all subject areas?
2. How should we teach and reinforce critical and creative thinking? Should they be covered at a separate time of the day or integrated into existing instruction?
3. How will we assess whether our students are becoming better thinkers?
4. How will we communicate these efforts to parents?
5. How should our efforts to promote critical and creative thinking be related to state tests?

At the second meeting, the group had a lively discussion about critical and creative thinking. One person saw the two types of thinking as opposites; another believed individuals tend to be better at one than the other. A teacher who did a lot of interdisciplinary instruction with a focus on science found that the state expectations for critical and creative thinking paralleled the scientific method. Another teacher utilized the same steps in teaching her students creative problem solving. The group brainstormed a list of skills associated with critical and creative

(Continued)

thinking and came up with over twenty-five skills. Topping the list were comparing and contrasting, finding similarities and differences, sequencing, classifying, predicting and hypothesizing, seeing things from multiple perspectives, identifying unique alternatives, observing and analyzing, interpreting data, weighing alternatives, making analogies, and making inferences. Everyone agreed that effective decision making and problem solving were broader goals for all students.

Prior to the next meeting, committee members met with other teachers at their grade levels and discussed how to address the teaching of critical and creative thinking. The committee unanimously agreed that teaching specific skills related to effective thinking was important and that decision making and problem solving should be incorporated into every subject whenever appropriate. They also agreed that these skills should be taught within the context of already existing curriculum, not during a separate block of time. The teachers thought it essential for all teachers to help students see how the thinking skills taught in one subject were applicable to others. For example, when a lesson focused on a particular thinking skill or strategy such as comparing and contrasting climates in different regions of the country, teachers would encourage students to reflect on examples of comparing and contrasting earlier in the year in social studies, in another subject, or perhaps in a prior year.

The third grade teacher suggested that teachers at each grade level brainstorm examples of lessons where they teach or reinforce the major thinking skills that were identified at the first meeting. She thought it would be interesting to see how teachers at lower and higher grade levels address the same skills she teaches. The fifth grade teacher added that it would be beneficial to hear about specific assignments at different grade levels that included these skills. The first grade teacher suggested that, at a future meeting, teachers bring in samples of student work that demonstrate effective thinking skills. The members of the committee agreed that a sharing session would be scheduled a month later and be open to all teachers of the school. Perhaps the next step would be to create a matrix of skills introduced and applied throughout the grade levels.

At the next committee meeting the teachers present began discussing how to assess students in the area of critical thinking and problem solving. They knew that this would be just the beginning of discussing this subject. Their prior year's in-service workshops on alternative and authentic assessment would certainly be of value here. The second grade teacher, who was new to the school that year, mentioned that the sharing session with samples of student work was extremely valuable to him in his understanding of the many dimensions of thinking skills as well as serving as a wealth of creative curriculum ideas. A discussion followed in which committee members debated the value of assessing students on specific thinking skills or on their overall skill in decision making and problem solving. One teacher believed that some of her students were more successful at certain thinking skills in some subjects than in others. She saw this as an opportunity to help her students apply their successes in subjects that they found more challenging, but she wondered how their assessments should address this. Would they assess students' application of thinking skills in specific subject areas or across the curriculum? One teacher thought that it would be interesting to see if there would be a discrepancy in skill level across the curriculum with regard to thinking

(Continued)

skills. Another teacher who had been using portfolios in her classroom for a number of years described how this would be a natural method for assessing students' growth in specific thinking skills as well as decision making and problem solving. A second-year teacher asked if she should begin writing specific assessments regarding thinking as she created new lessons that involved a focus on thinking skills. That led to a discussion on formative and summative assessment and what their overall goals were at this time. The committee agreed that they should continue to explore the variety of assessment options available to them and to generate a list to be discussed and prioritized at the next meeting. At that time, the teachers would also discuss piloting different assessment strategies according to grade level or their areas of interest.

Issues for Further Reflection and Application

You have now been appointed to be a member of this committee. Your charge is to respond to the following questions and to be prepared to participate in the next committee meeting.

1. List at least ten strategies you could utilize to assess aspects of critical thinking. Which do you believe would be the easiest to implement? Which do you believe would be the most complex? Why?

2. Since the teachers are revising their instruction in response to the new statewide standards and assessments, does this infer that they are "teaching to the test"? If so, is this a positive or a negative aspect of statewide educational reform?

3. Given the fact that letter grades are used on report cards, how will teachers be able to communicate to parents the emphasis on and assessment of critical thinking?

4. Would you prefer to be on a grade-level team or an interest-based team to develop critical thinking assessments? Why? What would be the advantages and disadvantages of each?

5. How might this case differ if the discussion occurred among middle school teachers? High school teachers?

Suggested Readings

Knodt, J. S. (1997). "A think tank cultivates kids." *Educational Leadership,* 55(1), 35–37.

McKernan, J. & Powers, E. (2000). "The action inquiry seminar and collaborative reflection: Forms of democratic pedagogy in teacher education." *Action in Teacher Education,* 21(4), 61–71.

Snow, R. E. (1997). "Aptitudes and symbol systems in adaptive classroom teaching." *Phi Delta Kappan,* 78(5), 354–360.

Trocco, F. (2000). "Encouraging students to study weird things." *Phi Delta Kappan,* 81(8), 628–631.

Evaluating Curricula

This case study concerns standards that cut across subjects and grade levels. As mentioned in Chapter 7, integrated themes facilitate constructivist lessons. This faculty believes that the most effective arena for such changes is the entire school. Effective school research supports this theory. Other factors in this case reflect the current understanding of practices that will best promote multiculturalism and constructivist themes. These teachers acknowledged that they were already teaching creative thinking and critical thinking, although not in a uniform way.

Likewise, most schools already use constructivist and multicultural practices. There is currently a reluctance among many education reform groups, particularly at the state level and particularly among pressure groups, to acknowledge the many good practices that are already in place in schools throughout the country. This reluctance is caused, at least in part, by a feeling that the reform group will not receive full credit for a school's improvement if people recognize that some of the practices were already being used. But teachers and administrators must receive credit for success at their school. The need to give students and teachers credit for progress is even greater in diverse classrooms where expectations in the homes and throughout the community can differ significantly from those at school.

Evaluating the Curriculum

A Need for Consistency and Teacher Involvement

Curriculum evaluations should be comprehensive and consistent. Unfortunately, many widely used programs today are not being evaluated consistently and comprehensively (Dusenburg & Falco 1997). As education reform and its required restructuring increases, the need for teachers to become involved in evaluating the school's curriculum will continue to increase. This book has reported on teachers' failure to use research and their failure to use the knowledge base on testing and evaluation, not as an attempt to engage in teacher bashing, for such practice for its own sake would prevent the success of education reform efforts the book promotes. Teacher education programs must share any blame directed at teachers, for they have failed to prepare teachers to conduct research and to provide an adequate knowledge base on evaluation and testing. The point of mentioning these shortcomings again is to stress the critical need for teachers to develop curriculum evaluation skills.

A Need for Curriculum Alignment

In addition to meeting the demands that education reform reports have made with regard to increased ongoing evaluation of the entire school program, evaluating the curriculum provides needed direction, security, and feedback for teachers. Consider, for example, the concept of *curriculum alignment.* Reporting on effective practices used by a dozen education reform programs, Wang, Haertel, and Walberg (1998) noted that all of these programs maximized the use of curriculum and assessment alignment. A faculty that is unaware of this concept is unlikely to align the taught curriculum with the tested curriculum and even more unlikely to try to align the implied curriculum with the taught and tested curricula. If caught teaching test items, these teachers are inclined to invent explanations or excuses to justify this practice.

When teachers understand the proper relationships among these curricula, however, they are apt to feel good about their efforts and to derive a sense of security from knowing that they are doing what they should be doing.

A Need to Involve Teachers

Chapter 8 stressed the need to involve teachers in curriculum matters of all types. Involving teachers in evaluating the curriculum requires early and continuous involvement. To understand the relationships among such curriculum components as philosophy, aims, goals, objectives, content, teacher activities, student activities, and evaluation, teachers must be involved in writing the school's mission statement and in writing their department or grade-level goals, so that they can see how the components are interrelated and understand the basis on which all curriculum decisions are made, that is, the school's philosophy.

Needless to say, historically most teachers have not been involved continuously with shaping the school's written philosophy. While it is clear that teacher involvement has increased in recent years (Latham, 1998), there is evidence that more involvement in curriculum decisions is needed (Shen, 1998). Nor have teachers been involved continuously in relating their grade-level objectives to the objectives in their subjects at the grade levels that immediately precede and follow their own grade level.

A Need for Integration

Teachers' inability to expand their understanding of the curriculum either vertically (to grades above or below their own) or horizontally (to other subjects) without working with teachers at these levels is obvious. Although this process will be discussed further in Chapter 11, it must be understood that effective curriculum evaluation begins in the classroom and spreads throughout the school. Curriculum evaluation cannot occur in isolated classrooms. Each individual teacher's curriculum must be assessed *always* in relation to the school's overall mission. Developing a mission statement, as discussed earlier in this book, is a major undertaking in itself. Weller, Hartley, and Brown (1994, p. 298) explain: "Developing vision, that seemingly mystical and sometimes elusive concept, is the most important element in making any organization highly effective in promoting quality products."

The CIPP Model

One of the most popular curriculum evaluation models developed in recent years is the *CIPP model* (shown in Figure 9.2). A Phi Delta Kappa committee chaired by Daniel Stufflebeam developed this comprehensive model (CIPP is an acronym for *c*ontext, *i*nput, *p*rocess, and *p*roduct). Context evaluation involves defining the environment of the curriculum. This part of the model is similar to the concept that Beauchamp called the *arena* in his curriculum theory model. It includes a needs assessment. The input part of the CIPP model involves determining appropriate and available resources to use to attain the objectives. Process evaluation is an ongoing monitoring of the evaluation to detect flaws. This information is used to revise the model. The evaluation stage refers to assessing the product to determine whether to continue the use of the model.

Evaluating Curriculum Components

Another way to evaluate a curriculum is to examine each of its components, beginning with the institution's mission statement (see Figure 9.3).

Perhaps the most underappreciated and certainly the most underused curriculum component is the mission statement, which reflects the institution's philosophy. The mission statement serves as a rudder to steer the ongoing curriculum. Usually dusted off and tinkered with only at those periods just preceding an accreditation visit, the school's written philosophy is then quickly put back on the shelf and thought of only as a document. As Schwahn and Spady (1998, p. 47) remind us, "Planning, compelling purposes, and inspiring visions mean nothing until something different and better happens for children."

FIGURE 9.3

University mission statement.

Eastern Kentucky University shall serve as a residential, regional university offering a broad range of traditional programs to the people of central, eastern, and southeastern Kentucky. Recognizing the needs of its region, the University should provide programs at the associate and baccalaureate degree levels, especially programs of a technological nature.

Subject to demonstrated need, selected master's degree programs should be offered, as well as the specialist programs in education. The elimination of duplicative or nonproductive programs is desirable, while development of new programs compatible with this mission is appropriate.

The University should continue to meet the needs in teacher education in its primary service region and should provide applied research, service, and continuing education programs directly related to the needs of its primary service region.

Because of the University's proximity to other higher education and post-secondary institutions, it should foster close working relationships and develop articulation agreements with those institutions. The University should develop cooperative applied research and teaching programs using resources such as Maywoods and Lilley Cornett Woods and Pilot Knob Sanctuary.

A school's philosophy, as stated in its mission statement, should give rise to the curriculum's aims (remember the Seven Cardinal Principles) and goals (remember the Goals for 2000). In most states, reform efforts are strong enough to require an evaluation and revision, if necessary, of a school's philosophy. Interestingly, the philosophy affects all components, and these components have an impact on the philosophy.

Curriculum evaluation is multidirectional. In Figure 9.2, the lines with arrows on both ends show an energy flow in both directions, and consequently, the element on each end of the arrow affects and is affected by its counterpart. Curriculum evaluation, then, is not a simple, one-way, linear process. Second, the figure shows an uninterrupted circular flow, representing the continuous nature of curriculum evaluation.

The amount of impact of each part of the curriculum on other parts can be minimal, or it can be monumental. For example, consider the effect that one part of society, such as the economy, has had on today's curricula. The success of education reform practices in each state hinges on that state's economy. Or consider the impact that a federal law such as Public Law 94-142 (now P.L. 101-476, *Education for All Handicapped Children*) has had on the curriculum in every school in the country. Influenced by the economic level in each state and community, technology is having varying degrees of impact on the schools. Innovative teaching practices and their accompanying philosophies (such as mastery learning or the nongraded primary program) can reshape an entire curriculum.

Evaluating Curriculum Sequence

The curriculum *sequence,* the order in which objectives, content, and activities are presented, can significantly determine the level of difficulty or ease with which students can comprehend the content. The attainment of some objectives would be impossible without first attaining some prerequisite objectives. Parallel sequence among schools prevents disruptions for students who move from one district to another. The children of migrant farm workers exemplify the need for consistency in sequence.

When curriculum sequence is disrupted, continuity cannot be maintained. Lack of sequence can also cause unintentional redundancy and omission.

Evaluating Curriculum Continuity

Continuity is the absence of disruptions in the curriculum. Failure to maintain continuity contributes to learning difficulty. To illustrate the need for continuity, consider the difficulty in remembering the following letters: NISEYLANNAPV. These letters lack continuity because they also lack sequence. There are two reasons why a curriculum lacks continuity: either it lacks sequence or it has gaps. The letters in our example lack sequence. Ordered correctly, they are much easier to remember: PENNSYLVANIA.

Evaluating Curriculum Scope

Curriculum evaluations should also examine the curriculum's scope. The *scope* of a curriculum refers to its breadth; it is a horizontal dimension or a snapshot of the curriculum. For example, one might wish to examine the number of subjects a middle school curriculum offers at the eighth grade level. Or when helping a high school student plan his or her curriculum for the senior year, the counselor might examine the number of subjects the student would have on Tuesday. Curriculum evaluation should consider, in addition to the number of subjects in a curriculum, the variety or breadth of content that each offers.

Evaluating Articulation

Curriculum developers want to be sure that each part of the curriculum fits the other parts. This "smoothness" quality is called *articulation.* When evaluating the curriculum for its articulation, the curriculum developer examines both the vertical dimension (through the grades) and also the horizontal dimensions (across the grades).

Evaluating Balance

One of the most important characteristics of any curriculum is *balance.* The balance of a curriculum should be examined from several perspectives. Since most schools have some graduates who enter the world of work, care should be taken to offer a balance between college preparation courses and vocational or business courses. College entrance examinations measure both quantitative and qualitative abilities, so care should also be taken to offer a balance between quantitative subjects such as mathematics and the hard sciences and qualitative subjects such as English, social studies, and the fine arts. Since good health requires exercise, each curriculum should offer some types of physical education.

Even within the disciplines, care should be taken to offer a balance of subjects. For example, the hard sciences curriculum is often expected to offer some physics, chemistry, biology, and earth science. A junior high earth science curriculum might be evaluated to ensure that it contains some geology, oceanography, meteorology, astronomy, and physical geography. Although some education reform programs are stressing the need to integrate the curriculum, increased integration of the disciplines will not negate the importance of balance among the subjects offered.

Curriculum balance is equally important to each student's individual curriculum. The need for a "well-rounded" education reflects a history of concern for curriculum balance.

Chapter 7 described a teacher who taught 28 times as much science as a colleague who did not feel comfortable with science. The education reform reports have consistently recommended more science and mathematics for public school curricula. Perhaps the imbalance of these subjects from one classroom to another will be rectified by their recommendations; however, most reform reports have consistently ignored the fine arts. Contemporary teachers and other curriculum directors have a shared responsibility for protecting these subjects and thus contributing to the maintenance of balance in the curriculum.

Evaluating Curriculum Coherence

A common flaw in curricula is the failure to connect or relate the components to each other. As stated earlier, the aims must flow from the philosophy or mission statements, and goals must flow from the aims. Such relationships among the curriculum components is called *coherence.*

An example that illustrate the common lack of coherence occurred in a college that offered a course in music appreciation. Some students elected the course because they wanted to increase their understanding and appreciation of classical music; others elected it because of its reputation for awarding an easy A. The word spread about the course's reputation for being easy, and adjustments were made to the course. Rigid, objective, pencil-paper exams were administered. Dissatisfied and discouraged with their first scores, some students dropped the course. Of those who remained, few students earned an A. Ironically, most students exited the course having developed a disdain for classical music.

Evaluating School Reform

School reform (or education reform) inevitably involves changing the curriculum, for by doing so, reformers can shape the nature of schools and, indeed, of entire communities. Cuban (1993, p. 183) explains the impact that curriculum change can have on society at large: "To change the curriculum is to fiddle with important values in American culture."

The primary tool for evaluating school reform has been and continues to be standardized exams. President Bill Clinton proposed a voluntary national testing program, and 71 percent of the public favor this proposal (Rose & Gallup, 1998).

School Transformation

Education reform can start at the top or at the bottom or anywhere that someone has the energy and commitment to work to make it happen. But, as Schlechty (1990, p. 8) says, "Change can be most effectively implemented when those whose energy, commitment, and goodwill are needed to support the change believe in, understand, and support the change." True education reform requires effecting substantial changes in the schools, and evaluation is needed to determine when schools need change and when schools have been transformed. Evaluation is essential to avoid the dead-end trap of rhetoric that characterizes so much of today's "reform." It is also needed because transformation itself is often part of the rhetoric and, when applied to schools, its meaning is unclear.

School transformation is more than changing the curriculum. Goodman (1992) says that school transformation is partly ethereal, referring to its temporary nature and also to its emotional or attitudinal quality. Like *curriculum* itself, school *transformation* should be defined at each school. Following are some questions that can be used to determine whether your school has been transformed.

What kinds of questions do we want our students to ask?

What kinds of attitudes do we want our students to have?

What are the desired values that our faculty agrees should be promoted at our school?

What is the teacher's role in promoting attitudes?

How can we help our students develop the sense of efficacy required for success?

How does our faculty define true success?

What is the future of our culture, and how can our curricula be adjusted to prepare students for the future?

What barriers does our school present to minority students, and what adjustments are needed to help them cope with these barriers?

What types of desirable and undesirable attitudes, beliefs, and behaviors does our evaluation system reward?

What kinds of real passions should our school promote, and how can we adjust the curriculum to promote them?

What kinds of values does our school's hidden curriculum promote?

What currently unused resources does our community have that can be tapped to achieve our school's major goals?

What evidence of constructivism can be seen in our school's curriculum plan?

Retreats

Measuring school transformation requires getting beyond surface answers. Retreats are a valuable transformation evaluation tool because they offer opportunity to assess difficult-to-measure feelings and impressions. Retreats give teachers time to think deeply about important questions such as the purpose of school. Goodman (1994) reported that, at the beginning of a two-day retreat, one fifth grade teacher responded to the question "What is the purpose of the fifth grade curriculum?" by saying that it was to prepare students for the sixth grade. At the end of the retreat, the same teacher said that the purpose of the fifth grade curriculum was to prepare students to live in a democracy.

Restructuring

Another term that is closely related to transformation is *restructuring*. Schlechty (1990, p. xvi) defines restructuring as "altering systems of rules, roles, and relationships so that schools can serve existing purposes more effectively or serve new purposes altogether."

Chapter Summary

In the past, teacher education programs have neglected to prepare teachers to construct, administer, and score tests. Most programs that require a measurement or evaluation course offer a course that deals almost exclusively with standardized tests, ignoring teacher-made tests.

Education reform has stressed accountability as measured by student performance on standardized exams. Education reform is also stimulating the restructuring of the school's curriculum. Maximum success with this process requires teacher involvement with evaluating the total curriculum. Effective evaluation is continuous and comprehensive, covering all parts of the curriculum.

Teachers have often been accused of teaching to the test. Today, teachers are taught to align the taught curriculum with the tested curriculum.

Historically, most tests used in elementary and secondary schools were summative tests administered at the end of the teaching unit. Today, teachers are learning that a far more powerful tool to promote learning is formative tests, which are administered prior to and throughout the unit and which can promote learning by improving instruction, study skills, and the curriculum.

Instead of using objective test scores exclusively as grade determiners, as has been a common practice, schools are being encouraged to use a combination of test scores and portfolios or other subjective criteria.

Curriculum evaluators should examine such qualities as articulation, balance, continuity, scope, and sequence; these must be tied to the school's philosophy or mission statement. The mission statement should produce the curriculum's aims, and the aims should produce the goals, which in turn produce the objectives. Unfortunately, the philosophy and mission statement has often been overlooked.

As noted in this chapter, teachers in multiculturally or socially or academically diverse classrooms must discover alternative ways to recognize achievement, both academic and social. The community at large may hold grades or scores on national or statewide exams as the ultimate purpose of schools; therefore, educators must relate the goals and objectives to the school's mission. They should, periodically, question the goals of the local, state, and national reformers.

Learning Questions

1. Why must teachers become more knowledgeable of curriculum evaluation?
2. What relationship should exist between the curriculum and the school's testing program?
3. Why have teachers ignored formative evaluation, and why is this important?

4. Why is criterion-referenced evaluation more appropriate for use in elementary and secondary schools than norm-referenced evaluation?

5. What impact is education reform having on testing, and how should teachers respond?

6. What advantages do progressive reporting systems have over traditional testing?

7. Why do curriculum developers need evaluation models?

8. Which of the following curriculum elements relate to the vertical curriculum and which elements relate to the horizontal curriculum: scope, sequence, articulation, continuity, balance, coherence?

9. What general advice would you give beginning college students to help them plan their curricula?

10. Why is continuous curriculum evaluation necessary.

11. Is it ever acceptable to sacrifice one discipline to achieve excellence in another? Why or why not?

12. If a school invested all its resources and time in academics at the expense of a physical education program, would that practice be more acceptable than Hillsboro Middle School's curriculum?

13. Usually when economic recessions occur, the first program to be eliminated is fine arts. Is this practice acceptable? Why or why not?

14. What do you suppose could have motivated the faculty members at Hillsboro to shape their curriculum as they did?

15. The current education reform programs are pressing for more math and science. What precautionary measures should school personnel take to ensure curriculum balance?

16. How does competition affect the attainment of multicultural goals?

17. What criteria can be used to evaluate a curriculum for its constructivist strengths and weaknesses?

Suggested Activities

1. Draw a diagram to show your own concept of the CIPP evaluation model and, for each part, write a descriptive paragraph.

2. Draw a chart and with it, contrast formative and summative evaluation according to when they occur and according to their purpose.

3. Make your own portfolio. Include at least *five* of the following *six* items: (*a*) formative test, (*b*) summative test, (*c*) objectives, (*d*) essay test, (*e*) your philosophy of evaluation (how you believe it should and should not be used), and (*f*) a sample simulation you will use to teach a future lesson.

4. Identify the two curriculum elements that you believe are most important and write a paper telling why you believe they are important. Explain how each can be used to develop and maintain (*a*) a constructivist classroom, and (*b*) a multicultural classroom.

5. Identify the major strengths in your curriculum model and identify relationships among its parts.

6. Critique your school's curriculum and explain any recent effects of educational reform efforts on its multicultural goals.

Works Cited and Suggested Readings

Abruscato, J. (1993, February). Early results and tentative implications from the Vermont portfolio project. *Phi Delta Kappan, 74*(6), 474–477.

Archbald, D., & Newmann, F. (1988). *Beyond standardized testing: Authentic academic achievement in the secondary school.* Reston, VA: NASSP Bulletin.

Aschbacher, P. R. (1992). Issues in performance assessment staff development. In J. R. Craig (Ed.), *New directions for education reform.* Bowling Green, KY: Western Kentucky University, pp. 51–62.

Banks, J. A. (1993). Multicultural education: Development, dimensions, and challenges. *Phi Delta Kappan, 75*(1), 22–28.

Barton, J., & Collins, A. (1993). Portfolios in teacher education. *The Journal of Teacher Education, 44*(3), 200–210.

Block, J. H., Efthim, H. E., & Burns, R. B. (1989). *Building effective mastery learning schools.* New York: Longman.

Block, J. H., & Henson, K. T. (1986). Mastery learning and middle school instruction. *American Middle School Education, 9,* 21–29.

Bloom, B. S., Hastings, J., & Madaus, G. F. (1971). *Handbook of formative and summative evaluation of student learning.* NewYork: McGraw-Hill.

Borko, H., & Elliott, R. (1999). Hands-on pedagogy versus hands-off accountability. *Phi Delta Kappan, 80*(5), 394–400.

Bracey, G. W. (1993). Restructuring: Achievement and engagement outcomes. *Phi Delta Kappan, 75*(2), 186–187.

Brandt, R. S. (1994). Overview: Is outcome based education dead?" *Educational Leadership, 51*(6), 5.

Brogdon, R. E. (1993). Darlene's story: When standards can hurt. *Educational Leadership, 50*(5), 76–77.

Brown, D. S. (1990). Middle level teachers' perceptions of action research. *Middle School Journal, 22*(1), 30–32.

Buschee, F., & Baron, M. A. (1994). OBE: Some answers for the uninitiated. *The Clearing House, 67*(4), 193–196.

Carroll, J. B. (1963). A model of school learning. *Teachers College Record, 64,* 723–733.

Chambers, D. L. (1993). Standardized testing impedes reform. *Educational Leadership, 50*(5), 80.

Craig, J. R. (1992). Performance assessment: A new direction in education reform. In J. R. Craig (Ed.), *New directions in education reform.* Bowling Green, KY: Western Kentucky University, pp. v–vii.

Cuban, L. (1993). The lure of curricular reform and its pitiful history. *Phi Delta Kappan, 75*(2), 182–185.

Dagley, D. L., & Orso, J. K. (1991, September). Integrating formative and summative modes of evaluation. *NASSP Bulletin, 75,* 72–82.

Delgado-Gaitan, C. (1991, November). Involving parents in the schools: A process of empowerment. *American Journal of Education, 100*(1), 20–46.

Dusenburg, L. A., & Falco, M. (1997). School-based drug abuse prevention strategies: From research to policy and practice. In R. P. Weissberg, T. G. Gullotta, R. L. Hampton, B. A. Ryan, & G. R. Adams (Eds.), *Healthy Children 2010: Enhancing children's wellness.* Thousand Oaks, CA: Sage.

Egbert, R. L. (1984). The role of research in teacher education. In R. L. Egbert & M. M. Kluender (Eds.), *Using research to improve teacher education.* Lincoln, NE: American Association of Colleges for Teacher Education.

Epstein, J. L., & MacIver, D. J. (1990, November). National practices and trends in the middle grades. *Middle School Journal, 22*(2), 36–40.

Fantini, M. D. (1986). *Regaining excellence in education.* Columbus, OH: Merrill.

Fever, M. J., & Fulton, K. (1993). The many faces of performance assessment. *Phi Delta Kappan, 74*(6), 478.

Fielding, G., & Shaughnessy, J. (1990, November). Improving student assessment: Overcoming the obstacles. *NASSP Bulletin,* 90–98.

Frymier, J. (1979, February). Keynote speech at Southwest Educational Research Association, Houston, TX.

Goldberg, M. R. (1992). Expressing and assessing understanding through the arts. *Phi Delta Kappan, 73*(8), 619–623.

Goodlad, J. I. (1984). *A place called school.* New York: McGraw-Hill.

Goodman, J. (1992). Towards a discourse of imagery: Critical curriculum theorizing. *The Educational Forum, 56*(3), 269–289.

Guskey, T. R. (1994). What you assess may not be what you get. *Educational Leadership, 51*(6), 51–54.

Habermann, M. (1992, November). The role of the classroom teacher as a curriculum leader. *NASSP Bulletin, 76*(547), 11–19.

Hill, J. C. (1986). *Curriculum evaluation for school improvement.* Springfield, IL: Charles C Thomas.

Huggest, A. J., & Stinnett, T. M. (1958). *Professional problems of teachers.* New York: Macmillan.

Kanpol, B. (1993). Critical curriculum theorizing as subjective imagery: Reply to Goodman. *The Educational Forum, 57*(3), 325–330.

Kennedy, R. (1992). What is performance assessment? In J. R. Craig (Ed.), *New directions for education reform.* Bowling Green, KY: Western Kentucky University.

Krause, S. (1996). Portfolios in teacher education: Effects of instruction on preservice teachers' early comprehension of the portfolio process. *Journal of Teacher Education, 47*(2), 130–138.

Latham, A. S. (1998). Gender differences on assessments. *Educational Leadership, 55*(4), 88–89.

Looman deWijk. (1996). Career and technology studies: Crossing the curriculum. *Educational Leadership, 53*(8), 50–53.

Markle, G., Johnston, J. H., Geer, C., & Meichtry, Y. (1990, November). Teaching for understanding. *Middle School Journal, 22*(2), 53–57.

Marshall, C. (1991, March–April). Teachers' learning styles: How they affect student learning. *The Clearing House, 64*(4), 225–227.

Marzano, R. J. (1994). Lessons from the field about outcome-based performance assessment.

Meek, A. (1998). America's teachers: Much to celebrate. *Educational Leadership, 55*(4), 88–89.

National Commission on Excellence in Education (1983). *A nation at risk: The imperative for educational reform.* Washington, DC: U.S. Government Printing Office.

Oliva, P. F. (1997). *Developing the curriculum.* (4th ed.). New York: HarperCollins.

Nelson, W. W. (1999). The emperor redux. *Phi Delta Kappan, 80*(5), 387–392.

Parsons, J., & Jones, C. (1990, September–October). Not another test. *The Clearing House, 64*(1), 17–20.

Perrone, V. (1994). How to engage students in learning. *Educational Leadership, 51*(5), 11–13.

Pitton, D. E. (1999). The naked truth isn't very revealing. *Phi Delta Kappan, 80*(5), 383–386.

Pratt, D. (1980). *Curriculum design and development.* New York: Harcourt Brace.

Rose, L. C., & Gallup, A. M., (1998). The 30th annual Phi Delta Kappa/Gallup poll of the public's attitudes toward the public schools. *Phi Delta Kappa, 80*(1), 41–56.

Schlechty, P. C. (1990). *Schools for the 21st century: Leadership imperatives for educational reform.* San Francisco: Jossey-Bass.

Schwahn, C., & Spady, W. (1998). Why change doesn't happen and how to make sure it does. *Educational Leadership, 55*(7), 45–47.

Shen, J. (1998). Do teachers feel empowered? *Educational Leadership, 55*(7), 35–36.

Smith, M. (1991, January). Evaluation as instruction: Using analytic scales to increase composing ability. *Middle School Journal, 22*(2), 21–25.

Spady, W. G. (1994). Choosing outcomes of significance. *Educational Leadership, 51*(6), 18–22.

Special Study Panel on Education Indicators for the National Center for Education Statistics. (1991). *Education counts.* Washington, DC: United States Department of Education.

Stefanich, G. P. (1990). Cycles of cognition. *Middle School Journal, 22*(2), 47–52.

Van Wangenen, L., & Hibbard, K. M. (1998). Building teacher portfolios. *Educational Leadership, 55*(5), 26–29.

Wade, R. K. (1997). Lifting a school's spirit. *Educational Leadership, 54*(8), 34–36.

Wang, M. C., Haertel, G. D., & Walberg, H. J. (1998). Models of reform: A comprehensive guide. *Educational Leadership, 55*(7), 66–71.

Weissberg, R. P., Shriver, T. P., Bose, S, & DeFalco, K. (1997). "Creating a districtwide social development project." Educational Leadership, 54(8), 37–39.

Weller, L. D., Jr., Hartley, S. H., & Brown, C. L. (1994). Principles and TMQ: Developing vision. *The Clearing House, 67*(5), 298–301.

Wiggins, G. (1989, April). Teaching to the authentic test. *Educational Leadership, 46*(7), 41–47.

Wiggins, G. (1992). Creating tests worth taking. *Educational Leadership, 49*(8), 26–35.

Wilcox, B., & Tomei, L. (1999). *Professional portfolios for teachers.* Norwood, MA: Christopher-Gordon Publishers, Inc.

Winograd, P., & Jones, D. L. (1992). The use of portfolios in performance assessment. In J. R. Craig (Ed.), *New directions in education reform.* Bowling Green, KY: Western Kentucky University, pp. 37–50.

Winton, J. J. (1991, January). You can win without competing. *Middle School Journal, 22*(3), 40.

Worthen, B. R., & Leopold, G. D. (1992). Impediments to implementing alternative assessment: Some emerging issues. In J. R. Craig (Ed.), *New directions in education reform.* Bowling Green, KY: Western Kentucky University, pp. 1–20.

10   PLANNING AND CONVERTING CURRICULUM INTO INSTRUCTION

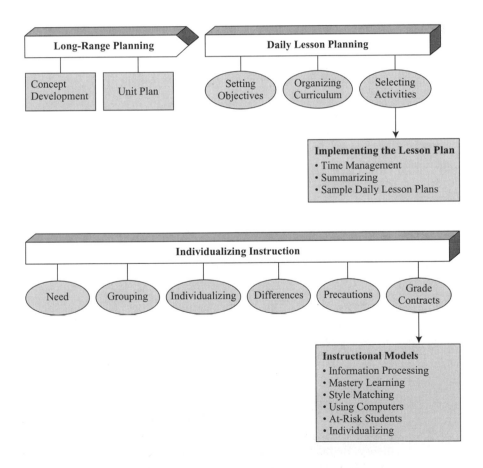

Objectives

This chapter should prepare you to:

- Explain the relationship between curriculum and instruction.
- Develop a plan for ensuring that the major concepts in each lesson will be understood by all students.
- Choose a lesson plan and adjust it to prepare students to discover new concepts and relate those to existing knowledge.
- Develop a multipurpose activity to achieve some of the daily objectives.
- Contrast the effectiveness of token rewards with that of student involvement in promoting interaction among students from different cultures.
- Develop a set of guidelines for assigning students to groups and for using group assignments to meet individual student needs.
- Develop a contract to be used with students whose needs differ significantly from those of their classmates.
- Make a list of the qualities and advantages of mastery learning and a similar list for matching teaching and learning styles. Using some of these qualities, design a lesson to meet the needs of a class of at-risk students.
- Explain how recent local reform practices are guided by and reflect constructivist theory.

"A teacher's greatest opportunity for growth is systematic inquiry into his or her own teaching and learning." (B. J. Stallworth, 1998, p. 77).

A WICHITA SCHOOL CASE

Traditionally, many teachers throughout the country have been expected to stay in their rooms, apply the "tried and proven" approaches, and keep things under control. With little or no encouragement to try new approaches, many teachers who have chosen to experiment with new educational theories have had to do so in the isolation of their classrooms, with little or no support. Nevertheless, some teachers are eager to use any technique they believe will improve their lessons.

Fortunately, today most districts are encouraging teachers to experiment. Such is the case here in Wichita. One Wichita junior high school teacher attended a district in-service meeting where he learned about learning styles theory. He then invited a consultant from the teacher center to visit one of his classes and explain the concept to his students.

The teacher administered a learning style preference questionnaire, and the students scored the survey, developed their profiles, and shared the results with the class. The students were then encouraged to contribute ideas for classroom organization that would take advantage of the variety of preferred learning modalities within the class. They helped set up areas where students could hold discussions and listen to tapes and areas where students could read or work on written assignments.

Student enthusiasm soon spread, and parents became interested, so at a parent meeting the teacher explained the learning styles concept and how he was implementing it. He then administered the survey to the parents and helped them interpret the results regarding their own preferences. To demonstrate the use of styles management and thus earn potential support, the teacher began using the parents' learning styles when he conducted parent-teacher conferences.

The results of this experiment were very positive; student-teacher shared planning increased, and tolerance for others' learning differences increased. Parent-teacher conferences became more effective, and soon other teachers began experimenting with the concept in their classrooms.

Because innovations often require additional facilities, materials, space, and program flexibility, success requires the support of administrators, teachers, students, and parents, all of whom must understand the importance of the change. A simple approach is first to inform others about the process and then to involve them with the innovation.

Districtwide implementation of an innovation shows support for the change; therefore, teachers who can persuade the district office to try a new approach are academically empowered. The teacher must establish the credibility of the proposed change. First, the teacher should provide evidence that the approach is effective. The literature can be used to show the success other teachers or districts have had with the innovation. Also, the teacher might ask permission to try the innovation at the classroom or department level, collecting test data to show whether the new approach is effective compared with the approach currently in use.

Experienced teachers know that many variables affect learning, including students' natural interests, skills, and aspirations (Latham, 1998). As Rinne (1998, p. 621) says, "What captures one student's attention might not affect another, and what appeals to one student today might miss the mark tomorrow." Some students learn best in the mornings; others learn best in the afternoons (Callahan, 1998). Johnston (1998, p. 82) was right in saying, "The first step in meeting the needs of learners is to understand how they learn." Teachers should develop and implement new approaches with these thoughts in mind. As mentioned in an earlier chapter, it is both ironic and unfortunate that some education reformers have increased the amount of research but have neglected the most important area of all—the amount of learning resulting from each new approach (Wang, Haerte., & Walberg, 1998).

An Introduction to Converting the Curriculum

This book began by examining a variety of definitions of *curriculum*. Although the perceptions of curriculum are many and diverse, the ultimate purpose of curriculum is universally accepted: all curricula exist to provide the basis for effective instruction, that is, instruction that maximizes learning. To the degree that any curriculum succeeds in improving instruction and learning, that curriculum is successful; conversely, any curriculum that fails to improve learning cannot claim success.

This interpretation of the role of the curriculum, predicated on the assumption that all children can learn, makes the curriculum accountable for the academic success of all students. An effective curriculum and effective instruction require effective planning.

This chapter begins by examining long-term curriculum strategies, followed by daily lesson planning. The chapter ends with a discussion of ways to adjust the curriculum to meet individual student needs.

Long-Range Planning

Concept Development

Sometimes students need help in focusing on the major concepts in a lesson. Just prior to or at the beginning of a lesson, teachers may ask questions, present a simple outline, or give students a few key words to help them focus on the major concepts. Such strategies, called *advance organizers,* can be an effective means of gaining student attention and directing it to the lesson. Snapp and Glover (1990, p. 270) found that middle school students who read and paraphrased an advance organizer prior to study correctly answered more lower-order and higher-order study questions than did students who did not encounter the organizer. They conclude, "The educational implications of the current study seem straightforward. If a reasonable academic goal is to improve the quality of answers that students construct for study questions, we recommend that one method of so aiding students is through the use of advance organizers."

Harrison (1990, pp. 503–504) offers the following 10 steps for teachers to use to help students identify and become familiar with each lesson's (or unit's) major concepts:

1. Present a nominal definition of a concept and give examples.

2. Emphasize the common attributes and ask students to name further attributes.

3. Ask students to generate examples.

4. Have students give totally opposite examples.

5. Have students name metaphors to compare and contrast to the original idea.

6. Have students review contexts in which the concept takes place.

7. Describe the overt application of the concept.

8. Identify factors in the environment that facilitate or hinder the application of the concept.

9. Formulate an operational definition involving the last steps of this process.

10. Discuss consequences in terms of viable solutions to a given problem.

Harrison (1990, p. 203) reminds teachers that just understanding concepts is not enough: "Instruction must focus on the use of the concepts and the context in which they occur in order to ascertain their practical connotations." Perkins (1994, p. 23) said that teachers must induct students into each discipline they study:

> Concepts and principles in a discipline are not understood in isolation. Grasping what a concept or principle means depends in considerable part on recognizing how it functions within the discipline. This requires a sense of how the discipline works as a system of thought.

One method that teachers can use to help students apply concepts is the case study (Kowalski, Henson, & Weaver, 1994), which enables students to separate relevant information from irrelevant information. In doing so, they can gain a clearer grasp of the concepts.

Van Gulick (1990) believes that the decline in performance on standardized tests is the result of the way our students store information. To be able to use newly learned information, students must see how the new information relates to a larger whole as they learn it.

The implications for teachers and other curriculum developers are significant. According to Von Glaserfeld (1998), "The teachers' role will no longer be to dispense 'truth' but rather to help and guide the student in the conceptual organization of certain areas of expertise." Such guidance is best achieved through the use of group assignments that require students to describe the process they use to explore the new content as it relates to what they already know (Markle et al., 1990, p. 54).

The Unit Plan

Chapter 6 focused on setting appropriate aims, goals, and objectives, and Chapter 7 focused on selecting the appropriate content and activities needed to reach the aims, goals and objectives. Reaching aims, goals, and objectives also requires a long-term plan, or *unit plan*. Long-term planning is often a defining attribute that distinguishes between the approaches of novice teachers and those of more experienced teachers. Roskos (1996, p. 120) explains, "Where experts engaged in long-range planning, the novices' approach was more short-term in nature, focused on preparing for tomorrow."

Planning the Unit

Unit planning should be a joint effort by the teacher and students, whose roles in curriculum planning are obviously different. Teachers' extensive study of their subjects gives them insights into what students need to know about the subject of the unit, which students by their very role cannot have.

Involving students in planning helps avoid the sequential approach that often limits learning. According to Hart (1983, p. 77), "Because the ordinary classroom does not provide this richness in learning and, in most instances, limits what the brain can do, students become addicted or habituated to this limited, sequential approach." Involving students can also increase their emotional commitment to the material, enhancing their learning of that material. According to Levy (1983, p. 70), "If students are engaged [in learning activities, as opposed to remaining passive], both sides of the brain will participate in the educational process regardless of the subject matter." Experiential curricula, the curricula that actively involve students, also have been found to rouse students to choose to associate with members of other cultures, where token reward systems have failed (Wade, 1997).

A third part of the teacher's role in planning a unit is to help students select activities necessary for learning the content. This does not mean that the teacher selects some of the activities and the students independently select other activities. When presenting the option of selecting class activities, teachers should have on hand a list of activities from which the class can choose and should permit students to add activities that are feasible, safe, and consistent with school policy. Student interest in a particular activity may of itself make that activity worthwhile by raising the level of motivation in the class.

Another group to include in curriculum planning is parents, because of their vested interest in the schools and their ability to influence students positively. The recent popularity of school-based decision making has intensified the need to include parents in all parts of schools, especially academics. O'Neal, Earley, and Snider (1991, p. 123) stress this need: "Research has constantly indicated that parent and family involvement is critical to the academic success of many children."

Reporting on a research and development study for the National Center for Education Statistics, Finn (1993, p. 72) said, "Overall, parents' direct involvement with their youngsters regarding school work is positively associated with academic performance." If parental involvement is to increase achievement, this involvement must occur during planning.

Another often neglected group is other teachers. Most planning is done without the input of other teachers, but collaborative planning changes the way teachers view their subjects. Roskos (1996, p. 127) explains: "The presence of a partner may have forced each teacher to explain her ideas, elaborate on her thinking, or attempt to articulate misgivings, concerns, and hunches left unsaid or not pursued in solitary planning."

Parts of the Unit Plan

The learning unit, or unit plan, is much more than an outline of the subject material to be explored within a certain topic. Although there are many variations, most unit plans contain a title, a statement of philosophy, goals, objectives, content to be covered, teacher and student activities to enhance the attainment of the objectives, and a method of evaluating the degree of understanding developed while studying the unit. The unit plan may also include a list of resource people (consultants) and resource materials (bibliography). See Figure 10.1.

A statement of philosophy is a declaration of a teacher's beliefs about such issues as the purposes of the school, the nature of youth, how youngsters learn, and the purposes of life in general. Because some teachers spend too little time reflecting on their beliefs about these all-important issues, the philosophy statement is perhaps the most neglected part of learning units. The first question teachers hear at the beginning of a new unit, however, is often "Why do we have to study this stuff?" Only by thinking through these broad issues can teachers prepare to answer this question intelligently.

The statement of purposes is a list of general expectations the teacher has of the unit. For example, the general expectations of a tenth grade unit in government may include an understanding of how a bill is introduced, increased tolerance of the opinions of others, or an appreciation of democracy as a type of government. Unlike the performance objectives used in daily planning, which are stated in specific, observable, and measurable terms, the purposes for a unit should be general.

The selection of content for any unit should be based on three broad considerations: (1) the significance of the content in attaining the purposes of the particular unit (in other words, it must be content that is necessary to master in order to reach the general objectives), (2) the importance of the content to society, and (3) the needs and interests of the learners.

Teachers need not feel obligated to select one activity for each objective, for some of the best activities serve multiple purposes and lead to the attainment of several objectives. For example, one activity for a senior English class might be to write a composition contrasting Shelley's poetry with that of Byron, which would provide students with opportunities for both gaining writing skills and sharpening concepts of an author's style by contrasting it with that of another author. Planning activities that have multiple objectives does not necessarily promote inefficiency. Each learning unit should include different types of measurement, such as written tests, oral tests, debates, term projects, homework

Figure 10.1

Anatomy of a learning unit.

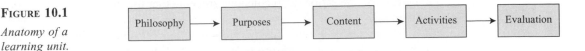

assignments, classwork, and perhaps performance in class or group discussions. This type of evaluation, which examines the quality of a product, is called *product evaluation.*

Another type of evaluation that can be applied to each learning unit is called *process evaluation.* This is a description of the effectiveness of the teaching or the unit. Process evaluation analyzes the various parts of the unit in isolation to determine whether the unit needs improvement. It also involves looking at all parts together to see how they relate to one another. Teachers should ask themselves such questions as, Is my philosophy sound? Does it convince these students that the unit is important? Are the purposes important? Am I being realistic in expecting students to achieve them in this length of time? Is the content in this unit what is needed to achieve the unit's stated purposes? Are these activities helpful in attaining these objectives? Is the evaluation fair to everyone? Does it discriminate between those who have met the objectives and those who have not?

Learning units should include certain practical information, including the title, subject, grade level, and a list of resources—consultants, equipment, facilities, and supplies—needed to teach the unit, especially audiovisual aids. Learning units should also include a list of references that support the unit and can be used to pursue the topic further. Each unit should contain performance objectives that (1) are stated in terms of student behavior, (2) describe the conditions, and (3) specify the minimum acceptable level of performance.

Sample Unit Plans

Following are several sample unit plans. The title of each unit describes the unit; the statement of purpose or objectives describes a desired change in the students; and the evaluation is related to the objectives stated at the beginning of the unit.

The unit plan in Box 10.1 was chosen for its brevity and simplicity. This does not make it a superior plan, but such brief units are often used. Perhaps the unit is too skimpy. What would you say about the format? Is the outline adequate? Figure 10.2 shows the parts commonly found in a unit. Notice that some of the parts in Figure 10.2 are not included in the sample unit given in Box 10.1.

The meteorology unit has neither a statement of philosophy nor a statement of rationale to show the significance of the unit. Many educators feel that a statement of philosophy is needed to help teachers clarify their basic beliefs about life, school, and adolescents and how adolescents learn. Goals and objectives should coincide and should reflect the teacher's basic beliefs. Other educators prefer to have a statement of rationale instead of a statement of philosophy. By writing a statement of rationale, teachers justify the unit to themselves; then they can use the rationale to convince students that the unit is worth their time and energy.

The meteorology unit has no sections titled "Teacher Activities" or "Student Activities." This is unfortunate, because at the time of planning the unit, the teacher should make decisions about activities, such as taking the class to

Box 10.1

Unit Plan—Meteorology

Meteorology Unit Plan: What Meterorology Means to You

I. Purpose
   A. Knowledge: To understand—
       1. The different types of weather
       2. The principles of weather formation
       3. The role of the weatherperson
       4. The names and principles of commonly used weather instruments
       5. Weather vocabulary
   B. Attitudes: To appreciate—
       1. The damage weather can do
       2. The advantage of good weather
       3. How weather affects our daily behavior
       4. The rate of accuracy of weather predictions
       5. The precision use of weather instruments
       6. The fallacies of superstitions about the weather
   C. Skills: To develop the ability to—
       1. Read and interpret weather instruments
       2. Read and interpret weather maps
       3. Predict future weather
II. Daily Lessons
   A. Definition of weather
   B. Precipitation
       1. The different types of precipitation
       2. How each type of precipitation is formed
   C. Reading the weather map
   D. Reading weather instruments
   E. Predicting weather
   F. Effects of geographic location on weather
   G. Effects of the earth's rotation on weather
   H. Effects of the earth's tilting on weather
   I. How to change weather that can hurt you
III. Materials
   A. Weather reports from newspapers
   B. Weather maps
   C. Equipment for making fog: air pump, water, jar
   D. Barometer, thermometer, anemometer, wind vane
   E. Graph paper for each student
IV. Evaluation
   Tests for each section of the unit: approximately one test per week's study of the topic

FIGURE 10.2

A learning-teaching unit.

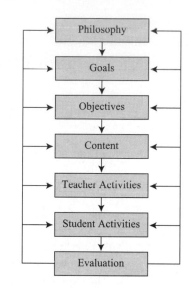

a weather station and showing films on meteorology. The weather station may need advance notice, and for field trips students will have to identify in advance what information they will attempt to obtain during the visit. Films must be scheduled and ordered in advance so that they will be available when they are needed, and time will be required to preview them. You can probably identify other weaknesses in this unit plan.

Box 10.2 contains a sample chemistry unit designed for use in an eleventh grade class. This more comprehensive plan has fewer weaknesses because it has most of the parts that educators consider essential to any unit. Examine its strengths and weaknesses. Pay particular attention to the unit's overall structure and organization, and you will probably be able to improve it.

Daily Lesson Planning

As essential as they are by themselves, aims and goals remain no more than elusive generalities. Making them attainable requires designing daily lesson plans that include the general expectations (goals) but that can also be translated into more specific terms. Each daily lesson plan should be developed to achieve a particular part of the unit; in fact, most units contain a series of daily lesson plans.

The Daily Lesson Plan

Because the teaching unit is usually content-oriented and may not specify the experiences needed for learning each day's lesson, daily strategies are required

Box 10.2

Chemistry Unit

Chemistry Unit Plan: The Organization of Chemistry

 I. Statement of Purpose: The chapters covered in this unit are designed to introduce the beginning chemistry student to the basic background and structural knowledge needed for further studies in chemistry. Topics include Atomic Theory and the Periodic Table.

 II. Performance Objectives
   A. Chapter I: Atomic Theory. The eleventh grade general chemistry student will be able to—

   Lesson 1
   1. Define an atom correctly in a closed-book test.
   2. Give the size of an atom in the unit posttest.
   3. Identify the parts of an atom by name and describe them, given an unlabeled diagram of the atom. Four or five parts must be correctly labeled and described.
   4. Match the mass of the parts of the atom to the correct path, given a list of masses.

   Lesson 2
   1. Define the atomic number of an atom.
   2. Define the mass number of an atom in a closed-book test.
   3. Utilize the concept of isotopes by correctly grouping given atoms into isotopic groups.
   4. Apply the concept of energy level shells by designating the number of electrons in each shell, given an atomic number.

   Lesson 3
   1. Correctly define atomic mass in a closed-book test.
   2. Define Avogadro's number in a closed-book test.
   3. Apply the concept of a mole by the amount of a substance in a mole of a given substance.
   4. Define the atomic weight of an atom in a closed-book test.
   5. Apply the concept of atomic number, Avogadro's number, mole, and gram atomic weight in solving simple stoichiometric problems. Given the problem and required information, the student must solve for the asked-for information, correctly answering 80 percent of the problems to receive credit. (Partial credit given for correct setups.)
   B. Chapter 2: Periodic Table. The eleventh grade general chemistry student will be able to—

   Lesson 1
   1. List at least three of the four basic elements.

(Continued)

Let's Talk

Each performance objective should contain four parts. Check the above objectives against these criteria. It is as simple as A, B, C, D.

Audience: The student should be the subject of each objective.

Behavior: The student's behavior should be the verb of each objective.

Conditions: The objective should describe the conditions under which the student is expected to perform.

Degree: The degree or level of performance required of the students should be specified.

2. Identify the common elements by symbol. This will be shown by correctly giving the elements or symbol asked for in 15 of 18 questions in two in-class quizzes.

Lesson 2
1. Obtain atomic numbers of elements from the periodic table with an accuracy level of 80 percent.
2. Obtain the mass number of elements from the periodic table with an accuracy level of 80 percent.
3. Obtain a given element's electron configuration from the periodic table.

Lesson 3
1. Define periodic law.
2. Define "group of elements."
3. Define "period of elements."
4. Distinguish the characteristics of families of elements by matching the correct family with the given characteristic with a minimum accuracy level of 80 percent.
5. With 80 percent or above accuracy, match the correct family with the given element.

III. Attitudinal Objective. The eleventh grade general chemistry student will be able to participate in class discussions. This objective will be met when 80 percent of the class answers general questions, directed to the class as whole, during the course of the discussion.

Let's Talk

Following are lists of concepts and content generalizations under topics to be studied. A check to see whether students know these terms can help the teacher begin at the appropriate level. The second list—generalizations—is even more important. These are the major understandings that should come from the unit. Notice that they are essential for achieving the preceding objectives.

(Continued)

IV. Concept and Generalizations
   A. Topic 1: Atomic Structure

Concepts	*Generalizations*
Atomic theory	Atomic theory has been developed
Atom	to support observations.
Proton	Each subparticle composing the
Neutron	atom (electron, neutron, proton)
Electron	has certain characteristics and is
Nucleus	unique in energy levels or shells.
Element	Each atom has its electrons arranged.
Mole	
Avogadro's number	
Angstrom A	

   B. Topic 2: Arrangement of Electrons in Atoms

Concepts	*Generalizations*
Orbitals	Quantum numbers describe
Orbital notation	the orientation of an electron in
Electron configuration notation	an atom in terms of (a) distance
Electron dot notation	from the nucleus; (b) shape;
	(c) position in space with
	respect to the three axes
	(x, y, z); and (d) direction
	of spin.

   C. Topic 3: Periodic Table

Concepts	*Generalizations*
Periodic table	The periodic table organizes
Series (period)	the elements; properties can
Group (family)	be predicted from the element's
Noble gas family	positions. Elements with similar
Sodium family	arrangements of outer shell
Calcium family	electrons have similar properties.
Nitrogen family	
Oxygen family	

to help students move nearer to the unit goals. For most teachers, this organized approach is the *daily lesson plan*. Like a map, the lesson plan gives direction to the lesson objectives. If the lesson begins to stray, the lesson plan brings it back on course. Staying on course is difficult without a lesson plan; however, despite the emphasis teacher education places on the ends-means approach, there is much evidence that experienced teachers do not begin the planning process by determining objectives. Even when teachers modify their teaching approaches, they seldom consider the lesson objectives (Clark & Peterson, 1986).

Lesson Plan Factors Affecting Achievement

Romberg and Carpenter (1986) reviewed studies of mathematics classes and discovered three significant variables associated with student achievement. First, instead of teaching the concepts needed to understand their subject, teachers of the same subject and grade level may cover very different materials.

A second factor in daily lesson planning is the amount of engaged time teachers spend on a topic or concept compared to the time that is allocated for the subject. The disparity between the time students are engaged in their subjects is enormous. Reinstein (1998) reported that one school where he taught provided 300 minutes of classroom instruction a week and another school where he taught provided only 200 minutes of instruction a week.

A third factor that affects achievement is the time students spend identifying and developing particular concepts, as opposed to the time they spend just studying the concepts. Des Dixon (1994, p. 362) criticizes schools for failing to involve students in meaningful curriculum development:

> We have Mickey Moused the lives of children by denying them control, the very thing we should be teaching them so they can find meaning in life and learn to survive in the real world of childhood.

In the developmental portion of a lesson, students spend time discussing such issues as why the concept is true, how skills or concepts are interrelated, and how to use broader relationships to estimate answers to problems. In other words, developmental time should put the important concepts and skills in a broader context in order to extend the students' understandings of those ideas.

Another variable that has been studied for over 50 years to determine its effect on achievement is class size. Although the research shows the positive effects of smaller classes to be minimal, over time, the cumulative effect may be significant. Johnston (1990) reports that one advantage of smaller classes is improved teacher morale. Fowler (1992) stresses the need for additional research to determine the effect of class size on the level of student participation, since participation directly correlates with achievement.

Traditionally, clear concepts in each discipline, and effective models and strategies for teaching them, have not been available because they have not been identified. As Armento (1986, pp. 948–949) states, "Methodological advances have outpaced conceptual advances in the last 10 years." Although Armento is referring to the field of social studies, the same is true of all disciplines. But there is hope, because more studies that identify important concepts in disciplines are being conducted today, and there is an increase in metacognitive studies, which will help determine more effective ways to teach students to analyze their individual conceptual development processes.

What Makes a Lesson Plan Good?

Lesson plans come in many sizes and varieties, and their the length or style does not make one plan better than another. A good lesson plan can be a comprehensive outline that is worded formally, neatly typed on bond paper, and enclosed in a plastic binder, or it can be a brief outline written in pencil on 3- by 5-inch cards. The styles of good lesson plans vary as much as their length. A good lesson plan contains material that will challenge and engage students throughout the class period with activities that involve every student, using a format the teacher can follow without having to stop the lesson to read it.

Setting Objectives

Planning a daily lesson should begin with the teacher asking, In what ways do I want this lesson to change my students? Or, What will they be able to do as a consequence of the lesson? When stated at the outset, these proposed behavioral changes can give direction to daily activities. Writing performance objectives was the focus of Chapter 6.

Organizing Materials

Chapter 5 provided assistance in organizing material. Having decided what material to include in the lesson, the teacher must next decide on the sequence in which students will experience it. Sometimes the nature of the subject dictates the order of presentation, so the teacher should check the major ideas to be covered to determine whether there is a natural sequence. For example, a physical education teacher who wants to provide experiences that are essential for learning to drive a golf ball will think, "What ideas are important to understanding this process?" The answer is: "Addressing the ball, the backswing, the downswing, and the follow-through," which is a natural sequence. Or, a lesson on how to bake a chiffon cake would follow the sequence of the recipe. A history teacher, too, would prepare many lessons involving historical events taught in chronological order.

If the four of five objectives of a day's lesson have no natural order, perhaps a particular sequence would make the lesson more easily understood. For instance, a chemistry teacher would probably not teach the formula of a compound until the students had learned to recognize the symbols of the elements contained in the compound.

Selecting Activities

Generally, more emphasis is placed on activities than on content, because today's educators recognize that classroom activities are major avenues for learning. For this reason, a lesson plan must describe those activities the teacher expects to use to teach the content. Because students learn more when they participate in lessons (Finn, 1993), each lesson plan should provide meaningful activities.

At this point the teacher should review the partially completed lesson plan. A statement of how the lesson should change the students—that is, the objectives of the lesson—has been made. Some major ideas to be developed have been selected and organized. The next step is to plan involvement by assigning a task that will require the students to use each of the major ideas in the lesson.

Questions can be used to focus students' attention on the lessons. Snapp and Glover (1990) found that questions can be used as advance organizers to improve student achievement.

The English teacher who is planning a lesson on "How to Capture the Reader's Attention" would assign tasks that make the students use what they have just learned. Presented with several compositions, the students could be asked to identify the principles of capturing the reader's attention each time they occur. Later in the class period, each student could write the lead paragraph of a composition, employing the techniques of capturing the reader's attention introduced earlier in the lesson.

The physical education teacher who wants to teach the correct procedure for driving a golf ball may demonstrate each step and ask students to identify mistakes that the teacher deliberately makes in each phase. Eventually, the students go through the process themselves, while other students critique. A vocational shop teacher would follow a similar process, as would math, science, history, English, music, and art teachers.

Each of these activities is an assigned task that requires students to do things they could not do correctly unless they understand the content taught in the earlier part of the lesson.

Implementing the Lesson Plan

The results of any lesson are likely to be no better than the daily lesson plan, yet the lesson plan does not guarantee learning success. Even the best plans may need modification as the students interact with the materials and activities (Green & Smith, 1982). In summarizing several studies on planning, Shavelson (1984) suggests that prolific planning may be counterproductive if the teacher becomes single-minded and does not adapt the lesson to the students' needs. As teachers develop planning skills, they should consider ways to alter their plans in case the plans are not effective with a particular group at a particular time.

Time Management

Ciscell (1990, p. 217) explains the importance of time management skills for teachers:

> Teachers' inefficient use of their professional time recently has become the focus of much attention within the educational community. What started out as simple efforts to measure the amount of on-task behavior have resulted in somewhat alarming reports concerning the ways elementary and secondary teachers manage the school day. In the last decade, educational time has taken on a vocabulary all its own: Researchers now talk in terms of allotted time, engaged time, and academic learning time. Almost inevitably, teachers' use of classroom time has been blamed for declining achievement in America's schools.

An important time management skill is to learn to say no. When asked to fill in for a friend on a committee or assignment, say either "I'm sorry, but I'm tied up at that time," or negotiate: "I'll be happy to if you will take my place selling football tickets Friday night." With practice, these strategies will become natural and easy, and your colleagues will learn to find an easier target elsewhere. As Ciscell, 1990, p. 218) emphasizes, "Benefits accrue not only for teachers themselves but also for students as they take on the responsibility and challenge of a well-planned assignment." The well-planned assignment takes time to design.

Effective teachers distinguish between important information and other information and simplify these major concepts for their students; less effective teachers attempt to deal with more issues. Because beginning teachers often lack the ability to simplify and make sense of classroom events, the time spent identifying the major principles and concepts in a discipline will be a wise investment.

Summarizing the Daily Lesson

The lesson plan should end with a review of the main ideas covered in the lesson, but the summary should not include every detail, nor should it merely list the main parts of the lesson. Harrison (1990, p. 503) makes an excellent suggestion for summarizing or reviewing a lesson: "Have students name analogies and metaphors, and compare and contrast these with the original idea." The review should show the relationships among the major ideas, tying together the parts of the lesson.

Returning to the earlier example, the physical education teacher planning a lesson on how to drive a golf ball would include in the review each of the major ideas—the address, the backswing, the downswing, and the follow-through—and go over the major issues related to each. The review would begin with the first idea—how to address the golf ball—and include the major points involved in the proper address as they were mentioned in the lesson. Likewise, the English lesson on "How to Capture the Reader's Attention" would include each point and its development.

Learning Cycle Theory

An instructional theory called the *learning cycle theory* uses a learning cycle approach to instruction to help students move through the levels of understanding. The program has three parts: exploration, concept introduction, and application. The hands-on introduction enables students to develop descriptive and qualitative understandings. The concept introduction stages let them talk about their experiences, with the teacher or in cooperative learning groups, where the teacher guides the discussion. During the application phase, students are given assignments that let them apply the concepts in different ways.

Markle et al. (1990) caution the teacher to guard against making assumptions about what students know. They advise teachers to provide a procedural structure that tells students in advance what they are going to do, what the key points are, and what they should know when the lesson is completed.

Sample Daily Lesson Plans

Boxes 10.3 and 10.4 show some sample daily lesson plans. They differ in style, but each contains a few major ideas and is arranged in a sequence that facilitates learning. Note that each major ideas is followed by an assigned task that requires students to use the idea. Note also that each sample lesson ends with a review that ties together the major ideas in the lesson.

The best curriculum planning seldom occurs when teachers are isolated from their colleagues. The following case study by MacNeil describes a school that has been converted into a learning community. As you read this case, consider the type of leadership that is needed to develop a learning community.

Box 10.3

Daily Lesson Plan—Business

I. Title of Lesson: How to Read and Analyze a Newspaper's Financial Page Effectively

II. Reason for Lesson: To show how a stock exchange allows people to put their capital to work whenever and however they choose.

III. Points to be reviewed
   A. Just what common stock is
   B. What common stock means to an issuing corporation
   C. What common stock ownership means to the investor
   D. Advantages and disadvantages of common stock

IV. Content and Activities

Content	*Activity*
A breakdown of the different headings contained in the stock quotes.	Each student will be asked in advance of my explanation as to their meanings.
The prices will be analyzed as to what they actually mean.	Different prices will be put on the board with students giving the answer in dollars and cents.
Actual examples from a newspaper will be analyzed as to their meanings in relation to other stock quotes.	Each student will recite the quotes from a newspaper handout and will tell what they mean.

(Continued)

Summarizing the concepts:

V.   Evaluation: A simple quiz on the material just covered and the review
     work will be given. A simulated paper quote will be provided so that I
     can test whether they understand all the aspects of the heading and the
     prices contained in the quotes.

VI. Assignment: They will be given a project of keeping the daily price
     quotes of a particular stock, which will be turned in at the end of the
     week and evaluated. Each student will be assigned a different stock.

Box 10.4

Daily Lesson Plan—Speech

1. Title: "How to Use *Time* When Reading with Expression." Establish set
    by reading a poem ("Richard Cory") aloud as monotonously and
    ineffectively as possible, with no pauses or variation in speed.

2. The essential concepts of time: pause, rate, duration. Introduce these
    concepts (pause, rate, and duration) in that order because we go from
    time where no words are involved to time that involves several words,
    down to time that involves just one word.

3. (a) Pause—the pregnant space of time when no sound is uttered, the
    dramatic pause after a heavy statement—give an example; the
    anticipating pause—slight hesitation before key word, often used both
    in dramatic and comedy punch line—give an example.

    (b) Duration—the amount of time spent on just one word. Used for
    emphasis and imagery. Show how one can stretch out a single word and
    how it highlights the meaning of a passage.

4. Assignment: Go around the room and have each one say "Give me
    liberty, or give me death" using the three concepts of time for more
    expression.

5. Summary: Read the same poem ("Richard Cory") as in beginning, only
    read it well and with expression. Then ask class if they've heard it
    before. Tell and then show how important the proper use of those three
    concepts is for effective communication. In the second reading,
    demonstrate how those three concepts worked.

Creating Community at North Campus Deer Park High School

Angus MacNeil
University of Houston–Clear Lake

Background Information

"Building a learning community is the most important and demanding responsibility of the principalship," according to Speck (1999, p. 5). Developing a learning community continues to be an important challenge for a principal's leadership (Sergiovanni, 1995). The notion of a school as a community has its roots in the traditions of the Greek academy and has remained true through monastic schools of the Middle Ages to the comprehensive schools of the twentieth century. *Community* is defined as a collection of individuals who are bonded together by natural will and by a set of shared ideals and ideas (Barth, 1990). Building or creating a community in school is not an easy process; it requires a great commitment, expertise, and leadership that reflects a profound understanding of the educational process. Unfortunately, the notion of school as community eludes many American schools, because such thinking requires a different focus than many of us were trained or have a disposition to develop.

Modern organizations with personnel whose relationships are formal and distant tend to focus on prescribed roles and expectations and evaluate by universal criteria as embodied in policies, rules, and protocols (Hodgetts, 1996). These organizations focus on rights, whereas organizations that build community focus on discretion, freedom, and responsibility. Building community requires us to put human needs before organizational needs. Administrators will not be successful in building a caring community for students without the support of teachers and staff members. The key to community building is involving and showing support for all members of the school, but the role played by teachers, who have the most direct relationship with students, is especially important.

Building a community requires leadership that is focused, flexible, fast, and friendly. The importance of informal interpersonal relationships is the most dynamic source of power in organizations today (Kanter, 1989). Schools that have this type of leadership are caring and nurturing places that create collegial teaching environments for teachers and successful learning environments for students.

The Deer Park Community

Located on the site of the historic battle of 1836, which ended Mexico's rule over Texas, is the city of Deer Park, "The Gracious Little City on the Golden Plains of the Great Gulf Coast." Lubrizol Corporation, Occidental Chemical Company, Rohm & Haas Texas, Inc., Shell Oil Company, and other industrial corporations

(Continued)

draw this city's 40,000 people to the area. These companies take advantage of Deer Park's location on the Houston Ship Channel.

The school district has 14 campuses housing seven elementary schools, four junior high schools, and one high school on three campuses. The district's 11,000 students are 76.2 percent Caucasian, 20.8 percent Hispanic, 1 percent Black, 1.8 percent Asian, and .3 percent American Indian. The Southern Association of Colleges and Schools accredits Deer Park Senior High School. Residents enjoy easy access to the benefits provided by Houston, yet they like the small-town atmosphere afforded them by Deer Park.

Deer Park students score consistently high on the Texas Educational Assessment of Minimal Skills. Students taking the SAT & ACT tests score above both national and state averages. Student participation is high in the co-curricular and extracurricular activities offered at the schools. Students from Deer Park consistently excel in athletics, band, choir, and orchestra. Deer Park Academic Decathlon and Science Olympiad teams rank among the highest in the state.

David Hicks, the school superintendent, says that the success of students in and out of the classroom is largely due to the excellence of the teachers. Currently the district employs over 750 teachers, giving Deer Park an average student-teacher ratio of 17 to 1. Almost 70 percent of Deer Park's teaching staff have masters degrees.

The School: Deer Park High School, North Campus

Deer Park High School is housed on three campuses: an alternative education center, Wolters Learning Center; a separate campus that houses strictly ninth graders, called the North Campus; and two miles away, a campus that serves tenth, eleventh, and twelfth graders, the South Campus. Approximately 100 personnel staff the North Campus. There are 68 full- or part-time teachers, 1 nurse, 1 librarian, 1 technological support teacher, 2 counselors, 3 administrators, 7 aides, and 10 clerical staff members. The 975 students are 78.7 percent Caucasian, 18.9 percent Hispanic, 0.6 percent African American, 1.5 percent Asian, and 0.3 percent Native American. To meet the needs of a diverse population fed by four separate junior high schools, the North Campus uses a unique arrangement that allows it to be a transitional school for these newly arrived high school students. The school offers these students a gradual adjustment to the pressures of high school, and it offers them an opportunity to become better academically, socially, and emotionally prepared for their eventual attendance at the South Campus.

A pilot program was established to create two separate academic teams—a team for 100 at-risk students and a "math" team for 125 math students. The students comprising the math team have daily work in a math lab as part of their regular curriculum. Due to the success of these "schools within a school" programs, and the freedom of site-based decision making, academic teaming was implemented for the entire student population.

The success of the efforts at the North Campus can be seen directly in the results of the TAAS test, which is given in the tenth grade. To receive a high school diploma from a Texas high school, students must pass the TAAS test, and the

(Continued)

results for the recent TAAS test showed that Deer Park High School exceeded the state high school averages. The continued improvement in all areas of this test reflects the success of the teaching and teaming techniques used on the North Campus.

Recently the school was assessed for its organizational health using the *Organizational Health: Diagnostic and Development Corporation* (1990) instrument. The following table shows the results for the North Campus:

Rank order by score	Percent
Resource Utilization	99
Morale	99
Power Equalization	99
Innovativeness	98
Cohesiveness	96
Adaptation	96
Autonomy	96
Goal Focus	94
Communications	94
Problem Solving Adequacy	92

The Case

The key to creating a community of learners resides in leadership, the kind of leadership demonstrated by Principal Gary Berry of Deer Park's North Campus High School. This rare situation of an entire school composed of one grade requires that a sense of belonging and commitment be created very quickly, and all evidence indicates that this is the case. It is evident that Gary cares for his students and teachers and that they in turn like and trust him as their principal. This compassion and understanding for his teachers and students is evident from Gary's kindly disposition and philosophy, which make students and teachers feel they are really important and wanted. He is genuinely happy to be with them. He delights when talking about the accomplishments of the teachers and students and is embarrassed when it is suggested that his leadership may have something to do with the school's achievements. His sense of fairness and his commitment to the notion that each student is important come through loud and clear in his words and his actions.

The teachers are involved in deciding the needs of the school and creating the action agenda for the school year. Using a participatory style of leadership, the principal realizes that he can build a caring school community only with the support of teachers, who have the most direct relationship with students. He is determined to have his teachers feel a sense of ownership for the North Campus. "If you feel you own something, you'll take care of it," he says. To foster this sense of ownership, he adjusts his daily schedule to make time for teachers. The major effort he has taken in making up work teams within the school reflects his priority

(Continued)

of providing teachers with opportunities to develop the curriculum together and support for peer instructional supervision. These are opportunities for teachers to interact and collaborate on community-building projects. The principal has made a strong commitment to professional development, and it takes a variety of forms. The principal's open-door policy makes it possible for teachers to participate.

In this school it is evident that the focus is on student success and achievement. Having the students in the math and at-risk student teams allows for smaller, more intimate settings that contribute to the feeling of school as community. The division into teams also promotes closer bonds between unit members, simplifies administration, and enhances a sense of place. A school is a reflection of the people who work there; the physical environment conveys messages to parents and other visitors about the school. More important, the physical surroundings affect teacher and student performance and relationships. The North Campus teachers can truly be proud of the physical appearance of the school. The building speaks volumes about the care and attention that is characteristic of schools that have a vital sense of community.

Because North Campus is only a one-year placement for students, the faculty make extraordinary efforts to develop a sense of community in the school. The lessons they have learned and the type of leadership practiced by this principal can be an inspiration for all schools to engage in community building.

Issues for Further Reflection and Application

1. Why is leadership so important in developing school as community?
2. What role does honesty play in creating a sense of community?
3. How is a friendly atmosphere created in a school?
4. Why must the school environment be clean and attractive to create a positive school community?
5. How does a principal create a feeling of ownership for the school with teachers? Students?
6. Why are visibility and accessibility essential components in developing a sense of community in school?
7. What are the advantages of creating teams in large school settings?
8. The role of the principal as a communicator is said to be critical: more specifically, it is important to make sure that misunderstandings don't prevail. Why is this critical?

Think of Your School
9. How could teachers be more involved in generating the notion of school as community?
10. How could your students be more involved and responsible for creating school community?
11. What are the attitudes that would have to be changed or improved in order to successfully develop your school as a community?

(Continued)

12. What are the areas of professional development that need to be planned in order to prepare and continue the journey toward the development of school as community?

13. What are the organizational requirements that would have to be established in order to develop the school as community?

14. Do you think that the development of school as community is a worthwhile concept, or do you think it is just another fad? Explain.

15. Describe what you would do if you were given the opportunity to lead your school, given the need for and the quality of leadership required.

Suggested Readings

Barth, R. S. (1990). *Improving schools from within: Teachers and students can make a difference.* San Francisco, Oxford: Jossey-Bass.

Hodgetts, R. M. (1996). *Modern human relations at work.* Forth Worth, Texas: The Dryden Press.

Kanter, R. M. (1989). The new managerial work. *Harvard Business Review, 66* (November–December) 85–92.

Sergiovanni, T. J. (1996). *Leadership for the school house.* San Francisco, Oxford: Jossey-Bass.

Speck, M. (1999). *The principalship: Building a learning community.* Upper Saddle River, NJ: Prentice-Hall.

Author. (1990). *Organizational Health Profile.* Highland Village, Texas: Organizational Health: Diagnostic and Development Corporation.

MacNeil's case study emphasizes the need for a sense of ownership in the promotion of any change. People are committed to and are thus willing to work for innovations that they consider their own. For this reason, it is important that schools develop diversity goals and academic goals and strategies for their attainment. What kind of philosophy facilitates the development of an attitude of ownership among teachers? Constructivism places teachers and students together as learners in an environment devoted to learning.

Individualizing Instruction

The Need to Individualize

Without adequate planning, teachers can be overwhelmed by the challenge of designing instruction for students who have a broad range of abilities and levels of motivation. The need for individualized instruction, that is, instruction that meets the needs of all students, is clarified in Marshall's statement (1991, p. 225), "If students do not learn the way we teach them, then we must teach them the way they learn." Individualized instruction is based on the premise that students are different and that each has unique learning needs that each teacher must make special efforts to meet; otherwise some students will become bored because they are inadequately challenged and others will become discouraged by expectations that are beyond their abilities. Following are some of the many approaches that schools and teachers use to individualize instruction.

In-Class Ability Grouping

A common approach to reducing the task of teaching 30 or so students of varying abilities and needs is to form subgroups of students who have abilities and interests in common. Simple arithmetic would suggest that dividing a class of 30 students into five groups of six students per group would reduce the range to which the instruction must be adapted to one-fifth the original range. Unfortunately, the results of ability grouping are not usually dramatically successful, though ability grouping does tend to improve student learning. An analysis of more than 40 studies of ability grouping found that grouping makes a small contribution to the improvement of learning and a larger contribution toward improvement of student motivation (Julik, 1981).

Individualizing Instruction

The effectiveness of ability grouping depends on the teacher's ability to adjust the instruction to each group. In general, less capable students need more concrete material and examples of ways to apply the newly learned concepts to real-world experiences, and more capable students need greater challenges, but challenges of different types. For example, rather than assigning a high-ability group of math students a much larger number of the same type of problems given to less capable groups, the teacher might assign this group more creative challenges that require divergent thinking. Advanced groups might even be assigned to develop problems instead of finding solutions, or to find a variety of solutions to a problem.

The teacher using ability grouping should expect to spend more time with the less capable students, especially after the more capable groups get on task. Slower students may require more careful monitoring and guidance. Good, Reys, Grouws, and Molyran (1990–1991) say that when working in groups, higher-ability students tend either to dominate the group or to not participate in the group. Furthermore, low-ability students perform less well when placed with other low-ability students (Calfee & Brown, 1979), probably partly because teachers usually spend less time with the less capable groups. Oakes (1990) reports that schools serving mainly non-English-speaking students offer less breadth and depth of content coverage.

Taking time to ask higher-order questions, encouraging students to ask each other questions, and giving students time and encouragement to reflect on their thinking are imperative. Sigel (see Ellsworth and Sindt, 1994) discovered that children's ability to move from the concrete to the symbolic level requires distancing themselves from the present. Higher-order questions can be used to make this necessary cognitive linking occur. Drawing can be used to help young children make this necessary time transition (Phillips, Phillips, Melton, & Moore, 1994).

Unintentional Differential Treatment

Ability grouping requires different treatment for different groups at different levels, but unintentional differential treatment must be avoided. For example, while it is realistic to expect high-ability students to cover more material faster than less capable groups, teachers often make unrealistically different demands of the groups. Shavelson (1984) found that high-ability groups were paced as much as 15 times faster than groups of lesser ability, increasing dramatically the difference in amounts of material covered by the two groups.

Teachers tend to treat students for whom they hold low expectations in several different ways. For example, Good and Brophy (1997, p. 90) report that teachers will:

1. Wait less time for lows to answer questions.
2. Give lows the answer or call on someone else.
3. Provide inappropriate reinforcement.
4. Criticize lows more than highs for failure
5. Praise lows less than highs for success.
6. Fail to give lows feedback on their public responses.
7. Interact with lows less and pay less attention to them overall.
8. Call on lows less often in class.
9. Ask for lower performance levels from lows.
10. Smile less, have less eye contact, have fewer attentive postures towards lows.

Teachers' tendency to treat low achievers differently without realizing they are doing so is a powerful message for teachers in diverse settings, because invariably this special treatment becomes a barrier to success for these students. The goal must be to always keep the standards high and find ways to help all students meet them.

Differences in Evaluation

The teacher may find it desirable to devise nontraditional ways to evaluate advanced students, because objective tests may not measure the kinds of growth anticipated for these groups. Such methodology as oral discussions or one-on-one questioning may be needed to discover the depth of insights developed by advanced students and to detect progress made by students with limited ability. Term projects may be preferable to exams. For example, the teacher of a student who accepts responsibility for writing a computer program to analyze data on breeding plants may find that the resulting product—that is, the computer program—is itself the best measure of success for this assignment.

Precautions

Whenever students are grouped by ability, the teacher must take certain precautions. Thee is a certain prestige in being affiliated with the upper group(s), whereas a certain disgrace befalls students who are assigned to the lower group(s). Attempts to disguise the ranking or ordering of groups usually fail. Indeed, students often know the level to which they are assigned even before their teachers know it. By making comments that allow comparisons among ability groups, and allowing students to make judgmental or derogatory comments about another group, teachers may unwittingly contribute to the caste problem.

The high premium set on peer approval in schools can exacerbate the emotional damage caused by ability grouping. Also, higher-ability groups tend to become snobbish and condescending toward members of lower-ability groups.

Interclass Ability Grouping

In some schools, ability grouping is done independently of teachers—standardized intelligence tests to determine the placement of students in groups. Under these circumstances, teachers are still responsible for protecting the members of lower-ability groups from ridicule.

Interclass grouping and intraclass grouping produce different types of competition. When grouped within the same class, students are forced to compete with classmates, but when the grouping is done externally the competition is between two or more classes causing students to cooperate while competing.

For several centuries schools in England have had "houses." A *house* is a group of students whose abilities are heterogeneous. The houses frequently compete in oral debates, encouraging cooperation, not competition, among the members of a house.

Other schools choose homogeneous ability grouping. For example, five groups of students with similar abilities may be formed, producing five "tracks," each representing a different level of general ability.

Grade Contracts

Grade contracting is a method that recognizes that students are more highly motivated by some topics than by others. It permits an individual to place more emphasis on certain topics.

At the beginning of each unit of study, students are issued contracts. According to the student's ability and interest in the topic, the student agrees to perform a certain amount of work in order to earn a certain grade. A sample contract is shown in Box 10.5. Contracts can also be used to provide students with opportunities to earn free time and other rewards.

Box 10.5

Student Contract for Art History

Grade	Requirements
A	Meet the requirements for the grade of B and visit a local art gallery. Sketch an example of a Gothic painting. Visit a carpenter Gothic house and sketch the house. Show at least three similarities in the two products.
B	Meet the requirements for the grade of C and name and draw an example of each of the major classes of columns used in buildings.
C	Meet the requirements for the grade of D and submit a notebook record of the major developments in art since 1900, naming at least six major painting styles and two authors of each style.
D	Attend class regularly and participate in all classroom activities.

I _____ agree to work for the grade of _____ as described in this contract.
  (Student's name)   (specify grade)

Using Instructional Models

Another way to organize lessons is to use the formats provided by instructional models. An advantage to using models is that models have been tested and proved to be theoretically and practically sound. Lewellen (1990, p. 63) says that a model should be "systematic, descriptive, explanatory, and widely applicable." Examples of instructional models include direct instruction, scientific inquiry, concept attainment, and the Socratic questioning model. Reyes (1990, p. 214) endorses the use of such models to plan lessons:

> Models provide a convenient organizer for teaching the precepts of effective teaching or for teaching the steps of lesson planning. For the teacher in the classroom at any level, models of instruction can structure his or her decision making. For example, the teacher's choice of classroom questions, homework assignments, introductions to lessons, and so on are typically influenced by the instructional model being used as an organizer.

Information Processing Model

A popular contemporary way to examine and describe learning is by viewing it mechanically, as you might describe the process that computers use to store and retrieve information. Using the five senses to gather information (see Figure 10.3), humans immediately decide which information to store. A perceptual screen is used to filter out unwanted information (see Figure 10.4)

FIGURE 10.3

The five sensors act as receptors.

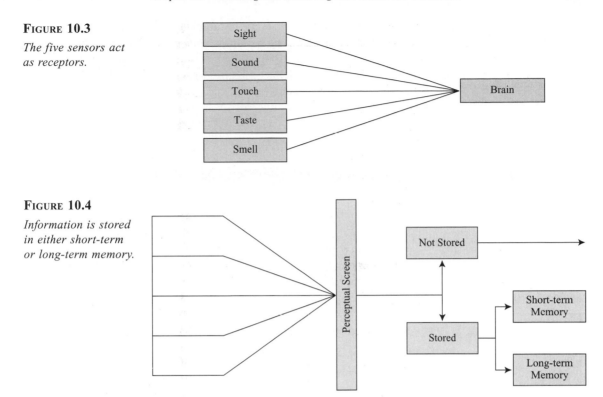

FIGURE 10.4

Information is stored in either short-term or long-term memory.

Information that is going to be used immediately or in the near future is stored in the short-term memory; the other information is stored in the long-term memory. Van Gulick (1990) believes that students cannot possess information unless it is stored in a manner that allows them to make use of it. He stresses the need for interconnections.

When introducing new information to students, advance organizers can be used to point students toward the most important information, thus affecting the information that is retained. Then, by relating this new information to previously acquired information, students can get meaning from new information that might otherwise be meaningless to them.

Mastery Learning

In 1963, J. B. Carroll, a professor at Harvard University, wrote an article titled "A Model of School Learning" in which he challenged the then-accepted belief that students' IQs are a major factor in determining academic success. Carroll hypothesized that if three conditions were met, at least 90 to 95 percent of all high school students could master class objectives. The three conditions were: (1) each student must be given enough time to complete a task, (2) each student must be properly motivated, and (3) the subject matter must be presented in a manner compatible with the individual student's learning style.

Using Carroll's model, Benjamin S. Bloom and his students at the University of Chicago developed an education system called *learning for mastery* (*LFM*) (see Block & Henson, 1986). This system is teacher-paced and group-based. In other words, the teacher leads the lessons and the class as a group follows. In contrast, most mastery learning programs are student-paced (that is, the students set the pace) and individually based. Each student pursues learning individually, at that student's own preferred pace (Guskey & Gates, 1986).

All mastery learning programs have several important characteristics in common. First, they provide students with different lengths of time to master each topic. Second, they give students opportunities to remediate or restudy material that proves difficult for them, and then to retest without penalty. Third, all mastery learning programs use formative evaluation—that is, evaluation designed to promote learning, not to be computed as part of the grading system. Short daily or weekly tests are given to diagnose learning weaknesses and teaching weaknesses, and then teachers and learners adjust to improve learning. Finally, all mastery learning uses criterion-based evaluation. This means that the criteria essential for success are revealed before the study unit begins. (For further discussion of formative evaluation and criterion-referenced evaluation, see Chapter 9.)

Finally, with mastery learning programs, as with all other programs, the success depends on how it is used. Cunningham (1991, p. 84) explains:

> There are two essential elements of the mastery learning process. The first is an extremely close congruence between the material being taught, the teaching strategies employed, and the content measured. The second essential element is the provision of formative assessment, opportunities for students followed by feedback, corrective and enrichment activities.

To determine the effectiveness of mastery learning compared with that of traditional programs, Burns (1979) examined results from 157 mastery learning studies and discovered that 107 studies found that mastery learning students significantly outscored their traditionally taught counterparts, while 47 of the studies showed no significant differences. Only 3 of the 157 studies reported that traditionally taught students outscored mastery learning students. One study of mastery learning, spanning 15 years in 3,000 schools, concluded that mastery learning was consistently more effective than traditional curriculums (Hyman & Cohen, 1979). Guskey and Gates (1986) reviewed 25 studies of group-based and teacher-paced mastery learning in elementary and secondary schools. In all 25 studies, the students in the mastery learning groups outlearned their counterpart control groups.

But mastery learning is not without its critics. In a review of studies on mastery learning, Arlin (1984) reports some of the more popular criticisms. Some critics say that the claim that mastery learning equalizes students' learning abilities is an overstatement. Some critics describe mastery learning as a "psychological trap" that does not have a proper conceptual base. Some critics even call mastery learning a "Robin Hood phenomenon" that takes from the advanced students and gives to the poor students. Arlin himself argues that studies that find all students equally capable should be interpreted more cautiously. Slavin (1989, p. 79) says that "if school districts expect that by introducing group-based mastery learning . . . they can measurably increase their students' achievement, there is little evidence to support them."

Readers of professional journal articles must remember that any innovation may experience either astounding success or total failure, depending on the conditions of the moment. The old adage "Never believe anything you hear, and believe only half of what you see" is good advice to remember as you interpret research findings. Proceed with caution. Curricularists must also carefully examine the studies being reported; many are so flawed that Bracey (1993, p. 85) was prompted to write, "Far too many flawed studies are getting through the seams of peer review and into print. Mislabeled and misleading graphs and figures abound."

Matching Teaching Styles and Learning Styles

For more than three decades, educators have conducted research to discover how to teach students with diverse learning styles with complementary instructional strategies. Figure 10.5 shows five major categories of characteristics that affect learning: environmental, emotional, sociological, physiological, and psychological. While the effects of the environment on learning may be obvious, the other elements may affect learning without the teacher's being aware of it.

FIGURE 10.5

Diagnosing learning styles.

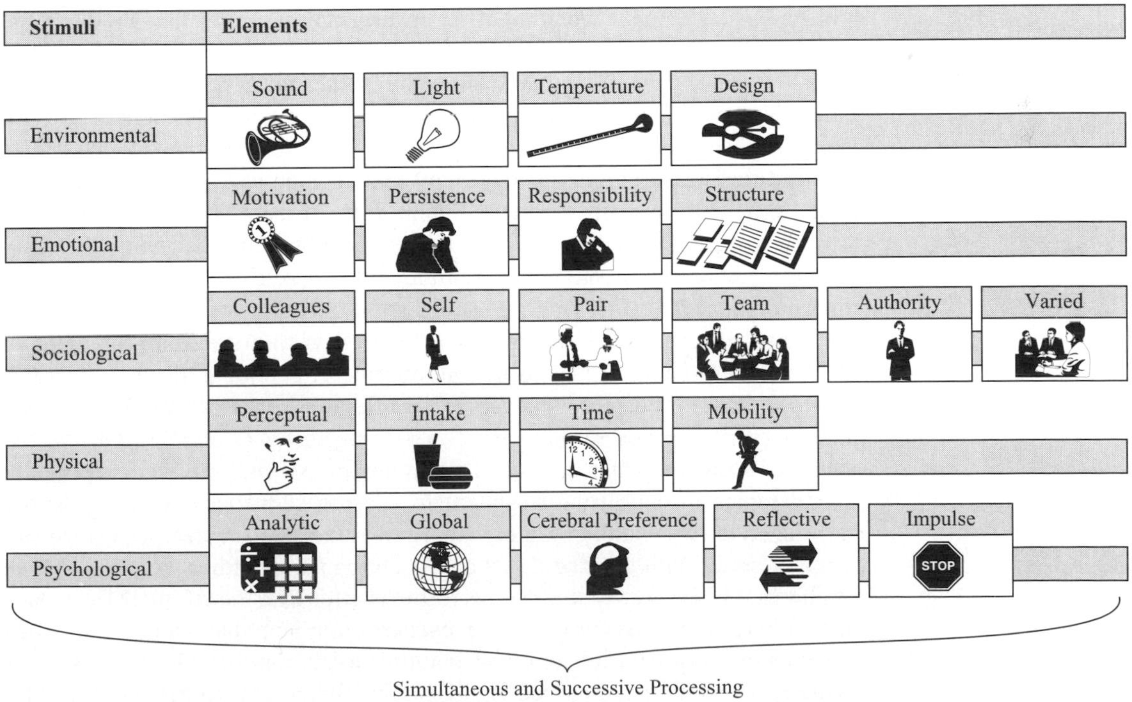

Simultaneous and Successive Processing

Research conducted with the Dunn and Dunn model of Figure 10.5 at more than 115 institutions of higher education has reported successful applications of their strategies for matching instructional approaches to students' learning style strengths at the primary, elementary, secondary, and college levels (*Research with the Dunn & Dunn Model,* 1999). For example, a meta-analysis of 42 experimental studies conducted with this model between 1980 and 1990 at 13 universities revealed that students whose learning styles are accommodated would be expected to achieve 75 percent of a standard deviation higher than students who have not had their learning styles accommodated (Dunn, Griggs, Olson, Gorman, & Beasley, 1995). This indicates that matching students' learning style preferences with educational interventions compatible with those preferences is beneficial to their academic achievement.

According to the Center for Research in Education (CRE), the 20-year period of extensive federal funding from 1970 to 1990 produced few programs that consistently resulted in statistically higher standardized achievement test scores for special education students (Alberg, Cook, Fiore, Friend, Sano et al., 1992). Prominent among those programs was the Dunn and Dunn model. The average students in the Dunn, Griggs, Olson, Gorman, and Beasley (1995) meta-analysis revealed the largest effects.

Dunn, Dunn and Perrin (1994) perceive knowledge of learning-style preferences as a tool teachers can use to design more effective instructional experiences. Dunn and Dunn (1992, 1993, 1999) report that difficult academic material needs to be introduced through each student's strongest perceptual modality, reinforced through his/her secondary or tertiary modality, and then applied by the student when creating an original resource that includes the information, such as a poem, a set of task cards or flip cards, a time line, or a kinesthetic floor game. Using these procedures, the Dunns developed guidelines (called Homework Disc prescriptions) for having students do their homework using their learning style strengths. At almost every grade level, students have achieved statistically higher achievement and attitude test scores by following those Homework Disc prescriptions (Dunn & Klavas, 1992). Studies show that such matching of learning style and instructional approach consistently increases academic achievement, improves attitudes toward school, and reduces discipline problems. This last finding is consistent with the often-heard statement that a well-planned lesson is the greatest deterrent to discipline problems.

Miller and Dunn (1997) tested the relative effects of traditional lectures, readings, and class discussions versus the affects of programmed learning sequences (PLS) in book format versus PLS using software on CD-ROM for the computer on students in a college of allied health. All students were exposed to several topics through each treatment in varying sequences. Students whose learning styles were auditory, motivated, and authority-oriented performed statistically better with the traditional approach than with either the book PLS or the CD-ROM PLS. Fewer students performed better with the CD-ROM approach than with the PLS book format; some teachers complained about the technology noises in the computer lab and their inability to sit comfortably, eat, and work privately. Most students earned significantly higher test scores with the PLS book format, and those students were highly visual, preferred informal seating, liked learning alone in a softly lit, quiet environment, and preferred snacking while studying.

How to Match Styles

There are several ways to attain a match between teaching style and learning style. First, teachers can be matched with students who have similar personalities, but there are mixed results with this method. For example, Thelan (1960) found that such personality matches produced more "manageable" classes and increased student satisfaction with classroom activities. Yet Jones (1971) matched introverted teachers with introverted students and extroverted teachers with extroverted students and found that these matchings failed to foster productive two-way interactions.

A second approach to matching is to have the teacher select teaching methods that correspond to student learning styles. The teacher who discovers that a particular class of students responds favorably to simulations and not to lectures would use more simulations than lectures with that class. Another way to match methods with learning styles is to administer a learning style inventory to the entire class, which usually results in a variety of preferences. The teacher can then group students according to their style preferences.

To provide students with opportunities to develop preferences, teachers may choose to expose students to a variety of styles. Of course, this means each teacher must master a variety of teaching styles. Changing styles may be difficult for many teachers, however, because it requires a change of attitudes. Marshall (1991, p. 226) explains:

> Consequently, for teachers to change their teaching styles, to understand and risk planning instruction on the basis of learning style patterns of students—and, therefore, to teach successfully a wider range of learners—[teachers] must come to recognize, respect, and support the learning differences of students.

Not everyone believes in the powers of matching teaching styles with learning styles. For example, consider the following hypothetical statement:

The Matching Learning and Teaching Styles Movement:
Much Ado About Nothing

The movement to match learning styles with teaching styles is a fluke that several educators dreamed up to get attention. Little quality research had been conducted in this area, and some of the limited studies on matching styles found little or no difference in learning. Some studies suggest that teachers should expose students to several styles, but teachers naturally tend to alter their approaches according to students' responses. So matching teaching and learning styles is nothing new—it's the same old wine in a new bottle. To quote Shakespeare, it's "much ado about nothing."

1. How consistent must research findings be to be considered conclusive? In other words, must all studies produce the same answer before the answer can be considered factual?

2. Choose one of your favorite teachers. Did this teacher use different teaching styles? If so, list three or four of this teacher's styles.

3. Do you have a single preferred style? To reach an intelligent answer to this question, draw a vertical line down the middle of a sheet of paper. On the left side, list variables that enhance learning for you. On the right side, list variables that impede learning for you.

4. Challenge or defend this statement: All teachers should purposely increase their repertoire of teaching styles.

5. Do you think teachers should spend more or less time developing new styles? Why?

Using Microcomputers to Individualize

Microcomputers offer teachers unprecedented opportunities to individualize instruction. As Magney (1990, pp. 55–56) so aptly notes, "Computer games can be a window [through] which students can enter many academic realities." Because of their versatility, computers offer a diverse array of ways to help teachers meet the needs of their individual students. First, computers are powerful student motivators (Alvestad & Wigfield, 1993). Computer simulations can help students integrate learned factual knowledge with abstract concepts (Sawyer, 1992) leading to higher learning levels. Software is readily available that enables students to develop their creative potential (Buckleitner, 1996). Increasingly quality software (Parette, Hourcades & Vanblerviet, 1993), for students with disabilities is becoming more available including non-English speaking students (Bruder et al, 1992). Former South Carolina Teacher of the Year, Nancy Townsend (1999), advises educators to use technology when it works best with your students and continue learning new ways to meet students' cognitive needs.

Future curriculum planners will have unlimited opportunities to improve services for all students if they keep an open mind toward unconventional uses of technology. For example, online communication makes possible almost continuous communications with parents and other school constituents (Armstrong, Henson, & Savage, 2001). This expanded level of involvement should include a variety of roles such as homework, curriculum planning, and advisory councils and committees (Buttery & Anderson, 1999).

Other Ways to Involve Students

In addition to varying lesson plans, a variety of learning avenues, such as textbooks, discussions, field trips, oral reports, term projects, and homework is necessary. We now turn to the use of these approaches and the teacher's role in each.

Textbooks

As discussed in Chapter 7, throughout the history of education in the United States, one type of textbook or another has dominated the curriculum. At first, the textbook determined the content to be studied. Lectures followed by rote memorization and recitation often resulted in a boring, irrelevant curriculum. Some teachers still consider the textbook to be the major source of content, and although it is no longer the sole determiner of content, the textbook still plays an important role in today's planning.

Another approach is to use the textbook along with other materials. Instead of letting the textbook lead the teacher and students in the selection of content and experiences, the teacher can take a proactive posture and lead the designing of the curriculum. For example, instead of following the textbook organization from Chapter 1 to Chapter 2, the teacher can determine the sequence of topics. The teacher may decide that some chapters are not worth including in the curriculum. Teachers are becoming increasingly competent in curriculum development, and more and more teachers are insisting on shaping the curricula in their classes as they see fit. Many reform programs provide teachers with curriculum frameworks (guidelines for selecting curriculum content and activities) and require teachers to design the curriculum.

Some teachers almost totally avoid using a textbook, substituting current problems, learning activity packages, or learning units they have developed themselves. But few teachers have total freedom to design their curricula. Concern that students may not "cover" all the content needed for the following year or for college is always present, and this concern is legitimate. School administrators must ensure that the total school curriculum does not have major content gaps. Many larger secondary schools hire a curriculum director, a curriculum supervisor, or an assistant principal who is directly responsible for this. Teachers should work with the curriculum leader and/or other teachers to avoid curriculum redundancy and gaps.

Discussions

Today's students want to be involved, and good discussions provide all participants opportunities to relate the topic to their own experiences. This sharing of various perspectives can enrich the knowledge and understanding of individual participants. Nicaise and Barnes (1996, p. 206) address the importance of providing students opportunities to discuss lessons:

> Discourse and dialogue are essential in learning. Discourse among students helps them construct hypotheses and tests them against what they believe to be reality; it helps people to view knowledge and information from multiple perspectives. Conceptual growth occurs when students and teachers share different viewpoints and understanding changes in response to new perspectives and experiences.

Grouping students according to their interest in the topic and letting students choose discussion topics can encourage total participation. Putting the reserved students together forces one or more of them to assume leadership, and placing aggressive students in the same group forces some of them to learn to yield the floor to others. Assigning roles, such as "discussion moderator" and "recorder," and then rotating the assignment of these roles, will prompt all group members to participate even further.

Selecting topics that have answers, even though there may be multiple answers, and letting students know that a definite outcome of their discussions is expected can give students a sense of purpose and responsibility.

A student moderator's failure to keep group discussion progressing and on target can prompt teacher intervention, but too much interference will cause a group to become dependent on the teacher's leadership. The group moderator must not dominate the discussion; she or he must communicate that all serious comments are worth hearing.

A free-flowing discussion provides a valuable opportunity to develop social skills, itself an important goal, and helps students identify with their peers. All adolescents need to belong, and all need positive recognition and approval from peers. Group discussions should help fill these needs.

The participants need to know that each person has a definite role in every discussion. First, each participant is obligated to read the assignment so the discussion will begin from a common base. Second, each person is responsible for contributing information to the discussion. Opinions and contributions of knowledge should be prized only when the participants can present evidence or knowledge to support them. Third, each participant is responsible for listening to others and, when possible, for referring to specific comments of others. This assures all participants that their comments are being considered.

The teacher keeps the environment informal, pleasant, and nonthreatening. The teacher is also a facilitator, helping students to locate appropriate resources and to plan and evaluate their discussion.

Oral Reports

Begin planning oral reports by first deciding each report's purpose. For example, oral reports can provide advanced students with the opportunity to share their expertise, they can provide a group of students of diverse backgrounds the opportunity to learn to work together cooperatively, or they can give shy and insecure students experience in public speaking.

Assigning a report to punish misbehavior and/or to substitute for effective planning are unacceptable. Students will quickly connect the report with those purposes and will not expect any significant learning to result. Similar results happen when reports are used at the end of a grading period to give students an opportunity to improve their grades.

Always communicate to the class the primary purposes of the assignment and what is expected of them during the report. Should they take notes? Ask questions? Take issue with the speaker? Should they ask for clarification when they do not understand? Should they interrupt the speaker with comments or wait until the end of the presentation? Will they be held accountable on the next test for the information presented orally by their peers? By answering these questions before the report is delivered, teachers can draw each student into the oral presentations, maximizing interest and involvement.

As a precaution against students' taking reports too lightly, credit might be given for oral reports—and perhaps to the rest of the students for their responses.

A positive reward system can let students earn credit for participation without penalizing those whose contributions are minimal.

The timing of oral reports can be critical, and care should be taken to avoid scheduling so many reports in succession that students are bored by the repetition. Because many secondary school students and some middle school students hold part-time jobs, and extracurricular activities consume much of their out-of-class time, class time should be allotted for preparing oral presentations.

Giving students time to prepare and an opportunity to present the results of their assignments tells students that the presentations are worthwhile.

Projects

Whatever subject a teacher teaches, assigning projects offers several valuable options: long-term projects, which may last for a grading period or even a semester; short-term projects; group projects; and individual projects. Not all projects must end with an oral presentation; some may conclude with written reports or concrete products. Regardless of the product, students need opportunities to show their creations. For example, a science teacher might want to arrange a local science fair to display students' insect collections, or a music teacher may want to set up a student recital.

Homework

According to Solomon (1989, p. 63), "The purpose of homework is to prepare the student for the next lesson and/or reinforce concepts and skills learned in the previous lesson." When used correctly, homework can "increase individual achievement."

Cooper (1990, p. 88) researched the effect of homework on achievement across grade levels and reported:

> Homework has a positive effect on achievement, but the effect varies dramatically with grade level. For high school students, homework has substantial positive effects. Junior high school students can benefit from homework, but only about half as much. For elementary school students, the effect of homework on achievement is negligible.
>
> The optimum amount of homework also varies with grade level. For elementary students, no amount of homework—large or small—affects achievement. For junior high school students, achievement continues to improve with more homework until assignments last between one and two hours a night. For high school students, the more homework, the better achievement—within reason, of course.
>
> I found no clear pattern indicating that homework is more effective in some subjects than in others. I did conclude, however, that homework probably works best when the material is not too complex or completely unfamiliar. Studies comparing alternative feedback strategies revealed no clearly superior approach.

The following suggestions should help teachers design and implement a system for assigning homework.

Homework Guidelines

Clarify the Assignment.   Homework assignments must be clear. Assignments that involve problem solving can be clarified and simplified by giving students an opportunity to work at least one problem of each type in class before asking them to do problems at home.

Individualize Homework Assignments.   Consider the abilities and needs of each student. Certain homework assignments for slower students will help them catch up with the rest of the class, while the more advanced students can explore areas of special interest to them in depth.

Make Homework Authentic.   Homework assignments are more interesting when they are authentic. Students could be asked to respond to something that is on the evening news, in the newspaper, or on an educational television program.

Be Reasonable.   Many secondary school students and some middle school students use after-school hours for part-time jobs on which their families depend for some essentials. For such students, homework assignments that require a few hours each evening are impossible to complete. Secondary school teachers must also remember that students have several other courses and may be receiving homework assignments in all of them.

Follow-Up.   Spending time and energy on an assignment, only to have the teacher forget about it, can be disheartening. By scheduling a follow-up at the time of the assignment, teachers can prevent these annoying situations. Follow-ups also let students know that they are expected to complete each assignment. According to Phelps (1991, p. 242), regular follow-ups result in improved results, "When students are held responsible for assigned work, they are more likely to do the work than when their efforts go unnoticed."

Parent Involvement.   The past decade has seen a definite trend toward increased parent involvement and an increasing desire among parents to have a greater role in controlling the future of their children's school. Half (53%) of all parents still want more say in the choice of curriculum offered (Rose & Gallup, 1998).

Site-based decision making, which is sweeping the country, offers much hope for garnering the support of family members. Most site-based teams include parents and are empowered to make decisions on curriculum, finance, and all other major school matters.

The power of involving the community in schoolwork is illustrated in a study by Reinstein (1998), who reported that a program featuring someone in the community who uses high-level math skills did more to motivate students than any action the school could take.

As parents in poor communities become more involved, curricula are being reconstructed to meet the needs of students from all segments of society. Kohl (see Scherer, 1998, p. 11) recognizes this change: "I'm happy that the curriculum is being fundamentally reconstructed to respond to the diversity on this nation."

Chapter Summary

This chapter encourages the matching of styles in the classroom. There are a number of advantages to matching teaching and learning styles, but this method is not a solution for all education problems, and teachers should be aware of the limitations and criticisms of this movement.

The general approach of grouping may present overwhelming problems. Studies show that many teachers, especially novices, find it impossible to monitor different groups in classrooms (Doyle, 1980; Good & Brophy, 1997). Studies show that if the major purpose of style grouping is to accommodate students, a degree of discomfort can be an asset in learning, rather than a problem to be circumvented (Harvey, Hunt, & Schroder, 1963; Piaget, 1952).

Even the term *learning styles* is not clearly defined in the literature, and a clear definition in terms of student performance would be helpful. Learning style is not static, because learning itself is highly complex. Indeed, learning is such a broad activity that it cannot be contained within the cognitive domain. The study of the effects of matching learning and teaching styles is still in its infancy. The findings hold promise, but these studies and their claims should be read with a critical eye.

Mastery learning has proven both successful and controversial. Some of its major strengths for learners include unlimited time on each topic, opportunities to remediate without penalty, and the absence of grades. Unfortunately, each of these strengths can also cause major administrative headaches. Flexible time for individual students doesn't fit the school calendar, and many parents insist on receiving traditional A–F grade reports based on competition.

Another approach to individualizing learning which has also been highly successful with many classes is grade contracts. Such successful approaches have some common elements. They spell out the expectations the teacher holds for students, and the teacher carefully monitors student behavior. Maximum success usually requires involving parents, and site-based decision-making teams are doing just that.

This chapter has introduced several curriculum structures that can be used to meet the multicultural goals of this text. Long-range planning, short-term planning, and individualizing instruction all contribute to the goal of helping each and every student succeed. Teachers who are empowered can, in turn, pass on this power to their students through helping them earn ownership of their education.

Learning Questions

1. What is the difference between long-range planning and unit planning?

2. What are some ways that a constructivist perception should affect (*a*) long-term planning? (*b*) daily planning?

3. How can assignments of students to groups be made to ensure that all students will participate?

4. What are some advantages of mastery learning, and what is one planning step teachers can use to ensure that a lesson realizes each advantage?

5. What new reform practices in local schools enhance students' self-images?

6. How would you relate the terms *individualized instruction, grouping, mastery learning,* and *academic contracts* to each other?

7. Is the current reform practice of providing a curriculum framework to introduce students to activities adequate, or must teachers also lead students to identify major concepts within each discipline? Explain your answer.

8. How do curricula for non-English-speaking students differ from curricula for mainstream students?

Suggested Activities

1. Develop three separate ways of using advance organizers to introduce one lesson.

2. Develop a set of guidelines for teachers to use to involve all students in planning.

3. Describe the strengths and limitations of the sample daily lesson plans given in this chapter in meeting the needs of at-risk students. Tell how each plan may be adjusted to reach the needs of these students.

4. Make a chart showing some obstacles to implementing mastery learning in K–12 schools. Describe a planning adjustment teachers and other curriculum developers can make to overcome each obstacle listed.

5. Draw a model to show your perception of the relationship between curriculum and instruction.

6. Develop a contract to be used in a class of students with diverse needs. Ensure that the conditions enable students to build on their previous experiences.

7. Choose a lesson plan and convert it into a mastery learning plan.

8. Make a list of positive multicultural features of recent reform practices in the schools in your area.

9. Having read pros and cons on the matching of teaching and learning styles, consider your own position. Some critics see the entire movement as a unilateral approach in which the teacher assesses the learning style of the student and prescribes or selects an acceptable teaching style to match with the learner's style. Perhaps the student should be involved in this selection. If you agree, identify some ways to make style matching a bilateral process.

Works Cited and Suggested Readings

Aksamit, D. (1990). Mildly handicapped and at-risk students: The greying of the line. *Academic Therapy, 25*(3), 227–289.

Alberg, J., Cook, L., Fiore, T., Friend, M., Sano, S., et al. (1992). *Educational approaches and options for integrating students with disabilities: A decision tool.* Triangle Park, NC: Research Triangle Institute, Post Office Box 12194, Research Triangle Park, North Carolina 27709.

Alvestad, K. A., & Wigfield, A. L. (1993, January). A matter of motivation. *Executive Educator, 1,* 12–13.

Arlin, M. (1984). Time, equality, and mastery of learning. *Review of Educational Research, 54,* 71–72.

Applebee, A. N., Langer, J. A., & Mullis, I. V. S. (1987). *The nation's report card: Literature and U.S. history.* Princeton, NJ: Educational Testing Service.

Armento, B. J. (1986). Research on teaching social studies. In M. C. Wittrock (Ed.), *Handbook of research on teaching* (3rd ed.). New York: Macmillan.

Armstrong, D. G., Henson, K. T., & Savage, T. V. (2001). *Teaching today* (6th ed.). New York: Prentice-Hall.

Bail, A. L. (1982, November). The secrets of learning style: Your child's and your own. *Redbook, 160,* 73–76.

Banks, R., Kopassi, R., & Wilson, A. M. (1991). Inter-agency networking and linking schools and agencies: A community based approach to at-risk students. In R. C. Morris (Ed.), *At-risk students.* Lancaster, PA: Technomic, pp. 106–107.

Beauchamp, G. A. (1975). *Curriculum theory* (3rd ed.). Wilmette, IL: Kagg.

Berliner, D. C. (1984). The half-full glass: A review of research on teaching. In P. A. Hosford (Ed.), *Using what we know about teaching.* Alexandria, VA: Association for Supervision and Curriculum Development.

Berry, K. (1977). Homework: Is it for elementary kids? *Instructor, 86,* 52.

Block, J. R., & Henson, K. T. (1986). Mastery learning and middle school instruction. *American Middle School Education, 9*(2), 21–29.

Blumenthal, C., Holmes, G. V., & Pound, L. (1991). Academic success for students at-risk. In R. C. Morris (Ed.), *Youth at risk.* Lancaster, PA: Technomic.

Bracey, G. W. (1993). Tips for researchers. *Phi Delta Kappan, 75*(1), 84–86.

Brophy, J. (1983). Classroom organization and management. *Elementary School Journal, 83,* 265–285.

Bruder, I., Buchsbaum, H., Hill, M., & Orlando, I. C. (1992, May–June). School reform: Why you need technology to get there. *Electronic Learning, 11,* 22–28.

Buckleitner, W. (1996, November–December). The best educational software for kids. *Consumer's Digest, 35*(28).

Burns, R. B. (1979). Mastery learning: Does it work? *Educational Leadership, 37,* 110–113.

Buttery, T. J., & Anderson, P. J. (1999). Community, school, and parent dynamics: A synthesis of literature and activities. *Teacher Education Quarterly, 26*(4), 111–122.

Calderhead, J. (1981). *Research into teachers' and student teachers' cognitions: Exploring the nature of classroom practice.* Paper presented at the annual meeting of the American Educational Research Association, Montreal, Quebec, Canada.

Calfee, R., & Brown, R. (1979). Grouping students for instruction. *National Society for the Study of Education, Yearbook 78,* Pt. 2, 144–148.

Callahan, R. J. (1998). Giving students the (right) time of day. *Educational Leadership, 55*(4), 84–87.

Carnahan, R. S. (1980). *The effects of teacher planning on classroom processes.* Doctoral dissertation. University of Wisconsin at Madison.

Carroll, J. B. (1963). A model of school learning. *Teachers College Record, 64,* 723–733.

Carson, M. D., & Badarack, G. (1989). *How changing class size affects classrooms and students.* Riverside, CA: University of California at Riverside, California Educational Research Cooperative.

Centra, J., & Potter, D. (1980). School and teacher effects: An interrelational model. *Review of Educational Research, 50,* 273–291.

Ciscell, R. E. (1990). A matter of minutes: Making better use of teacher time. *The Clearing House, 63*(5), 217–218.

Clark, C. M., & Peterson, P. L. (1986). Teachers' thought process. In C. M. Whittrock (Ed.), *Handbook of research on teaching* (3rd ed.). New York: Macmillan.

Clark, S. N., Clark, D. C., & Irvin, J. I. (1997, May). Collaborative decision making. *Middle School Journal, 28*(5), 54–56.

Coleman, J. G. (1991). Risky business: The library's role in dropout prevention. In R. C. Morris (Ed.), *Youth at risk.* Lancaster, PA: Technomic, pp. 61–62.

Cooper, H. (1990). Synthesis of research on homework. *Educational Leadership, 47*(3), 85–91.

Copenhaver, R. (1979). *The consistency of student learning as students move from English to mathematics.* Doctoral dissertation. Indiana University.

Corno, L. (1981). Cognitive organizing classrooms. *Curriculum Inquiry, 11,* 359–377.

Cunningham, R. D., Jr. (1991). Modeling mastery teaching through classroom supervision. *NASSP Bulletin, 75*(536), 83–87.

Des Dixon, R. G. (1994). Future schools and how to get there from here. *Phi Delta Kappan, 75*(5), 360–365.

Doll, R. C. (1978). *Curriculum improvement: Decision making and process* (4th ed.). Boston: Allyn & Bacon.

Doyle, W. (1979). Making managerial decisions in classrooms. In D. L. Duke (Ed.), *Classroom management.* 78th Yearbook of the National Association for the Study of Education, part II, Chicago: University of Chicago Press.

Doyle, W. (1980). *Classroom management.* West Lafayette, IN: Kappa Delta Pi.

Doyle, W. (1983). Academic work. Review of educational research. *American Educational Research Assoc., 53*(2), 176–177.

Drucker, P. F. (1954). *The practice of management.* New York: Harper.

Dunn, K. (1981). Madison prep: Alternative to teenage disaster. *Educational Leadership, 39*(5), 386–387.

Dunn, R., (1999). *Research on the Dunn and Dunn Model.* Jamaica, NY: St. John's University's Center for the Study of Learning and Teaching Styles.

Dunn, R., Brennan, P., DeBello, T., & Hodges, H. (1984, Winter). Learning style: State of the science. In K. T. Henson (Ed.), *Theory into Practice, 23,* 10–19.

Dunn, R., & Dunn, K. (l992). *Teaching elementary students through their individual learning styles: Practical approaches for grades 3–6.* Boston: Allyn & Bacon.

Dunn, R., & Dunn, K. (l993). *Teaching secondary students through their individual learning styles: Practical approaches for grades 7–12.* Boston: Allyn & Bacon.

Dunn, R., & Dunn K. (1999). *The complete guide to the learning styles inservice system.* Boston: Allyn & Bacon.

Dunn, R., Dunn, K., & Perrin, J. (1994). *Teaching young children through their individual learning styles.* Boston: Allyn & Bacon.

Dunn, R., Griggs, S. A., Olson, J., Gorman, B., & Beasley, M. (1995). A meta-analytic validation of the Dunn and Dunn learning styles model. *Journal of Educational Research, 88*(6), 353–362.

Dunn, R., & Klavas, A. (1992). Homework disc. Jamaica, NY: St. John's University's Center for the Study of Learning and Teaching Styles.

Elam, S. M. (1979, June). Gallup finds teenagers generally like their schools. Report taken in November 1978. *Phi Delta Kappan, 60,* 700.

Elkind, R. (1991). Success in American education. In R. C. Morris (Ed.), *Youth at risk.* Lancaster, PA: Technomic.

Ellsworth, P. C., & Sindt, V. G. (1994). Helping "Aha" to happen: The contributions of Irving Sigel. *Educational Leadership, 51*(5), 40–44.

Finn, J. D. (1993). *School engagement and students at risk.* Washington, DC: National Center for Education Statistics, U.S. Department of Education.

Finn, J. D., & Pannozzo, G. M. (1992). *Classroom behaviors that detract from learning.* Unpublished manuscript.

Flantzer, H. (1993). What we say and what we do. *Phi Delta Kappan, 75*(1), 75–76.

Fowler, W. J., Jr. (1992, April). What do we know about school size? What should we know? Paper presented at the annual meeting of the America Educational Research Association, San Francisco.

Friedman, R. S. (1991). Murray High School: A nontraditional approach to meeting the needs of an at-risk population. In R. C. Morris (Ed.), *Youth at risk.* Lancaster, PA: Technomic.

Friesen, C. D. (1979, January). The results of homework versus no homework research studies. ERIC 167–508.

Frymier, J., & Gansneder, B. (1989, October). The Phi Delta Kappa study of students at risk. *Phi Delta Kappan, 71,* 142–146.

Geisert, G., & Dunn, R. (1991). Effective use of computers: Assignments based on individual learning style. *The Clearing House, 64*(4), 219–223.

Good, T. L., & Brophy, J. (1997). *Looking in classrooms* (7th ed.). New York: Harper & Row.

Good, T. L., Reys, B. J., Grouws, D. A., & Molryan, C. M. (1990–1991). Using work-groups in mathematics instruction. *Educational Leadership, 47*(4), 56–62.

Good, T. L., & Stipek, D. J. (1983). Individual differences in the classroom: A psychological perspective. In G. D. Fenstermacher (Ed.), *Individual differences and common curriculum.* Eighty-Second Yearbook of the National Society for the Study of Education, Part I, Chicago: University of Chicago Press.

Green, J., & Smith, D. (1982). *Teaching and learning: A linguistic perspective.* A paper presented to the Conference on Research and Teaching, Airlie House, VA.

Guskey, T. R., & Gates, S. L. (1986). Synthesis of research on the effects of mastery learning in elementary and secondary classrooms. *Educational Leadership, 43*(8), 73–80.

Harrison, C. J. (1990). Concepts, operational definitions, and case studies in instruction. *Education, 110*(4), 502–505.

Hart, L. A. (1983). *How the brain works.* New York: Basic Books.

Harvey, O. J., Hunt, D. E., & Schroder, H. M. (1963). *Conceptual systems and personality organization.* New York: Wiley.

Hunter, M. (1984). Knowing, teaching and supervising. In P. L. Hosford (Ed.), *Using what we know about teaching.* Alexandria, VA: Association for Supervision and Curriculum Development, pp. 175–176. Abstracted with the author's permission.

Hubbuch, S. M. (1989, April–May). The trouble with textbooks. *The High School Journal, 72*(4), 203–209.

Hyman, J. S., & Cohen, A. (1979). Learning for mastery: Ten conclusions after fifteen years and 3,000 schools. *Educational Leadership, 37,* 104–109.

Hyman, R. T., & Rosoff, B. (1984, Winter). Matching learning and theory styles: The jug and what's in it. In K. T. Henson (Ed.), Matching learning and teaching styles. *Theory into Practice, 23,* 35–43.

Johnston, C. A. (1998). Using the learning combination inventory. *Educational Leadership, 55*(4), 88–89.

Johnston, J. M. (1990, April). *What are teachers perceptions of teaching in different classroom contexts?* Paper presented at the annual convention of the American Educational Research Association, Boston, MA.

Jones, V. (1971). *The influence of teacher-student introversion achievement, and similarity on teacher-student dyadic classroom interactions.* Doctoral dissertation, University of Texas at Austin.

Julik, J. A. (1981, April). *The effect of ability grouping on secondary school students.* Paper presented at the American Educational Research Association, Los Angeles.

Joyce, B. (1979). Toward a theory of information processing in teaching. *Educational Research Quarterly, 3,* 66–77.

Karweit, N. (1987). *Effective kindergarten programs and practices for students at risk.* Report No. 21. Baltimore: The Johns Hopkins University, Center for Research on Elementary and Middle Schools.

Keefe, J. W. (1979). *School applications of the learning style concept: Student learning styles.* Reston, VA: National Association of Secondary School Principals, pp. 123–132.

Kohl, H. (1998) in M. Scherer. A conversation with Herbert Kohl. *Educational Leadership, 56*(1), 8–13.

Kowalski, T. J., Weaver, R. A., & Henson, K. T. (1990). *Case studies on teaching.* New York: Longman.

Kowalski, T. J., Henson, K. T., & Weaver, R. A. (1994). *Case studies on beginning teachers.* New York: Longman.

Latham, A. S. (1998). Gender differences on assessments. *Educational Leadership, 55*(4), 88–89.

Lawson, A. E., Abraham, M. R., & Renner, J. W. (1989). *A theory of instruction: Using the learning cycle to teach science concepts and thinking skills* (NARST Monograph No. 1). Cincinnati, OH: University of Cincinnati, National Association for Research in Science Teaching.

Lee, J., & Pruitt, K. W. (1978). Homework assignments: Classroom games or teaching tools? *Clearing House, 53,* 31.

Levin, H. M. (1987). *New schools for the disadvantaged.* Unpublished manuscript. Stanford, CT: Mid-Continent Regional Laboratory.

Levy, J. (1983). Research synthesis on right and left hemispheres: We think with both sides of the brain. *Educational Leadership, 40*(4), 66–71.

Lewellen, J. R. (1990). Systematic and effective teaching. *The High School Journal, 63*(1), 57–63.

Lile, B., Lile, G., & Jefferies, B. (1991). "Project rebound: Effective intervention for rural elementary at-risk students. In R. C. Morris (Ed.), *Youth at risk* (pp. 40–41). Lancaster, PA: Technomic.

Little, D. (1985). *An investigation of cooperative small-group instruction and the use of advance organizers on the self-concept and social studies achievement of third-grade students.* Doctoral dissertation, University of Alabama.

Magney, J. (1990). Game-based teaching. *The Education Digest, 60*(5), 54–57.

Markle, G., Johnson, J. H., Geer, C., & Meichtry, Y. (1990, November). Teaching for understanding. *Middle School Journal, 22*(2), 53–57.

Marshall, C. (1991, March–April). Teachers' learning styles: How they affect student learning. *The Clearing House, 64*(4), 225–227.

McDonald, C. (1972). *The influence of pupil liking the teacher, pupil perception of being liked, and pupil socioeconomic status on classroom behavior.* Doctoral dissertation. University of Texas at Austin.

Miller, J. A., & Dunn, R. (1997, November/December). The use of learning styles in sonography. *Journal of Diagnostic Medical Sonography, 13*(6), 304–308.

Morine, G., & Vallance, E. (1975). *Special study B: A study of teacher and pupil perceptions of classroom instruction* (Technical Report No. 75–11–6). San Francisco: Far West Laboratory.

Morris, R. C. (1991). (Ed.). *Youth at risk.* Lancaster, PA: Technomic.

Nicaise, M., & Barnes, D. (1996). The union of technology, constructivism, and teacher education. *Journal of Teacher Education, 47*(3), 205–212.

Oakes, J. (1990). *Multiplying inequalities. The effects of race, social class and tracking on opportunities to learn mathematics and science.* Santa Monica, CA: The Rand Corporation.

Oliva, P. F. (1992). *Developing the curriculum,* (2nd ed.). New York: HarperCollins.

O'Neal, M., Earley, B., & Snider, M. (1991). Addressing the needs of at-risk students: A local school program that works. In Robert C. Morris (Ed.), *Youth at risk.* Lancaster, PA: Technomic, pp. 122–125.

Orlich, D. C. (1980). *Teaching strategies: A guide to better instruction.* Lexington, MA: D. C. Heath.

Parette, H. P., Hourcade, H. P., & Vanblerviet, A. (1993, Spring). Selection of appropriate technology for children with disabilities. *Teaching Exceptional Children, 4,* 18–22.

Perkins, D. (1994). "Do students understand understanding?" *Education Digest, 59*(5), 21–25.

Peterson, P. L., Marx, R. W., & Clark, C. M. (1978). Teacher planning, teacher behavior, and student achievement. *American Educational Research Journal, 15,* 555–565.

Phelps, P. H. (1991). Helping teachers excel as classroom managers. *The Clearing House, 14*(3), 241–242.

Phillips, D. R., Phillips, D. G., Melton, G., & Moore, P. (1994). Beans, blocks, and buttons: Developing thinking. *Educational Leadership, 51*(5), 50–53.

Piaget, J. (1952). *The origins of intelligence in children.* New York: International University Press.

Pizzo, J. (1981). *An investigation of the relationships between selected acoustic environments and sound, an element of learning style, as they affect sixth grade students' reading achievement and attitudes.* Doctoral dissertation. St. John's University.

Prescott, C., Rinard, B., Cockerill, J., & Baker, N. (1996). Science through workplace lenses. *Educational Leadership, 53*(8), 10–13.

Reinstein, D. (1998). Crossing the economic divide. *Educational Leadership, 55*(4), 28–29.

Reyes, D. J. (1990). Models of instruction: Some light on the model muddle. *The Clearing House, 63*(1), 214–216.

Rinne, C. H. (1998). Motivating students is a percentage game. *Phi Delta Kappan, 79*(8), 620–628.

Romberg, T. A. (1983). *Allocated time and content covered in mathematics.* Paper presented at the annual meeting of the American Educational Research Association, Montreal, Canada.

Romberg, T. A., & Carpenter, T. P. (1986). Research on teaching mathematics: Two disciplines of scientific inquiry. In M. C. Wittrock (Ed.), *Handbook of research on teaching* (3rd ed.). American Educational Research Association. New York: Macmillan.

Rose, L. C., & Gallup, A. M. (1998). "The 30th annual Phi Delta Kappan/Gallup poll of the pubic's attitudes toward the public schools." *Phi Delta Kappan, 80*(1), 41–56.

Roskos, K. (1996). When two heads are better than one: Beginning teachers' planning processes in an integrated instruction planning task. *Journal of Teacher Education, 47*(2), 120–129.

Sawyer, W. D. M. (1992). The virtual computer: A new paradigm for educational computing. *Educational Psychology, 32*(1), 7–14.

Schville, J., Porter, A., Billi, G., Floden, R., Freeman, D., Knappan, L., Kuhs, T., & Schmidt, W. (1983). Teachers as policy brokers in the content of elementary school mathematics. In L. S. Schulman & E. G. Sykes (Eds.), *Handbook of teaching and policy.* New York: Longman.

Shavelson, R. J. (1984). Review of research on teachers' pedagogical judgments, plans, and decisions. Los Angeles: Rand Corporation and University of California. Reported in R. L. Egbert & M. M. Kluender (Eds.), *Using research to improve teacher education.* Lincoln, NE: American Association of Colleges for Teacher Education/Teachers College, University of Nebraska–Lincoln, pp. 132–133.

Shavelson, R. J., & Stern, P. (1981). Research on teachers' pedagogical thoughts, judgements, decisions, and behavior. *Review of Educational Research, 51,* 455–498.

Shea, T. C. (1983). *An investigation of the relationship between preferences for the learning style element of design, selected instructional environments, and reading test achievement of ninth-grade students to improve administrative determinations concerning effective educational facilities.* Doctoral dissertation, St. John's University.

Slavin, R. (1980). Cooperative learning. *Review of Educational Research, 50,* 503–527.

Slavin, R. E. (1989). On mastery learning and mastery teaching. *Educational Leadership, 46*(7), 77–79.

Slavin, R. E. (1998). Can education reduce social inequity? *Educational Leadership, 55*(4), 6–10.

Snapp, J. C., & Glover, J. A. (1990). Advance organizers and study questions. *The Journal of Educational Research, 83*(5), 266–271.

Solomon, S. (1989). Homework: The great reinforcer. *The Clearing House, 63*(2), 63.

Stefanich, G. P. (1990). Cycles of cognition. *Middle School Journal, 22*(2), 47–52.

Stinnett, T., & Henson, K. T. (1982). Chapter 16, The Human Equation and School Reform. In *America's public schools in transition: Future trends and issues.* New York: Teachers College Press.

Taba, H. (1962). *Curriculum development: Theory and practice.* Orlando, FL: Harcourt Brace.

Thelan, H. (1960). *Education and the human quest.* New York: Harper & Row.

Townsend, N. C. (1999). A teacher's class. In K. T. Henson & B. F. Eller (Eds.), *Educational psychology for effective teaching.* Belmont, CA Wadsworth.

Trachtenberg, D. (1974). Student tasks in text material: What cognitive skills do they tap? *Peabody Journal of Education, 52,* 54–57.

Trump, J. L., & Miller, D. F. (1979). *Secondary school curriculum improvement: Meeting challenges of the times* (3rd ed.). Boston: Allyn & Bacon.

Tyler, R. W. (1984). Curriculum development and research. In P. A. Hosford (Ed.), *Using what we know about teaching.* Alexandria, VA: Association for Supervision and Curriculum Development

Tyson, H., & Toodward, A. (1989). Why students aren't learning very much from textbooks. *Educational Leadership,* 14–17.

Van Gulick, R. (1990). Functionalism, information, and content. In W. G. Lylcan (Ed.), *Mind and cognition.* Cambridge, MA: Basil Blackwell.

Von Glasersfeld, E. (1988). *Environment and communication.* Paper presented at the Sixth International Congress on Mathematics Education. Budapest. As cited by Tobin, K., Bugler, K., & Fraser, B. (1990). *Windows into science classrooms: Problems with higher-level cognitive learning.* New York: Falmer Press.

Wade, R. K. (1997). Lifting a school's spirit. *Educational Leadership, 54*(8), 34–36.

Walter, L. J. (1979). How teachers plan for curriculum and instruction. *Catalyst, 2, 3.*

Walter, L. J. (1984). A synthesis of research findings on teaching, planning, and decision making. In R. L. Egbert & M. M. Kluender (Eds.), *Using research to improve teacher education,* Lincoln, NE: American Association of Colleges for Teacher Education.

Wang, M. C., Haertel, G. D., & Walberg, H. J. (1998). Models of reform: A comprehensive guide. *Educational Leadership,* 66–71.

Wellington, P., & Perlin, C. (1991). Palimpsest probability and the writing process: Mega-change for at-risk students. In R. C. Morris (Ed.), *Youth at risk,* Lancaster, PA: Technomic.

Wuthrick, M. A. (1990). Blue says win: Crows go down in defeat. *Phi Delta Kappan, 71*(7), 553–556.

Zahorik, J. A. (1975). Teacher planning models. *Educational Leadership, 33,* 134–139.

Zais, R. S. (1976). *Curriculum: Principles and foundations.* New York: Crowell.

11 CURRENT AND FUTURE CURRICULUM TRENDS

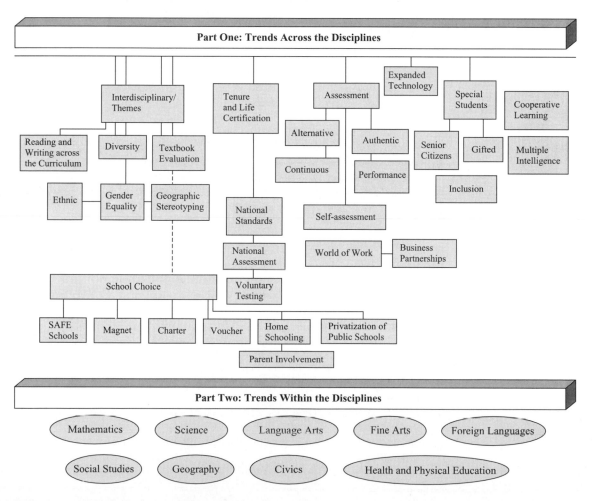

Part One: Trends Across the Disciplines

Interdisciplinary/ Themes

Tenure and Life Certification

Assessment

Expanded Technology

Special Students

Cooperative Learning

Reading and Writing across the Curriculum

Diversity

Textbook Evaluation

Alternative

Authentic

Senior Citizens

Gifted

Multiple Intelligence

Ethnic

Gender Equality

Geographic Stereotyping

Continuous

Performance

Inclusion

National Standards

Self-assessment

National Assessment

World of Work

Business Partnerships

School Choice

Voluntary Testing

SAFE Schools

Magnet

Charter

Voucher

Home Schooling

Privatization of Public Schools

Parent Involvement

Part Two: Trends Within the Disciplines

Mathematics

Science

Language Arts

Fine Arts

Foreign Languages

Social Studies

Geography

Civics

Health and Physical Education

Objectives

This chapter should prepare you to:

- Name and define several types of assessment and describe some impacts of assessment on school reform.
- Using a definite knowledge base, and citing references, debate the tenure and lifelong certification issue.
- Explain the impact that school-to-work programs are having on today's curriculum.
- Discuss some pros and cons of inclusion.
- Choose one of the following topics and explain its impact on education today: multiple intelligences, magnet schools, charter schools.
- Develop a set of guidelines to use to evaluate textbooks in your field for their contribution to (1) multiculturalism and (2) constructivist curriculum.
- Describe two trends in your subject area, including the work that has been done to date on national standards and benchmarks.

INTRODUCTION

The rapid rate at which education is changing demands that curriculum planners attempt to stay abreast of new changes and, furthermore, develop the ability to anticipate future changes. This chapter should enable the reader to review current major trends and identify emerging trends. The first part of the chapter focuses on trends across the disciplines, and the second part focuses on trends within the disciplines.

TRENDS ACROSS THE DISCIPLINES

Safe Schools

The twenty-first century began with the public expressing great concern over the need to provide children with safe schools. As Kenney and Watson (1996, p. 453) state, "Students are interested in a safer, more orderly school environment." The U.S. Department of Justice reports that three million crimes, or about 11 percent of all crimes, occur each year in public schools (Sautter, 1995). Williams et al. (1999) describe an approach to discipline that involves the local community with the school. Several state legislatures are providing major funding to support school safety centers, which will be prepared to work with schools to promote safety.

About one-third of American parents fear for the safety of their children while at school (Rose and Gallup, 1998). This number has increased from about one-fourth (25 percent to 36 percent) over the past two decades. Thirty-one percent of parents say they fear for the safety of their children when the children are not in school, and this number has remained stable over the past two decades.

Some schools have formulated safety teams. Skiba, & Peterson (1999, p. 382) say that such approaches characterize schools with effective discipline:

> School safety teams or behavior support teams—composed of regular and special education teachers, personnel from related services, administrators, and parents— ensure a consistent and individualized response to disruptive students.

But a more common approach has been to increase the harshness of school policies, which Hyman & Snook (2000, p. 489) warn is the wrong approach, not one that is educationally based but one that is based on the use of force and punishment: "Even in those exceptional cases where police involvement remains necessary, an overdependence on police intervention can have a variety of unintended negative consequences, but all these approaches focus on violence committed by students and do not address the conditions of schools and the acts of educators that may increase school disruptions." These researchers suggest that schools step up the use of democratic principles which they say has always been more effective in reducing crime than the traditional punishment and constraint approach, which schools in the United States have always favored.

Home Schooling

In recent years many parents have chosen to educate their children at home, and the number that make this choice is growing annually, with between 100,000 and 300,000 children being home schooled each year. Home schooling has some clear advantages. The teacher, often a parent, is usually highly dedicated. Home-schooled children get plenty of attention and the process is learner-centered (Day, 1999). The main disadvantage of home schooling is the lack of opportunities for these students to socialize with peers (Williams, et al., 1999).

Multidisciplinary/Thematic Approach

Elementary and secondary school curricula of the 1980s experienced a swing toward the use of themes that cut across the disciplines. This shift came more unintentionally than by design, as teachers searched for ways to make learning more authentic and move students up the learning hierarchies. As educators examined the schools of the early 1980s, they found that students were generally passive listeners as many teachers taught from the text. Even activities-oriented classes often found students engaged physically without understanding or caring deeply about the exercises or the understanding these exercises were designed to promote.

To give the assignments more meaning to students, teachers invited students to become involved in choosing problems—not from the textbook, not from a list of problems by the author at the end of the chapter, but real problems that existed in their communities. Few real problems exist within the boundaries of a single discipline; therefore, the move to make schooling more authentic automatically changed curricula, making it integrated and multidisciplinary.

Multidisciplinary education is supported by learning theory. As noted in Chapter 1, constructivists say that grasping an in-depth understanding of a subject requires that the students themselves create understanding. Rather than being told about the relationships between bodies of knowledge, students must discover these relationships and must tie newly acquired information to their own previously acquired understanding. Williams and Reynolds (1993, p. 13), report that "When teachers build interdisciplinary units around hot local issues, said one student, the result is 'learn, learn learn.'"

It should be noted, however, that designing activities that cut across traditional discipline boundaries will not ensure that in-depth learning occurs. Williams and Reynolds (1993, p. 14) report:

> Throughout the implementation of the unit, the teachers made a point of not differentiating among the subject areas. During the planning phase, though, each of the teachers represented his or her discipline, and each had two clear-cut responsibilities: to make sure that content and skills from each subject were developed during the unit and to provide suggestions as to how this might be done.

These teachers also say that a key to success in multidisciplinary learning is choosing a theme that will excite all students. Consequently, they recommend choosing controversial local problems, which allows the teacher and students to bring the community into the classroom.

Keller (1995, pp. 11–12) says that such problems lead to accelerated learning:

> The term "accelerated" may be somewhat misleading, because the lessons are not really fast-track, but designed to enrich students' learning experience through higher expectations, relevant content, and stimulating instructions. The approach has three underlying principles:
>
> 1. Unity of purpose—the whole school community has a unified focus.
> 2. Empowerment with responsibility—the entire school community makes important educational decisions and takes responsibility for them.
> 3. An effort to build on the strengths of the entire school community.

Curriculum planners should understand that terms such as *interdisciplinary, multidisciplinary, integrated learning, authentic learning, problem-solving,* and *accelerated learning* tend to run together. A good program may, and indeed should, contain a mix of these characteristics and approaches. Gardner and Boix-Mansilla (1994, pp. 16 17) point out that in-depth learning can occur either within a discipline or across disciplines but that it is not likely to occur either place unless teachers understand that each discipline has become a discipline because it has its own preferred ways of organizing content. These authors state:

> Disciplines constitute the most sophisticated ways yet developed for thinking about and investigating issues that have long fascinated and perplexed thoughtful individuals: Subject matters are devices for organizing schedules and catalogs. Second, disciplines represent the principal ways individuals transcend ignorance. While disciplines can blind or sway, they become, when used relevantly, our keenest lenses on the world.

These authors remind curriculum planners that while much interdisciplinary work is vital and impressive, such results can occur only after teachers have mastered at least portions of their specific disciplines.

As with teaching within the disciplines, teachers' success with multidisciplinary units hinges on their ability to help students understand the analytic styles and problem-solving approaches that work best within each discipline and across disciplines and craft these into their own personal learning methodologies. These are both areas that have been barely scratched by research, and future curriculum planners should continue to strive to learn more about the key relationships within and across disciplines that lead to better understanding of how the content can best be understood. Teachers must remember that involvement in any curricular approaches, regardless of how highly tauted the approach may be, does not diminish their responsibility to ensure that their students master those parts of a discipline essential to operating successfully in twenty-first-century society and those areas of a discipline needed to pursue further study in that discipline.

Reading and Writing across the Curriculum

Historically, curricula have been departmentalized into content areas or disciplines. As we approach the twenty-first century, a strong push to integrate the disciplines is complemented by the practice of ensuring that students also read and write across the curriculum.

At least two advantages can be derived from reading and writing across the curriculum. Obviously, reading strengthens students' understanding of the discipline being studied; understanding is enriched further when the subjects cross the discipline boundaries. Writing also offers an avenue for enriching understanding. Writing forces students to ascend the learning hierarchy, for having to write about a subject is an invitation to internalize otherwise possibly random-seeming information, making it personal and meaningful to the individual.

Perrone (1994, p. 13) expresses his belief in the importance of having students write across the curriculum and a belief that writing is an indispensable part of self-evaluation when he says, "If students are not regularly writing across a variety of topics and in a variety of styles for diverse purposes, then promoting self-evaluation has a limited value."

Alternative Assessment

Assessment could well be called the paradox of education reform. Like Dickens' "age of enlightenment" and "season of hope," assessment offers unprecedented opportunity to improve schooling. Yet, also quoting Dickens, the ways that we have used assessment can cast us into a "season of darkness and an age of foolishness."

The significance of assessment to contemporary teachers is reflected in the amount of time they spend on it. Contemporary teachers spend as much as a third to half of their professional time on assessment-related activities, yet current teacher education programs are practically void in covering basic assessment techniques (Stiggins, 1995; Stiggins & Conklin, 1992). In effect, we have used assessment almost exclusively as an indicator of success, even though it has the potential of being so much more—an instrument of improvement.

The educational critics of the late 1980s and 1990s were aware of the awesome power that assessment can have in shaping the curriculum. Critics often complain that the curriculum is test driven or that teachers teach to the test. Wiggins (1989, p. 703) believes that teachers owe no apology for such practice, claiming that "To talk with disdain of 'teaching to the test' is to misunderstand how we learn."

Alternative assessment is a general term that refers to a variety of types of assessment designed to replace traditional testing, including performance assessment, authentic assessment, continuous assessment, progressive reporting, and self-assessment.

Performance Assessment

Performance assessment is an attempt to escape the simple testing that required only the recalling of information, which was the most popular form of testing until the 1980s. Performance assessment requires instead that students use the information and knowledge they acquire. Because students must use this knowledge to solve problems, performance evaluation leads students to develop higher-order thinking skills.

Authentic Assessment

During the education reform movement of the late 1980s and early 1990s, the schools attributed students' failure to perform at least in part to a dysfunctional testing system. At that time, true-false, multiple choice, and fill-in-the-blank tests dominated elementary and secondary assessment. The curricula offered teachers very limited options for measuring those skills students needed to function in an information-based society. Students had trouble perceiving those tests as being related to real life.

Authentic assessment is designed to measure students' ability to apply the knowledge they acquire to their real-life experiences (Spady, 1994). Armstrong et al. (1997, p. 8) state, "Authentic assessment requires learners to demonstrate what they have learned in a way that has much in common with how a proficient adult might deal with the content that has been learned." Because authentic assessment deals with real-life problems, these tests prompt students to raise their thinking to higher levels. As Hargrove (1999, p. 91) explains, authentic assessment uses a variety of instruments to assess student progress: "Authentic assessment encompasses the use of portfolios, exhibitions, performances, learning logs, and experiments as measures of student progress." Some educators fail to recognize that multiple-choice tests can be one of several methods of authentic testing so long as they are not the only or dominant means. Some proponents of authentic assessment question whether authentic learning can ever be measured accurately and argue persuasively that if it can be measured it would require years (Campbell, 2000).

Continuous Assessment and Progressive Reporting

As the name implies, continuous assessment is on going. The term also implies that the assessments are related to one another, which makes sense: just as students' education program should be a continuous effort as opposed to sporadic, unrelated exercises and unrelated sessions, proponents of continuous assessment argue that the assessment program should be a series of assessments, each leading to the next.

A type of testing that is included in continuous assessment is formative evaluation. Formative evaluation is defined as "the designing and using of tests for only one specific purpose—to promote learning" (Henson & Eller, 1999). Formative evaluation consists of a series of short tests given at short intervals to provide students with ongoing feedback on their progress. Formative evaluation never affects students' grades. A second use of formative evaluation is to inform teachers about how effective their teaching and curriculum are, thereby, helping teachers improve their instruction.

Progressive reporting is a term often used in conjunction with continuous assessment, and it refers to the popular practice of reporting student progress.

On a continuing basis, student progress is systematically reported to the students themselves or to the students and their parents. Although progress reports can take various shapes, parents find written descriptions of student behavior to be the most useful (Elam, Rose, & Gallup, 1994, p. 55).

Self-Assessment

Self-assessment is the practice of involving students with the assessment of their own work. It has the benefit of motivating students by promoting a sense of ownership over their education program (Barton & Collins, 1993). Ironically, the national role that assessment plays in education reform involves the opposite: no willingness to involve local educators in the design of these tests or in deciding how they are to be used. Gallagher (2000, pp. 502–503) attributes this unwillingness to involve teachers to the fact that today assessment is a billion dollar business, "Schools are cast as damsels in distress, remote experts are cast as heroic saviors, and teachers are written out of the production altogether." Gallagher further points out that while schools and teachers are held accountable, the testing industry is not held accountable but is allowed to cloak itself in secrecy (p. 504).

Tenure and Life Certification

Of all the issues that face educators at the turn of the century, probably none is more volatile than the issue of tenure. Some legislators are dedicating their full time and energy to attempting to craft, introduce, and pass legislation in their state that would completely abolish teacher tenure. These legislators maintain that not only does tenure not serve education but that, indeed, it does just the opposite. They say that tenure protects incompetent teachers, making reform difficult or impossible. Whether these legislators really believe this or whether they are using this issue to garner votes is impossible to know.

Perhaps no other issue has the power to rally teachers and provoke strikes more than attempts to abolish tenure. Teachers often remind those who would rid their schools of tenure that tenure was created to protect competent teachers from the whims of administrators and pressure groups. They argue that such protection is essential if they are to experiment with new methods and openly exchange ideas and practices, in particular those ideas and practices needed to bring positive reform to their schools.

Even tenured teachers can be dismissed, but usually only for the following reasons (Armstrong et al., 1997, pp. 325–326).

1. *Incompetence:* The conditions that have been used to dismiss teachers for incompetence include lack of knowledge, failure to adapt to new teaching methods, violation of school rules, lack of

cooperation, persistent negligence, lack of ability to impart knowledge, physical mistreatment of learners, and failure to maintain discipline. Failure to maintain discipline is one of the most common causes for dismissal actions filed against tenured teachers.

2. *Incapacity:* This standard includes any physical or mental condition that keeps a teacher from performing his or her assigned duties.

3. *Insubordination:* This is most commonly applied to teachers who stubbornly and willfully violate reasonable school rules and policies. Usually several insubordinate acts are required before dismissal can occur.

4. *Conduct:* This is a broad standard that can embrace behaviors as varied as insulting fellow teachers, espousing personal political causes in the classroom, taking time off without permission, and even shoplifting. Some specific instances where school districts have successfully dismissed teachers for inappropriate conduct have involved drinking to excess, serving alcohol to learners in the teacher's home, and telling wrestling team members to lie about their weights when registering for a tournament.

5. *Immorality:* The courts have consistently ruled that moral fitness is a standard that teachers must meet. Dismissal actions related to this category may include such things as criminal activity, sexual misconduct, drug use, and dishonesty.

6. *Other causes:* Many tenure laws provide for dismissal for a number of other reasons that include such things as intemperance, neglect of duty, cruelty, and willful misconduct.

Although there are varied reasons for firing teachers, their administrators must prove that a teacher has behaved in one or more of these specified ways. School districts can dismiss nontenured teachers much more easily than they can dismiss tenured teachers.

Ethnic Diversity

Historically, teachers have been poorly prepared to address the increasingly diverse nature of our society. Not only have textbooks failed to address this issue, but in their failure to do so they have contributed to the problem by promoting unacceptable stereotypes and prejudices. Although for decades educators have known that a large number of nonmainstream Americans have experienced low academic achievement, they have chosen not to try to help these students because they have believed them less capable, a perception known as the "genetic deficit" view (Savage & Armstrong, 1996). By the 1960s, this view was replaced by a "cultural deficit" view, which was the belief that nonmainstream students perform poorly because they receive less intellectual stimulation at home than mainstream students receive.

These views have limited teachers' efforts to help all students achieve, and they have damaged the self-images of these students. Banks (1994) affirms that the curriculum ought to describe ways different cultural groups have contributed to Western civilization. Vargas and Kellam (see Bracey, 1999) have noted that immigrants are well represented in occupations that, while perhaps not requiring a higher education, require much skill (for example, chefs, tailors, and jewelers). When selecting textbooks and ancillary materials, teachers should choose those that represent nonmainstream persons positively.

Another major limiting factor for many nonmainstream students is the language barrier. An increasing number of students come from homes where English is not the primary spoken language. For example, one of every four students in the California schools last year was a learner with limited English proficiency (Schnalberg, 1995). Studying in their primary language improves students' self-images and enhances their understanding of their own worth (Macedo, 1995). In selecting textbooks and ancillary materials, teachers should consider the potential language barrier and avoid those texts and other materials that are poorly written and difficult to understand.

Fortunately, even with all the mistakes our nation has made in dealing with the needs of its people, in general Americans are now committed to serving the needs of all students. A mid 1990s Gallup poll found that three-fourths of the public think that the schools should promote both a common cultural tradition and the diverse cultural traditions of the nation's different population groups (Elam, Rose, & Gallup, 1994). Unfortunately, there are major differences in achievement among students of different ethnic groups, and student drop-out rates vary from group to group. For example, in the mid 1990s the percentage of eighth grade age students who had already dropped out of school was 9.4 percent for white learners, 14.5 percent for African American students, and 18.3 percent for Hispanic students (Smith et al., 1994).

Gender Equity

Age-old stereotypes about women have produced ongoing limiting effects on the futures of women. Our schools have been guilty of sustaining and even promoting these ideas. For example, generally, girls have not been encouraged to take advanced mathematics. This pattern continues in college, where "relatively few (females) elect to pursue advanced work in mathematics and the sciences" (Armstrong et al., 1997, p. 195).

Pollina (1995) suggests that for years we have tried to give girls tougher subjects such as math and the sciences to make them more masculine when, instead, math teachers should nurture girls' unique strengths. This would include such things as encouraging girls to use mathematics to discuss decorative designs, to participate in collaboration, to assume the role of expert, and to use technology to solve problems as opposed to playing games, which is a method preferred by boys. Mathematics teachers could also give girls assignments that require more writing, because girls' verbal scores on achievement tests are higher than boys' scores.

Teachers of co-ed science and mathematics classes should use some strategies that acknowledge the strengths of students of each gender. Because the culture in any class is an important variable, this practice could hold considerable promise to the teaching of math and science.

Teachers at all levels, and especially at the preschool and early elementary levels, should be careful to choose textbooks and other educational materials for their classes that portray females in roles that once were held only or mainly by males, and vice versa. For example, seeing pictures of male and female secretaries, flight attendants, nurses, doctors, and law officers can help dispel the myth that these jobs are appropriate for members of only one gender.

In addition to using this awareness when selecting texts and ancillary materials, teachers should use this awareness when making role-playing assignments. When planning to use consultants, efforts should be made to use this opportunity to break gender stereotypes.

Geographic Stereotyping

As a nation, we have held enduring stereotypes about people because of where they live. Rural people have been thought of as hayseeds, yet a substantial portion of today's farmers use advanced technology to run multimillion-dollar farms and ranches. People dwelling in the mountains are sometimes portrayed as ignorant and backward, yet improved communications, transportation, and technology have put many mountain people on the cutting edge of their businesses.

Special Students

About 12 percent of all elementary and secondary students have disabilities, and almost half of this group (45 percent) have disabilities that inhibit their learning (Smith et al., 1994). One approach to helping these students is through redesigning the curriculum to meet their needs. If we accept the premise that all children can and will learn, then teachers and schools are responsible for seeing that this happens (Bradley & Fisher, 1995). The following questions by Hoover (1990, pp. 410–411) can help ensure that this goal is reached:

1. Content: Does student possess sufficient reading level?
   a. Has student demonstrated mastery of prerequisite skills?
   b. Does student possess sufficient language abilities?
   c. Does student possess appropriate prior experience?

2. Instructional strategy: Is student motivated to learn through strategy?
   a. Does strategy facilitate active participation?
   b. Is strategy effectiveness relative to content to be learned?
   c. In what conditions is strategy effective/ineffective?

3. Instructional setting: Does setting facilitate active participation?
   a. Is student able to complete tasks in selected setting?
   b. Is student able to learn in selected setting?
   c. Is setting appropriate for learning selected?

4. Student behavior: What types of behaviors are exhibited by the learner?
   a. Time on task?
   b. Attention to task?
   c. Self-control abilities?
   d. Time-management skills?
   e. What are the most appropriate behaviors exhibited in selecting a strategy?

The teacher can also help students with disabilities by carefully choosing the textbook and other materials. Once selected, the following strategies can be used with these materials (Cheney, 1989):

1. Change the nature of the learning task from one that requires reading and written responses to one that requires listening with oral responses (for example, use a cassette tape or peer tutor).
2. Allow the student to demonstrate understanding through group projects or oral reports.
3. Allow the student to complete smaller amounts of material in a given time.
4. Have the student circle or underline the correct responses rather than write them.
5. Fasten the student's materials to the desk to help with coordination problems.
6. Provide extra drill-and-practice materials for those students who understand the material but need more time to master it.
7. Present information using graphs, illustrations, or diagrams.
8. Incorporate rhyming, rhythm, music, or movement into lessons.
9. Lessen distractions from other sources within the learning environment.

Another approach to helping students with disabilities is through the use of technology (Bradley & Fisher, 1995), which can improve students' achievement levels and attitudes. Some educators believe that the possibility for improvement through the use of assistive technology (i.e., technology designed especially to help students overcome their disabilities) will be so profound that it will require educators to rethink the scope of instructional opportunities for children with disabilities (Parette, Hourcade, & Vanbiervliet, 1993).

Inclusion

The opposite of the concept of ability grouping is the concept of inclusion, which has been defined as "the formal name for an educational arrangement in which all students are given the opportunity to participate in general education with their typical age peers to the greatest extent possible" (Bradley & Fisher, 1995). Proponents of inclusion say that it involves keeping special education students in a classroom and bringing support services to the child, rather than bringing the child to the services (Smelter, Rasch, & Yudewitz, 1994).

Inclusion differs from mainstreaming in that mainstreamed students spend only part of their days in regular classrooms, whereas students in inclusion curricula spend their entire day in regular classrooms. Inclusion differs further from mainstreaming in that mainstreamed students may not receive special services in the regular classroom, while students in inclusion curricula are given whatever special services they require within the regular classroom.

Students with disabilities tend to achieve a modest to moderate amount more when placed in classrooms with nondisabled students. Baker, Wang, and Walberg (1995) compared three metanalysis studies of the effect of placing disabled students in inclusive classrooms (see Table 11.1).

These effects show a small-to-moderate benefit of inclusion over noninclusive education on both academics and social behavior. The academic scores are based on standardized achievement test scores and the social effect is based on

Table 11.1   Effects of Inclusive Placement

Author(s)	*Carlberg & Kavale*	*Wang & Baker*	*Baker*
Year Published	1980	1985–1986	1994
Time Period	Pre-1980	1975–1984	1984–1992
Number of Studies	50	11	13
Academic Effect Size	0.15	0.44	0.08
Social Effect Size	0.11	0.11	0.28

observations and ratings made by the students (self-evaluations), their teachers, their peers, and classroom observers.

Inclusion is a highly controversial issue across the country. About two-thirds (66 percent) of the public oppose inclusion (Rose & Gallup, 1998) because they believe it is disruptive and it lowers the quality of education for nonchallenged students; yet inclusion is required by federal law. Undoubtedly, the controversy over this practice will continue.

Currently, federal law requires schools to offer disabled students the right to be educated with their nondisabled peers. School officials who remove disabled students from inclusive classrooms must be capable of proving that such placements benefit the disabled students.

Gifted Students

Historically, little has been done to ensure that the needs of gifted students have been met. One popular approach to helping gifted students is through grouping. Feldheusen (1989, p. 9) says that grouping can enable teachers to enrich the curriculum used with these students:

> Gifted and talented children complain a great deal about the boredom of their classroom experiences; they are forced to spend a lot of time being taught things they already know, doing repetitive drill sheets and activities, and receiving instructions on new material at too slow a pace. These experiences probably cause gifted youth to lose motivation to learn, to get by with minimum effort, or to reject school as a worthwhile experience. Grouping gifted and talented youth for all or part of the school day or week also serves as a stimulus or motivator. Interaction with other students who are enthusiastic about astronomy, robotics, Shakespeare, or algebra motivates gifted and talented students.

Gifted students need opportunities to use their creative abilities. Burns (1990, pp. 35–36) tested 515 subjects and concluded:

> This study indicates that there is value in teaching students how to manage, focus, and plan a project or investigation. . . . Along with the development of lessons to teach strategies for creative productivity, gifted education teachers might also become more aware of the importance of self-efficacy; in increasing the likelihood that students will begin creative investigations.

The creative needs of these students can also be met through the fine arts; they may benefit from opportunities to hold discussions with artists and opportunities to create their own projects. The alternative curriculum shown in Chapter 7 offers a variety of classes that challenge students to use their creative abilities. Although such programs are motivating and fun, it is important that they be profoundly academically challenging if they are to be used by gifted students.

Senior Citizens

Perhaps the most overlooked members of American society are its senior citizens. In most countries, the senior members of a society maintain high status in that society because they are respected for their knowledge and wisdom. Even the most primitive societies have organized education systems that use senior citizens as teachers. Unfortunately, the United States has not adhered to this practice.

Service learning programs offer teachers an excellent opportunity to bring students and senior citizens together. Projects can be planned that encourage senior citizens to share their wealth of knowledge and their wisdom with students at all grade levels. One effective vehicle that can be used to transfer knowledge and values is storytelling (Jalongo and Isenberg, 1995). Through storytelling, senior citizens can share a wealth of knowledge about the values and lifestyles of earlier generations. Such knowledge can give youth a much needed anchor for their own values and beliefs.

Magnet Schools

Magnet schools have a specialized curriculum that generally is not available in other schools in their community, for example, an auto mechanics school in Indianapolis or a fine arts school in Houston. Most magnet schools are secondary schools, but some offer K–12 curricula. Students in schools located throughout the city can opt to spend part of their week in one of these magnet schools.

Overall, magnet schools have been successful in providing many students educational opportunities that they otherwise would not have had, but these schools have not escaped criticism. Critics say that had the enormous amount of dollars required to build and operate these schools been instead spread out among the other schools in the district, then tremendous improvement could have been made in the other schools. Another major criticism of magnet schools is accessibility. At many magnet schools students are required to furnish their own transportation, thus eliminating attendance by many poorer students.

Charter Schools

Charter schools are schools that have been given special permission (usually for a period of five years) to experiment with unique curricula. For example, by law, schools with twenty or more students whose first language is not English are required to offer instruction in each non-English language for which there is a large enough population; however a charter school located in an Hispanic community might receive permission to teach only in Spanish.

A two-year, national study of charter schools (Manno, Finn, Bierlein, & Vanourek, 1998) reported that two-thirds of the founders of these schools gave their reason for establishing the school as a desire to create a school that matched their vision. Families who sent their children to charter schools did so because of the charter school's small school size (53 percent), higher standards (46 percent), educational philosophy (44 percent), greater opportunity for parent involvement (43 percent), and better teachers (42 percent). Teachers reported that they chose to work at a charter school because of its educational philosophy (77 percent), because they wanted to work at a good school (65 percent), because they wanted to work with like-minded colleagues (63 percent), because they wanted to work for good administrators (55 percent), and because charter schools have smaller class sizes (54 percent). A basic belief about charter schools is that a higher-quality education can be offered when the micro-management and bureaucracy that characterizes traditional public schools can be eliminated. It is not surprising to learn that most charter school members come from families who were dissatisfied with traditional schools. Perhaps it is also not surprising to learn that these customers want higher standards and a louder voice in the running of the school. Some may be surprised to learn that charter schools often attract low-income families and minority parents (Manno, Finn, Bierlein, & Vanourek, 1998). For example, in Minnesota, most members of charter schools are from low-income groups and communities of color (Minnesota Charter Schools Evaluation, Interim Report, December 1996. Minneapolis: Center for Applied Research and Educational Improvement of Minnesota).

The number of charter schools has grown from one in 1992 to 800 in 1998. This suggests that many people are ready to change to a nontraditional system to educate their children (Nathan, 1998). Although there is much evidence that charter schools work (Hall 1998; Pitton 1999), resistance to change has slowed their development. Wagner (1998, p. 513) says, "In most school or district change efforts with which I am familiar, a single individual—the principal or the superintendent—or perhaps a small committee determines the goals of change . . . There is rarely any discussion of the need for the change or what its goals should be among the groups most directly affected—teachers, parents, and students."

Like all other curricula, those at charter schools have both advantages and limitations and, therefore, have both supporters and critics (Rael, 1995). At their best, these schools have stimulating curricula and enthusiastic teachers. Consider a fine arts charter school in Houston which uses performing artists to teach. Where else could such teachers find a school that is dedicated to the arts alone? Where else could students find teachers who are professional artists? It isn't surprising that by the mid 1990s three-fifths of the states had already established charter schools or were enacting legislation to start offering them (Mauhs-Pugh, 1995).

Some states are proceeding slowly with legislation and are taking various precautions. California has set a limit of no more than 100 charter schools for the state and no more than 10 for any district (Sinis & Roda, 1995). Some states issue charters only to existing schools to prevent the use of funds to pay for new buildings (Eggleston, 1995).

Business Partnership Programs

Business people have always taken interest in the schools because the schools are vital to a prospering community, and their level of interest has been further kindled by education reform reports of the 1980s and 1990s. Many businesses have participated in adopt-a-school programs, taking special responsibility for helping a single school. This help has come in a variety of ways, including financial support, providing consultants to the schools, and providing students on-the-job experience to see whether they wish to pursue various careers.

Like all partnerships, business-school partnerships must offer advantages to both partners if they are to succeed. To the participating students, these programs provide income, opportunities to explore careers (Hartoonian & Van Scotter, 1996), experience needed to develop expertise in the job role, and an inside track to a permanent job at a time when employment opportunities are becoming increasingly scarce.

The participating business must also realize meaningful benefits. Partnerships with schools have become a politically correct practice. In addition to benefiting from positive publicity, a major enticement for many businesses to join partnership programs is the opportunity to train students, some of whom will become lifetime employees who have grown up in the culture of the company, taking on the characteristics of the successful supervisors/trainers who are role models for these future employees. Goldberger and Kazis (1996, p. 554) address a less obvious advantage, the positive shaping that occurs to these supervisors as a consequence of their leadership roles: "These benefits include improved management skills, greater enjoyment of their jobs (and hence better employee retention), and increased attention to improving the development of their own skills."

Partnerships have the power to bring dramatic improvement, but Day (1999, p. 6) warns of a possible down side: "The potential for promoting self-serving interests that are not beneficial for students can be a negative aspect for such partnerships." To reduce the likelihood for such damage, Hopkins and Wendel (1997) suggest that the roles of both parties be carefully delineated.

National Standards

During the 1980s and 1990s the public showed a renewed interest in and demand for schools and teachers to be held accountable for learning. For some people, such concerns are usually accompanied by the felt need to have national standards. Proponents say that without national standards, many states will not provide adequate education for their youth (Noddings, 1997). Those who oppose the movement, however, argue that the "teaching and learning we all desire cannot be imposed by the state" (Pitton, 1999, p. 392), and that such standards limit the learning of the best students by lowering the level of expectancy.

Ostrom (1997, p. 2) observes, "These standards hold student learning and demonstrations of work constant." This leveling effect can be argued to be either good or bad. Perhaps a more important observation is that merely setting high standards will not improve student learning. Covington (1996, p. 24) points out that, "If students cannot now measure up to old, presumably less demanding standards, increased demands seem pointless." According to Darling-Hammond and Falk (1997, p. 191), "Few have examined how schools and teaching practices might need to succeed or how a closer look at student learning might trigger more effective responses."

Another argument against national standards is that they tend to stifle creativity among students and teachers, and that the encouragement and opportunity for students to be creative is of importance to the student and the nation. But the advocates for national standards argue that these standards are not dictates of specific student and teacher behavior, nor are they prescriptions for specific information to be dictated by the government. Marzano & Kendall (1996) say that standards are not a narrow description of information to be learned and skills to be performed under a particular set of conditions, but rather are broad enough to be articulated with benchmarks.

Quality education cannot be guaranteed by legislation, and this includes setting national standards. Indeed, as one educator has noted with skepticism, "Externally mandated goals seldom result in either meaningful improvement or the development of organizational capacity for effecting improvement" (Bernauer, 1999, p. 69). Rather than continuing to argue the pros and cons of having national standards or spending a lot of time searching for ideal standards, Fullan (1998, p. 8) says it is time to refocus our attention: "Giving up the futile search for the silver bullet is the basic precondition for overcoming dependency and for beginning to take actions that do matter." As the twentieth century ended, national standards were either already set or had almost been completed by the learned societies in each discipline. These will be discussed in the second part of this chapter. Meanwhile, Pitton (1999, p. 386) gives good advice in advocating that wherever and at whatever level standards are developed, teachers must be involved early in their development: "As standards projects continue to develop across the nation, state directors and legislators need to be sure that teachers are involved from the beginning." The movement toward national standards has significantly raised the level of involvement of teachers. Hall (1998, unpublished address) states, "There is more discussion about curriculum now than ever before, and teachers are coming together across grade levels and buildings to talk about what students should know and be able to do."

Teachers may need help in wrestling with the standards issue. Perhaps the best approach is to step away and review the potentials and limitations of the standards and of how they are used. Sweeny (1999, p. 64) cautions:

> Previous reform efforts show standards typically serve one or two means: (1) a challenging gate through which only some students can pass or (2) a bridge by which "only" means more, then teachers will face an unwelcome standards explosion that reflects the knowledge explosion.

Table 11.2   Guidelines for Adopting and Crafting Standards

We need standards that	*We don't need standards if*
• Help ensure opportunities for all students to master the essentials.	• Better only means more.
• Lead to objectives that are attainable by all students.	• They do not represent what educators know is best practice.
• Define attainable essentials and help educators guide students in achieving them.	• They are handed down from above (top-down) and teachers are not involved in setting them.
	• They are specific dictates of content and classroom procedures.

Table 11.2 has been developed to assist teachers who have responsibility for choosing whether their school will either create their own set of standards or adopt an existing set of standards.

Many states have taken the initiative to set their own standards (Sweeny, 1999). As you continue to study the national standards movement, you will probably discover that attempts to generalize either the importance of standards in one state or the techniques used to implement them in other states have usually failed. Pitton (1999, p. 384) says, "If we compare standards in one state with those of another, or if we compare standards to behavioral objectives or outcome-based education, we are looking at the standards out of context."

Increased Parental Involvement and Control

Parents will continue to demand an increased role in determining the direction the local schools are taking. As mentioned in Chapter 10, this trend was strong throughout the 1990s. As the 1990s ended, half (53 percent) of American parents said they want even more control of their schools (Rose & Gallup, 1998), especially in how the schools spend their funds. The second most frequently mentioned desire was for more input into hiring administrators, and the third most frequently voiced desire was greater control over the types of curriculum offered.

There is increased evidence that parents can significantly increase their children's cognitive attainment. For example, Palmer and Pugalee (1999, pp. 95–104) report that "parents can provide useful insights into students' literacy behaviors in the home setting." They predict that "parent-teacher conferences will be more centered around portfolios, and the focus will be to communicate student developmental progress, growth in independent reading, the development of attitudes and interests, and the ability to use reading and writing for a variety of purposes."

Teachers tend to draw the line when parents make suggestions about daily classroom operations such as teaching methodology and classroom management methods. Teachers generally feel that most parents lack the expertise required to make decisions of this nature. Keeping parents from interfering while honoring the fact that the schools belong to the parents and other members of the community is a skill that twenty-first-century administrators and teachers will need to hone as the trend toward increased desire for parental control continues. Administrators and teachers will need to continue improving communications with parents. A review of research and literature shows that teachers use specific strategies to involve parents (Buttery & Tichner, 1996). Table 11.3 shows seven of the most common communications strategies and their relative effectiveness.

As shown in Table 11.3, newsletters continue to be viewed as one of the most effective ways to communicate with parents. However, there is no substitution for regularly scheduled events that bring teachers face-to-face with parents. As Claus (1999, p. 14) points out:

> The literature suggests that the more teachers and parents know each other on a personal basis, and the more educators understand and appreciate the perspectives of parents, the greater the likelihood the two groups will be able to collaborate and, in times of disagreement, achieve constructive compromise.

It is interesting to note that email and Internet chat rooms have become a major strategy for communicating with parents.

Table 11.3   Relative Effectiveness of Common Strategies Used to Communicate with Parents

	Very and Somewhat Effective %	*Very Effective %*	*Somewhat Effective %*	*Not Very Effective %*	*Not At All Effective %*	*Don't Know %*
Public school open houses	89	54	35	6	3	2
Public school newsletters	87	47	40	9	3	1
Open hearings	85	48	37	8	4	3
Neighborhood discussion groups	81	43	38	12	5	2
Public school news hotlines	77	35	42	13	4	6
Televised school board meetings	74	39	35	15	9	2
Internet "chat rooms" set up by your local school	63	25	38	19	9	9

Another way that parents are being involved in some parts of the country is through the forming of parent-teacher-administrator networks, which may involve several schools, joining to form "families." For example, the Los Angeles public school district has more than two dozen such school families. An investigation of an in-depth study of four of these school families (Wohlstetter & Smith, 2000, p. 515), concluded that such networks, when connected appropriately, can "generate a sense of efficiency that any organization needs in order to sustain its efforts to give schools the reform at a level that is otherwise impossible."

A Move to Privatize Public Schools

The country's fascination with privatizing its schools grew out of its dissatisfaction with the public schools. Among the many arguments for turning the public schools over to private organizations, the two most common are the beliefs that (1) anyone can do better with the schools than the public sector has been doing, and (2) private firms can do the job at less cost.

Those who prefer to retain the public schools argue that both of these proposed benefits are really not benefits because they are based on false premises. First, the argument that anyone could do better than the public schools have done is based on the assumption that the single purpose of schools is to raise test scores. Houston (1994, p. 134) reminds critics that the goal of education is much greater: "The fact is that education's role in production is to produce a better society." Few authors who support the privatization of public schools have considered any of the many important services that public schools render except the improving of test scores. Moffett (1994, p. 587) captured this idea in his observation that "Business should indeed participate in school reform, but it has too narrow a perspective to guide it."

The World of Work

As the current millennium gives way to a new millennium, Americans are vitally concerned with ensuring that students acquire those skills and understandings essential to performing successfully on the job. In 1991, the Secretary of Labor's Commission on Achieving Necessary Skills (SCANS) produced the document *What Work Requires of Schools,* focusing on standards that address higher-order thinking, interpersonal skills, personal traits, and communication skills.

The American Society for Training and Development (ASTD) polled its 50,000 members to identify those skills most desired by employers. The result was a list of 16 skill areas including traditional, academic skills and also nontraditional skills and traits such as high self-esteem, negotiation skills, and interpersonal skills. The results of this work are published in the pamphlet *Workplace Basics: the Essential Skills Employers Want* (Carnevale, Gainer, & Meltzer, 1990).

Although preparing graduates with the skills needed to get a job is important, critics are quick to point to the shortsightedness of this goal—those skills needed to get a job become obsolescent before the new employee has settled comfortably into the new position. As Goodlad (1997, p. 17) says about putting job preparation at the top of our reasons for having schools, "We confound their purpose with expectations for social engineering." To combat this problem of viewing the purpose of schools as being only job preparation, the Carl Perkins Act, which funds vocational education, was amended to require that all funded programs "integrate academic and vocational education . . . through coherent sequences of courses so that students achieve both academic and occupational competencies" (Grubb, 1996).

Such integrated approaches have the power to motivate many students to become involved with the academic side of their education, students who otherwise might remain turned off to all academics. These include students who suffer from cultural dissonance. As Grubb (1996, p. 544) explains:

> Changing teaching so that intrinsic motivation is improved by producing meaningful contexts for students themselves has rarely been proposed. However, a recent analysis of teaching and learning for disadvantaged children has concluded that more active, student-centered approaches are the most promising ways of teaching such students. And these methods are consistent with contextualized and integrated teaching.

This current approach of integrating academics and work skills, coupled with authentic assessment and broad theme approaches, offers a promising route to diverse student populations of the twenty-first century.

Vouchers and School Choice

Since the landing of the pilgrims, Americans have always had a voice in public education. The idea that no single type of schooling is best for all locales led the writers of the constitution, through purposeful omission, to grant the power to each state to establish and maintain its own school programs.

The voucher movement reflects Americans' desire to choose their children's schools (public or private) and use public school allocations to pay the tuition. Vouchers are "government-issued notes that parents can use to pay all or part of the tuition at a private or church-related school" (Rose & Gallup, 1998, p. 41).

Traditionally, some parents have chosen to send their children to private schools, at their own expense. Proponents of voucher plans argue that those parents who choose to send their children to private schools should be able to take the tax money that is currently allotted to the local public schools to educate their children and use that money to pay the school of their choice to do the job. Voucher plans are not a new idea; Canada has been a leader in their use during recent decades. In 1999 Florida became the first state to issue a statewide voucher plan that allows public funding of private schools (McCarthy, 2000).

Since 1990, parents in Milwaukee, Wisconsin, have had the option of using vouchers to send their children to private schools. During the 1994–1995 school year, vouchers averaging $3,200 for each student were used in 12 Milwaukee private schools (Witte & Thorn, 1994). The academic achievement of these students has not differed significantly from that of their counterparts who remained in the public schools, but the parents are much more pleased with the private schools.

Although they have recently gained political and legal support, vouchers remain highly controversial (McCarthy, 2000). Critics of the voucher plan worry that it will exacerbate the inequality of educational opportunities, hurting most those children who attend the poorest schools. This concern is based on the fact that a disproportionate number of children in the poorest schools come from broken homes, or homes where parents cannot afford to take off from work to attend school meetings, or homes with parents who lack the ability to choose wisely among the options available. Put succinctly, these critics worry that vouchers will improve opportunities for the fortunate but will grossly worsen opportunities for the less fortunate.

Proponents of the voucher system say that this system will force all schools to compete for students and that the competition will bring improvement to all schools. They say that teachers will have to cooperate to save their jobs and that teachers will not be able to afford to ever give up on a student (Hill, 1996). Furthermore, advocates for voucher programs point out that since the school is chosen by the parents, this gives the parents leverage to entice their children to perform well. Conversely, the school can eject students who fail to perform properly. Viewed positively, giving students some choice in the schools they attend should increase their satisfaction with their school and entice them to work hard to continue as a member of the school.

The early twenty-first century is characterized by hot debates over whether public taxes should be spent this way. In fact, the public is almost evenly split on this issue. Vouchers that would pay all the tuition are supported by 48 percent and opposed by 46 percent of the public. Vouchers that would pay for part of the tuition are supported by 52 percent and opposed by 41 percent of the public (Rose & Gallup, 1998).

At least for the near future, the use of vouchers will continue to occur here and there throughout the country and debates over their value will also continue.

Cooperative Learning

The literature is replete with definitions of cooperative learning, and these definitions vary from general to specific. Lindblad (1994, p. 292) offers a general definition when he says, "In its purest form, cooperative learning is merely a few people getting together to study something and produce a single product." At the opposite end of the continuum, Johnson and Johnson (1989–1990) list five specific basic elements of all cooperative learning programs: positive interdependence, face-to-face interaction, individual accountability, collaborative skills, and group processing.

Cooperative learning offers several advantages. Because the success of each member is contingent upon the other members succeeding, this technique has strong motivation potential and, consequently, promotes higher achievement. Cooperative learning also increases students' self-esteem (Manning & Lucking, 1991).

When implementing cooperative learning, teachers need to play a guiding role rather than a dominating, leadership role. Lindblad (1994, p. 293) explains:

> Too often the traditional teacher feels the need to be part of everything going on in the class. Let students handle their own team progress. When the teacher stays removed from minor discord, the team members are forced to deal with those problems themselves.

The following guidelines can be used to implement cooperative learning:

1. Give students the freedom they need to run their groups.
2. Plan a short group assignment and introduce it early in the lesson.
3. Assign three or four students to each group.
4. Put dominating students together so that they will be forced to listen part of the time.
5. Put reserved students together so that they will be forced to assume leadership roles part of the time.
6. Explain that it is to everyone's advantage to help other group members.
7. Consider teaming with another teacher when implementing cooperative learning.
8. Help students learn how to ask productive questions.
9. Encourage students to ask questions.
10. Listen carefully to student-generated questions.

Multiple Intelligences

Most of our understanding about intelligence comes from work done at the end of the nineteenth century and the beginning of the twentieth century. Even many of the tests we are using almost a century later were developed at that time.

Recently, though, an increasing number of educational psychologists have been accepting and promoting the idea of multiple intelligences (Armstrong et al., 1997). Howard Gardner (1993) believes that humans possess the following seven distinct and separate kinds of intelligence:

- logical-mathematical
- linguistic, musical
- spatial
- bodily-kinesthetic
- interpersonal
- intrapersonal

Other theories of multiple intelligences have also been proposed. For example, Robert Sternberg (see Woolfolk, 1995) proposed a triarchic theory of intelligence, which includes *componential intelligence* (the ability to learn by separating relevant and irrelevant information), *contextual intelligence* (the ability to adapt to new experiences and solve problems in new situations), and *experiential intelligence* (the ability to deal with novel situations and the ability to turn new situations into routine procedures.

Teachers who accept the multiple intelligences concept do not restrict their classroom activities to the goal of acquiring information. Such teachers have the ability to see and appreciate potentials in their students that were not recognized by most teachers only a few years ago. Perhaps most important, multiple intelligences theory is causing teachers to appreciate and promote a wide range of abilities among their students.

The old narrow concept of giftedness has taken on additional dimensions, too. As new theories continually emerge, new types of human potentials are being discovered that should provoke teachers to continuously search for potentials among their students, never giving up on a student who a few years ago might have been typecast as a slow student. An awareness of multiple intelligences theory should provoke teachers to expand their planning to include using a variety of ways to help students use their creativity to discover and understand important content introduced in the classroom.

Evaluating Textbooks and Ancillary Materials

Other sections of this text have warned against the overuse of textbooks, a proclivity of many teachers to let the textbook virtually determine the curriculum. While this has been a prevailing problem over the years, such practice will be more flagrant and visible in the future since we now have content standards that teachers, through their representatives in their learned societies, have agreed to accept. Although overreliance on the textbook for determining curriculum direction is a major problem, there are other concerns about textbooks that also demand attention. Among these is the need to help teachers select textbooks and ancillary materials that promote the acceptance of ethnic diversity; people from all geographic regions, both outside and within the country; gender equity; physically, mentally, and emotionally challenged students; gifted students; and senior citizens.

Textbook Selection

One of the most controversial issues in education today is textbook selection. Typically, teachers play a variety of roles in selecting textbooks for their local district and state. Dr. Connie Mather, a nationally recognized expert on textbook selection provides the following information and advice.

The most important thing to know in evaluating instructional materials is having a clear picture of what you want. This means you evaluate only selected content that fulfills one or more of the following criteria:

- Essential to your curriculum
- Coverage of your students' weakest areas
- Something you personally dislike teaching, but you must
- Something controversial
- Something small enough so that a thorough examination can be made without you becoming confused

Have the committee define and describe the ideal. What is quality instruction or content in the desired new materials? How are the current materials being used? Remember, the committee is selecting materials for those who are not on the committee; those not serving may not teach the same way. A change in materials will not change how those materials are used—especially with those who have no voice in the selection.

Once the topic, concept, or skill is selected, based upon the above listed criteria, compare three publisher's materials at the same time and select the best match to what you have described as ideal. If you look at only one publisher, what are you comparing it to? Your old publisher? Then the new materials look pretty good. If you compare with two publishers, one is either good or bad. Three publishers gives you a nice comfortable triad. With four, you become confused.

You can remove publisher bias and make your study more scientific if you assign each publisher a color and duplicate that publisher's lesson in its designated color. Next, cut and tape the comparative lesson on a three-column form. You can immediately see differences (see Tables 11.4 and 11.5).

Label each publisher by its color, and you can show these cut-and-tape evaluations to anyone: to other teachers who are not on the committee or even to students. Save your comparison charts, and if your district is ever challenged, you have clear evidence you selected the best materials to match your major curriculum goals.

There are many different evaluations strategies to use, but all are based on this same principle of choosing a topic, comparing three publishers, selecting the best, and photocopying the evidence. If your materials are hands-on programs, photocopy the teacher's editions. Whether it is audio, video, or software, you again try to compare apples to apples. I often ask three committee members to videotape the news for a specific evening on different stations. We then select the same story and compare the coverage. It's amazing the differences that can be seen quickly when comparing the same items.

The best evaluation strategy is what I call the "horizontal trace." However, this method is extremely time consuming, so I usually have the committee do the cut-and-tape small topic evaluations first. To do the horizontal trace, select the topic,

**Table 11.4   A Comparison of Three Publishers' Coverage of Discrimination
Against Japanese Americans**

Social Studies • Japanese Americans • Grade 8

	Pink, p.615
Title	*The Relocation of Japanese Americans*
Introduction	At the start of the war, about 120,000 Japanese Americans lived on the West Coast of the United States. At least two-thirds of them were American-born citizens, known as Nisei. After the surprise attack by Japan on Pearl Harbor, many people believed rumors that Japanese Americans were involved in acts to aid the enemy. Although false, the rumors led to widespread mistreatment of West Coast Japanese Americans.
Roosevelt	On February 20, 1942, President Roosevelt gave in to public pressure and issued an order allowing the army to move West Coast Japanese Americans to "relocation camps." Forced to sell their homes, farms, and businesses quickly, many families suffered heavy losses.
Living Conditions	The relocation camps proved to be little better than prison camps, mostly in isolated desert areas. They were surrounded by barbed wire and patrolled by armed troops. Families were crowded into small wooden barracks covered with tar paper. *(See Reading 24A.)*
Supreme Court Ruling	None
Japanese Americans in the Armed Services	Despite this mistreatment, Japanese Americans remained loyal to the United States. Over 33,000 of them volunteered to serve in the armed forces. Japanese Americans made up the 442nd Regimental Combat Team, the most decorated unit in American military history.

Gray, p.634	Blue, p.839
Tragedy for Japanese Americans	*None*

The worst discrimination, however, was felt by Japanese Americans. Most Japanese Americans lived on the West Coast. Many were successful farmers and business people. For years, they had faced racial prejudice in part because of their success. After the attack on Pearl Harbor, many white Americans distrusted Japanese Americans. They warned that Japanese Americans on the West Coast could act as spies and help Japan invade the United States.	The demand for weapons and supplies finally ended the Great Depression. American industry had slowly been climbing out of the depression, helped by European war needs. Now greatly expanded production was needed. Hundreds of thousands of new workers were needed to produce the tools of war. Men and women flocked from farms, towns, and great cities to jobs in shipyards, steel plants, former automobile factories, and aircraft plants. About 6 million women were employed during the war. Farmers also experienced boom times. The demand for food to feed American and Allied troops was enormous. Farm income more than doubled during the war. World War II had great popular support. Almost no one questioned the decision to fight the Axis powers.
The President agreed to an order to move Japanese Americans away from the coast to "relocation" camps farther inland. Over 100,000 Japanese Americans on the West Coast were ordered to sell their homes, land, and belongings.	This enthusiasm led to a serious blot on the Roosevelt record of civil liberties: treatment of Japanese Americans. Unfounded suspicion forced about 112,000 living on the West Coast to move to internment camps in a barren section of the country. There was absolutely no evidence that the Japanese Americans were less loyal than other Americans.
In relocation camps, Japanese Americans had to live behind barbed wire. Housing was poor.	None
The people did not understand why they, as American citizens, were singled out. Americans of German and Italian backgrounds were not sent to camps. In 1944, the Supreme Court ruled that the camps were a necessary wartime measure.	None
Only when an Allied victory seemed certain were Japanese Americans allowed to return to their homes. At first, Japanese Americans were barred from serving in the military. Later, this policy was changed. More than 10,000 Japanese Americans volunteered for service. Many were cited for their bravery. One unit of Japanese Americans used the slogan "Go for broke!" It became a popular rallying cry across the nation.	None

concept, or skill exactly as you did before; however, instead of beginning with the instruction you begin with the measurement. How does your district test this item? How is it measured on state testing? The procedure is as follows:

- Take the test yourself.
- List everything the students will need to know or be able to do in order to succeed with the test.
- Go to the indices at the end of the first publisher's program and read (or photocopy) every page reference listed.
- Determine whether the instruction and content match what you're measuring.

Again, always compare three publishers, selecting the best match. (When you try to do more you'll forget what was in each publisher's version.) Photocopy evidence to support which publisher's material was best aligned with the test material. Share your results with others. Again, you'll have documentation in case you are challenged several years later.

Table 11.5   A Comparison of Three Publishers' Coverage of the Boston Massacre

Social Studies • Boston Massacre • Grade 5

	White, '91
Introduction	*The Boston Massacre* In 1767, Parliament ordered a tax on British glass, paint, paper, silk, and tea. British tax collectors, with soldiers to guard them, arrived in the colonies. Again the colonists protested. This time the protests led to violence.
Chronology of Event	The first incident took place in Boston. For years, Boston colonists had made fun of the red-coated British soldiers by calling them lobsterbacks. In 1770, however, this sport turned ugly. A crowd of colonists gathered around a lobsterback who was guarding the tax office. Colonists began shouting and throwing snowballs, some packed around ice or rocks. Other soldiers rushed to help the guard. In the confusion, soldiers fired into the crowd, killing five people including a black sailor named Crispus Attucks.

Why do these evaluations work? What most people do not know is that authors do not necessarily write instructional materials. Most major publishers create their programs using "development houses" whose freelance authors write to each publisher's specifications. Ironically, development houses do not work with exclusivity contracts, which means they can be working for competing publishers at the same time. Since there are so many writers involved (which means a greater chance of error), and the materials all have to sound like they're written by one person in one voice, many instructional materials are boring. New programs must be created quickly in order to meet printer deadlines, for there are only about five major printers used by most companies. The pressure builds from adoption states, who preselect the instructional materials that can be purchased by teachers in that state. Deadlines are critical, for if a publisher misses getting material to the printer, the books are not submitted in time for state adoption, which automatically disqualifies them. Typically a publisher's program is written in one year, edited the next year, and then rushed to the printer. This leaves little or no time for field testing with students. Production is high-pressured and sales-driven, with some authors barely having time to read the text they are credited with writing. There are exceptions to all this, which is why comparing three publishers with your ideal will identify the best product.

Yellow '91	*Green '91*

The Boston Massacre

In 1768, during the argument over the Townshend duties, Parliament got worried. They feared that the colonial protests were out of control. They sent soldiers to Boston. Some colonists welcomed the soldiers. They believed the soldiers might help keep order. Other colonists were angry. They charged that the soldiers were a danger to the rights of colonists.

B. Tempers Flare in Boston

British Troops   After the French and Indian War, the British government had sent thousands of troops to the colonies. They said that the soldiers were needed to defend the colonists against Indian attack. However, instead of going to the frontier where the Indians were, most of the soldiers remained in the cities near the coast.

The colonists were angered by the sight of soldiers on their streets day and night. They jeered at the soldiers, made fun of them, and made their lives miserable. In several cities, fights broke out between colonists and soldiers.

Anger over the soldiers finally exploded in violence. On March 5, 1770, about 100 Bostonians moved toward some soldiers guarding the customs house. One of the Bostonians' leaders was a black man named Crispus Attucks. The crowd yelled, then threw rocks and snowballs. Fearing for their safety, the soldiers opened fire. They killed Attucks and four other colonists.

On the evening of March 5, 1770, a crowd of men and boys in Boston gathered around a lone British soldier on guard duty. They shouted insults and threw snowballs at him. Some of the snowballs had rocks inside them. The frightened soldier called for help. Then more British soldiers arrived. The crowd grew larger. And the shouts, dares, and insults grew louder and angrier.

Boston Massacre   Suddenly someone—no one knows who—called out "Fire!" The soldiers turned their guns on the crowd and shot. When the smoke cleared, five colonists lay dead, their blood staining the snow-covered street. One of them was Crispus Attucks, a runaway slave who worked as a sailor. Attucks was the first African American to die for the cause of American liberty, but not the last.

Increased and Expanded Use of Technology

The twenty-first century will experience increase in the number of people using technology and an increase in the number of ways of using technology. Paramount among these uses will be the expanded use of hypertext and hypermedia. Nelson (1999, p. 387) defines hypertext as follows: "By 'hypertext' I mean nonsequential writing text that branches and allows choices on an interactive screen." As popularly conceived, this is a series of text chunks connected by links which offers readers different pathways.

Some new ways that we can expect technology to change homework have already been discussed under the reading partnerships. For an imaginative scenario of some future uses of technology see Morisund (1999).

National Voluntary Testing

As mentioned in Chapter 9, President Bill Clinton proposed a voluntary national testing program. As proposed, this program would involve administering exams to fourth graders and eighth graders. Seventy-one percent of the public support such a program, and the support is uniform across all demographic groups (Rose & Gallup, 1998).

Summary: Trends across the Disciplines

Due to space limitations, this discussion of trends across the disciplines has been cursory and far from exhaustive. Most curriculum workers find the ever-changing nature of their profession exciting. Some choose one or two trends and follow these in their literature throughout their professional lives. Now let's examine several trends that are occurring within the disciplines.

TRENDS WITHIN THE DISCIPLINES

The landmark education reform report, *A Nation at Risk* (National Commission on Excellence in Education, 1983) exposed the enduring practice of letting textbooks shape (and in many instances determine) elementary and secondary curricula, pointing to the absolute unreliability and failure of textbooks to contain the essential content in their respective fields (for further elaboration on the failure of textbooks to cover essential content, see Chapter 1).

Various segments of society, including educational societies, are calling for national standards (Cohen, 1995; Jennings, 1995). Although there is national agreement across content areas that elementary and secondary schools need help in upgrading the content in their curricula, and that some sort of national minimum standards should be set, the learned societies representing the disciplines do not agree on what those standards should be designed to do. A major area of disagreement is over whether the standards should be designed to pre-pare high school graduates to pursue further study in their chosen disciplines or whether the standards should be designed to bring all students to a minimum level required to function in our society.

Although disagreements exist, the nation vigorously embraces the call for national educational standards. Currently, 48 states and the District of Columbia are developing standards. Iowa and Wyoming are leaving the decision to local districts (Associated Press, Aug. 5, 1996, p. 3a).

Mathematics

The National Council of Teachers of Mathematics (NCTM) set a precedent for other content organizations when it took leadership in publishing a document setting forth what students should know at the various levels (K–4, 5–8, and 9–12). The publication, titled *Curriculum and Evaluation Standards for School Mathematics,* also tells how students might best demonstrate this knowledge in the classroom. In May 1995, NCTM published another document, titled *Assessment Standards for School Mathematics.* This document is organized around six important standards: important mathematics, enhanced learning, equity, open-ness, valid inferences, and coherence. It provides guidelines to help teachers use assessment to make instructional decisions, monitor student progress, evaluate student achievement, and evaluate programs.

In general, mathematics programs are demanding increasingly higher levels of thinking (Ballew 1999). This change is reflected in a discussion of the Inter-active Mathematics Program, a National Science Foundation funded program. Alper, Fendel, Fraser, and Resck (1996, p. 19) say:

> A major premise of the Interactive Mathematics Program (IMP) is that most stu-dents are capable of thinking about Mathematics and Understanding. This is a change from the philosophy of many traditional programs in which students do mostly rote work. . . . One of the features of the program . . . is the expansion of the curriculum to include new topics. For example, students learn about normal distri-bution and standard deviation, regression and curve fitting, and matrix algebra for both equation solving and geometric transformations   areas of mathematics that most high school students never see.

Twenty-first-century mathematics teachers will continue to use a variety of programs such as the IMP. But, instead of focusing their attention on trying new programs, many teachers will be striving to continuously experiment with new approaches and continue learning more about teaching. Schifter (1996, p. 499) explains:

> For many teachers, this approach implies a change in their relationship to their own profession. Instead of concentrating on technique and strategy—keeping up with the latest trends—the new pedagogy means developing an attitude of inquiry to-ward classroom processes.

Teachers of young children must be cognizant of their developmental limitations. Elkind (1999) has identified three common barriers to teaching mathematics to young children: (1) the futility of using logical analysis to determine how young children learn, (2) the inability to use inductive and deductive reasoning, and (3) the fact that young children have their own priorities. To overcome these barriers, Elkind suggests that teachers observe children, encourage their unlimited imagination, and involve parents in modeling and question asking.

Science

Efforts to develop content standards in the sciences have been both vigorous and diverse. Leading this drive as major sources are the National Committee on Science Education Standards, and Assessment (NCSESA), the American Association for the Advancement of Science (AAAS), and the National Science Teachers Association (NSTA).

NCSESA produced the document titled *National Science Education Standards;* AAAS's Project 2061 produced *Benchmarks for Science Literacy,* providing more than 60 literacy goals in science, math, and social studies; and NSTA published *The Content Core: A Guide for Curriculum Designers* (1993) with an addendum entitled *Scope, Sequence, and Coordination of National Science Education Standards* (1995).

Trends in science include a continuing emphasis on covering less content while using a multidisciplinary hands-on approach with the goal of developing deeper understanding. Inquiry or problem solving are used in the constructivist vein to enable students to tie newly discovered information to previously learned knowledge and to content across the curriculum.

Research-tested science programs in the form of kits continue to be popular, but only when teachers have received the necessary staff development required for the understanding and implementation of such programs. The early twenty-first century should see plenty of staff development for science teachers.

Koba (1996, p. 17), who used an NSF-funded, constructivist, community-based project titled "Solving Problems and Revitalizing Curriculum" (SPARCS), reports:

> Clearly . . . student achievement has risen, with fewer failures among African-American students who were formally tracked in fundamentals classes. In addition, our own attitudinal surveys indicate that students now enjoy science more, feel more comfortable in the science classes, and perceive science as being more important than they ever did before. Most important, we now see learning as a way to make a difference—in our own lives, in our community, and in our world.

As the twenty-first century proceeds, expect to see more interdisciplinary, integrated, community-based science programs in both elementary and secondary schools. Although the terms *interdisciplinary* and *integrated* are used sometimes interchangeably, they are different. According to Huntley (1999, p. 58),

"An interdisciplinary curriculum has the focus on one discipline, and other discipline(s) support or facilitate content in the first domain. An integrated curriculum is one with explicit assimilation of concepts from more than one discipline . . . (with) . . . equal attention to two (or more) disciplines." Both the National Council of Teachers of Mathematics and the National Science Education standards emphasize constructivist teaching and learning techniques (Wise, Spiegel, & Bruning, 1999).

While we tend to think of integrated curriculum as a horizontal concept, in the following case study Buzzell shows how true integration of the curriculum involves a major challenge—the ability to integrate vertically through generations of educators.

Case Study

The Arts in the Curriculum

Judith B. Buzzell
Southern Connecticut State University

Susannah Lerner, an art teacher, and Jennifer Dobner, a staff developer, hugged each other with exhilaration. They had just learned that their school, Remington, had been awarded a new grant. It required the staff to revise their curriculum and expand the integration of the arts into the ongoing program. Although excited by this prospect, Susannah and Jennifer recognized that changing the traditional instructional strategies that had long characterized their school would not be easy.

The Community

Centerville, a Northeastern city with many socioeconomic problems and a population of approximately 150,000, was located in one of the richest states. Once a thriving industrial city, Centerville's employment rate was now at only 50 percent. There were great disparities in state school funding for the rich and poor districts, and residential patterns had led to de facto school desegregation. In fact, the state supreme court had recently ruled on a landmark seven-year case, ordering the state to develop an effective plan for statewide integration. School districts throughout the state were reeling from the ruling: some saw it as opportunity; others were threatened by the prospect of such change.

The School

Remington Elementary School had about 375 students in its kindergarten through sixth grades. Located in the southern corner of the city, the school's neighborhood was characterized by well-kept, single-family homes. To achieve greater racial balance within the city schools, students were bused to Remington from other neighborhoods, and the minority population of the school had grown in the last

(Continued)

ten years. About 85 percent of the school population consisted of minority students, primarily African Americans and Hispanics. The average income of school families had dropped during that ten years.

Remington's veteran staff was proud to be part of a school once acclaimed for its excellent reputation. Most of the teachers used traditional approaches, such as whole class instruction, basal readers, and standard textbooks. There was little collaboration among the teachers. The school had a long-standing history of supporting the arts.

A few years ago, however, a group of neighborhood parents began to complain that the quality of the school had declined. They pointed to the apparent lack of a clear educational mission, the perceived decline in the students' standardized test scores, and the demoralizing school climate. The school was dirty, paint was peeling, and the teachers seemed defeated. Backstabbing among the staff was rampant.

The hard data did not necessarily support these parents' perceptions. For example, two years before these parents organized, a group of Remington students had done exceptionally well on the state's mastery tests in reading, writing, and mathematics. This was the school's first class made up of primarily minority students (60 percent were African American and Hispanic; 40 percent were white).

However, the strong impression of declining excellence weighed more heavily on these parents than did the actual evidence. As a result, neighborhood parents had stopped sending their children to the school. Instead, they vied to get their children into a magnet school with a clearly articulated constructivist approach and a racially balanced population.

Parents whose children remained at Remington began storming the superintendent's office and lobbying other central office administrators to demand changes at the school. They were considered racist by some members of the school and city communities. Others refuted this, pointing out that the parents had chosen to live in an integrated neighborhood and to send their children to the diverse city schools. Instead, they saw the parents as educational innovators.

Leaders

At this point in Remington's history, Jennifer Dobner had just been promoted to staff developer. In this position, she would assist teachers in developing curriculum and learning new instructional strategies. Jennifer had been a first, second, and third grade classroom teacher for twenty years. Having majored in mathematics as an undergraduate, she was known for her hands-on, inductive approach. She was also recognized as a dynamic, caring teacher.

In her new role, Jennifer felt that it was important to develop trusting relationships with her colleagues, so they would turn to her for support and assistance. As a personal credo, she resolved never to speak badly of any teacher to the principal, unless, of course, a child's physical or psychological well-being was at stake.

Larry Evans, Remington's principal, was pleased to have Jennifer take the major role as the school's educational leader. He was good at delegating authority and never blocked change. He focused on the operational administration of the

(Continued)

school, for example managing the physical plant and lobbying for building improvements, freeing Jennifer to be creative with the curriculum.

Curriculum Concerns

In response to parents' concerns about the quality of the school, a steering committee was convened, consisting of Larry, Jennifer, a district curriculum director, some classroom teachers, and several parents of diverse racial and ethnic backgrounds. The committee's initial meetings were shouting matches. Parents were unhappy but couldn't identify the causes. The curriculum director helped by suggesting that the steering committee visit some model schools to help them develop a common vision. He wanted them to see a city school, based on a constructivist model, where parents had painted a mural and were transforming the atmosphere of the building in other ways as well.

After the visit, Jennifer commented, "We weren't struck by the building but rather by what was going on in the classrooms. Children were treated with such dignity and respect, not just socially but intellectually. For example, children in one class were working on a difficult math concept, expanded notation. One child shared what he thought was the correct answer, but one part wasn't quite right. Instead of jumping in to correct the child, the teacher patiently encouraged other children to explain their thinking about the problem to him and each other until the original child understood. They were given the space to think, to form decisions, and to make and learn from their mistakes. We wanted our children to be treated like this."

The steering committee still needed to identify what model the school should follow. Visiting various schools had helped members to envision an array of choices. Some parents wanted to adopt the model of the nearby magnet school, although Jennifer wasn't sure that they really knew what a constructivist approach was. Others were interested in a focus on science and technology; they considered the arts as fluff.

Eventually, the steering committee had to weigh the competing interests of its members. What tipped the balance was that there was possible funding to develop an "ARTS (Arts Reflective Teaching Style) School," a kind of arts-integrated magnet school. The focus would be not on teaching the arts but on teaching the curriculum *through* the arts.

With Jennifer at the helm, a small group worked hard to prepare the grant. Two months after submitting it, they were thrilled to be awarded $25,000, designated for a rotating group of teachers and the principal to attend a week-long training institute on the ARTS School approach every summer for five years. The grant also paid for three resident part-time artists during the five years.

During the first year of the grant, school-wide assemblies were held twice a month on Wednesday afternoons to celebrate what students had accomplished in their classrooms. At Remington, the meetings became primarily a time to appreciate students' writing. Jennifer headed an editorial board of ten students and trained them to review and evaluate writing submitted by their peers. The board then developed a script for each assembly. Sometimes, the music teacher and students would create songs from student writings.

(Continued)

During the second year of the grant, the school focused on classroom experiences. Two artists-in-residence, a storyteller and a photographer, were hired. In addition, an art teacher, Susannah Lerner, was hired.

Susannah was trained as an artist at the undergraduate level; her specialty was painting. She commented on the advantages of being a working artist when teaching youngsters: "I'm confident of my own artistic abilities. I'm not nervous when drawing in front of people or mixing a color. I'm knowledgeable about the materials and the processes, so I can be instinctive in my teaching. Although I'm a new teacher, I don't second-guess myself a lot when it comes to the art curriculum."

Susannah saw her role as providing support to the other teachers and felt her art curriculum needed to fit into the various curricula in the grades. Within that framework, she could carry out any activity she wanted. For example, in kindergarten, the teachers taught a "letter of the week," so Susannah offered a weekly art project that provided a visual representation for the chosen letter. For the letter "B," for example, children created butterflies, using colored tissue paper to pattern the wings. One fourth grade class was studying carnivorous plants. Susannah had them invent their own carnivorous plants using found objects such as cereal boxes, toilet paper rolls, and other items from home. After constructing and painting the plants, students gave oral presentations describing their plant's food and how it ate. The sculptures had to be accurate working models. Susannah enhanced students' learning by showing them photographs of "organic abstract" art, plant-oriented yet abstract sculpture by artists such as Joan Snyder and Marisol. She started to build a library of art books and magazines as a resource for the children.

Susannah's art projects supplemented the ongoing curriculum and often provided a culminating activity. She hoped eventually her projects, instead of being an add-on, would be fully integrated into the curriculum, so that she and the teachers could build on and expand each other's projects. For Black History Month, she taught the third graders about Jacob Lawrence, an African American artist who created a series of paintings titled *The Great Migration,* about the migration of African Americans from the South to the North. She first showed the students the illustrations. Her philosophy of education included a strong belief that learning is more meaningful if it relates to students' lives and experiences. So, to help students to understand the illustrations and connect these to their own background, she told them to ask their family members where their own recent ancestors had come from. This was in preparation for paintings they would do in the style of Jacob Lawrence, depicting families en route to homes in new locales. Unfortunately, only a few of the students remembered to collect the information at home. Susannah explained, "Because I didn't see these students until the following week, it would have helped if the teachers had followed through with this and reminded them about the assignment."

When the students finished their paintings, Susannah asked them to write a brief statement about what was happening to the characters in the paintings. These statements could describe fictitious events or real ones based on their own families' experiences. One of the three third grade teachers proofread her students' writings and asked the students to type them on the computer. These were hung with the paintings, in an appealing mixed-media display. The other two teachers didn't follow through with the writing experience.

(Continued)

Still, this project involved greater collaboration than had occurred previously, and Susannah wanted to move further in this direction. It wasn't feasible for her to require much writing in her 45-minute art lessons with her students, but it wasn't clear how much more the teachers could be expected to do either. "I think the teachers feel overwhelmed by the mandated curriculum and the various grant-funded activities. They feel pressured and don't really have the time," she observed sympathetically. Then she continued, "We're at such baby steps with this that the teachers aren't really aware of how much a part I could play in their classrooms."

By the end of the second year, the school achieved another success. It was awarded funds from the city's magnet school grant to develop a curriculum and align it with state and district goals (including integration) over a five-year period.

That summer 13 people eagerly signed up to attend the ARTS School training. Moreover, during the summer break, teachers began to write thematic teaching-learning units to integrate a variety of curriculum areas and the arts. They planned to develop three thematic units for each grade level. For example, the kindergarten teachers were developing a unit called "All About Me," the first grade teachers were creating one on transportation, and the fourth grade teachers were planning a unit on the rain forest. In the upper grades, there would be an attempt to raise the level of inquiry and require students to conduct primary research related to particular themes. Each theme would provide an umbrella for integrating reading and writing experiences, as well as include hands-on learning opportunities in math, science, and social studies. Ideally, the arts would be used to promote understanding in every area.

In planning the units, Jennifer urged the teachers to ask themselves, "What am I trying to teach?" and "How can I do that in an alternative fashion?" She wanted to nudge them away from commercially produced materials and their heavy reliance on standard texts. Although the texts could still be valuable resources, the themes should provide the driving force of the curriculum. Thus, in addition to curriculum development, Jennifer viewed this coming third year as the year to improve instruction.

She saw the forthcoming year as both an exciting opportunity and a challenge. "I think trying to change instruction is going to create a great deal of tension," she commented. The first two steps of the school reform had been easier, because the problems could be identified outside of the teachers. In attacking the school climate, Jennifer had pointed out various issues but did not question the teachers' instructional strategies. In addressing the curriculum, she again suggested that they were doing a fine job, although some changes were needed. Now, in focusing on instruction, she would need to address considerations closer to teachers' personal styles and philosophies. "It might feel to them like I'm saying, 'Guess what? There may be problems with aspects of what you're doing.' I'll have to find ways to say this diplomatically so people don't feel threatened," she said. Then she sighed, adding, "But how do we change people trained in one generation to transform their teaching styles to accommodate our new understandings of the nature of knowledge and how children learn—to move away from a model that at its extreme implies, 'I tell you and you spit it back?'"

(Continued)

Issues for Further Reflection and Application

1. At the end of the case, Jennifer refers to "our new understandings of the nature of knowledge and how children learn." What research might she be referring to, and what are its findings?

2. Consider the steering committee's reaction to observing mathematics instruction during a school visit. In what ways, if any, was this reaction an indication of educators' new understandings of how children learn? Relate this to Taba's approach to curriculum development.

3. Evaluate the advantages and disadvantages of implementing an integrated approach to curriculum development as seen in this case and in general. How can an integrated approach be achieved through teaching-learning units?

4. It is Remington's goal to emphasize the role of the arts in the curriculum. In what ways were the arts used to enhance the curriculum in this case? What are the advantages of this approach for students? How might the role of the arts have been expanded?

5. If test scores actually were declining at Remington, would it be more advantageous for students to concentrate on basic skills? Are the arts just fluff? Consider this in terms of your own philosophy of education.

6. Consider the questions that Jennifer asked the teachers to consider in planning their teaching-learning units. What other questions do you think they should ask themselves?

7. Susannah comments sympathetically that the teachers may feel overwhelmed by the mandated curriculum and the various grant-funded activities. How can teachers and administrators cope with overloaded curricula? Some might say, "Less is more." Do you agree? Is too much being expected of the teachers in this case?

8. How might teachers' reactions to professional collaboration differ? How important is collaboration in your opinion? How might professional collaboration have been improved in this case?

9. How would you respond to Jennifer's question at the end of the case?

Suggested Readings

DeVries, R., & Kohlberg, L. (1990). *Constructivist early education: Overview and comparison with other programs.* Washington, DC: National Association of Early Childhood Education.

Fredericks, A. D., Meinbach, A. M., & Rothlein, L. (1993). *Thematic units: An integrated approach to teaching science and social studies.* New York: HarperCollins.

Gardner, H. (1993). *Multiple intelligences: The theory in practice.* New York: Basic Books.

Jones, E., & Minno, J. (1994). *Emergent curriculum.* Washington, DC: National Association for the Education of Young Children.

Lowenfeld, V. (1987). *Creative and mental growth of the child* (8th ed.). New York: Macmillan.

Seefeldt, C. (1995, March). Art: A serious work. *Young Children,* pp. 39–44.

Van Scoy, I. J. (1995). Trading the three R's for the four E's: Transforming curriculum. *Childhood Education, 72*(1), 19–23.

Language Arts

In 1992, the Office of Research and Improvement funded a three-year project entitled the Standards Project for the English Language Arts (SPELA). The National Council of Teachers of English (NCTE), the International Reading Association (IRA), and the Center for the Study of Reading (CSR) proposed to conduct SPELA as a collaborative program, but because they failed to make substantial progress, the support was withdrawn. IRA and NCTE planned to continue the project even without federal support. An article in *Education Daily* (October 25, 1995, p. 1) criticizes the new standards set by the IRA and NCTE, saying they "deliberately say little more than that students should be able to read a wide range of texts and write effectively using various strategies."

Although not purporting to write standards, the National Assessment of Educational Progress (NAEP) has produced several documents describing the nature of and format for writing language arts standards. For example, NAEP's *Description of Writing Achievement Levels—Setting Process and Proposal Achievement Level Definitions* (1993) gives examples of basic, proficient, and advanced performance in writing. In the area of reading, NAEP's project *Assessment and Exercise Specifications: NAEP Reading Consensus Project: 1992 NAEP Reading Assessment* (NAEP, 1990) provides a detailed description of what students should know and be able to do at various levels and details the types of materials students should be able to read.

Fine Arts

Substantial and successful efforts have been made to provide content standards in the fine arts. The U.S. Department of Education funded a grant to the National Endowment for the Arts and the National Endowment for the Humanities to identify standards for the arts. In 1994, the Consortium of National Arts Education Associations published *What Every Young American Should Know and Be Able to Do in the Arts.* This document gives standards for dance, music, theatre, and the visual arts organized into K–4, 5–8, and 9–12 grade clusters.

As the trend toward multidisciplinary programs continues, art is the perfect discipline to blend with all other disciplines. Unfortunately, funds to support the arts continue to dwindle, forcing art teachers to use some of their creative talents to garner support from the local community. As pointed out by Aschbacher (1996, p. 40), involving the arts with other disciplines produces positive changes in student attitudes:

> Infusing art into the curriculum provides students with therapy and motivation. It also gives students important tools for learning from, and communicating with, their world. Most important, it nurtures a sense of confidence that they can succeed in school and in life.

The potential that the arts offer to help students develop their creative talents (Nelson, 1999) has already been discussed (see Chapter 9). Unfortunately, the importance of the arts is not realized by many, especially early twenty-first-century education reformers, and therefore people who believe in the importance of teaching the arts must continue to fight to maintain a place in the curricula for the arts in schools throughout the country.

Foreign Language

The American Council on the Teaching of Foreign Language (ACTFL) and several foreign language associations produced *National Standards for Foreign Language Education* (April, 1995). The document gives standards under five goal areas for students: communicate in languages other than English; gain knowledge and understanding of other cultures; connect with other disciplines and acquire information; develop insight into own language and culture; and participate in multilingual communities.

English Language Arts

The English language arts include speaking, listening, reading, writing, and viewing. In recent years, educators have recognized that students draw meaning from the integration of these arts. Concerned with the narrowness of traditional standardized tests, especially objectively scored tests, Palmer and Pugalee (1999) emphasize the need for new assessment measures in the English language arts curriculum. Some future trends predicted by Palmer and Pugalee include:

1. Continued use of standardized tests

2. Improved efficiency in the use of standardized tests

3. Greater scrutiny of unfair test use

4. Continued exploration of better ways to measure multiple ways students learn

5. Increased use of bibliotherapy (use of reading and writing for therapeutic value)

6. Increased use of story writing, reading, and telling to improve critical, creative, and reflective thinking

7. Increased parental involvement in portfolio assessment

Social Studies

The National Council for the Social Studies (NCSS) has taken responsibility for setting broad social studies curriculum standards and has designated the setting of content standards to the individual disciplines within the social studies. In its 1994 publication *Expectations of Excellence: Curriculum Standards for Social Studies,* NCSS lists 10 thematic strands, including Culture, Time, Continuity and Change, and Individual Development and Identity. For these 10 strands, 241 performance expectations are described.

According to Parker (1996), the use of performance assessment in social studies will continue. Because many of the social studies activities involve discourse (for example, participation in mock trial teams), future social studies teachers will need to be skilled in developing rubrics to evaluate or score discourse. Parker (1996) offers the performance criteria shown in Figure 11.1 for civic discourse activities and then offers the corresponding rubric shown in Figure 11.2 for scoring such discourse.

History

The National Center for History in the Schools (NCHS), through its History Standards Project, has published three sets of standards: National Standards for History K–4, National Standards for United States History, and National Standards for World History. This work grew out of a 1992 document, *Lessons from History: Essential Understandings and Historical Perspectives Students Should*

FIGURE 11.1

Performance Criteria for Civic Discourse.

Substantive

- States and identifies issues
- Uses foundational knowledge
- Stipulates claims or definitions
- Elaborates statements with explanations, reasons, or evidence
- Recognizes values or value conflict
- Argues by analogy

Procedural

Positive

- Acknowledges the statements of others
- Challenges the accuracy, logic, relevance, or clarity of statements
- Summarizes points of agreement and disagreement

Negative

- Makes irrelevant, distracting statements
- Interrupts
- Monopolizes the conversation
- Engages in personal attack

Substantive			
Exemplary (3)	**Adequate (2)**	**Minimal (1)**	**Unacceptable (0)**
Weighs multiple perspectives on a policy issue and considers the public good; or uses relevant knowledge to analyze an issue; or employs a higher-order discussion strategy, such as argument by analogy, stipulation, or resolution of a value conflict.	Demonstrates knowledge of important ideas related to the issue, or explicitly states an issue for the group to consider, or presents more than one viewpoint, or supports a position with reasons or evidence.	Makes statements about the issue that express only personal attitudes, or mentions a potentially important idea but does not pursue it in a way that advances the group's understanding.	Remains silent, or contributes no thoughts of his or her own, or makes only irrelevant comments.

Procedural			
Exemplary (3)	**Adequate (2)**	**Minimal (1)**	**Unacceptable (0)**
Engages in more than one sustained interchange, or summarizes and assesses the progress of the discussion. Makes no comments that inhibit others's contributions, and intervenes only if others do this.	Engages in an extended interchange with at least one other person, or paraphrases important statements as a transition or summary, or asks another person for an explanation or clarification germane to the discussion. Does not inhibit others' contributions.	Invites contributions implicitly or explicitly, or responds constructively to ideas expressed by at least one other person. Tends not to make negative statements.	Makes no comments that facilitate dialogue, or makes statements that are primarily negative in character.

FIGURE 11.2

Scoring Rubric for Assessing Civic Discourse.

Acquire (Crabtree, Nash, Gagnon, & Waugh, 1992). Some history standards documents that are currently in progress include *Building a U.S. History Curriculum* and companion booklets in Western civilization and world history and also a guide for history in the early grades.

Geography

Teachers who enjoy teaching geography are more fortunate than other social studies teachers in that the Geography Education Standards Project has delineated 18 standards articulated for grades K–4, 5–8, and 9–12. The standards are organized into six areas: The World in Spatial Terms, Places and Regions, Physical Systems, Human Systems, the Environment and Society, and the Uses of Geography. These standards are published in *Geography for Life: National Geography Standards* (1994).

Another source for standards in geography is NAEP's *Item Specifications* (1992) for its *Geography Assessment Framework for the 1994 National Assessment of Educational Progress* (1993).

Civics

In 1994, the Center for Civic Education (CCE) published *National Standards for Civics and Government.* This document gives some 70 standards for K–4, 5–8, and 9–12 students. Each content standard lists key concepts essential to meeting the standard. These standards are organized into the following areas: civic life, politics and government, the foundations of the U.S. political system, the values and principles of U.S. constitutional democracy, the relationship of U.S. polities to world affairs, and the role of the citizen.

Butts (1999) stressed the need for national standards to be used in all schools, including private schools. In 1996, the second president's education summit of governors and business leaders pressed for high academic standards, not at the national level but at the state and local levels, and for all teachers, not just teachers of history, social studies, geography, government, and civics.

Health and Physical Education

In 1995, the Joint Health Education Standards Committee published *National Health Education Standards: Achieving Health Literacy,* which identifies seven standards. Each has "performance indicators" for students at grades K–4, 5–8, and 9–11. The document also provides a table that maps the topics covered to related adolescent risk behaviors.

In 1995, the National Association for Sports and Physical Education (NASPE) published *Moving into the Future: National Standards for Physical Education: A Guide to Content and Assessment.* This document identifies seven standards with benchmarks at grades K, 2, 4, 6, 8, 10, and 12. Included are sample benchmarks and assessments.

Chapter Summary

As the twenty-first century unfolds, a time when education is being radically reformed, curriculum planners must be aware of current trends and major changes.

Authentic assessment is playing an important role in shaping curricula; it is designed to measure students' ability to apply what they have learned to real-life problems. Some of the new assessments include performance evaluation, self-assessment, and continuous assessment, all known as alternative assessments.

Because the reform report writers of the 1980s succeeded in convincing society that the education system in this country was inferior, it is not surprising that the issues of tenure and certification processes were viewed as systems that protect inept teachers and promote an inferior education system. This conflict between education critics and teachers is one to be watched as the new century proceeds.

Concern for ethnic diversity and gender equity continue to grow. Concerns about fairness to all citizens are broadening to include attempts to eliminate geographic stereotyping and to promote the fair treatment of senior citizens.

Several new programs have been developed in response to the criticisms of schools. Included among these are magnet schools with unique curricula, charter schools with permission to ignore restrictions that limit other schools, and vouchers that let students and parents choose their schools.

Concern for children with disabilities continues as these students are being placed in classrooms with students who do not have disabilities, a process called "inclusion." Inclusion differs from mainstreaming in that included students are given special help through individually designed education programs. Some programs that will continue into the near future include cooperative learning and concern for multiple intelligences.

The various disciplines are being shaped by national standards and benchmarks, currently being developed. Although the teachers developing these standards disagree on whether the purpose of school is to prepare all students for citizenship or to prepare students to become experts in the disciplines, there is widespread agreement that national standards are needed.

Learning Questions

1. How does teaching interdisciplinary curricula contribute to implementing constructivism?

2. Of the several curriculum programs introduced during the 1980s and 1990s to respond to educational criticisms, which do you believe will improve the system most?

3. What do you believe will be the result of attempts to abolish teacher tenure, and upon what do you base your belief?

4. Do you believe it wise to take funds away from some schools in order to support magnet schools?

5. On what basis would you defend teacher tenure?

6. What is the social injustice that you would most like to see corrected, and how can the schools contribute to this adjustment?

7. What are the major liabilities of having national standards, and how can these be overcome?

Suggested Activities

1. Choose the current curriculum trend that you believe will have the greatest impact on twenty-first-century schools, research this trend, and prepare a written report on it.

2. Curriculum innovations are seldom pure and detached from one another. Select two contemporary trends in education and explain how they interact with each other.

3. Prepare a statement that both challenges and defends the concept of national educational standards.

4. Develop a strategy that teachers can use to affirm ethnic diversity in the classroom and in teachers' broader professional arena.

5. For each of the national standards in your discipline, select those benchmarks that you believe adequately represent and ensure attainment of the standards.

6. Reexamine the trends that this chapter has identified in each discipline and identify those trends that reflect constructivist philosophy.

Works Cited and Suggested Readings

Acquarelli, K., & Mumme, J. (1996). A renaissance in mathematics education reform. *Phi Delta Kappan, 77*(8), 478–484.

American Association for the Advancement of Science (1993). *Benchmarks for science literacy.* New York: Oxford University Press.

Armstrong, D. G., Henson, K. T., & Savage, T. V. (1997). *Teaching today: An Introduction to education,* (5th ed.) Upper Saddle River, NJ: Prentice-Hall.

Aschbacher, P. (1996). A flare for the arts. *Educational Leadership, 53*(8), 40–43.

Associated Press. (August 5, 1996). Report warns against vague school standards. *St. Petersburg Times,* p. 3a.

Baker, E. T., Wang, M. C., & Walberg, H. J. (1995). The effects of inclusion on learning. *Educational Leadership, 52*(4), 33–35.

Ballew, H. (1999). Mathematics in the next century. In B. Day (Ed.), *Teaching and learning in the new millennium.* Indianapolis, IN: Kappa Delta Pi.

Banks, J. (1994). *An Introduction to multicultural education.* Boston: Allyn & Bacon.

Barton, J., & Collins, A. (1993). Portfolios in teacher education. *The Journal of Teacher Education, 44*(3), 200–210.

Bernauer, J. A. (1999). Emerging standards: Empowerment with purpose. *Kappa Delta Pi Record, 35*(2), 68–70, 74.

Block, J. H., Everson, S. T., & Guskey, T. R. (Eds.) (1995). *School improvement programs: A handbook for education leaders.* New York: Scholastic.

Bradley, D. F., & Fisher, J. F. (1995). The inclusion process: Role changes at the middle level. *Middle School Journal, 26*(3), 13–17.

Bracey, G. W. (1999). The impact of immigration. *Phi Delta Kappan, 80*(5), 407–408.

Burns, D. E. (1990). The effects of group training activities on students' initiation of creative investigations. *Gifted Child Quarterly, 34*(1), 31–36.

Buttery, T. J., & Anderson, P. J. (1999). Community, school and parent dynamics: A synthesis of literature and activities. *Teacher Education Quarterly, 26*(4), 111–122.

Buttery, T. J., & Tichenor, M. (1996). Parent involvement and teacher education. *SRATE Journal, 5*(1), 42–50.

Butts, R. F. (1999). The politics of national education standards. In B. Day (Ed.), *Teaching and learning in the new millennium.* Indianapolis, IN: Kappa Delta Pi.

Campbell, D. (2000). Authentic assessment and authentic standards. *Phi Delta Kappan, 81*(5), 405–407.

Carnevale, A. P., Gainer, L. J., & Meltzer, A. S. (1990). *Workplace basics: The essential skills employers want.* San Francisco: Jossey-Bass.

Carnine, D., Grossen, B., & Silbert, J. (1995). Direct instruction to accelerate cognitive growth. In J. H. Block, S. T. Everson, & T. R. Guskey (Eds.), *School improvement programs: A handbook for educational leaders.* New York: Scholastic.

Cheney, C. D. (1989). The systematic adaption of instructional materials and techniques for problem learners. *Academic Theory, 25*(1), 25–30

Claus, J. (1999). You can't avoid the politics: Lessons for teacher education from a case study of teacher-initiated tracking reform. *Journal of Teacher Education, 50*(1), 5–16.

Cohen, D. (1995). What standards for national standards? *Phi Delta Kappan, 76*(10), 751–757.

Consortium of National Arts Education Associations (1994). *National standards for arts education: What every young American should know and be able to do in the arts.* Reston, VA: Music Educators National Conference.

Covington, M. V. (1996, November). The myth of intensification: Section 3, Higher Standards. *Educational Researcher,* 25(8), 24–27.

Crabtree, C., Nash, G., Gagnon, P., & Waugh, S. (Eds.) (1992). *Lessons from history: Essential understandings and historical perspectives students should acquire.* Los Angeles: National Center for History in the Schools Education Daily.

Darling-Hammond, L., & Falk, B. (1997). Using standards and assessment to support student learning. *Phi Delta Kappan, 79*(3), 190–199.

Day, B. (1999). Participatory education: A proactive approach to U.S. education in the 21st century. In B. Day (Ed.), *Teaching and learning in the new millennium.* Indianapolis, IN: Kappa Delta Pi.

Dixon, C., & Horn, H. (1995). Writing across the curriculum. In J. H. Block, S. T. Everson, & T. R. Guskey (Eds.), *School improvement programs: A handbook for educational leaders.* New York: Scholastic.

Eggleston, L., Jr. (1995). Why no charter schools have been formed in some states that have passed legislation. In T. J. Mauhs-Pugh (Ed.), Charter schools 1995: A survey and analysis of the laws and practices of the states. *Education Policy Analysis Archives, 3*(12).

Elam, S. M., Rose, L. C., & Gallup, A. M. (1994). The 26th annual Phi Delta Kappa/Gallup poll of the public's attitudes toward the public schools. *Phi Delta Kappan, 76*(1), 41–56.

Elkind, D. (1999). Educating young children in mathematics, science, and technology. In B. Day (Ed.), *Teaching in the new millennium.* Indianapolis, IN: Kappa Delta Pi.

Everson, S. T. (1995). Selecting school improvement programs. In J. H. Block, S. T. Everson, & T. R. Guskey (Eds.), *School improvement programs: A handbook for educational leaders.* New York: Scholastic.

Feldheusen, J. F. (1989). Synthesis of research on gifted youth. *Educational Leadership, 46*(6), 6–11.

Fullan, M. (1998). Breaking the bonds of dependency. *Educational Leadership, 55*(7), 8.

Gallager, C. (2000). A seat at the table: Teachers reclaiming assessment through rethinking accountability. *Phi Delta Kappan, 81*(7), 502–507.

Gardner, H. (1993). Multiple intelligences: The theory in practice. New York: Basic Books.

Gardner, H., & Boix-Mansilla, V. (1994). Teaching understanding: Within and across the disciplines. *Educational Leadership, 51*(5), 14–18.

Geography Education Standards Project. (1994). *Geography for life: National geography standards.* Washington, DC: National Geographic Research and Exploration.

Goldberger, S., & Kazis, R. (1996). Revitalizing high schools: What the school-to-career movement can contribute. *Phi Delta Kappan, 77*(8), 547–554.

Goodlad, T. I. (1997). *In praise of education.* San Francisco: Jossey-Bass.

Grubb, W. N. (1996). The new vocationalism: What it is, what it could be. *Phi Delta Kappan, 77*(8), 535–546.

Guskey, T. R. (1995). Integrating school improvement programs. In J. H. Block, S. T. Everson, & T. R. Guskey (Eds.), *School improvement programs: A handbook for educational leaders.* New York: Scholastic.

Gutherie, L. F., & Richardson, S. (1995). Turned on language arts: Computer literacy in the primary grades. *Educational Leadership, 53*(2), 14–17.

Hargrove, T. Y. (1999). Assessment: Past practices, future expectations. In B. Day (Ed.), *Teaching and learning in the new millennium.* Indianapolis, IN: Kappa Delta Pi.

Hartoonian, M., & Van Scotter, R. (1996). School-to-work: A model for learning a living. *Phi Delta Kappan, 77*(8), 555–560.

Henson, K. T. (1996). *Methods and strategies for teaching in secondary and middle schools* (3rd ed.). New York: Longman.

Henson, K. T., & Eller, B. F. (1999). *Educational psychology for effective teaching.* Belmont, CA: Wadsworth.

Hill, P. T. (1996). The educational consequences of choice. *Phi Delta Kappan, 77*(10), 671–675.

Hoover, J. J. (1990, March). Curriculum adaptation: A five step process for classroom implementation. *Academic Therapy, 25*(4), 407–416.

Hopkins, B. J., & Wendel, F. C. (1997). *Creating school-community business partnerships.* Bloomington, IN: Phi Delta Kappa Educational Foundation.

Houston, P. D. (1994). Making watches or making music. *Phi Delta Kappan, 76*(2), 133–135.

Huntley, M. A. (1999). Theoretical and empirical investigations of integrated mathematics and science education in the middle grades with implications for teacher education. *Journal of Teacher Education, 50*(1), 57–67.

Hyman, I. A., & Snook, P. A. (2000). Dangerous schools and what you can do about them. *Phi Delta Kappan, 81*(7), 489–501.

Jalongo, M. R., & Isenberg, J. P. (1995). *Teachers' stories.* San Francisco: Jossey-Bass.

Jennings, J. (1995). School reform based on what is taught and learned. *Phi Delta Kappan, 76*(10), 765–769.

Johnson, D. W., & Johnson, R. (1989–1990). Social skills for successful group work. *Educational Leadership, 47*(4), 29–33.

Johnson-Gentile, K., & Gentile, J. R. (1996). Integrating music into the elementary school. *Kappa Delta Pi Record, 32*(2), 66–68.

Keller, B. M. (1995). Accelerated schools: Hands-on learning in a unified community. *Educational Leadership, 52*(5), 10–13.

Kendall, J. S., & Marzano, R. J. (1995). *The systematic identification and articulation of content standards and benchmarks: Update,* March 1995, Aurora, CO: Mid-continent Regional Educational Laboratory.

Kendall, J. S., & Marzano, R. J. (1996). *Content knowledge: A compendium of standards and benchmarks for K–12 education.* Aurora, CO: Mid-continent Regional Educational Laboratory.

Kenney, D. J., & Watson, T. S. (1996). Reducing fear in the schools: Managing conflict through problem solving. *Education and Urban Society, 28*(4), 436–455.

Koba, S. B. (1996). Narrowing the achievement gap in science. *Educational Leadership, 53*(8), 14–17.

Lindblad, A. H., Jr. (1994). You can avoid the traps of cooperative learning. *The Clearing House, 67*(5), 291–293.

Lopez, R. E. (1996). Trends in science. *Educational Leadership, 52*(8), 78–79.

Macedo, D. (1995). English only: The tongue-tying of America. In T. J. Noll (Ed.), *Taking sides: Clashing views on controversial educational issues* (8th ed.). Guilford, CT: Dushkin, pp. 249–258.

Manning, M. L., & Lucking, R. (1991, January–February). The what, why, and how of cooperative learning. *The Clearing House, 64*(3), 152–156.

Manno, B. V., Finn, C. E., Bierlein, L. A., & Vanourek, G. (1998). How charter schools are different. *Phi Delta Kappan, 79*(7), 489–498.

Marzano, R. J., & Kendall, J. S. (1995). The McREL database: A tool for constructing local standards. *Educational Leadership, 52*(6), 42–47.

Marzano, R. J., & Kendall, J. S. (1996). *A comprehensive guide to designing standards-based districts, schools, and classrooms.* Aurora, CO: McReel.

Mauhs-Pugh, T. J. (Ed.). (1995). Charter schools 1995. A survey and analysis of the laws and practices of the states. *Education Policy Analysis Archives, 3*(12).

McCarthy, M. M. (2000). What is the verdict on school vouchers? *Phi Delta Kappan, 81*(5), 371–377.

Minnesota Charter Schools Evaluation, *Interim Report.* (December 1996). Minneapolis: Center for Applied Research and Educational Improvement, University of Minnesota.

Moffett, J. (1994). On to the past: Wrong-headed school reform. *Phi Delta Kappan, 75*(8), 584–590.

Morisund, D. (1999). Digital technology: Transforming schools and improving learning. In B. Day (Ed.), *Teaching and learning in the millennium.* Indianapolis: Kappa Delta Pi.

Nathan, J. (1998). Heat and light in the charter school movement. *Phi Delta Kappan, 79*(7), 499–505.

National Assessment of Education Progress Science Consensus Project. (1993). *Science assessment and exercise specifications for the 1994 national assessment of educational progress.* Washington, DC: National Assessment Governing Board.

National Commission on Excellence in Education. (1983). *A nation at risk: The imperatives for educational reform.* Washington, DC: U.S. Department of Education.

National Committee on Science Education Standards and Assessment. (1994, November). *National science education standards (draft).* Washington, DC: National Academy Press.

National Council of Teachers of Mathematics. (1989). *Curriculum and Evaluation Standards for School Mathematics.* Reston, VA: Author.

National Education Standards and Improvement Council. (1993). *Promises to keep: Creating high standards for American students.* Report on the review of education standards from the Goals 3 and 4 Technical Planning Group to the National Education Goals Panel. Washington, DC: National Goals Panel.

National History Standards Project. (1993, March). *Progress report and sample standards.* Los Angeles; National Center for History.

National Science Teachers Association. (1993). *Scope, sequence, and coordination of secondary school science. Vol. 1. The content core: A guide for curriculum designers.* Washington, DC: Author.

Nelson, W. W. (1999). The emperor redux. *Phi Delta Kappan, 80*(5), 387–392.

Noddings, N. (1997). Thinking about standards. *Phi Delta Kappan, 79*(3), 184–189.

Ostrom, C. (1997). *Graduation standards facilitator's manual.* St. Paul, MN: Minnesota Department of Children, Families, and Learning.

Palmer, W. S., & Pugalee, D. K. (1999). Assessment and the English language arts: Present and future perspectives. In B. Day (Ed.), *Teaching and learning in the new millennium.* Indianapolis, IN: Kappa Delta Pi.

Parker, W. C. (1996). Trends in social studies. *Educational Leadership 52*(8), 84–85.

Parette, II. P., Hourcade, H. P., & Vanbiervliet, A. (1993). Selection of appropriate technology for children with disabilities. *Teaching Exceptional Children, 4,* 18–22.

Perrone, V. (1994). How to engage students in learning. *Educational Leadership, 51*(5), 11–13.

Pitton, D. E. (1999). The naked truth isn't very revealing. In Interview with Howard Hall, director of curriculum, Minnesota District 191, June 5. *Phi Delta Kappan, 80*(5), 383–386.

Pollina, A. (1995). Gender balance: Lessons from girls in science and mathematics. *Educational Leadership, 53*(1), 30–33.

Pressley, M., Brown, R., Van Meter, P., & Shuder, T. (1996). Trends in reading. *Educational Leadership, 52*(8), 84–85.

Rael, E. J. (1995). A summary of arguments for and against charter schools. In T. J. Mauhs-Pugh (Ed.), Charter schools 1995: A survey and analysis of the laws and practices of the states. *Education Policy Analysis Archives, 3*(86).

Raphael, J., & Greenberg, R. (1995). Image processing: A state-of-the-art way to learn science. *Educational Leadership, 53*(2), 34–37.

Rose, L. C., & Gallup, A. M. (1998). The 30th annual Phi Delta Kappa/Gallup poll of the public's attitudes toward the public schools. *Phi Delta Kappan, 80*(1), 41–56.

Sautter, R. C. (1995, January). Standing up to violence. *Phi Delta Kappan, 76*(5), K1–K12.

Savage, T. V., & Armstrong, D. G. (1996). *Effective teaching in elementary social studies* (3rd ed.). New York: Macmillan.

Schnalberg, L. (1995, August). Board relaxes bilingual-ed. policy in California. *Education Week*, p. 1.

Schifter, D. (1996). A constructivist perspective on teaching and learning mathematics. *Phi Delta Kappan, 77*(7), 492–499.

Smelter, R. W., Rasch, B. W., & Yudewitz, G. J. (1994). Thinking of inclusion for all special needs students? Better think again. *Phi Delta Kappan, 76*(1), 35–38.

Sinis, P., & Roda, K. (1995). California. In T. J. Mauhs-Pugh, (Ed.), Charter schools 1995: A survey and analysis of the laws and practices of the states. *Education Policy Analysis Archives, 3*(12).

Skiba, R., & Peterson, R. (1999). The dark side of zero tolerance: Can punishment lead to safe schools? *Phi Delta Kappa, 80*(5), 372–372 + 381–382.

Spady, W. G. (1994). Allowing for thinking styles. *Educational Leadership, 52*(3), 36–40.

Sternberg, R. (1990). *Metaphors of mind: Conceptions of the nature of intelligence.* New York: Cambridge University Press.

Stiggins, R. J. (1995). Assessment as a school improvement innovation. In J. H. Block, S. T. Everson, & T. R. Guskey (Eds.), *School improvement programs: A handbook for educational leaders.* New York: Scholastic.

Stiggins, R. J., & Conklin, N. F. (1992). *In teachers' hands: Investigating the practice of classroom assessment.* Albany: SUNY Press.

Sweeny, B. (1999). Content standards: Gate or bridge? *Kappa Delta Pi Record, 35*(2), 64–67.

Wagner, T. (1998). Change as collaborative inquiry: A "constructivist" methodology for reinventing schools. *Phi Delta Kappan, 79*(7), 512–517.

Wiggins, G. (1989). A true test: Toward more authentic and equitable measurement. *Phi Delta Kappan, 70*(9), 703–713.

Williams, J., & Reynolds, T. D. (1993). Courting controversy: How to build interdisciplinary units. *Educational Leadership, 50*(7), 13–15.

Williams, P., Alley, R., & Henson, K. T. (1999). *Managing secondary classrooms.* Boston: Allyn & Bacon.

Williams, T. (1998). *Home schooling: An overview.* Online at http:11www.ohioline.ag.ohio_state.edu.

Wise, V. L., Spiegel, A. N., & Bruning, R. H. (1999). Using teacher reflective practice to evaluate professional development in mathematics and science. *Journal of Teacher Education, 50*(1), 42–49.

Witte, J. F., & Thorn, C. A. (1994, December). *Fourth-year report: Milwaukee Parental Choice Program.* Madison, WI: University of Wisconsin, Department of Political Science and the Robert La Follette Institute of Public Affairs.

Wohlstetter, P. (2000). A different approach to systematic reform: Network structures in Los Angeles. *Phi Delta Kappan, 81*(7), 508–515.

Woolfolk, A. (1995). *Educational psychology* (6th ed.). Boston: Allyn & Bacon.

Preface to Glossary

This book has emphasized the perspective of the constructivists, which holds that no knowledge is permanent. As an experienced educator, you may already have a basic level of understanding of all of these terms, however, as your understanding grows, your vocabulary must be revised accordingly, therefore, you may wish to compare and contrast your definitions with those offered here, paying particular attention to the ways in which your definitions of many of these terms are changing.

abstraction   Something that is not concrete; a theoretical construct.

achievement test   Standardized test designed to measure how much has been learned about a particular subject.

action research   Classroom-based or school-based research aimed at improving educational practices. Usually teacher conducted.

affective domain   The part of human learning that involves changes in interests, attitudes, and values.

aims, educational   Aspirations so broad that they can never be fully achieved.

algorithm   Step-by-step procedure for solving problems.

alignment, curriculum   Matching learning activities with desired outcomes, or matching what is taught to what is tested.

alternative assessment   Any of many types of assessment that replace traditional testing.

alternative curriculum   A curriculum that offers students choices from a menu of courses.

analysis-level objective   Requires students to work with concepts and principles.

armchair case   A contrived case study, as opposed to real experiences.

arena, curriculum   Location and level at which curriculum decisions are made.

articulation   The flow (absence of disruptions) of a curriculum either vertically or horizontally.

assigned time   Time allocated to study a topic.

at-risk students   Students whose probability of dropping out of school is above average.

authentic tests   Assessment that requires students to apply new knowledge to solve lifelike problems.

axiology   The philosophical structure concerned with pursuing the study of values and ethics.

axiom   Universally accepted truth.

balanced curriculum   Equal emphasis on disciplines; for example the arts and sciences, or vocational courses and college preparatory courses.

Boston English Classical School   The first public high school in America, established in 1821.

broad-fields curriculum   A curriculum designed to replace the subject-centered curriculum and lead to understanding the broad content generalizations that spread among two or more subjects.

Cardinal Principles of Secondary Education, Seven   The National Education Association's aims for elementary and secondary schools.

Carnegie unit   120 clock hours of instruction.

case study   Method of using actual or contrived classroom experiences to connect theory and practice.

catechisms   Religious rhymes used extensively in Colonial times to teach morality.

charter schools   Schools given special permission to experiment with unique curricula.

CIPP model   A curriculum evaluation model that focuses on the content, input, process, and product.

coercive power   Power based on the ability to punish or give rewards.

cognitive domain   The part of human learning that involves changes in intellectual skills, such as assimilation of information.

cognitive objectives   Instructional objectives that stress knowledge and intellectual abilities and skills.

coherence, curriculum   The fitting together or meshing of curriculum components.

collaborative research   Professors and teachers working together as equal action research partners.

common sense approach   The unscientific practice of drawing conclusions based only on personal experience.

components, curriculum   Any of the following: aims, goals, objectives, philosophy statement, student activities, teacher activities, content, and tests.

comprehensive-level objective   Requires students to translate, interpret, or predict.

comprehensive schools   Large secondary schools with diversified curricula.

concepts   Those major understandings within each discipline characterized by recurring patterns such as a common physical characteristic or common utility.

concrete operations level of development   Stage in Piaget's developmental learning theories that precedes the ability to think abstractly; roughly includes the elementary school years. Ages seven to eleven.

connectionism   A learning theory which says that the most effective approach to learning and therefore to curriculum development is to connect newly acquired information to prior understandings.

connectionists psychologists   Psychologists who perceive learning occurring in a step-by-step fashion.

consortium, educational   A group of schools that join together, usually led by a university or other organization. By uniting their resources, these schools can afford programs that, by themselves, none of the schools could afford.

content, curriculum   Information that has been selected for inclusion in the curriculum.

constructivism   A philosophy of curriculum as connected concepts.

constructivists   Psychologists who believe that new information must be related to previously acquired understanding (knowledge) before it can become meaningful.

continuity, curriculum   The quality of a curriculum that links parts together in a sequence for easier learning. Vertical articulation.

cooperative learning   Students working in groups to learn. The success of each member depends on the success of all members.

core curriculum   A curriculum design that has a common core of content and/or activities required of all students and other content and activities that are electives.

criterion-referenced evaluation   Evaluation that measures success by the attainment of established levels of performance. Individual success is based wholly on performance of the individual without regard to the performance of others.

criterion-referenced test   Measure of a student's performance with reference to specified criteria or to that individual's previous level of performance.

cultural discontinuity   Problems that minority students face caused by conflicting expectations of family and school.

culture   The capacity for constantly expanding the range and accuracy of one's perception of meanings. An attempt to prepare human beings to continuously add to the meaning of their experiences.

culture, school   A school's somewhat permanent climate or ethos. The way things are done at a particular school.

curriculum   The total experiences planned for a school or students.

curriculum alignment   Matching learning activities with desired outcomes, or matching what is taught to what is tested.

curriculum compacting   Strengthening parts of the curriculum for gifted students.

curriculum guide   A written statement of objectives, content, and activities to be used with a particular subject at specified grade levels; usually produced by state departments of education or local education agencies.

Dalton plan   An early twentieth-century school that had a highly individualized curriculum.

dame schools   Private homes where the colonial mother taught her children and her neighbors' children. Also called *kitchen schools*.

deductive logic   Reasoning that starts with the general and moves to the specific.

developmental hierarchy   Specified levels of development of youths.

dilectic logic   Reasoning that begins with a thesis, moves to an antitheses, and then moves to synthesis.

dissatisfier   A factor that is a prerequisite to the operation of motivators but which itself does not motivate.

eclecticism   Incorporating into a learning-teaching unit ideas from several learning theories.

education   The process through which individuals learn to cope with life.

Education for All Handicapped Children Act   A 1977 legislative act requiring all states to provide special services for handicapped students at public expense and under supervision and direction.

education reform   An organized attempt to substantially improve the schools in a district, state, or nation.

educational taxonomy   An hierarchical system for classifying educational objectives.

effective schools   Those schools whose students are high academic achievers.

effective teaching   Teaching that results in high learner achievement.

Eight-year study   A study from 1933 to 1941 conducted by Harvard University to compare the success of child-centered education with the success of traditional education.

electronic bulletin board   Tool that enables individuals to use the computer to read computer-transferred group messages.

Emile   Book written by Jean Jacques Rousseau on child rearing the natural way.

empowerment, teacher   Giving teachers a broader role in the operation of the school.

ends-means planning   Beginning curriculum planning by determining the desired outcomes. Also called the Tylerian curriculum model.

engaged time   Time actually spent in the classroom learning a topic.

epistemology   That structure which pursues the study of truth.

essentialism   That structure which focuses on the knowledge that is needed for a successful adult life.

evaluation   Making measurements plus providing value judgments.

evaluation-level objective   The highest-level cognitive objective. Requires students to define criteria and then assess how well they were met.

existentialism   That structure that focuses on the present, promoting the belief that life is only what you make of it and you must live for the moment.

expert power   Power that derives from the possession of specialized skills or knowledge.

faculty psychology   A learning theory that considers the brain as a muscle whose growth requires rigorous and boring exercise.

formal operations level of development   Piaget's highest level of thinking, involving abstractions. Usually from age 11 to age 16.

formative evaluation   Evaluation that occurs before or during instruction and whose sole purpose is to promote learning by improving study skills, instructional strategies, or the curriculum.

Franklin Academy   A pragmatic school that by the end of the Revolutionary War replaced the Boston Latin Grammar School as the most important secondary school in America.

Gary plan   Early twentieth-century experimental school that operated as a miniature community.

gender equity   Treating females and males fairly, having similar expectations for both.

gestalt psychology   A learning theory that says we learn by seeing new patterns or insights.

goal displacement   Inadvertently letting the attainment of the goal replace the purpose for having the goal.

goals, educational   Desired learning outcomes stated for a group of students and requiring from several weeks to several years to attain.

Goals for 2000   A list of goals set by the president and governors in 1990 to be reached by all American schools by the year 2000.

grading   The act of using a combination of types of student performance to indicate a student's overall level of success.

grassroots curriculum change   Change that is introduced and conducted at schools.

heterogeneous grouping   Grouping high-ability students with low-ability students.

hidden curriculum   The messages given by schools and teachers via the school climate and the teachers' behavior.

home schooling   When a parent assumes responsibility for teaching his or her children at home.

homogeneous grouping   Grouping students with similar abilities.

hornbook   A board with Biblical rhymes (catechisms) and other simple curriculum content, covered by a thin, transparent material, used in the dame schools.

human development   The idea that schools should improve society by improving individual learners.

idealism   A belief that reality lies in ideas and that there are universal truths and values.

inclusion Placing challenged students in classrooms with their nonchallenged peers and giving them special instructional support.

individualized guided education   An individualized education program developed in Wisconsin.

individualized instruction   Instruction designed to meet the needs of all students.

inductive logic   Reasoning that moves from the specific to the general.

information   Rather random facts that have not been connected to the learner's prior knowledge.

in-service teachers   Teachers who have graduated and are teaching full time.

insight   Learning that occurs when an individual perceives new relationships.

integration of disciplines   Uniting two or more disciplines through the use of conceptual themes.

Interactive distance learning   Computer-based teaching that enables students to interact with their own teachers and other teachers.

interactive video discs   Video discs that let members of the audience interact with each other.

interclass ability grouping   Matching the performance of one class against another class of similar ability.

intraclass ability grouping   Grouping students of similar ability within a class.

intrinsic motivator   Incentive that comes from within or from one's own values.

Kalamazoo Case   A law passed in 1874 giving state legislatures the right to levy taxes to support schools.

kitchen school   See *dame school.*

knowledge   Meaningful information that the learner has related to prior understanding.

knowledge base   The research-derived knowledge and other knowledge that supports the practice of a profession.

knowledge-level objectives   Lowest level of cognitive objectives, requiring only memorization.

Latin Grammar School   Forerunner of modern high schools that prepared young men for entrance to Harvard College.

learning   More or less permanent change in behavior as a result of experiences.

learning activities   Ways to involve students in the curriculum to help them relate newly acquired information to prior knowledge.

learning for mastery (LFM)   A particular type of teacher-paced, group-based mastery learning program.

learning experiences   Student activities that are made meaningful by tying these activities to prior experiences.

learning cycle theory   A learning approach that involves exploration, concept introduction, and application.

learning unit   A curriculum plan that usually covers 1 or 2 weeks of elementary study or 6 to 18 weeks of middle school or high school program.

legitimate power   Organizationally sanctioned ability to influence others.

long-range planning   Curriculum planning that covers several days, weeks, or years.

magnet school   School with special curricula not available in other local schools. Attended part of each school week by students from neighboring schools.

mastery learning   Technique of instruction whereby pupils are given multiple opportunities to learn using criterion-based objectives, flexible time, remediation, and instruction that matches the learners' styles.

measurement   The nonqualitative part of evaluation.

metanalysis An organized process for analyzing many studies on a common topic.

metaphysical explanation A proposition that cannot be tested.

metaphysics The study of existence; the study of concepts.

metacognition Knowledge of how one's mind works; thinking about ways to improve one's own ability to think and learn. The study of one's own learning processes.

metaphysics The philosophical structure that studies the supernatural. Also called ontology.

mission statement A statement of an institution's purpose.

model A written or drawn description used to improve the understanding of its subject.

motivation Arousal, selection, direction, and continuation of behavior.

multicultural perspective Commitment to helping students learn to appreciate and work with members of other cultures.

multidisciplinary education Education directed at themes that cover two or more disciplines.

multiple intelligences, theory of The idea that individuals have more than one type of intelligence.

multipurpose activity An activity that serves to attain two or more objectives.

NCATE National Council for the Accreditation of Teacher Education.

national standards Minimal educational standards set at the national level for all schools.

nature of knowledge A study of how information is related to form knowledge.

naysayers A group of workers who oppose all changes, especially those that would require them to retrain to improve their job performance.

need hierarchy model Abraham Maslow's model of human motivation; it assumes that people are primarily motivated by a desire to satisfy specific needs, which are arranged in a hierarchy.

needs assessment A questionnaire given to a school or school district to determine its educational needs. For example, a test to determine faculty development needs.

nongraded primary curriculum The multiage grouping of students in the same classroom. Usually ages 5 to 8.

norm-referenced grading A student's performance is evaluated by comparing it to the performance of others.

normal learning curve A symmetrical, bell-shaped curve that shows the distributions of learners' abilities.

Norman Rockwell family Two siblings with a working father and a stay-at-home mother, which is the makeup of many scenes painted by the American artist Norman Rockwell.

Northwest Ordinance of 1787 A law requiring that one section (one-sixteenth) of every township be set aside to be used to support public schools.

objectives, educational   Desired learning outcomes stated for a single student, specifying a minimum acceptable level of behavior and the conditions under which the behavior must be demonstrated. Also called behavioral objectives, performance objectives, instructional objectives, or learning objectives.

official curriculum   A school's planned curriculum.

Old Deluder Satan Act   A Massachusetts Colony law passed in 1647 which required every town of 50 or more families to hire a teacher and every town of 100 or more households to build a school.

ontology   The philosophical structure which studies the supernatural. Also called metaphysics.

open education   Curriculum that stresses student activity and student freedom, multiage grouping, self-selection, and individualized teaching. Also called *open classroom.*

operational objective   Objective written with active verb and specified criteria; also called behavioral objective and performance objective because it requires the student to perform specific behaviors.

outcomes-based education   Curriculum design that begins by determining or identifying desired learning outcomes.

perennialism   The structure that focuses on the knowledge that is retained through the years.

perfect arena for curriculum planning   The school.

performance assessment   Assessment that requires students to apply information, as opposed to testing only for recall of information.

performance-based assessment   The practice of basing grades on measured performance.

performance objective   Objective that requires students to perform at specific levels under specified conditions; also called behavioral objective or instructional objective.

pertinent concepts   Those concepts whose understanding is a prerequisite to understanding the discipline being studied.

philosophy   The love, study, and pursuit of wisdom.

portfolio, learners'   A diversified combination of samples of a student's quantitative and qualitative work.

pragmatism   The structure that emphasizes the practical.

praxis theory   Curriculum theory that brings together theory and practice.

preoperations stage of development   That state in Piaget's learning theory when children attend to or focus on only one characteristic. The period when language development is the most rapid. Two to seven years.

pressure groups   Any of a wide variety of groups of people who unite to influence the curriculum.

privatization movement   The practice of a school district contracting with a private business or industry to educate its students.

professionalism   Putting the client's welfare first.

progress reports   Ongoing assessment to promote learning.

progressive education era   From the early 1920s to the early 1940s when the curriculum was student-centered and activities-centered.

psychomotor domain   The part of human learning that involves motor skills.

Public Law 94-142   See the *Education for All Handicapped Children Act.*

punishment power   The ability to punish others who fail to comply with your requests.

Quincy system   The nation's first school district to use a child-centered curriculum.

rationale, curriculum   A statement that uses students' values to convince them of the worth of a topic of study.

readiness   The stage of development required to perform mental and physical operations.

reading across the curriculum   Giving multidisciplinary reading assignments to enhance learning.

realism   The belief that people should pursue truth through using the scientific method.

reconstructionism   That philosophical structure which is dedicated to using education to rid society of its ills.

referent power   The ability to influence others because they identify with you or want to be like you.

research-based teaching   Using methods that have been validated by research.

restructuring   Changing a school's entire program and procedure, as opposed to changing only one part of the curriculum.

reward power   The ability to reward others when they do what you want them to.

safe schools   Schools that have taken formal, proactive measures to reduce the probability of violence.

satisfier   Motivator.

science   An organized way to study the world or any part of it.

scientism   Placing faith in science to do everything.

scientific method   A systematic approach to pursue truth through using the five senses.

scope, curriculum   The breadth of a curriculum.

sensorimotor stage of development   Piaget's earliest stage of development. Birth to age two.

sequence, curriculum   The order in which content and activities in a curriculum are arranged.

self-assessment   Requiring students to maintain an ongoing record of their academic progress.

spiral curriculum A curriculum that introduces the same topic at different levels because students were not able to deal with some of the abstractions at a lower level (younger age).

site-based decision making The practice of using a council of teachers, administrators, and parents to run the school.

social contract A written agreement signed by teacher and student to improve student behavior.

special students Students who are either unusually challenged or who are unusually gifted.

Sputnik World's first satellite, launched by U.S.S.R. in 1957.

staff development workshops Workshops for in-service educators.

stanine scores Reporting scores in categories of one-ninth of the normal curve.

stimulus-response psychology A learning theory that views all behavior as responses to stimuli.

structure of disciplines learning theory A learning theory that emphasizes the need to understand the unique structure of the discipline being studied.

styles, learning Conditions that favor learning for an individual student.

subject-centered curricula Curricula consisting of specific courses usually delivered by using lectures and textbooks.

summative Evaluation Evaluation that occurs following instruction and is used to determine grades and promotion.

Summerhill A famous English school that practices almost complete permissiveness.

synthesis-level objectives Cognitive objectives that require students to take parts of a whole and reassemble them to form an new whole.

Taba's inverted model A curriculum model that begins with teachers who design learning units; considered opposite or inverted from traditional top-down models.

table of specifications Chart to ensure coverage of varying levels of desired objectives, knowledge, and skills.

tabula rasa Literally "blank slate." The idea that everyone is born with a blank mind and the only way to fill it is through direct experience.

Taylorism Applying efficiency engineering theory to education.

teacher empowerment An attempt, associated with education reform, to increase teachers' involvement in decisions that affect the entire school.

testing Measuring student performance or measuring the degree to which students meet a curriculum's objectives.

transformation, school Changing the very basic nature of schools.

transesence Preadolescent development stage.

Trump Plan A curriculum design by Lloyd Trump which requires all students to use a combination of large group instruction, small group instruction, and independent study.

two-factor motivation theory   Herzberg's theory that there is a set of factors that when absent can block performance but when present do not motivate performance.

Tyler's ends-means model   A curriculum model that begins by identifying desired learning outcomes and designing the curriculum accordingly.

values clarification   Techniques of humanistic education designed to help students understand the basis of their beliefs and to teach them to choose, prize, and act on their beliefs.

values education   The purposeful teaching of certain attitudes.

vouchers   Government-issued notes that parents can use to pay all or part of the tuition for their children at a private or church-related school.

Winnetka plan   An early twentieth-century curriculum planning model that involved teachers.

wisdom   The knowledge of things beautiful, first, divine, pure, and eternal.

Woods Hole Conference   A meeting of 35 scientists, educators, and business leaders in 1959 to redesign the curricula in American schools.

world of work   Purposefully designing curricula to prepare students to work.

writing across the curriculum   Giving multidisciplinary writing assignments to enhance learning in other disciplines.

Chapter 1

Excerpt from Gough: From "A view from the outside" by P. B. Gough (1993) in *Kappan* 74, p. 669. Reprinted by permission of Phi Delta Kappa International.

Exerpt from Hodgkinson: From "Reform vs. reality" by H. Hodgkinson (1990) *Kappan* 73(1), pp. 9–16. Reprinted by permission of Phi Delta Kappa International.

Excerpt from Oliva (interpretations of curriculum): From *Developing the Curriculum*, 3/e by Peter F. Oliva. Copyright 1992 by Peter F. Oliva. Reprinted by permission of Addison-Wesley Educational Publishers, Inc.

Chapter 2

Excerpt from Wirth: From "Educational work: the choice we face" by A. C. Wirth (1993), *Kappan* 74(5), pp. 361–366. Reprinted by permission of Phi Delta Kappa International.

Box 2.1, Social contract: From *Kappa Delta Pi Record* ©1994. Reprinted by permission of Kappa Delta Pi International Honor Society in Education.

Chapter 4

Figure 4.3, Oliva's 1976 model of curriculum development, and Figure 4.4, Oliva's 1992 model for curriculum development: From *Developing the Curriculum*, 3/e by Peter F. Oliva. Copyright 1992 by Peter F. Oliva. Reprinted by permission of Addison-Wesley Educational Publishers, Inc.

Figure 4.5, The Saylor-Alexander curriculum model: From *Curriculum Planning for Modern Schools* by J. G. Saylor & W. M. Alexander, 1966.

Figure 4.6, Macdonald's curriculum model: From James B. Macdonald & Robert R. Leepers (Eds.), *Theories of Instruction*, Alexandria, VA, Association for Supervision and Curriculum Development.

Figure 4.7, The Zais model of the curriculum and its foundations: From *Curriculum Principles and Foundations* by Robert S. Zais. Copyright 1976 by Thomas Y. Crowell Company, Inc. Reprinted by permission of Addison-Wesley Educational Publishers, Inc.

Figures 4.11–4.27: Reprinted by permission of Rex W. Bolinger/Angola High School, Angola IN.

Table 4.1, Percentage of Individuals in Piagetian Stages: From *Middle School Journal*, 22(2), p. 49. Used with permission from National Middle School Association.

Table 4.3, Sample Rationale Statement: Elementary and Secondary Education Act of 1965. Terre Haute, IN, Vigo County School System, Indiana State University.

Short quotes from Ozmon, H. O. & Craver, S. M.: From *Philosophical Foundations of Education* 2/e by Ozmon/Craver, ©1990. Reprinted by permission of Prentice-Hall, Inc., Upper Saddle River, NJ.

Chapter 5

Excerpt (Oliva, six characteristics of core curricula): From *Developing the Curriculum*, 3/e by Peter F. Oliva. Reprinted by permission of Addison-Wesley Educational Publishers, Inc.

Chapter 8

Figure 8.3, A strategy for helping teachers become researchers in the classroom (chart): From Cardelle-Elawar, M. (1993) "The teacher as researcher in the classroom" in *Action in Teacher Education*, pp. 15, 17, 49–57.

Excerpt from Kowalski and Reitzug: From *Contemporary School Administration and Introduction* by Theodore J.

Kowalski and Ulrich C. Reitzug. Copyright 1993 by Longman. Reprinted by permission of Addison-Wesley Educational Publishers, Inc.

Chapter 9

Figure 9.3, The CIPP model: From Blaine R. Worthern and James Sanders, *Educational Evaluation and Decision Making*, ©1971. Reprinted by permission of Phi Delta Kappa International.

Figure 9.4, University mission statement: Reprinted by permission of Eastern Kentucky University.

Box 9.3, A Sample Portfolio, Box 9.4, An Oral History Project for Ninth-Graders, and Box 9.5, The Writing Portfolio: From "Teaching to the authentic test" by G. Wiggins in *Educational Leadership* 46(7), April 1989, pp. 44–47.

Excerpt (special need for teachers to be involved with whole school curriculum): From *Developing the Curriculum*, 3/e by Peter F. Oliva.

Chapter 10

Figure 10.5, Diagnosing learning styles: Reprinted by permission of Drs. Rita and Kenneth Dunn

Chapter 11

Excerpt from Armstrong et al.: From *Teaching Today: An Introduction to Education*, 5/e by Armstrong, Henson, and Savage, ©1997. Reprinted by permission of Prentice-Hall, Inc., Upper Saddle River, NJ.

Excerpt from Hoover: From "Curriculum adaptation: A five step process for classroom implementation" by J. J. Hoover, 1990, *Academic Therapy*, 25(4), pp. 410–411. Copyright ©1990 by PRO-ED, Inc. Reprinted by permission.

Excerpt from Grubb: From Grubb, W. N. (1996) "The New Vocationalism: What it is, what it could be" in *Kappan*, 77(8), pp. 547–554.

Case Studies

Action Research as an Instrument of Change: Reprinted by permission of David O. Stine, California State University.

Accessing the Internet: Reprinted by permission of Bob Lucking, Old Dominion University.

Curriculum for the Real World: Reprinted by permission of Leonard Kaplan, Wayne State University.

Angola High School: Reprinted by permission of Rex W. Bolinger, Angola High School, Angola, IN.

Developing Aims, Goals,, and Objectives for an Afrocentric Elementary School: Reprinted by permission of Johnnie Thompson, Wichita State University.

Integrating and Assessing Critical Thinking Across the Curriculum: Reprinted by permission of Christy L. Faison, Rowan University.

The Arts in the Curriculum: Reprinted by permission of Judith B. Buzzell, Associate Professor in the Education Department at Southern Connecticut State University.

Creating Community North Campus Deer Park High School: Reprinted by permission of Angus J. MacNeil, University of Houston–Clearlake.

The Role of Collaboration in Curriculum Decisions: Reprinted by permission of Charles Evans, Western Kentucky University.

An Interdisciplinary Team Approach: Reprinted by permission of Dr. Irma Guadarrama, University of Houston.

Abruscato, J., 339
Adler, M., 109
Alberg, J., 392
Alexander, W. M., 8, 152, 153
Alley, R., 57, 411, 412
Alper, L., 198, 441
Alvarez, M. C., 266
Alvestad, K. A., 395
Ambrosie, F., 291
American Association for the Advancement of Science, 442
Anderson, D., 266
Anderson, P. J., 45, 46, 395
Anderson, R., 65, 242, 268
Antin, Mary, 43
Apple, M. W., 12, 41, 43
Applebaum, K., 93
Applebee, A. N., 248
Aquinas, T., 107
Aristotle, 107
Arlin, M., 197, 391, 392
Armento, B. J., 375–376
Armstrong, D. G., 68, 84–85, 110, 395, 416, 417–418, 419, 433
Aschbacher, P. R., 343, 449
Associated Press, 441
Association for Supervision and Curriculum Development, 271–272
Astuto, T. A., 22, 23
Augustine, St., 110
Ayers, W., 269

Bacon, F., 82, 106–107
Bagley, W., 108
Baker, E. T., 9, 11, 422, 455

Baker, N., 130
Ballew, H., 6, 441
Bank, M. A., 125
Banks, J. A., 6, 12, 335, 419
Banks, L., 63
Barnes, D., 30, 64, 71, 73, 147, 252, 396–397
Baron, M. A., 344
Barth, R. S., 290
Barton, J., 336, 417
Basom, R. E., 311–312
Beasley, M., 392
Beauchamp, G. A., 145, 351
Bell, T. H., 15, 22, 23
Bellanca, J., 103
Bellon, E. C., 125, 131, 242, 289
Bellon, J. J., 131, 242, 289
Bennett, C. K., 44, 295, 297
Berliner, D. C., 248, 249
Bernauer, J. A., 14, 17, 64, 131, 295–296, 314, 427
Bestor, A., 90
Bickel, W. E., 307
Biddle, B., 266
Bierlein, L. A., 424–425
Bjork, L., 190
Blank, M. A., 131, 242, 289
Block, J. H., 328, 391
Bloom, B. S., 91, 197, 216–221, 225–227, 328
Blythe, T., 128, 130, 146, 252
Boix-Mansilla, V., 130, 252, 257, 413–414
Boleyn, A., 83
Bolinger, R., 133–145 (case study)
Bonar, B., 235–241
Bondi, J., 10–11

Bondy, E., 51
Boren, L. C., 308–309
Borko, H., 15, 115, 336
Boyer, E., 295
Bracey, G. W., 13, 17, 18, 126, 392, 419
Bradley, D. F., 420, 422
Bradley, M. J., 63
Brameld, T., 110
Brandt, R. S., 200, 344
Brimfield, R. M. B., 267
Brogdon, R. E., 334, 335
Brophy, J., 387, 400
Brown, C. L., 351
Brown, D. S., 24, 125, 167, 327
Brown, R., 386
Bruder, I., 395
Bruning, R. H., 443
Brunner, J. S., 91, 148, 181
Buchsbaum, H., 395
Buckleitner, W., 395
Bunny, S., 295
Burke, W. J., 50
Burns, R. B., 197, 328, 391, 423
Buschee, F., 344
Buttery, T. J., 45, 46, 395, 429
Butts, R. F., 453
Buzzell, J., 443–448 (case study)
Byrne, S., 210, 212
Byron, Lord, 369

Caine, G., 103
Caine, N., 103
Calfee, R., 386
Callahan, R., 365

Campbell, D., 9, 11, 416
Campbell, J. K., 88
Campbell, L. P., 58
Canady, R. L., 145
Canfield, J., 271
Cardelle-Elawar, M., 307
Carnevale, A. P., 430
Carnine, D., 55
Carpenter, T. P., 375
Carroll, J. B., 328, 390–391
Carroll, M. A., 129, 132
Carson, T., 294, 295, 296
Caswell, H. L., 9, 11
Cavazos, L., 44
Chambers, D. L., 328
Chattin-McNichols, J., 295, 307
Cheney, C. D., 421
Cherniss, C., 93
Chodorow, S., 63
Ciscell, R. E., 377–378
Clandinin, D., 103
Clark, C. M., 375
Clark, D. C., 91, 212
Clark, D. L., 22, 23
Clark, S. N., 91, 212
Claus, J., 287, 294, 429
Clinchy, E., 15, 251
Clinton, Pres. Bill, 355, 440
Cloud, N., 93
Cochran-Smith, M., 295
Cockerill, J., 130
Cohen, A., 49, 180, 391
Cohen, D., 40, 49, 54, 440
Cole, R. W., 215
Collins, A., 336, 417
Conally, M., 103
Conant, J. B., 91, 127, 254
Confer, C. B., 125

Conklin, N. F., 415
Conroy, P., 41
Conte, C., 63
Cook, A., 14
Cook, L., 392
Cooper, H., 46, 398–399
Costa, A. A., 103
Counts, G. S., 110–111
Covingon, M. V., 427
Crabtree, C., 452
Crandall, D. P., 311–312
Craver, S. M., 127, 128, 131
Crawford, J., 190
Crew, A. B., 162
Cross, C. T., 93
Csikszentmihalyi, M., 313
Cuban, L., 267, 291, 295, 355
Cunningham, R. D., Jr., 391
Curtis, A. C., 66

Dagenais, R. J., 65, 128, 211–212, 268
Dagley, D. L., 328, 329
Dansereau, D. F., 265
Darling-Hammond, L., 45–51, 92, 182, 246, 427
Davidman, P. T., 12
Davis, D. M., 65
Davis, G. A., 49
Day, B., 7, 294, 412, 426
Decker, L. E., 266–267
Delgado-Gaitan, C., 335
Denee, J., 267
Des Dixon, R. G., 13, 14, 375
Dewey, John, 89, 107, 110, 131, 148, 176–177, 253, 254, 257, 310
Dickens, C., 415
Doak, S. C., 11
Doll, R., 9, 11
Dormody, T. J., 265–266
Dosch, D., 128
Doyle, W., 400
Dunn, K., 392
Dunn, R., 66, 69, 180, 392, 393
Duran, R., 190, 393
Dusenburg, L. A., 350

Earley, B., 45, 368
Efthim, H. E., 328
Egbert, R. L., 24, 125, 167, 289, 327
Eggebrecht, J., 128
Eggleston, L., Jr., 425

Einstein, A., 129
Eisner, E. W., 50, 182, 270, 290
Elam, S. M., 43, 45, 64, 417, 419
Elkind, R., 442
Eller, B. F., 201, 212, 416
Elliott, R., 15, 336
Ellsworth, P. C., 386
English, F., 211
Epstein, J. L., 339
Erb, T., 40, 93
Essex, N. L., 211
Evans, C. S., 257, 258–265 (case study)
Everts-Danielson, K., 215

Faidley, R., 219–220
Faison, C., 345–349 (case study)
Falco, M., 350
Falk, B., 246, 427
Fantini, M. D., 334, 340
Farson, R., 164
Feldheusen, J. F., 423
Fendel, D., 198, 441
Fenstermacher, G. D., 48
Fever, M. J., 343
Fielding, L., 255, 327
Fillion, B., 220–224 (case study)
Finn, C. E., 424–425
Finn, J. D., 368, 377, 425
Fiore, T., 392
Fisher, J. F., 420, 422
Foshay, A. W., 8
Fowler, W. J., Jr., 75
Fowlkes, J., 296
Franklin, B., 85
Fraser, S., 198, 441
Friend, M., 392
Frymier, J., 327, 332
Fullan, M. G., 288, 291–292, 294, 315, 427
Fulton, K., 343

Gagnon, E., 69
Gagnon, P., 452
Gallager, C., 417
Gallup, G. H., 355, 399, 412, 417, 419, 423, 428, 431, 432, 440
Garcia, J., 257
Garcia, R. L., 52
Gardner, H., 103, 130, 252, 257, 413, 414, 433–434

Garmston, R., 243–244
Gates, S. L., 197, 391
Gay, G., 9
Geer, C., 30, 58, 252, 328, 379
Geisert, G., 66, 69, 180
Genesee, F., 93
Geography Education Standards Project, 452
Gibson, S., 72
Glasser, W., 103
Glatthorn, A. A., 51
Glover, J. A., 366, 377
Goldberg, M. R., 343
Goldberger, S., 426
Good, T. L., 125, 126, 386, 387, 400
Goodlad, J. I., 5, 40, 48, 210–211, 219, 431
Goodman, J., 355–356, 357
Gordon, K., 287
Gorman, B., 392
Gough, P. B., 17–18
Granada, J., 297–306 (case study)
Green, J., 377
Greenlaw, M., 270
Gregg, L., 7, 8, 9, 91, 288
Griggs, S. A., 392
Grondel, M., 201, 212
Grossen, B., 55
Grouws, D. A., 386
Grubb, W. N., 431
Guadramma, Irma, 182–190 (case study)
Guskey, T. R., 133, 145, 197, 343, 344, 345, 391

Haberman, M., 13, 211, 290, 291, 292, 326
Haertel, G. D., 24, 54, 126, 146, 192, 351, 365
Haffner, J. E., 97–103 (case study)
Hakim, D., 125
Hall, G. S., 21
Halperin, R., 39
Hanley, P. W., 291
Hargrove, T. Y., 416
Harrison, C. J., 181, 366–367, 378
Hart, L. A., 368
Hartley, S. H., 351
Hartoonian, M., 426
Harvard, J., 84
Harvey, O. J., 400

Hastings, J. T., 197, 328
Hatch, T., 17
Hattrup, V., 307
Heckman, P. E., 125
Henry, VIII, King, 83
Henson, K. T., 57, 68, 84–85, 110, 162, 201, 212, 266, 294, 296, 367, 391, 395, 411, 412, 416, 417–418, 419, 433
Herbart, J. F., 107
Herzberg, F., 292
Hibbard, K. M., 339
Hill, J. C., 145, 326–327, 432
Hill, M., 395
Hill, P. T., 432
Hodgkinson, H., 20–21
Holmes, K. M., 255, 268
Holzman, M., 314
Hoole, E., 181
Hoover, J. J., 420–421
Hopkins, D., 264, 426
Houck, J. W., 93
Hourcade, H. P., 395, 422
Houston, P. D., 430
Howe, L. W., 226
Huggest, A. J., 335
Hunt, D. E., 400
Huntley, M. A., 442–443
Hutchens, R., 11
Hutchins, W., 109
Hyman, I. A., 412
Hyman, J. S., 391

Ingram, J., 162
Ireton, E., 92
Irvin, J. I., 91, 212
Isenberg, J. P., 424

Jacobs, H., 103
Jalongo, M. R., 424
James, I., King, 83
James, W., 107
Jefferson, T., Pres., 42, 86
Jennings, J., 440
Jensen, E., 103
Johnson, D. W., 432
Johnson, R., 432
Johnston, C. A., 365
Johnston, J. H., 30, 58, 252, 328, 379
Johnston, J. M., 375
Jones, C., 327, 328, 341–342
Jones, D. L., 343
Jones, R., 309
Jones, V., 394

Joyce, B., 145, 264, 293, 311
Julik, J. A., 386
Jung, B., 295
Justiz, J., 190

Kant, I., 107, 114, 123, 128
Kaplan, L., 97–103
  (case study)
Kazis, R., 426
Kearns, D. T., 210
Keller, B. M., 413
Kendall, J. S., 427
Kennedy, R., 343
Kenney, D. J., 411
Kenny, M. S., 40, 57
Kerlinger, F., 127, 130–131
King, A., 181, 252, 265, 266
King, M., 289
Kirby, K. L., 97–103
  (case study)
Kirk, D., 291, 295
Kirschenbaum, H., 226
Klavis, A., 393
Klein, M. F., 269, 292
Kletzien, S., 42, 126
Knapp, M. S., 57
Knovac, J. D., 265
Koba, S. B., 93, 442
Kobrin, D., 338
Kopassi, R., 9
Kovalik, S., 103
Kowal, J., 201
Kowalski, T. J., 40, 89,
  124, 244, 266, 288,
  310–311, 367
Kozol, J., 8
Krashen, S., 57
Krathwohl, D. R., 225–227
Kyle, D. W., 51

LaBonty, J., 215
Langer, J. A., 248
Langholz, J., 296
Lapan, S., 297–308
  (case study)
Latham, A. S., 89, 351, 365
Laud, L. E., 287
LeDoux, J., 200
Leeper, R. R., 154
Leopold, G. D., 344
Levy, J., 368
Lewellen, J. R., 389
Lewis, C., 256
Lieberman, A., 40
Linblad, A. H., Jr., 432, 433
Lindsay, J. J., 46

Little, J., 293
Little, W., 64
Lobkowicz, N., 104
Locke, J., 89, 107, 115, 257
Loeffler, M. H., 295, 307
Looman de Wijk, 345
Lounsbury, J. H., 37, 49
Lowery, L., 294
Lucking, R., 59–64,
  (case study) 433
Lytle, S. L., 295

McCarthy, M. M., 431, 432
McCutcheon, C., 295
Macdonald, J. B., 8, 10, 11,
  152, 154
Macedo, D., 419
McElroy, L., 296
McIlvich, A., 257, 258–263
  (case study)
MacIver, D. J., 339
McIver, M. C., 288
McKenzie, J., 63
McKernan, J., 294
McKowen, C., 164
MacNeil, A., 345–349
  (case study)
McNeil, J. D., 11, 47, 310
Madaus, G. F., 197,
  225–227, 328
Maddox, H., 18
Magney, J., 395
Manning, M. L., 244, 433
Manno, B. V., 424–425
Markle, G., 30, 58, 252,
  328, 379
Marshall, C., 102, 125, 136,
  154, 167, 180, 276, 326,
  327, 394
Martin, N. K., 125, 131, 269
Martinez, M. E., 198
Marzano, R. J., 96, 97,
  344, 427
Maslow, A., 268
Mather, C., 435–439
Matisse, H., 145
Mauhs-Pugh, T. J., 425
Mausner, B., 292
Maxon, S., 93
Means, B., 63
Mecklenburger, 69
Meek, A., 336
Meichtry, Y., 58, 252,
  328, 379
Melton, G., 387
Merczak, N. J., 128

Michael, W. B., 63
Miller, J. A., 393
Moffett, J., 430
Mohrman, S. A., 89
Moilryan, C. M., 386
Moore, P., 387
Morisund, D., 440
Morrison, G. R., 63
Moss, J., 345–349
  (case study)
Mowday, R. T., 313, 314
Muillis, I. V. S., 248
Musser, S., 219–220
Myrick, P., 309

Nagel, G. K., 66
Nash, G., 452
Nathan, J., 425
National Assessment
  of Education Progress
  Science Consensus
  Project, 449
National Committee on
  Excellence in Education,
  344, 440
National Committee
  on Science Education
  Standards and
  Assessment, 442
National Science Teachers
  Association, 442
Neal, L., 63
Neil, A. S., 253
Neilsen, L., 295
Nelson, W. W., 14, 16, 19, 24,
  51, 125, 182, 288, 326,
  327, 328, 344, 440, 450
Newton, B. T., 254
Newton, Sir I., 254
Nicaise, 30, 64, 71, 73, 147,
  252, 396–397
Nixon, J., 295
Noddings, N., 426
Northrup, P. T., 64
Nye, B., 46

Oakes, J., 386
Oana, R. G., 40
Obermier, D., 201
Obispo, S. L., 313
O'Donneill, T., 265
Oliva, P. F., 10, 12, 13, 149–
  152, 192, 244, 287, 307,
  312, 326, 328
Olson, K., 392
O'Neil, M., 45, 199, 368

Orlando, I. C., 395
Orlich, D., 15–16, 181,
  219, 249
Orso, J. K., 328
Ostrom, C., 427
Ovando, C., 54
Ozmon, H., 127, 128, 131

Palmer, W. S., 428, 450
Parette, H. P., 395, 422
Park, M. N., 128
Parker, Col. F., 88, 89,
  111, 115
Parker, W. C., 451
Parsons, J., 327, 328,
  341–342
Patrick, D., 66
Pavan, B. N., 242
Pawlas, G. E., 244, 287, 307,
  312
Paxton, S., 296
Pearson, P. D., 255
Pepi, D., 71
Perkins, C., 431
Perkins, D., 128, 130, 146,
  252, 367
Perrin, J., 393
Perrone, V., 328, 329,
  336, 415
Peterson, P. L., 375
Peterson, R., 412
Phelps, P. H., 399
Phillips, D. G., 387
Phillips, D. R., 387
Piaget, J., 268, 400
Pierce, C., 107
Pinal, J., 190
Pitton, D. E., 326, 425, 426,
  427, 428
Pollina, A., 419
Ponder, G. A., 255, 268
Popham, W. J., 9, 11
Poplin, M. S., 309
Pratt, D., 132, 336, 341
Prescott, C., 130
Price, H. B., 42, 52
Pugalee, D. K., 428, 450
Purvis, J. R., 308–309
Puryear, H., 145
Pythagoras, 104

Rael, E. J., 425
Rafferty, M., 91
Rappoport, A. L., 42, 126
Rasch, B. W., 422
Ravitch, D., 291–292

Reich, R. B., 44
Reinhartz, J., 66
Reinstein, D., 375, 400
Reitzug, V. C., 40, 124, 244, 288, 310–311
Renwick, L., 63
Resek, D., 198, 441
Rettig, M. D., 145
Reyes, D. J., 389
Reynolds, T. D., 413
Richards, P. M., 265
Rickover, Adm. H., 91
Rinard, B., 130
Rinne, C. H., 253, 365
Rivett, P., 145
Robertson, P. J., 89
Roda, K., 425
Rodriguez, E., 103
Rhomberg, T. A., 375
Roosevelt, Pres. F. D., 437
Roosevelt, T., 49
Rose, L. C., 47, 355, 399, 412, 417, 419, 423, 428, 431, 432, 440
Rosenholtz, S. J., 293
Rosenshine, B., 252, 265, 266
Roskos, K., 367, 368
Ross, D. D., 51
Rousseau, J. J., 253
Rugg, H., 110
Ryan, K., 13

Sagor, R. D., 311
Saddlemire, R., 244
Sanger, J., 296–297
Sano, S., 392
Sardo-Brown, D., 295
Sautter, R. C., 12, 17, 411
Saylor, J. G., 8, 11, 152, 153
Savage, T. V., 68, 84, 85, 110, 178, 395, 416, 417–418, 419, 433
Sawyer, W. D. M., 395
Schane, B., 214
Scherer, M., 92, 256, 400
Scheurman, G., 71
Schifter, D., 441
Schlechty, P. C., 16, 50, 215, 355–356, 357
Schmidt, W. II., 97
Schmoker, M., 96, 97, 313
Schnalberg, L., 419
Schroder, H. M., 400
Schubert, W. H., 11

Schwahn, C., 293–294, 352
Scott, P., 54
Selekman, H. R., 177, 212
Seligmann, J., 57
Sergiovanni, T. J., 145, 314–315
Shalaway, L., 295, 307
Shane, H., 93
Shaughnessy, J., 327
Shavelson, R. J., 377, 387
Shelly, P., 369
Shen, J., 212, 269, 351
Shields, P. M., 57
Shores, J. H., 8, 11
Shouse, J. B., 39
Showers, B., 311
Siegel, M. A., 65
Siegel, P., 210, 212
Silbert, I., 55
Silbert, J., 430
Simon, S., 226
Simpson, E. J., 227–229
Sinis, P., 425
Sizer, T. R., 54
Skiba, R., 412
Slaton, D. B., 295
Slavin, R. E., 392
Smelter, R. W., 422
Smith, B. O., 8, 11
Smith, D., 377
Smith, M., 343
Snapp, J. C., 366, 377
Snider, M., 40, 368
Snidt, V. G., 386
Snook, P. A., 412
Snyder, D., 145
Snyderman, B., 292
Solomon, S., 45, 398
Spady, W., 293–294, 344, 352, 416
Spencer, H., 112, 241, 249
Spiegel, A. N., 443
Stallworth, B. J., 131, 364
Stanley, W. O., 8, 11
Stedman, P., 296
Steers, R. M., 313, 314
Stefanich, G. P., 24, 130, 147, 181, 218–219, 328
Steffs, L., 296
Stevens, K. B., 295
Stiggins, R. J., 415
Stine, D., 25–29 (case study)
Stinnett, T. M., 335
Stlegelbauer, S., 288

Stringfield, J. K., 51–52
Stroot, S. A., 296
Stutflebeam, D., 351
Styer, S. C., 128
Sweeny, B., 427, 428

Taba, H., 9, 14, 147
Tanner, D., 9, 15–17
Tanner, L. N., 9
Tatum, B. D., 12
Taylor, F., 43–44
Tewel, K. J., 312
Thames, W. R., 284–287
Thelan, H., 394
Thompson, J., 133–145 (case study), 220–224 (case study)
Thompson, S., 7, 8, 9, 91, 288
Thorn, C. A., 32
Tice, T. N., 40
Tichenor, M., 429
Townsend, N. C., 395
Trachtenberg, D., 249
Tripp, D. H., 295–296
Tsuchida, I., 256
Tyack, D., 288
Tyler, R., 148, 149, 150, 167
Tyson, H., 129, 132, 249
Tyson, J. C., 129, 132

Unger, C., 214
Ungson, G. R., 313, 314

Vanblerviet, A., 395, 422
Van Buren, Pres. M., 163
Van Gulick, R., 367, 390
Van Kirk, A. N., 89
Vanourek, G., 424–425
Van Scotter, R., 426
Van Wangenen, L., 339
Vars, G. F., 16, 213
Von Glaserfeld, E., 367
Vygotsky, L., 6

Wade, R. K., 292, 366, 368
Wagner, T., 17, 425
Walberg, H. J., 24, 54, 126, 146, 192, 351, 365, 422
Walker, B. F., 87
Wanat, C. L., 256
Wang, M. C., 24, 54, 126, 146, 192, 351, 365, 422
Ward, M. W., 129

Warren, R. P., 163
Washburne, C., 88
Watson, T. S., 40, 411
Waugh, S., 452
Weaver, R. A., 266, 367
Weil, J., 145
Weller, L. D., Jr., 351
Wellman, B., 243–244
Wendel, F. C., 426
Whitehead, A. N., 107, 127
Wigfield, A. L., 395
Wiggins, G., 326, 327, 336, 337, 338, 415
Wiles, J., 10–11
Williams, J., 413
Williams, P. A., 57, 411, 412
Wilmont, J., 107
Wilson, B., 92
Wilson, R., 190
Winograd, P., 343
Winter, W., 14
Winton, J. J., 326, 328, 329, 330, 340
Wirt, W. A., 88
Wirth, A. C., 44
Wise, A., 44
Wise, V. L., 443
Wiske, M. S., 124, 129
Witte, J. F., 432
Wohlstetter, P., 89, 430
Wolf, S. A., 288
Wolf, S. S., 288
Wolfe, M., 200
Wolfe, P., 200
Wolfgramm, H. F., 255
Wood, G. H., 39
Wood, J. A., 92
Woods, R. K., 125
Woodward, A., 249
Woolfolk, A., 434
Workman, D., 128
Worley, D., 81–84
Worthen, B. R., 344
Wright, J., 218
Wright, R., 292
Wulf, K. M., 214
Wynne, E. A., 13

Young, J. H., 290, 292
Yudewitz, G. J., 422

Zais, R. S., 8, 154–155, 192
Zlatos, B., 211
Zubrick, P. R., 266

"A Model of School Learning," 390

A Nation at Risk, 15–17, 19, 266

A Place Called School, 219

Ability grouping, 386–388

    heterogeneous, 388

    homogeneous, 388

    in-class, 386

    inter-class, 388

    intra-class, 386

Accountability and reform, 366

Accountability in Instructional Management. *See* AIM Program

Accreditation visits. *See* case study, 323–325

"Achievement," 128–129

    definition of, 295

    factors affecting, 375–376, 398

    narrow definition, 128

Acknowledging victories, 312

Action for Excellence, 19

Action research, 289. *See also* Research; Teachers, as researchers

Activities. *See also* Involvement of students; Selecting content and activities; Students' role

    multipurpose activities, 147, 265–266

Actors in curriculum development, 242–248

Administrators, educational. *See also* Leadership

    case writing, 312

    changing role, 287, 309

    keys to curriculum improvement, 21–22

    mushroom analogy, 290

    protector of teachers' time, 309

    providing teachers with latitude, 311

Advance organizers, 366, 379

Affective domain, 194–195. *See also* Taxonomy of Educational Objectives

    list of levels, 225

African-American students, effect of competition on, 335–336

Agents of change, 40, 113, 287, 292

AIM Model, 146

AIM Program, 14

Aims, educational, 212–213

Alignment. *See* Curriculum alignment

"All children can learn," 344, 366, 387

Alternative assessment, 415

Alternative curriculum, sample, 238–242

Alternative scheduling, 237, 270

Alverno College, 164, 167

American education, 17

    creativity, emphasis on, 47, 256

    free for all, 43

    strengths, 17, 43

    uniqueness, 16

    weaknesses, 12–13, 23–24

American High School, The, 254

American Studies Program, 162–164

Anti-intellectualism, 90

Apathy, curriculum of, 267

Application of information, students' inability to relate new information to previously acquired knowledge, 343, 367

Appreciation for diversity, 52

Arena, teachers' curriculum development, 21, 28, 126, 242–248, 269, 290

Articulation, evaluation of, 199

Arts, 17, 93. *See also* Fine arts curriculum, trends in

Asian education, 47, 256

Assessment

    authentic, 345

    formative, 328

    performance, 343–344

    self-, 336

Assessment role of philosophy, 112. *See also* Tests, teacher-made

    change agent, 113

clarifier, 114

influencing teachers, 112–113

moral guide, 113–114

Assigned time. *See under* Time

Assignments for extra credit, 340–341

Association for Supervision and Curriculum Development, 247, 264, 271

At-risk students, 256, 335–336

characteristics of, 256

contributing social conditions, 256

definition, 51

Attitudes of Americans toward

intellectualism, 42

technology, 66

Attitudes of teachers toward

content coverage, 28

education reform, 22–23, 271, 288

integrated disciplines, 270

multicultural classrooms, 92

personal experience, 28

test scores, 16

Authentic tests, 345

Authenticity, increasing teacher, 296

Autobiographic essays to achieve multicultural goals, 66

Awareness, increasing teacher, 296

Axiology, 106

Back to basics, 33

Balance, curriculum, 200

need for, 16–17

Barriers to change. *See* Change

Bell curve, 330–331

Benchmarks, establishing, 307

Bible, 85

Biological Science Curriculum Study, 91

Blaming teachers for student failure, 23, 294

Block scheduling. *See* Alternative scheduling

Blue Back Speller, 87

Bonus credit, 340–341

Boston English Classical School, 86

Bottom-up reform. *See* Grassroots reform

Bracey Reports, 17–18

Broad-fields curriculum, 180–82, 199

Brown v. Board of Education, 48

Business, effects on schools, 43

Cardinal Principles of Secondary Education, 42, 43, 87, 212–213, 250

Carnegie Corporation, 254

Case studies in this book

THE CASE OF EASTWOOD MIDDLE SCHOOL, 2–5

ACTION RESEARCH AS AN INSTRUMENT OF CHANGE, 22–25

THE CASE OF LINDA BLEVINS AND MARVIN WATTS, 37–39

ASSESSING THE INTERNET, 59–64

THE CASE OF DIANE WORLEY, 81–83

CURRICULUM FOR THE REAL WORLD, 97–103

THE CASE OF A DISAPPOINTED STUDENT, 123–124

ANGOLA HIGH SCHOOL, 133–145

THE CASE OF THE LITTLE SCHOOL THAT GREW, 173–176

AN INTERDISCIPLINARY TEAM APPROACH, 182–190

THE CASE OF SAN SONA ELEMENTARY SCHOOL, 209–210

DEVELOPING AIMS, GOALS, AND OBJECTIVES FOR AN AFROCENTRIC ELEMENTARY SCHOOL, 220–224

THE CASE OF BUILDING BRIDGES TO REFORM, 235–241

THE ROLE OF COLLABORATION IN CURRICULUM REFORM, 258–263

TEAMING AND COLLABORATING FOR CHANGE, 297–306

THE CASE OF THE ACCREDITATION VISIT, 323–325

INTEGRATING AND ASSESSING CRITICAL THINKING, 345–349

A WICHITA SCHOOL CASE, 364–365

CREATING COMMUNITY AT DEER PARK HIGH SCHOOL, 381–385

THE ARTS IN THE CURRICULUM, 443–448

Case Study method, 266, 367

Catechisms, 87

CD-ROM, 67

Celebrating diversity, 268

Centers

child care, 45

teen, 45

Certification of teachers. *See* Life certification

Challenge, need for curricula to, 91

Change, 282–321

agent, 40, 113, 287, 292

barriers to, 289, 311–312

for change's sake. *See* "Little School that Grew, The"

forces, list of, 289

nature of, 287, 296

philosophy as, 113

rules for effecting, 293

Changing nature of
schools, 44
society, 44

Charter schools, 424–425

Citizenship role of education, 42, 48

Civics, trends in, 453

Clarifier, philosophy as, 114

Class size, 375

Classroom-bound behavior of
teachers
limitations, 242
reasons, 290

Classroom-level planning, 242

Climate, 91, 310–311
of future schools, 268. *See also*
Ethos of schools
school. *See* Ethos of schools

Cognitive domain, 216. *See also*
Taxonomy of Educational
Objectives

Cognitive mapping, 70

Cognitive styles, 268

Coherence, curriculum, 355

Collaboration, 268, 368
in curriculum development. *See*
AIM Program; case studies,
258–263; 297–306

Collaborative decision making, 91

Colonial laws, 84

Colonial schools, purpose of, 83–84

Commission on the Reorganization
of Secondary Education, 86

Committee of Fifteen, NEA, 86

Committee of Ten, NEA, 86

Committee on College Entrance
Requirements, 87

Common curriculum designs,
176–199

Common sense, role in determining
teacher behavior, 126–128

Community's effects on schools,
39–40. *See also* case study,
381–385

Competency-based programs, 92–93

Competition
versus cooperation, 47, 265, 333
effect on at-risk students,
335–336
effect on minorities, 336
evaluation, 334–335

Components, curriculum, 176–199

Comprehensive high school, 254

Computer, 65–66. *See also*
Technology
assignments, 65–66
limitations, 71

Concepts, 129–130, 366–367, 375.
See also case study, 81–83
definitions, 198
developmental time, 375
identifying via studying, 375
role in learning, 91, 252
students' failure to learn major,
252
teachers' role, 367

Conflict resolution programs, 93

Confluent education, 268

Connections, 30, 177, 256, 334

Consortium, 307–308. *See also*
Educational Excellence
Laboratory Consortium

Consortium proposal, sample,
284–287

Constructivism, 5–6, 70, 270, 289,
306, 413

Constructivists, 30–31, 130, 198, 252

Content
coverage, 28–48
definition of, 251
versus information and
knowledge, 251
selection of, 248, 249

Continuity, curriculum, 200

Continuous assessment. *See*
Assessment

Contracts, grade, 388–389
sample, 284–287

Cooperation, 266
versus competition, 265

Cooperative learning, 432–433

Coral reef analogy to change, 296

Core curriculum, 90, 191–197

Core standards, 95

Creativity. *See* case study, 345–349
gifted students, 423
role in education, 47, 49
using technology to promote, 395
using tests to promote, 345

Criterion-referenced objectives, 256

Critical thinking, 266, 295

Critics, school, 90–91

Cultural discontinuity, 51

Cultural diversity. *See* Ethnic
diversity

Culture, 39–40
definition of, 39–40
of schools, 268

Culture, school, 310. *See also*
Climate; Ethos of schools

Curiosity, failure of curricula to
promote, 266, 307

Curriculum
alignment, 48, 211, 337, 350–
351. *See also* case study,
133–145
articulation, 354
definition of, 7–10
evaluation, 322–356
ever-changing nature, 13, 291
hidden, 10–13
plan, 8
program of studies, 8
sample definitions, social, 6–7
"Teacher-proof," 180–182
Victorian, 13

Curriculum alignment, 188, 211. *See
also* case study, 133–145

Curriculum balance
evaluation of, 355

Curriculum coherence, evaluation of, 355

Curriculum components, 176–177, 355

evaluation of, 351–356

Curriculum content, definition of, 30

Curriculum continuity, evaluation of, 354–355

Curriculum designs, 176–199

Curriculum evaluation, 350–356

Curriculum planning

administrators' role, 289, 309

continuous nature of, 242, 287

sloppy nature of, 13, 231

teacher involvement in, 23, 242, 367

Curriculum renewal, 291

Curriculum scope

evaluation of, 354–356

Cycles of cognition, 147

Daily lesson planning, 372–400

concepts, 375

sample plans, 379–380

Dalton Plan, 88

Dame Schools, 84–85

Decentralization, 7

Decision-making. *See* IDEA Model

Democratic function of schools, 48

Democratic principles in schools, 412

Demographic shifts, 57–58

Designing curricula, 176–199

Designs, curriculum

broad-fields, 180–182, 199

core, 90, 191–197

mastery reaming, 390–392

need for continuous, 176

spiral, 195–196

subject-centered, 178–180

Trump Plan, 194–195

Dialoguing, teacher, 212

Differential treatment of

high-ability and low-ability students, 387

minority students, 386

Direct instruction, 54–56

Discontinuity, cultural, 51

Discussion teaching method, 396–397

Distance learning. *See* Interactive strategies

District-wide planning, 244–245

Diversity. *See* Cultural diversity; Multicultural

"Drowning in a rising tide of mediocrity," 19

Drug abuse, 45

Earth Science Curriculum Project, 91

Educate America Act, 94

Education for All Handicapped Children Act, 48

Education reform, history of, 14–30

Education reform reports. *See* Reform reports

Education reform theme of this book, xx

Education reform, top-down, 14

Educational Excellence Laboratory Consortium, 284–287

Educational taxonomies. *See* Taxonomy of Educational Objcctives

Effective schools research, 29

Efficacy, 256

Eight-year study, 90

Electronic bulletin boards, 68

Elementary and Secondary Education Act of 1965, 48

Emile, 253

Emotions, role and learning, 200–201, 255

Empathy, 267

Empowerment

goal of in-service education, 268–269

role of encouragement, 58

students, need for, 7, 269, 375

teachers of, 212, 268, 269, 292, 295, 309

Engaged time, 375

English Classical School, 86

English language arts, trends in, 450

Epistemology, 105–106

Errors, role in learning, 198, 268, 271

ESCAPE Modules, samples, 157

Essentialism, 108

Ethnic diversity, 418–419

Ethos of schools, 310–311

Evaluating instruction, 322–356

Evaluating school reform, 355–356

Evaluating textbooks and other materials, 434–439

Evaluation of curriculum. *See* Curriculum evaluation

Evaluation of teachers, history of, 327–328

Expanded arena of curriculum development, teachers', 21, 28, 126, 242–248, 269, 290

Expectations teachers hold of high *versus* low achievers, 57

Exploration, 268

Extrinsic motivators, 292

Family, American

changing concept of, 40, 57–58

deterioration of, 45, 256

Norman Rockwell, 20

Feelings, 357. *See also* Emotions, role and learning

Financial support for education, 246

Fine arts curriculum, trends in, 449

Flexibility in curricula, need for, 70, 267–268. *See also* Intellectual flexibility

Flowchart, sample, 158

Forces that shape curricula, 46

Foreign language, trends in, 450

Formative assessment, 328

Franklin Academy, 57, 85–86

Free education, 86

Freedom, students'. *See Summerhill*

Friendliness, need for. *See* Personalization

Future Farmers of America, 294

Future Homemakers of America, 294

Future role of research, 50–51

Future schools, curriculum needed for, 93, 268

Futuristic planning, 93

Gallup Poll. *See* Phi Delta Kappa

Games, 395

Gary Plan, 88

Generalizability, 129–130, 131, 181, 266. *See also* Teakettle experiment

Geographic stereotyping, 420

Geography, trends in, 452–453

Gifted learners, 386, 423

Global awareness. *See* Goals for 2000

Goals for 2000, Educate America Act, 94

   public's views, 94

Grade contracts. *See* Contracts, grade

Grades, converting raw scores into, 341–343

Grading *versus* testing, 339–340

Grassroots reform, 23, 291

Guest speakers, use to promote multiculturalism, 66

Health curricula, trends in, 453

Herzberg's Two-Factor Motivation Theory, 293

Hidden curriculum, 10–13

High ability students, high expectations on, 57

High school, comprehensive, 254

Higher order questions, 386–387

Higher order thinking
   influence of textbooks on, 249
   use of computers to promote, 65–66
   use of objectives to promote, 220, 344–345
   use of other technology to promote, 395

Historical Foundations, 83–97

History curriculum trends, 451–452

Home life, effect on student achievement, 335

Home schooling, 412

Homeostatic balance, 58

Homework, 398–399
   effect on achievement, 398–399
   guidelines, 399
   need for reasonableness, 57–58
   purpose, 398

Hornbook, 87

"House" concept in British schools, 388

Hub of community, school as, 294

Human development, 254

Human relations skills, 256

Humanizing curriculum, 92

Humor, 255

Hypertext, 70, 440

IDEA Model, 307–308

Incentives to promote teacher changes, 292–293

In-class ability grouping, 386

Inclusion, 422–423

Indiana University, 93

Individualized education, 92, 386–387. *See also* Trump Plan

Individualized Guided Education (IGE), 92

Individualized programs, 92–93, 256

Individualizing instruction, 385–395
   using microcomputers, 395

Individually Prescribed Instruction (IPI), 92

Influence of school on society, 42–44

Influence of society on schools, 44–52

Information
   versus content, 251
   versus knowledge, 251

Information Processing Model, 389–390

Infrastructure, 296

Inquiry, 54, 91, 131

Inquiry training, 92

In-service programs, 265

Instructional models, 389–392

Instructional supervisors, 244–246

Integrated curricula, 198, 270. *See also* case studies, 182–190; 443–448
   need for, 57

Integration of disciplines, need for, 57

Intellectual flexibility, 307

Interactive strategies, 66

Interclass ability grouping, 388

Interdisciplinary curricula, 90–91

Interdisciplinary programs, 91, 414–416

Intermediate Science Curriculum Study, 91

International competition, 16, 161, 268. *See also* case studies, 182–190; 443–448

International Reading Association, 307

Internet. *See* World Wide Web

Interstate New Teacher Assessment and Support Consortium, 95–96

Intrinsic motivators, 292

Inviting climates, 22

Involvement of parents, 45, 46, 57, 70–71, 212, 368

Involvement of students, 336, 368

Involvement of teachers. *See* Arena, teachers' curriculum development
  curriculum planning, 242, 291
  reform, 291–292, 326
  research, 16
Islands of safety, schools as, 47. *See also* Status-quo, teachers' need to protect

Japanese education, 47, 256
Journals, need to read, 264–265, 289, 307
Joy of learning, 201, 255

Kalamazoo case, 86
Kappa Delta Pi, International, 247
Kentucky Education Reform Act, 235–236
Keys to successful reform, 23, 212, 242, 244–245, 287
King Henry VIII, 83
Knowledge
  explosion, 248
  versus information, 251
  nature of, 251–252, 265
  use in discussions, 397
Knowledge base, xxvi, 264–265

Laboratory schools, 89–90. *See also* case study, 235–241
Lackluster leadership, 22
Language barriers, 54
Language myths, 54
Latch-key children, 20–21
Latin Grammar School, 84, 178
Latitude, need for teacher, 309, 311
Laws. *See also* Colonial laws influencing curriculum, 48
Leadership, 287–290
  definition, 287
  education, 308–309
  future of, 309, 315

Learned societies, 246, 312–315
Learners' needs, list of, 253
Learning communities, 269
Learning Cycle Theory, 378–379
Learning for Mastery, 391
Learning modules. *See* Project ESCAPE
Learning styles, 392–395
Learning tracks, 256
Lecturing, 48
Lesson planning, 372–400. *See also* Daily lesson planning
Life certification, 417–418
Listservs, 70
"Little School that Grew, The," 173–176
Long-range planning, 366–372
Low-ability students, teaching, 387

Macdonald's Curriculum Model, 152, 154
Maslow's Needs Hierarchy, 292
Magnet schools, 424
Mainstreaming, 422
Mastery learning, 196–197, 390–392
  criticisms of, 391–392
  research on effectiveness, 391
Matching learning styles and teaching styles. *See* Styles
Mathematics, trends in, 441–442
Messy process, curriculum planning as a, 13
Metacognition, 70
Metaphors, 378
"Mickey Mousing of students," 375
Microcomputers, 395. *See also* Technology
Microcosm of community, school as a, 39–40
Missions, 7, 45, 288
Mistakes, need for tolerance, 198, 268, 271
Model Laboratory School's alternative curriculum, 235–241

Models, curriculum planning, 146–164
Models, instructional, 489–492
Moral education
  decline in society, 49–50
  values, 49
Moral guide, philosophy as a, 113–114
Moral leukemia, 49
Motivation, 58, 291, 310, 353. *See also* Herzberg's Two-Factor Motivation Theory
  use of computers, 291
Motivators, teacher, 292, 344
Multicultural, 51–52. *See also* case studies, 209–210, 220–224, 345–349, 381–385
  concerns, 51–52, 92
  education, 51
  goals, 66
  hidden curriculum, 12–13
Multipurpose activities, 147, 265–266
Mushroom analogy, 290

Nation at Risk, A, 15–17, 19, 266
National Board for Professional Teaching Standards, 96
National Center for Educational Statistics, 368
National Commission on Excellence in Education, 15. *See also A Nation at Risk*
National Council for Accreditation of Teacher Education, 67
National Council for the Teaching of Mathematics, 246
National Council of Teachers of English, 246
National Education Association, 86–87, 254
National educational standards, 246, 292, 426–428
  criticisms of, 94–97
National goals, 250–251

National level planning, 246

National School Boards Association, 69

National School Boards Association Institute for the Transfer of Technology in Education, 69

National Science Teachers Association, 246

National standards, 426–428. *See also* National educational standards

National voluntary testing, 440

Natural education. *See* Emile

Nature of knowledge, 251–252, 265

Nature of teaching, 255

Naysayers, 312–313

New basics, 93

New England Primer, 87

Normal curve, 330–331

Norman Rockwell Family, 20

Norm-referenced *versus* criterion-referenced evaluation, 329–330

Northwest Ordinance of 1787, 86

Oasis, School as an, 255

Objective-based education. *See* Alverno College; Outcomes-based education; Tyler's Ends-Means Model

Objectives, 213–214

Official curriculum, 267

Old Deluder Satan Act, 85

Oliva Model, 149–152

On-line data systems, 68

Open-ended assignments, 65, 71, 265

Organizing content, 376

Organizing materials, 376

Outcomes-based education, 344–345

Ownership, student, 182

Parent involvement via use of computers, 70–71

Parents, involving, 45, 46, 57, 70–71, 212, 368, 399, 428–450

Parents' role in education, 29, 45–46, 71, 399

Perceptions of students toward tests for promoting learning, 328

Perceptions of teachers, 290

Perceptual modality, 393

Perennialism, 109

Performance assessment. *See* Objectives, Performance objectives

Performance evaluation, 343–344, 345

Performance objective terms, list of, 215

Performance objectives, 213–214
    guidelines for writing, 219–229

Performance-based assessment, 414. *See also* Outcomes-based education

Permissive curricula, 253

Personalization, 255–256. *See also* Humanizing curriculum

Personalized curricula, 92–93

Personalizing education, 92, 268

Phi Delta Kappa, 17–18, 247

Philosophical foundations, 104–115

Philosophy
    definition of, 105
    role in education, 112–114

Physical Science Study Group, 91

Piagetian stages percentage chart, 147

Planned curriculum, 267

Planning
    daily, 372–400
    long-range, 366–372
    sample daily lesson plans, 379–380

Platoons, 88

Political controversy, 40

Portfolios, 336–337

Poverty, 45, 57

Power of involvement, 292

Power of teachers, 23, 212

Power, types of, 313–314

Practical education, 107

Practical role of philosophy, 112–114

Pragmatism, 107–108

Pressure groups, 247–248

Privitization of schools, 430

Proactive teaching, 44–45, 256

Problem-solving, 28, 47, 197–198, 215, 266, 270. *See also* IDEA Model

Process of Education, The, 91

Product evaluation, 370

Professionalism, 6, 124–125, 291

Progress grades, 336

Progressive education, 89–90

Progressive Education Era, 90, 253

Progressive reporting, 329

Progressivism. *See* Progressive education

Project ESCAPE, 156–161

Protestants, 83–85

Psychomotor domain, 227–229. *See also* Taxonomy of Educational Objectives

Public Law, 94–142, 48

Public school, history of, 86–93. *See also* Education for All Handicapped Children Act

Puritans, 84

Purpose of American schools, 18, 23

Quality, 210

Quincy School System, 88–89

Reading across the curriculum, 414–415

Reading, effect of poverty on, 57

Reading, role in research, 307

Real world curriculum. *See* case study, 97–103

Realism, 106–107

Reconstructionism, social, 28, 40, 109–112, 326

Reflective assignments, 66

Reflective thinking, 295, 386

Reform. *See* Grassroots reform; Top down regulations

Reform, need for evaluation, 267

Reform reports

    positive outcomes, 21

    purposes of, 19

    rhetoric, 43, 48, 91

    unsound recommendations, 19 21

    weaknesses, 18–21

Regional education offices, 245

Reluctance to change, teachers', 22–23, 271, 288

Reorganization. *See* Commission on the Reorganization of Secondary Education

Reports, oral, 396, 397

Research

    collaborative, 296

    in-service faculty development, 265

    involving teachers with, 294–297

    need for, 14, 45

    role in curriculum development, 50, 124–125

    role in education, 50

    source of ideas for projects, 307

    teachers' failure to use, 23–24, 124–125, 289

Research base. *See* Knowledge base

Researchers, helping teachers become, 306–307

Researchers, teachers as, 294–297

Resistance to change

    schools, 288

Respect for students, 255, 256

Restructuring

    definition, 288, 356

    purpose of, 210

Retreats, 356

Revising curricula, checklist for, 271

Revoludonism, 110

Rhetoric, reform report, 43, 91

    "rigor," 43, 91

    "rising tide of mediocrity," 19, 266

Risk taking, 198, 268

Role of schools

    conserve society, 40

    national security, 43

    problem solving, 47

    serve students, 41

    shape society, 40

    socialization, 12

    vocational preparation, 41, 43–44

Role of students

    in group discussions, 392

    in planning, 368

Role of teachers

    changing, 242, 367

    counseling, 255

    facilitator, 397

    group discussions, 397

    reform, 23

    research, 306–307

Safe schools, 255, 256, 269, 411–412

Saylor-Alexander Model, 152, 153

Scenarios, 65

Scheduling. *See* Alternative scheduling

School choice, 431–432

School climate, 22, 39, 256

School reform, 355–356

    evaluation of, 355–356

School-based decision making, 400

Schools as communities, 39–40

Schools as community centers, 294

School-wide planning, 243–244

Science

    importance in curriculum development, 127

    trends, 448

Science Mathematics Study Group, 91

Science *versus* common sense, 127–128

Scientific method, 106–107

Scientism, 50

Scope, 199

Scopes trial, 49

Security, teachers' need for, 270–271

Selecting content and activities

    bases for, 369

    problems in, 248–251

Self-acceptance, 270

Self-assessment, 417

Self-concepts learners', 104

Self-development of students, role of the arts in, 17

Self-development of teachers, 295

Self-esteem programs, 271

Self-evaluation of teachers, 309, 364

Self-understanding, 256

Separate subjects curriculum, 199

Sequence, curriculum, 199

Sequential learning, 368

Service centers, 245

Seven Cardinal Principles of Secondary Education. *See* Cardinal Principles of Secondary Education

Slow students

    treatment by teachers, 387

    ways to evaluate, 387–388

Social collaboration, 252

Social contract, 52

    sample, 53

Social foundations, 39–40

Social reconstruction. *See also* Reconstructionism, social

Social studies trends, 451

Societal forces that affect curriculum, 48–49

Special students, 420–422

Spiral curriculum, 195–196

Spirit of inquiry, 54

Sports, effects on curricula, 244

Sputnik, 252

Stable schools, 256

Stabilizer, 50

Staff development, 284–287, 292

Standardized Achievement Test, 17, 330

Standards, 292

   harm in overemphasizing national, 16

Stanine scores, 331–332

Status-quo, teachers' need to protect, 288. *See also* Islands of safety, schools as

Structure of the disciplines theory, 91, 148

   use in lesson planning, 376

Student learning styles instrument, 393

Student opinions, 255

Student ownership, 255

Student-centered curriculum, 88–89, 215, 255. *See also* Progressive education

Students as purposes of schools, 215

Students' role. *See* Role of students

Styles, 392–395

   criticisms of styles theory, 394–395

   learning, 392–395

Subject content, power to motivate, 253

Subject-centered curriculum, 178–180

Summary, lesson plan, 378

Summative evaluation, 328

Summerhill, 253

Symbiotic relationship between school and community, 44

Taba's Inverted Model, 146–148

Tables of specifications, 272–274

   samples, 273

"Tabula Rasa," 257

Take-home tests, 329

Taxonomy of Educational Objectives, 91

Taylorism, 43–44

Teacher education colleges, 22–23

   failure to require research, 24

   role in education reform, 22–23

Teacher education models, 156–164

Teacher empowerment, 14, 21, 28, 126, 212, 268, 269, 292, 295, 309. *See also* Empowerment, of teachers

Teacher feelings, assessing, 357–358

Teacher involvement in curriculum development. *See* Arena, teachers' curriculum development

Teacher-proof curricula, 182, 290

Teachers

   as researchers, 294–297

   competence levels of, 344–345

Teachers' influence, 112–113, 212

Teachers' role in reform, 23. *See also* Role of teachers

   shift in, 242

"Teachers' world" *versus* "researchers' world" concept, 295

Teaching and learning styles, 392–395

Teaching and learning units. *See* Unit plans

Teaching, using objective-based tests to improve, 345

Teakettle experiment, 129–130

Technological foundations, 59–72

Technology

   instructional management, 66

   limitations of, 71

   need for flexibility, 70

   unconventional use, 395, 440

   used to enhance self-concepts, 66

   used to individualize, 395

Teen center, 45

Temporary nature of knowledge. *See* Nature of knowledge

Tenure, 417

Term projects, 387

Tests. *See also* Assessment

   authentic, 345

   power of, 58

   teacher-made, 326

Textbooks

   evaluating, 434–439

   influence on schools, 44, 248–249

   strengths of, 44

   weaknesses, 44, 249

Thematic approach, 412

Themes, integrated, xx–xxii, 5—7

Theories, 91, 130–133

   samples, 132

Theory

   common sense, 126–128

   imperfect nature, 131

   role in curriculum development, 132

   temporary nature, 132

Theory of education, 91

Time management, 297, 377–378, 386, 398. *See also* case study, 297–306

Time, need to protect teachers', 309

Time to plan, need for, 309

Time to reflect, 295, 386

Time-on-task, 57

Top down regulations, 14, 19, 44, 96, 270, 291, 311. *See also* Grassroots reform

Tracking, 256. *See also* Ability grouping

Tradition

   effect on schools, 32

   role in curriculum development, 10

Transformation of schools, 356

Treatment of slow students, 387

Trends across the disciplines, 411–440

Trends within the disciplines, 440

Trump Plan, 194–195

Two-Factor Motivation Theory, 293

Tyler's Ends-Means Model, 148–149, 268

Uniqueness of schools, 39

Unit plan, 367–373
  parts, 373
  samples, 373–374, 379–380

Unit planning, 367–372

U.S. Department of Education, 292

U.S. Department of Justice, 411

Valued outcomes, 58, 210

Values education *versus* moral education, 49

Values need for emphasizing, 49
  need to teach, 49
  universally accepted, 49

Variety, need for. *See* Grading *versus* testing

Vertical articulation, 200

"Very standard error, A," 332

Victorian curriculum, 13

Vocational preparation, 18

Voluntary testing, 440

Vouchers, 431–432

Wait-time studies, 387

Water Is Wide, The, 41

Weaknesses of schools, 23

Wholistic learning theory, 367

Wichita, Kansas programs, 364–365

Winnelka Plan, 88

Wisdom, definition of, 104

Woods Hole Conference, 91, 265

World of work, 430–431

World Wide Web, 69–72

World-class workers, 41

Word traps, 128–129

Work of Nations: Preparing Ourselves for 21st Century Capitalism, 44

Work role of education, 41, 43–44

Work skills needed in future, 44

Writing across the curriculum, 65, 336, 414–415

Zais Eclectic Model, 154–155